Film Noir Guide

Film Noir Guide

745 Films of the Classic Era, 1940–1959

MICHAEL F. KEANEY

McFarland & Company, Inc., Publishers
Jefferson, North Carolina, and London

Library of Congress Cataloguing-in-Publication Data

Keaney, Michael F., 1947–
Film noir guide : 745 films of the classic era, 1940–1959 / Michael F.
Keaney.
p.   cm.
Includes bibliographical references and index.

ISBN 0-7864-1547-9 (illustrated case binding : 50# alkaline paper) ♾

1. Film noir — Catalogs.   2. Film noir.   I. Title.
PN1995.9.F54K43   2003   016.79143'655 — dc21   2002156655

British Library cataloguing data are available

On the cover: Lauren Bacall and Charles Boyer in *Confidential Angel* (1945)

Manufactured in the United States of America

McFarland & Company, Inc., Publishers
Box 611, Jefferson, North Carolina 28640
www.mcfarlandpub.com

To Doreen
my loyal moll of 32 years
for not kicking me out
after the many hundreds of hours I spent with
Lizabeth, Ava, Ida, Veronica, Audrey, Barbara, Joan, Marilyn
and scores of other gorgeous dames
during the planning of this caper

Acknowledgments

Special thanks to my wife, Doreen Keaney, for reading the entire manuscript and finding a number of errors that would have been embarrassing if not caught, and for helping me double-check my lists; and to Charlie Mitchell of Darker Images Videos, who was so helpful in answering my many questions.

Contents

Preface

From 1956, when I was nine years old, through 1963, when my family moved away from my beloved Bronx to Queens (at the time a more suburban area of New York City), I made weekly pilgrimages to three neighborhood movie theaters — the Spooner, the Boulevard and the Star — all located on the same street within walking distance of my home.

The Spooner and the Boulevard were quality theaters that showed double features (a first-run A film plus a new or re-released B film), an occasional cartoon, and coming attractions. I don't recall the price of admission for matinees in the 1950s, but I do remember that by the early 1960s the price was a whopping fifty cents for kids over twelve and thirty-five cents for the younger children.

I can recall my mother taking me to see *The Ten Commandments* at the Boulevard. We sat in the non-smoking section of the balcony, an unusual treat for me because during matinees kids unaccompanied by an adult had to sit in the children's section, which was patrolled by an ornery matron who carried a flashlight and barked orders to disruptive children, warning them to be quiet or be evicted. Some of the other films I saw at the Boulevard and the Spooner were *Tom Thumb* with Russ Tamblyn, *The Buccaneer* with Charlton Heston and Yul Brynner, *The Delicate Delinquent* with Jerry Lewis, *Al Capone* with Rod Steiger, *The Alamo* with John Wayne and teen idol Frankie Avalon, *Rodan* with Japanese actors nobody ever heard of, and *Godzilla* with some more unknown Japanese and Raymond Burr, who would soon become famous playing Perry Mason on television. I could easily list a hundred films like these without taxing my memory.

While I appreciated the classy atmosphere of these two theaters, with their cushiony seats, plush carpets and super-wide screens, I really preferred their smaller, somewhat dingy competitor, the Star, which showed, count 'em, *three* movies on Saturdays — at half the price. A triple feature for a quarter! Plus cartoons, newsreels and coming attractions. Sure, the screen was smaller, the seats were harder and the carpets were dirtier, but do hundreds of boisterous twelve-year-olds really care about

1

such luxuries? And moms and dads were quicker to part with twenty-five cents than half a dollar, especially since their little darlings were sure to be out of their hair for a good five or six hours.

The Star never showed first-run A films. All three movies were usually re-released Bs, with an occasional newer B film that management always saved for the evening shows. While I never saw a Hollywood blockbuster at the Star, the films were different every week. I saw plenty of old Abbott and Costello comedies; Three Stooges shorts; Johnny Mack Brown Westerns; decade-old Frankenstein, Dracula and Wolf Man movies; science fiction flicks (many in 3-D); and scores of old, low-budget crime films that I didn't understand. Oh, sure, once in a while they'd show one I could follow. What wasn't there to understand about *Split Second*? An escaped killer (Stephen McNally) holds some hostages in a ghost town where the Army has scheduled an A-bomb test. Every kid in the theater understood that. Weren't the Russians going to drop one of those bombs on us any day now? Then there was *Baby Face Nelson* with Mickey Rooney. That certainly wasn't difficult to follow: a short, angry guy blasting away with a tommy gun.

The previous week's coming attractions, however, always seemed to sucker me back — gangsters shooting it out with rivals, hold-up men fleeing with bags of money stolen from an armored car, a killer shooting a cop in the back (and vice versa), or a guy kissing (or slapping) his scantily clad girlfriend. But more often than not I was disappointed and, frankly, bored. There seemed to be an awful lot of talking going on in these dark and dreary, black-and-white films. And all that talk bored me. I remember being puzzled as to why Sterling Hayden was spending so much time *planning* the race track heist in *The Killing* instead of skipping right to the good part, the robbery itself, and why they had to show that TV doctor Ben Casey (Vince Edwards) snuggling up with Elisha Cook's wife (Marie Windsor). A lot of familiar TV faces kept popping up in these types of moves. There was that Perry Mason guy (Raymond Burr) and that cowboy from *The Restless Gun* (John Payne). And the heavyset cop in *Highway Patrol* (Broderick Crawford).

Evidently, the rest of the kids felt as I did because it was during these talky "cops and robbers" movies that we usually decided to act up (throwing popcorn and water balloons at each other, or creating flatulent sound effects by blowing through our cupped hands). We quieted down only when somebody on the screen was about to get shot or beaten up. The Star's manager was crafty, though, because these types of films always seemed to be run last, after the monster movies and Abbott and Costello romps, and many of the kids just gave up in the middle and went home.

It wasn't until years later, in the 1970s, when I began seeing reruns of these old crime movies on TV, that I finally realized that all that dialogue and character development actually were quite interesting. The films no longer bored me. I soon discovered that there was even a name for these types of movies. They called them *films noirs*, French for "black films."

The term "film noir" had been applied by French critics to a number of American films that, over a six-week period, made their way to France at the end of World War II. These films (*The Maltese Falcon*, *The Big Sleep*, *Laura*, *The Woman in the*

Window, Double Indemnity, This Gun for Hire, Lady in the Lake, Gilda, The Killers and *Murder, My Sweet*) had some common elements that fascinated the entertainment-starved French filmgoers. One of these elements was crime, especially murder. Not the gangster-type murders that were commonplace in such 1930s films as *The Public Enemy, Little Caesar* and *The Roaring Twenties*, in which the bad guys were expected to behave as they did because they were, after all, killers. These newer films and the ones following them presented the viewer with new breeds of criminals—love-starved husbands and wives, local business owners, writers, gamblers, small-time hoods, private eyes, mental patients, cynical war veterans, rebellious teenagers and corrupt lawyers, politicians, judges and cops. Of course, unlike the cold-blooded 1930s gangsters, these middle-class criminals often suffered guilt and felt alienated from the rest of society as a result of their crimes. But even more often, these feelings were the *cause* of their criminal activity. Watching these film noir characters was like secretly watching neighbors or friends indulging in illegal and immoral behavior.

What could be more exciting and provocative than that?

Many of these films were based on the works of hard-boiled American mystery writers such as Raymond Chandler, Dashiell Hammett and James M. Cain, whose views of society were certainly less than cheerful. As a matter of fact, they were downright bleak. The characters in their novels were obsessed with money, power and sex, and would stop at nothing to achieve their desires, including murder. And this translated nicely, but carefully, to the big screen. Postwar Hollywood directors, producers, writers, actors and actresses, if they didn't realize or care that the French loved their films, surely recognized from box office receipts that the average American moviegoer did.

Film noir, in addition to its thematic criminal content with an emphasis on obsession, desperation, alienation and paranoia, is also noted for its dark visual style. European directors like Max Ophuls, Fritz Lang, Robert Siodmak, William Dieterle, John Brahm, Billy Wilder and Boris Ingster brought with them from the old country an artistic style called German expressionism, which played an important role in the development of film noir. "Dark" is a key word when describing this style, as indicated by the number of film noir titles that contain the word: *Dark City, The Dark Corner, The Dark Mirror, Dark Passage, The Dark Past, Dark Waters, Man in the Dark, So Dark the Night, Spin a Dark Web.* "Shadow" is also used often: *Cast a Dark Shadow, Chase a Crooked Shadow, City of Shadows, Man in the Shadow, Shadow of a Doubt, Shadow of a Woman, Shadow on the Wall, Shadow on the Window.* Many films noirs take place in urban settings: *The Captive City, City Across the River, City of Shadows, The City That Never Sleeps, Cry of the City, Dark City, Edge of the City, The Naked City, Night and the City, The Phenix City Story, The Sleeping City, While the City Sleeps, Whispering City.*

There are exceptions to the rules, of course, with a number of films noirs having been shot in a flat, uninteresting style—for example, *Cause for Alarm*, which is reminiscent of an old television drama, and *High Sierra*, an outdoor crime drama with most of the action taking place in the daylight. While film noir is known mostly for its black and white photography (as were most films prior to the late 1950s), some, such as *Leave Her to Heaven, I Died a Thousand Times* (a remake of *High Sierra*), *Vertigo*, *Playgirl* and *House of Bamboo*, were filmed in color.

While it's not within the scope of this book to go into detail about the ongoing controversy over the definition of "film noir," I will say a few words about it. (A few of the many books that cover this in great detail are included in the bibliography for those who want to delve further into this interesting, but futile, debate.) Some film historians and critics believe that film noir is a genre, while others believe it's simply a style. Some squeeze themselves right into the middle, claiming it's a genre in which style plays an important part. Others say it began as a style within the B film genre and developed into a genre itself. Still others believe it's a "movement" or a "cycle." Most film noir fans I speak with tell me that they don't really care whether it's a genre or a style or a cycle. It's all very interesting, they say, but they'd rather leave the argument to the professors and critics to iron out. It takes time away from collecting and viewing these incredible films, some of which are masterpieces of American moviemaking and some of which are turkeys.

An equally controversial topic is when this genre or style or movement actually began and when, or even if, it ended. Here is just a sampling of some of the opinions that prominent authors hold on this subject:

- Alain Silver, in his introduction to his *Film Noir Reader,* and Paul Schrader, in his 1972 "Notes on Film Noir," say that it began in 1941 with *The Maltese Falcon* and ended in 1958 with *Touch of Evil.*

- Michael Stephens (*Film Noir: A Comprehensive Illustrated Reference to Movies, Terms, and Persons*) believes that *Stranger on the Third Floor* (1940) was "the first true film noir" and that "film noir has never really gone away, but evolved into new sub-genres."

- Forster Hirsch states in *The Dark Side of the Screen* that the most sensible view has film noir "extending from the early forties to the late fifties."

- Lee Server, in his introduction to *Hard-Boiled (Great Lines from Classic Noir Films)* by Peggy Thompson and Saeko Usukawa, points to *Citizen Kane* (1941) and *The Maltese Falcon* (1941) as the "true catalysts for the genre." (The authors, though, include a line from 1940's *Stranger on the Third Floor.*) Server has the classic period ending with *Touch of Evil* and *Vertigo* (both 1958).

- Paul Duncan, in *Film Noir: Films of Trust and Betrayal*, says that the film noir classic period ran from 1940 through 1960, but none of the more than 500 films he lists are from 1960.

- David N. Meyer (*A Girl and a Gun: The Complete Guide to Film Noir on Video*) believes the classic period began with *The Maltese Falcon* (1941) and ended with *Touch of Evil* (1958)

- Spencer Selby, in *Dark City: The Film Noir*, says the classic period started with *Rebecca* (1940) and ended with *Odds Against Tomorrow* (1959).

• Arthur Lyons, in *Death on the Cheap: The Lost B Movies of Film Noir!* believes that "1939 was actually the year that inaugurated the film noir with the release of three prototypical films: *Let Us Live, Rio* and *Blind Alley.*"

In any event, for roughly twenty years, from the early 1940s to the late 1950s, Hollywood churned out these new and unusual crime dramas, psychological thrillers and "women's melodramas," which in the 1970s were finally labeled as "films noirs."

In *Film Noir Guide*, I have gone with the 1940–59 scenario (sometimes called the classic period), giving the benefit of the doubt to such 1940 films as *Angels Over Broadway, City for Conquest, The Letter, Rebecca, Stranger on the Third Floor* and *They Drive by Night* and such 1959 films as *The Crimson Kimono, The Beat Generation, The Last Mile* and *Odds Against Tomorrow*. Films noirs made after 1959 have been referred to by some film historians and critics as "post-noirs" and "neo-noirs" and include *Cape Fear* (1961), *Death Wish* (1974), *Dog Day Afternoon* (1975), *The Postman Always Rings Twice* (1981), *Internal Affairs* (1990), *Reservoir Dogs* (1992) and many others. Many of the post- or neo-noirs were made by directors whose intention was to create a film noir. Not so during the classic period, when money restraints were the reasons for the dark sets (this way the viewer couldn't tell how cheap they really were), and when the technological advances in cinematography allowed more inventive and creative camerawork and on-location, outdoor shooting, which allowed for the more realistic urban settings.

The films I have included in this book are from the classic period. I collected the titles from various sources—the films noirs covered by the authors mentioned above, those of other authors listed in the Bibliography, some Internet lists, personal recommendations, films advertised by video dealers as films noirs, and films described by film historians and critics as being in "the noir style." Some purists may disagree with some of my inclusions. I'm not too convinced about a few of them myself, but I've tried to include everything that a reasonable person might consider a genuine film noir. I have included an assortment of genres (crime, thriller, suspense, Western, adventure, horror, melodrama and even one science fiction, *Invasion of the Body Snatchers*) because I agree with the theory that film noir is essentially a style that can be fit into any genre.

There were many obscure B films that I wanted to include but couldn't because I was unable to find them in time, and my goal was to view each film personally before writing about it. (The film noir collector should not miss Appendix D, where I give some hints on how to build an affordable film noir library.)

While film noir was highly influenced by European filmmakers who fled Europe before and during World War II, the film noir is mostly an American art form. Of the 745 films in *Film Noir Guide*, 699 are American-made. Because they can be obtained easily by the determined fan, and for variety, I've included some foreign-made films noirs—thirty-three British, three French, four Italian, one Canadian and one Japanese—and a few joint ventures (i.e., U.S.–French, U.S.–Danish and U.S.–Italian).

Each writeup contains the title of the film, its release date, the main performers (not necessarily in the original credits order), the screenwriter(s) (not including those credited with "additional dialogue" or "contributions"), the director(s), the type of noir (my own highly subjective classification — see Appendix B), the film's thematic content, and a rating based on the familiar five-star system:

> ★ = Poor (for the die-hard film noir fan only)
> ★★ = Fair
> ★★★ = Good
> ★★★★ = Very Good
> ★★★★★ = Excellent

I've used half-stars to help give some distinction to the definitions.

In the main body of the writeup, I describe the plot, without divulging the ending, and comment on the quality of the acting from my own (again, highly subjective) point of view. I make no pretense at analyzing a film, trying to find some hidden meaning that the director or writer may never have had in mind.

Within the writeup, a title in **bold italics** indicates a film that has its own entry in the book.

Two additional features follow many of the reviews—"Familiar Faces from Television" and "Memorable Noir Moment."

Under the former, I include sightings of actors and actresses (usually in minor or bit roles) who went on to star or play in television series. For instance, Ray Teal, the sheriff in the long-running TV western *Bonanza*, appears in thirty-five of the films reviewed in *Film Noir Guide*, usually typecast as a uniformed cop. I didn't notice him in all thirty-five films because some of his roles were so minor that if you blinked an eye you'd miss him. But I managed to spot him in twenty-six of them. Some of the other performers you might recognize are Billy Gray (Bud in *Father Knows Best*), Ellen Corby (Grandma Walton in *The Waltons*), Frank Cady from *Petticoat Junction* and *Green Acres*, and even Jay North (*Dennis the Menace*). While I know I missed many familiar faces while viewing these 745 films noirs, I did manage to sight some whose names are not to be found on any cast list.

Under "Memorable Noir Moment," I've described scenes that I thought were either interesting or humorous and that reflected the noirish character of the film. I've also included some negative features (e.g., Hollywood's stereotypical portrayal of women and minorities) that, unfortunately, were not limited to films noirs but were commonplace in the films of the forties and fifties. If a film writeup doesn't include a memorable noir moment, it may be because that mentioning it would ruin the ending for the viewer, or because I may not have picked up on a particularly interesting scene, even in some of the better films. Some of the highlights I've included may not seem particularly interesting or humorous to some viewers. If that's the case, all I can say is, you had to be there.

At the end of the book are four appendices that I hope will be of some interest to the reader:

• Appendix A contains a list of films noirs by director.

• Appendix B is a list of the films by "Film Noir Type." This is my attempt to classify the films in order to help fans who want to find a movie that is similar to one they have seen and enjoyed. It was a difficult and highly subjective task because many of the noirs could fit easily into two and sometimes three types. (For example, *I Confess*, which I classified as a "Religion" noir, would also fit easily into the "Wrong Man" category. *Kansas City Confidential* would fare equally well in the "Heist" or "Troubled Veteran" categories).

• Appendix C contains the films noirs sorted by date.

• Appendix D gives some hints on how to build an affordable film noir video library.

There is also an annotated bibliography of recommended reading for fan and serious student alike.

In the following pages, the reader will find the largest collection of films noirs from the classic period to be included in a single volume (as of this writing). There were no "contributors" who watched and submitted reviews. I viewed each of the book's 745 films, and I enjoyed the experience tremendously—from the eleven films noirs that are on the American Film Institute's List of America's 100 Greatest Movies* to the one-star noirs that could only be described as "bombs." I hope you'll enjoy reading about them all.

I look forward to and invite reader comments (send them in care of the publisher). Feel free to disagree with me as to whether or not a film should be considered noir, to complain about an unreasonable rating, to point out any errors or glaring omissions or, best of all, to let me know that you enjoyed the book.

---

*Films noirs that made AFI's List of America's 100 Greatest Movies are *Citizen Kane* (#1), *Casablanca* (#2), *On the Waterfront* (#8), *Sunset Blvd.* (#12), *The Maltese Falcon* (#23), *The Treasure of the Sierra Madre* (#30), *Double Indemnity* (#38), *Rear Window* (#42), *The Third Man* (#57), *Vertigo* (#61) and *A Place in the Sun* (#92).

THE FILMS

Abandoned (1949) 79 min. Dennis O'Keefe, Gale Storm, Jeff Chandler, Raymond Burr, Marjorie Rambeau, Will Kuluva, Mike Mazurki. **Screenplay by:** Irwin Gielgud. **Directed by:** Joseph M. Newman. **Noir Type:** Undercover. **Noir Themes:** Social reform, woman in jeopardy, child in jeopardy. ★★★

A small-town Pennsylvania girl (Storm) arrives in Los Angeles looking for her missing sister, who recently had an illegitimate baby (did that really happen in 1949?). Unfortunately, the sister turns up in the morgue and the baby has disappeared. Storm and newspaper reporter O'Keefe, teamed up to find the killers, stumble across an infant-for-sale gang led by a pair of evil baby brokers (Rambeau and Kuluva). The amateur detectives turn over the information they have collected to a sympathetic cop (Chandler) who initiates a sting operation, using as bait a pregnant girl from a Salvation Army home and O'Keefe and Storm as potential adopters. Burr is terrific as usual, this time playing a shady but nervous P.I. ("I'd have been just as happy if we committed our murders in a state that doesn't have capital punishment"). There's only a little action, notably when Kuluva's goon (noir veteran Mazurki) takes on Burr, but it's still a fast-moving crime drama.

Familiar Faces from Television:
❏ Billy Gray (Bud in *Father Knows Best*) as a tough little kid in the park.
❏ Jeanette Nolan (Annette Devereaux of the *Hotel de Paree* and Holly Grainger in *The Virginian*) as a major in the Salvation Army.

Memorable Noir Moments:
❏ O'Keefe doubts Burr's sincerity about going straight. "You going legitimate," he says, "is like a vulture going vegetarian."
❏ Kuluva, losing patience with the arrogant Burr, warns him, "There's a rumor going around town that I'm getting soft. Whenever that happens, I always cut a couple of throats just to prove a point."

Accomplice (1946) 66 min. Richard Arlen, Veda Ann Borg, Tom Dugan, Archie Twitchell, Earle Hodgins. **Screenplay by:** Irving Elman and Frank Gruber. **Directed by:** Walter Colmes. **Noir Type:** Missing Person. **Noir Themes:** Betrayal, greed, corruption. ★½

A bookworm P.I. (Arlen) is hired by his ex-fiancée (Borg) to find her missing husband, a banker who she says has been known to suffer from amnesia. Figuring that the old guy has probably embezzled bank funds and run off with a girlfriend, Arlen investigates. A couple of murders later, he begins to realize that there are more holes in Borg's story than in a wedge of Swiss cheese. Dugan plays Arlen's wise-cracking employee, and Twitchell and Hodgins are yokel lawmen. Cheaply and badly made, this B film does, however, boast of a spectacular castle in the middle of the Arizona desert that serves as a hideout for crooks on the lam.

Memorable Noir Moment:
❑ Arlen takes aim with a rifle and misses two bad guys on the other side of the room, but later turns sharpshooter, picking off two others hundreds of feet away.

The Accused (1948) 101 min. Loretta Young, Robert Cummings, Wendell Corey, Sam Jaffe, Douglas Dick. **Screenplay by:** Ketti Frings. **Directed by:** William Dieterle. **Noir Type:** Cover-Up. **Noir Themes:** Sexual hostility, paranoia, guilt. ★★★½

Young plays a spinster college professor who, in a state of panic, clobbers a student (Dick) when he gets a bit too frisky at a secluded spot overlooking the ocean.

A psychology professor (Loretta Young) fights off a student (Douglas Dick) who is making some overly aggressive romantic moves in *The Accused* (Paramount, 1949).

Checking herself in a moment of unexpected passion, she grabs an iron pipe and beans Dick about five or six times and then tries to make it look like a diving accident. Coincidentally, the student's uncle (Cummings) shows up the next day to talk with Young about his nephew's scholastic difficulties and also becomes romantically interested in her. When Dick's body is discovered, homicide detective Corey (who, believe it or not, also has designs on Young) begins an exhaustive investigation that eventually points to the professor. This is a compelling though slow-moving drama, with Young excellent as the conscience-stricken killer trapped in her own cover-up. Jaffe's portrayal of an insensitive police scientist is enjoyable, and Corey, as a cop with a guilt complex about his own investigative tactics, gives his usual solid performance.

Memorable Noir Moment:

❑ Sensitivity Training Required: When Corey becomes annoyed because Young keeps interrupting his interrogation of a student, Cummings helpfully explains that Young, after all, is a psychology professor. Unimpressed, Corey replies, "Does that make her any less gabby than most women?"

Accused of Murder (1956) 74 min. David Brian, Vera Ralston, Warren Stevens, Lee Van Cleef, Virginia Grey, Sidney Blackmer, Frank Puglia. **Screenplay by:** Bob Williams and W.R.

A homicide detective (David Brian) arrests a hit man (Warren Stevens) in *Accused of Murder* (Republic Pictures, 1956).

Burnett. **Directed by**: Joseph Kane. **Noir Type**: Hit Man. **Noir Themes**: Victim of fate, woman in jeopardy, obsession. ★★

Brian is a homicide detective investigating the shooting death of a crooked lawyer (Blackmer). Brian's partner (Van Cleef) believes that the lawyer's girlfriend, nightclub singer Ralston, is the killer, but Brian, smitten with the suspect, downplays Van Cleef's suspicions. Meanwhile, a hit man (Stevens) has been spotted leaving the scene of the crime by an over-the-hill barfly (Grey) who sees an opportunity to shake him down and make a few bucks. Big mistake. This B noir sounds exciting but don't be fooled. It's for the patient noir enthusiast only. Brian was TV's *Mr. District Attorney*, and Stevens was the star of the adventure series *Tales of the 77th Bengal Lancers*.

Familiar Faces from Television:
❑ Victor Sen Yung (Hop Sing in *Bonanza*) as a gangster's house servant.
❑ Barry Kelley (Harry Morgan's boss in *Pete and Gladys*) as a police captain.
❑ Robert Shayne (Inspector Henderson in *The Adventures of Superman*) as a hospital surgeon.

Memorable Noir Moments:
❑ A doctor diagnoses a suspect's gunshot wound as "only a flesh wound, nothing to worry about." See also *Jail Bait*, *Guilty Bystander*, *The Enforcer*, *New York Confidential*, *Riot in Cell Block 11* and *Sleep, My Love*.
❑ Grey, in her first attempt at blackmailing Stevens, receives a hundred-dollar bill down her blouse and a terrific right cross that would flatten a prizefighter. She fares even worse in her second try.
❑ When Brian shows up to arrest Stevens for pummeling Grey, the hit man is flabbergasted: "That tramp. That dirty little tramp. She's still alive. She must have a head like an anvil."

Ace in the Hole *see* The Big Carnival

An Act of Murder (1948) 91 min. Fredric March, Edmond O'Brien, Florence Eldridge, Geraldine Brooks, Stanley Ridges. **Screenplay by**: Michael Blankfort and Robert Thoeren. **Directed by**: Michael Gordon. **Noir Type**: Trial. **Noir Themes**: Fatalism, guilt. ★★★½

When a no-nonsense judge (March), a "talking law book," learns that his loving wife (Eldridge) of twenty years is suffering from a painful and fatal disease, he helps her along with a mercy killing. After turning himself in, the depressed judge finds himself standing in the shoes of those he's so apathetically sentenced over the years. Acting as his own lawyer, March decides to plead guilty to first degree murder. But an upstart young attorney (O'Brien)—who is also the boyfriend of the judge's daughter (Brooks)—convinces the court to allow him to represent March. Outstanding performances (especially by March and Eldridge as the loving couple) and an intelligent, sensitively written script make this tearjerker noir one that you won't want to miss.

Familiar Faces from Television:
❑ John McIntire (Lt. Dan Muldoon in *Naked City* and Chris Hale in *Wagon Train*) as the judge in March's trial.
❑ Ray Teal (Sheriff Roy Coffee in *Bonanza*) as a consulting physician.

Act of Violence (1949) 82 min. Van Heflin, Robert Ryan, Janet Leigh, Mary Astor, Phyllis Thaxter, Berry Kroeger. **Screenplay by:** Robert L. Richards. **Directed by:** Fred Zinnemann. **Noir Type:** Troubled Veteran. **Noir Themes:** Revenge, guilt, paranoia. ★★★★½

Heflin, a war veteran and pillar of the community, has a dark secret. While a prisoner in a German P.O.W. camp, he betrayed his men's escape plans. Believing he would be saving lives, he instead caused his friends to be bayoneted by German soldiers and left for dead. Of the eleven escapees, only the disabled Ryan has survived and now he's out for revenge. Heflin's wife (Leigh), though shocked by her husband's past, stands by her man, and Ryan's girl (Thaxter) tries in vain to convince hers to give up his deadly mission. Astor is excellent as the whore with a heart who, in a misguided attempt to help Heflin, unwittingly hooks him up with a vicious hit man (Kroeger). Heflin gives a bravura performance as the guilt-ridden veteran who seeks redemption in a final act of atonement, and Ryan is convincingly sinister as the limping, avenging angel. A film noir classic.

Familiar Face from Television:

❏ Connie Gilchrist (Purity, pub proprietress and girlfriend of *Long John Silver*) as Heflin's next door neighbor.

Memorable Noir Moment:

❏ Astor's "lawyer" friend gives Heflin some questionable advice about how to handle Ryan: "Get rid of this guy. Be sorry later."

Affair in Havana (1957) 71 min. John Cassavetes, Raymond Burr, Sara Shane. **Screenplay by:** Burton Lane and Maurice Zimm. **Directed by:** Laslo Benedek. **Noir Type:** Triangle. **Noir Themes:** Greed, betrayal, jealousy, guilt. ★½

Cassavetes, an American jazz musician working in a pre–Castro Havana nightclub, falls in love with Shane, wife of a crippled sugar plantation owner (Burr). Burr, who has hired a private eye to obtain evidence of their affair, threatens to divorce Shane and leave her penniless unless she drops Cassavetes. With twenty million dollars at stake, Shane, who was responsible for the boating accident that confined Burr to a wheelchair, must choose between her lover and her husband's riches. But then again, maybe she can have both. Only the presence of noir icon Burr (getting in some good practice for his future role of the wheelchair-bound TV detective *Ironside*) makes this boring melodrama tolerable. Salsa fans, look for Celia Cruz, the Queen of Latin Music, as a singer at Burr's annual fiesta.

Affair in Trinidad (1952) 98 min. Rita Hayworth, Glenn Ford, Alexander Scourby, Steven Geray. **Screenplay by:** James Gunn and Oscar Saul. **Directed by:** Vincent Sherman. **Noir Type:** Undercover. **Noir Themes:** Obsession, jealousy, revenge. ★★½

The *Gilda* crew (Hayworth, Ford and Geray) reunites in this minor film noir. Ford arrives in Trinidad days after his brother has been murdered, just in time to hear the coroner declare the death a suicide. He doesn't buy it. He meets his sister-in-law, nightclub dancer Hayworth, for the first time and suspects that she may have been involved in her husband's death. But, with his brother in the grave less than a week, he gives in to temptation and starts romancing her. Unbeknownst to Ford, however, Hayworth is working undercover for the British police to find out more about a nefarious international rogue (Scourby). While playing amateur detective, she finds herself embroiled in a hotbed of spies and Nazis. This was supposed to be Hayworth's comeback film after a four-year screen hiatus, during which she ran around with, married and eventually divorced Aly Khan, playboy son of the Aga Kahn, the spiritual leader of millions of Moslems.

Memorable Noir Moment:

❑ The American ambassador catches Hayworth's sexy act just before delivering the bad news that she's a widow. "Why would a man kill himself," he wonders aloud, during a moment of understandable indecorum, "when he had…" A disapproving glance from the British chief inspector abruptly silences him.

Alias Nick Beal (1949) 92 min. Ray Milland, Audrey Totter, Thomas Mitchell, Geraldine Wall, George Macready. **Screenplay by:** Jonathan Latimer. **Directed by:** John Farrow. **Noir Type:** Fantasy. **Noir Themes:** Character deterioration, betrayal, guilt. ★★★★

A resolute D.A. (Mitchell) swears that he would sell his soul for the opportunity to convict a slippery crime lord. The Devil (Milland), using the alias Nick Beal, arrives on the scene to lend a helping hand, miraculously supplying Mitchell with the evidence he needs for a conviction, which earns Mitchell his party's gubernatorial nomination. Still unaware of Milland's identity, Mitchell allows him to run his campaign and to forge an alliance with unscrupulous politicians who deliver the votes Mitchell needs to win the election. Meanwhile, the double-crossing Devil has enlisted a down-and-out hooker (Totter) to help destroy Mitchell's reputation and his happy marriage to Wall. Events culminate in murder and the inevitable showdown between good, represented by a Protestant minister (Macready), and evil. Topnotch performances by Milland as the seemingly amiable prince of darkness, Totter as the softhearted femme fatale and Macready, who is delightfully cast against type, make this film noir oddity a must-see.

Familiar Faces from Television:

❑ King Donovan (Harvey Helm in *Love That Bob* and Herb Thornton in *Please Don't Eat the Daisies*) as an assistant district attorney.
❑ Darryl Hickman (Darvey in *The Many Loves of Dobie Gillis* and Ben Canfield in *The Americans*) as a juvenile delinquent.
❑ Fred Clark (Harry Morton in *The George Burns and Gracie Allen Show*) as a dishonest political bigwig.
❑ Percy Helton (Homer Cratchit in *The Beverly Hillbillies*), always the toady, as one of the Devil's henchmen.

Memorable Noir Moments:

❑ While passing a religious street gathering, Milland and Mitchell hear a former wrestler give his testimony about defeating the Devil. "I've pinned his shoulders to the mat," the man boasts, causing Milland to smile and comment, "I wonder if he knows it's two falls out of three."
❑ Plagued by a guilty conscience, Mitchell reacts to his wife's call to honesty. "You're not a wife," he snaps. "You're a missionary!"

Alimony (1949) 71 min. Martha Vickers, John Beal, Hillary Brooke, Laurie Lind, Douglass Dumbrille. **Screenplay by:** Lawrence Lipton, George Bricker and Sherman L. Lowe. **Directed by:** Alfred Zeisler. **Noir Type:** Femme Fatale. **Noir Themes:** Betrayal, obsession, greed. ★

Vickers is a callous, ambitious beauty who hooks up with a shady lawyer (Dumbrille) and an ex-model (Lind) in a scheme to photograph wealthy husbands in sexual dalliances and split the eventual alimony awards with the men's greedy wives. Between suckers, Vickers seduces a struggling songwriter (Beal) away from his fiancée (Brooke). She thinks he's about to hit the big time but quickly drops him when his big deal falls through. With his tail between his legs, Beal crawls back to the forgiving Brooke, who marries him and soon becomes pregnant. But when one of Beal's songs climbs the charts, Vickers shows up again; the blockhead composer is putty in her femme fatale hands. A real bomb.

Familiar Faces from Television:
❑ Leonid Kinskey (Pierre in *The People's Choice*) as Beal's agent.
❑ Harry Lauter (Jim Herrick in *Waterfront*) as the hospital intern treating Vickers.

All My Sons (1948) 93 min. Edward G. Robinson, Burt Lancaster, Mady Christians, Louisa Horton, Howard Duff, Frank Conroy. **Screenplay by:** Chester Erskine. **Directed by:** Irving Reis. **Noir Type:** Cover-Up. **Noir Themes:** Betrayal, fatalism, guilt, paranoia. ★★★½

War veteran Lancaster plans on marrying his brother's former fiancée (Horton) despite opposition from his mother (Christians), who unrealistically expects her other son, who's been missing in action for three years, to show up alive and well. Complicating things is the suspicion that Lancaster's father (Robinson) may have knowingly provided the war effort with defective airplane parts, resulting in a number of American casualties, a crime for which Horton's father (Conroy), Robinson's business partner, is serving time in a federal penitentiary. Horton's embittered brother (Duff) is determined to prevent her from marrying into the family he believes is responsible for their father's imprisonment. Lancaster, meanwhile, is beginning to have doubts about his father's innocence, and swears that he will kill him if he finds out he's guilty. Based on the play by Arthur Miller, *All My Sons* still packs an impressive punch thanks to dynamic performances by Robinson and Lancaster.

Familiar Faces from Television:
❑ Harry Morgan (Col. Potter in *M*A*S*H*) as Robinson's neighbor.
❑ Elisabeth Fraser (Sgt. Joan Hogan in *The Phil Silvers Show*) as Morgan's wife.
❑ Lloyd Gough (crime reporter Mike Axford in *The Green Hornet*) as Robinson's family doctor.
❑ Arlene Francis (long-time panelist on *What's My Line?*) as the doctor's wife.

Memorable Noir Moment:
❑ Family doctor Gough dispenses a noirish prescription for the severely depressed Robinson and Christians: "Sleep's a wonderful thing — best thing about living."

All That Money Can Buy *see* **The Devil and Daniel Webster**

All the King's Men (1949) 109 min. Broderick Crawford, John Ireland, Joanne Dru, Mercedes McCambridge, John Derek, Shepperd Strudwick, Anne Seymour. **Screenplay by:** Robert Rossen. **Directed by:** Robert Rossen. **Noir Type:** Politics. **Noir Themes:** Corruption, betrayal, revenge. ★★★★★

"Well, I guess that's the end of Willie Stark." Newspaper reporter Ireland proves a poor psychic after inept politician Crawford loses a local election. Honest and well intentioned, the charismatic yokel bounces back, clawing his way up the ladder of small town politics to the governor's mansion of his unnamed southern state and, along the way, succumbing to the usual temptations of power. Ireland falls under Crawford's spell and quits his job in protest when his newspaper withdraws its support for the gubernatorial candidate. He lands a position with Crawford's campaign and, after the election, becomes part of his staff. Meanwhile, Ireland's girl (Dru) has an affair with the governor, while Crawford's assistant (McCambridge) seethes with jealousy and rage. Crawford's wife (Seymour) by now has developed a bad case of apathy, even as her rebellious son (Derek) seems determined to ruin the his father's career. Strudwick plays Dru's physician brother, who cracks under the political and emotional strain. Based on the Pulitzer Prize–winning novel by Robert Penn Warren, which, in turn, was inspired by the rise and fall of Governor Huey Long of Louisiana, this classic film won an Academy Award for Best Picture. Crawford's great performance won him the award for Best Actor, and McCambridge, in her film debut, won for Best Supporting Actress.

Familiar Faces from Television:
❏ Paul Ford (Sgt. Bilko's befuddled commanding officer Colonel Hall in *The Phil Silvers Show*) as a state legislator.
❏ King Donovan (Bob Cummings' Air Force buddy Harvey Helm in *Love That Bob* and lawyer Herb Thornton in *Please Don't Eat the Daisies*) as a reporter.

Memorable Noir Moment:
❏ When candidate Crawford offers to hire Ireland at four hundred dollars a month, the impressed ex-reporter comments, "You throw money around like it was money."

The Amazing Mr. X (1948) 78 min. Turhan Bey, Lynn Bari, Cathy O'Donnell, Richard Carlson. **Screenplay by:** Muriel Roy Bolton and Ian McClellan Hunter. **Directed by:** Bernard Vorhaus. **Noir Type:** Con Artist. **Noir Themes:** Woman in jeopardy, betrayal. ★★★

Bey is a fake psychic who preys on lonely people wishing to contact their dear departed loved ones. A widow (Bari) who has been hearing her dead husband's voice seeks Bey's help instead of a psychiatrist's. Her worried younger sister (O'Donnell) joins Bari's fiancé (Carlson) in a plan to expose the charlatan but eventually falls in love with him. A well acted and engaging little film, also known as *The Spiritualist*, its opening sequences are genuinely frightening and guaranteed to cause goose bumps.

Memorable Noir Moment:
❏ Huckster Bey gives his accomplice an economics lesson on how inflation has forced him to raise the price of his three-dollar crystal balls from twenty-five to fifty dollars.

A seductress (Susan Hayward) and a psychopath (Albert Dekker) team up in *Among the Living* (Paramount, 1941).

Among the Living (1941) 68 min. Albert Dekker, Susan Hayward, Harry Carey, Frances Farmer. **Screenplay by:** Lester Cole and Garrett Fort. **Directed by:** Stuart Heisler. **Noir Type:** Good twin–bad twin. **Noir Themes:** Paranoia, guilt, greed, corruption. ★★★★

Dekker plays a dual role in this suspenseful thriller about a man who arrives home for his father's funeral only to find that his twin brother, who he thought had died at age 10, is alive and insane and a prisoner in the basement of their rundown mansion. Carey is the family doctor who, at the request of the boys' wealthy father, had falsified the boy's death certificate in return for a contribution to build a local medical center. When the lunatic escapes after killing a family servant, Carey convinces the sane brother to remain silent until they can find and institutionalize the killer. Unfortunately, the killings continue and the townspeople are beginning to get nervous. Hayward plays a flirtatious and greedy nymph who has hooked onto the psychopath, and Farmer is the sane brother's wife. Fast-paced, well-acted (Dekker is terrific) and beautifully photographed, this early noir is a classic.

Memorable Noir Moment:

❑ You'll forget all about Jason Voorhees and Michael Myers when you witness the wild-eyed Paul Raden (Dekker) chasing a terrified bargirl through the town's shadowy alleys.

Femme fatale Jean Simmons makes a play for ambulance driver Robert Mitchum in *Angel Face* (RKO, 1953).

Angel Face (1953) 91 min. Robert Mitchum, Jean Simmons, Herbert Marshall, Mona Freeman, Barbara O'Neil, Leon Ames, Kenneth Tobey. **Screenplay by:** Frank Nugent and Oscar Millard. **Directed by:** Otto Preminger. **Noir Type:** Femme Fatale. **Noir Themes:** Obsession, betrayal, jealousy. ★★★½

When casting directors needed someone who could play a handsome but gullible sucker for a dame, did they always check first to see if Bob Mitchum was available? (See especially *Out of the Past* and *Where Danger Lives*, which is remarkably similar to this film.) Simmons plays a psychologically disturbed young woman who hates her rich stepmother (O'Neil) so much that she attempts to murder her. The attractive psychopath then becomes involved with ambulance driver Mitchum and hires him as the family chauffeur. The two begin a torrid relationship, causing Mitchum's usually understanding girlfriend (Freeman) to drop him and start seeing his friend (Tobey). Meanwhile, Mitchum begins to suspect that Simmons isn't all there and decides (too late) to end their relationship. By then, nothing can stop Simmons' evil plans, and the poor sap ends up an unwilling accomplice to murder. Cast against type, Simmons is excellent as the unbalanced femme fatale, and Mitchum gives his usual standout, low-key performance. *Angel Face* gives us not one but two sensational car crashes and an extraordinary ending that will leave you shaking your heads over the unfairness of life.

Familiar Face from Television:

❑ Jim Backus (Thurston Howell III of *Gilligan's Island*) as the D.A.

Memorable Noir Moment:

❑ Sensitivity Training Required: A juror questions an expert witness on the difficulty of rigging an automobile so that it's always in reverse. "Can anyone do it?" he asks. "Even a woman?"

Angela (1955-Italian) 81 min. Dennis O'Keefe, Mara Lane, Rossano Brazzi, Arnoldo Foa. **Screenplay by:** Jonathan Rix and Edoardo Anton. **Directed by:** Dennis O'Keefe. **Noir Type:** Femme Fatale. **Noir Themes:** Betrayal, obsession. ★★

This Italian-made cheapie stars O'Keefe as an American G.I. who remained in Italy after the war to manage a car dealership. After falling in love with a voluptuous secretary (Lane), he soon finds himself trying to dispose of her boss' body after the man evidently dies of a heart attack in her apartment. After placing the body in the trunk of the wrong car and watching helplessly as Lane drives away with it, O'Keefe tries to rectify the situation, but police inspector Foa and Lane's husband (Brazzi) have different plans for him. O'Keefe is okay as the American patsy, as is Italian romantic lead Brazzi as Lane's sadistic husband, but the all-too-familiar plot doesn't make the grade.

Angels Over Broadway (1940) 78 min. Douglas Fairbanks, Jr., Rita Hayworth, Thomas Mitchell, John Qualen. **Screenplay by:** Ben Hecht. **Directed by:** Ben Hecht and Lee Garmes. **Noir Type:** Comedy. **Noir Themes:** Fatalism, greed, betrayal. ★★★½

Fairbanks is a penniless hustler who mistakes a suicidal embezzler (Qualen) for a rich mark. Hayworth is a showgirl wannabe with a big heart, and Mitchell is a former Pulitzer Prize playwright whose recent literary failures have driven him to the bottle. The three concoct a dangerous plan to place Qualen in a crooked poker game with dangerous hoods so he can win enough money to pay back the three grand he embezzled from his boss and avoid a prison term. This is an enjoyable film thanks to screenwriter Hecht's snappy dialogue and solid performances by the three "angels." Fairbanks and Hayworth have just the right amount of chemistry, and Mitchell is excellent as the witty, inebriated playwright. Qualen nicely underplays his role as the meek, cuckolded husband with suicidal tendencies. Look for screenwriter Hecht in a cameo as a night court judge.

Memorable Noir Moments:
❏ Sensitivity Training Required: Penniless Fairbanks lectures an equally broke Hayworth: "I used to be like you — two bits and I'd start bowing like a Chinaman."
❏ When Fairbanks compliments Hayworth, the surprised beauty asks, "You're not trying to make love to me, by any chance?" The suave con man replies, "Listen, baby, when I start making love to you, it won't be any guessing game."

Another Man's Poison (1951-British) 91 min. Bette Davis, Gary Merrill, Emlyn Williams, Anthony Steel. **Screenplay by:** Val Guest. **Directed by:** Irving Rapper. **Noir Type:** Femme Fatale. **Noir Themes:** Betrayal, jealousy, distrust, paranoia. ★★★½

Davis is a British mystery writer who poisons her estranged husband with a healthy dose of horse medicine when he shows up at her Yorkshire estate, on the run after killing a guard during a flubbed bank robbery. When his accomplice (Merrill) arrives a little later, he helps Davis dispose of the body and then blackmails her into pretending that *he's* her husband so that he'll have a place to hide out until the heat's off. Complicating things, Davis' secretary returns unexpectedly with her fiancé (Steel), who is also Davis' lover, causing the already desperate Merrill to become dangerously agitated. Davis has had just about enough of the fugitive when he does the unimaginable, killing her favorite horse. Davis is sensational as the scheming murderess and seems to be having fun with the role. Merrill, her real-life husband at the time, is good as the unfortunate bank robber who makes the mistake of messing with the wrong femme. The ending is delightfully ironic.

Memorable Noir Moment:
❏ When Merrill sarcastically suggests that a chair under the doorknob of their adjoining bedrooms might work better than a lock, Davis responds, "A man who knows his place is better than either of them."

Apology for Murder (1945) 67 min. Ann Savage, Hugh Beaumont, Charles D. Brown, Russell Hicks, Pierre Watkin. **Screenplay by:** Fred Myton. **Directed by:** Sam Newfield. **Noir Type:** Femme Fatale. **Noir Themes:** Lust, betrayal, guilt, character deterioration. ★½

This *Double Indemnity* clone stars Savage as the greedy wife of a wealthy older man (Hicks). She latches on to a happy-go-lucky newspaper reporter (*Leave it to Beaver*'s Beaumont) and convinces him to help her do away with her husband, who she claims is going to divorce her and leave her without a cent. Sucker Beaumont is initially appalled but eventually takes to the idea, killing Hicks and trying to make it look like a car accident. But not only is Beaumont a sucker, he's dimwitted, too. Pushing Hicks' car over a cliff, he forgets to turn on the ignition and put the car in gear, causing cops to conclude it's a homicide. Beaumont's wily editor (Brown) smells a story and assigns Beaumont to cover Hicks' death. Straying a bit from *Double*

Indemnity, cops arrest Hicks' business associate (Watkin), who is quickly convicted and sentenced to hang. Remorseful, Beaumont turns to the bottle, while his sociopathic lover turns to the lawyer she hired to contest her husband's will. Savage doesn't approach her gritty performance in *Detour*, and Beaumont is much too Ward Cleaver–ish to be believable. There are plenty of good reasons why everyone remembers *Double Indemnity* and few people have ever heard of *Apology for Murder*.

Memorable Noir Moment:

❑ When Savage teases Beaumont about not being able to get a human-interest story from her stodgy husband, the flirtatious reporter says, "I'm human and plenty interested."

Appointment with Danger (1951) 89 min. Alan Ladd, Phyllis Calvert, Paul Stewart, Jan Sterling, Jack Webb, Henry (Harry) Morgan. **Screenplay by:** Richard Breen and Warren Duff. **Directed by:** Lewis Allen. **Noir Type:** Undercover. **Noir Themes:** Greed, paranoia, woman in jeopardy. ★★★

Ladd plays a hard-as-nails postal inspector trying to find the hoods who strangled one of his colleagues. His search leads him to a nun (Calvert) who witnessed the murder and can identify the killers (Webb and Morgan), henchmen of gangster Stewart. Ladd, pretending to be on the take, infiltrates Stewart's gang and becomes

An undercover G-Man (Alan Ladd) talks with a gangster's moll (Jan Sterling) in *Appointment with Danger* (Paramount, 1951).

involved in their plan to rob a mail truck of a million dollars. Ladd is excellent as the cynical G-man with a reputation for being cold and impersonal, and Sterling is enjoyable as Stewart's sympathetic, beebop loving moll. Webb's performance as the psychopathic hit man, however, is the highlight of this violent film noir. Webb and Morgan also appeared in 1950's **Dark City** and co-starred from 1967 to 1970 as in the hit TV series *Dragnet*.

Familiar Face from Television:
❑ Ann Tyrrell (Vi in *Private Secretary* and Olive in *The Ann Sothern Show*) as a secretary.

Memorable Noir Moments:
❑ A resourceful killer uses a bronzed baby shoe to bludgeon a victim. See *C-Man* for another murderous innovation.
❑ When a colleague accuses Ladd of not knowing what love is, the tough cop replies, "Sure I do. It's something that goes on between a man and a forty-five that doesn't jam."
❑ Ladd agrees with the suggestion that he doesn't have a heart. "When a cop dies," he says, "they don't list it as heart failure. It's charley horse of the chest."

Armored Car Robbery (1950) 67 min. Charles McGraw, William Talman, Adele Jergens, Steve Brodie, Don McGuire, Douglas Fowley, Gene Evans. **Screenplay by**: Earl Felton

Gang members (Gene Evans, left and Steve Brodie) look on as their wounded partner (Douglas Fowley) gets the drop on the gang's double-crossing mastermind (William Talman) in *Armored Car Robbery* (RKO, 1950).

and Gerald Drayson Adams. **Directed by:** Richard Fleischer. **Noir Type:** Heist. **Noir Themes:** Greed, Lust, betrayal. ★★★★

McGraw and Talman give standout performances in this early heist noir, which was released the same day as its more famous noir cousin, *The Asphalt Jungle*. Talman, a vicious killer, is the brains behind the planned heist of an armored car during its stop at Chicago's Wrigley Field. Fowley, Brodie and Evans are his accomplices. Things go wrong (as they inevitably do in a noir heist) and one of the gang is wounded in a shoot-out with police detective McGraw and his partner, who is killed by Talman. The robbers get away, but there's dissension over the split and (surprise!) Talman winds up with all of the dough. In an attempt to trap the cop killer, McGraw and his new partner (McGuire) stake out Fowley's stripper wife (Jergens), who is also Talman's lover. A guaranteed no-snoozer.

Memorable Noir Moment:

❑ The exciting climax at the airport, where the unlucky Talman catches *two* planes, anticipates the famous ending of another great heist noir, *The Killing*.

The Arnelo Affair (1947) 86 min. John Hodiak, Frances Gifford, George Murphy, Dean Stockwell, Eve Arden, Warner Anderson. **Screenplay by:** Arch Oboler. **Directed by:** Arch Oboler. **Noir Type:** Blackmail. **Noir Themes:** Woman in jeopardy, lust, betrayal. ★★★

Hodiak and Gifford are perfectly cast in this enjoyable noir melodrama. Gifford, the neglected wife of a workaholic lawyer (Murphy) and the mother of a precocious nine-year-old (Stockwell), finds herself irresistibly drawn to an all-around cad, nightclub owner Hodiak. She narrowly avoids a fling with Hodiak but winds up being involved in a murder. When the real killer blackmails her and homicide detective Anderson starts snooping around, the guilt-ridden Gifford snatches a bottle of sleeping pills from her doctor. Murphy gives a nicely subdued performance as the nearly cuckolded husband, who learns just a little too late that his family is more important than his career. Arden (TV's *Our Miss Brooks*) plays Gifford's wisecracking chum. Child star and future leading man Stockwell went on to co-star in the successful TV series *Quantum Leap*.

Familiar Face from Television:

❑ Ruby Dandridge (Oriole in *Beulah* and Delilah in *Father of the Bride*), real-life mother of famed African-American actress Dorothy Dandridge, as Gifford's maid.

Memorable Noir Moment:

❑ During breakfast, Arden confides in Gifford. "Just give me a plate of bacon and eggs, a full pocketbook, a chinchilla coat and a man and I'm happy," she says.

The Asphalt Jungle (1950) 112 min. Sterling Hayden, Louis Calhern, Jean Hagen, James Whitmore, Sam Jaffe, John McIntire, Marc Lawrence, Barry Kelley, Anthony Caruso, Marilyn Monroe. **Screenplay by:** Ben Maddow and John Huston. **Directed by:** John Huston. **Noir Type:** Heist. **Noir Themes:** Greed, betrayal, lust, corruption, fatalism. ★★★★★

When an aging criminal genius (Jaffe) is released from prison, he goes straight to a small-time bookie (Lawrence) to seek financial backing for a jewelry caper he

Jean Hagen and her wounded boyfriend (Sterling Hayden) attempt a getaway in *The Asphalt Jungle* (MGM, 1950).

had planned before he was sent up. Lawrence introduces him to a "big fixer," corrupt lawyer Calhern, who has squandered his fortune on his lusty young mistress (Monroe). Calhern agrees to fence the jewels after the job but secretly plans a double cross. Meanwhile, the nervous Lawrence must dish out his own dough to put together a gang—box man (i.e., safe cracker) Caruso, getaway driver Whitmore and hooligan Hayden. Inevitably things go noirishly awry. McIntire plays the crusading police commissioner, Kelley is a corrupt cop and Hagen is Hayden's on-again, off-again girlfriend. A sensational film noir classic and one of the greatest crime films of all time, *The Asphalt Jungle* gave a big boost to the struggling career of Sterling Hayden, once billed as "the most beautiful man in the movies," and was a spark that helped ignite Monroe's meteoric rise to stardom. Marc Lawrence is terrific as the weasely middleman, and Jaffe earned a Best Supporting Actor nomination for his role as the luckless criminal mastermind with a costly penchant for young girls. He lost the Oscar but went on to co-star in the successful TV medical series *Ben Casey*.

Familiar Faces from Television:
❑ Ray Teal (Sheriff Roy Coffee in *Bonanza*) as a uniformed cop knocked out by Hayden.

❑ Frank Cady (Doc Williams in *The Adventures of Ozzie and Harriet* and Sam Drucker in *Petticoat Junction* and *Green Acres*) as a witness in a police lineup.
❑ Strother Martin (Aaron Donager in *Hotel de Paree* and Jimmy Stewart's cousin R.J. Hawkins in *Hawkins*) as a suspect in a police lineup.

Memorable Noir Moments:

❑ Bookie Lawrence vouches for a corrupt cop, but Jaffe is unconvinced. "Experience has taught me never to trust a policeman," Jaffe explains. "Just when you think one's all right, he turns legit."
❑ Lawrence's opinion of hooligans matches Jaffe's feelings about cops: "They're like left-handed pitchers. They all have a screw loose somewhere."
❑ Calhern's sickly wife is concerned about her husband's criminal chums. "Nothing so different about them," the attorney assures her. "After all, crime is only a left-handed form of human endeavor."

Attack (1956) 107 min. Jack Palance, Eddie Albert, Lee Marvin, William Smithers, Robert Strauss, Buddy Ebsen, Richard Jaeckel. **Screenplay by:** James Poe. **Directed by:** Robert Aldrich. **Noir Type:** Combat. **Noir Themes:** Betrayal, paranoia, revenge. ★★★★

Palance, an American platoon leader in World War II, loses fourteen men to the Germans because of his commanding officer's incompetence and cowardice. The C.O. (Albert) gets the opportunity to redeem himself when the company commander (Marvin) orders him to take an abandoned town held by the enemy. When Albert sends Palance and his platoon (including Ebsen, Strauss and Jaeckel) into what could be an enemy trap, the combat veteran swears that if he loses just one more man because of Albert's cowardice, he'll drop a grenade down his throat and pull the pin. Smithers plays a lieutenant who naively hopes to have Albert removed from command by filing an unofficial complaint with Marvin, Albert's protective but self-serving buddy from back home. Palance gives a powerful performance, one of his best, as the warrior who has little sympathy for his sniveling C.O. Albert is impressive as the "gutless wonder" and "putrid piece of trash," whose bravura is limited to the safe confines of his office and the solace of his bourbon bottle. Marvin also is excellent as the opportunistic colonel whose political aspirations come before the safety of his men. Former song and dance man Ebsen later hit the jackpot on TV, starring in the smash hit series *The Beverly Hillbillies* and *Barnaby Jones.*

Familiar Face from Television:

❑ Strother Martin (Aaron Donager in *Hotel de Paree* and Jimmy Stewart's cousin R.J. Hawkins in *Hawkins)* as a radioman in the opening sequence.

Memorable Noir Moment:

❑ A soldier who wonders why the Germans hate him is told by Strauss that it's because he's the enemy. "Whaddya mean I'm the enemy?" the bewildered youngster complains. "I'm an American, for cryin' out loud. *They're* the enemy!"

Autumn Leaves (1956) 108 min. Joan Crawford, Cliff Robertson, Vera Miles, Lorne Greene. **Screenplay by:** Robert Blees, Jack Jevne and Lewis Meltzer. **Directed by:** Robert Aldrich. **Noir Type:** Newlywed. **Noir Themes:** Paranoia, betrayal. ★★★

A work-at-home typist (Crawford) meets a charming but flaky young man

(Robertson) who sweeps her off her spinster feet and causes her to forget her fear of romantic involvement. After a whirlwind May–December romance, the couple tie the knot in Mexico and return home to start their new life together. But the honeymoon has barely begun before Crawford starts catching her groom in little lies, and a woman (Miles) shows up claiming to be his ex-wife. When Crawford looks into the matter, she discovers some hanky panky going on between Miles and Robertson's father (Greene) and determines that this could be the cause of Robertson's obvious schizophrenic behavior. Crawford gives a good performance as the middle-aged newlywed who tries to save her floundering marriage despite her husband's increasingly violent behavior. Robertson is downright frightening at times as her troubled husband.

Familiar Face from Television:
❑ Marjorie Bennett (Mrs. Blossom Kennedy in *The Many Loves of Dobie Gillis*) as a waitress in desperate need of customer service training.

Memorable Noir Moments:
❑ Crawford's landlady attempts to cheer her up by telling her she has her whole future ahead of her. Crawford responds sadly, "The only trouble with the future is it comes so much sooner than it used to." See *Playgirl*, where *Autumn Leaves* screenwriter Blees has Shelley Winters using the same line.
❑ Crawford gives Greene and his "slut" a piece of her mind, adding "Your filthy souls are too evil for Hell itself."

Baby Face Nelson (1957) 85 min. Mickey Rooney, Carolyn Jones, Cedric Hardwicke, Leo Gordon, Ted de Corsia, Anthony Caruso, Jack Elam, Elisha Cook, Jr., John Hoyt. **Screenplay by:** Daniel Mainwaring. **Directed by:** Don Siegel. **Noir Type:** Gangster. **Noir Themes:** Law breaking for kicks, betrayal. ★★½

Rooney, in a frenzied, hard-boiled performance, stars as Lester Gillis (a.k.a. Baby Face Nelson), the diminutive killer and bank robber. Recently released from prison, Rooney is hired by mob chieftain de Corsia to knock off a union organizer, but he can't bring himself to kill a working stiff. De Corsia finds someone else to do the hit and frames Rooney, who ends up back in jail, no longer Mr. Nice Guy. After his moll (Jones) helps him to escape, they join up with Public Enemy Number 1, John Dillinger (Gordon). Caruso and Cook are members of Dillinger's gang, Elam is a shady businessman who provides the gang with blueprints of banks and Hoyt is the F.B.I. agent tracking Rooney. Hardwicke plays the gang's alcoholic doctor who, unfortunately for him, fouls up Rooney's fingerprint operation. This low budget, highly fictionalized, violent account of the real-life 1930s outlaw was condemned by F.B.I. Director J. Edgar Hoover as glorifying criminals.

Memorable Noir Moment:
❑ Rooney asks his pint-sized hostage, "You ever try wearing lifts?" "I do wear them," the frightened bank manager replies, amusing Rooney. Later, the banker tells F.B.I. agents that he believes he was spared because he, like the gangster, is short.

Baby Face Nelson (Mickey Rooney) is about to give a fellow short guy a break. Gang member Elisha Cook, Jr., looks on (United Artists, 1957).

Backfire (1950) 91 min. Gordon MacRae, Edmond O'Brien, Virginia Mayo, Dane Clark, Viveca Lindfors, Ed Begley. **Screenplay by:** Larry Marcus, Ivan Goff and Ben Roberts. **Directed by:** Vincent Sherman. **Noir Type:** Missing Person. **Noir Themes:** Obsession, betrayal. ★★½

Buddies MacRae and O'Brien are war veterans who plan to buy a ranch together. While MacRae is in the hospital recuperating from his wounds, O'Brien gets himself into a jam involving small-time, but dangerous, gamblers and finds himself wanted for murder. Lindfors is a mysterious nightclub singer who visits a heavily sedated MacRae to tell him that his missing buddy has suffered a severe spinal injury and wants to end it all. Hospital staff, including girlfriend Mayo, believe that MacRae has imagined the whole incident, but that doesn't stop him from searching for O'Brien after being released from the hospital. Begley is the homicide detective warning MacRae to stay off the case, and Clark is a war buddy who has become a successful mortician (conveniently, too, because there are a lot of bodies in this film). This noir mystery rises above mediocrity thanks to a fairly interesting, if convoluted, plot and solid performances by O'Brien and Clark.

Familiar Face from Television:

❑ John Dehner (reporter Duke Williams in *The Roaring Twenties*) as a homicide detective.

Memorable Noir Moments:

❑ Lindfors comes on to O'Brien. "You're amusing, Mr. Connor," she says. "And hard." "It's a hard world," replies the tough war hero.
❑ Begley admonishes a cop firing at a fleeing, unarmed suspect: "Hold it. You're liable to hit a taxpayer."
❑ A nurse complains to her frisky but sleepy boyfriend: "Why do you always get romantic *after* your hypo?"

Backlash (1947) 66 min. Jean Rogers, Richard Travis, Larry Blake, John Eldredge, Douglas Fowley, Robert Shayne, Richard Benedict, Louise Currie. **Screenplay by:** Irving Elman. **Directed by:** Eugene Forde. **Noir Type:** Whodunit. **Noir Themes:** Paranoia, revenge. ★

A wrecked car contains a charred body that police determine was once a well-known attorney (Eldredge). Homicide detectives Blake and Benedict suspect foul play. Everybody's a suspect: Eldredge's wife (Rogers), his law partner (Shayne), an escaped convict (Fowley), the con's moll (Currie) and even the D.A. (Travis). Pretty awful stuff.

The Bad and the Beautiful (1952) 116 min. Lana Turner, Kirk Douglas, Walter Pidgeon, Dick Powell, Barry Sullivan, Gloria Grahame, Gilbert Roland. **Screenplay by:** Charles Schnee. **Directed by:** Vincente Minnelli. **Noir Type:** Show Biz. **Noir Themes:** Obsession, betrayal, jealousy, revenge. ★★★★½

While a successful director (Sullivan), a movie star (Turner) and a Pulitzer Prize–winning novelist (Powell) wait in the office of a studio executive (Pidgeon) for a telephone call from a has-been Hollywood producer (Douglas), each reminisces about their experiences with the man who made and broke careers during his meteoric rise to the top. Via flashback, we witness Sullivan, a wannabe director, as he teams up with Douglas to produce moneymaking B pictures and winds up fending for himself when they graduate to A films. Turner, the alcoholic daughter of a famous actor, allows Douglas to turn her into a star. She falls hopelessly in love with him but is unceremoniously dropped. Writer Powell visits Hollywood with his Southern belle wife (Grahame) to work on a Douglas screenplay, only to experience tragedy as the result of the producer's callous scheming. A sardonic, hard-hitting look at the inner workings of Tinseltown, the film won five Academy Awards, including Best Screenplay and Best Supporting Actress (Grahame). Douglas was nominated for Best Actor but lost out to Gary Cooper in *High Noon*. Many feel that Turner should have received a Best Actress nomination for this, her best performance.

Familiar Faces from Television:

❑ Leo G. Carroll (Cosmo Topper in *Topper* and Mr. Waverly in *The Man from U.N.C.L.E.*) as a British director.
❑ Kathleen Freeman (Katie the maid in *Topper* and Flo Shafer in *The Beverly Hillbillies*) as Carroll's assistant.
❑ Madge Blake (Dick Grayson's Aunt Harriet in *Batman* and Flora MacMichael in *The Real McCoys*) as Powell's autograph-seeking guest.
❑ Barbara Billingsley (June Cleaver in *Leave It to Beaver*) as a costume designer.
❑ Ned Glass (Sgt. Andy Pendleton on *The Phil Silvers Show*) as a wardrobe man hawking his "cat men" costumes.

❑ Jeff Richards (*Jefferson Drum*, Old West newspaper editor) as a Douglas flunky showing Powell and Grahame around the studio.

Memorable Noir Moments:

❑ Douglas has to pay Hollywood extras to attend the funeral of his despised producer father. "He lived in a crowd," he explains. "I couldn't let him be buried alone."
❑ A bitter starlet responds noirishly to Roland's suggestion that Douglas is a great man, saying, "There are no great men, buster. There's only men."

Bad Blonde (1953-British) 80 min. Barbara Payton, Tony Wright, Frederick Valk, John Slater, Sidney James. **Screenplay by:** Guy Elmes and Richard Landau. **Directed by:** Reginald LeBorg. **Noir Type:** Femme Fatale. **Noir Themes:** Lust, obsession, betrayal, greed. ★★

This cheapie British noir stars Payton as a former taxi dancer married to an older man, boxing manager Valk. Valk's newest boxing sensation (Wright), who was discovered by trainers Slater and James, develops a bad case of the hots for Payton. Before he knows what hits him, Wright becomes involved in Payton's bizarre plot to murder her husband. LeBorg's twist on *The Postman Always Rings Twice* is mildly entertaining and reminiscent of fellow director Hugo Haas' similarly themed noirs (see *Pickup*, *Hit and Run* and *Bait*).

A boxer (Tony Wright) is asking for a kayo playing around with a deceitful femme fatale (Barbara Payton) in *Bad Blonde* (Lippert Pictures, 1953).

Memorable Noir Moment:

❏ While Valk is talking to him, Wright ogles his future manager's scantily clad wife as she adjusts her nylons. Valk asks him congenially, "Have you seen all the sights in London yet?" Without taking his eyes off of Payton, the young boxer replies, "Just about."

Bait (1954) 79 min. Cleo Moore, Hugo Haas, John Agar, Cedric Hardwicke. **Screenplay by:** Samuel W. Taylor. **Directed by:** Hugo Haas. **Noir Type:** Gold Fever. **Noir Themes:** Greed, lust, obsession, betrayal. ★½

Director Haas has chosen a unique setting for his favorite theme (the older man-younger woman-younger man triangle)—a cabin in the wilderness. Prospectors Haas and Agar search for the gold mine that Haas and a former partner had worked fifteen years earlier. Haas' first partner died in a violent snowstorm, and rumors quickly spread that Haas killed him to avoid splitting the gold. When Haas and Agar finally find the lost mine, greed rears its ugly head once again and, with some egging on by the Devil (yes, the literal Devil!), Haas concocts an outlandish plan so he won't have to share the bonanza with his new partner. Haas marries the local "bad girl" (Moore), moves her into the cabin and proceeds to push her and Agar together, actually encouraging hanky panky. Agar, of course, is more than happy to comply. Unless they succumb

Miners (John Agar, seated, and Hugo Haas) experience gold fever in *Bait* (Columbia, 1954).

to cabin fever first, viewers will have to endure the entire seventy-nine minutes to discover Haas' diabolical motive. Hardwicke, the film's only saving grace, makes an appearance as the Devil in the prologue and is the voice of temptation for the Bible-reading Haas.

Battle Shock *see* A Woman's Devotion

The Beast with Five Fingers (1946) 88 min. Robert Alda, Andrea King, Peter Lorre, Victor Francen, J. Carrol Naish, Charles Dingle, John Alvin, David Hoffman. **Screenplay by:** Curt Siodmak. **Directed by:** Robert Florey. **Noir Type:** Horror. **Noir Themes:** Character deterioration, paranoia. ★★½

In the little turn-of-the-century Italian village of San Stefano, a wheelchair-bound, one-handed pianist (Francen) takes a tumble down a flight of stairs and dies. Coincidentally, the wealthy man had just finalized his new will, leaving all of his possessions to his gorgeous caregiver (King). Francen's only relatives (Dingle and Alvin) seek to contest the will, hiring a lawyer (Hoffman), who is promptly strangled, seemingly by the dead man's disembodied hand. A composer-turned-con man (Alda) and a superstitious police commissioner (Naish) investigate, while Francen's secretary (Lorre), a bug-eyed astrologist, tries to find "the keys to the future" in his cherished books. A dark and eerily foreboding atmosphere, some fine special effects and a wonderfully hammy performance by noir icon Lorre help make the silly plot more palatable.

Memorable Noir Moments:
❏ While in his wheelchair, Francen takes an amazing spill down a flight of stairs. (For more wheelchair acrobatics see *Kiss of Death, The Lineup* and *Whiplash*.)
❏ Speaking with a ludicrous Italian accent, which he would use again in **The Black Hand, A Voice in the Wind** and numerous other films, policeman Naish announces the unusual results of his murder investigation: "In my mind, there is-a no doubt a hand is walking around."

The Beat Generation (1959) 93 min. Steve Cochran, Mamie Van Doren, Ray Danton, Fay Spain, Jim Mitchum. **Screenplay by:** Richard Matheson and Lewis Meltzer. **Directed by:** Charles Haas. **Noir Type:** Psycho. **Noir Themes:** Sexual hostility, paranoia, lawbreaking for kicks. ★★

Cochran plays a misogynistic vice squad cop whose wife (Spain) is raped by a serial rapist/pseudo-beatnik (Danton). When Spain becomes pregnant, there's no telling who the father is, so she opts for an abortion. This causes by-the-book cop Cochran to behave badly because abortion, after all, is against the law. Mitchum (noir icon Robert Mitchum's son) is Danton's unenthusiastic accomplice, and blonde bombshell Van Doren plays an intended victim. Van Doren and Cochran join forces, tracking the murderers to an inane "beatnik hootenanny," which turns into an even more ridiculous scuba diving battle between Cochran and Danton. The silly backdrop (the beatnik lifestyle) of this crime drama ruins what might have been an intriguing little film. Although spousal abuse is handled in the typical, lighthearted manner of the day, a number of other controversial issues (especially for the 1950s), such as rape and abortion, are presented almost intelligently. Worth viewing mostly for the interesting cultural oddities (hula-hoops, beat poetry, jazz and hep talk) and the many familiar movie and TV faces. Jazz great Louis Armstrong appears in a cameo as himself.

Undercover cops (Jackie Coogan in drag and Steve Cochran) try to trap the Lover's Lane Bandit in *The Beat Generation* (MGM, 1959).

Familiar Faces from Television:

❑ Jackie Coogan (Uncle Fester in *The Addams Family*) as Cochran's partner.
❑ William Schallert (Patty's dad in *The Patty Duke Show*) as a Catholic priest.
❑ Sid Melton (Ichabod Mudd, assistant to *Captain Midnight*, and Charlie Halper, owner of the Copa Club, in *Make Room for Daddy*) as a vice squad detective
❑ Guy Stockwell (Chris Parker in *Adventures in Paradise*) as a vice squad detective.
❑ Vampira (late-night horror movie hostess) as a beatnik poet

Memorable Noir Moments:

❑ Danton lets a marriage-minded beatnik chick down easily. "You're the most," he explains. "But there's no tomorrow. Not while the sky drools radioactive gumdrops. I mean, you gotta live for kicks."
❑ Sympathetic cop Coogan asks a victim of spousal abuse, "Why won't you prosecute when he keeps beating you up?" The heavily bruised woman replies, "Oh, well. He's got to go to work."
❑ Sexpot Van Doren comes on to Cochran, cooing, "You're a pretty little policeman."
❑ Coogan and Melton go undercover — in drag — and are forced to snuggle up to Cochran and Stockwell, while waiting for the Lover's Lane Bandit to make an appearance.

Beat the Devil (1953) 100 min. Humphrey Bogart, Gina Lollobrigida, Jennifer Jones, Robert Morley, Peter Lorre, Edward Underdown, Ivor Barnard, Marco Tulli. **Screenplay by:** Truman Capote and John Huston. **Directed by:** John Huston. **Noir Type:** Comedy. **Noir Themes:** Greed, betrayal, paranoia, sexual hostility. ★★★½

Bogart, a "middle-aged roustabout" in Italy, works for a quartet of bumbling but murderous international criminals (Morley, Lorre, Barnard and Tulli) who are conspiring to gain control of uranium-rich land in Africa. Bogey becomes romantically involved with Jones, the idiosyncratic wife of a British hypochondriac (Underdown). Bogey's employers suspect that he and his wife (Lollobrigida) are trying to double-cross them by allying themselves with the mysterious couple, who, according to pathological liar Jones, are either members of the British upper class or Africa-bound missionaries. The plot, which takes a series of bizarre twists and turns, including the group's capture by an Arab chieftain in love with American sex goddess Rita Hayworth, is difficult to follow at times. The enjoyment, however, comes from the terrific cast and the sophisticated, low-key comedy, which was not appreciated by the early 1950s movie-going public; the film bombed at the box office. Look for Bernard Lee (nine years before his debut as James Bond's boss, "M," in *Dr. No*) as a Scotland Yard inspector.

Memorable Noir Moments:

❑ Sensitivity Training Required: The pint-sized and belligerent Barnard refuses to drink a toast to women, saying, "Hitler had the right idea. Keep them in their place ... babies and the kitchen."

❑ Sensitivity Training Required: An Arab chieftain, reacting to Jones' righteous indignation over her captivity, comments that "in my country, a female's lips may move but her words are not heard."

Beautiful Stranger *see* Twist of Fate

Bedlam (1946) 78 min. Boris Karloff, Anna Lee, Billy House, Richard Fraser, Leyland Hodgson. **Screenplay by:** Val Lewton (as Carlos Keith) and Mark Robson. **Directed by:** Mark Robson. **Noir Type:** Asylum. **Noir Themes:** Woman in danger, corruption, paranoia, social reform. ★★★½

Karloff is the evil and corrupt Apothecary General of St. Mary's of Bethlehem Asylum, a.k.a. Bedlam, in mid-eighteenth century London. When a former actress (Lee), the companion of a hedonistic Tory politician (House), decides to make life more comfortable for the abused inmates of Bedlam, Karloff sees to it that she's committed, putting her avowed compassion to the test. Her only allies, kindly Quaker Fraser and Whig Party member Hodgson, are unaware of her predicament. Meanwhile, her new friends at St. Mary's, whose plight is ignored by the apathetic ruling class because "loonies don't vote," are getting fed up with their cruel caretaker. Karloff gives a masterly performance in this chilling Val Lewton production as a lunatic on the wrong side of the asylum bars.

Familiar Face from Television:

❑ Ellen Corby (Grandma Walton from *The Waltons*) as inmate Betty.

Memorable Noir Moment:

❑ The outspoken but eloquent Lee complains that Karloff is "a stench in the nostrils, a sewer of ugliness and a gutter brimming with slop."

Behind Locked Doors (1948) 62 min. Richard Carlson, Lucille Bremer, Douglas Fowley, Thomas Browne Henry, Herbert Heyes, Ralf Harolde, Tor Johnson, Dickie Moore. **Screenplay by:** Martin Wald and Eugene Ling. **Directed by:** Oscar (Budd) Boetticher, Jr. **Noir Type:** Asylum. **Noir Themes:** Corruption, paranoia. ★★★

This is an enjoyable little noir about a private investigator (Carlson) hired by an ambitious reporter (Bremer) to infiltrate La Siesta Sanitarium, an insane asylum, to find an on-the-lam ex-judge (Heyes). While La Siesta certainly isn't the place you'd choose to put your crazy Uncle Ralph, it has its good points: It's not overcrowded (but that could be because of Boetticher's minuscule budget), and there's a caring orderly (Harolde) who seems to have a "special" relationship with a young patient (Moore), whom he calls "my boy." Its negative features include a sadistic orderly (Fowley) and a zombie-like ex-boxer (Johnson), whom Fowley uses to punish smart-mouthed inmates like Carlson. Some film historians and reviewers don't hold this film in high regard. But, despite with the presence of Tor Johnson, who later played similar roles for the notorious Ed Wood, Jr., in *Bride of the Monster* and *Plan 9 from Outer Space*, this is an entertaining and decently acted noir.

Familiar Face from Television:
❑ Kathleen Freeman (Katie the maid in *Topper* and Flo Shafer in *The Beverly Hillbillies*) as a nurse at the asylum.

Memorable Noir Moments:
❑ Professionally trained psychiatric orderly Fowley, smacking a hysterical patient, shrieks: "Shut up, you screaming monkey."
❑ Fowley throws the fearful Carlson into a cell with the gargantuan Johnson and clangs on the fire extinguisher to start Round 1.

Berlin Express (1948) 86 min. Robert Ryan, Merle Oberon, Charles Korvin, Paul Lukas, Charles McGraw. **Screenplay by:** Harold Medford. **Directed by:** Jacques Tourneur. **Noir Type:** Missing Person. **Noir Themes:** Conspiracy, betrayal. ★★½

An important West German diplomat (Lukas), on his way to present a plan for the unification of Germany, is kidnapped by a group of postwar Nazis as he boards an American troop train in Frankfurt. Ryan, a U.S. Agriculture Department employee, and three other passengers (an Englishman, a Frenchman and a Russian soldier) join the diplomat's secretary (Oberon) in the search for her missing boss. Ryan does a good job as an American who isn't crazy about Germans but is ripe for an attitude adjustment (especially if it's administered by the delectable Oberon). Mostly unexciting, *Express* contains many sobering shots of the bombed-out ruins in Frankfurt and Berlin. Filmed during the earliest stages of the Cold War, the moral of the story is, "Can't we all just get along?"

Memorable Noir Moment:
❑ Over drinks, Ryan tells Oberon that he can't figure out whether he's concerned about Lukas' disappearance because he's interested in her or because he realizes the diplomat's importance to the world. A smiling Oberon suggests that it's understandable that a stranger in an unfamiliar country would feel close to a "reasonably attractive girl." Ryan promptly informs her that he never said she was attractive. What he said was "not bad-looking" and there's a difference. He then points out women who are *really* attractive. American diplomacy at work.

Betrayed *see* **When Strangers Marry**

Between Midnight and Dawn (1950) 89 min. Mark Stevens, Edmond O'Brien, Gale

Storm, Donald Buka, Gale Robbins. **Screenplay by:** Eugene Ling. **Directed by:** Gordon Douglas. **Noir Type:** Payback. **Noir Themes:** Revenge. ★★★

Unfairly underrated, this exciting noir boasts of fine performances by Stevens and O'Brien as patrolmen who fall in love with Storm, a police department secretary. O'Brien, the hardened, cynical cop, and Stevens, the happy-go-lucky sort, have been buddies since the war. So they take their romantic rivalry lightly, and when Storm makes her choice, the loser is genuinely glad for his friend. Standing in the way of a happy ending, however, is gangster Buka, whom they arrested for viciously gunning down a rival and who has vowed revenge. After being convicted of murder, Buka escapes from prison and heads back to town. Robbins plays Buka's kind-hearted moll, whom O'Brien unfairly labels a "no-good filthy tramp." Unlike other directors of his time, Douglas seemed to know that when somebody gets shot, there's bound to be plenty of blood. Roland Winters, who starred as the great Chinese detective in six Charlie Chan films, plays Buka's henchman.

Familiar Faces from Television:
- ❏ Madge Blake (Dick Grayson's Aunt Harriet in *Batman* and Flora MacMichael in *The Real McCoys*) as Storm's widowed mother.
- ❏ Billy Gray (Bud in *Father Knows Best*) as a pre-teen juvenile delinquent.
- ❏ Jim Brown (Lt. Rip Masters in *The Adventures of Rin Tin Tin*) as a uniformed cop.

Memorable Noir Moments:
- ❏ Gray tells O'Brien and Stevens that the freckle-faced kid in the back seat of the police car is his brother. "He doesn't look like you," Stevens observes. "I ain't complainin'," cracks Gray.
- ❏ When O'Brien and Stevens show up at Storm's doorstep, it's like Lenny and Squiggy arriving at Laverne and Shirley's apartment. "Hello," they croon, grinning stupidly and carrying all of their worldly possessions.

Beware, My Lovely (1952) 77 min. Ida Lupino, Robert Ryan, Taylor Holmes, Barbara Whiting. **Screenplay by:** Mel Dinelli. **Directed by:** Harry Horner. **Noir Type:** Psycho. **Noir Themes:** Woman in jeopardy, paranoia. ★★★

A paranoid-schizophrenic handyman (Ryan) hops a freight train after killing a housewife and lands a job with homeowner Lupino in a nearby town. He isn't on the job five minutes before he starts behaving strangely, turning the widow's Christmas holiday into a film noir nightmare. Holmes plays Lupino's boarder and Whiting is her annoying teenage niece. Although Ryan is chilling, and Lupino is convincing enough, *Beware* is a bit dated, managing only an occasional fright. The film was based on the successful Broadway play *The Man,* which starred Dorothy Gish.

Memorable Noir Moments:
- ❏ After being harassed by Lupino's perceptive canine Corky, Ryan confesses, "I've never seen a dog yet that liked me."
- ❏ "I don't think I've ever loved anyone," the psychopath confides to his frightened victim, "and I *know* that no one has ever loved me."

A psychopathic handyman (Robert Ryan) and his latest victim (Ida Lupino) in *Beware, My Lovely* (RKO, 1952).

Bewitched (1945) 65 min. Phyllis Thaxter, Edmund Gwenn, Horace (Stephen) McNally, Henry H. Daniels, Jr. **Screenplay by:** Arch Oboler. **Directed by:** Arch Oboler. **Noir Type:** Psycho. **Noir Themes:** Fatalism, victim of fate. ★★★½

Thaxter, suffering from what we now call Multiple Personality Disorder, is a good girl fighting the femme fatale inside. Daniels is her unlucky hometown fiancé, whom she drops to go to New York. There she meets lawyer McNally, who falls in love with her better half. This is convenient because she soon requires his professional services when her psychotic dominant personality stabs a man in the back with scissors. At her trial, the state's expert psychiatric witness (Gwenn) testifies that she's sane but eventually discovers her true condition. Is he too late to save her? This is a genuinely eerie film with Thaxter giving an excellent performance as the haunted schizophrenic. The plot might be a bit hokey, but considering the film was made years before the classic split personality flick *The Three Faces of Eve*, it's impressive. Noir icon Audrey Totter does the beast-like voice of Thaxter's evil personality.

Memorable Noir Moment:
❏ An impatient prison guard, assigned to wait with Thaxter while the jury considers her fate, remarks indifferently, "I'm supposed to be having a spaghetti dinner at six."

Beyond a Reasonable Doubt (1956) 80 min. Dana Andrews, Joan Fontaine, Sidney Blackmer, Philip Bourneuf, Arthur Franz. **Screenplay by:** Douglas Morrow. **Directed by:** Fritz Lang. **Noir Type:** Whodunit. **Noir Themes:** Victim of fate, social reform. ★★½

A successful novelist (Andrews) and an anti-capital punishment editor (Blackmer) concoct a hare-brained, downright illegal scheme to prove that an innocent man can be convicted of murder and sent to the chair, especially when a top-notch lawyer (Bourneuf) with political aspirations is the prosecutor. After a stripper is murdered, the conspirators plant circumstantial evidence implicating Andrews in the crime. For Andrews' protection, they carefully document each piece of phony evidence with photographs and notes and lock everything in Blackmer's office safe. After Andrews is convicted and sentenced to death, fate intervenes, causing the plan to backfire. Andrews' fiancée (Fontaine) must now prove his innocence. Despite the presence of noir icons Andrews and Fontaine, Lang's last American film is disappointing. Even he is said to have hated it. The good acting and the enjoyable ending compensate for the hard-to-swallow plot.

Familiar Face from Television:
❑ Edward Binns (Detective Lt. Roy Brenner in *Brenner* and Dr. Anson Kiley in *The Nurses*) as a police lieutenant.

Memorable Noir Moment:
❑ "This guy's got a lot of class," a stripper remarks about her new boyfriend. "Yeah? If he's got so much class, what's he doing with you?" asks her friend.

Beyond the Forest (1949) 96 min. Bette Davis, Joseph Cotten, David Brian, Ruth Roman, Regis Toomey. **Screenplay by:** Lenore Coffee. **Directed by:** King Vidor. **Noir Type:** Triangle. **Noir Themes:** Greed, obsession, lust. ★★

Davis has a field day overacting her role as the bitch-goddess/bored housewife married to a do-gooder country doctor (Cotten). With strains of *Chicago* playing annoyingly in the background, she skulks around, longing to visit the big city and marry her millionaire lover (Brian). But her deepest noir yearnings lead her nowhere, of course, except to murder and tragedy. Cotten is okay as the dedicated doctor, but Roman is wasted in a role that has nothing to do with the plot. Even Bette Davis fans might be disappointed.

Memorable Noir Moments:
❑ Sensitivity Training Required: Davis lashes out at her abused Native American maid, calling her a "red Indian" and complaining that the girl is standing around like a cigar store Indian.
❑ Sensitivity Training Required: Davis gets kicked out of a Chicago nightclub because, as a woman, she requires an escort.
❑ Davis utters the familiar line that Davis impersonators have been having fun with for decades: "What a dump," she says about her house, the nicest in town.

The Big Bluff (1955) 70 min. John Bromfield, Martha Vickers, Rosemarie Bowe, Robert Hutton, Eve Miller. **Screenplay by:** Fred Freiberger. **Directed by:** W. Lee Wilder. **Noir Type:** Newlywed. **Noir Themes:** Woman in jeopardy, greed, betrayal, lust. ★★

A bored housewife (Bette Davis) and her country doctor husband (Joseph Cotten) in *Beyond the Forest* (Warner Bros., 1949).

Director Wilder should have left well enough alone. This uninspired rehash of his much better 1946 film ***The Glass Alibi*** stars Vickers as a rich, terminally ill widow victimized by fortune hunter Bromfield. Hutton is her doctor and Miller is her loyal assistant, who suspects that Bromfield has married Vickers for her money and, worse, is conspiring with his lover (Bowe) to murder her. After substituting a placebo for her heart medicine, Bromfield, believing that strenuous activity will cause a heart attack, takes his wife dancing, encourages her to play tennis and tricks her into climbing stairs. To his dismay, however, her condition actually *improves*, so he decides to rush things along, with unexpected results. Bromfield later starred in TV's long-running (1956–60) syndicated police drama *The Sheriff of Cochise*.

Memorable Noir Moment:
❏ Bromfield resorts to clichés in his attempts to seduce and placate the jealous Bowe, saying, "You know, you're very beautiful when you're mad."

The Big Caper (1957) 84 min. Rory Calhoun, Mary Costa, James Gregory, Robert Harris, Corey Allen, Paul Picerni. **Screenplay by:** Martin Berkeley. **Directed by:** Robert Stevens. **Noir Type:** Heist. **Noir Themes:** Greed, jealousy, betrayal. ✫✫

This is definitely one of the weirder heist films. A small-time hood (Calhoun) talks his reluctant boss (Gregory) into pulling a bank job that will net them a cool million. Calhoun and Gregory's moll (Costa), posing as husband and wife, purchase a gas station and set up house for four months to stake out the bank. Ironically, they begin to enjoy the "straight" life—playing Scrabble with the neighbors, attending neighborhood barbecues and babysitting kids. It isn't long before Costa starts wishing that she and Calhoun could make this lifestyle a permanent one. The rigid Calhoun, once fiercely loyal to his boss, begins to soften under her influence. Other members of the team include a psychopathic muscleman (Allen), a pyromaniac (Harris) and ladies' man (Picerni). Nothing special, but enjoyably camp. Calhoun went on to star in TV's *The Texan*, Picerni co-starred in *The Untouchables* and Gregory played Inspector Frank Luger in *Barney Miller*.

Familiar Face from Television:
❏ Ray Teal (Sheriff Roy Coffee in *Bonanza*) as a real estate agent.

The Big Carnival (1951) 111 min. Kirk Douglas, Jan Sterling, Robert Arthur, Porter Hall, Richard Benedict, Ray Teal, Lewis Martin. **Screenplay by:** Walter Newman, Lesser Samuels and Billy Wilder. **Directed by:** Billy Wilder. **Noir Type:** Newspaper. **Noir Themes:** Corruption, betrayal, guilt. ★★★★½

An unethical, hotshot New York journalist (Douglas), down on his luck, takes a job as a sixty-dollar-a-week reporter for a small town, by-the-book newspaper editor (Hall). On their way to cover a "news" story (a rattlesnake hunt), Douglas and his photographer (Hall) stumble upon a mishap at a tourist attraction just off the main highway. A cave-in has trapped Benedict, the owner of a roadside general store, inside an ancient Indian cave dwelling, pinning his legs under heavy rocks. Douglas, smelling a great story, perhaps even a Pulitzer Prize, brazenly takes charge of the rescue operations. Promising unlimited publicity to the crooked sheriff (Teal), who is up for reelection, the reporter manages to prevent competing journalists from getting too close to the story. He and Teal then do the unimaginable: To milk the tragedy for all its worth, they coerce the construction contractor (Martin) into taking a longer route to the victim, ensuring that the rescue operation will go on for at least a week instead of the estimated twelve hours. Douglas also convinces Benedict's unloving wife (Sterling), who's about to take a powder, to hang around to collect the dough that's sure to start pouring in. His prediction proves accurate, as thousands of spectators and campers show up to enjoy the circus atmosphere—a Ferris wheel and other rides are trucked in by a traveling carnival, hawkers push their goods and the frenzied news media set up camp. Business at the general store is booming, prompting the grateful Sterling to throw herself at Douglas, even as her dying husband daydreams about their upcoming wedding anniversary. Douglas, the only one authorized to enter the cave for a daily visit with Benedict, uses the visits as a bargaining tool in his bid to be rehired by his former boss at a large New York newspaper. This is a grim but enjoyable film, with Douglas and Sterling giving outstanding performances. Originally released as *Ace in the Hole*, the film was a smash in the rest of the world but did not do well in the U.S. Douglas, in his autobiography *The Ragman's Son*, surmises that this was because the American press didn't appreciate being portrayed in such a negative fashion. "Critics love to criticize," he wrote, "but they don't like being criticized."

Familiar Face from Television:
❑ Frank Cady (Doc Williams in *The Adventures of Ozzie and Harriet* and Sam Drucker in *Petticoat Junction* and *Green Acres*) as an insurance salesman on vacation with his family.

Memorable Noir Moments:
❑ "Bad news sells best," Douglas tells an aspiring reporter, "because good news is no news."
❑ Sterling can't hide her admiration for the way Douglas has taken advantage of the catastrophe. "I met a lot of hard-boiled eggs in my life," she tells him. "But you, you're twenty minutes."
❑ When Douglas suggests that Sterling go to a rosary service with the other ladies to pray for her husband, she replies, "I don't go to church. Kneeling bags my nylons."

The Big Clock (1948) 95 min. Ray Milland, Charles Laughton, Maureen O'Sullivan, George Macready, Elsa Lanchester, Rita Johnson, Harry Morgan. **Screenplay by:** Jonathan Latimer. **Directed by:** John Farrow. **Noir Type:** On the Run. **Noir Themes:** Victim of fate, paranoia. ★★★★

Milland is on the run (sort of) for a murder committed by his tyrannical boss (Laughton). All of the running takes place in the skyscraper headquarters of Laughton's publishing empire, where Milland manages the true crime magazine. While evading cops, co-workers and witnesses who can place him with the victim (Johnson) on the night she was killed, Milland comes to believe that it was Laughton who, in a fit of rage, bludgeoned his girlfriend to death. Proving it before he's collared, however, turns out to be a challenge. O'Sullivan plays Milland's impatient wife, tired of his broken promises to spend more time with her and their little boy; Macready is Laughton's sycophantic right-hand man and possibly his gay lover; Lanchester is a wacky artist who has been hired to draw a sketch of the man last seen with the victim; and Morgan is Laughton's mute bodyguard. More farce than thriller, *The Big Clock* (which refers to a master timepiece that synchronizes all of the clocks in Laughton's organization) is a sardonic and suspenseful look at murder and the dog-eat-dog world of big business, as seen through the eyes of a self-confessed workaholic. Laughton scores big as the bullying executive with a big ego problem, and Lancaster is delightful as the eccentric artist.

Familiar Faces from Television:
❑ Noel Neill (Lois Lane in *The Adventures of Superman*) as an elevator operator.
❑ Richard Webb (*Captain Midnight*) as a junior executive.
❑ Lloyd Corrigan (Prof. McKillup in *Hank*, Charlie Dooley in *Happy* and Ned Buntline in *The Life and Legend of Wyatt Earp*) as "President McKinley."

Memorable Noir Moment:
❑ When a woman in a bar identifies herself as Laughton's "friend," Milland is surprised to hear that his boss *has* a friend. "I thought all he was crazy about was clocks," he says. "Maybe I have a clock," the woman replies suggestively.

The Big Combo (1955) 89 min. Cornel Wilde, Richard Conte, Brian Donlevy, Jean Wallace,

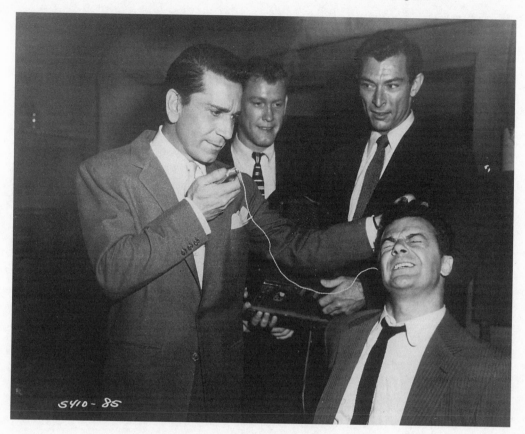

A crime boss (Richard Conte) tortures a cop (Cornel Wilde) to the amusement of his hit men (Earl Holliman, left, and Lee Van Cleef) in *The Big Combo* (Allied Artists, 1955).

Lee Van Cleef, Earl Holliman, Helene Stanton. **Screenplay by:** Philip Yordan. **Directed by:** Joseph H. Lewis. **Noir Type:** Gangster. **Noir Themes:** Lust, obsession, guilt. ★★★★

A police lieutenant (Wilde), obsessed with arresting Conte, the head of a local mob called simply "the organization," pines for Conte's moll (Wallace). But it's burlesque star Stanton he turns to when he needs some TLC. Wallace, meanwhile, seemingly tormented with guilt about her lustful feelings for Conte, makes a feeble attempt at suicide. Two hit men roommates (Van Cleef and Holliman) seem to be romantically involved with each other, while Donlevy, once Conte's boss but now his hearing-impaired underling, makes the mistake of trying to take over. With its talented cast and top-notch direction, the sexy and violent *Combo* is an excellent noir choice for fans who enjoy the films of director Quentin Tarantino.

Memorable Noir Moments:

❏ Conte excites Wallace in a steamy love scene that will cause you to ask, "Where's he going?" It's been reported that Wilde, Wallace's real-life husband, was not happy about this scene, which was deliberately filmed at a time when he was away from the set.

❏ Sensitivity Training Required: Conte advises Wallace on her wardrobe, saying, "A woman dresses for a man."

❑ When a concerned Van Cleef tries to convince his ill partner to eat some food, Holliman refuses, replying, "I can't swallow any more salami." (Like married couples in other films of the fifties, the hit men sleep in separate beds in the same room and show obvious affection for each other. When one is killed, the other cries out in anguish, "Don't leave me.")

The Big Heat (1953) 90 min. Glenn Ford, Gloria Grahame, Jocelyn Brando, Alexander Scourby, Lee Marvin. **Screenplay by:** Sydney Boehm. **Directed by:** Fritz Lang. **Noir Type:** Payback. **Noir Themes:** Revenge, obsession, sexual hostility, corruption. ★★★★

Ford plays a homicide detective who turns vigilante after his wife (Brando) is mistakenly killed by gangsters as a result of his investigation into a corrupt cop's suicide. Obsessed with taking vengeance against syndicate chieftain Scourby and his sadistic goon Marvin, Ford quits the force after being warned by the corrupt police commissioner to lay off. Marvin's estranged moll (Grahame) becomes an invaluable ally for Ford, whose crusade ultimately ends in tragedy for almost every woman he meets. Marvin is sensational as the loathsome mobster who gets a kick out of torturing and disfiguring the ladies, and Grahame is terrific as the big-hearted femme fatale. Don't miss this film noir classic.

Familiar Face from Television:

❑ Carolyn Jones (Morticia of *The Addams Family*) in a bit part as Marvin's ashtray.

Memorable Noir Moments:

❑ "I've been rich and I've been poor," Grahame tells Ford. "Believe me, rich is better."
❑ Grahame looks around Ford's hotel room appreciatively. "Hey," she says, "I like this. Early nothing."

The Big Knife (1955) 111 min. Jack Palance, Ida Lupino, Wendell Corey, Shelley Winters, Rod Steiger, Jean Hagen, Everett Sloane, Wesley Addy, Paul Langton. **Screenplay by:** James Poe. **Directed by:** Robert Aldrich. **Noir Type:** Show Biz. **Noir Themes:** Fatalism, betrayal, paranoia, corruption, guilt. ★★★★

Palance, a popular Hollywood star, wants to quit the business to save his crumbling marriage to Lupino, but ruthless producer Steiger and his henchman Corey blackmail him into signing a new seven-year contract. With a possible jail sentence hanging over Palance's head if it becomes known that the studio P.R. man (Langton) took the blame for his drunk driving accident, which killed a young girl, the actor gives in to Steiger's demands. Lupino, who's considering running off with her husband's best friend (Addy), isn't thrilled with the prospect of seven more years in Tinseltown. Complicating matters, a dipso bit player (Winters), who was in the car with Palance on the night of the accident, has been blabbing about the cover-up. When Corey decides that she should be shut up for good, the horrified actor feels he must take a stand. Hagen plays Langton's libidinous wife, who can't resist Palance, and Sloane is the actor's sympathetic agent. Steiger gives his usual boisterous but enjoyable performance, and Palance is so compelling that noir icon Lupino is hardly noticeable as his indecisive wife. Based on the play by Clifford Odets, *The Big Knife* presents a grim look at the darker (albeit fictional) side of Hollywood life. The film wasn't a big hit with audiences, who couldn't drum up much sympathy for the pathetic life of an alcoholic, millionaire actor living in a Bel Air mansion. They also had difficulty accepting the hard-featured Palance as a sex symbol adored by millions of women.

Familiar Faces from Television:

❑ Strother Martin (Aaron Donager in *Hotel de Paree* and Jimmy Stewart's cousin R.J. Hawkins in *Hawkins)*, shown only from the back, as a studio photographer.
❑ Richard Boone (Paladin in *Have Gun Will Travel*) as the opening scene narrator.

Memorable Noir Moments:

❑ Sensitivity Training Required: Misogynist producer Steiger informs Palance of "one essential fact of life — the woman must stay out of her husband's work when he earns her bread and butter."
❑ A repentant Palance pleads with Lupino for another chance. "Am I world's biggest oaf?" he asks. "The world's a big place," she replies, "but you're the biggest one in *my* life."
❑ Corey responds angrily to the threat that big-mouthed Winters poses to the security of the studio. "She's a stupid little tramp," he says. "Two bits worth of nothing with a little power."

The Big Night (1951) 75 min. John Barrymore, Jr., Preston Foster, Howard St. John, Philip Bourneuf, Joan Lorring. **Screenplay by:** Stanley Ellin and Joseph Losey. **Directed by:** Joseph Losey. **Noir Type:** Payback. **Noir Themes:** Revenge, character deterioration. ★★½

Barrymore (a.k.a. John Drew Barrymore, Drew's dad) plays an awkward 17-year-old high school student who's teased by his peers because he's different. His macho father (Foster) is the owner of a bar where the boy hangs out after school. Shortly after a disappointed Foster witnesses his son taking a "birthday beating" from other students, he himself submits to a vicious caning by a crippled sportswriter (St. John) in front his customers and son. Barrymore, humiliated by his father's behavior and hell-bent on vengeance, steals Foster's gun and goes hunting for St. John. During the course of a mystifying evening, he hooks up with a happy-go-lucky drunk (Bourneuf), commits an unconscious but hurtful racial gaffe and romances a sensitive older woman (Lorring) who hides his gun and tries to talk him out of his plan. At the end of the evening, the disturbed boy learns the reason for his father's beating. Painfully slow at times but interesting.

Familiar Face from Television:

❑ Myron Healey (Doc Holliday in *The Life and Legend of Wyatt Earp*) as a uniformed police officer.

Memorable Noir Moment:

❑ Twenty-five years before Scorsese placed a gun-brandishing DeNiro in front of a mirror in *Taxi Driver* ("You talkin' to *me*?"), Losey did it for Barrymore ("You're gonna sit there and take orders from *me*").

The Big Operator (1959) 90 min. Mickey Rooney, Steve Cochran, Mamie Van Doren, Ray Danton, Mel Torme, Jay North. **Screenplay by:** Robert Smith and Allen Rivkin. **Directed by:** Charles Haas. **Noir Type:** Union. **Noir Themes:** Corruption, paranoia, child in jeopardy. ★★½

Director Haas brings back much of his cast from *The Beat Generation* and throws in Mickey Rooney (who gives an enjoyable, hard-boiled performance) as icing on the cake. Rooney, a corrupt union leader who's already had a stool pigeon tossed into a cement mixer, is concerned about straight-laced union members Cochran and Torme because they witnessed him being chummy with hit man Danton (whom Rooney has denied knowing under oath at a Senate hearing). Fearing a perjury charge, Rooney tries bribing the two men; when that fails he calls in the sadistic Danton, whose bag of tricks includes a gasoline can and a book of matches. But Rooney goes too far when he threatens Cochran's little boy (North, TV's *Dennis the Menace*) to prevent Cochran from testifying against him. Sex kitten Van Doren (cast way against type as a housemaker complete with apron) plays Cochran's wife. The film's climax, considerably better than *Beat Generation*'s lame ending, is an enjoyable brawl where the good guys, carrying makeshift weapons (a tire iron, hammer, trophy cup and a mop stick!) take on the gun-wielding bad guys. Rooney keeps this one interesting.

Familiar Faces from Television:
❑ Vampira (late-night horror movie hostess) as a owner of a night spot.
❑ Jackie Coogan (Uncle Fester in *The Addams Family*) as one of Rooney's corrupt union officials.
❑ Peter Leeds (George Colton in *Pete and Gladys*) as a senator questioning Rooney.
❑ Joey Forman (Freddie in *The Mickey Rooney Show* and Dr. Sam Nolan in *The Joey Bishop Show*) as a shop steward.
❑ Jim Backus (Thurston Howell III of *Gilligan's Island*) as a state labor board official.
❑ Leo Gordon (Hank Miller in *Circus Boy* and Sgt. Kick in *Enos*) as one of Rooney's thugs.

Memorable Noir Moments:
❑ When Torme speaks his mind at a union meeting to the annoyance of Rooney and his goons, the more subdued Cochran warns him, "How do you think you're gonna look without teeth?" "A lot better than I'd look without guts," replies his hotheaded friend.
❑ After being sucker-punched by Torme at a union meeting, Rooney calls for order. "Let's try to conduct the meet with a little dignity," he shouts before spitting up blood on the speaker's platform.

The Big Punch (1948) 50 min. Wayne Morris, Lois Maxwell, Gordon MacRae, Mary Stuart, Eddie Dunn. **Screenplay by:** Bernard Girard. **Directed by:** Sherry Shourds. **Noir Type:** Boxing. **Noir Themes:** Corruption, paranoia, revenge, betrayal. ★½

MacRae, a "tanker" (i.e., a boxer known for throwing fights), double-crosses his manager and knocks out an opponent. To get even, the manager kills a cop and frames it on the boxer, who flees New York and hides out in preacher Morris' parsonage in a small Pennsylvania town. After Morris helps him land a job at the local bank, MacRae reluctantly becomes involved in a heist scheme. Maxwell plays a former Army nurse, the romantic interest for both boxer and pastor. Stuart is the double-crossing dame whom MacRae stupidly trusts, and Dunn is the wary chief of police. Try to stay awake to witness pastor Morris pummeling a crook into repentance. Stuart later played in three TV soap operas—*Search for Tomorrow*, *The Guiding Light* and *One Life to Live*.

Memorable Noir Moment:
❑ The Reverend Morris is concerned about Maxwell's safety when she leaves her New York hotel room all dolled up to seduce a crook. "I can take care of myself," she says. "I didn't

spend two years in the Army for nothing." "Yeah," Morris replies, "but you were invading Europe then. This is *New York*." You may have a point there, Rev.

The Big Sleep (1946) 114 min. Humphrey Bogart, Lauren Bacall, John Ridgely, Martha Vickers, Regis Toomey, Charles Waldron, Louis Jean Heydt. **Screenplay by**: William Faulkner, Leigh Brackett and Jules Furthman. **Directed by**: Howard Hawks. **Noir Type**: P.I. **Noir Themes**: Paranoia, jealousy, betrayal. ★★★★

Bogart stars as Raymond Chandler's famous private eye Philip Marlowe in this sordid tale of murder, blackmail, illicit sex and gambling. Bogey is hired by wealthy invalid Waldron to find out who's blackmailing his wild younger daughter (Vickers). While investigating, Bogey falls for Vickers' sultry sibling (Bacall), covers up a murder, shoots a few bad guys, wards off the sexual advances of several cuties and takes a couple of vicious beatings. All in a day's work (for twenty-five bucks plus expenses). Ridgely plays a gambler whose wife seems to have run away with an Irish revolutionary; Toomey is Bogey's homicide detective pal; and Heydt is a blackmailer who runs afoul of both Ridgely and Bogart. The plot is borderline incomprehensible (even Chandler is said to have been unsure of the identity of a murderer), but the real attraction of this film is the chemistry between Bogey and Bacall, who heat up the screen with their thinly disguised sexual banter. Bogart's gritty portray of the

P.I. Philip Marlowe (Humphrey Bogart) and his wealthy client's daughter (Lauren Bacall) get ready to greet some late night visitors in *The Big Sleep* (Warner Bros., 1946).

tough but foursquare private eye was a hint of things to come in film noir. Look for B western star Bob Steele as Ridgely's hit man.

Familiar Faces from Television:

❏ Dorothy Malone (Constance Mackenzie in *Peyton Place*) as a bookstore clerk with an eye for Bogey.

❏ Tom Fadden (Duffield in *Broken Arrow* and Silas Perry in *Cimarron City*) as one of Ridgely's goons.

Memorable Noir Moments:

❏ When blackmailer Heydt gets the drop on him, a grinning Bogey says, "My, my, my. Such a lot of guns around town and so few brains."

❏ Bogart finds Vickers waiting for him in his apartment and wonders how she got in. "You came in through the keyhole like Peter Pan," he suggests. "Who's he?" Vickers asks. "A guy I used to know around the pool room," replies Bogey.

The Big Steal (1949) 71 min. Robert Mitchum, Jane Greer, William Bendix, Patric Knowles, Ramon Novarro, John Qualen. **Screenplay by:** Gerald Drayson Adams and Daniel Mainwaring (as Geoffrey Homes). **Directed by:** Don Siegel. **Noir Type:** South of the Border. **Noir Themes:** Corruption, greed, betrayal. ★★★½

Army lieutenant Mitchum is hunted by his superior officer (Bendix) after being falsely accused of participating in a military payroll heist. The real thief (Knowles) is in Mexico to launder the hot dough through an art-loving fence (Qualen). Along the way, Mitchum meets up with Knowles' ex-fiancée (Greer), who's trying to get back the two grand that Knowles stole from her. Unwilling allies, Mitchum and Greer track Knowles through rural Mexico, while they in turn are pursued by an increasingly frustrated Bendix. It's a wild and enjoyable ride, full of plot twists, witty dialogue, nicely staged fistfights and some hysterical slapstick. The usually laid-back and droopy-eyed Mitchum is remarkably energetic. Greer is delightful as his equally dynamic partner. Silent film star Novarro plays a savvy Mexican police inspector who enjoys practicing his English. (The inept attempts at Spanish by Mitchum and Bendix are hysterical).

Memorable Noir Moments:

❏ *The Big Steal* contains some fairly racy humor for its time. When Mitchum remarks that Knowles is a "good-looking fellow," she quips, "Is that why you're interested in him?" Later, G.I. Mitchum acknowledges that his Spanish isn't as good as Greer's. "You know where *I* learned *my* Spanish," he says, obviously referring to the brothels where many American soldiers hone their linguistic skills. She smiles knowingly.

❏ Trying to elude Bendix, Mitchum takes refuge in a barbershop and waits for his pursuer to leave. When the coast is clear, he tosses the surprised barber a coin and quickly leaves. "Loco," the barber comments to another customer, who's wearing a what-else-can-you-expect grin. "*Americano*," the customer explains.

Big Town (1947) 59 min. Philip Reed, Hillary Brooke, Robert Lowery, Byron Barr, Veda Ann Borg, Charles Arnt. **Screenplay by:** Daniel Mainwaring (as Geoffrey Homes). **Directed by:** William C. Thomas. **Noir Type:** Newspaper. **Noir Themes:** Corruption, obsession, greed, betrayal. ★½

With increased circulation and more advertising as his highest priorities, a callous reporter (Reed) takes over as the editor of a respected but unsuccessful big-city newspaper owned by publisher Arnt and turns it into a notorious scandal sheet. Reporters Brooke and Lowery learn the pros and cons of being hotshot reporters as they cover spectacular news stories like "The Pistol Packin' Mama" (Borg) and "The Vampire Killer" (Barr) cases. Reed's obsession with circulation, however, leads to tragedy. Also known as *Guilty Assignment*, this low-budget B movie tries hard to be entertaining while making a social statement about "yellow journalism." Unfortunately, it fails at both.

Familiar Faces from Television:
❑ John Dehner (reporter Duke Williams in *The Roaring Twenties*) as a TV advertising man involved in a train wreck.

Memorable Noir Moment:
❑ Editor Reed disapproves of Lowery's treatment of a news story about a young murder suspect whom the reporter believes is innocent. "You're not writing," Reed complains, "you're bleeding all over the joint."

Black Angel (1946) 80 min. Dan Duryea, June Vincent, Peter Lorre, Broderick Crawford, Constance Dowling, Wallace Ford, John Phillips. **Screenplay by**: Roy Chanslor. **Directed by**: Roy William Neill. **Noir Type**: Boozer. **Noir Themes**: Betrayal, obsession, jealousy. ★★★½

A club manager (Freddie Steele, left) talks to amateur detectives (Dan Duryea, second from left, and June Vincent) as they take a break from their undercover nightclub act in *Black Angel* (Universal, 1946).

A singer and part-time extortionist (Dowling) is found strangled by one of her victims (Phillips), a former lover. He's seen leaving the scene and then quickly arrested, convicted and sentenced to death. His faithful and forgiving wife (Vincent) is determined to find the real killer and clear her husband before his execution. A tough homicide detective (Crawford) has already investigated the only other suspect, the murdered woman's estranged husband (Duryea), an alcoholic pianist and songwriter. Duryea, however, has an airtight alibi: His friend (Ford) locked him in his room on the night of the murder, as is his habit whenever Duryea is on a particularly nasty binge. Hoping to find evidence that will save Phillips, Vincent teams up with Duryea to go undercover as a musical team at a nightclub owned by another of Dowling's blackmail victims (Lorre). Of course, Duryea, who's trying hard to stay on the wagon, finds himself falling for Vincent, but the feeling isn't mutual. Based on a novel by pulp writer Cornell Woolrich, this intriguing film is notable for its fast pace, enjoyable musical numbers and distinctive performances by Lorre and noir icon Duryea, cast against his usual villainous type.

Memorable Noir Moments:

❏ When murder suspect Phillips complains that he's innocent, homicide detective Crawford utters a common noir platitude that offers little consolation. "Then you've got nothing to worry about," he lies.

❏ After accusing Duryea of murdering his wife and then discovering he's been cleared by police, a regretful Dowling says, "I seem to have said all the wrong things." Ford, Duryea's friend, replies gruffly, "Yeah, most women do."

The Black Book *see* Reign of Terror

The Black Hand (1950) 93 min. Gene Kelly, J. Carrol Naish, Teresa Celli, Marc Lawrence. **Screenplay by:** Luther Davis. **Directed by:** Richard Thorpe. **Noir Type:** Gangster. **Noir Themes:** Economic repression, revenge. ★★½

Between his more familiar musical roles, Irishman Kelly takes on the difficult job of convincing you that he's Italian. The setting is Little Italy, New York, in 1900. Kelly, whose father was killed by an extortionist gang called the Black Hand (Mafia), seeks vengeance against the murderers. But when he concludes that violence is useless, he tries to organize the neighbors to cooperate with the police. Naish (another Irishman) plays the Italian-American cop who's been fighting the Black Hand for years and who sees in Kelly the spark that might ignite a fire under his fearful neighbors. Celli plays Kelly's love interest and the sensational Marc Lawrence is the mob boss. The acting is good (except for Naish and his phony accent) but the film drags on too long before anything really happens. In addition to the Irishman-as-Italian problem, we also are supposed to believe that Kelly, who was 38 at the time, is about 23. Robert Taylor was considered for the lead role, but it was decided that he didn't look enough like an Italian. Go figure. Naish's character (and that of Ernest Borgnine ten years later in *Pay or Die*) was based on the exploits of real-life New York detective Lt. Joseph Petrosino, who was killed in Italy by vengeful mobsters.

Memorable Noir Moment:

❏ A witness gets several "death signs" (the finger across the neck) from Mafiosi in the courtroom and, despite the nationalistic pleadings of Naish, refuses to identify the hood who blew up his store. He leaves the stand, head slumped in shame, and is comforted by the wife whose life he just saved.

Black Magic (1949) 105 min. Orson Welles, Nancy Guild, Akim Tamiroff, Frank Latimore, Valentina Cortese, Margot Grahame, Stephen Bekassy, Charles Goldner, Berry Kroeger. **Screenplay by:** Charles Bennett. **Directed by:** Gregory Ratoff and Orson Welles (uncredited). **Noir Type:** Period. **Noir Themes:** Obsession, lust, jealousy, betrayal, conspiracy. ★★

Welles plays Cagliostro, gypsy and master eighteenth century hypnotist, who becomes embroiled in a political conspiracy that would prevent France's Marie Antoinette (Guild), the king's daughter-in-law, from ascending to the throne. Guild, in a dual role, also plays Marie Antoinette's innocent lookalike; Bekassy is a corrupt, low-level court official; and Grahame is Madame DuBarry, the king's girlfriend. Welles, who hates Bekassy because he executed his parents on witchcraft charges years earlier, is obsessed with the beautiful lookalike, who loves only the captain of the guard (Latimore). Romantic rivalry, however, is no obstacle for the powerful hypnotist, who has only to look into a woman's eyes to make her his slave. A subplot has Welles meeting with Franz Antoine Mesmer, the real-life figure credited with developing and promoting hypnotism for medical uses. Based on a novel by Alexandre Dumas (Kroeger, who narrates), this one is strictly for Welles fans; they might get a kick out of watching him give his best Vincent Price impersonation, hamming it up as an "insolent devil-may-care vagabond" who is out to capture the throne of France.

Familiar Face from Television:

❏ Raymond Burr (*Perry Mason* and *Ironside*) as Dumas' son.

Memorable Noir Moment:

❏ Welles, commenting on the "hysterical faith and emotional instability" of the lower classes, notes, "They cheer you and lash you to death with the same emotion."

Black Tuesday (1955) 80 min. Edward G. Robinson, Peter Graves, Jean Parker, Milburn Stone, Warren Stevens, Jack Kelly, Sylvia Findley, Vic Perrin, Hal Baylor. **Screenplay by:** Sydney Boehm. **Directed by:** Hugo Fregonese. **Noir Type:** Gangster. **Noir Themes:** Fatalism, greed. ★★★½

Convicted murderer Robinson, with help from his moll (Parker) and gang member (Stevens), escapes from death row minutes before his scheduled execution, taking along fellow inmate Graves, who has two hundred Gs stashed away from a bank heist. They take hostages—the prison chaplain (Stone), a newspaper reporter (Kelly), a guard (Baylor), a prison guard's daughter (Findley) and a doctor (Perrin) to treat the wounded Graves—and hole up in a warehouse, where they try to fend off cops. A throwback to the 1930s gangster genre, *Black Tuesday* is fast-moving and exciting, with Robinson giving a volatile performance as the psychopathic rackets czar with seventeen murders to his credit.

Familiar Faces from Television:

❑ Frank Ferguson (Gus the ranch hand in *My Friend Flicka*) as a determined police inspector.
❑ William Schallert (Patty's dad from *The Patty Duke Show*) as a reporter covering Robinson's execution.

Memorable Noir Moments:

❑ When an attorney tells his Death Row client that he may have one more trick up his sleeve, Robinson shouts from his cell, "All you got up your sleeve, shyster, is your filthy, hairy arm."
❑ Graves, when asked how he feels about having escaped Death Row, replies spiritually, "Like being born again."

Blackmail (1947) 67 min. William Marshall, Adele Mara, Ricardo Cortez, Grant Withers, Richard Fraser, Stephanie Bachelor, George J. Lewis. **Screenplay by:** Royal Cole and Albert DeMond. **Directed by:** Lesley Selander. **Noir Type:** P.I. **Noir Themes:** Greed, betrayal. ★★½

A tough-as-shoe-leather private eye (Marshall) is hired by a Hollywood playboy (Cortez) who is being blackmailed over a few indiscreet photographs taken of him and a former gal pal (Bachelor). Mara plays Cortez's fiancée, Fraser is his phony French chauffeur and Withers is the police inspector investigating the case. This low-budget movie falls into the so-bad-it's-good category. The plot is predictable, of course, but the film is enjoyable anyway, with a plethora of nicely staged fistfights and an amusing car chase. The actors, even the expressionless Marshall, aren't *that* bad, proving at least that they're not graduates of the Ed Wood, Jr., school of acting (see *Jail Bait*). When Marshall speaks, he has the strange habit of adding little handles to the end of his sentences (sucker, sweetheart, bright boy, pally, baby) despite the gender of the person he's addressing. He, in turn, is addressed as Sherlock, gumshoe and, mysteriously, Samson. The dialogue is so camp that, if the film hadn't been made in 1947, one might suspect that the screenwriters were alumni of the 1960s TV series *Batman*. The intentionally humorous dialogue delivered by the deadpan Marshall and his co-stars is mostly incomprehensible, but that's what makes it amusing. This must be seen to be believed.

Memorable Noir Moments:

❑ Cortez: "I hope you know what you're doing." Marshall: "I hope you get your hope."
❑ After Cortez pulls out a telephone wire from the exterior of his house, he informs Marshall, "You can't call the police over a dead wire." Undeterred, our hero replies, "Well, maybe, there's *another* telephone in California."
❑ "Don't move, sweetheart," Lewis warns as he points his gun at Marshall. "This thing doesn't shoot marshmallows."
❑ Marshall to blackmailer Lewis, who is holding a gun on him and his client Ziggy Cranston: "There are several reasons why Mr. Cranston won't be able to play with you. Five to be exact." When straight man Lewis asks, "What are they?," Marshall shouts "Four fingers and a thumb" and sucker punches him (was this film made by a 12-year-old?). A rousing fistfight follows and Marshall gets knocked out not once, but twice.

Blackout (1954-British) 87 min. Dane Clark, Belinda Lee, Betty Ann Davies, Andrew Osborn. **Screenplay by:** Richard Landau. **Directed by:** Terence Fisher. **Noir Type:** Amnesia. **Noir Themes:** Betrayal, woman in jeopardy, dysfunctional family, greed. ★½

Blackout is a disappointing British noir with Clark playing a down-and-out American in London. While intoxicated, he meets a rich English girl (Lee) who offers him 500 pounds if he'll marry her. He wakes up the next morning suffering from booze-induced amnesia and finds blood on his clothes and a pocketful of dough. He reads that the girl is missing and that her father has been murdered. Guess who the bobbies are looking for? On the run and trying to prove his innocence, he eventually finds Lee, who claims that they're married. Of course, the poor sap winds up falling in love with his "wife," who may be the real killer. Or is it her former fiancé (Osborne)? Or her mother (Davies)? By the time this confusing mess is over, you'll be asking yourself a more appropriate question: Huh? Released in Great Britain as *Murder by Proxy*.

Blind Spot (1947) 73 min. Chester Morris, Constance Dowling, Steven Geray, Sid Tomack, William Forrest. **Screenplay by:** Martin Goldsmith. **Directed by:** Robert Gordon. **Noir Type:** Boozer. **Noir Themes:** Victim of fate. ★★★

Narrator Morris plays a has-been novelist accused of murdering his conniving publisher (Forrest) in this tightly plotted, locked-room murder mystery. Stewed to the gills, Morris shows up at the publisher's office and demands an advance on his royalties. The publisher refuses and suggests that Morris start writing more marketable books, *a la* the company's best-selling mystery writer (Geray), who witnesses the confrontation. When Forrest is found dead, Morris, who's experiencing hangover memory loss, is arrested and later released. The publisher's glamorous secretary (Dowling) offers to help him prove his innocence. It's not difficult to figure out who the killer is, but the question of how the murderer got out of a room bolted from the inside will have the viewer thinking. Between 1941 and 1949, Morris starred in a string of *Boston Blackie* films and later had a role in the short-lived 1960 TV series *Diagnosis: Unknown*.

Memorable Noir Moment:

❑ Morris, on his way to ask his publisher for an advance, tells the viewer, "It isn't easy to borrow money from a man you'd rather kick in the teeth."

Blonde Alibi (1946) 62 min. Tom Neal, Martha O'Driscoll, Donald MacBride, Robert Armstrong, Elisha Cook, Jr., Peter Whitney, John Berkes. **Screenplay by:** George Bricker. **Directed by:** Will Jason. **Noir Type:** Whodunit. **Noir Themes:** Victim of fate. ★★

This is a mildly entertaining noir with Kurt Russell look-alike Neal playing a pilot accused of murdering ex-girlfriend Driscoll's sugar daddy. MacBride, Whitney and Armstrong are the Keystone Cops investigating the case, and noir veteran Cook is a cab driver who runs over the murdered man. Berkes gives a humorous performance as Louie the Stool Pigeon, who's uncharacteristically silent about the theft of a Guttenburg Bible. The plot is foolish, but the film's short length may help the viewer get through it all.

Memorable Noir Moment:

❑ Detective Armstrong gets the drop on a bad guy and warns, "Get away from that gun or I'll kill you good."

The Blonde Bandit (1950) 60 min. Dorothy Patrick, Gerald Mohr, Robert Rockwell, Larry Blake, Charles Cane, Argentina Brunetti. **Screenplay by:** John K. Butler. **Directed by:** Harry Keller. **Noir Type:** Femme Fatale. **Noir Themes:** Betrayal, corruption, obsession, woman in jeopardy. ★★

A small-town Kansas girl (Patrick) arrives in the big city to meet her fiancé pen pal for the first time and discovers that the man, who had "too many wives and a solo ticket to Cleveland," has been arrested for bigamy. Broke, she sells her phony engagement ring to a shady jeweler, who pays her a grand and then cleans out his own safe, reporting to the cops that Patrick held him up. Mohr, the head of a local gambling syndicate, comes to her rescue, bailing her out and giving her a job. He falls in love with her and even brings her home to meet his old-fashioned Italian mama (Brunetti). Unfortunately for Mohr, Patrick has been coerced by an unethical D.A. (Rockwell) to spy on the gangster and collect evidence of his illegal activities. When two cops on Mohr's payroll (Blake and Cane) discover that this reluctant femme fatale is working undercover, her life expectancy is shortened considerably. The humdrum plot is offset by the decent acting and the film's mercifully short length.

Memorable Noir Moment:
❑ Like most lovesick noir saps, syndicate chief Mohr doesn't know women as well as he thinks. "You know, baby," he tells Patrick, "you're probably the one dame in the world who can make a sucker out of me. But I don't think you would."

Blonde Ice (1948) 78 min. Leslie Brooks, Robert Paige, Walter Sande, John Holland, Emory Parnell, Michael Whalen, Russ Vincent. **Screenplay by:** Kenneth Gamet. **Directed by:** Jack Bernhard. **Noir Type:** Femme Fatale. **Noir Themes:** Sexual hostility, betrayal, jealousy, greed. ★½

Brooks stars as a society columnist, a former "eighteen-dollar-a-week steno," who has a bad habit of murdering the men who reject her. A shameless social climber, she weds the wealthy Holland and, while still on their honeymoon, kills him because he threatens to divorce her after finding a love letter she wrote to her former sportswriter boyfriend (Paige). She establishes an ingenious alibi for herself, seeing to it that Paige is with her when Holland's body is discovered. Naturally, homicide detective Parnell suspects that Paige is the murderer. Sande plays Paige's editor and Vincent is an airplane pilot who helps Brooks establish her alibi and then blackmails her. Bad move, Russ. Whalen is a wannabe Congressman who could wind up being the black widow's next victim. A cheapie noir with not much going for it, *Blonde Ice* is for hardcore noir fans only.

Familiar Face from Television:
❑ James Griffith (Deputy Tom Ferguson in *The Sheriff of Cochise*) as a newspaper reporter.

Memorable Noir Moments:
❑ Newlywed Brooks is asked by homicide detective Parnell if she and her murdered husband were happy. "Throughout every minute of our married life we were supremely happy," she claims. "The entire week, huh?" Parnell responds.
❑ After being dumped a second time by Brooks, Paige finally wises up. "You're like a poison," he tells her. "Take a little bit and you're finished. But too much becomes an antidote."

Blonde Sinner (1956-British) 99 min. Diana Dors, Yvonne Mitchell, Michael Craig, Marie Ney, Harry Locke. **Screenplay by:** John Cresswell and Joan Henry. **Directed by:** J. Lee Thompson. **Noir Type:** Prison. **Noir Themes:** Obsession, revenge, jealousy. ★½

Dors, obsessed with her pianist boyfriend (Mitchell), who is in love with another married woman, drops her kind but boring husband (Locke) and eventually kills her romantic rival. This dull British noir opens promisingly enough with Dors emptying her revolver into her victim but rapidly deteriorates into a thinly disguised, overly melodramatic social commentary on capital punishment. While waiting several excruciating weeks on Death Row for the prison governor (Ney) to bring word of a reprieve and being waited on by the kindly Mitchell and other prison guards assigned to her cell, the killer recalls the incidents that led to her crime. Dors, whose self-pitying character has a tough time evoking viewer sympathy, does a poor acting job, walking around in a zombie-like trance for most of the film. Anyone interested in the woman-awaiting-execution theme is referred to the even worse, but shorter, *Lady in the Death House* with Jean Parker and the far superior *I Want to Live!* with Susan Hayward, who won an Oscar for her portrayal of a death row inmate.

Memorable Noir Moment:
❑ When Craig makes a negative comment about marriage, Dors questions how he could know so much about the subject since he never married. Craig responds, "You don't have to go *down* a coal mine to know it's dark and dirty."

Blood on the Moon (1948) 88 min. Robert Mitchum, Robert Preston, Barbara Bel Geddes, Walter Brennan, Phyllis Thaxter, Frank Faylen, Tom Tully. **Screenplay by:** Lillie Hayward. **Directed by:** Robert Wise. **Noir Type:** Horse Opera. **Noir Themes:** Greed, betrayal, guilt. ★★★½

Mitchum arrives on the scene of an escalating range war ("a little argument over grazing land") between the deluded landowners following schemer Preston, and his nemesis, wealthy rancher Tully. Hired as a gunman by his old buddy Preston, Mitchum finds he hasn't the stomach for all the cheating and killing. He decides to switch sides in the middle of the fight (with a little encouragement from Tully's pretty young daughter, Bel Geddes), throwing a monkey wrench into the plans of Preston and corrupt Indian agent Faylen. Brennan plays a landowner who loses his son in the war and Thaxter is Tully's older daughter, who betrays her father for a scoundrel's false love. Mitchum, acknowledged by some as the first noir cowboy (see *Pursued*) is dandy as the hired gun with a conscience. Preston is appropriately evil as the villain, and Bel Geddes and Thaxter do well as the womenfolk. *Blood on the Moon* is dark and dismal, a well-acted adult Western with enough action to satisfy noir and Western fans alike. Look for noir veteran Charles McGraw, barely recognizable (except for that familiar gruff voice) with bearded face and bearskin coat, as an angry landowner.

Memorable Noir Moment:
❑ Screenwriter Hayward finds an interesting way for Mitchum to call Preston an S.O.B. and avoid the censors' ire: "I've seen dogs wouldn't claim you for a son."

The Blue Dahlia (1946) 99 min. Alan Ladd, Veronica Lake, William Bendix, Howard da Silva, Doris Dowling, Hugh Beaumont, Tom Powers, Will Wright. **Screenplay by:** Raymond Chandler. **Directed by:** George Marshall. **Noir Type:** Wrong Man. **Noir Themes:** Victim of fate, betrayal, paranoia. ★★★½

When Navy pilot Ladd returns to Los Angeles after the War with buddies Bendix and Beaumont, he discovers that he's been cuckolded: His wife (Dowling) has been having an affair with a local hood (da Silva), the owner of the Blue Dahlia

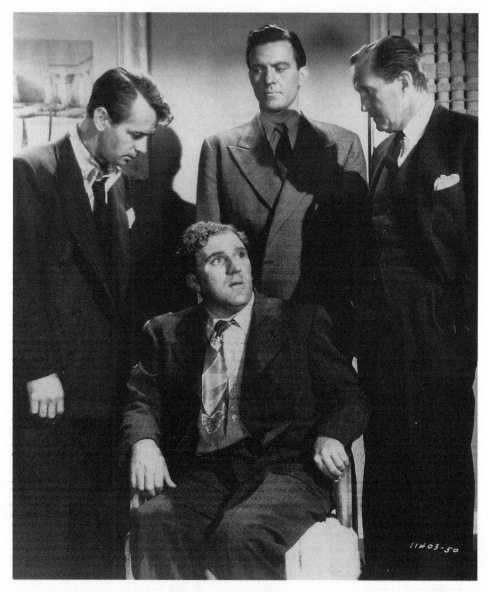

A World War II Navy veteran (William Bendix) is grilled by a homicide cop (Tom Powers, right), while war buddies (Alan Ladd, left, and Hugh Beaumont) provide moral support in *The Blue Dahlia* (Paramount, 1946).

nightclub. Even though she's completely unrepentant ("I go where I want, with any-body I want"), he's willing to forgive and forget. But when she reveals that their child, who Ladd thought had died from diphtheria, was killed as a result of her drunken driving, he leaves her. While walking in the rain, he's offered a ride by, coinciden-tally, da Silva's estranged wife (Lake), who drives him to Malibu. There he hears on the radio that Dowling has been found dead and that he's the chief suspect. Homi-cide detective Powers scours the city for Ladd, who's busy trying to prove that da Silva is the real murderer. Written by pulp fiction writer Raymond Chandler, *The Blue Dahlia* is fast-paced and hard-hitting, with Ladd and Lake terrific as usual. Ben-dix gives an amusing (and, at times, terrifying) performance as the war veteran with a metal plate in his head, experiencing bouts of amnesia, pounding headaches and fits of rage whenever he hears what he calls "monkey music." You can thank the Navy for the cop-out ending.

Familiar Faces from Television:
❑ Noel Neill (Lois Lane in *The Adventures of Superman*) as a Blue Dahlia hat check girl.
❑ Frank Faylen (Herbert T. Gillis in *The Many Loves of Dobie Gillis*) as a con man out to bilk Ladd.

Memorable Noir Moments:
❑ Sensitivity Training Required: House dick Wright gladly accepts a payoff from da Silva, saying, "That sure is white of you." See *Detour*, *The Devil and Daniel Webster* and *Strange Illusion*.
❑ Da Silva's nightclub partner shares his opinion about Ladd's wife and dames in general. "I told you she was poison," he says. "They're all poison sooner or later."

The Blue Gardenia (1953) 90 min. Anne Baxter, Richard Conte, Ann Sothern, Ray-mond Burr, Jeff Donnell, George Reeves. **Screenplay by:** Charles Hoffman. **Directed by:** Fritz Lang. **Noir Type:** Cover-Up. **Noir Themes:** Guilt, paranoia, woman in jeopardy. ★★★½

Commercial artist Burr thinks he died and went to Heaven (he turns out to be half right, anyway) when a pretty switchboard operator (Baxter), depressed after receiving a "Dear Jane" letter from her G.I. boyfriend in Korea, accepts his invita-tion for dinner and drinks at the Blue Gardenia Restaurant. After plying Baxter with Polynesian Pearl Divers all evening, he takes her to his apartment, where he attempts to seduce her. When she drunkenly responds, thinking that he's her boyfriend, Burr becomes emboldened to go further. When she regains her senses, however, he learns the hard way that no means no— she beans him with a fireplace poker before pass-ing out. Later, she manages to make it home to the apartment she shares with two co-workers (Sothern and Donnell, who provide the comedy relief). The next morn-ing, homicide detective Reeves (TV's *Superman*) shows up at the telephone company asking questions. Suffering from booze-induced amnesia, Baxter eventually learns that Burr has been bludgeoned to death with a fireplace poker and that the cops are searching for the blonde he was seen with at the Blue Gardenia. Ace reporter Conte, smelling a scoop, writes a column asking the "The Blue Gardenia Murderess" to sur-render to him and his newspaper. While this isn't one of Lang's best efforts, *The Blue Gardenia* is a gem thanks to Baxter's superb performance as the sweet working girl whose happy-go-lucky life has been turned upside down by a faithless boyfriend and an unscrupulous Lothario. Nat King Cole plays himself and sings the title song.

Familiar Faces from Television:
❑ Richard Erdman (Peter Fairfield III in *The Tab Hunter Show*) as Conte's tag-along photographer.
❑ Robert Shayne (Inspector Henderson in *The Adventures of Superman*) as a doctor.
❑ Frank Ferguson (Gus the ranch hand in *My Friend Flicka*) as a drunken reporter.
❑ Victor Sen Yung (Hop Sing in *Bonanza*) as a Blue Gardenia waiter.
❑ Jim Brown (Lt. Rip Masters of *The Adventures of Rin Tin Tin*) as a photographer.

Memorable Noir Moments:
❑ Baxter comments on the tastiness of her Polynesian Pearl Diver. "Mainly ice and pineapple," Burr lies.
❑ From the Some-Things-Never-Change Department: Burr's 1953 date-rape drug of choice is alcohol, which he pours into Baxter's coffee to ensure that the already smashed girl is ready for his amorous advances.

Bluebeard (1944) 73 min. John Carradine. Jean Parker, Nils Asther, Ludwig Stossel. **Screenplay by:** Pierre Gendron. **Directed by:** Edgar G. Ulmer. **Noir Type:** Period. **Noir Themes:** Character deterioration, obsession, lust. ★★★★½

Edgar G. Ulmer, that master of the low-budget film, struck gold with this minor masterpiece. Carradine, in the title role, gives one of his best performances as a painter, puppeteer and strangler of young girls in nineteenth century Paris. Parker plays the beautiful dressmaker who makes him want to stop killing, difficult as that is for the conscience-stricken psychopath. Asther is the police inspector who's hunting the strangler, and Stossel is the sleazy art dealer who, even though he knows that painting young girls causes the artist to kill, pressures Carradine to create more portraits. Brilliant camerawork, skillful direction and excellent acting make this classic a must-see.

Memorable Noir Moments:
❑ A pathetic looking messenger barges in on several young women trying on clothes in Parker's shop. "We don't allow beggars," complains one of the ladies. He smiles and replies, "I did not come here professionally."
❑ For a guy as skinny as a stick, Carradine sure can fight. He fends off at least a dozen of Paris' finest in the film's exciting climax. Five years later, Dean Jagger should have asked co-star Carradine for some pointers in *C-Man*.

A Blueprint for Murder (1953) 76 min. Joseph Cotten, Jean Peters, Gary Merrill, Catherine McLeod, Freddy Ridgeway, Jack Kruschen, Barney Phillips, Walter Sande. **Screenplay by:** Andrew L. Stone. **Directed by:** Andrew L. Stone. **Noir Type:** High Seas. **Noir Themes:** Child in jeopardy, betrayal. ★★★½

When Cotten's young niece dies unexpectedly, his friends Merrill and McLeod convince him that she was poisoned with strychnine. They suspect the girl's stepmother (Peters), Cotten's widowed sister-in-law, who stands to collect a huge inheritance if Cotten's surviving nephew dies also. Cotten, unconvinced of Peters' guilt, nevertheless is worried about Ridgeway's safety. Detectives Kruschen and Phillips and

D.A. Sande are concerned that the evidence against Peters is too flimsy and a judge confirms this when he finds there's no probable cause to bring her to trial. When Cotten learns that his sister-in-law is taking the boy on a cruise to Europe, he concocts a risky plan to protect his nephew and to discover if she is indeed a killer. This is a tense and stimulating film noir with an enjoyable, but somewhat flamboyant, ending.

Memorable Noir Moment:

❑ Cotten reminisces about his noirish scheme to uncover a possible murderer. "There were moments when I was horrified by the enormity of my plan," he says. "Cold fear would come over me."

Blues in the Night (1941) 89 min. Richard Whorf, Priscilla Lane, Betty Field, Lloyd Nolan, Jack Carson, Elia Kazan, Peter Whitney, Billy Halop, Wallace Ford, Howard da Silva. **Screenplay by:** Robert Rossen. **Directed by:** Anatole Litvak. **Noir Type:** Show Biz. **Noir Themes**: Fatalism, character deterioration. ★★★½

And now for something completely different. An idealistic jazz and blues quintet (Whorf, Carson, Kazan, Whitney and Halop) and their singer (Lane) struggle to make a name for themselves in the music world. After hopping a freight train on their way to a gig, the almost penniless band meets up with an escaped convict (Nolan) who robs them of their few remaining dollars. Taking a liking to them, he hires them to play at a jazz joint which he runs with his partners in crime (Field, Ford and da Silva). Femme fatale Field (who is almost as despicable as *Detour*'s Ann Savage), angry at having been dropped by Nolan, tries to make him jealous by making a play for Carson. Carson is more than receptive until he finds out that his wife, Lane, is pregnant. Field then sets her sights on the bandleader (Whorf), who's willing to sacrifice even his music for the unappreciative temptress. A couple of murders and a double suicide later, everybody's playing those "real, low-down New Orleans blues." If you enjoy swing music, daring photography and a storyline that emphasizes characterization, this noir's for you. Halop was one of the original *East Side Kids* and was a regular on TV's *All in the Family* from 1972 to 1976. Whorf and Kazan later turned their attention to directing.

Memorable Noir Moments:

❑ Whorf describes "our kind of music" to his wannabe band members: "Blues, real blues, the kind that come out of people, real people — their hopes and their dreams, what they've got and what they want, the whole U.S.A. in one chorus."

❑ When Kazan yells for a doctor after the tubercular Halop begins one of his coughing fits, a black prisoner from the segregated cell across the hall shouts, "What's the matter with that white boy? Has he got the miseries? We all got the miseries in here, all of us. Don't make no difference what you're in for. Don't make no difference where the jail is. Come nights ya start to thinkin', then the miseries get ya."

Body and Soul (1947) 104 min. John Garfield, Lilli Palmer, Hazel Brooks, William Conrad. Lloyd Goff, Anne Revere, Joseph Pevney, Canada Lee. **Screenplay by:** Abraham Polonsky. **Directed by:** Robert Rossen. **Noir Type:** Boxing. **Noir Themes:** Corruption, greed. ★★★★★

A shady nightclub owner (Lloyd Nolan) manages to resist the advances of a cagey femme fatale (Betty Field) in *Blues in the Night* (Warner Bros., 1941).

A heavyweight champion in the boxing noir category, *Body and Soul* has been hailed by some as the greatest of all boxing movies. Although ***The Set-Up*** has the more exciting boxing scenes, *Body and Soul* has Garfield and that's enough to make it a winner on any judge's card. Garfield plays a hungry young pugilist whose only motive is the dough. Like most poor kids who make it big, he learns how to spend it quickly and frivolously. After years of living the wild life as the undefeated world champion, his mettle is tested when he's given sixty grand and ordered to bet against himself in an upcoming championship fight. This film has loads of interesting characters: Garfield's mother (Revere), who hates that her son is mixed up in such a savage business; his loyal girlfriend (Palmer), seemingly willing to wait forever for her man to straighten out; a femme fatale (Brooks) out to get what she can for as long as the ride lasts; Garfield's conniving manager (Conrad); a crooked fight promoter (Goff); Garfield's trainer and childhood pal (Pevney), who hates the monster his best friend is becoming; and African-American ex-champ Lee, whose career was cut short because of a brain clot. None of the boxing clichés are missing from *Body and Soul* and its impact has been blunted by time, but the acting is great. Director Rossen was himself a professional boxer for a short time.

Memorable Noir Moments:

❑ Palmer, standing with Garfield outside her apartment, shouts to her roommate inside: "Irma, are you decent?" "Not particularly," Irma answers, adding, "Bring him in."
❑ Brooks advises former boyfriend Conrad, "Don't romance me, Quinn. You're getting old." "You could use a new paint job yourself," he replies.

The Body Snatcher (1945) 79 min. Boris Karloff, Bela Lugosi, Henry Daniell, Edith Atwater, Russell Wade. **Screenplay by:** Philip MacDonald and Val Lewton (as Carlos Keith). **Directed by:** Robert Wise. **Noir Type:** Horror. **Noir Themes:** Corruption, character deterioration, paranoia, guilt, greed, revenge. ★★★★

Based on a short story by Robert Louis Stevenson, *The Body Snatcher* stars Karloff as a nineteenth century Edinburgh grave robber and murderer who supplies bodies to a medical school operated by Daniell. The two men, who share a mysterious past, hate each other fiercely. Wade is Daniell's top student and assistant, unwillingly caught up in the ghastly bodies-for-sale business. Atwater plays Daniell's housekeeper with a secret of her own, and Lugosi is the school's greedy handyman. Karloff gives his best performance since *Frankenstein* in this, his first of three films for B horror producer Val Lewton (see also *Isle of the Dead* and *Bedlam*). Lugosi's role is small but effective, especially his scene with Karloff, in which he foolishly attempts to blackmail the killer. Daniell also gives a standout performance as the callous doctor desperately seeking to rid himself of the heinous body snatcher.

Familiar Face from Television:

❑ Bill Williams (Kit Carson in *The Adventures of Kit Carson*) as a medical student playing with a pair of skeletons.

Memorable Noir Moments:

❑ A slightly tipsy Daniell forgets whom he's talking to and asks Karloff, "You know something about the human body?" The grave robber smiles evilly and replies, "I've had some experience."
❑ Preparing for the inevitable showdown with Karloff, Daniell can't restrain his invective: "You've become a cancer, a malignant evil cancer rotting my mind."

Bodyguard (1948) 62 min. Lawrence Tierney, Priscilla Lane, Philip Reed, Steve Brodie, Elizabeth Risdon. **Screenplay by:** Fred Niblo, Sr., and Harry Essex. **Directed by:** Richard Fleischer. **Noir Type:** Wrong Man. **Noir Themes:** Corruption, greed. ★★★

Tierney, a hotheaded, hard-hitting cop, socks a superior officer then resigns from the force rather than accept a suspension. He takes a job as bodyguard for a meat packing heiress (Risdon) and soon finds himself framed for the murder of the cop he assaulted. His fiancée (Lane) is a police department secretary and his inside contact for information that may clear him. Reed plays the shady nephew of the meat packing company owner, and Brodie is the ex-con who works as a meat cutter. Tierney is fine in a good-guy role for a change, but Lane is much too cutesy. This is a fast-moving film (at sixty-two minutes, it has to be).

Memorable Noir Moments:
❑ Risdon's stiff butler keeps insisting that no one is home and tries to close the door in Tierney's face. The impatient ex-cop brushes past him, saying, "Just a minute, Dracula, I'll wait."
❑ When bodyguard Tierney is introduced as a night watchman, he quips, "Thanks for the promotion."

The Bonnie Parker Story (1958) 79 min. Dorothy Provine, Jack Hogan, Richard Bakalyan, Joseph Turkel, William Stevens, Douglas Kennedy, Patricia Huston. **Screenplay by:** Stan Shpetner. **Directed by:** William Witney. **Noir Type:** Gangster. **Noir Themes:** Greed, lust, sexual hostility, jealousy. ★★½

Before Dunaway and Beatty (*Bonnie and Clyde*) there was Provine and Hogan (Bonnie and Guy), in this fictionalized account of the famous outlaw couple. Sexy waitress Provine teams up with small-time hood Hogan while her husband (Bakalyan) is serving a 175-year stretch in the pen. Hogan teaches her how to use a tommy gun and the two, who are eventually joined by Hogan's brother (Turkel) and his moll (Huston), go on a murder and robbery spree throughout the Midwest, sticking up filling stations, general stores and freight offices before moving on to bigger things— an armored car carrying a hundred Gs. Kennedy, a lawman obsessed with their capture, gets lucky during one of his ambushes. After Provine and Hogan break Bakalyan out of jail, the two men become rivals for entry into Provine's frigid bedroom, but she spurns the both of them and becomes infatuated with a "sweet" architectural student. There's no romanticizing of the killers, as in the technically superior and better acted *Bonnie and Clyde*, only a violent portrayal of a pair of ruthless and sociopathic outcasts, who are doomed before they really get going.

Familiar Face from Television:
❑ Stanley Livingston (Chip in *My Three Sons*) as a gun-toting little boy who gets the drop on the gang.

Memorable Noir Moment:
❑ Provine expresses her distaste for men in general. "You're a punk," she tells Hogan. "You could stand on your head and you'd still be a punk. You. Duke. All of you."

Boomerang (1947) 88 min. Dana Andrews, Arthur Kennedy, Jane Wyatt, Lee J. Cobb, Ed Begley, Karl Malden. **Screenplay by:** Richard Murphy. **Directed by:** Elia Kazan. **Noir Type:** Wrong Man. **Noir Themes:** Corruption, victim of the law. ★★★★

This first-rate film noir dramatizes the brutal murder of an elderly Episcopal

A district attorney (Dana Andrews) and his wife (Jane Wyatt) discuss his faltering political future in *Boomerang* (20th Century–Fox, 1947).

priest in Bridgeport, Connecticut, and the victimization of an innocent man by corrupt politicians. Andrews plays an honest D.A. who is offered his party's gubernatorial nomination if he will bring a murder suspect (Kennedy) to trial. Andrews believes the man is innocent. Cobb and Malden are detectives who, under political and media pressure, psychologically brutalize their suspect until they wring a confession out of him. Begley, a political hack and nervous real estate developer, tries to force Andrews' hand by threatening to expose his wife's (Wyatt) unwitting involvement in a shady land deal. Andrews is excellent as the embattled D.A., and Kennedy shines as the troubled war veteran who gets a bum deal instead of his nation's thanks. Filmed in semi-documentary style a year before the innovative technique was made famous by *The Naked City*, *Boomerang* is based on real-life events. Andrews, we learn at the end of the film, portrayed Homer Cummings, who went on to become the U.S. Attorney General in Franklin Roosevelt's administration. Playwright Arthur Miller has a small role as a suspect in a police lineup. Screenwriter Murphy was nominated for an Oscar for Best Screenplay.

Familiar Face from Television:

❏ Cara Williams (Gladys Porter in *Pete and Gladys*) as a vengeful waitress.

Memorable Noir Moment:

❑ After a corrupt city official commits suicide, the savvy newspaper reporter who was about to expose him comments, "It's always the same. You look around long enough you'll find some guy with his fingers in the till."

Border Incident (1949) 94 min. Ricardo Montalban, George Murphy, Howard da Silva, Charles McGraw, James Mitchell. **Screenplay by:** John C. Higgins. **Directed by:** Anthony Mann. **Noir Type:** Undercover. **Noir Themes:** Economic repression, greed, social reform. ★★★

An American immigration official (Murphy) and a Mexican law enforcement agent (Montalban) go undercover to break up an illegal immigration ring headed by a crooked farmer (da Silva). Tough guy McGraw is one of da Silva's henchmen, and Mitchell is a Mexican *bracero* seeking to enter the U.S. to find work to support his family. While the U.S. and Mexican governments are cooperating on the illegal alien problem, so are the Mexican and American bad guys, who use the *braceros* as cheap labor and then rob and murder them as they try to return to their homeland with their earnings. This is an extremely violent and fast-paced film noir. The thrilling climax takes place, appropriately enough, in the "Canyon of Death." Montalban, breaking away from his "Latin lover" image, is excellent as the Mexican G-man. Look for Alfonso Bedoya, the grinning bandit in *The Treasure of the Sierra Madre*, playing yet another *bandido*.

Memorable Noir Moment:

❑ After being ordered to kill a fed and make it look like an *accident*, the innovative McGraw shoots and rifle butts his victim and then runs him over with a tractor!

Born to Be Bad (1950) 93 min. Joan Fontaine, Zachary Scott, Robert Ryan, Joan Leslie, Mel Ferrer. **Screenplay by:** Edith Sommer. **Directed by:** Nicholas Ray. **Noir Type:** Femme Fatale. **Noir Themes:** Greed, obsession, greed. ★★½

Millionaire Scott's unfortunate fiancée (Leslie) doesn't stand a chance against shameless, man-stealing femme fatale Fontaine. While Fontaine would rather be with novelist Ryan, her social aspirations win out over her libido and emotions, and she goes after Scott with a fierce determination. Ferrer is a wisecracking painter who knows the society crowd and, it seems, their darkest secrets. Fontaine plays her shrewd and heartless character to the hilt, but her constant smiley face is really maddening. Ryan also has an irritating habit — grabbing Fontaine at the slightest whim and fiercely kissing her. It's an okay melodrama but the hard core crime fan might not enjoy it.

Memorable Noir Moments:

❑ Having lost her man thanks to Fontaine, Leslie complains, "Someone should have told the birds and bees about *you*."
❑ Sensitivity Training Required: The chairperson of the women's club advises Fontaine that their membership fee is a thousand dollars. Fontaine tells her to discuss the fee with hubby Ferrer. Fontaine's Aunt Clara pipes up, "Exactly as it should be. I must say, I disapprove of women having anything to do with finances."
❑ Ryan, who finally sees through Fontaine, storms off, exclaiming, "I love you so much I wish I could like you."

Born to Kill (1947) 92 min. Claire Trevor, Lawrence Tierney, Walter Slezak, Elisha Cook, Jr., Audrey Long, Esther Howard. **Screenplay by:** Eve Greene and Richard Macaulay. **Directed by:** Robert Wise. **Noir Type:** Psycho. **Noir Themes:** Lust, sexual hostility, betrayal, paranoia. ★★★★

This one is all Tierney. He's outstanding as one of the most violently disturbed psychos in all of film noir, giving even Robert Ryan in *Crossfire* a run for his money. Trevor, a recent divorcee, is a visitor to Las Vegas who discovers the bodies of a man and a woman at a Reno rooming house — two bodies left by you-know-who in a fit of jealous rage. Without contacting the police, she leaves for home but, coincidentally, ends up on the same train with Tierney, whom she had been ogling in a casino that evening. The hard-to-swallow plot develops slowly, with Tierney eventually dropping Trevor to marry her wealthy half-sister (Long). Soon he's suffering from the delusion that he can run his wife's newspaper (something he wants to do so he can crush other people's lives) and is hurt when sister-in-law Trevor won't support his dream. Trevor, meanwhile, is becoming more and more attracted to Tierney, and the sexual tension is almost unbearable for her. Tierney's pal (Cook) is the only controlling influence in his life, and even *his* hold is tenuous. Slezak plays a portly, Bible-quoting P.I. hired by Howard to find the murderer of her only friend. *Born to Kill,*

A jealous psychopath (Lawrence Tierney) takes care of a romantic rival (Tony Barrett) in *Born to Kill* (RKO, 1947).

also known as *Deadlier than the Male*, has become a cult classic thanks to the excellent performances of Tierney and Howard and Wise's brilliant direction.

Familiar Face from Television:
❑ Ellen Corby (Grandma Walton from *The Waltons*) as a maid.

Memorable Noir Moments:
❑ Tierney's love-smitten girlfriend dreamily tells Howard and Trevor about her newest beau. "He's a quiet sort," she says, "and yet ya get the feelin' if you stepped out of line, he'd kick your teeth down your throat." "Ain't that wonderful," sighs Howard.
❑ Cook gives his pal Tierney a word of practical advice: "You can't just go around killing people whenever the notion strikes you," he says. "It's not feasible."

The Boss (1956) 88 min. John Payne, William Bishop, Gloria McGhee, Doe Avedon, Roy Roberts, Robin Morse. **Screenplay by**: Ben L. Perry. **Directed by**: Byron Haskin. **Noir Type**: Politics. **Noir Themes**: Corruption, betrayal, greed. ★★★½

The Boss chronicles the rise and fall of the head of a powerful political machine in an unnamed "middle class city." At the end of World War I, G.I. buddies Payne and Bishop go on a wild drunk. After an argument with his fiancée (Avedon), Payne marries a complete stranger (McGhee), who warns him in advance that he'll wake up the next morning and hate her forever. She proves a capable psychic when the now sober Payne takes a gander at the plain Jane sleeping in the hotel bed next to his. Fiercely proud and independent, Payne refuses to divorce McGhee when ordered to do so by his older brother (Roberts), the city's aging political boss. Roberts drops dead of a heart attack on the spot, and Payne takes over the city, proving more ruthless than his predecessor, even threatening to place his wife in an insane asylum if she tries to divorce him. Meanwhile, Bishop, who's since become an attorney and married Avedon, hires on as Payne's right-hand man. Together they run Payne's powerful, now statewide political empire. When the stock market crashes in 1929, they team up with the city's vicious crime lord (Morse) to get the dough they need to stay in power. The alliance, of course, leads to tragedy. Payne, in his finest performance, is impressive as the ferocious political boss bent on self-destruction, and McGhee is excellent as his loyal but frustrated wife. Ben L. Perry was a front for the film's real screenwriter Dalton Trumbo, who had been blacklisted during Hollywood's Red scare.

Familiar Faces from Television:
❑ Joe Flynn (Captain Binghamton in *McHale's Navy*) as Payne's only honest political appointee.
❑ Percy Helton (Homer Cratchit in *The Beverly Hillbillies*) as a hotel clerk.

Memorable Noir Moment:
❑ The film's melodramatic opening statement warns viewers that "only you, a vigilant people, can combat the menace of a boss."

The Boy with Green Hair (1948) 92 min. Pat O'Brien, Dean Stockwell, Robert Ryan, Barbara Hale. **Screenplay by**: Ben Barzman and Alfred Lewis Levitt. **Directed by**: Joseph

Losey. **Noir Type:** Fantasy. **Noir Themes:** Bigotry, betrayal, victim of fate, guilt child in jeopardy. ★★½

The film opens in a police station with cops trying to determine the identity of a tight-lipped runaway (Stockwell). Psychologist Ryan, bearing sandwiches and malted milk, gets him to open up, and, via flashback, we discover that Stockwell is a war orphan who, after being passed from relative to relative, winds up living with a former vaudevillian (O'Brien), whom he calls "gramps." One morning Stockwell wakes up to find that his hair has turned green. At first, his new hair is a source of embarrassment because of all the negative attention and his classmates' taunts. But, after an eerie vision of European and Asian war orphans who encourage him to be their spokesman, the boy begins to spread the message that "war is very bad for children." Unfortunately, the townspeople are more concerned about whether or not his condition has been caused by a problem with the town's milk and if it's contagious. While the good citizens pressure O'Brien to have the boy's head shaved, some of Stockwell's classmates lie in wait with a pair of scissors. The film does well as an indictment against prejudice but flounders in its overly preachy anti-war message. O'Brien is entertaining as the singing waiter whose love for the orphan is put to the test by his angry and fearful neighbors. Hale (Della Street in TV's *Perry Mason*) is good as Stockwell's sympathetic teacher. Crime fans, don't bother.

Familiar Faces from Television:
❑ Dale Robertson (Jim Hardie in *Tales of Wells Fargo*) as a cop trying to learn Stockwell's name.
❑ Dwayne Hickman (Dobie in *The Many Loves of Dobie Gillis*) as Stockwell's bespectacled, scissors-wielding classmate.
❑ Russ Tamblyn (Dr. Lawrence Jacoby in *Twin Peaks*), in his film debut, as Stockwell acrobatic classmate.

Memorable Noir Moment:
❑ When a young student asks his peers, "What's wrong with green hair?," another classmate responds, "How'd ya like your sister to marry somebody with green hair?"

The Brasher Doubloon (1947) 72 min. George Montgomery, Nancy Guild, Roy Roberts, Florence Bates, Marvin Miller. **Screenplay by:** Dorothy Hannah. **Directed by:** John Brahm. **Noir Type:** P.I. **Noir Themes:** Greed. ★★★

Montgomery plays Raymond Chandler's hard-boiled sleuth Philip Marlowe on a case involving a missing gold coin (the Brasher Doubloon). Hired by a crusty old eccentric (Bates), Montgomery uses "Marlowe's muddled method" of investigation and soon finds himself entangled in a nasty web of murder and blackmail. Guild (a young Cybill Shepherd look-alike) plays Bates' man-fearing secretary, whose phobia Montgomery is more than eager to cure. Roberts is the homicide detective losing patience with the troublesome P.I., and Miller is a nightclub owner who wants the doubloon for other than numismatic reasons. The grotesque world of Chandler's pulp fiction character translates uneasily in this mild but enjoyable film noir. While the boyish Montgomery can't approach the gritty performances of Dick Powell and Humphrey Bogart (***Murder, My Sweet*** and ***The Big Sleep***), or even the more genteel

Robert Montgomery (*Lady in the Lake*), he's still fairly entertaining. Montgomery (George, that is) went on to star in the TV Western series *Cimarron City*, which co-starred film noir icon Audrey Totter.

Memorable Noir Moments:

❑ The elderly Bates sends a nervous Guild to Montgomery's house to seduce him into turning over the gold coin. "Capitalize on what you've got, girl," she advises, and boasts, "It wouldn't have been difficult for me when I was your age."
❑ "I don't like to have men touch me," Guild tells Montgomery. Examining her perfume bottle, he notes the brand, "Night of Bliss," and remarks, "You just can't seem to make up your mind."
❑ Montgomery, after being beaten silly by Miller's gang, dives through a closed window, but not before grabbing his hat from the floor. At twenty-five bucks a day plus expenses, a struggling P.I. can't afford to lose too many hats.

The Breaking Point (1950) 97 min. John Garfield, Patricia Neal, Phyllis Thaxter, Juano Hernandez, Wallace Ford. **Screenplay by:** Ranald MacDougall. **Directed by:** Michael Curtiz. **Noir Type:** High Seas. **Noir Themes:** Fatalism. ★★★½

More faithful to the Hemingway story than Howard Hawks' *To Have and Have Not* (1944), *The Breaking Point* stars Garfield as a charter boat skipper forced by economic pressures to smuggle a boatload of illegal Chinese immigrants from Mexico into the U.S. When he's double-crossed, Garfield accidentally kills the smuggler who hired him and drops the illegals off in shallow waters to be picked up by immigration agents. His boat is impounded by the Coast Guard while the Mexican government investigates the incident, further worsening his financial situation. Thaxter, his loving wife, wants him to retire from the failed business venture and take a job on her uncle's lettuce farm. Garfield understandably resists that career move and soon finds himself involved with a shady lawyer (Ford) in yet another illegal charter — this time for a gang of stick-up men who are planning a race track heist. Hernandez plays Garfield's friend and first mate, and Neal is the femme fatale who falls for the skipper — who *almost* gives her the time of day. Garfield is terrific and so is the climactic shoot-out on board the *Sea Queen*.

Familiar Faces from Television:

❑ Sherry Jackson (Danny Thomas' first TV daughter in *Make Room for Daddy* a.k.a. *The Danny Thomas Show*) as Garfield's younger daughter.
❑ Victor Sen Yung (Hop Sing on *Bonanza*) as the smuggler of illegal aliens.

Memorable Noir Moments:

❑ Responding to Garfield's remarks that she's an unwanted passenger on his boat, Neal says, "Maybe I should have swam back to Newport. Or is it swum?" Garfield replies, "Either way it could still happen."
❑ When a bartender tells Garfield that lawyer Ford is harmless, the skipper replies, "He's two pounds in a one-pound bag. That's what he is."

The Bribe (1949) 98 min. Robert Taylor, Ava Gardner, Charles Laughton, Vincent Price, John Hodiak, John Hoyt. **Screenplay by:** Marguerite Roberts. **Directed by:** Robert Z. Leonard. **Noir Type:** South of the Border. **Noir Themes:** Obsession, betrayal. ★★★

A "pie-shaped man" (Charles Laughton, left) listens attentively to a federal agent (Robert Taylor) while a nightclub singer (Ava Gardner) stands by in *The Bribe* (MGM, 1949).

Taylor is a U.S. federal agent assigned by his boss (Hoyt) to find out who is smuggling airplane motors into Central America. His primary suspects include nightclub singer Gardner, her alcoholic husband (Hodiak), a seedy "pie-shaped man" with podiatric problems (Laughton) and an American businessman (Price). After Taylor falls for Gardner, he's forced to choose between honor and love when arrest time comes around. The beautiful Gardner is terrific, but it's Laughton, managing to out-ham even Price, who steals the film. Don't miss the exciting climax — a shootout in the midst of a spectacular fireworks display.

Memorable Noir Moments:

❑ From the Some-Things-Never-Change Department: Price and Taylor chat about the current generation gap. "You young men — the world is falling apart and you go fishing," Price chides. "The world just got through falling apart," Taylor says, referring to World War II. "This is the 'brave new world,' the one you guys promised."

❑ A nervous Laughton balks at Price's suggestion that he kill Taylor. "They get the chair twice as hot for bumping off a fed," he says.

The Brothers Rico (1957) 92 min. Richard Conte, Dianne Foster, Larry Gates, Paul

Picerni, James Darren. **Screenplay by:** Lewis Meltzer and Dalton Trumbo (as Ben Perry). **Directed by:** Phil Karlson. **Noir Type:** Gangster. **Noir Themes:** Betrayal. ★★½

Conte, a former accountant for the mob, is now a legitimate businessman. He and his wife (Foster), unable to have their own children, are desperately trying to adopt. The adoption process comes to a screeching halt when Conte's kid brothers (Picerni and Darren), who recently performed a hit for their boss (Gates), ask for Conte's help because they're afraid that Gates now wants *them* dead. Not a lot of action here, but Conte is excellent as usual. Teen idol Darren went on to star in the TV sci-fi series *The Time Tunnel.*

Familiar Face from Television:
❏ Harry Bellaver (Sgt. Arcaro in *Naked City*) as a mob goon in El Camino.

Memorable Noir Moment:
❏ Conte begs a syndicate underling to spare his brother's life. The unmoved hood replies, "You're like the guy in the death house arguing with the warden."

Brute Force (1947) 94 min. Burt Lancaster, Hume Cronyn, Charles Bickford, Yvonne De Carlo, Ann Blyth, Ella Raines, Anita Colby, Howard Duff, Art Smith, Roman Bohnen, John Hoyt, Jeff Corey, Jack Overman. **Screenplay by:** Richard Brooks. **Directed by:** Jules Dassin. **Noir Type:** Prison. **Noir Themes:** Betrayal, obsession, revenge, corruption, fatalism, social reform. ★★★★★

Lancaster and his cellmates (Duff, Hoyt, Corey and Overman) plan a daring prison break escape, but a sadistic prison captain (Cronyn) catches wind of the scheme. Lancaster, desperate for freedom because his girl (Blyth) needs a cancer operation, convinces trusty Bickford, the prison newspaper editor, to start a riot to keep the tower guards occupied while he and his men attack them from a work station outside the wall. Meanwhile, the sympathetic warden (Bohnen) is under political pressure to crack down. Cronyn is waiting in the wings for his chance to take over—and killing a bunch of inmates during an escape attempt seems like a good first step toward a promotion. Smith is the reform-minded, rum-dum prison doctor; De Carlo plays Duff's Italian war bride; Raines is the wife of a con (Bissell) who went to prison for embezzling money to buy her a fur coat; and Colby is a wily femme fatale who teaches Hoyt a valuable lesson about dames ("I wonder who Flossie's fleecing now?"). One of the best prison break movies ever made, *Brute Force* is a bleak film about hopelessness, betrayal and violence. While Lancaster is powerful as the breakout leader, and Duff, in his film debut, gives a solid performance, Cronyn, cast way against type, is the top attraction. His psychopathic guard, with a penchant for classical music and rubber hoses, is one of the most despicable villains in movie history. Look for at least a dozen familiar noir faces, including noir veteran Charles McGraw as a con working in the prison auto shop.

Familiar Faces from Television:
❏ Ray Teal (Sheriff Roy Coffee in *Bonanza*) as Cronyn's right-hand man.
❏ Jay C. Flippen (Chief Nelson in *Ensign O'Toole*) as a prison guard.

Wannabe escapees (Howard Duff, Jeff Corey, Jack Overman, Burt Lancaster and John Hoyt, left to right) pretend to play dominos while a guard makes his rounds in *Brute Force* (Universal-International, 1947).

Memorable Noir Moments:

❏ When Lancaster returns to his cell from solitary confinement, he's told by his cellmates that everything's okay now. "Nothing's okay," he responds through gritted teeth. "It never was and it never will be. Not 'til we're out."

❏ A terrified stoolie in the prison workshop becomes the recipient of convict justice when blowtorch-wielding Duff, Hoyt and Overman slowly back him toward a giant, pounding press.

A Bullet for Joey (1955) 86 min. Edward G. Robinson, George Raft, Audrey Totter, George Dolenz, Peter Van Eyck. **Screenplay by:** Daniel Mainwaring (as Geoffrey Homes) and A.I. Bezzerides. **Directed by:** Lewis Allen. **Noir Type:** Nuclear. **Noir Themes:** Betrayal, obsession, jealousy. ★★½

A Canadian police inspector (Robinson) investigating the murder of a cop by an organ grinder finds the trail leading to a Commie spy (Van Eyck). Van Eyck has hired a deported American gangster (Raft) to kidnap an atomic physicist (Dolenz). Raft calls in members of his old gang and his former moll (Totter), now a legitimate business owner, whom he forces to seduce Dolenz. Unfortunately for Raft, Totter falls for the scientist, endangering the operation. Slow moving, but Robinson and Raft are enjoyable, and Totter does a good job as the reluctant femme fatale.

Memorable Noir Moments:

❑ Robinson promises Raft a fair trial if he cooperates. "Listen to him," Raft tells his goons. "If I get a fair trial I'm dead. What I need is an *un*fair trial."

❑ Spy ringleader Van Eyck balks at Raft's suggestion that they get a doll to seduce the physicist, calling the idea primitive. "Wait 'til you see this dame I've got in mind," says Raft, referring to Totter. "She'd make anyone turn primitive."

The Burglar (1957) 90 min. Dan Duryea, Jayne Mansfield, Martha Vickers, Peter Capell, Mickey Shaughnessy, Stewart Bradley. **Screenplay by:** David Goodis. **Directed by:** Paul Wendkos. **Noir Type:** On the Run. **Noir Themes:** Greed, sexual hostility, betrayal, corruption. ★★

Duryea and his gang (Mansfield, Capell and Shaughnessy) burglarize a wealthy spiritualist's mansion and make off with a necklace worth 150 Gs. They have to stay holed up in their claustrophobic apartment until the heat is off, when they'll be able to fence the necklace for half its value. Mansfield is in love with Duryea, but all he's interested in is keeping his word to her father, his late mentor, that he'll watch out for her. Shaughnessy, who has the unrequited hots for the blonde bombshell, attacks her, forcing Duryea to send her away for her own protection. The remaining gang member, Capell, simply wants his share of the dough so he can realize his dream — a luxurious and carefree life in Central America. To complicate matters, a crooked cop (Bradley) and a femme fatale (Vickers) begin to romance Mansfield and Duryea in a plot to pinch the necklace. This is an unsatisfying noir with too many weird camera angles and close-ups, little character development and even less action. The heist at the beginning of the film and the climax on Atlantic City's boardwalk are enjoyable, however. Mansfield is surprisingly good (compared to her lame performance the previous year in *Female Jungle*).

Memorable Noir Moments:

❑ Vickers tells Duryea about her vicious father, drunken mother and four brothers: "We were a close family. We had to be close. We lived in two rooms."

❑ Duryea plans to escape Atlantic City by stealing a yacht. "What do *you* know about boats?" Capell asks sarcastically. "They float," replies landlubber Duryea.

Bury Me Dead (1947) 68 min. June Lockhart, Hugh Beaumont, Cathy O'Donnell, Mark Daniels, Greg McClure, Sonia Darrin. **Screenplay by:** Dwight V. Babcock. **Directed by:** Bernard Vorhaus. **Noir Type:** Whodunit. **Noir Themes:** Woman in jeopardy, lust, jealousy. ★½

Despite its fascinating title and premise, this low-budget noir is a big disappointment. Wealthy Lockhart shows up at her own funeral, leaving everyone to wonder (via flashbacks) whose charred body was discovered after a fire in her stable. Murder is suspected, and Lockhart begins to worry that the killer might try to rectify the mistake. Suspects include Lockhart's husband (Daniels), who's been having an affair with femme fatale Darrin; O'Donnell, Lockhart's disturbed teenaged sister; Beaumont, the family lawyer; and boxer McClure, a "muscle-bound meatball." Beaumont gives a decent performance, but the film's numerous attempts at light comedy ruin what could have been a suspenseful and intriguing mystery. (One enjoyable exception: Lockhart and Darrin go toe to toe in a pretty intense slapping contest.) If you like lengthy films, try this one for size — its sixty-eight minutes seem more like two hours.

Familiar Face from Television:

❏ John Dehner (reporter Duke Williams in The Roaring Twenties) as a reporter covering the stable fire.

Memorable Noir Moments:

❏ "You mean you actually came here for purposes of extortion?" a stunned Beaumont asks McClure. The dim-witted boxer replies, "Oh, no. Nothing violent like that."
❏ Sensitivity Training Required: After Lockhart fakes not being able to pull an ice tray from the freezer, the manly Beaumont does so easily. "I guess I'm not very strong," Lockhart remarks. "Of course you're not," replies Beaumont. "You're a woman."

C-Man (1949) 75 min. Dean Jagger, John Carradine, Lottie Elwen, Harry Landers, Rene Paul. **Screenplay by:** Berne Giler. **Directed by:** Joseph Lerner. **Noir Type:** Police Procedural. **Noir Themes:** Greed. ★★½

Jagger is a U.S. Customs agent on the trail of the jewel smugglers who murdered

A U.S. customs agent (Dean Jagger, right) gets the evil eye from a psychopathic hood (Harry Landers) in *C-Man* (Film Classics, 1949).

his best friend, a fellow C-Man. Paul is the ringleader of the gang; Carradine is the drunken, has-been surgeon on Paul's payroll; and Elwen is a Dutch war bride who unwittingly smuggles a valuable necklace into the U.S. Jagger, who takes quite a few beatings, is perhaps the worst fighter in all of film noir. The only brawl he wins is the one in which his opponent is accidentally shot by a cohort with a bad aim. *C-Man*, like the groundbreaking *The Naked City* filmed a year earlier, makes good use of its New York City locations, and Landers spices up the bland moments with his portrayal of a sadistic hood.

Memorable Noir Moment:

❑ An imaginative killer discovers a new weapon to take care of an unconscious squealer: a bedpost knob. See *Appointment with Danger* for another inventive killer's weapon of choice.

Caged (1950) 97 min. Eleanor Parker, Agnes Moorehead, Hope Emerson, Betty Garde, Jan Sterling, Ellen Corby. **Screenplay by**: Virginia Kellogg and Bernard C. Schoenfeld. **Directed by**: John Cromwell. **Noir Type**: Prison. **Noir Themes**: Victim of fate, corruption, fatalism, social reform. ★★★★

A 19-year-old, pregnant newlywed (Parker), wrongly convicted of being an accessory to a forty dollar stick-up committed by her husband, is sentenced to one to fifteen years in a women's prison. The film tracks her rapid descent from bewildered innocent to hardened con, who learns early on that "in this cage, you get tough or you get killed." Moorehead plays the kindly warden trying to protect Parker from a particularly vicious matron (Emerson). Garde plays the tough cellblock leader, who is serving time for murder and can exercise some control over Emerson with meager bribes from her shoplifting ring on the outside. Sterling is a savvy blonde inmate, and dimwitted Corby ("Who's this Pearl Harbor anyway? Is she an inmate?") plays a husband killer. Highly enjoyable, if somewhat dated, *Caged* is a powerful prison noir and a daring, socially conscious drama that earned well-deserved Oscar nominations for Best Writing (Story and Screenplay), Best Actress (Parker) and Best Supporting Actress (Emerson).

Familiar Faces from Television:

❑ Gertrude Hoffman (Mrs. Odetts of *My Little Margie*) as an elderly lifer.
❑ Ann Tyrrell (Vi in *Private Secretary* and Olive in *The Ann Sothern Show*) as a sickly inmate in isolation.
❑ Lee Patrick (Cosmo's wife, Henrietta in *Topper*) as a big-time vice queen serving a six-month term.

Memorable Noir Moments:

❑ Inmate Corby, who attempted to kill her abusive husband three times before succeeding, blames the judge for her predicament. "If he'd a nabbed me the first three times when I was just practicin', I wouldn't be here now for murder," she complains.
❑ During new inmate processing, Parker is told by a lazy civil servant, "I'll skip the mental test. You look normal enough."
❑ A frail, elderly killer warns Emerson, who's about to strike her, "Lay your hand on me and I'll put your lights out. I'm in for life and one more like you is just so much velvet."

Pilot buddies (Alan Ladd, left, and William Bendix) fly the Chungking-to-Calcutta route in *Calcutta* **(Paramount, 1947).**

Calcutta (1947) 83 min. Alan Ladd, Gail Russell, William Bendix, June Duprez, John Whitney, Lowell Gilmore. **Screenplay by:** Seton I. Miller. **Directed by:** John Farrow. **Noir Type:** Adventure. **Noir Themes:** Revenge, betrayal, greed. ★★½

When their buddy Whitney is strangled after a barroom brawl, commercial pilots Ladd and Bendix go looking for payback. They find themselves involved with Whitney's mysterious fiancée (Russell), the owner of a gambling casino (Gilmore), some nasty jewel smugglers and the British police, who suspect them of having committed a murder. Duprez plays a worried nightclub singer, who is afraid that boyfriend Ladd may be falling for the beautiful Russell. Who can blame him? A pretty standard action flick with some interesting noir elements to spice it up somewhat.

Memorable Noir Moments:
❑ When Whitney tells Ladd of his engagement to Russell, the committed bachelor scolds him: "You've combed enough dames out of your hair to know what they want — stability, settle down."
❑ Russell can't see what Ladd and her murdered fiancé had in common. "You're cold, sadistic, egotistical," she accuses. "Maybe," he agrees, "but I'm still alive."

Call Northside 777 (1948) 111 min. James Stewart, Richard Conte, Lee J. Cobb, Helen Walker, John McIntire, Kasia Orzazewski. **Screenplay by:** Jerome Cady and Jay Dratler.

Directed by: Henry Hathaway. **Noir Type**: Wrong Man. **Noir Themes**: Victim of the law, obsession. ★★★★

This interesting semi-documentary, shot on location in Chicago, is based on actual events. Stewart is cast against type as a tough, outspoken reporter assigned to follow up on a story about a man (Conte) convicted of killing a cop eleven years earlier. He interviews the con's mother (Orzazewski), a Polish scrubwoman who has scrimped and saved enough money to be able to offer a five thousand dollar reward for information that will prove her son's innocence. Knowing a hot human interest story when he sees one, Stewart's editor (Cobb) sends his reluctant ace reporter to Illinois State Prison to interview Conte, who's serving a ninety-nine-year term. The skeptical reporter finds himself believing Conte's story and starts investigating more thoroughly, running into numerous obstacles—a police department covering up its mistakes, a missing witness, a dead judge and politicians worried about being the fall guys for a previous administration's screw-ups. Walker plays Stewart's wife and McIntire is a frightened politician. The film is thoroughly entertaining thanks in large part to Stewart's solid performance as the methodical investigative reporter.

Familiar Faces from Television:
- ❏ E.G. Marshall (Lawrence Preston in *The Defenders*) as the man who married Conte's ex-wife.
- ❏ Charles Lane (Homer Bedloe in *Petticoat Junction* and Mr. Barnsdahl in *The Lucy Show*) as the prosecutor at Conte's trial.
- ❏ Percy Helton (Homer Cratchit in *The Beverly Hillbillies*) as a mailman.
- ❏ Henry Kulky (Otto Schmidlap in *The Life of Riley*) as the bartender in Drazynski's Place.

Memorable Noir Moment:
- ❏ Reporter Stewart is not confident that the reward offered by Conte's mother will help her son's case. "This is sucker bait," he says. "Every drifter and moocher in town is after that five grand. They'll frame their brothers to get it."

Calling Homicide (1956) 60 min. Bill Elliott, Don Haggerty, Kathleen Case, Myron Healey, Jeanne Cooper, Thomas Browne Henry, Lyle Talbot. **Screenplay by**: Edward Bernds. **Directed by**: Edward Bernds. **Noir Type**: Police Procedural. **Noir Themes**: Greed, obsession. ★★

Los Angeles Sheriff's Department detectives Elliott and Haggerty investigate the killing of a colleague who had been working on an important case. Unfortunately, all of the cop's paperwork was lost in the car bombing that took his life. The detectives' only clue leads them to a modeling agency owner, whose strangled body is discovered on a construction site. The hated woman's death goes unmourned by her employees (Case, Cooper, Henry and Talbot) and former lover (Healey), all of whom are suspects in her murder. This was the second in the bland series of "Lt. Doyle" crime dramas starring Elliott (see *Sudden Danger* and *Footsteps in the Night*). Another Lt. Doyle film, *Chain of Evidence*, was not available for review by the author at the time of writing.

Familiar Faces from Television:
- ❏ James Best (Sheriff Roscoe P. Coltrane in *The Dukes of Hazzard*) as a detective.
- ❏ Mary Treen (Hilda the maid on *The Joey Bishop Show*) as a studio script girl.

Convict Scott Brady borrows a uniform from an obliging guard in *Canon City* (Eagle-Lion, 1948).

Canon City (1948) 82 min. Scott Brady, Jeff Corey, Whit Bissell, Charles Russell. **Screenplay by:** Crane Wilbur. **Directed by:** Crane Wilbur. **Noir Type:** Prison. **Noir Themes:** Fatalism, distrust. ★★★

This documentary-style noir, narrated by Reed Hadley (of TV's *Racket Squad*), is based on the true story of an actual prison break. Twelve convicts escape from Colorado State Penitentiary ("a grim place of gray stone walls") during a heavy winter storm, terrorizing local residents. Brady does well in his film debut as the repentant cop-killer, as do noir veterans Corey and Bissell as his fellow cons. The film was shot on location at the penitentiary, and the warden, some prison guards and a number of inmates played themselves. An interesting gimmick, but don't leave your day jobs, boys.

Familiar Face from Television:
❏ DeForest Kelley (Dr. Bones McCoy in *Star Trek*) as a convict.

Memorable Noir Moment:
❏ A senior citizen (veteran character actress Mabel Paige) kicks some convict butt.

The Captive City (1952) 90 min. John Forsythe, Joan Camden, Harold J. Kennedy, Ray Teal, Hal K. Dawson. **Screenplay by:** Alvin M. Josephy, Sr., and Karl Kamb. **Directed by:** Robert Wise. **Noir Type:** Newspaper. **Noir Themes:** Corruption, paranoia. ★★½

John Forsythe (of TV's *Bachelor Father* and *Dynasty*) plays a crusading newspaper editor battling the Mafia in his small town. When a terrified private eye (Dawson) contacts Forsythe and tells him that he's being harassed by the police and followed by a car with out-of-state plates, Forsythe doesn't pay much attention ... until the man turns up dead, a hit-and-run victim. Forsythe finally decides to investigate but finds the townsfolk strangely uncooperative. He's resisted at every turn by the police chief (Teal), the town's business and religious leaders and even his partner (Kennedy) at the newspaper. It isn't long before Forsythe and his wife (Camden) notice a car with out-of-state plates following them, too. Forsythe gives an enjoyable, low-key performance, but the film is slow moving and lacking suspense. Senator Estes Kefauver (see *Mad at the World*), the chairman of the Senate Crime Investigating Committee, makes an appearance to warn the American public of the dangers of ignoring seemingly victimless crimes such as gambling. United Artists was careful to point out that Kefauver's salary for his part in the film went to charity.

Familiar Face from Television:
❏ Martin Milner (Officer Pete Malloy in *Adam 12*) as a newspaper photographer.

Memorable Noir Moment:
❏ A discouraged Forsythe hits the bottle and comments cynically, "They say that alcohol never cured anybody of anything. But when you're legs have been cut off at the knees, believe me, it helps."

The Capture (1950) 67 min. Lew Ayres, Teresa Wright, Victor Jory, Jacqueline White, Barry Kelley, Edwin Rand. **Screenplay by:** Niven Busch. **Directed by:** John Sturges. **Noir Type:** South of the Border. **Noir Themes:** Victim of fate, guilt, paranoia. ★★½

A wounded man (Ayres), the former field manager of an American oil rigging company in Mexico and now a fugitive, tells a village priest (Jory) the story of how he tracked down and shot a man suspected of killing several guards during a payroll robbery. Via flashback, we follow Ayres into the mountains while a fellow oil rigger

(Kelley) leads a posse into the desert. Ayres eventually finds the suspect (Rand) and orders him to raise his hands. Rand, whose arm is broken, cannot comply and the nervous Ayres, unaware of the man's disability, doesn't hesitate to shoot him. Rand, protesting his innocence, later dies of his wounds. Even though the payroll was not recovered, Ayres' superiors offer him a two thousand dollar reward, which the conscience-stricken man refuses. This angers Ayres' greedy fiancée (White), who breaks off their engagement. Ayres quits his job and soon finds himself working as a handyman on a ranch owned by Rand's widow (Wright), who doesn't know that he's the man who killed her husband. After falling in love with Wright, Ayres becomes determined to prove her late husband's innocence. He winds up wounded and wanted for murder, fearing that his karma is to be shot by the Mexican *federales* because he, too, will not be able to raise his wounded arm to surrender. This unusual noir, with a Western backdrop, is well-acted and occasionally exciting, but too much time is spent establishing the unlikely romance between Ayres and Wright.

Familiar Face from Television:
❑ Duncan Renaldo (*The Cisco Kid*) as Ayres' Mexican amigo.

Casablanca (1942) 102 min. Humphrey Bogart, Ingrid Bergman, Paul Henreid, Claude Rains, Conrad Veidt, Sydney Greenstreet, Peter Lorre. **Screenplay by:** Julius J. Epstein, Philip G. Epstein and Howard Koch. **Directed by:** Michael Curtiz. **Noir Type:** Triangle. **Noir Themes:** Fatalism, conspiracy, corruption, betrayal. ★★★★★

Bogart is the cynical owner of a Casablanca nightclub-casino called Rick's Café Américain, a gathering place for Nazis, French resistance fighters, thieves and desperate refugees seeking to purchase exit papers that will allow them to continue on to America. When asked by small-time crook Lorre to safeguard two letters of transit signed by General De Gaulle, Bogey agrees, not realizing that the letters are intended for his former lover (Bergman) and her resistance leader husband (Henreid). When the couple arrives in Casablanca, a vicious Gestapo major (Veidt) begins plotting with the city's French police captain (Rains) to arrest Henreid before he can flee to the United States, where he's expected to rally support for his fight against the Nazis. Still smarting from being dropped by Bergman several years earlier without a word of explanation, Bogart is tempted to stand by his life philosophy ("I stick my neck out for nobody") and withhold the precious transit letters, for which another nightclub owner (Greenstreet) will pay a pretty penny. Long considered *the* perfect film, *Casablanca* is a genuine American masterpiece of romance, mystery and intrigue. Outstanding performances by Bogart and Bergman as the star-crossed lovers, and Henreid as the unselfish patriot, helped earn *Casablanca* an Academy Award for Best Film. Curtiz took home the Best Director Oscar, and the Epstein brothers and Koch won for Best Screenplay. The film was nominated for five other Academy Awards, including Best Actor (Bogart) and Best Supporting Actor (Rains). Rated number two on the American Film Institute's List of America's 100 Greatest Movies, *Casablanca* spawned two unsuccessful television series (a 1955-56 version with noir veteran Charles McGraw and a 1983 version with *Starsky and Hutch* star David Soul).

Memorable Noir Moments:

❑ An inebriated, self-pitying Bogey complains bitterly to his piano player, "Of all the gin joints in all the towns in all the world, she walks into mine."
❑ Bogey can't hide his disdain for petty thief Lorre, telling him, "I don't mind a parasite, but I object to a cut-rate one."

Cast a Dark Shadow (1957(?)-British) 88 min. Dirk Bogarde, Mona Washbourne, Margaret Lockwood, Kay Walsh. **Screenplay by:** John Cresswell. **Directed by:** Lewis Gilbert. **Noir Type:** Con Artist. **Noir Themes:** Greed, woman in jeopardy. ★★½

Sociopath Bogarde has developed a nice little scam: He marries wealthy widows and murders them for their money. His current wife (Washbourne), having fallen for his evil charm, intends to change her will, leaving everything to Bogarde. Believing that she's planning to disinherit him, he kills her before she can sign the paperwork, and winds up with only the house and no cash. Broke, he next weds a saloonkeeper's street-smart widow (Lockwood), who he thinks is wealthy. The joke is on him when he discovers that she's a con artist who married *him* for *his* money. When Bogarde meets Walsh, an eligible lady with money, it seems that the cycle will start all over. Lockwood, however, isn't a willing victim. This British noir entry is a bit confusing, but Bogarde is terrific as the charismatic (but unlucky) schemer. Sources differ as to the actual date that this film was released. Some say 1955 while others put it at 1957 and 1958. The film itself shows no date in its credits.

Memorable Noir Moment:

❑ Lockwood informs the interested Bogarde that she's a recent widow. "I buried him six months ago," she says. "Oh, I'm sorry," replies Bogarde. "What was wrong with him?" "He was dead," she answers.

Cat People (1942) 73 min. Simone Simon, Kent Smith, Tom Conway, Jane Randolph. **Screenplay by:** DeWitt Bodeen. **Directed by:** Jacques Tourneur. **Noir Type:** Horror. **Noir Themes:** Fatalism, character deterioration, jealousy, paranoia, betrayal. ★★★★

Believing herself to be the victim of an old Serbian curse, shy émigré–Manhattanite Simon takes a chance on love. Fully expecting to turn into a panther and rend her groom (Smith) to pieces the moment he kisses her, Simon subjects her extremely patient husband to an even worse fate — no intimate contact. Smith's patience has its limit, however, and after a frustrating month of wedded non-bliss, he sends her to a libidinous psychiatrist (Conway) who wants to test the curse for himself. Meanwhile, Smith's lovesick co-worker (Randolph) is starting to look better and better to the deprived newlywed. Unfortunately for Randolph, it seems that the curse ignites just as easily with the fuel of jealousy as it does with passion. There's not much horror here, but tons of atmosphere and subtle terror, thanks to the dark imagination of director Tourneur and the beautiful cinematography of Nicholas Musuraca. Simon does a fine job as the pitiable immigrant bride, who seems to spend more time at the zoo than in her unconsummated bed. This was the first in a series of sophisticated low-budget horror films by producer Val Lewton. A dismal 1982 remake starred Nastassia Kinski and was directed by Paul Schrader.

Memorable Noir Moment:
❑ When a mysterious "cat woman" stops at Smith and Simon's wedding reception table in a Serbian restaurant to greet her feline "sister," Smith reacts to his bride's obvious fear by chucking her on the chin and giving her an encouraging, "You crazy kid."

Caught (1949) 88 min. James Mason, Barbara Bel Geddes, Robert Ryan, Curt Bois. **Screenplay by:** Arthur Laurents. **Directed by:** Max Ophüls. **Noir Type:** Soap Opera. **Noir Themes:** Obsession, greed, sexual hostility. ★★

Bel Geddes is a carhop who dreams of someday marrying a millionaire. After graduating from charm school, where she learns that "marrying well is the most important thing for a girl," she realizes her goal. The marriage turns out to be no Cinderella story, however, when she discovers that her wealthy catch (Ryan) is abusive and psychologically disturbed. In one of her saner moments, Bel Geddes leaves her new husband and goes to work for a dedicated city doctor (Mason) who, between house calls, falls in love with her. Ahead of its time in its portrayal of psychological spousal abuse, the film is considered by many to be powerful and compelling. Despite fine performances, especially by Bois as Ryan's effeminate toady, the melodrama wears thin after a while. The ending might leave some scratching their heads over Bel Geddes' and Mason's unusual, almost gleeful response to what many women would consider a tragedy. This is film noir at its most bland.

Familiar Faces from Television:
❑ Natalie Schafer (Mrs. Howell on *Gilligan's Island*) as the charm school owner.
❑ Barbara Billingsley (June Cleaver in *Leave it to Beaver*) as a department store customer.

Memorable Noir Moments:
❑ Ryan shares with his psychiatrist his opinion about women in general and Bel Geddes in particular. "They're a dime a dozen," he says. The puzzled doctor remarks, "I thought you said before she was sweeter than most of the girls." "Psychoanalysts and elephants— they never forget," Ryan complains.
❑ Sensitivity Training Required: The help-wanted ad under the one that Bel Geddes circles reads, "Female Singer — American preferred."

Cause for Alarm (1951) 74 min. Loretta Young, Barry Sullivan, Bruce Cowling, Irving Bacon, Art Baker. **Screenplay by:** Mel Dinelli and Tom Lewis. **Directed by:** Tay Garnett. **Noir Type:** Newlywed. **Noir Themes:** Paranoia, jealousy, revenge, woman in jeopardy, character deterioration. ★★★

A dashing, young naval officer (Sullivan) sweeps a beautiful volunteer hospital worker (Young) off her feet and steals her away from her doctor boyfriend (Cowling). After they settle down into a fairy tale, Ward-and-June-Cleaver existence, things go horribly awry. Sullivan, suffering from heart disease, begins exhibiting paranoid schizophrenic behavior and writes a letter to the District Attorney claiming that Young and Cowling are trying to kill him by tampering with his medication. Nothing could be further from the truth, but the letter gets mailed just before Sullivan suffers a fatal heart attack. The frantic housewife desperately tries to retrieve the incriminating letter from an obstinate postman (Bacon) and a by-the-book postal superintendent (Baker). This is a suspenseful and well-acted noir with an enjoyable

A paranoid schizophrenic (Barry Sullivan) and his unsuspecting wife (Loretta Young) during happier times in *Cause for Alarm* (MGM, 1951).

surprise ending. Keep an eye out for former Little Rascal Carl "Alfalfa" Switzer, sans the hair lick, as a jalopy mechanic.

Familiar Face from Television:

❑ Richard Anderson (Oscar Goldman in *The Six Million Dollar Man*) as a sailor hospitalized with a broken leg.

Champion (1949) 99-min. Kirk Douglas, Marilyn Maxwell, Arthur Kennedy, Paul Stewart, Ruth Roman, Luis Van Rooten, Lola Albright. **Screenplay by**: Carl Foreman. **Directed by**: Mark Robson. **Noir Type**: Boxing. **Noir Themes**: Character deterioration, betrayal, corruption. ★★★★½

This sensational boxing noir ranks right up there with *Body and Soul* and *The Set-Up*. Douglas, who was nominated for an Academy Award for his performance, stars as "a boy who rose from the depths of poverty to become champion of the world," and who leaves behind a trail of broken spirits on his road to self-destruction. A hero in the public eye, behind the scenes he's a vicious conniver willing to knock out anybody, inside or outside the ring, who tries to stop his dream ("I wanna hear people call me 'Mister'"). We witness the cad's transformation from fun-loving freight car hobo to callous middleweight champ, and meet the people whom he double-crosses along the way—his loving wife (Roman), his crippled brother (Kennedy), his loyal manager (Stewart), the unfaithful wife (Albright) of a disreputable promoter (Van Rooten) and his femme fatale lover (Maxwell). Douglas, whose film career began as a spineless district attorney in *The Strange Love of Martha Ivers*, is terrific in the powerful role that changed his image and helped make him a star. Veteran character actor Kennedy, whose film debut was in another boxing noir (*City for Conquest*), earned an Oscar nomination for Best Supporting Actor. Albright later co-starred in the successful TV detective series *Peter Gunn*.

Memorable Noir Moments:
❑ Stewart, attempting to discourage boxer wannabe Douglas, rationalizes his retirement from the boxing world. "This is the only sport in the world," he says, "where two guys get paid for doing something they'd be arrested for if they got drunk and did it for nothing."
❑ Double-dealing Maxwell tries to convince Douglas to leave Stewart for a new manager. "I've *got* a manager," he protests. "Ya got an appendix, too," she retorts, "but it'll never make you rich."
❑ Douglas, in an argument with Kennedy, who's had a bellyful of boxing, defends his chosen profession. "It's like any other business," he claims, adding, "only the blood shows."

The Chase (1946) 86 min. Robert Cummings, Michèle Morgan, Steve Cochran, Peter Lorre, Lloyd Corrigan. **Screenplay by**: Philip Yordan. **Directed by**: Arthur Ripley. **Noir Type**: Troubled Veteran. **Noir Themes**: Sexual hostility, obsession, betrayal. ★★½

Navy war veteran Cummings is a shock case suffering from "anxiety neurosis." Down on his luck, he finds a wallet on the street, uses some of the money for breakfast and then returns it to its grateful owner, mobster Cochran, who hires him as his chauffeur. Morgan, Cochran's melancholy wife, desperately wants to run away from her husband and go to Cuba. Cummings falls for her and, with no sense of loyalty to the man who gave him a job, runs off with her to Havana. This is where the plot strays wildly, as the luckless Cummings is accused of murder, escapes from Cuban police and attempts to find the real killer. However, like so many other films noirs, not everything is as it seems. Lorre plays Cochran's creepy right-hand man and Corrigan is a competitor who foolishly turns down Cochran's offer to buy his business. The always enjoyable Cochran is the film's main attraction.

Memorable Noir Moments:
❑ Misogynist Cochran badgers his female barber about her sexual motivation for cutting men's hair and then slaps the clumsy manicurist when she accidentally digs the nail file too deep.
❑ Cochran asks Cummings if Morgan has confided in him about her plans. Cummings, feigning surprised, asks why he thinks she would. "You've got the kind of face women like to talk to," Cochran tells him.

Chase a Crooked Shadow (1957-British) 92 min. Richard Todd, Anne Baxter, Herbert Lom, Alexander Knox, Faith Brook, Alan Tilvern. **Screenplay by**: David Osborn and

Charles Sinclair. **Directed by**: Michael Anderson. **Noir Type**: Impersonator. **Noir Themes**: Woman in jeopardy, betrayal. ★★★★

A mysterious stranger (Todd) arrives at Baxter's Barcelona villa claiming to be her brother, who supposedly died in an auto accident several years earlier. He seems to know everything, even the most personal details, about Baxter and her family, so much so that Spanish cop Lom buys his story, despite Baxter's denials. Once established in the villa, Todd fires all the servants and brings in his own staff (Brook and Tilvern). The terrorized Baxter tries desperately to get Lom to believe that her real brother is dead. Meanwhile, the only person who can verify her story, her "uncle" (Knox), has mysteriously disappeared. This is a well-crafted and highly suspenseful British thriller, with Baxter excellent as the frantic woman who believes she will be killed once Todd and his cohorts get what they're after.

Memorable Noir Moment:
❑ The producer, actor Douglas Fairbanks, Jr., appears briefly at the end of the film to plead with viewers not to disclose the surprise ending.

Chicago Confidential (1957) 75 min. Brian Keith, Beverly Garland, Dick Foran, Elisha Cook, Jr., Paul Langton, Beverly Tyler. **Screenplay by**: Bernard Gordon (as Raymond T. Marcus). **Directed by**: Sidney Salkow. **Noir Type**: Union. **Noir Themes**: Corruption, greed. ★★½

A two-fisted D.A. (Keith) with his eye on the Illinois governorship convicts an innocent union leader (Foran) of murder. When pressured by Foran's girl (Garland) to reopen the case, Keith comes to believe he's sent an innocent man to Death Row. Along with homicide detective Langton, Keith tries to track down the real killers, but the clues lead them only to dead bodies and live B-girls. Noir veteran Cook plays a rum-dum hobo called "Candymouth," who stumbles on the murder weapon and sells his false testimony for a bottle of hooch. Tyler is the defense witness forced to change her testimony by union thugs. This standard crime drama works thanks to a competent cast and a nicely crafted script. Many of the stars of this B film continued their careers on television — Keith (most notably in *Family Affair* and *Hardcastle and McCormick*), Garland (*Decoy*, *My Three Sons*, *Scarecrow and Mrs. King*), Foran (*O.K. Crackerby*), Cook (*Magnum P.I.*), Langton (*Peyton Place*) and Tyler (*Big Town*).

Familiar Faces from Television:
❑ Anthony George (Agent Allison in *The Untouchables* and Don Corey in *Checkmate*) and Jack Lambert (first mate Joshua in *Riverboat*) as union hit men.
❑ Phyllis Coates (the original Lois Lane in *The Adventures of Superman*) as Keith's wife.
❑ John Hamilton (editor Perry White in *The Adventures of Superman*) as Foran's defense attorney.
❑ Jim Bannon (Sandy North in *The Adventures of Champion*) as an airplane pilot.

Chicago Deadline (1949) 86 min. Alan Ladd, Donna Reed, June Havoc, Irene Hervey, Arthur Kennedy, Berry Kroeger, Shepperd Strudwick, Gavin Muir. **Screenplay by**: Warren Duff. **Directed by**: Lewis Allen. **Noir Type**: Newspaper. **Noir Themes**: Obsession, jealousy, guilt, betrayal. ★★★½

When hard-boiled reporter Ladd finds the tuberculosis-ridden body of a mysterious young woman in a flea-bag Chicago hotel, he steals her address book before the cops arrive and, smelling a story, begins contacting the people listed in it. Fearful and hesitant, each person has a tale to tell him about Reed. Via flashback, we learn that the circumstances that preceded her death are as mysterious as the woman herself. Kennedy plays Reed's devoted brother, angry about the newspaper stories that have been portraying his sister as a cheap femme fatale. Strudwick is the small-time hood who was in love with Reed. Havoc, Ladd's love interest, plays Reed's ex-roommate. Sinister gangster Kroeger and nervous banker Muir seem to have had some connection to the dead girl, and the obsessed Ladd is determined to find out what it was. And a couple of murders later, he does. *Chicago Deadline* is reminiscent of **Laura**, but with its seedy, big-city locale and its malignant inhabitants, it is much darker than its 1944 noir predecessor. Ladd gives a good performance as the journalist driven by a strange fascination, and Strudwick is a pleasant surprise as the violent thug with a romantic streak.

Familiar Faces from Television:
❏ Dave Willock (Harvey Clayton in *Margie*) as the reporter helping Ladd.
❏ Roy Roberts (Captain Huxley in *Oh Susanna*) as a boxing manager.
❏ Arthur Space (Doc Weaver on *Lassie* and Velvet's dad in *National Velvet*) as a homicide detective questioning a wheelchair-bound witness.

Memorable Noir Moment:
❏ Ladd tells Havoc what he's learned about the dead woman from the people listed in her little black book. "Fifty-four names," he says. "Each one with a different picture of her. She was a dame, a saint, a gangster's girl and a sister who remembered birthdays."

Christmas Holiday (1944) 92 min. Deanna Durbin, Gene Kelly, Richard Whorf, Gail Sondergaard. **Screenplay by:** Herman J. Mankiewicz. **Directed by:** Robert Siodmak. **Noir Type:** Newlywed. **Noir Themes:** Jealousy, woman in jeopardy. ★★★

Gene Kelly, Deanna Durbin and Christmas time ... a light and cheerful musical? Hardly. Whorf is a despondent Army lieutenant who's just received a "Dear John" letter from his fiancée. On the flight home to San Francisco, he's stranded in New Orleans because of bad weather. On Christmas Eve, he meets Durbin, a sultry nightclub singer who begs him to take her to midnight Mass. After the service, she tells him the depressing story of how she fell in love with and married mama's boy Kelly, a charming, ne'er-do-well gambler now serving a stretch in the pen for murdering a bookie. Via flashback, we witness Kelly and Durbin marrying after his overly protective mother (Sondergaard) gives her blessing because she thinks Durbin can make him "stronger." Sondergaard eventually blames her daughter-in-law for Kelly's murder conviction, causing the guilt-ridden Durbin to leave home and take a job singing at an unsavory nightclub. For Whorf, Durbin's tale ends here, but for the viewer there's still an exciting climax. Kelly and Durbin, both ingeniously cast way out of type, are so good that they make the viewer forget their goody-two-shoes images. Kelly doesn't dance or sing at all, but Durbin performs a moving rendition of the movie's theme song, Irving Berlin's *Always*. Whorf nicely underplays his role as the depressed soldier who desperately needs to hear a story sadder than his, and Sondergaard is perfect as Kelly's strange mother. Hollywood in the 1940s had a strict

A mama's boy (Gene Kelly) takes his date (Deanna Durbin) only to the best places in *Christmas Holiday* (Universal, 1944).

production code, so there are only subtle hints of the homosexuality and incest that were more obvious in the W. Somerset Maugham novel on which the film was based.

Memorable Noir Moments:

❑ In a noirish understatement, Durbin describes Kelly to Whorf: "He was so gay, so charming, so *different*."
❑ From the Some-Things-Never-Change Department: When Whorf's airplane is grounded in New Orleans because of bad weather, a reporter seeking a scoop questions him: "Nobody hurt?" Whorf responds that there were no injuries, causing the reporter to complain, "I was afraid of that."

Circumstantial Evidence (1945) 67 min. Michael O'Shea, Lloyd Nolan, Billy Cummings, Roy Roberts. **Screenplay by:** Robert Metzler. **Directed by:** John Larkin. **Noir Type:** Wrong Man. **Noir Themes:** Victim of the law, paranoia. ★★½

Three witnesses swear that widower O'Shea, angry because a grocer slapped his son, killed the man by hitting him in the head with the blunt end of a hatchet. O'Shea swears that the grocer hit his head on the stove while the two men struggled for the weapon. When he tries to hightail it out of town, his best friend (Nolan), whose life he saved during the war, informs on him in a misguided an attempt to protect him. Nolan once again causes problems when he's tricked into testifying in court that O'Shea had once threatened to bash in the grocer's head. With friends like this.... O'Shea, of course, is found guilty and sentenced to death, leaving Cummings and the regretful Nolan to figure out how to save him. Despite its shortcomings, *Circumstantial Evidence* works well, with Nolan and O'Shea giving good accounts of themselves.

Familiar Faces from Television:
❑ John Hamilton (Perry White in *The Adventures of Superman*) as the governor.
❑ Reed Hadley (Capt. John Braddock in *Racket Squad*) as the prosecutor.
❑ Ray Teal (Sheriff Roy Coffee in *Bonanza*) as a cop.

Memorable Noir Moment:
❑ A Death Row inmate actually breaks back *into* prison after finding out that the governor is going to grant him a stay of execution and that his appeal for a new trial has been approved. See *House of Numbers* for more prison break-in weirdness.

Citizen Kane (1941) 119 min. Orson Welles, Joseph Cotten, Dorothy Comingore, Everett Sloane, Ruth Warrick, Paul Stewart, George Coulouris, William Alland. **Screenplay by:** Herman J. Mankiewicz and Orson Welles. **Directed by:** Orson Welles. **Noir Type:** Ambition. **Noir Themes:** Character deterioration, obsession, corruption. ★★★★★

Welles stars as Charles Foster Kane, a publishing tycoon with unfulfilled political aspirations, who, with his dying breath, utters a word that ignites a journalistic investigation into his past to discover the meaning of the word and, perhaps, the man's life. A reporter (Alland) interviews those who were closest to Welles—his guardian and family attorney (Coulouris), his business manager (Sloane), his only friend (Cotten), his second wife (Comingore) and the butler (Stewart) at Welles' isolated, palatial estate, Xanadu—but their recollections, while shedding light on the mysterious nature of the man, bring Alland no closer to his goal. The privileged viewer, however, will discover the secret meaning of the most famous word in American cinema, "Rosebud." Boy wonder Welles was only twenty-five when he created this masterpiece, which, more than sixty years later, is still considered an amazing cinematic achievement and is rated number 1 on the American Film Institute's List of America's 100 Greatest Movies. The film was nominated for nine Academy Awards, including Best Picture and Best Actor (Welles), and Mankiewicz and Welles won Oscars for Best Original Screenplay. While *Citizen Kane*'s thematic content is questionably noir, the unusual camera angles, flashbacks, deep focus photography and exceptionally dark sets certainly qualify it as such.

Familiar Faces from Television:
❑ Agnes Moorehead (Endora in *Bewitched*) as Kane's mother.
❑ Ray Collins (Lieutenant Tragg in *Perry Mason*) as a corrupt gubernatorial candidate.

Memorable Noir Moments:
❑ Attorney Coulouris points out that Welles' newspaper lost a million dollars the previous year. The tycoon smiles and comments, "At the rate of a million dollars a year, I'll have to close this place in sixty years."

❑ At a boisterous office party, complete with dancing girls, Welles calls Cotten a "long-faced, overdressed anarchist." Cotten answers, "I am *not* overdressed."

❑ The elderly chairman of Welles' newspaper discusses old age with a reporter. "It's the only disease that you don't look forward to being cured of," he says.

City Across the River (1949) 90 min. Stephen McNally, Peter Fernandez, Thelma Ritter, Jeff Corey, Tony Curtis, Al Ramsen. **Screenplay by:** Maxwell Shane and Dennis J. Cooper. **Directed by:** Maxwell Shane. **Noir Type:** Troubled Youth. **Noir Themes:** Paranoia, character deterioration, betrayal, social reform, fatalism. ★★½

Based on *The Amboy Dukes*, Irving Shulman's novel about juvenile delinquents, and narrated by columnist Drew Pearson, *City Across the River* stars McNally as a dedicated social worker dealing with tough youngsters in the slums of Brooklyn. For the most part he's successful at his job, except when it comes to a neighborhood gang, the Dukes. A non-violent gang member (Fernandez) who is "going down a confused road, toward gangsterdom, toward murder," turns nasty when his family's dream of buying their own home in a nice neighborhood goes sour because his working mom (Ritter) has to be hospitalized. When he and a fellow gang member (Ramsen) rough up their shop teacher, killing him, homicide detective Corey tries to find enough evidence to arrest them. A bit dated, with the Brooklynese being laid on kind of thick ("I can only boin once"), it's still entertaining. Curtis, in an early role, plays a gang member.

Familiar Face from Television:

❑ Richard Jaeckel (Lt. Martin Quirk in *Spenser: For Hire* and Lt. Ben Edwards in *Baywatch*) as one of the Dukes.

Memorable Noir Moment:

❑ A gang member shares a helpful hint with birthday boy Fernandez, who's wearing his parents' present. "Never slug a guy while wearin' a good watch," he advises. "Take it off foist and put it in your pocket. But remember, ya gotta do it fast."

City for Conquest (1940) 105 min. James Cagney, Ann Sheridan, Donald Crisp, Arthur Kennedy, Frank McHugh, Elia Kazan, Anthony Quinn. **Screenplay by:** John Wexley. **Directed by:** Anatole Litvak. **Noir Type:** Boxing. **Noir Themes:** Corruption, sexual hostility, betrayal. ★★★★

Cagney plays a kindhearted $27.50-a-week truck driver who turns to boxing to help his kid brother (Kennedy, in his film debut) make it as a composer. Along the way, Cagney loses his girl (Sheridan), who has teamed up with a roguish dancer (Quinn) in an attempt to become the next Fred Astaire and Ginger Rogers. Fate is unkind to both Sheridan and Cagney, but the boxer never loses his positive attitude or his love for the wayward Sheridan. Crisp plays Cagney's manager, and McHugh is his former truck-driving partner, more than happy to bask in his buddy's limelight as his corner man. Kazan, before he became a famous director, plays Cagney's neighborhood chum, an impoverished jailbird who becomes a big-time gangster. Litvak's film may be overly melodramatic, but Cagney is so outstanding (and the swing music so cool) that even the hard-core crime fan won't mind sitting through this tearjerker. Cagney is said to have loved the book but hated the film (and the director).

Familiar Faces from Television:

❑ Lee Patrick (Cosmo's wife Henrietta in *Topper*) as a burlesque dancer.
❑ Thurston Hall (Mr. Schuyler, Cosmos's boss, in *Topper*) as a Broadway producer.
❑ Charles Lane (Homer Bedloe in *Petticoat Junction* and Mr. Barnsdahal in *The Lucy Show*) as Quinn's booking agent.
❑ Frank Faylen (Herbert T. Gillis in *The Many Loves of Dobie Gillis*) as a bandleader.
❑ Frank Wilcox (John Brewster in *The Beverly Hillbillies*) as a party guest enjoying Kennedy's music.

Memorable Noir Moments:

❑ Truck driver Cagney, explaining why he's reluctant to become a boxer, says, "I think I need a good reason to sock a guy." Later, the sleazy Quinn manages to give him one.
❑ A newspaper headline, "50 More Millionaires Reported Last Year," causes burlesque dancer Patrick to remark, "I wish some of them would report to me."

City of Shadows (1955) 70 min. Victor McLaglen, John Baer, Kathleen Crowley, Anthony Caruso, Richard Reeves, June Vincent, Frank Ferguson. **Screenplay by:** Houston Branch. **Directed by:** William Witney. **Noir Type:** Gangster. **Noir Themes:** Betrayal, greed, guilt. ★★

McLaglen is a small-time slot machine entrepreneur who's almost pushed out of the business by two ruthless competitors (Caruso and Reeves). After a feisty lad gives him the idea of feeding slugs into his rivals' slot machines, McLaglen gains control of the gambling syndicate, and sore losers Caruso and Reeves wind up working for him. The grateful McLaglen puts the now-grown boy (Baer) through college and law school where, as an ace student, he finds legal loopholes to keep his benefactor out of jail. When Baer meets a judge's daughter (Crowley), he decides to go straight and turns McLaglen's protection racket into a legal security and insurance business. But, unknown to him, McLaglen and his hoods still have their dirty hands in the enterprise, and the D.A. (Ferguson) is out to bust them all. Vincent plays Baer's femme fatale secretary, who's spying for Caruso. The 69-year-old McLaglen, looking comfortable in a role so familiar to him — the big-hearted, somewhat dimwitted giant of a man — saves the silly but inoffensive film.

Familiar Faces from Television:

❑ Paul Maxey (Mayor Peoples in *The People's Choice* and Matt Brockway in *Lassie*) as the mob's attorney.
❑ Kay E. Kuter (Newt Kiley in *Petticoat Junction* and *Green Acres*) as a diner counterman who rides to the top on McLaglen's shirttail.
❑ Nicolas Coster (Chief Carson in *Lobo*) as Baer's law school buddy.

The City That Never Sleeps (1953) 90 min. Gig Young, Mala Powers, William Talman, Edward Arnold, Chill Wills, Marie Windsor, Paula Raymond. **Screenplay by:** Steve Fisher. **Directed by:** John H. Auer. **Noir Type:** Triangle. **Noir Themes:** Lust, obsession, betrayal. ★★★

Young, a uniformed police officer tired of his job and his working wife (Raymond), is planning to quit the force to run off with a stripper (Powers). Chicago and some of its shadier inhabitants — Arnold, Talman and Windsor — have different plans for Young. During what he hopes will be his final shift, Young delivers a baby, investigates a robbery and chases a murderer across Chicago's tenement roofs and elevated subway tracks. All in a night's work. Raymond's 1950s guilt trip over earning more than her husband is the film's unintentional comedic moment. Although this suspenseful noir has its weaknesses (e.g., the dark and menacing mood doesn't fit with the overly cheerful narration of Wills as the voice of Chicago), Young's gritty performance overshadows them. Talman is excellent as the menacing former stage magician.

Familiar Face from Television:
❑ Comedian Tom Poston (Franklin Delano Bickely in *Mork & Mindy*, George Utley in *Newhart* and Floyd Norton in *Grace Under Fire*) as a cop.

Memorable Noir Moment:
❑ The voice of Chicago diplomatically describes stripper Powers as "free, *wise* and 21." See *Fall Guy*, *The Glass Key* and *Out of the Fog* memorable noir moments for more variations of the cliché.

Clash by Night (1952) 104 min. Barbara Stanwyck, Paul Douglas, Robert Ryan, Marilyn Monroe, J. Carrol Naish, Keith Andes. **Screenplay by:** Alfred Hayes. **Directed by:** Fritz Lang. **Noir Type:** Soap Opera. **Noir Themes:** Betrayal, lust, jealousy, fatalism, guilt, sexual hostility. ★★★½

A top-notch cast brings new life to this screen version of Clifford Odets' failed Broadway play. Stanwyck plays a world-weary woman who returns home to her fishing community after a decade of big-city disillusionment. A bulky, big-hearted fisherman (Douglas) quickly falls in love with her. During their courtship, Douglas makes the mistake of introducing Stanwyck to his buddy (Ryan), an embittered misogynist, who spends his free time hitting the bottle and worrying about his faithless stripper wife. Stanwyck, who is looking for "a man who isn't mean and doesn't hate women," takes an instant dislike to Ryan, and when she becomes aware of the sexual tension between them, she agrees to marry the dumbfounded Douglas, who can't believe his good luck. After Ryan's wife divorces him, he makes his move on Stanwyck, who by now is bored with playing housewife and mother. Andes is Stanwyck's brother, unenthusiastic about her sudden return, especially since his gorgeous steady (Monroe) is an admirer of Stanwyck's daring and independence. Veteran character actor Naish plays Douglas' moocher uncle. Stanwyck is good as the faithless but guilt-stricken wife, as is Douglas as the overly trusting and quick-to-forgive cuckold. But the film belongs to Ryan, as Douglas' cynical "friend." Fans who prefer a dash of crime with their noir might not enjoy this soap opera.

Memorable Noir Moments:
❑ "Home is where you come when you run out of places," remarks Stanwyck when asked if she's glad to be back home.
❑ Douglas, agonizing that his double-crossing best friend is making time with his (Douglas') wife, cries out, "Why doesn't God stop him?"

The Clay Pigeon (1949) 63 min. Bill Williams, Barbara Hale, Richard Quine, Richard Loo. **Screenplay by:** Carl Foreman. **Directed by:** Richard Fleischer. **Noir Type:** Amnesia. **Noir Themes:** Betrayal, greed. ★★½

Williams is an amnesiac sailor. (What, again? See *Deadline at Dawn*.) A former Japanese prisoner of war, he awakens from a coma in a Navy hospital to learn that he faces a court martial for treason and that he stands accused of causing the death of his buddy. He escapes from the hospital and teams up with Hale, his friend's widow, to search for another ex–P.O.W. (Quine), who may be able to shed some light on what really happened. Loo plays a sadistic Japanese guard whom the inmates called "The Weasel," and who is now living in Los Angeles. *The Clay Pigeon*, with its fairly interesting (if predictable) plot and good acting by real-life husband and wife Williams and Hale, works well. (If you look closely at Williams' face, you might be amazed to see their son, actor William Katt.) Look for Martha Hyer in a bit role as receptionist.

Cloak and Dagger (1946) 106 min. Gary Cooper, Lilli Palmer, Robert Alda, Vladimir Sokoloff, James Flavin, Marc Lawrence. **Screenplay by:** Ring Lardner, Jr. and Albert Maltz. **Directed by:** Fritz Lang. **Noir Type:** Nuclear. **Noir Themes:** Paranoia, betrayal. ★★★

Director Lang applies the film noir treatment to what might have been just an average Hollywood spy story, turning it into an enjoyably bleak tale of love, war and nuclear fission. Cooper is a German-speaking American scientist working on the Manhattan Project. He's recruited by a college chum (Flavin), now an O.S.S. bigwheel, to travel undercover to neutral Switzerland to find out from a nuclear scientist who recently escaped from Germany if the Nazis are developing an atomic bomb. The scientist is murdered by the Gestapo, but before she dies she informs Cooper that Germany and its ally Italy are both working on the bomb. Amateur spy Cooper and professional spy Alda travel to Italy to convince the Fascists' only nuclear scientist (Sokoloff) to escape to America. While ensuring that it is safe for us to drop an A-bomb on Hiroshima and Nagasaki without fear of retaliation, Cooper falls in love with Palmer, a beautiful member of the Italian underground. Not one of Lang's best efforts, but enjoyable nevertheless, with Cooper and German-born Palmer giving good performances. Particularly memorable is Cooper's exciting fight scene with veteran film heavy Marc Lawrence.

Memorable Noir Moments:

❑ When feline fancier Cooper expresses sympathy for a hungry cat, Palmer sets him straight. "The American likes cats, hmm? Only you're in Europe now," she tells him. "Here you find cats in butcher shops."

❑ When Cooper expresses a romantic interest in Palmer, she informs him that next week she might have to play up to "a fat Gestapo pig," and forewarns him, "In my job, I kiss without feeling."

Cloudburst (1951-British) 106 min. Robert Preston, Elizabeth Sellars, Colin Tapley, Sheila Burrell, Harold Lang. **Screenplay by:** Francis Searle and Leo Marks. **Directed by:** Francis Searle. **Noir Type:** Payback. **Noir Themes:** Revenge, obsession, fatalism. ★★★

A Canadian cryptographer (Preston) working for British intelligence in postwar London plans to buy some land and start a family with his loving wife (Sellars), who suffered torture during the war at the hands of the Gestapo rather than betray him. After leaving their car to look at the property, Sellars is run down by a has-been boxer (Lang) and his girlfriend (Burrell), who are on the run after killing a watchman during a robbery attempt. As Preston tries to prevent the panicky driver from backing up over his critically injured wife, Burrell stabs his hand with a pair of scissors, permitting Lang to speed away, running over Sellars once again and killing her. After deliberately withholding information from the police about the crime, Preston, a highly skilled commando, goes looking for payback. A suspicious Scotland Yard inspector (Tapley) is his only obstacle. Preston is excellent as the laid-back vigilante in this violent British noir.

Memorable Noir Moment:
❑ Preston doesn't buy the story he's hearing from the man he's torturing. "When you're being tortured, remember the first lie's the most important," he advises. "You may never get a chance to tell another."

The Clouded Yellow (1951-British) 95 min. Jean Simmons, Trevor Howard, Kenneth More, Sonia Dresdel, Barry Jones. **Screenplay by**: Janet Green. **Directed by**: Ralph Thomas. **Noir Type**: On the Run. **Noir Themes**: Betrayal, woman in jeopardy. ★★½

A recently fired British secret service agent takes a live-in job cataloguing butterflies for an eccentric lepidopterist (Jones) and his wife (Dresdel). There he falls in love with the couple's emotionally troubled ward (Simmons), who has been fending off the advances of a lecherous handyman. After the handyman is founded murdered and Simmons is about to be arrested by Scotland Yard, Howard and the girl go on the lam, where the reason for her psychological problems becomes evident. Meanwhile, the Yard and a secret service agent (Moore) join forces to capture them. Simmons and Howard make an unlikely but entertaining romantic team in this suspenseful British noir, whose title refers to a species of butterfly.

Memorable Noir Moment:
❑ Manhandled in the street by a secret service agent seeking information, a Chinese thug who knows his civil rights exclaims, "Third degree. Third degree. Not allowed. England." "Fourth degree if you don't talk," the unimpressed agent warns.

The Come-On (1956) 82 min. Anne Baxter, Sterling Hayden, John Hoyt, Jesse White. **Screenplay by**: Whitman Chambers and Warren Douglas. **Directed by**: Russell Birdwell. **Noir Type**: Con Artist. **Noir Themes**: Obsession, betrayal, greed. ★★

A seafaring wanderer (Hayden) falls in love with a gorgeous con artist (Baxter). She pressures him to help her do away with her insanely jealous partner in crime (Hoyt), who has threatened to turn her over to the police if she leaves him. When Hoyt slugs Baxter during one of their frequent arguments, Hayden stops straddling the fence and agrees that the abusive Hoyt must go. Meanwhile, a shady private eye (White, TV's original "Maytag Repairman"), hired by Hoyt to keep an eye on the lovers, has some ideas of his own. Noir veterans Hayden and Baxter are enjoyable to watch but neither they nor the deliciously evil Hoyt can do much to help the superficial plot.

Familiar Face from Television:
❑ Paul Picerni (Agent Lee Hobson of *The Untouchables*) as an assistant D.A.

Memorable Noir Moments:

❑ Con man Hoyt, when reprimanded by a mark about his abusive treatment of Baxter, gives the man some drunken advice: "Respect everything you've got. Your money, position, reputation. Never respect a woman."
❑ Sensitivity Training Required: Hoyt, sharing with Baxter the philosophy that has made him such a hit with the ladies, says, "A woman like you needs a good beating at least once a week."
❑ Baxter gives Hayden a reason to help her kill Hoyt. "It's the only way we can be together," she says. "We can go to the chair together," he reminds her.

The Company She Keeps (1950) 82 min. Lizabeth Scott, Jane Greer, Dennis O'Keefe, Fay Baker. **Screenplay by:** Ketti Frings. **Directed by:** John Cromwell. **Noir Type:** Jailbird. **Noir Themes:** Paranoia, fatalism, distrust. ★★½

Scott is a parole officer whose most recent assignment (Greer) has just been released after spending two years in prison for passing bad checks. Greer, sporting a huge chip on her shoulder, pursues Scott's boyfriend, newspaper columnist O'Keefe, and falls in love with him. Scott is faced with a difficult choice when she must recommend for or against their marriage, especially after Greer gets into hot water by associating with fellow parolee Baker, who has been stealing medical supplies from the hospital where they are both employed as nurses aides. Scott and Greer are, as usual, a pleasure to watch, and O'Keefe does a good job as the ladies' love interest. Lloyd Bridges' kids, Beau and Jeff, appear as a young boy and an infant, respectively, at the railroad station with their real-life mom, Dorothy.

Familiar Faces from Television:

❑ Gertrude Hoffman (Mrs. Odetts of *My Little Margie*) as a member of the parole board.
❑ Kenneth Tobey (Chuck Martin in *The Whirlybirds*) as a diner counterman.
❑ Kathleen Freeman (Katie the maid in *Topper* and Flo Shafer in *The Beverly Hillbillies*) as a parolee with two kids.

Memorable Noir Moment:

❑ A parolee filling out a form asks, "How do you spell indisposed? The reason I was off the job so much last month." "D-r-u-n-k," another parolee offers.

Compulsion (1959) 103 min. Orson Welles, Diane Varsi, Dean Stockwell, Bradford Dillman, E.G. Marshall, Martin Milner. **Screenplay by:** Richard Murphy. **Directed by:** Richard Fleischer. **Noir Type:** Trial. **Noir Themes:** Lawbreaking for kicks, paranoia, sexual hostility, jealousy, fatalism. ★★★★

Dillman and Stockwell play sociopathic college students who kill a young boy — Dillman for the thrill of it and Stockwell as a "test of the superior intellect." When their dream of committing the perfect crime falls apart because of a pair of eyeglasses dropped by Stockwell while disposing of the body, the two turn on each other and sign confessions, each fingering the other as the killer. Their wealthy families hire a flamboyant attorney (Welles) to defend them, but even he sees the futility of pleading insanity before a hostile jury and a state's attorney eager for a hanging. Varsi plays a college student sympathetic to the friendless Stockwell, and Milner is her newspaper reporter boyfriend, who is not thrilled about his girl's feelings for the killer. Welles is outstanding in his relatively brief appearance, but stealing the film as the obviously gay murderers are Dillman, the arrogant, schizophrenic "momsy's" boy, and Stockwell, his weaker-willed, eager-to-please companion. Based on the real-life 1924 Loeb-Leopold murder case, *Compulsion* is highly suspenseful at times but hits a painful snag in the courtroom, where Welles delivers a nearly 15-minute-long anti-capital punishment speech.

Familiar Faces from Television:
❑ Richard Anderson (Oscar Goldman in *The Six Million Dollar Man*) as Stockwell's brother.
❑ Gavin MacLeod (Murray Slaughter in *The Mary Tyler Moore Show* and Captain Merrill Stubing in *The Love Boat*) as an assistant state's attorney.
❑ Edward Binns (Detective Lt. Roy Brenner in *Brenner* and Dr. Anson Kiley in *The Nurses*) as a reporter at Milner's newspaper.
❑ Robert F. Simon (copy editor Dave Tabak in *Saints and Sinners* and General Mitchell in *M*A*S*H*) as the homicide detective investigating the murder.

Memorable Noir Moments:
❑ An exuberant Dillman, who has just tried to run down a hitchhiking drunk, explains to Stockwell why he did it: "Because I damn well felt like it, that's why."
❑ Dillman is pleased when he finds out that Stockwell is going to take Varsi on a bird watching date in the woods and encourages him to rape her in the safety of the isolated location, where she can scream her head off without being heard. As further inducement, he adds, "Girls never talk about it afterwards."

Confidential Agent (1945) 113 min. Charles Boyer, Lauren Bacall, Victor Francen, Wanda Hendrix, Peter Lorre, Katina Paxinou. **Screenplay by:** Robert Buckner. **Directed by:** Herman Shumlin. **Noir Type:** On the Run. **Noir Themes:** Betrayal, conspiracy, paranoia. ★★½

A Spanish patriot (Boyer) travels secretly to England to purchase coal for the Loyalist cause in Spain, but his every move is thwarted by his Fascist nemesis (Francen). Fortunately for Boyer, he meets up with the coal mining company owner's daughter (Bacall); she falls hard for him and helps him elude police, who wrongly suspect he's a murderer. Hendrix is the 14-year-old girl whose crush on Boyer leads to tragedy, and Lorre and Paxinou are the Spanish quislings who are interested more in gold than coal. Bacall, who made no attempt to disguise her American accent, isn't believable as the aristocratic English girl who falls for the Spaniard. Boyer gives an enjoyable, low-key performance, but Lorre and Paxinou, both of whom brazenly ham it up, are the top attractions.

Memorable Noir Moments:
❑ When a Scotland Yard inspector advises Bacall that "this isn't a case for a lady's ears," the independent-minded Bacall takes justifiable offense. "Oh, don't be an ass," she scolds.
❑ A desperate Boyer pulls a gun as a couple of British coppers approach and is given some excellent, but peculiarly worded, advice from Bacall's suitor: "Drop that gun, you fool. This is London."

Confidential Report *see* **Mr. Arkadin**

A suspected murderer and Spanish patriot (Charles Boyer) has a quick one in a pub with a new friend (Lauren Bacall) in *Confidential Agent* (Warner Bros., 1945).

Conflict (1945) 86 min. Humphrey Bogart, Alexis Smith, Sydney Greenstreet, Rose Hobart. **Screenplay by:** Arthur T. Horman and Dwight Taylor. **Directed by:** Curtis Bernhardt. **Noir Type:** Missing Person. **Noir Themes:** Obsession, betrayal, paranoia. ★★★

Based on a story written by veteran noir director Robert Siodmak, *Conflict* finds Bogart desperately in love with his sister-in-law (Smith). His wife (Hobart) knows about his unrequited love for her sister but refuses to divorce him. This being film noir, Bogey attempts to solve that little problem by strangling Hobart, dumping her body and reporting her missing. With Hobart out of the way, he begins to pursue Smith, who is not the slightest bit interested. Unluckily for Bogey, however, some of the things Hobart was last seen wearing begin showing up, leading him to believe that she's still alive. The ending is no big surprise — his growing doubt and paranoia lead to his downfall — but all the fun is in getting there. Greenstreet nicely underplays his role as a psychiatrist friend of the family, and Bogart, who also played a wife killer in 1947's **The Two Mrs. Carrolls**, is terrific.

Familiar Face from Television:
❑ Frank Wilcox (John Brewster in *The Beverly Hillbillies*) as Bogey's business associate.

Memorable Noir Moment:

❏ Psychiatrist Greenstreet expounds on his job description for an inquisitive guest. "Sometimes a thought can be like a malignant disease that starts to eat away the willpower," he explains. "When that happens, it's my job to remove the thought before it can cause destruction."

Convicted (1950) 91 min. Glenn Ford, Broderick Crawford, Millard Mitchell, Dorothy Malone, Carl Benton Reid. **Screenplay by:** William Bowers, Fred Niblo, Jr., and Seton I. Miller. **Directed by:** Henry Levin. **Noir Type:** Prison. **Noir Themes:** Fatalism, revenge. ★★½

Army veteran Ford, defending a barfly's honor, accidentally kills a big-wheel's son, and D.A. Crawford, despite his sympathy for the young man's predicament, prosecutes him fiercely. Ford, with an incompetent corporation attorney defending him, is convicted of manslaughter and sent to the pen for a one- to ten-year stretch. Ironically, during Ford's fifth year of imprisonment, Crawford becomes warden and, surprisingly, makes Ford a trusty, assigning him the job of chauffeuring his daughter (Malone) back and forth to town. As Ford's parole hearing nears, things begin to heat up among the other cons, with Ford's cellmate (Mitchell) seeking revenge against a snitch and a sadistic guard (Reid). Ford gives a capable, low-key performance in this better-than-average prison noir, while Mitchell is a fireball as the con whose minor parole infraction sent him back to the pen to serve "twelve years for one little beer."

Familiar Faces from Television:

❏ Will Geer (Grandpa Walton in *The Waltons*) as one of Ford's cellmates.
❏ Frank Cady (Doc Williams in *The Adventures of Ozzie and Harriet* and Sam Drucker in *Petticoat Junction* and *Green Acres*) as Crawford's assistant.
❏ John Doucette (Jim Weston in *Lock Up* and Captain Andrews in *The Partners*) as a con.
❏ Ray Teal (Sheriff Roy Coffee in *Bonanza*) as a prison guard.
❏ Jimmy Dodd (the head Mouseketeer in *The Mickey Mouse Club*) as the warden's chauffeur.
❏ Whit Bissell (Gen. Heywood Kirk in *The Time Tunnel*) as a prosecutor.
❏ Frank Faylen (Herbert T. Gillis in *The Many Loves of Dobie Gillis*) as the squealer.

Memorable Noir Moment:

❏ A guard, listening in as several cons discuss their imaginary dates in high society circles, suggests that they invite him along on their next outing. "These dames require character references," replies one of the cons.

Cop Hater (1958) 75 min. Robert Loggia, Gerald S. O'Loughlin, Ellen Parker, Shirley Ballard, Russell Hardie. **Screenplay by:** Henry Kane. **Directed by:** William Berke. **Noir Type:** Police Procedural. **Noir Themes:** Betrayal. ★★½

Somebody is "blasting bulls" in New York's 87th Precinct. Based on Ed McBain's novel, *Cop Hater* stars Loggia and O'Loughlin as homicide detectives trying to track down a cop killer while keeping the women in their lives happy. Hardie is their boss, Ballard plays O'Loughlin's complaining wife and Parker is Loggia's deaf-mute girlfriend. Worth viewing thanks to a fast-paced script, an enjoyable surprise ending and good performances by Loggia and O'Loughlin. Loggia went on to star in TV's *Mancuso, FBI* and *T.H.E. Cat.* O'Loughlin is best known for his role in *The Rookies*, a hit 1970s police drama.

Homicide cops (Robert Loggia, left, and Gerald O'Loughlin, center) discuss a line-up suspect with their boss (Russell Hardie) in *Cop Hater* (United Artists, 1958).

Familiar Faces from Television:

❏ Jerry Orbach (Detective Lennie Briscoe in *Law & Order*) as a teen-aged gang leader.
❏ Vincent Gardenia (Frank Lorenzo in *All in the Family*) as a sleazy police informant.
❏ Lincoln Kilpatrick (Detective Lieutenant Michael Hoyt in *Matt Houston* and Reverend Deal in *Frank's Place*) as the cop killer's second victim.
❏ Steve Franken (Chatsworth Osborne, Jr., in *The Many Loves of Dobie Gillis*) as a suspect in a police lineup.

Memorable Noir Moment:

❏ When O'Loughlin's wife asks him why somebody would put three slugs into the back of a cop's head, he responds, "Who knows what motives are pumping inside somebody's black heart?"

Cornered (1945) 102 min. Dick Powell, Walter Slezak, Micheline Cheirel, Morris Carnovsky, Luther Adler. **Screenplay by:** John Paxton. **Directed by:** Edward Dmytryk. **Noir Type:** Payback. **Noir Themes:** Revenge. ★★★★

A former Canadian flyer and newly released prisoner of war, Powell is searching for the man responsible for his French bride's death. Hellbent on vengeance, he travels to France, Switzerland and, finally, Argentina, where he encounters French patriots, Vichy collaborators and Nazis conspirators. His frustrating, grief-inspired mission to find and destroy a man who may not even be alive plays havoc with his intelligence and common sense, causing him to make foolish blunders. In the end, though, it's not his brain but his brawn that pulls him through. Character actor Adler plays a mysterious Nazi collaborator who already longs for the next war when, of course, the outcome will be different. Slezak is just right as the slimy, detestable cad who will work for anyone as long as the price is right. Song-and-dance man Powell, who proved in **Murder, My Sweet** that he could play a tough guy with the best of them, turns in another fine performance and ensures his place in the annals of hard-boiled film noir.

Familiar Face from Television:

❏ Ellen Corby (Grandma Walton in *The Waltons*) as a maid.

Memorable Noir Moments:

❏ "I've got a tradition too," Powell tells Nazi hunters. "As far back as I can remember, the men in my family have gotten mad when their wives were murdered."
❏ "What are you?" Powell asks Slezak, "French or German?" Slezak, loading up on free food and drink, replies, "I'm an epicure."
❏ When a Nazi collaborator tells Powell, "I like the life; I like the money." Powell replies, "What do you do for morals?"

Crack-Up (1946) 93 min. Pat O'Brien, Claire Trevor, Herbert Marshall, Wallace Ford, Ray Collins. **Screenplay by**: Ray Spencer, Ben Bengal and John Paxton. **Directed by**: Irving Reis. **Noir Type**: Nightmare. **Noir Themes**: Paranoia. ★★★

Ex–G.I. O'Brien, who served as an art expert in postwar Germany exposing Nazi forgeries, now conducts art appreciation seminars at a New York museum. After he's arrested for breaking into the museum, seemingly while intoxicated, he tells detective Ford that he was aboard a train that was involved in a head-on collision with an oncoming train. After being dismissed as a kook because there have been no recent train wrecks, O'Brien investigates on his own and discovers that he holds the key to breaking up an art smuggling ring. Trevor plays his newspaper reporter girlfriend, Marshall is a mysterious art expert visiting the States from England, and Collins is a physician employed by the museum. The convoluted plot is difficult to follow, but O'Brien and Trevor are so enjoyable and the photography so wonderfully eerie that you might not notice the holes in the script. Or if you do, you won't care.

Familiar Face from Television:

❏ Ellen Corby (Grandma Walton in *The Waltons*) as a maid at a cocktail party.

Crashout (1955) 88 min. William Bendix, Arthur Kennedy, William Talman, Luther Adler, Gene Evans, Marshall Thompson. **Screenplay by**: Hal E. Chester and Lewis R. Foster. **Directed by**: Lewis R. Foster. **Noir Type**: On the Run. **Noir Themes**: Greed, betrayal. ★★½

Six cons, part of a mass breakout, hide in a cave while the rest of the escapees get shot down or captured. Ringleader Bendix has been wounded and promises equal shares of his hidden loot to his fellow escapees if they care for his wounds and take him along when the coast is clear. With dollar signs in their eyes and Bendix in tow, the desperate cons (Talman, Adler, Evans, Thompson and Kennedy) begin their trek through several states to retrieve the dough. It's pretty standard stuff, but the acting is good and the action scenes satisfying. Talman is especially enjoyable as a knife-wielding religious fanatic.

Memorable Noir Moments:

❑ Reacting to radio coverage of the manhunt, convict Adler asks, "They want us back? Why? We give them nothing but trouble."
❑ After kissing a reluctant and frightened hostage, Adler remarks, "After eight years, a little chicken like you tastes good."
❑ Talman, concerned that Bendix will die without being baptized, drags him into a stream and almost drowns the wounded man during a lengthy prayer service.

Crime Against Joe (1956) 69 min. John Bromfield, Julie London, Henry Calvin, Alika Louis. **Screenplay by:** Robert C. Dennis. **Directed by:** Lee Sholem. **Noir Type:** Wrong Man. **Noir Themes:** Betrayal, sexual hostility, jealousy. ★★★

Bromfield, a Korean War veteran and struggling artist, goes on a drunken binge and winds up as the chief suspect in an attack on a local woman and the murder of a nightclub singer (Louis). When London, the carhop girlfriend of Bromfield's best friend (Calvin), provides a phony alibi for the jailed artist, he and London team up to find the real killer. Their only clue is a high school class pin found next to the body. Having determined that the murderer has to be someone from his 1945 graduating class, Bromfield narrows the list down to four suspects. Fast-paced and well-acted, this enjoyable, low-budget noir will keep you guessing to the end. Bromfield, London and Calvin all wound up in popular television shows (*The Sheriff of Cochise, Emergency,* and *Zorro,* respectively). Calvin played Zorro's comic foil, the portly Sgt. Garcia.

Familiar Faces from Television:

❑ Rhodes Reason (John Hunter in *White Hunter* and Sheriff Will Mayberry in *Bus Stop*) as a wannabe cowboy.
❑ Joyce Jameson (Colleen Middleton in *General Hospital*) as the attack victim.

Crime in the Streets (1956) 91 min. James Whitmore, John Cassavetes, Sal Mineo, Mark Rydell, Malcolm Atterbury, Peter Votrian. **Screenplay by:** Reginald Rose. **Directed by:** Don Siegel. **Noir Type:** Troubled Youth. **Noir Themes:** Law breaking for kicks, revenge, fatalism, paranoia, social reform. ★★★

Originally telecast live on TV's *Eglin Playhouse, Crime in the Streets* is the familiar story about inner city boys who turn to crime because they are starving for attention. Reprising his TV role, Cassavetes is the leader of a neighborhood gang called the Hornets. A middle-aged neighbor (Atterbury) makes the mistake of slapping Cassavetes, who has a habit of freaking out whenever anyone lays a hand on him. Cassavetes decides to murder Atterbury (using a switchblade, naturally), and recruits gang members Rydell and baby faced Mineo (both of whom appeared in the original TV play) to help him. Whitmore plays the well-intentioned but ineffective social worker, and Votrian is Cassavetes' sensitive younger brother. Despite good performances by Cassavetes and Votrian, the film failed to capitalize on the commercial success of 1955's *Rebel Without a Cause* and *The Blackboard Jungle*. A few good New York location shots could have given this otherwise enjoyable film a desperately needed touch of realism. Rydell, who plays a limp-wristed psycho, went on to become a successful film director (*The Rose, Cinderella Liberty, On Golden Pond*) and TV director (episodes of *Gunsmoke, Ben Casey, I Spy*). The future was not so bright for the unfortunate Mineo, who was best known for his sensational performance as a disturbed delinquent in *Rebel Without a Cause*. His career was a turbulent roller-coaster ride until it ended tragically one night in 1976, when he was stabbed to death outside his Hollywood home.

Memorable Noir Moment:
❑ Law and order advocate Atterbury espouses a familiar, if questionable, tactic to control the neighborhood delinquents: "The only way they're going to be good is if they're scared to be bad."

Crime of Passion (1957) 84 min. Barbara Stanwyck, Sterling Hayden, Raymond Burr, Fay Wray, Royal Dano. **Screenplay by:** Jo Eisinger. **Directed by:** Gerd Oswald. **Noir Type:** Femme Fatale. **Noir Themes:** Greed, lust, obsession. ★★★

Stanwyck, an advice-to-the-lovelorn columnist, cracks a murder case and is offered a lucrative position on a New York newspaper. She turns the job down after falling in love with a cop (Hayden), whom she marries after a whirlwind romance. She soon discovers that married life is boring and tires of her new circle of friends (other lower echelon cops' snobby wives) and pressures her complacent husband to start climbing the departmental ladder more quickly. Her scheming takes her on a suspenseful rollercoaster ride that starts with a planned fender bender to meet the police chief's wife (Wray) and ends with murder. Burr plays the chief, a cad who is more than amenable to Stanwyck's sexual advances. Dano is Hayden's boss and, in Stanwyck's eyes, his biggest competitor for advancement. Stanwyck has always excelled in femme fatale roles (see especially *Double Indemnity*) and she doesn't disappoint here. Keep an eye out for Robert Quarry (the star of the 1970 cult hit *Count Yorga, Vampire*), who has a small role as a reporter.

Familiar Face from Television:
❑ Stuart Whitman (Marshal Jim Crown on *Cimarron Strip*) as a crime lab technician.

Memorable Noir Moments:
❑ Sensitivity Training Required: When homicide detective Dano withholds information from the press, reporter Stanwyck complains that she has a job to do. He replies, "Your work should be raising a family, having dinner ready for your husband when he gets home."
❑ Reporters seem to have been as well thought of in 1957 as they are today. A note scrawled on the Press Room sign at the police station reads: "Do not feed the animals."

Crime Wave (1954) 73 min. Sterling Hayden, Gene Nelson, Phyllis Kirk, Ted de Corsia, Charles Bronson, Timothy Carey. **Screenplay by:** Bernard Gordon, Crane Wilbur and Richard Wormser. **Directed by:** André De Toth. **Noir Type:** Jailbird. **Noir Themes:** Betrayal, woman in jeopardy. ★★★

Hayden is a tough, no-nonsense homicide detective with a major distaste for

An escaped con (Charles Buchinsky, a.k.a. Charles Bronson) convinces a jailbird doctor (Jay Novello) not to call the cops in *Crime Wave* (Warner Bros., 1954).

felons ("once a crook, always a crook"). The cop comes down hard on ex-con Nelson, who's trying to go straight, after one of Nelson's former prison pals, a cop killer, is found dead in the small apartment the parolee shares with his wife (Kirk). Thanks to his kindly parole officer, Nelson is released, but the couple is visited by the dead man's partners (San Quentin escapees de Corsia and Bronson), who have been on a robbery spree since their escape. They want Nelson, a former pilot, to be the getaway driver for a bank heist and to fly them out of the country. Fearful for Kirk, who's being held hostage by another gang member (Carey), Nelson reluctantly agrees. Of course, despite de Corsia's seven years of meticulous planning, the heist goes horribly wrong. The craggy-faced Bronson (billed as Charles Buchinsky) and the perpetually grinning Carey are especially enjoyable as demented psychos who ogle and paw at the terrified Kirk. The independent-minded De Toth, who took all of fourteen days to make this enjoyable B movie, refused Warner Bros.' offer of Humphrey Bogart and Ava Gardner for the lead roles and went with Hayden and Kirk. Several years later, Kirk went on to play Nora Charles opposite Peter Lawford in the popular TV series *The Thin Man*.

Familiar Faces from Television:

❑ Harry Lauter (Jim Herrick in *Waterfront*) as a cop at a roadblock.
❑ Dub Taylor (Ed Hewley in *Please Don't Eat the Daisies* and a *Hee Haw* regular from 1985 to 1991) as a gas station attendant.

Memorable Noir Moment:

❑ "Once you do a stretch, you're never clean again," Nelson complains to Kirk. "You're never free. They've always got a string on you and they tug, tug, tug! Before you know it, you're back again."

Criminal Court (1946) 63 min. Tom Conway, Martha O'Driscoll, June Clayworth, Robert Armstrong, Steve Brodie, Robert Warwick. **Screenplay by:** Lawrence Kimble. **Directed by:** Robert Wise. **Noir Type:** Cover-Up. **Noir Themes:** Woman in jeopardy, corruption. ★★

Conway, a successful lawyer with a history of flamboyant courtroom theatrics, is running for district attorney. As part of his campaign, he gathers filmed evidence of gangster Brodie bribing police and government officials. Brodie's brother, nightclub owner Armstrong, unsuccessfully tries to blackmail Conway into destroying the evidence. Things get complicated when Conway gets into a fight with Armstrong, whose dropped gun goes off, killing the unlucky club owner. When his girlfriend (O'Driscoll), a singer at the club, gets the blame, Conway comes clean but nobody believes him because of his past courtroom ploys. Conway's secretary (Clayworth), who was secretly on Armstrong's payroll, was a witness to the deed, but she has orders from Mr. Big (Warwick) to keep her mouth shut. The acting is okay, but this noir is a big yawn. Conway, actor George Sanders' real-life older brother, was a heavy drinker and died broke in 1967 of liver cirrhosis. His last movie was the ironically titled *What a Way to Go!* (1964).

The Crimson Kimono (1959) 82 min. Glenn Corbett, James Shigeta, Victoria Shaw. **Screenplay by:** Samuel Fuller. **Directed by:** Samuel Fuller. **Noir Type:** Whodunit. **Noir Themes:** Paranoia, jealousy. ★★★

Corbett and Shigeta are Los Angeles homicide detectives investigating a stripper's murder. While searching for the killer, the former war buddies both fall in love with a pretty artist (Shaw) who ultimately chooses Shigeta. This standard murder mystery is enhanced by the love triangle subplot, the interracial affair between Shigeta and Shaw, and Shigeta's paranoia after he mistakes his best friend's jealousy for racism. The exciting jazz score and the Los Angeles backdrop add a realistic dimension to the film. Fuller relates in an interview published in *Film Noir Reader 3* (see Bibliography) that the opening nighttime sequence, in which a stripper is shot to death after being chased through a heavily trafficked downtown street, was filmed without the knowledge of the real-life pedestrians, most of whom ignored the nearly naked actress racing past them. A neighborhood shopkeeper, however, did call the police when a shot rang out and the actress fell to the ground. Fuller and his crew quickly packed up and left before the cops arrived.

Familiar Face from Television:

❑ Stafford Repp (Chief O'Hara in *Batman*) as the City Librarian.

Memorable Noir Moments:

❑ When Shaw refers to Corbett as a "cop," he corrects her: "We don't like being called cops, like girls don't like being called broads."

❑ Film noir detective Shigeta, instead of plugging a fleeing suspect in the back, surprisingly fires two warning shots into the air. See *The Red House* for another considerate noir cop.

Crisis (1950) 95 min. Cary Grant, José Ferrer, Paula Raymond, Signe Hasso, Ramon Novarro, Gilbert Roland, Leon Ames. **Screenplay by:** Richard Brooks. **Directed by:** Richard Brooks. **Noir Type:** South of the Border. **Noir Themes:** Corruption, conspiracy, betrayal, paranoia, social reform. ★★½

A gringo brain surgeon (Grant) and his wife (Raymond), vacationing in an unnamed South American country, are kidnapped by an Army colonel (Novarro) and brought to the presidential palace, where Grant is asked to perform surgery to remove a brain tumor from the hated dictator (Ferrer). The country is on the verge of a revolution, and the rebels, led by Novarro, ask Grant to let his scalpel slip "accidentally." When Grant refuses, Novarro takes Raymond hostage and threatens to kill her if *el presidente* survives the operation. Femme fatale Hasso is the Eva Perón–like first lady, and Ames is an American oil company executive. Grant seems too blasé about the whole experience, and the film moves too slowly before reaching its exciting but unsurprising climax.

Memorable Noir Moment:

❑ When Grant asks Ferrer if he's afraid to die, the macho dictator replies, "I'm only afraid to die badly."

Criss Cross (1949) 88 min. Burt Lancaster, Yvonne De Carlo, Dan Duryea, Stephen McNally, Alan Napier, Percy Helton. **Screenplay by:** Daniel Fuchs. **Directed by:** Robert Siodmak. **Noir Type:** Heist. **Noir Themes:** Obsession, lust, greed, betrayal. ★★★★

Lancaster is terribly miscast as the "prize sucker of all time," but this powerful film noir entry has other things going for it, namely, impressive performances by De Carlo as his femme fatale ex-wife, and noir icon Duryea as De Carlo's gangster husband. When Lancaster returns home from a self-imposed exile after his divorce from the beautiful De Carlo, he finds himself irresistibly drawn back into her web, despite his mother's concerns. ("Out of all the girls in Los Angeles, why did you have to pick her?") De Carlo seems interested in renewing their relationship but, after being frightened off by Lancaster's well-meaning detective friend (McNally), she marries the abusive Duryea. But even the dangerous gangster can't keep the lovers apart, and, when he catches them together, armored car driver Lancaster comes up with an ingenious lie about being there to talk about a six-figure payroll heist. Duryea, putting aside his jealousy for the time being, assembles his gang and recruits an alcoholic heist expert (Napier) to devise the perfect plan which, in typical noir fashion, goes tragically awry. Veteran character actor Helton, playing a bartender, is actually likable for a change. Remade in 1995 as *The Underneath*, *Criss Cross* is a must-see for all noir fans. Tony Curtis, in his film debut, has a non-speaking role as De Carlo's rhumba partner.

An amorous armored car driver (Burt Lancaster, right) tries to bluff his way out of a dangerous predicament with a jealous gangster (Dan Duryea, left). Duryea's cheating wife (Yvonne De Carlo) and a member of his gang (Tom Pedi) await the outcome in *Criss Cross* (Universal-International, 1949).

Familiar Faces from Television:
- ❏ Richard Long (Rex Randolph in *Bourbon Street Beat*, Professor Everett in *Nanny and the Professor* and Jarrold Barkley in *The Big Valley*) as Lancaster's kid brother.
- ❏ Tom Pedi (Julius in *Arnie*) as a member of Duryea's gang.
- ❏ Gene Evans (Rob McLaughlin in *My Friend Flicka*) as an armored car driver.

Memorable Noir Moments:
- ❏ Lancaster, understandably annoyed that De Carlo has married Duryea, resorts to name calling: "You cheap little no-good tramp."
- ❏ When Lancaster tells Duryea about his idea for a heist, the gangster asks, "Why come to me?" Lancaster replies, "Because you're the only crooks I know." Duryea, feigning hurt, turns to his thugs and asks, "Is that polite?"

The Crooked Circle (1958) 72 min. John Smith, Fay Spain, Steve Brodie, Don Kelly, Robert Armstrong. **Screenplay by:** Jack Townley. **Directed by:** Joseph Kane. **Noir Type:** Boxing. **Noir Themes:** Corruption, betrayal, revenge. ★★

A former boxer (Kelly) tries to keep his baby brother (Smith) out of the boxing racket. But Smith, egged on by his girlfriend (Spain), asks a sportswriter (Brodie) for help in finding a manager. Brodie introduces the young hopeful to an honest manager (Armstrong), but the desire for a quick buck soon causes Smith to sign up with the same crooks who once managed his brother. After a string of victories, he's offered a grand to throw his next fight. And a grand would buy a nice engagement ring for his girl. This is a boring film that compensates for its trite plot with some nicely choreographed boxing scenes. Smith later co-starred in two TV westerns, *Cimarron City* (1958–60) and *Laramie* (1959–63).

The Crooked Way (1949) 87 min. John Payne, Sonny Tufts, Ellen Drew, Rhys Williams, Percy Helton, John Doucette. **Screenplay by**: Richard H. Landau. **Directed by**: Robert Florey. **Noir Type**: Amnesia. **Noir Themes**: Betrayal, revenge. ★★½

Silver Star winner Payne, with a piece of shrapnel still embedded in his head, is released from a military hospital after doctors have told him he has "organic amnesia," for which there is no cure. Military paperwork shows only his name and his hometown, so Payne decides to return to Los Angeles in the hope that someone will recognize him. He gets his wish at the airport when he runs into a couple of cops (Williams and Doucette), who call him by a different name and take him to the police station for questioning. (As it turns out, the war hero was a racketeer who turned state's evidence against his partner, Tufts, who ended up serving time.) After being released by the no-nonsense cops and advised that he's no longer welcome in L.A., Payne runs into his ex-wife (Drew), who immediately informs the vengeance-minded Tufts that Payne is back in town. Payne gives a solid performance as the amnesiac war hero, and Drew is good as his ex-wife, who has started noticing some pleasant changes in him since his return. Tufts hams it up as Payne's sinister ex-partner, and girly-voiced Helton is wonderfully typecast as a wretched flunky.

Memorable Noir Moment:
❑ Tufts says goodbye to a squealer as two goons drag the unlucky man to his fate: "When you get to where you're goin', have 'em give ya a nice even burn. Don't let 'em just fry ya on one side."

The Crooked Web (1955) 77 min. Frank Lovejoy, Mari Blanchard, Richard Denning, John Mylong. **Screenplay by**: Lou Breslow. **Directed by**: Nathan Juran. **Noir Type**: Undercover. **Noir Themes**: Greed, betrayal, obsession, revenge. ★★

Ex–G.I. Lovejoy, who was stationed in Germany after World War II, now owns a drive-in diner in the States. He's in love with his sexy waitress (Blanchard). When Denning, claiming to be her brother, shows up with a get-rich-quick scheme that involves buried treasure in Frankfurt, Lovejoy is eager to finance it. What he doesn't know is that Denning and Blanchard are lovers, not siblings, and have a special motive for tricking him into returning to Germany. Mylong plays a German policeman. The stupidity of the three main characters ruin what could have been an interesting *Mission Impossible*–type plot.

Familiar Face from Television:
❑ Harry Lauter (Jim Herrick in *Waterfront*) as an Air Force Master Sergeant in charge of reenlistment.

Memorable Noir Moment:

❑ Pretending to be interested in marriage and security, Blanchard tells horseplayer Lovejoy, "The only ponies I want to hear about are the Shetlands for the kids."

Crossfire (1947) 85 min. Robert Young, Robert Mitchum, Robert Ryan, Gloria Grahame, Sam Levene, Steve Brodie, George Cooper, Jacqueline White. **Screenplay by:** John Paxton. **Directed by:** Edward Dmytryk. **Noir Type:** Racist. **Noir Themes:** Bigotry, social reform, betrayal. ★★★★

Ryan plays a recently discharged G.I., a psychotic bigot who, in a drunken fury, beats a stranger (Levene) to death simply because he's Jewish, and then tries to pin the murder on one of his buddies (Cooper). Mitchum is the cynical sergeant who helps Cooper elude a homicide detective (Young, in a nicely restrained performance), and then cooperates with the cops as they attempt to sniff out the real killer. Grahame has a small role as the hardened taxi dancer who, in a moment of uncharacteristic sweetness, takes a shine to the murder suspect and is rewarded for her kindness with an embarrassing confrontation with the man's wife (White). Noir veteran Brodie plays another unfortunate war buddy of the double-crossing Ryan. The three Bobs are terrific but Ryan's performance is electrifying, earning him an Academy Award for Best Supporting Actor. The film received four other nominations—Best Picture,

G.I. buddies (Steve Brodie, right, and Robert Ryan, left) with a murder victim-to-be (Sam Levene) in *Crossfire* (RKO, 1947).

Best Director, Best Screenplay and Best Supporting Actress (Grahame)— but won no Oscars, losing Best Picture to *Gentleman's Agreement*, another film about anti–Semitism. *Crossfire* was based on a novel (*The Brick Foxhole* by Richard Brooks, who served in the Marines with Ryan) about the murder of a homosexual by a vicious, homophobic soldier.

Memorable Noir Moments:

❑ Mitchum responds to Young's question about where Cooper went on the night of the murder: "Soldiers don't have anywhere to go unless you tell 'em where to go."

❑ A sneering Mitchum reacts to a Marine's comment about how Ryan has been so helpful to their buddy, murder suspect Cooper. "Every time he opens his mouth," Mitchum notes, "he hangs him a foot higher."

Crossroads (1942) 82 min. William Powell, Hedy Lamarr, Claire Trevor, Basil Rathbone. **Screenplay by:** Guy Trosper. **Directed by:** Jack Conway. **Noir Type:** Blackmail. **Noir Themes:** Victim of fate, paranoia. ★★★½

Powell, a member of the war French Foreign Office and in line for an ambassadorship to Brazil, finds himself being blackmailed by Rathbone and nightclub singer Trevor. The extortionists inform Powell, who's been suffering from amnesia for the past fifteen years, that at one time he was romantically involved with Trevor, that he helped Rathbone commit an armed robbery, and that he ruthlessly killed a guard during that robbery. After investigating their claim, Powell reluctantly comes to the conclusion that he must pay the one million francs they demand in order to save his reputation, his political career and his three-month-old marriage to the beautiful Lamarr. Powell is terrific as the dumbfounded civil servant, while Trevor makes the best of her small role as a femme fatale. But it's Rathbone, best known for his Sherlock Holmes films, who really shines as the scoundrelly extortionist.

Memorable Noir Moment:

❑ During a courtroom trial, Powell's eccentric psychiatrist loudly voices his opinion of lawyers. "That defense attorney!" he shouts, " I thought the *medical schools* turned out all the idiots."

Cry Danger (1951) 79 min. Dick Powell, Rhonda Fleming, William Conrad, Regis Toomey, Richard Erdman, Jay Adler. **Screenplay by:** William Bowers. **Directed by:** Robert Parrish. **Noir Type:** Payback. **Noir Themes:** Victim of the law, betrayal, greed, revenge. ★★★

Tough guy Powell, imprisoned for a murder and robbery he had nothing to do with, is released after five years when an alcoholic, disabled Marine (Erdman) provides him with a false alibi. Erdman's motive for the big fib is the hope that Powell will cut him in for a share of the hidden loot. Powell breaks the bad news to him that he's really innocent, but Erdman hangs around anyway, seemingly content with Powell's company and his free booze. Meanwhile, Powell's best pal is still serving one to twenty for the robbery so Powell goes after the real culprit (Conrad). Fleming is Powell's ex-girl, now married to his imprisoned friend. Sparks still fly, but Powell, loyal to his buddy, considers her off limits. Toomey is the detective who believes that Powell will lead him to the hidden money, and Adler is the ukulele-playing manager of Fleming's trailer park. There's not much action, but the story is interesting and has a decent surprise ending. Powell, who shares the best lines of the film with Erdman, is fine as the stoic hero. Most enjoyable scene? An angry Powell plays Russian roulette with a terrified Conrad.

Familiar Face from Television:

❑ Kathleen Freeman (Katie the maid in *Topper* and Flo Shafer in *The Beverly Hillbillies*) as a cigarette counter girl.

Memorable Noir Moments:

❑ Powell admonishes a sexy pickpocket for taking advantage of the inebriated Erdman. "I was only going to keep his money for him until he sobered up," she lies. "That's like tying it up permanently," replies Powell.
❑ When Erdman expresses sympathy over Powell's lost years behind bars, Powell quips, "I would have just wasted time having fun."

A Cry in the Night (1956) 75 min. Edmund O'Brien, Brian Donlevy, Natalie Wood, Raymond Burr, Richard Anderson, Carol Veazie. **Screenplay by:** David Dortort. **Directed by:** Frank Tuttle. **Noir Type:** Psycho. **Noir Themes:** Woman in jeopardy, obsession. ★★

Burr plays a simple-minded psycho who likes hiding in the woods near Lover's Loop and spying on the local guys and gals. The Loop is also a favorite necking place for sweethearts Wood and Anderson. When Anderson spots the peeping tom, he confronts him and gets a concussion for his trouble. Burr then takes off with Anderson's car *and* his girl, hiding out in an abandoned brickyard. Wood's concerned father, police detective O'Brien, and fellow cop Donlevy begin a search, starting with Burr's overprotective mother (Veazie), who's almost as daft as her son. Burr spices up the all-too-predictable plot. Noir icon Alan Ladd narrates.

Memorable Noir Moments:

❑ Sensitivity Training Required: When Burr attacks Wood at Lover's Loop, she screams for help, causing one of the busy young lovers to yell out, to the understandable annoyance of his girl, "Sock her again. They love it!"
❑ The narrator explains that kids go to Lover's Loops because they're rebelling against their old-fashioned parents, who worry too much about them. "What's there to worry about?" he asks. The camera pans to the dense woods and, in a disturbing close-up, reveals a wild-eyed peeper, who the following year would become America's favorite TV lawyer, *Perry Mason.*

Cry of the City (1948) 96 min. Victor Mature, Richard Conte, Fred Clark, Shelley Winters, Betty Garde, Berry Kroeger, Tommy Cook, Debra Paget, Hope Emerson. **Screenplay by:** Richard Murphy. **Directed by:** Robert Siodmak. **Noir Type:** Gangster. **Noir Themes:** Fatalism, betrayal, obsession. ★★★★

Director Siodmak gives the noir treatment to this familiar tale of two Italian-American kids who grew up on the same side of the tracks, one becoming a cop (Mature), the other a cheap hoodlum (Conte). Conte gives an impressive performance as the vicious cop killer who escapes from jail and risks his freedom and his life for Paget (making her film debut at 15), the nice girl he wants to marry. Mature is the homicide detective who, despite his affection for Conte's family, must bring in his old friend even though he faces the electric chair for his crime. Clark is Mature's partner and Winters is Conte's former girlfriend, who gamely drives the wounded murderer around New York while an unlicensed, immigrant physician works desperately in the back seat to save his life. Garde is Conte's sympathetic nurse and Emerson is the wicked, Amazonian masseuse, who desperately wants the jewels that Conte has stolen from crooked lawyer Kroeger. Cook plays Conte's cop-hating kid brother, who is already exhibiting signs that he'll wind up just like his idol. Excellent performances and some terrific New York City location shots make this grim crime noir a must see. Garde and the delightfully evil Emerson would work together again in the 1950 prison drama *Caged*. From 1958 to 1959, Emerson played "Mother" in TV's *Peter Gunn*, and Garde went on to play in *The Real McCoys* and the daytime soap operas *The Edge of Night* and *As the World Turns*. Look for Roland Winters (one of Hollywood's Charlie Chans) as a shady prison guard.

Memorable Noir Moment:

❑ Conte taunts Mature over his $94.43 weekly paycheck. "Ever go to Florida for a couple of weeks?" he asks. "Ever bet a hundred bucks on a horse? Or maybe give a girl a big bunch of orchards just because you like her smile?" "No," replies the unimpressed cop, "but I sleep good at night."

Cry of the Hunted (1953) 78 min. Barry Sullivan, Vittorio Gassman, Polly Bergen, William Conrad. **Screenplay by:** Jack Leonard. **Directed by:** Joseph H. Lewis. **Noir Type:** On the Run. **Noir Themes:** Paranoia, fatalism. ★½

A bit of boring swamp noir with Sullivan as a prison security chief determined to bring back an escaped con (Gassman) from Louisiana's dangerous bayous. Conrad plays Sullivan's conniving assistant, who hopes his boss will fall flat on his face during the manhunt so he can inherit his job. Bergen is Sullivan's wisecracking cutie-pie wife who packs him a martini thermos and sandwiches tied with ribbons for his trek into the swamp. Director Lewis tries to keep things interesting by throwing in a couple of fistfights and a quasi-suspenseful quicksand scene that's supposed to make the viewer worry that Gassman will allow Sullivan to sink. A real snoozer.

Cry Terror! (1958) 96 min. James Mason, Rod Steiger, Inger Stevens, Neville Brand, Angie Dickinson, Jack Klugman, Kenneth Tobey. **Screenplay by:** Andrew L. Stone. **Directed by:** Andrew L. Stone. **Noir Type:** Hostage. **Noir Themes:** Greed, woman in jeopardy, child in jeopardy, sexual hostility. ★★★

Ex-Army demolition expert Steiger and his gang (Brand, Dickinson and Klugman) try to extort a half million dollars from a large airline, claiming that they have planted several bombs aboard one of its planes. The terrorists kidnap Mason, his wife (Stevens) and their little girl as extra insurance. Brand gives a first-rate performance as a psychopathic, bennie-popping rapist. (Guess who Steiger puts in charge of watching the nervous Stevens.) Dickinson (TV's *Police Woman*) is terrific as the sexy moll, who wouldn't think twice about sticking Mason's four-year-old daughter with a shiv if push came to shove. Tobey plays the F.B.I. agent in charge of the investigation. The plot is implausible and Stevens gives a whiny performance, but the suspense never lets up and there's an exciting climax in the foreboding tunnels of New York City's

A fed-up hostage (James Mason, left) gets tough with one of his captors (Jack Klugman) in *Cry Terror!* (MGM, 1958).

subway system. Stevens starred in the TV comedy series *The Farmer's Daughter* from 1963 to 1966 and committed suicide in 1970.

Familiar Faces from Television:
- ❑ Newscaster Chet Huntley as himself.
- ❑ Ed Hinton (Special Agent Henderson in *I Led Three Lives*) as an F.B.I. agent.
- ❑ William Schallert (Patty's dad from *The Patty Duke Show*) as a banker.
- ❑ Jack Kruschen (Tully in *Hong Kong* and Sam Markowitz in *Busting Loose*) as an F.B.I. agent.
- ❑ Barney Phillips (Sgt. Ed Jacobs in *Dragnet*, Capt. Franks in *Felony Squad* and Maj. Kaiser in *Twelve O'Clock High*) as the airline's security man.

Memorable Noir Moment:
- ❑ A compassionate airline bigwig, when told that a little girl's life depends on the airline's cooperation, responds, "I'm not going to gamble with lives even if it means busting the company." Those were the days.

Cry Tough (1959) 84 min. John Saxon, Linda Cristal, Joseph Calleia, Joe De Santis, Harry Townes, Don Gordon, Paul Clarke. **Screenplay by:** Harry Kleiner. **Directed by:** Paul Stanley. **Noir Type:** Troubled Youth. **Noir Themes:** Lust, corruption, social reform. ★★★

This screen adaptation of Irving Shulman's novel *Children of the Dark* details the rise and fall of a small-time Puerto Rican hood (Saxon) in New York's Spanish Harlem. After serving a year in the pen, Saxon returns home to his proud, unforgiving father (Calleia) and his overcrowded tenement apartment. Determined to go straight, Saxon shuns his former hoodlum associates (Townes, Clarke and Gordon), who have been pressuring him to pick up where he left off. Engaged to a nice girl from a good family, he's soon led astray by an illegal Cuban immigrant, femme fatale Cristal, who marries him to avoid deportation. He takes a job at a laundry owned by a crooked politician (De Santis) and, because he has a wife to support and he's being paid less than workers without criminal records, he finds himself pulling heists with the old gang. *Cry Tough* is an intelligent character study of a poor minority youth who feels he's one generation too early to get his slice of the American pie, and takes a violent shortcut that leads only to tragedy. The film's major weakness (indicative of the era) is that, with the exception of Argentina-born Cristal (best known for her role in the popular TV western series *High Chaparral*), the major Latino characters are played by Anglos. Saxon, however, who was born in Brooklyn, New York, to immigrant Italian parents, does a fine job as the young Puerto Rican hood.

Memorable Noir Moment:

❑ A young man flirts with Cristal as she sashays across the dance floor. "Hey, what's shakin'?" he asks. "Nothin's shakin' but the bacon," she replies, adding, "But the bacon's taken."

Cry Vengeance (1954) 81 min. Mark Stevens, Martha Hyer, Skip Homeier, Joan Vohs, Douglas Kennedy, Lewis Martin. **Screenplay by:** Warren Douglas and George Bricker. **Directed by:** Mark Stevens. **Noir Type:** Payback. **Noir Themes:** Revenge, child in jeopardy, sexual hostility. ★★★

Ex-cop, ex-con Stevens judo chops his way from San Francisco to Alaska in search of the crime lord (Kennedy) he believes framed him and killed his wife and child. Kennedy is now a respectable businessman living in Ketchican, Alaska ("the salmon capitol of the world"), with his young daughter. Unbeknownst to Stevens, Kennedy's former underlings (Martin and woman-beating wimp Homeier) are the real killers. Homeier's abused dipso moll (Vohs) wants to help Stevens but is afraid for her life. Hyer is the Alaskan bar owner who falls for Stevens and tries to convince him to give up his plan. This is a fast-paced action film with Stevens giving a good performance as the scar-faced avenger whose devious plot includes Kennedy's six-year-old daughter. Homeier later starred in the short-lived TV police drama *Dan Raven*.

Memorable Noir Moments:

❑ Vohs philosophizes about life. "One way or another," she says, "we're all on a merry-go-round … none of us can get off until they push us off."
❑ A somber Stevens is contemplating his next move when Hyer approaches. "A penny for your thoughts," she offers. "Might scare you," he replies. "I don't scare easy," she brags.

Cry Wolf (1947) 83 min. Barbara Stanwyck, Errol Flynn, Richard Basehart, Geraldine Brooks, Jerome Cowan. **Screenplay by:** Catherine Turney. **Directed by:** Peter Godfrey. **Noir Type:** Newlywed. **Noir Themes:** Dysfunctional family, woman in jeopardy, paranoia. ★★½

A psychopatic misogynist (Skip Homeier) gets tough with his girlfriend (Joan Vohs) in *Cry Vengeance* (Allied Artists, 1954).

Stanwyck shows up at Flynn's mansion claiming to be the widow of his nephew (Basehart), whose funeral is the next day. She advises Flynn that Basehart paid her to marry him because he had to have a wife before turning thirty in order to collect his inheritance, which he claimed Flynn was planning to steal by choosing a wife for him. Suspecting that Flynn is a mad scientist who's either killed her husband or is keeping him locked up in his laboratory, the inquisitive Stanwyck skulks around looking for ways into Flynn's mysterious lab. Brooks is Basehart's neurotic sister, afraid that Uncle Errol is out to get her, too. Cowan, Flynn's brother, is a U.S. senator who wisely tries to keep his distance from his kooky family. The talented Stanwyck manages to make this tedious melodrama somewhat enjoyable, but swashbuckler Flynn is badly cast against type.

The Curse of the Cat People (1944) 70 min. Simone Simon, Kent Smith, Jane Randolph, Ann Carter, Elizabeth Russell, Eve March, Julia Dean. **Screenplay by:** DeWitt Bodeen. **Directed by:** Gunther von Fritsch and Robert Wise. **Noir Type:** Fantasy. **Noir Themes:** Child in jeopardy, jealousy, paranoia. ★★★

In this ethereal sequel to *Cat People*, producer Val Lewton surprised everyone with a film vastly different from the original. Smith and Randolph reprise their roles, only they're married now and have a lonely, sensitive six-year-old daughter (Carter) who, according to the disappointed Smith, has "too many fantasies and too few friends." Smith encourages her to be more outgoing, but the girl is already disliked by her schoolmates and the neighborhood kids. A near senile former actress (Dean), who refuses to recognize her own daughter (Russell), takes a shine to Carter and gives her a "magic" ring, which the girl promptly uses to wish upon for a friend. And who shows up to make her wish come true? Simon, Smith's deceased first wife, the cat woman herself. Meanwhile, the jealous Russell swears that she'll kill Carter the next time she shows up at her mother's house. Charming and eerie, *Curse* works nicely, thanks to Nicholas Musuraca's atmospheric cinematography and fine performances by the entire cast. "Different" says it all.

D.O.A. (1950) 83 min. Edmond O'Brien, Pamela Britton, Beverly Campbell (Beverly Garland), Luther Adler, Neville Brand. **Screenplay by:** Russell Rouse and Clarence Greene. **Directed by:** Rudolph Maté. **Noir Type:** Payback. **Noir Themes:** Victim of fate, revenge. ★★★★

Businessman O'Brien travels to San Francisco for a week's vacation to get away

While his partner (Michael Ross) looks on, a gun-toting psycho (Neville Brand) indulges in his favorite pastime — roughing up a dying poison victim (Edmond O'Brien) — in *D.O.A.* (United Artists, 1950).

from his annoyingly clingy girlfriend (Britton). At a jazz club, he's involved in a flirtatious moment with an attractive woman when somebody spikes his drink. The next day doctors tell him that he's suffering from "luminous poisoning" and that he has only a day or two to live. He does a lot of running around through the streets of San Francisco (pretty nimbly, too, for a big boy) before the fear and panic subside and anger sets in. He spends what little time he has left searching for the killer. After more frantic running around (this time in Los Angeles) and further attempts on his life, he gets closer to solving the puzzle and exacting his vengeance. Brand, in his film debut, is sensational as a grinning psycho who gets a sick kick out of viciously punching the dying man in the stomach. Some of Dimitri Tiomkin's score is silly (the wolf whistle effects as O'Brien eyes all the lovelies at a convention), but the feverish music at the jazz club is terrific. Remade in 1969 as *Color Me Dead* and in 1988 as *D.O.A.* Avoid both.

Familiar Face from Television:
❑ Jerry Paris (dentist Jerry Helper on *The Dick Van Dyke Show* and Agent Flaherty in *The Untouchables*) as a bellhop.

Memorable Noir Moments:
❑ O'Brien staggers into a police station and reports a murder to homicide detectives. "Who was murdered?" a detective asks. "I was," O'Brien answers.
❑ "He's an unfortunate boy," Adler says of his chief goon, Brand. "He's psychopathic. He's unhappy unless he gives pain. He likes to see blood."
❑ At the end of the film, a physician serving as the film's technical advisor assures the skeptical viewer that the medical facts presented in the film are authentic and that "luminous toxin" is indeed a descriptive term for an actual poison.

Daisy Kenyon (1947) 100 min. Joan Crawford, Dana Andrews, Henry Fonda, Ruth Warrick, Martha Stewart, Peggy Ann Garner, Connie Marshall. **Screenplay by:** David Hertz. **Directed by:** Otto Preminger. **Noir Type:** Soap Opera. **Noir Themes:** Obsession, betrayal, fatalism, jealousy, dysfunctional family. ★★½

Crawford is in top form as the "other woman" in Andrews' life. Andrews, a prominent New York attorney, is unhappily married to the boss' daughter (Warrick), whose frustration leads her to physically abuse their youngest child (Marshall). Crawford, a successful commercial artist, is becoming more and more distressed over her pathetic situation and eagerly accepts the attention given her by a widowed war veteran (Fonda), whom she eventually marries. She hopes this will finally break Andrews' hold over her, but her confident ex-lover won't let go, forcing her to make a choice between him and the laid-back war hero. Stewart plays Crawford's wisecracking friend and Garner is Andrews' older daughter. This stylish soap opera is a showcase for Crawford, who plays it to the hilt, but poor Andrews and Fonda are barely noticeable as the annoyingly civilized rivals. Look among the patrons at the Stork Club for cameos by John Garfield (seated at the bar) and gossip columnist Walter Winchell, who plays himself.

Familiar Face from Television:
❑ Roy Roberts (Captain Huxley in *Oh Susanna*) as Andrews' attorney.

The Damned Don't Cry (1950) 103 min. Joan Crawford, David Brian, Steve Cochran, Kent Smith. **Screenplay by:** Harold Medford and Jerome Weidman. **Directed by:** Vincent Sherman. **Noir Type:** Femme Fatale. **Noir Themes:** Character deterioration, greed, obsession, lust, betrayal. ★★★

A bored housewife (Crawford) leaves her working stiff husband after their son is killed in an accident and moves to the big city in search of more of everything. She befriends a romantically interested, 60-bucks-a-week CPA (Smith) and convinces him to take a job as bookkeeper for a mobster (Brian). She soon dumps Smith and becomes Brian's mistress because he promises her the world, and that's all she ever really wanted. Cochran, Brian's rival, also falls hard for Crawford, who plays him for a sucker. It's a complicated but interesting film, and Crawford fans will revel in her tough performance as a small-town girl who chooses a dangerous road to money and social position.

Familiar Face from Television:
❑ Richard Egan (Jim Redigo on *Empire*), in his film debut, as Crawford's husband.

Memorable Noir Moments:
❑ An experienced "model" talks Crawford into going out with the customers. "It's still modeling," she lies, "but it pays better at night."
❑ Sensitivity Training Required: Brian puts Crawford in her noir place, saying, "There's one thing I never do in the presence of women — discuss business."
❑ When Smith explains to Crawford why he won't work for the mob, she chastises him. "Don't talk to me about self-respect," she says. "That's something you tell yourself you've got when you've got nothing else."
❑ Brian finds himself turned on by Crawford. "I admire a woman with brains," he tells her. "But a woman with brains *and* spirit excites me."

Danger Signal (1945) 78 min. Zachary Scott, Faye Emerson, Rosemary DeCamp, Bruce Bennett, Mona Freeman. **Screenplay by:** Graham Baker and Adele Comandini. **Directed by:** Robert Florey. **Noir Type:** Con Artist. **Noir Themes:** Woman in jeopardy, betrayal. ★★

What little this film has going for it belongs to Scott, who's sensational as a contemptible but charming scoundrel. He woos public stenographer Emerson and then drops her for her younger sister (Freeman) when he learns that sis will inherit twenty-five thousand dollars when she marries. Unknown to the siblings, Scott is being hunted by police in connection with the supposed suicide of a married woman he had been seeing. Unfortunately, it takes forever for anything really interesting to happen, but watching smooth operator Scott at work compensates for having to sit through such a tedious film. DeCamp plays Emerson's psychiatrist friend and Bennett is an absent-minded professor, too shy to make a play for the lovely stenographer.

Familiar Face from Television:
❑ Richard Erdman (Peter Fairfield III in *The Tab Hunter Show*) as Freeman's ardent, teenaged admirer.

Memorable Noir Moment:
❑ Scott ingeniously tricks the lovesick Emerson into writing a suicide note by pretending it's

part of the story he's writing. See *The Unsuspected* and *A Kiss Before Dying* for two equally cunning killers.

Danger Zone (1951) 55 min. Hugh Beaumont, Edward Brophy, Richard Travis, Tom Neal, Pamela Blake, Virginia Dale, Ralph Sanford, Paul Drew. **Screenplay by**: Julian Harmon. **Directed by**: William Berke. **Noir Type**: Whodunit. **Noir Themes**: Greed, betrayal, jealousy. ✫

This stinker stars Beaumont as a boat storeowner–amateur detective whose "sideline is trouble." For some reason, the film centers around two unrelated cases, one involving a missing saxophone that showgirl Dale and the mysterious Sanford are willing to pay big bucks for, and another a divorce scam operated by a shady P.I. (Neal). Blake plays the wife of one of Neal's pigeons and Dale is her niece. Both cases lead to murder, with Beaumont playing the patsy and homicide detective Travis trying to get enough evidence to arrest him. For "comedy relief," Brophy plays Beaumont's boozing pal. This low-budget B film is so badly made that at one point, Dale addresses Blake by her own character's name. If your taste includes mediocre acting and appalling dialogue, then you can double your pleasure with this two-plots-in-one bomb.

Memorable Noir Moment:
❏ Beaumont responds sarcastically to a desperate, gun-toting man looking for answers. "What are you doing, writing a gossip column?" he asks. "No," the man replies. "The obituary. And you're going to make the morning deadline."

Dangerous Crossing (1953) 75 min. Jeanne Crain, Michael Rennie, Carl Betz, Willis Bouchey. **Screenplay by**: Leo Townsend. **Directed by**: Joseph M. Newman. **Noir Type**: High Seas. **Noir Themes**: Woman in jeopardy, betrayal, paranoia, fatalism. ✫✫½

Dangerous Crossing is a well-acted film noir in a unique setting — a cruise ship. Crain plays a honeymooning newlywed whose husband (Betz) disappears soon after boarding. When Crain reports the disappearance to ship authorities, she discovers that she has no proof that Betz ever was on board or that she's even married to him. Already depressed and emotionally unstable because of her father's recent death, she gradually descends into paranoia and despair. She scours the ship for her husband, who, she says, has telephoned her stateroom advising her to trust no one on board. The mystery is easily solved, but the enjoyment comes from watching Crain make a fool out of herself in front of the ship's passengers and crew. Rennie plays the ship doctor who tries to help her and, of course, falls in love with her. And don't worry, she'll take off that annoying fur coat eventually.

Dangerous Intruder (1945) 58 min. Charles Arnt, Veda Ann Borg, Tom Keene, Fay Helm, John Rogers, Jo Ann Marlowe. **Screenplay by**: Martin Goldsmith. **Directed by**: Vernon Keays. **Noir Type**: Psycho. **Noir Themes**: Woman in jeopardy, paranoia, greed. ✫½

While hitchhiking to New York, showgirl Borg is struck by a car driven by a loony art collector (Arnt) who brings her to his mansion to recuperate. While there, she becomes involved in a murder or two and falls in love with Arnt's golf-crazy brother-in-law (Keene). Helm plays Arnt's sickly wife, Marlowe is his precocious stepdaughter and Rogers is his weird assistant. The only entertainment to be gotten out of this mercifully short noir is from the overacting of Arnt and Rogers.

A Dangerous Profession (1949) 79 min. George Raft, Ella Raines, Pat O'Brien, Bill Williams, Jim Backus. **Screenplay by:** Martin Rackin and Warren Duff. **Directed by:** Ted Tetzlaff. **Noir Type:** Whodunit. **Noir Themes:** Betrayal, revenge. ★★

A bail bondsman (Raft) puts up company dough to bail out embezzler Williams, who's married to Raft's former girlfriend (Raines), a gal who ran out on him two years earlier. Raft's business partner (O'Brien) and a police detective (Backus) are perturbed with Raft because they expect Williams to go on the lam rather than face charges. Instead, the embezzler is murdered, and Raft sets out to trap the killer. The talented cast is wasted in this mediocre crime drama.

Memorable Noir Moment:
❑ Raft explains to his date why Backus, the cop sitting next to her, doesn't go for girls. "The only one he ever went for poisoned him," he says. "Pity he recovered," replies the cop-hating dame. "I didn't," Backus admits.

Dark City (1950) 98 min. Charlton Heston, Lizabeth Scott, Viveca Lindfors, Dean Jagger, Don DeFore, Jack Webb, Henry (Harry) Morgan, Ed Begley, Mike Mazurki. **Screenplay by:**

A patsy (Don DeFore, second from right) loses his shirt to conniving card sharks (Jack Webb, Charlton Heston and Ed Begley, left to right) while a nightclub singer (Lizabeth Scott) refrains from kibitzing in *Dark City* (Paramount, 1950).

John Meredyth Lucas and Larry Marcus. **Directed by:** William Dieterle. **Noir Type:** Payback. **Noir Themes:** Revenge, paranoia, guilt, fatalism. ★★★½

Heston, Webb and Begley, who run a gambling joint, are down on their luck because of recent police raids. When DeFore shows up with a five thousand-dollar cashier's check in his wallet, the crooks smell a patsy. It's not long before they sucker him into a crooked poker game and win all of his cash *and* the check, which had been entrusted to him by an organization back home. Ashamed and conscience-stricken, DeFore hangs himself, but not before leaving a note for his psychopathic big brother (Mazurki), who shows up looking for revenge. Heston, in his Hollywood film debut, is first-rate as the fatalistic gambler whose conscience won't allow him to forget DeFore or his family. Morgan plays the slightly punchy "Soldier," the butt of Webb's vicious sense of humor. Noir icon Scott is the torch singer in love with Heston, and Lindfors is DeFore's widow, who falls for Heston, unaware that he's one of the gamblers who fleeced her husband. Jagger plays the cop investigating the killings. Not exactly a noir classic, but enjoyable, nonetheless. Morgan and Webb would appear together in 1951's ***Appointment with Danger*** and in the revived TV series *Dragnet* (1967–70).

Memorable Noir Moments:

❑ After Heston expounds on the meaning of the River Styx to a bewildered, but captivated, Scott, she gushes, "I don't know what you're talking about. It doesn't matter. I love you, Danny."
❑ A patrolman rushes Heston and Webb out of his boss' office, saying, "All right, you two, let's go." "We've got names," Heston complains. "Yeah, how many?" replies the quick-witted cop.

The Dark Corner (1946) 99 min. Mark Stevens, Lucille Ball, William Bendix, Clifton Webb, Kurt Kreuger, Cathy Downs. **Screenplay by:** Jay Dratler and Bernard C. Schoenfeld. **Directed by:** Henry Hathaway. **Noir Type:** P.I. **Noir Themes:** Betrayal, revenge. ★★★

Recently released from prison after serving time for manslaughter, a crime he didn't commit, Stevens is trying desperately to make a go of his new private eye business. When he catches a man in a white suit (Bendix) tailing him, the two-fisted P.I. convinces him to talk by smashing his fingers with the butt of his gun. Bendix claims that he's also a private dick and that Stevens' former partner (Krueger), the man who framed Stevens, hired him. It soon becomes evident to Stevens that Krueger wants him out of the way. But things aren't always what they seem to be. Webb plays the stuffed-shirt art dealer whose wife (Downs) is having an affair with Krueger. Ball, as Stevens' secretary, doesn't have much to do except look beautiful. A good example of the film noir with Stevens handling the self-pitying P.I. role nicely and Bendix enjoyable as the crafty hired killer.

Familiar Faces from Television:

❑ Ellen Corby (Grandma Walton in *The Waltons*) as a cleaning lady.
❑ John Russell (Tim Kelly in *Soldiers of Fortune* and Marshal Dan Troop in *The Lawman*) as a uniformed cop.
❑ Reed Hadley (Capt. John Braddock in *Racket Squad*) as a detective.

A movie theater cashier (Mary Field) seems a bit shocked as a P.I. (Mark Stevens) flirts with his secretary (Lucille Ball) in *The Dark Corner* (20th Century–Fox, 1946).

Memorable Noir Moments:

❏ Stevens, enjoying a pity party, tells Ball, "I feel all dead inside. I'm backed up in a dark corner and I don't know who's hitting me."

❏ "How I detest the dawn," Webb tells Krueger. "The grass always looks like it's been left out all night."

❏ After Ball notices that Bendix has been following them, she confides in Stevens that she's never been followed before. "That's a terrible reflection on American manhood," the flirtatious P.I. replies.

The Dark Mirror (1946) 85 min. Olivia de Havilland, Lew Ayres, Thomas Mitchell. **Screenplay by:** Nunnally Johnson. **Directed by:** Robert Siodmak. **Noir Type:** Good Twin, Bad Twin. **Noir Themes:** Woman in jeopardy, betrayal, jealousy, paranoia. ★★★★

Twin sisters (de Havilland in a dual role) confuse the hell out of a homicide detective (Mitchell) investigating the murder of one of their boyfriends. He knows that one of the twins is guilty, but he's in the dark as to which one. And the ladies aren't cooperating. Forced to release them after several equally bewildered witnesses can't identify the killer, Mitchell turns to a psychologist (Ayres) who specializes in twins to help determine which of the siblings is the nutcase. Ayres falls in love with the good twin. The evil one, allowing jealousy to get the best of her once again, decides to drive her sister to suicide. De Havilland has a field day playing the two sisters, and Ayres is wonderfully low-key as the lemon drop–loving psychologist.

Familiar Face from Television:

❑ Richard Long (Rex Randolph in *Bourbon Street Beat*, Professor Everett in *Nanny and the Professor* and Jarrold Barkley in *The Big Valley*) as a uniformed lobby attendant.

Memorable Noir Moment:

❑ After welcoming de Havilland to his bachelor pad, the fastidious Ayres says, "I apologize for its neatness but I have no woman around to keep it messed up all the time."

Dark Passage (1947) 106 min. Humphrey Bogart, Lauren Bacall, Agnes Moorehead, Clifton Young, Houseley Stevenson. **Screenplay by:** Delmer Daves. **Directed by:** Delmer Daves. **Noir Type:** Plastic Surgery. **Noir Themes:** Victim of the law. ★★½

Bogart is an escaped convict wrongly convicted of murdering his wife and Bacall is the oh-so-helpful gal who hides him from the cops. Moorehead plays the shrew whose hearsay testimony was responsible for sending Bogey to prison, Young is a blackmailing hood and Stevenson is the plastic surgeon providing Bogey with a new

A blackmailer (Clifton Young) explains his demands to his victim (Humphrey Bogart) in *Dark Passage* (Warner Bros., 1947).

face. The acting is okay, with Bogart and Bacall the film's saving grace, but the plot is unbelievable — populated with overly helpful strangers and unlikely coincidences. We don't see Bogart's face for most of the film because, for a time, the camera is his eyes (a technique used earlier by Robert Montgomery in *Lady in the Lake*), and later his face is entirely wrapped in bandages. Anybody else but Bogey, please! The real killer's fate is enjoyable to watch, but the ending is disappointing.

Familiar Face from Television:
❑ Tom D'Andrea (Riley's best pal Gillis in *The Life of Riley*) as an amiable cab driver.

Memorable Noir Moment:
❑ Bogart asks blackmailer Young, "What are you?" Young grins and answers, "I was a small-time crook until this very minute, and now I'm a big-time crook. And I like it."
❑ Bogey stops at a diner for a meal and to escape the rain. A suspicious cop grills him about why he isn't wearing a raincoat and threatens to run him in. Probable cause in 1947?

The Dark Past (1948) 74 min. William Holden, Nina Foch, Lee J. Cobb. **Screenplay by:** Philip MacDonald, Michael Blankfort and Albert Duffy. **Directed by:** Rudolph Maté. **Noir Type:** Hostage. **Noir Themes:** Character deterioration, social reform. ★★★

Psychopathic killer Holden escapes from prison and, along with his gang and moll (Foch), invades psychiatrist Cobb's weekend retreat, holding his family, house guests and servants hostage while waiting for a getaway boat to arrive. Cobb makes the best of a bad situation by psychoanalyzing Holden and, displaying little concern for the safety of his wife and young son, spends his time trying to help the killer unravel the mystery of a recurring nightmare and, thus, his criminal mind. Talk about workaholics! Although director Maté overuses some common noir techniques (narration, flashback, a flashback within a flashback and a weird dream sequence), they work well, making the mundane plot more interesting. This remake of 1939's *Blind Alley* offers a controversial solution to society's violent criminals— send young offenders to psychiatric hospitals instead of jail before they turn into mad-dog killers.

Familiar Face from Television:
❑ Ellen Corby (Grandma Walton in *The Waltons*) as a maid.

Memorable Noir Moment:
❑ Cobb draws a picture of a human head and attempts to explain the conscious and subconscious minds to a bewildered Holden. "This is where you do your thinking," the psychiatrist says. "All the everyday stuff— eating, smoking, pulling jobs, planning getaways."

Dark Waters (1944) 90 min. Merle Oberon, Franchot Tone, Thomas Mitchell, Elisha Cook, Jr., John Qualen, Fay Bainter. **Screenplay by:** Joan Harrison and Marion Cockrell. **Directed by:** André De Toth. **Noir Type:** Impersonator. **Noir Themes:** Woman in jeopardy. ★½

Oberon plays a survivor of a ship disaster that has left her orphaned and a bit neurotic. She seeks refuge at the Louisiana plantation of her uncle and aunt but instead finds a household of weird and possibly dangerous people (Mitchell, Cook,

Qualen and Bainter). Tone plays the country doctor who falls in love with her. The acting is good, especially by the dependable Cook, but the film is boring and insufferably long.

Date with Death (1959) 81 min. Gerald Mohr, Liz Renay, Harry Lauter, Robert Clarke. **Screenplay by:** Robert C. Dennis. **Directed by:** Harold Daniels. **Noir Type:** Impersonator. **Noir Themes:** Corruption, victim of fate. ★

Veteran character actors Mohr and Lauter sink pretty low in this laughable low-budget flick. Mohr plays a hobo kicked off a freight train in the middle of the desert. After flipping a con to let fate decide which road he should take, Mohr stumbles on a car containing the body of a New York City cop. After stealing the car and the dead man's identity papers, he's mistaken for the new police commissioner recently hired to clean up a nearby town which has been overrun by mobster Clarke and his syndicate. Cool customer Mohr plays right along. Lauter is the crooked police lieutenant who wants the commissioner job, and Renay is the singer who falls for Mohr. The plot is ridiculous and the acting is terrible. *Date with Death* was filmed in "Psychorama," a subliminal image process that supposedly was banned from television for being too potent.

Memorable Noir Moment:
❑ When Mohr is exposed at a town council meeting as an impersonator, one of the politicians ponders a difficult question: "A hobo sworn in as chief of police — how does a thing like this happen?" Viewers might find themselves asking the same thing about the production of this film.

Dead Reckoning (1947) 100 min. Humphrey Bogart, Lizabeth Scott, Morris Carnovsky, Marvin Miller, Wallace Ford, William Prince. **Screenplay by:** Oliver H.P. Garrett and Steve Fisher. **Directed by:** John Cromwell. **Noir Type:** Whodunit. **Noir Themes:** Betrayal, lust. ★★★

Bogey stars as an Army captain whose publicity-shy buddy (Prince) deliberately disappears just before he is to be awarded the Congressional Medal of Honor. Bogey tracks him to his hometown, where he discovers that Prince has been murdered. Determined to find the murderer ("When a guy's buddy is killed, he ought to do something about it"), he soon runs into Prince's ex-girlfriend (Scott), a former nightclub singer whose husband was supposedly killed by Prince several years earlier. Suspicious at first of this "Cinderella with a husky voice," Bogey finds himself falling in love with the sexy widow, but not before being drugged, beaten and framed for murder by nightclub owner Carnovsky and his psychopathic goon (Miller). Ford plays an obliging safecracker whose skills come in handy. Bogart's gritty performance compensates for the convoluted plot, told mostly in flashback, and Miller is in top form as the repugnant henchman. Look for a grown-up Stymie Beard, former *Little Rascal* Stymie, as a bellhop in Bogey's hotel.

Familiar Faces from Television:
❑ Frank Wilcox (John Brewster in *The Beverly Hillbillies*) as a hotel clerk.
❑ Ruby Dandridge (Oriole in *Beulah* and Delilah in *Father of the Bride*) as Scott's maid.

Memorable Noir Moment:

❏ Bogey slams the door of a telephone booth in a beautiful girl's face and apologies as only he can: "Sorry, gorgeous, I didn't see what you looked like."

Deadlier Than the Male *see* Born to Kill

Deadline at Dawn (1946) 83 min. Susan Hayward, Paul Lukas, Bill Williams, Lola Lane, Marvin Miller, Joseph Calleia, Steven Geray, Joe Sawyer, Osa Massen. **Screenplay by:** Clifford Odets. **Directed by:** Harold Clurman. **Noir Type:** Whodunit. **Noir Themes:** Victim of fate, sexual hostility, revenge. ★★½

A small-town sailor (Williams) on liberty in New York finds a wad of bills in his pocket and believes that, while drunk, he must have stolen the money from the older woman who had plied him with booze earlier in the evening. When Williams and his new friend, taxi dancer Hayward, try to return the money, they discover the woman's body. Williams, suffering from hangover amnesia, thinks he must have killed her. Street-wise Hayward, taking pity on the naive young sailor, helps him search for the real murderer and, of course, falls in love with him in the process. Suspects include the dead woman's gangster brother (Calleia); her blind ex-husband (Miller); a cab driver (Lukas); a lovesick, new American citizen (Geray); a tipsy baseball player

A taxi dancer, taxi driver and puzzled sailor (Susan Hayward, Paul Lukas and Bill Williams) hunt for a murderer in New York in *Deadline at Dawn* (RKO, 1946).

(Sawyer); and a mysterious lame woman (Massen), to name just a few. Implausible but fun.

Familiar Face from Television:

❏ Peter Breck (Nick Barkley in *The Big Valley* and Clay Culhane in *Black Saddle*) as a counterman.

Memorable Noir Moment:

❏ Williams makes small talk as he dances with Hayward. "There's a lot of nice people dancing here, isn't there?" he remarks. Hayward replies cynically, "This is a post office ... a lot of second-class matter."

The Deadly Game (1955-British) 70 min. Lloyd Bridges, Finlay Currie, Maureen Swanson, Peter Dyneley. **Screenplay by:** Robert Dunbar and Daniel Birt. **Directed by:** Daniel Birt. **Noir Type:** Blackmail. **Noir Themes:** Victim of fate, greed. ★½

While in Spain to record Spanish folk music, Bridges runs across an old RAF buddy (Dyneley) and meets a beautiful folk dancer (Swanson) and her suspicious uncle (Currie). When Dyneley leaves Spain in a hurry, Bridges promises to drive his friend's car to London and deliver an envelope to him. When he arrives in London, he discovers that Dyneley has been murdered and soon becomes Scotland Yard's main suspect. Bridges learns that Dyneley was a blackmailer and that his murderer had been trying to steal the contents of the mysterious envelope — microfilm containing a new antibiotic drug formula. Slow-moving and confusing, this British programmer, also known as *Third Party Risk*, is interesting only for the presence of American actor Bridges, who would soon become a household name in the States as the star of the popular TV series *Sea Hunt*.

Deadly Is the Female *see* Gun Crazy

Death in Small Doses (1957) 78 min. Peter Graves, Mala Powers, Chuck Connors, Merry Anders, Roy Engel. **Screenplay by:** John McGreevey. **Directed by:** Joseph M. Newman. **Noir Type:** Undercover. **Noir Themes:** Greed, betrayal, social reform. ★★½

Graves (from TV's *Mission Impossible*) is a Food and Drug Administration agent assigned to discover who has been selling illegal amphetamines (stay-awake pills) to truck drivers. Posing as a student driver, he moves into a rooming house owned by sexy landlady Powers, whose husband was killed in a driving accident after consuming "bennies," also known as "co-pilots" by drivers. Graves' investigation leads him to a roadside diner waitress (Anders) who pushes the pills as side orders to support her own habit. After his driving teacher (Engel) is murdered by drug pushers for playing amateur detective, Graves finds himself teamed up with trucker Connors, a pill-popping hep-cat who seems determined to be benny's next victim. Will the stalwart FDA agent bust the drug ring and help make the American highways safe once again? What do you think? Entertaining, high-camp B movie with Connors (former Brooklyn Dodgers pitcher and TV's *The Rifleman*) giving an incredibly hyperactive performance.

Familiar Faces from Television:

A truck driver (Chuck Connors), hyped up on bennies, jitterbugs with an admirer in *Death in Small Doses* (Allied Artists, 1957).

❑ Harry Lauter (Jim Herrick in *Waterfront*) as Power's out-of-town friend.
❑ Robert Shayne (Inspector Henderson in *The Adventures of Superman*) as Graves' FDA boss.

Death of a Salesman (1951) 115 min. Fredric March, Mildred Dunnock, Kevin McCarthy, Cameron Mitchell, Howard Smith. **Screenplay by:** Stanley Roberts. **Directed by:** Laslo Benedek. **Noir Type:** Ambition. **Noir Themes:** Dysfunctional family, fatalism, betrayal, guilt. ★★★★½

March stars as the pathetic Willie Loman in this powerful screen adaptation of Arthur Miller's classic play. Having reached the end of the road in a mediocre sales career and having failed as a father, March has only one thing going for him — a loving wife (Dunnock) — but even she's not enough to redeem a wasted life of unfulfilled dreams. Having survived "riding on a smile and a shoeshine" for so long, March now faces the prospect of his golden years being spent in poverty and having to be supported by his two less-than-capable adult sons, one a kleptomaniac (McCarthy) and the other a playboy (Mitchell). Lately, the boys have noticed that the old man has been exhibiting some strange behavior — talking to himself and his long-dead brother, and tampering with the gas furnace in the basement. Adding to the tension is the dark secret at the root of the bitter antagonism between March and McCarthy for the past sixteen years. Smith plays a kindly neighbor providing March with small handouts to help keep his head above water. March, Dunnock and McCarthy received Academy Award nominations for their extraordinary performances in this American classic. Remade as a TV movie in 1985 with Dustin Hoffman as Loman and John Malkovich as his troubled son Biff.

Familiar Faces from Television:
❑ Jesse White (Jesse Leeds in *The Danny Thomas Show* and the bored Maytag repairman in commercials) as a waiter.
❑ Elisabeth Fraser (Sgt. Bilko's WAC girlfriend, Sgt. Joan Hogan, in *The Phil Silvers Show*) as a girl in a restaurant.
❑ Don Keefer (George in *Angel*) as Smith's geeky son.

Memorable Noir Moment:
❑ March, disgusted with McCarthy's vagabond lifestyle, complains bitterly to Dunnock, "Not finding yourself at the age of thirty-four is a disgrace."

Death of a Scoundrel (1956) 119 min. George Sanders, Yvonne De Carlo, Zsa Zsa Gabor, Coleen Gray, John Hoyt, Nancy Gates, Tom Conway. **Screenplay by:** Charles Martin. **Directed by:** Charles Martin. **Noir Type:** Ambition. **Noir Themes:** Greed, betrayal, revenge, guilt. ★★½

A conniving businessman (George Sanders) gets frisky with his assistant (Yvonne De Carlo) in *Death of a Scoundrel* (RKO, 1956).

Sanders, "the most hated man on earth" and "an evil genius," is found shot to death in his luxurious New York mansion. His assistant (De Carlo) tells homicide detectives about the Czech immigrant's swift, unethical rise in the world of American big business. Via flashback, we see witness Sanders, after his release from a Nazi concentration camp, discovering that his brother (Conway, Sanders' real-life brother) has stolen his girl. When he learns that Conway is without identity papers, Sanders informs on him to the police, who promptly execute the man, rewarding Sanders with a passport to the U.S. There, aided by the equally despicable Hoyt, he begins his ruthless climb to the top. Along the way he romances a wealthy widow (Gabor, Sanders' real-life wife), cozies up to a businessman's wife (Gray) in a plot to steal the man's fortune, and attempts to ruin the career of a struggling actress (Gates) because she spurned his romantic overtures. Sanders seems to be enjoying his role, hamming it up royally.

Familiar Face from Television:
❑ Werner Klemperer (Col. Klink in *Hogan's Heroes*) as Sanders' lawyer.

Memorable Noir Moment:
❑ Sanders stoops pretty low when he asks his elderly mother to claim he's the illegitimate son of a Swiss sailor so that in case he's deported it will be to Switzerland, where he'd be able to keep his money, and not to Czechoslovakia, where he'd be thrown into a Communist prison. Needless to say, the old girl is taken aback and even *she* finally realizes what a heel her boy has become.

Deception (1946) 111 min. Bette Davis, Claude Rains, Paul Henreid, John Abbott, Benson Fong. **Screenplay by:** John Collier and Joseph Than. **Directed by:** Irving Rapper. **Noir Type:** Triangle. **Noir Themes:** Jealousy, betrayal. ★★½

A New York pianist (Davis) runs into former lover Henreid, who she thought had died in Europe during the war. The out-of-work cellist suspects that something isn't quite right when he sees the luxurious lifestyle that Davis is enjoying and grills her about it. Knowing that he can be violently jealous, Davis allays his suspicions, explaining that she's been teaching music to wealthy clients. She sidetracks him further by suggesting that they get married, which they do, and rather quickly, before Davis' sugar daddy (Rains) returns to town. Rains, a famous composer, offers Henreid the opportunity to play his latest composition during a recital, and the unemployed musician enthusiastically accepts. But Davis knows her former lover, who has a mean streak a mile long, only too well and expects him pull the rug out from under Henreid at the last minute, replacing him with a stand-by cellist (Abbott). But what Rains has in mind is even worse, and somebody will be killed as a result. Fong, a semi-regular on TV's *Bachelor Father* and *Kung Fu* in the 1960s and 1970s, plays Rains' butler. Rains' excellent performance makes this slow-mover worth viewing.

Familiar Face from Television:
❑ Richard Erdman (Peter Fairfield III in *The Tab Hunter Show*) as the music editor of a college newspaper.

Deep Valley (1947) 104 min. Ida Lupino, Dane Clark, Wayne Morris, Henry Hull, Fay Bainter. **Screenplay by:** Stephen Morehouse Avery and Salka Viertel. **Directed by:** Jean Negulesco. **Noir Type:** On the Run. **Noir Themes:** Fatalism, guilt, paranoia. ★★★½

Lupino plays a shy farm girl disabled by a stutter because, as a child, she witnessed her father brutalize her mother. Her parents (Hull and Bainter) haven't slept in the same room for seven years, and Lupino has been suffering the consequences of their mutual disdain. Near their farm, a new highway is being built by a chain gang from San Quentin, and Lupino enjoys spying on the cons from the woods. She particularly enjoys watching one muscular prisoner (Clark) as he swings his pick. After Clark escapes thanks to a convenient landslide, Lupino runs into him at her secret hideaway, an abandoned cabin in the woods, and the two fall in love. Before long, Lupino's stutter disappears and the blissful couple make plans to run off to San Francisco to get married. As a posse searches for the escaped con, the romance-minded highway engineer (Morris) asks Hull to fix him up with Lupino. A top-notch tearjerker thanks to a sterling performance by Lupino, *Deep Valley* originally was planned as a vehicle for Humphrey Bogart, John Garfield and Ann Sheridan. It was Lupino's last film for Warner Bros. and it won her critical acclaim. When she turned down Jack Warner's offer of an exclusive four-year contract, the studio mogul swore she'd never make another movie for Warner Bros. After playing second fiddle to Warners' top star, Bette Davis, for seven long years, Lupino couldn't have cared less.

Familiar Face from Television:

❑ Ray Teal (Sheriff Roy Coffee in *Bonanza*) as a prison official visiting the sight of a landslide.

Memorable Noir Moments:

❑ The bad-tempered Clark, who was imprisoned for killing a man in a barroom brawl, complains to Lupino that "I always find out I didn't mean to when it's all over."
❑ From the Some-Things-Never-Change Department: Responding to Lupino's request to lower the neckline of her new dress, Bainter remarks, "All you young girls want everything lower in the front and tighter in the back. What are you so proud of?"

The Depraved (1957-British) 70 min. Anne Heywood, Robert Arden, Carroll Levis, Basil Dignam, Denis Shaw. **Screenplay by:** Brian Clemens and Edith Dell. **Directed by:** Paul Dickson. **Noir Type:** Femme Fatale. **Noir Themes:** Obsession, lust, betrayal, greed. ★★½

Yet another **Double Indemnity** clone, this British noir is about an American Army officer (Arden) in England who becomes involved with Heywood, the wife of an obnoxious alcoholic (Dignam). Heywood wants to get rid of the abusive Dignam, a self-proclaimed pacifist, and collect on his substantial life insurance policy. After seducing the unsuspecting Arden, she tries to enlist him in the murder plot. Horrified at first, like so many other weak-willed film noir patsies before him, Arden eventually dives into the project with a passion. After making Dignam's death look like an automobile accident, the two lovers sweat it out as an American major (Levis) and a British inspector (Shaw) investigate. Meanwhile, a handsome Italian chauffeur waits in the wings. Predictable and hackneyed, yet strangely entertaining.

Memorable Noir Moment:
- ❏ Sensitivity Training Required: As he watches Heywood on her hands and knees cleaning up a mess he's made, Dignam remarks, "That's how a woman should be."

Desert Fury (1947) 94 min. John Hodiak, Lizabeth Scott, Burt Lancaster, Wendell Corey, Mary Astor. **Screenplay by:** Robert Rossen. **Directed by:** Lewis Allen. **Noir Type:** Triangle. **Noir Themes:** Obsession, jealousy, betrayal, corruption. ★★½

Lots of desert, not much fury here. Scott plays the rebellious daughter of Arizona casino owner Astor, who also owns the judge and the sheriff. Against her mother's wishes, Scott starts seeing an out-of-town hood (Hodiak) whose previous wife died under mysterious circumstances. Deputy Sheriff Lancaster, who's in love with Scott, isn't happy about the situation but balks when Astor offers him a bribe to marry her wayward daughter. Corey, in his film debut, plays Hodiak's goon and companion-housekeeper, who has been with him for "a long time, a long, long time." Corey's jealousy of Scott, his rival for Hodiak's affection, is what makes this tedious film interesting. There appears to be more than meets the eye in the crooks' strained relationship, which explodes during the film's exciting climax. Lancaster, straight from his sensational debut in **The Killers**, is wasted as the affable lawman. Scott is okay, and Hodiak does a good job as the weak-kneed hood, but newcomer Corey steals the show.

Familiar Faces from Television:
- ❏ Ray Teal (Sheriff Roy Coffee in *Bonanza*) as a surly bus driver in a cafe.
- ❏ James Flavin (Lt. Donovan in *Man with a Camera*) as a town's sheriff.

Memorable Noir Moments:
- ❏ Sensitivity Training Required: When Scott notices Hodiak's gun, the crook tries to put her in her place. "Carpet sweeper's in the kitchen closet if you want it," he advises.
- ❏ Corey, bitten by the green-eyed monster, warns Scott to "get away from here or I'll kill you. So help me, I'll kill you where you stand."

Desperate (1947) 73 min. Steve Brodie, Audrey Long, Raymond Burr, Douglas Fowley, Jason Robards, Sr. **Screenplay by:** Harry Essex. **Directed by:** Anthony Mann. **Noir Type:** On the Run. **Noir Themes:** Victim of fate, paranoia, revenge, woman in jeopardy, child in jeopardy. ★★★½

Newlywed truck driver Brodie unwittingly becomes involved in a warehouse robbery after being hired by mobster Burr to do a hauling job. During the robbery, Brodie alerts a passing patrolman, who is killed in a shootout with Burr's brother. Brodie gets away but Burr's brother is caught by the cops. Burr tries to get the trucker to take the rap by threatening his pregnant wife (Long), so Brodie and Long go on the lam. Unfortunately for them, Burr, whose brother has been sentenced to death, has hired a shady P.I. (Fowley) to find them. Robards plays a crafty detective who uses Brodie as bait, hoping to reel in Burr and his gang. This is director Mann's first film noir and it's as hard-boiled and violent as they come. Brodie is excellent as the hapless war hero whose main concern is for his wife and newborn child. Burr, as usual, is a terrific villain.

A hood (William Challee) restrains an angry truck driver (Steve Brodie) from socking his gangster boss (Raymond Burr) in *Desperate* (RKO, 1947).

Memorable Noir Moment:

❑ When one of Burr's goons reports that he screwed up and let Brodie escape, Burr snaps, "You must have studied to get *that* stupid."

The Desperate Hours (1955) 112 min. Humphrey Bogart, Fredric March, Arthur Kennedy, Martha Scott, Gig Young, Mary Murphy, Richard Eyer, Dewey Martin, Robert Middleton. **Screenplay by:** Joseph Hayes. **Directed by:** William Wyler. **Noir Type:** Hostage. **Noir Themes:** Victim of fate, paranoia, revenge, child in jeopardy. ★★★★½

This classic noir still packs a terrific punch nearly a half-century later. Bogart stars as a psychopathic escaped con who, together with his brother (Martin) and an even worse psycho (Middleton), hides out from the law in the suburban Indianapolis home of businessman March and his family (wife Scott and kids Murphy and Eyer). While Bogey taunts and threatens the frightened family, the shy Martin tries to make friends with the attractive Murphy. Lecherous Middleton, however, has other ideas (like searching her for hidden weapons). Defending his family from the trio of armed intruders becomes March's number one priority, even if it's in ways that make him look like a coward in his son's eyes. Kennedy is the cop conducting the manhunt and fending off interference from bureaucrats, and Young is Murphy's bewildered boyfriend. Bogey's sensational in his next-to-last role, released the

An escaped killer (Humphrey Bogart) frisks his captive (Frederic March) in *The Desperate Hours* (Paramount, 1955).

year before he died (his final film being the equally terrific noir ***The Harder They Fall***). March and Scott also do great jobs as parents faced with the unbelievable horror that their children might be murdered in front of their eyes. Terrific acting, a great script, a fine directing job and lots of familiar faces. Remade in 1990 with Mickey Roarke in Bogey's role and Anthony Hopkins as the father. Stick with the original, noir fans.

Familiar Faces from Television:
- ❑ Ray Collins (Lieutenant Tragg in *Perry Mason*) as the uneasy County Sheriff.
- ❑ Whit Bissell (Gen. Heywood Kirk in *The Time Tunnel*) as an F.B.I. agent.
- ❑ Beverly Garland (Casey Jones in *Decoy*, Barbara Harper Douglas in *My Three Sons* and Dotty West in *Scarecrow and Mrs. King*) as Eyer's teacher.
- ❑ Ann Doran (Mrs. Kingston in *Longstreet*) as March's next-door neighbor.
- ❑ Joe Flynn (Captain Binghamton in *McHale's Navy*) as a carjack victim.
- ❑ Burt Mustin (Fireman Gus in *Leave it to Beaver* and Mr. Quigley in *All in the Family*) as a night watchman.

Memorable Noir Moments:
- ❑ Bogey lets the panic-stricken Scott know the score right from the get-go. "You scream," he warns, "and the kid'll come home and find you in a pool of blood."

❏ When March gets the drop on Bogey, the sneering killer dares him to use the gun. "You ain't got it in ya," he taunts. "I've got it in me," March warns. "You put it there."

Destination Murder (1950) 72 min. Joyce Mackenzie, Stanley Clements, Hurd Hatfield, Albert Dekker, James Flavin, Myrna Dell. **Screenplay by:** Don Martin. **Directed by:** Edward L. Cahn. **Noir Type:** Payback. **Noir Themes:** Woman in jeopardy, betrayal, revenge. ★★½

A messenger boy (Clements) has a deadly delivery for Mackenzie's father—two bullets—compliments of a sadistic hood (Dekker). Mackenzie, who got a glimpse of Clements as he was fleeing the scene, romances the killer to find out more about her father's murder. Later, she goes undercover as a cigarette girl at Dekker's nightclub. Dekker's femme fatale moll (Dell), who has the unrequited hots for the club's manager (Hatfield), joins Clements in a badly thought-out blackmail plot against Dekker. Mackenzie, meanwhile, makes the rounds—dating Clements, flirting with Dekker and falling in love with Hatfield, a dame hater from way back. At times, *Destination Murder* is a complicated mess that might leave you scratching your head, but it's still enjoyable if you play close attention (or watch it twice). The diminutive Clements enjoyed a tumultuous marriage to noir icon Gloria Grahame from 1945 to 1948.

Familiar Face from Television:

❏ John Dehner (reporter Duke Williams in *The Roaring Twenties*) as a suspect in the murder case.

Memorable Noir Moments:

❏ Dell spins her wheels trying to seduce the sexually ambiguous Hatfield. "Haven't you heard?" he asks. "I don't like dames." She walks off in a huff, complaining, "And you call yourself a man."
❏ When Dell tells Mackenzie that Hatfield has been bothering her, Mackenzie scoffs at the thought of it. "He never bothered you," she says. "That's what bothers me," Dell replies.
❏ Sadist Dekker, who has the annoying habit of referring to himself in the third person, removes his belt and announces, "Armitage is in the mood for music." Hatfield, who knows the routine by now, turns on the player piano and watches as Dekker viciously beats a would-be blackmailer.

Destiny (1944) 65 min. Alan Curtis, Gloria Jean, Frank Craven, Grace McDonald, Vivian Austin, Frank Fenton. **Screenplay by:** Roy Chanslor and Ernest Pascal. **Directed by:** Julien Duvivier and Reginald LeBorg. **Noir Type:** Jailbird. **Noir Themes:** Victim of fate, betrayal, greed. ★★½

After his nightclub singer girlfriend (Austin) runs off with his ten grand, Curtis gets nabbed by the cops for his part in a robbery that resulted in the wounding of a night watchman. Released after three years in San Quentin, the ex-con gets a job and a car and tries to go straight. Unfortunately, he runs into former accomplice Fenton, the guy who shot the guard. Curtis reluctantly gives him a lift, dropping him off to make a quick "transaction" at the bank. Before he knows what's happened, the patsy is on the lam again. He seeks shelter at an isolated cottage belonging to the kindly Craven and his mysterious blind daughter (Jean), a diviner who seems to have a magical kinship with nature. Before long, he must make a decision that could cost him his freedom. McDonald and Austin play the dames Curtis meets while on the run. *Destiny* was originally filmed as a thirty-minute episode of **Flesh and Fantasy** but was released separately after additional footage was added. Some viewers might find this eerie noir entertaining; others will nap.

Memorable Noir Moment:
- ❏ Experiencing dejá vu all over again, Curtis reminisces about a song playing on the radio. "I'll never forget the first time I heard that number," he tells McDonald. "It was new to me then."

Detective Story (1951) 103 min. Kirk Douglas, Eleanor Parker, William Bendix, Cathy O'Donnell, George Macready, Horace McMahon, Craig Hill. **Screenplay by:** Philip Yordan and Robert Wyler. **Directed by:** William Wyler. **Noir Type:** Police Procedural. **Noir Themes:** Fatalism, paranoia, jealousy. ★★★★

Douglas stars as a violent, self-righteous detective who hates criminals because his old man was one. Uncompromising to the point of being merciless, Douglas antagonizes even his easygoing partner (Bendix), who futilely begs him to give a young war hero, arrested for small-time embezzlement, a second chance. Douglas' short temper causes him to hospitalize an abortionist (Macready) who may not make it out of intensive care. And if things aren't bad enough, the beleaguered cop discovers a dark secret that his wife (Parker) has been keeping from him, a secret that could destroy his marriage and his career. McMahon (from TV's *Naked City*) plays Douglas' no-nonsense superior, and O'Donnell is the young extortionist's wannabe girlfriend, rightly astounded by Douglas' lack of compassion. Based on the Broadway play of the same title, *Detective Story* remains a compelling drama a half century later, thanks to the outstanding cast. Douglas is powerful as the tortured cop, and veteran character actor Bendix turns in one of his best performances. The film received four Academy Awards nominations—Best Actress (Parker), Best Direction (Wyler), Best Screenplay (Wyler and Yordan) and Best Supporting Actress (Lee Grant, in her screen debut, for her portrayal of a quirky shoplifter).

Familiar Faces from Television:
- ❏ Joseph Wiseman (Manny Weisbord in *Crime Story*), in his film debut, as a psychoneurotic burglar.
- ❏ Gerald Mohr (Christopher Storm in *Foreign Intrigue*) as Parker's ex-lover.
- ❏ Frank Faylen (Herbert T. Gillis in *The Many Loves of Dobie Gillis*) as a Don Juan detective.
- ❏ Warner Anderson (Lt. Ben Guthrie in *The Lineup* and Matthew Swain in *Peyton Place*) as Macready's attorney.
- ❏ Burt Mustin (Fireman Gus in *Leave it to Beaver* and Mr. Quigley in *All in the Family*) as the precinct's janitor.
- ❏ James Maloney (Jim, the handyman, in *21 Beacon Street*) as the embezzler's boss.

Memorable Noir Moments:
- ❏ A kook, or ahead of her time? An elderly, neighborhood crazy makes one of her frequent reports to Detective Faylen. "Atom bombs," she whispers. "That's what they're making. The foreigners next door."
- ❏ The self-destructive Douglas makes a sad admission: "I built my whole life on hating my father and all the time he was inside of me laughing."

A victim of fate (Tom Neal) and a femme fatale (Ann Savage) in the cult classic *Detour* (PRC, 1945).

Detour (1945) 68 min. Tom Neal, Ann Savage, Edmund MacDonald, Claudia Drake. **Screenplay by:** Martin Goldsmith. **Directed by:** Edgar G. Ulmer. **Noir Type:** Femme Fatale. **Noir Themes:** Victim of fate, fatalism. ★★★★

Filmed in just six days on a shoestring (it shows), *Detour* is worthy of its reputation as one of the best low-budget films ever made and has become a cult favorite of film noir fans. Director Ulmer deserves much of the credit for this B masterpiece, but the lion's share of the glory must go to the two stars, Neal and Savage, who give the best performances of their less-than-sensational careers. Wallowing in self-pity at a roadside diner, Neal ponders the events that brought him to the lowest point in his life. Via flashback, we meet the accomplished pianist as he performs at a New York nightspot (the Break O' Dawn Club) along with his torch singing girlfriend (Drake). After Drake packs up and heads for Hollywood and fame (she winds up slinging hash), the despondent Neal starts hitchhiking across the country to join her. Fate gives him a lift in the guise of a friendly motorist (MacDonald) on his way to L.A. But what seems like a stroke of luck is actually the beginning of Neal's tragic downfall. When MacDonald begins to feel ill, they pull over on the side of the road. The man keels over (probably as a result of the pills he's been popping) and falls to the ground, hitting his head on a rock. Convinced he'll be charged with murder, Neal disposes of the body and takes off with the man's car and wallet. Seemingly oblivious to his predicament, he stupidly picks up a cagey hitchhiker (Savage) who soon figures out what's happened and uses the opportunity to keep the poor sap on a tight leash, while attempting to blackmail him into participating in a hare-brained scheme in which he would impersonate the long-lost son of a dying millionaire. Fatally ill herself, and with no motivation to be nice, Savage makes life a living hell for the pitiable Neal, who's oddly repulsed by her sexual advances and yet fascinated by her beauty, which is "almost homely because it's so real." This rejection, of course, doesn't sit well with the femme fatale from Hell, whose cruelty seems to have no bounds. Despite some unintentional humor, *Detour* is a skillfully directed and competently acted film. You'll either hate it or love it.

Memorable Noir Moments:

❑ Sensitivity Training Required: MacDonald offers to buy a meal for hitchhiker Neal, who replies gratefully, "That's white of you." (See *The Blue Dahlia*, *The Devil and Daniel Webster* and *Strange Illusion*.)
❑ Pianist Neal hits the jackpot when a drunk tips him a ten spot for playing a request, but he can't seem to get excited about it. "What *was* it, I asked myself—a piece of paper crawling with germs. It couldn't buy anything *I* wanted."
❑ In the film's final scene, Neal sums up life with the noirish complaint that "fate or some mysterious force can put the finger on you or me for no good reason at all."

The Devil and Daniel Webster (1941) 107 min. Edward Arnold, Walter Huston, James Craig, Jane Darwell, Simone Simon, Anne Shirley, John Qualen. **Screenplay by:** Dan Totheroth and Stephen Vincent Benet. **Directed by:** William Dieterle. **Noir Type:** Fantasy. **Noir Themes:** Character deterioration, greed, betrayal. ★★★★

The Devil (Huston), calling himself "Mr. Scratch," arrives in mid-nineteenth century New England to offer a deal to a poverty-stricken farmer (Craig) that will make him the richest man in the country. When Craig, experiencing his usual run of bad luck, casually swears he would sell his soul to the Devil for two cents, Huston pops up with contract in hand offering Craig seven years of good luck in exchange for his "unnecessary" appendage. After Huston magically uncovers a bag of gold hidden in the farmer's barn, Craig readily agrees and signs the deal in blood. At first, the happy-go-lucky Craig is eager to share his good fortune with his struggling neighbors, but it isn't long before he starts behaving like the town loan shark (Qualen), whom the farmers have grown to hate. When Craig's good Christian wife (Shirley) has a baby, Huston dispatches Simon, a sexy nursemaid from hell, who seduces the farmer and takes over the household, to the dismay of Craig's elderly mother (Darwell). Meanwhile, with the contract's expiration date fast approaching, Shirley seeks help from her son's godfather, the famous New England lawyer and politician Daniel Webster (Arnold), who quickly agrees to defend Craig ("I'd fight ten thousand devils to save a New Hampshire man"). Arnold soon finds himself presenting his case before "a jury of the damned" and fighting to keep his own soul from falling into the Devil's hands. Arnold and Huston, who was nominated for an Academy Award for Best Actor, are delightful as the almost friendly combatants engaged in a battle of wits for a farmer's soul. Based on the short story by Stephen Vincent Benet, *The Devil and Daniel Webster* (also known as *All That Money Can Buy*) is a classic American film that's guaranteed to entertain even after multiple viewings.

Familiar Face from Television:

❑ Walter Baldwin (Grandpappy Miller in *Petticoat Junction*) as one of Craig's neighbors.

Memorable Noir Moments:

❑ Sensitivity Training Required: When Craig offers a farmer friend a bag of quality wheat seed, the grateful man replies, "That's mighty white of you." (See *Detour*, *The Blue Dahlia* and *Strange Illusion*.)
❑ Craig's wise old mother gives him a word of encouragement during his bout with depression over the devilish deal. "A man can always change things," she says. "That's what makes him different from the barnyard critters."

The Devil Thumbs a Ride (1947) 63 min. Lawrence Tierney, Ted North, Nan Leslie, Betty Lawford, Marian Carr. **Screenplay by:** Felix E. Feist. **Directed by:** Felix E. Feist. **Noir Type:** Psycho. **Noir Themes:** Victim of fate, paranoia. ★★★★

A friendly (but slightly inebriated) motorist (North) picks up a hitchhiker (Tierney), not realizing that the man has just committed robbery and murder. Along the way, the lecherous Tierney convinces North to give a lift to two women (Leslie and Lawford), who are thumbing their way to Los Angeles. Happily married North, who just wants to get home to his loving wife (Carr), reluctantly sets out with the three strangers and goes on the ride of his life. Before it's all over, psychopath Tierney cripples a motorcycle cop, murders a woman, steals North's identity, wounds a gas station attendant and hijacks a police car. The plot is silly but never boring, and the dialogue is incredibly snappy. Tierney is magnificent as evil incarnate, and if you thought he was bad in **Born to Kill**, wait until you meet the devil in this classic B noir.

Memorable Noir Moment:

❑ North asks a gas station attendant about his little girl's picture, and the proud father brags a bit about her. Tierney throws in his two cents, remarking, "From the looks of those ears,

A friendly motorist (Ted North, center) tries to calm psycho Lawrence Tierney in *The Devil Thumbs a Ride* (RKO, 1947). Hitchhikers (Betty Lawford, left, and Nan Leslie) look on.

she's gonna fly before she'll walk." When North tells the attendant to keep the change and buy something for the kid, Tierney adds, "Yeah, a parachute."

Devil's Doorway (1950) 84 min. Robert Taylor, Louis Calhern, Paula Raymond, Marshall Thompson, Edgar Buchanan. **Screenplay by:** Guy Trosper. **Directed by:** Anthony Mann. **Noir Type:** Horse Opera. **Noir Themes:** Betrayal, bigotry, revenge. ★★½

When Shoshone Indian Taylor returns home after winning the Congressional Medal of Honor for fighting against the Confederacy during the Civil War, he discovers that things aren't as he remembered them. Discrimination is the order of the day now that Wyoming has become a U.S. territory, and homesteaders are allowed to stake claims to untitled land. When Taylor, who owns a nice chunk of land called "Sweet Meadows," hires lawyer Raymond to help him homestead a parcel of his own land for his tribe, she discovers that, as an Indian, he's considered to be a ward of the government and isn't allowed to own land. When Thompson and his fellow sheep farmers try to lay claim to portions of Taylor's land, the Indian organizes his braves and readies for war. Calhern is the Indian-hating lawyer instigating the sheepmen for his own nefarious schemes, and Buchanan is the U.S. marshal friendly to the Shoshone. A heavily made-up Taylor gives a good performance, but the disillusioned war veteran theme translates uneasily in this talky Western noir.

Familiar Faces from Television:

❑ Spring Byington (Lily Ruskin in *December Bride* and Daisy Cooper in *Laramie*) as Raymond's rifle-toting mother.

Diabolique (1955-French) 107 min. Simone Signoret, Vera Clouzot, Paul Meurisse, Charles Vanel. **Screenplay by**: Henri-Georges Clouzot, Jérôme Géronimi, René Masson, and Frédéric Grendel. **Directed by**: Henri-Georges Clouzot. **Noir Type**: Triangle. **Noir Themes**: Betrayal, sexual hostility, guilt, paranoia. ★★★★

Signoret and Clouzot, teachers at a boys' private boarding school, plot the murder of the tyrannical principal (Meurisse), who is Signoret's lover and Clouzot's husband. Hesitant at first, the sickly and physically abused Clouzot allows herself to be pressured into the scheme by the domineering Signoret (who sports a black eye from a recent tussle with Meurisse). Their meticulous planning is for naught, however, when Meurisse's body inexplicably disappears from the school's putrid swimming pool, where they dumped it after drowning him in a bathtub. The panicky Clouzot soon starts blaming Signoret for the murder and threatens to call the police. Meanwhile, a retired police commissioner (Vanel) has offered Clouzot his assistance in finding her "missing" husband, and one of the students is claiming to have seen the principal around the school. This French noir, originally titled *Les Diaboliques* ("The Devils"), is slow going at times but builds to an almost unbearably suspenseful climax. Signoret and Clouzot are excellent as the unlikely conspirators, and Meurisse is enjoyably despicable as the abusive, penny-pinching school administrator. An inferior remake with Sharon Stone in the Signoret role was released in 1996.

Memorable Noir Moment:

❑ With fellow teachers and the entire student body looking on, Meurisse forces his wife to swallow the rotten fish he's purchased for the day's lunch. It's said that realism-minded director Clouzet, husband of co-star Clouzet, used real spoiled fish to get just the right effect. He succeeded.

Dial 1119 (1950) 74 min. Marshall Thompson, Virginia Field, Andrea King, Sam Levene, Leon Ames, Keefe Brasselle, William Conrad, James Bell. **Screenplay by**: John Monks, Jr. **Directed by**: Gerald Mayer. **Noir Type**: Hostage. **Noir Themes**: Paranoia, victim of fate. ★★★½

Thompson stars as an escaped lunatic heading for the town where he was arrested. After ruthlessly gunning down a bus driver, he holes up in a bar across the street from police psychiatrist Levene's apartment, waiting for the good doctor to come home so he can kill him. When the bartender (Conrad) recognizes him from a TV newscast, the gunman takes the employees and customers hostage, demanding that the police send in the doctor. His terrified hostages (Brasselle, Field, King, Ames and Bell) wait nervously while police surround the establishment. This suspenseful and innovative film contains interesting similarities to modern-day hostage films—the news-hungry TV reporters and their live coverage of the crisis, the hostage negotiator, the argument over whether to storm the place or talk the killer out, an ice cream truck peddling its goods to curious thrill seekers, and the killer viewing events on,

An escaped mental patient (Marshall Thompson) threatens his hostages (Leon Ames, Andrea King, Virginia Field, Keefe Brasselle and James Bell, left to right) in *Dial 1119* (MGM, 1950).

believe it or not, the bar's 3 × 4–foot projection TV screen (in 1950!). A lot happens in 74 minutes. Thompson is believable as the psycho with an ax to grind.

Familiar Face from Television:

❏ Barbara Billingsley (the Beaver's mom in *Leave it to Beaver*) as a newspaper reporter.

Memorable Noir Moments:

❏ Barfly Field responds to senior citizen Bell's proposition, saying, "Aw, you couldn't go the distance."
❏ Did 1950 bus drivers actually drive with pistols hanging above their rear view mirrors? And did they really leave passengers alone on the bus with a gun hanging there in full view? Lucky break for criminally insane Thompson, who grabs the weapon at the first opportunity. When asked by the driver, "Will you give it to me?," Thompson does. Right in the belly.

Don't Bother to Knock (1952) 76 min. Richard Widmark, Marilyn Monroe, Anne Bancroft, Elisha Cook, Jr., Jim Backus, Lurene Tuttle. **Screenplay by:** Daniel Taradash. **Directed by:** Roy Ward Baker. **Noir Type:** Psycho. **Noir Themes:** Child in jeopardy, paranoia, betrayal. ★★★½

The setting is a large New York City hotel. Monroe is a suicidal mental patient whom the hotel's elevator operator (Cook) has referred to hotel guests (Backus and Tuttle) as a reliable babysitter. Widmark plays the callous boyfriend of the hotel's torch singer (Bancroft), who has just given him the boot. Depressed, Widmark hooks up with Monroe and attempts a little hanky panky, but she starts calling him by her dead boyfriend's name and he rightly suspects that she's not all there. This is an exciting little thriller, tightly scripted and well acted (especially by Monroe). Bancroft, in her film debut, manages to look more glamorous than the dowdy Monroe (*sans* makeup).

Familiar Face from Television:
❑ Gloria Blondell (Honeybee Gillis in *The Life of Riley*) as a lounge photographer.

Memorable Noir Moments:
❑ A nosy hotel guest, suspicious of the goings-on in Monroe's room, suggests that her husband call the house detective. "Him?" he replies. "He couldn't detect a monk in a convent."
❑ Monroe's nervous young charge leans out of the window. Widmark is sitting on the bed looking the other way. Monroe slowly places her hand on the girl's back. A hotel guest looking out a window across the way screams.
❑ After an argument with Bancroft, Widmark asks a bartender if he and his wife fight all the time. "Some of the time she sleeps," replies the man.

Doorway to Suspicion (1954) 75 min. Jeffrey Lynn, Linda Caroll, Fred Baker, Dagmar Diaz, Bill Hickenboatham. **Screenplay by:** Hans Jacoby and Paul Tabori. **Directed by:** Dallas Bower. **Noir Type:** Show Biz. **Noir Themes:** Betrayal, woman in jeopardy. ★½

An obscure film that will probably remain so, *Doorway* stars Lynn as an American bandleader touring postwar Europe with his orchestra. He meets a beautiful woman (Caroll) in Munich, falls in love with her the next day in Hamburg, and marries her on his way to Amsterdam. The marriage seems to be working out well until his sax players (Baker and Hickenboatham) become suspicious of her behavior and start following her around. They think she might be cheating, but (unfortunately for Lynn) it looks like it's much more than that. Diaz plays a popular singer who happens to be a Russian general's girlfriend. It's simple-minded stuff and questionably noir.

Double Indemnity (1944) 106 min. Fred MacMurray, Barbara Stanwyck, Edward G. Robinson, Tom Powers. **Screenplay by:** Raymond Chandler and Billy Wilder. **Directed by:** Billy Wilder. **Noir Type:** Femme Fatale. **Noir Themes:** Obsession, lust, betrayal. ★★★★½

Despite the handicap of a stiff leading man and a leading lady with a laughable blonde wig, director Wilder and screenwriter Raymond Chandler were wildly successful in translating pulp fiction writer James M. Cain's novel into a masterpiece of film noir suspense. Insurance salesman MacMurray becomes involved with Stanwyck, the scheming wife of a rich businessman (Powers), and soon finds himself entangled in a plot to murder the man and collect on the large insurance policy. MacMurray and Stanwyck's icy romance matches the entire atmosphere of the film, and

A murderer (Fred MacMurray) hides his partner-in-crime (Barbara Stanwyck) from a wily insurance investigator (Edward G. Robinson) in *Double Indemnity* (Paramount, 1944).

even MacMurray's annoying overuse of the word "baby" can't spoil it. The brilliant screenplay and Robinson's sensational portrayal of an ace insurance investigator more than overcome the film's few shortcomings. Wilder's first choice for the lead was Alan Ladd; MacMurray, who was concerned about his good-guy persona, had to be convinced to take it. He never regretted the decision. Film historians disagree on whether *Double Indemnity* should have the honor of being labeled the first film noir. Some believe that distinction belongs to **The Maltese Falcon;** others think it was **Stranger on the Third Floor.** No matter. *Double Indemnity*, which is rated number 38 on the American Film Institute's List of America's 100 Greatest Movies, is still one of the best American films ever made — in any genre.

Memorable Noir Moments:

❏ MacMurray leaves a recording for his friend, Robinson: "As I was walking down the street to the drug store, suddenly it came over me that everything would go wrong. It sounds crazy, but it's true, so help me. I couldn't hear my own footsteps. It was the walk of a dead man."

❏ MacMurray, *sans* designated driver, stops at a *drive-in* cafe for *a beer*! Oh, those 1940s!

Double Jeopardy (1955) 70 min. Rod Cameron, Gale Robbins, Allison Hayes, Jack Kelly, Robert Armstrong, John Litel. **Screenplay by:** Don Martin. **Directed by:** R.G. Springsteen. **Noir Type:** Wrong Man. **Noir Themes:** Greed, distrust, betrayal, lust. ★½

When a rum-dum ex-con (Armstrong) is killed by his wife's lover (Kelly), a real estate developer (Litel) is arrested for the murder. Litel's attorney (Cameron) and pretty daughter (Hayes) investigate and find that Armstrong's wife (Robbins) and Kelly were planning to run off to Mexico with the ten Gs they thought the ex-con had extorted from Litel. The lovers' greed and distrust are their downfall. Yawn.

Familiar Faces from Television:

❑ Minerva Urecal (Annie in *The Adventures of Tugboat Annie* and "Mother" in *Peter Gunn*) as Armstrong's nosy landlady.
❑ Robert Shayne (Inspector Henderson in *The Adventures of Superman*) as a government real estate appraiser.

A Double Life (1947) 104 min. Ronald Colman, Signe Hasso, Edmond O'Brien, Shelley Winters. **Screenplay by:** Ruth Gordon and Garson Kanin. **Directed by:** George Cukor. **Noir Type:** Psycho. **Noir Themes:** Character deterioration, sexual hostility, woman in danger ★★★★

Colman won an Oscar for his brilliant portrayal of a mentally disturbed actor who takes his parts much too seriously. To the chagrin of a seductive waitress (Winters), his most recent role is Shakespeare's murderous Moor, Othello. Hasso, Colman's ex-wife, plays the unfortunate Desdemona opposite him in their new Broadway production. O'Brien, a publicist in love with Hasso, begins to suspect that Colman may be linked to the recent strangling of a local girl and conspires with a homicide detective to spring a trap for the actor. Colman is remarkable, horrifying the viewer with the ferocity of his transformations from likable actor to lunatic murderer. Director Cukor was nominated for Best Director but lost to Elia Kazan for *Gentleman's Agreement*. Winters, in her first big break, is excellent as the sexy waitress with the hots for older men. Look for Elmo Lincoln (the screen's first Tarzan) as a detective, John Derek as a police stenographer and playwright Paddy Chayevsky as a photographer.

Familiar Faces from Television:

❑ Joe Sawyer (Sgt. Biff O'Hara in *The Adventures of Rin Tin Tin*) as a homicide detective.
❑ Ray Collins (Lt. Tragg in *Perry Mason*) as a Broadway producer.
❑ Whit Bissell (Gen. Heywood Kirk in *The Time Tunnel*) as a medical examiner.

Memorable Noir Moment:

❑ Like her waitress sister in **Mad at the World**, Shelley Winters tries hard to impress a man she's interested in. "I'm a masseuse," she brags. "You don't say," remarks her customer. "You don't believe me?" she asks. "I can show you a certificate. I took a course."

Dragonwyck (1946) 104 min. Gene Tierney, Walter Huston, Vincent Price, Glenn Langan, Anne Revere, Vivienne Osborne, Jessica Tandy. **Screenplay by:** Joseph L. Mankiewicz. **Directed by:** Joseph L. Mankiewicz. **Noir Type:** Period. **Noir Themes:** Obsession, betrayal, woman in jeopardy. ★★★

In the mid–1840s, a Connecticut farm girl (Tierney) takes a job caring for the daughter of a wealthy New Yorker and his wife at their estate, Dragonwyck. The master of the house (Price), who longs for a son to carry on the family name and the baronial tradition, isn't happy that his hypochondriac, pastry-addicted wife (Osborne) is no longer able to bear children, so he takes an interest in the lovely Tierney. The town doctor (Langan) also has fallen for the new servant girl but loses out to Price when Osborne dies under mysterious circumstances and the widow proposes to Tierney. After marrying him, Tierney learns that her snobby neighbors want nothing to do with a girl from the Connecticut river bottom area. Price's tenants are caught up in the anti-rent movement that is spreading across the young nation, but the arrogant landlord has no sympathy for their demands. Huston plays Tierney's strict, Bible-believing father, and Revere is her somber but sympathetic mother. Price is excellent as the Dutch-American land baron with a penchant for narcotics and a distaste for imperfection, as Tierney's crippled maid (Tandy) soon discovers. Tierney does an admirable job as the simple farm girl who is a bit too impressed with the grandeur of Dragonwyck.

Familiar Faces from Television:
- Harry Morgan (Col. Potter in *M*A*S*H*) as the first tenant farmer to refuse to pay his tribute to Price.
- Spring Byington (Lily Ruskin in *December Bride* and Daisy Cooper in *Laramie*) as a busybody maid.
- Walter Baldwin (Grandpappy Miller in *Petticoat Junction*) as a tenant farmer.

Memorable Noir Moment:
- When Osborne complains about the mansion being miserable and drab, the offended Price retorts, "I cannot imagine that Dragonwyck could be either miserable or drab except to those who reflect misery or drabness from within themselves."

Drive a Crooked Road (1954) 83 min. Mickey Rooney, Dianne Foster, Kevin McCarthy, Jack Kelly. **Screenplay by:** Blake Edwards. **Directed by:** Richard Quine. **Noir Type:** Heist. **Noir Themes:** Betrayal, greed. ★★★

Rooney plays a shy, lonely auto mechanic who dreams of becoming a professional race car driver. Capitalizing on his loneliness, Foster, sexy girlfriend of bank robber McCarthy, lures Rooney into joining the planned heist of a Palm Beach bank. After refusing McCarthy's offer of fifteen grand to drive the getaway car, Rooney relents when Foster drops him. Rooney gives a surprisingly sensitive performance as the lovesick mechanic, and Foster is excellent as the femme fatale whose conscience pangs might cost Rooney his life. Kelly (brother Bart TV's *Maverick*) plays McCarthy's partner.

Familiar Faces from Television:
- Paul Picerni (Agent Lee Hobson of *The Untouchables*) as Rooney's antagonistic coworker.
- Jerry Paris (dentist Jerry Helper on *The Dick Van Dyke Show* and Agent Flaherty in *The Untouchables*) as Rooney's buddy.

Edge of Doom (1950) 99 min. Dana Andrews, Farley Granger, Mala Powers, Harold Vermilyea, Paul Stewart. **Screenplay by:** Philip Yordan and Ben Hecht. **Directed by:** Mark Robson. **Noir Type:** Religion. **Noir Themes:** Fatalism, paranoia. ★★½

A Catholic priest (Andrews) tells a young cleric the story of a murderer, "a youth with blood and sin on him," who helped bring him closer to God. Via flashback, the viewer is introduced to Granger, a flower deliveryman who wants to give his recently deceased mother a big send-off. Unfortunately, he's broke and his boss refuses him an advance. So he visits the elderly parish priest (Vermilyea) who denied his father a Christian burial because he committed suicide. The priest refuses the young man's demands that the church pay for an expensive funeral, and Granger, in a psychotic rage, clubs him with a heavy crucifix, killing him instantly. Granger flees into the streets, hoping he wasn't seen entering the rectory. But there may have been a witness. Powers plays Granger's marriage-minded girlfriend, Stewart is a small-time crook and Jergens is Stewart's sexy wife. The film is tedious at times, but Granger's competent portrayal of the tormented youth keeps it interesting.

Familiar Faces from Television:
- ❏ Ellen Corby (Grandma Walton in *The Waltons*) as a wife seeking shelter in the rectory from her abusive husband.

A priest killer (**Farley Granger**) and a two-bit thief's wife (**Adele Jergens**) are visited by a parish priest (**Dana Andrews**) in *Edge of Doom* (RKO, 1950).

❑ Ray Teal (Sheriff Roy Coffee in *Bonanza*) as Corby's irate husband.

Memorable Noir Moment:

❑ A discouraged priest who has failed to connect with his parishioners requests a transfer. "Poor people are difficult to serve," his superior tells him." "It isn't their poverty, Father," the priest replies. "They're weary and small, without a spark in them. There's no reaching them."

Edge of the City (1957) 85 min. John Cassavetes, Sidney Poitier, Jack Warden, Ruby Dee, Kathleen Maguire. **Screenplay by:** Robert Alan Aurthur. **Directed by:** Martin Ritt. **Noir Type:** Union. **Noir Themes:** Guilt, corruption, bigotry, revenge. ★★★★

Cassavetes stars as a disturbed Army deserter who gets a job as a dockworker on New York's waterfront. Forced to pay a bullying foreman (Warden) a percentage of his hourly wage, Cassavetes switches supervisors, going to work for an amiable black man (Poitier), and they become good friends. Poitier and his wife (Dee) are soon playing Cupid, nudging the painfully shy Cassavetes into a romantic relationship with a neighborhood schoolteacher (Maguire). Racist Warden, itching for a showdown with Poitier, discovers that Cassavetes is a deserter and threatens to turn him in unless he comes back to work for him. This is a tough, realistic account of waterfront corruption and prejudice, with Cassavetes and Poitier outstanding as friends who conquer racial barriers. Warden is wonderfully despicable as a bigot who really knows how to handle a stevedore's hook.

Memorable Noir Moment:

❑ Cassavetes opens up to Poitier about his relationship with his father. "In my whole life," he says, "we maybe said three things to each other — *good morning, good night,* and *go to hell.*"

The Enforcer (1951) 87 min. Humphrey Bogart, Roy Roberts, Zero Mostel, Ted de Corsia, Everett Sloane, Bob Steele. **Screenplay by:** Martin Rackin. **Directed by:** Bretaigne Windust and Raoul Walsh (uncredited). **Noir Type:** Hit Man. **Noir Themes:** Betrayal. ★★★★

Assistant D.A. Bogart investigates a murder-for-hire gang in this fast-moving, suspenseful noir. Multiple flashbacks tell the story of Bogart and police detective Roberts as they search for evidence that will allow them to bring mob boss Sloane to trial. Veteran character actor de Corsia is convincing as Sloane's nervous underling, who has been having second thoughts about testifying against his boss. Mostel does a great job as a novice hit man forced to spill his guts after Bogart threatens to jail his wife and put his child in a state institution. Veteran B western actor Steele is menacing as Herman the hit man, a specialist in rubbing out other hit men. Loosely based on the work of the real-life New York D.A. who took on Murder, Inc., this entertaining film will keep you away from the fridge until the very end.

Memorable Noir Moments:

❑ Roberts, in a pre–Miranda interrogation, tells a suspect: "Answer me straight or I'll blow your head off. Where are the bodies?"
❑ De Corsia gives fledgling hit man Mostel a fashion tip: "Burn that tent you're wearin' and get yourself a suit."

A wannabe hit man (Zero Mostel) gets the evil eye from an assistant D.A. (Humphrey Bogart) in *The Enforcer* (Warner Bros., 1951).

❏ After being shot, a police officer, asked about his condition, actually says, "It's only a flesh wound." (For more variations of the cliché, see *Accused of Murder, Guilty Bystander, Jail Bait, New York Confidential, Riot in Cell Block 11* and *Sleep, My Love*.)

Escape in the Fog (1945) 65 min. Nina Foch, William Wright, Otto Kruger. **Screenplay by:** Aubrey Wisberg. **Directed by:** Oscar (Budd) Boetticher, Jr. **Noir Type:** Nightmare. **Noir Themes:** Woman in jeopardy, victim of fate. ★★½

An ex–Navy nurse (Foch) is suffering from shell shock as a result of her hospital ship being attacked. Recuperating at an inn outside of San Francisco, she has a nightmare in which she witnesses a man being attacked. When her screams awaken the other guests, she's surprised to see that one of them is Wright, the man in her dream. They fall in love, but what she doesn't know is that Wright is an undercover federal agent ready to embark on a dangerous mission to Singapore, where the information he's carrying will do irreparable damage to the Japanese war effort. Fearing that her dream is becoming a reality, she infiltrates a German spy ring (led by Kruger). Despite the far-fetched premise of the premonitory nightmare, this is a fairly enjoyable noir with good performances by Foch and Wright. Keep a sharp eye out for the young and lovely Shelley Winters as a cab driver.

Memorable Noir Moments:

❑ Two spies, surrounded by cops, are desperately trying to get out of Chinatown. Despite their dangerous predicament, one spy manages to see the humor in it: "There seems to be more police around here than Chinese."

❑ From the Stupid Criminal Department: It's so foggy that two spies trapped in a crossfire end up shooting each other. See *Raw Deal*, *Knock On Any Door*, *The Long Wait* and *Sealed Lips* for more incompetent hoods.

Escape Route *see* I'll Get You

Experiment Perilous (1944) 90 min. Hedy Lamarr, George Brent, Paul Lukas, Albert Dekker, Olive Blakeney. **Screenplay by:** Warren Duff. **Directed by:** Jacques Tourneur. **Noir Type:** Period. **Noir Themes:** Woman in jeopardy, betrayal, jealousy. ★★½

In the winter of 1903, a psychiatrist (Brent) befriends a strange woman (Blakeney) on a train headed for New York City. Unfortunately, it's a short friendship. While visiting her brother (Brent), Blakeney dies of a suspicious heart attack. Brent investigates and, along with almost every other young man in New York, falls pathetically in love with Lukas' beautiful wife (Lamarr). Lukas confides in him that Lamarr may be going insane and that their five-year-old boy has been experiencing terrible nightmares. Brent decides to help and finds more than he bargained for. This standard melodrama might not interest the hardcore crime fan, but Lamarr certainly is lovely to look at, and Dekker turns in a good performance as a sculptor with a drinking problem.

Memorable Noir Moment:

❑ In describing Lukas, psychiatrist Brent remarks, "There's something out of tune with him. Like a chord of music with a basic note missing."

F.B.I. Girl (1951) 74 min. Cesar Romero, George Brent, Audrey Totter, Tom Drake, Raymond Burr, Raymond Greenleaf. **Screenplay by:** Dwight V. Babcock and Richard Landau. **Directed by:** William Berke. **Noir Type:** Blackmail. **Noir Themes:** Women in danger, corruption, betrayal, guilt. ★★

Burr plays a public relations man for Greenleaf, the governor of an unnamed state who is really a murderer wanted by police. Greenleaf's fingerprints are on file at F.B.I. headquarters and, with a statewide political housecleaning approaching, Burr must retrieve the fingerprint record to protect his client and his own influence. After the first attempt fails, resulting in the murder of a reluctant Bureau accomplice, Burr blackmails a lobbyist (Drake) into pressuring his fiancée (Totter), another F.B.I employee, to retrieve the file. Romero and Brent are the G-men trying to figure out who's behind the plot. Pretty tame stuff despite the presence of noir icons Burr and Totter.

Familiar Faces from Television:

❑ Peter Marshall (the host of *Hollywood Squares*) as one-half of a television comedy act. (His partner is Tommy Noonan, real-life half-brother of John Ireland and a regular panelist on *Stump the Stars*.)

❑ Byron Foulger (Wendell Gibbs in *Petticoat Junction*) as a county morgue supervisor.

Memorable Noir Moment:

❏ When a morgue employee is told that his latest "customer" was wanted for murder, he replies, "You'd never think it to look at him. But, of course, you lay in that icebox for 24 hours, they all come out peaceful and innocent looking."

The Falcon in San Francisco (1945) 66 min. Tom Conway, Rita Corday, Edward Brophy, Sharyn Moffett, Fay Helm, Robert Armstrong. **Screenplay by:** Robert E. Kent and Ben Markson. **Directed by:** Joseph H. Lewis. **Noir Type:** P.I. **Noir Themes:** Betrayal, greed. ★★

Private eye Conway, on vacation in San Francisco with his sidekick (Brophy, providing the comedy relief), becomes involved with a murderous gang of silk smugglers led by femme fatale Helm, who thinks the Falcon has been hired to investigate her gang. Swiss-born Corday, who can't seem to control her on-again, off-again accent, plays the older sister of little Moffett, whom Conway has been accused of kidnapping. Armstrong is the mysterious owner of a shipping line. Director Lewis gives this eleventh entry in the Falcon series the noir treatment, but the film lacks suspense. Conway took over the role of mystery writer Michael Arlen's suave private detective from George Sanders, his real-life brother, who starred in the first four Falcon films.

Memorable Noir Moment:

❏ From the Some-Things-Never-Change Department: Brophy, agonizing over an IRS income tax form, comments, "These things can ask more questions than a third degree."

Fall Guy (1947) 64 min. Clifford Penn, Teala Loring, Robert Armstrong, Elisha Cook, Jr., Virginia Dale. **Screenplay by:** Jerry Warner. **Directed by:** Reginald LeBorg. **Noir Type:** Amnesia. **Noir Themes:** Lust, jealousy. ★★½

Ex–G.I. Penn, depressed over an argument with his girlfriend (Loring), accompanies elevator operator Cook to a party where a dame (Dale) slips him a Mickey. He wakes up with a knife in his bloodstained hand and finds a woman's body in the closet. Suffering from drug-induced memory loss, he's taken in by the police after collapsing on the street. He later escapes and seeks help from his brother-in-law cop (Armstrong), who helps him trace the events of that fateful night. Fowley plays the homicide detective who doesn't buy his amnesia story. Pretty standard stuff, but noir veteran Cook is always enjoyable. Armstrong, who was 57 at the time (and looked it), is described in a newspaper story as a 36-year-old police officer.

Memorable Noir Moments:

❏ Sensitivity Training Required: When Loring expresses regrets about getting Armstrong involved in the murder case, he shrugs it off, saying, "I'm free, white and old enough." (See *The City That Never Sleeps, The Glass Key* and *Out of the Fog*.)
❏ Sensitivity Training Required: Penn and Montgomery, searching for Cook, know only that he's an elevator operator who works for a woman. Montgomery suggests that they check out a nearby office building, causing Penn to remark, "Nah, it couldn't be an office building and have a woman manager."

Fallen Angel (1945) 98 min. Alice Faye, Dana Andrews, Linda Darnell, Charles Bickford, Bruce Cabot, Anne Revere, John Carradine, Percy Kilbride. **Screenplay by:** Harry Kleiner.

Directed by: Otto Preminger. **Noir Type:** Con Artist. **Noir Themes:** Obsession, lust, betrayal, jealousy. ★★½

Director Preminger was hoping for another **Laura** with this nicely acted, but mostly dull, film noir. Andrews plays a has-been publicity agent, a self-described "washout at 30," forced to get off the bus in a small town on his way to San Francisco because he doesn't have enough money to continue the trip. He takes a job publicizing a séance for phony medium (Carradine) and falls for a sultry waitress (Darnell), who has a collection of suckers drooling over her, including a slot machine operator (Cabot), her fawning boss (Kilbride) and a tough former New York City cop (Bickford). Carradine, who has collected information on almost everyone in town, including two wealthy sisters (Faye and Revere), leaves for San Francisco after a successful show. Andrews stays behind hoping to use that information to bilk the two spinsters out of their dough so he can marry Darnell, who desperately wants to be made an honest woman. Of course, his plan backfires and he finds himself a murder suspect. Noir veteran Andrews is convincing as the good guy–bad guy, and Darnell is red hot as the femme fatale. This was Faye's first starring role in a non-musical, but Darnell got the rave reviews. Faye retired soon after the film's release, and didn't appear on screen again until 1962 when she played Pat Boone's mother in *State Fair*.

Familiar Face from Television:
❑ Olin Howlin (Swifty in *Circus Boy*) as the diner's elderly owner, who has eyes for Darnell.

Memorable Noir Moment:
❑ When Andrews jealously observes that Bickford seems to know just what Darnell likes, the waitress replies, "That's for his wife to worry about."

The Fallen Sparrow (1943) 94 min. John Garfield, Maureen O'Hara, Walter Slezak, Patricia Morison, Martha O'Driscoll. **Screenplay by:** Warren Duff. **Directed by:** Richard Wallace. **Noir Type:** Nazi. **Noir Themes:** Fatalism, paranoia, betrayal. ★★★

Garfield returns to the U.S. after helping the Spaniards in their fight against Franco. As a prisoner in Spain, he had been tortured by a Gestapo agent whose face he never saw but whose pronounced limp caused a dragging sound outside his cell — a sound he still hears in his disturbed mind. Once home, he discovers that his best friend, the man responsible for freeing him from the Spanish prison, has been killed and that authorities suspect his death was an accident or suicide. Determined to find the truth, he becomes entangled with Nazi spies eager for information that only he can provide. Clothing store model O'Hara, society dame Morison and nightclub singer O'Driscoll are the beautiful women who are involved, wittingly or unwittingly, with the spy ring. Slezak is a wheelchair-bound aristocrat with an unusual interest in Garfield's tale of physical and mental torture. Garfield gives a gripping performance as the haunted revolutionary.

Familiar Face from Television:
❑ Hugh Beaumont (Ward Cleaver in *Leave it to Beaver*) as a suspicious aristocrat.

Memorable Noir Moment:

❑ When Garfield files an application for a gun permit, a cop asks him why he wants to carry a gun. The former revolutionary smirks and replies, "To shoot people with, sweetheart."

The Family Secret (1951) 85 min. John Derek, Lee J. Cobb, Jody Lawrance, Erin O'Brien-Moore, Santos Ortega. **Screenplay by:** Francis Cockrell and Andrew Solt. **Directed by:** Henry Levin. **Noir Type:** Cover-Up. **Noir Themes:** Fatalism, paranoia, guilt. ★½

After a law student (Derek) accidentally kills his best friend, his parents (Cobb and O'Brien-Moore) reluctantly agree to help him cover it up. But when a local bookie is arrested for the murder, attorney Cobb feels obligated to defend the man. Lawrance plays Derek's love interest, and Ortega is the D.A. It's difficult to sympathize with Derek's character, although that's what the writers of this potentially intriguing film intend us to do. Rather, sympathy should go to the viewer who sits through the film's entirety, expecting it to improve. Ortega went on to play Grandpa Hughes in the long-running TV soap opera *As The World Turns*.

Familiar Faces from Television:
❑ Percy Helton (Homer Cratchit in *The Beverly Hillbillies*) as a shopkeeper.
❑ Whit Bissell (Gen. Heywood Kirk in *The Time Tunnel*) as the bookie wrongly charged with murder.

Fear (1946) 68 min. Warren William, Peter Cookson, Anne Gwynne, Nestor Paiva, Francis Pierlot. **Screenplay by:** Dennis J. Cooper and Alfred Zeisler. **Directed by:** Alfred Zeisler. **Noir Type:** Cover-up. **Noir Themes:** Character deterioration, guilt. ★★★

Medical student Cookson has just lost his scholarship and is about to be evicted from his seedy apartment. The only way he can obtain his rent money, he thinks, is to rob and kill a cantankerous and miserly professor (Pierlot) who secretly acts as a pawnbroker for the students. Cookson goes to Pierlot's apartment pretending he has something to pawn and strikes the man with a fireplace poker. Unfortunately for him, two students show up at the apartment door and he leaves in a panic, forgetting to take the money. Ironically, he receives a $1000 check the next day — payment for a magazine article he submitted about the intellectually superior man being above the law. The article attracts the attention of detectives William and Paiva, who suspect that Cookson might be the killer. Gwynne is the pretty waitress with whom Cookson falls in love. This is a skillfully acted little noir that sustains interest despite its low production values. The ending, however, is disappointing.

Familiar Face from Television:
❑ Darren McGavin (star of *Crime Photographer*, *Mike Hammer*, *Riverboat* and *Kolchak, The Night Stalker*) as a blonde, pipe-smoking student.

Fear in the Night (1947) 72 min. DeForest Kelley, Paul Kelly, Ann Doran, Kay Scott. **Screenplay by:** Maxwell Shane. **Directed by:** Maxwell Shane. **Noir Type:** Nightmare. **Noir Themes:** Victim of fate, paranoia. ★★★½

Opposite, top: A murderer (Peter Cookson) returns to his apartment to find a college beer party in *Fear* (Monogram, 1946). That's future TV star Darren McGavin on the right. *Bottom:* A possible killer (DeForest Kelley, left) and his brother-in-law cop (Paul Kelly) have a slight difference of opinion in *Fear in the Night* (Paramount, 1947).

In a scene reminiscent of a bad LSD trip, bank teller Kelley (Dr. McCoy of *Star Trek*) enters a room of mirrored closets and sees a man and woman trying to open a safe with a drill. During a struggle with the man, he grabs a drill bore that the woman is trying to hand to his opponent and stabs him. When the woman runs away, he hides the man's body in one of the closets. In the morning, he awakens in his hotel room, grateful that it was all a bad dream. Until he finds thumbprints on his neck and blood on his wrist. He goes to his brother-in-law (Kelly) with the story, but the homicide detective believes it was nothing more than a nightmare. Later, when Kelley leads him to a mansion containing the mirrored room of his "dream," the cop begins to suspect the worst. Doran plays Kelley's sister and Scott is his girlfriend. Kelley does a fine job in this suspenseful, eerily photographed noir, but you may have difficulty forgetting that you're not watching Dr. McCoy in some sort of time warp. Remade in 1956 as **Nightmare** with Kevin McCarthy and Edward G. Robinson.

Familiar Face from Television:
❏ Jeff York (Reno McKee in *The Alaskans*) as a deputy sheriff.

Female Jungle (1956) 73 min. Lawrence Tierney, John Carradine, Kathleen Crowley, Burt Kaiser, Jayne Mansfield. **Screenplay by:** Burt Kaiser and Bruno VeSota. **Directed by:** Bruno VeSota. **Noir Type:** Whodunit. **Noir Themes:** Women in danger, lust. ✶

This ultra-low-budget bomb has Tierney playing an off-duty cop who's in hot water because, while he was busy tying one on at the neighborhood bar, an actress was being strangled outside. A subplot has the cop wondering if he, while in a drunken stupor, killed the woman. Silver-haired gossip columnist Carradine, driving a convertible and dressed in his best Dracula tux and white ascot, is a prime suspect. Crowley is a waitress and screenwriter Kaiser is her alcoholic husband. Mansfield, early in her career, is terrible as a nymphomaniac. A big disappointment for fans of the usually dependable Tierney.

Memorable Noir Moment:
❏ Tierney walks in on Mansfield, who's fast asleep on a sofa. Our hero, suspecting she might be dead, puts his ear to her legendary chest to listen for a heartbeat. Ever hear of checking for a pulse, Larry?

Female on the Beach (1955) 97 min. Joan Crawford, Jeff Chandler, Jan Sterling, Natalie Schafer, Cecil Kellaway, Charles Drake, Judith Evelyn. **Screenplay by:** Robert Hill. **Directed by:** Joseph Pevney. **Noir Type:** Con Artist. **Noir Themes:** Woman in jeopardy, jealousy, paranoia. ✶✶

A wealthy, reclusive widow and former Las Vegas "specialty dancer" (Crawford) falls for a beach bum (Chandler) even after learning that he's in cahoots with con artists (Schaffer and Kellaway) who are after her money. When a homicide detective (Drake) warns her that the couple's last mark (Evelyn) may have been murdered, Crawford, paying more attention to her hormones than her instincts, continues to see Chandler. Sterling plays Crawford's real estate agent, who also has the hots for the misogynistic Romeo. At 50, Crawford still looks pretty good, but her penchant for overacting has gotten worse with age. A boring film with no surprises.

Memorable Noir Moments:

❑ "How do you like your coffee?" Chandler asks the surprised Crawford when she finds him in her kitchen. "Alone," she replies icily.

❑ Chandler frightens the usually unflappable Crawford when he comes on too strong. "That's right," he tells her. "Be afraid of me. A *little* afraid of me, at least. A woman's no good to a man unless she's afraid of him." See *Gilda* and *Witness to Murder* for other scary words of love.

The File on Thelma Jordon (1950) 100 min. Barbara Stanwyck, Wendell Corey, Joan Tetzel, Richard Rober. **Screenplay by:** Ketti Frings. **Directed by:** Robert Siodmak. **Noir Type:** Femme Fatale. **Noir Themes:** Obsession, lust, betrayal. ★★★½

Stanwyck plays yet another femme fatale (see *Double Indemnity* and *The Strange Love of Martha Ivers*). This time it's assistant D.A. Corey who's caught in her web. Corey, boozing it up lately because of an unhappy marriage to Tetzel, falls hard when Stanwyck walks into his office to report a possible burglary attempt. Soon Corey, who's ready to abandon his wife and two kids, finds himself covering up a murder that Stanwyck or her brutal lover (Rober) may have committed. The film is a bit slow at first, but Stanwyck and Corey manage to pull it off. Stanwyck, one of film noir's top icons, is terrific in a role that suits her perfectly, and Corey gives a first-class performance as a good public servant gone bad over a tantalizing dame.

Familiar Faces from Television:

❑ Gertrude Hoffman (Mrs. Odetts of *My Little Margie*) as Stanwyck's aunt.

❑ Kenneth Tobey (Chuck Martin in *The Whirlybirds*) as a police photographer.

Memorable Noir Moment:

❑ A killer tells a sucker, "That's the convenient part about a fall guy — once you've got him hooked, you've always got him hooked."

Finger Man (1955) 81 min. Frank Lovejoy, Forrest Tucker, Peggie Castle, Timothy Carey, Evelyn Eaton. **Screenplay by:** Warren Douglas. **Directed by:** Harold Schuster. **Noir Type:** Undercover. **Noir Themes:** Fatalism, paranoia, betrayal. ★½

When T-men arrest three-time loser Lovejoy for commercial hijacking, they give him a choice — go undercover to help them nab a local crime lord (Tucker) or go to prison for the rest of his life. The ex-con chooses the first option after he finds out that Tucker is responsible for turning his sister (Eaton) into a pathetic drug addict. Lovejoy convinces his girlfriend (Castle) to introduce him to Tucker and makes a good impression on the mobster by smacking his flunkies around, especially his right-hand man (Carey), a psychopath who enjoys turning dames' faces into mashed potatoes. This low-budget noir is downright boring, with the only real entertainment being Carey's weird performance.

Memorable Noir Moment:

❑ After Lovejoy and Castle compare hard luck stories, he concludes, "We're two of a kind. You never got a break and I never asked for one."

5 Against the House (1955) 85 min. Guy Madison, Kim Novak, Brian Keith, Alvy Moore, Kerwin Mathews. **Screenplay by:** John Barnwell, William Bowers and Stirling Sil-

p. 404-5

A three-time-loser (Frank Lovejoy) tickles the ivories for his girlfriend (Peggie Castle) in *Finger Man* (Allied Artists, 1955).

liphant. **Directed by**: Phil Karlson. **Noir Type**: Heist. **Noir Themes**: Paranoia, betrayal, law breaking for kicks. ★★★

Four law students (Madison, Keith, Moore and Mathews) and a nightclub singer (Novak) attempt to hold up a Reno gambling joint. It's all a lark at first, the brain-child of the rich but bored Mathews. Madison and Novak, planning a Reno wedding, don't even realize they're involved until it's too late. But Keith, an unstable Korean War veteran who swears he'll never go back to the Army's psycho ward, is taking the plan seriously. It's slow going at first and the dialogue borders on silly, but Keith (*Family Affair*'s Uncle Bill like you've never seen him) makes it a pleasurable experience. Madison took time off from his role as TV's *Wild Bill Hickok* to make this enjoyable noir. Moore went on to be a regular in TV's *Green Acres*.

Familiar Faces from Television:
❑ William Conrad (TV's *Cannon*) as the guy rolling the casino's money cart.
❑ John Larch (Deputy D.A. Jerry Miller in *Arrest and Trial*) as a Reno plainclothes detective.

Memorable Noir Moment:
❑ From the Some-Things-Never-Change Department: College student and war veteran Keith

complains, "Any guy who wants to lead himself a quiet, peaceful and uneventful life picked himself the wrong time to get born."

Fixed Bayonets (1951) 92 min. Richard Basehart, Gene Evans, Michael O'Shea, Craig Hill, Skip Homeier, Richard Hylton. **Screenplay by:** Samuel Fuller. **Directed by:** Samuel Fuller. **Noir Type:** Combat. **Noir Themes:** Fatalism, paranoia. ★★★★

During the Korean War, an American regiment retreats from the snow-covered South Korean mountains. A platoon led by a young lieutenant (Hill) and two experienced NCOs (O'Shea and Evans) stays behind to hold their position against the Red Chinese Army so their comrades will have a chance to escape. During sporadic mortar attacks and sniper fire, Basehart, a corporal with buck fever (he can't pull the trigger when the enemy is in his sights), spends his time worrying that his three superiors will be killed, leaving him to command the platoon by default. Early on, Hill is shot by a sniper, and tough GIs O'Shea and Evans take command. One down and two to go, the corporal worries, despite Evans' reassurance that he's too ornery to die. Homeier plays an intellectual private with an opinion on everything, and Hylton is the litter bearer who uses a bayonet to dig a bullet out of his own leg, leading him to fantasize about becoming a surgeon when the war ends. Basehart's sensitive portrayal of a soldier with a fear of responsibility, coupled with tough, gritty performances by Evans and O'Shea, make this action-packed combat film a must-see (as is *The Steel Helmet*, also from writer-director Fuller). If you have eagle eyes, try finding James Dean in a bit role as one of 50 soldiers cloaked in white, hooded parkas.

Familiar Faces from Television:
❏ Henry Kulky (Otto Schmidlap in *The Life of Riley*) as a lookout.
❏ John Doucette (Jim Weston in *Lock Up* and Captain Andrews in *The Partners*) as a soldier in the general's tent.

Memorable Noir Moment:
❏ During a bombardment, two men in a foxhole engage in favorite pastime of GIs—griping. "They told me this was gonna be a police action," says one. "Why didn't they send cops?" the other wonders.

The Flame (1948) 96 min. John Carroll, Vera Ralston, Robert Paige, Broderick Crawford, Constance Dowling. **Screenplay by:** Lawrence Kimble. **Directed by:** John H. Auer. **Noir Type:** Triangle. **Noir Themes:** Betrayal, jealousy, obsession, guilt. ★★½

A shiftless loafer (Carroll) and his lover (Ralston) plot to get their hands on the millions belonging to Carroll's critically ill half-brother (Paige) by tricking him into marrying Ralston. Things seem to be going according to plan when Paige proposes to the French nurse, but the plot backfires when she begins to fall in love with him and his health starts to improve. Making matter worse for Carroll is a blackmailer (Crawford) looking for enough dough to impress his nightclub singer girlfriend (Dowling), who's romantically involved with Carroll. Meanwhile, Carroll, who is beginning to have second thoughts about having pushed the girl he loves into marrying his brother, has started drinking heavily and is carrying a gun. Not a bad drama with plenty of atmosphere, including organ music, ocean waves crashing against rocks and a couple of killings. Former ice skater Ralston gives one of her better performances, although her Czechoslovakian accent makes some of her lines incomprehensible. B-veterans Carroll and Paige handle themselves nicely.

Familiar Face from Television:
❑ Victor Sen Yung (Hop Sing in *Bonanza*) as Carroll's house servant.

Memorable Noir Moments:
❑ Ralston expresses misgivings about taking advantage of Carroll's dying brother. "Is it our fault," Carroll asks, "that he's got a body that doesn't want to stay wrapped around that penny-pinching, shriveled-up little soul of his any longer?"
❑ Crawford tells Carroll that the reason he's standing on the street corner is because he's keeping an eye on his girlfriend. "What are you watching her for?" Carroll asks. "She's a dame that needs watching," Crawford explains.

Flamingo Road (1949) 94 min. Joan Crawford, Zachary Scott, Sydney Greenstreet, David Brian, Virginia Huston. **Screenplay by**: Edmund H. North and Robert Wilder. **Directed by**: Michael Curtiz. **Noir Type**: Politics. **Noir Themes**: Politics corruption, woman in jeopardy. ✭✭✭

Crawford is a performer (one of the sultan's dancing girls) in a traveling carnival. When Sheriff Greenstreet runs the show out of town, she stays on, falling in love

A carnival dancing girl-turned-waitress (Joan Crawford, left) gives a fellow performer a critical once over in *Flamingo Road* (Warner Bros., 1949).

with deputy sheriff Scott. She soon finds herself framed on a prostitution charge by Greenstreet, who has political plans for Scott and doesn't want Crawford around to ruin them. The spineless Scott, drinking heavily, allows the malignant sheriff to force him into a loveless marriage with socialite Huston, which helps him get elected state senator. Next stop, if Greenstreet gets his way, is the governor's mansion. Meanwhile, Crawford returns to town and marries political boss Brian, causing the depressed Scott to hit the bottle even harder. Crawford, at 45, isn't believable as a veiled, exotic dancer, but once the carnival leaves town, she's back on her own turf — playing a tough, sensible and, at times, fragile woman choosing to settle down in a town that doesn't want her. Greenstreet is at his nastiest as the fat old sheriff grasping at political power from behind closed doors and willing to do whatever it takes to get it.

Familiar Faces from Television:
❑ Dale Robertson (Jim Hardie in *Tales of Wells Fargo*) as a cafe patron who asks a waitress for a date.
❑ Fred Clark (one of several actors to play Harry Morton, George and Gracie's neighbor in *The George Burns and Gracie Allen Show*) as a newspaper editor.

Memorable Noir Moments:
❑ Greenstreet gives Scott some sound political advice. "All you need to know is two words," he says. "Yep and nope. You can't go wrong if you say yep to the right people and nope to the rest of them."
❑ Crawford asks her cellmate what crime she committed. "My boyfriend cut himself on a knife I was holdin'," the woman replies.
❑ When leviathan Greenstreet climbs a staircase at a local club, the owner stares up at him in disbelief. "No matter how many times you see it, you just can't believe it's real," she says loudly, referring to Greenstreet's sizable butt. The sinister lawman, stepping out of character momentarily, smiles agreeably.

Flaxy Martin (1949) 86 min. Virginia Mayo, Zachary Scott, Dorothy Malone, Douglas Kennedy, Elisha Cook, Jr., Helen Westcott, Jack Overman. **Screenplay by:** David Lang. **Directed by:** Richard Bare. **Noir Type:** Femme Fatale. **Noir Themes:** Betrayal, obsession. ★★★

Crime boss Kennedy's moll (Mayo) pretends to be in love with the mob's lawyer (Scott) to keep him in line. Scott, sick of being on the wrong side of the law, balks at defending one of Kennedy's goons (Overman) on a murder charge because he believes the man is guilty. Kennedy and Mayo hire a dipso (Westcott) to testify that the hood was with her the night of the murder, influencing the unwitting Scott to change his opinion about Overman's guilt. He takes and the case and succeeds in getting the killer off. Westcott, meanwhile, emboldened by the hooch, tries to blackmail Kennedy, who has her bumped off by Overman, the man she helped free. When Mayo gets implicated in the murder, Scott, the biggest sucker for a dame since Bob Mitchum (see *Angel Face, Out of the Past* and *Where Danger Lives*), confesses to the crime to protect her. He pleads self-defense but, thanks to a double-cross by Kennedy and Mayo, he's convicted and sentenced to twenty years. Malone plays the pretty librarian who tries to help Scott prove his innocence after he escapes from police custody. Noir veteran Cook is entertaining as a small-time hood, and Mayo is terrific as a femme fatale without an ounce of goodness in her. It's a pleasure hating her.

A fall-guy attorney (Zachary Scott) gets physical with a double-crossing femme fatale (Virginia Mayo) in *Flaxy Martin* (Warner Bros., 1949).

Familiar Face from Television:
- ❏ Tom D'Andrea (Gillis on *The Life of Riley*) as a garage mechanic.

Memorable Noir Moment:
- ❏ When dumb hood Cook expresses his legal opinion on a case, attorney Scott asks him, "Will you kindly take your legal advice back to the sixth grade?," thus bestowing upon the crook the hated nickname, "Sixth Grade."

Flesh and Fantasy (1943) 92 min. Edward G. Robinson, Charles Boyer, Barbara Stanwyck, Robert Cummings, Betty Field, Thomas Mitchell. **Screenplay by:** Samuel Hoffenstein, Ernest Pascal and Ellis St. Joseph. **Directed by:** Julien Duvivier. **Noir Type:** Fantasy. **Noir Themes:** Paranoia, betrayal, character deterioration. ★★★

This fanciful noir is composed of three supernatural tales about dreams and fortunetellers and their effects on the innocent and not-so-innocent. Cummings and Field star in the first episode, which takes place during Mardi Gras in New Orleans. It's about a homely seamstress with a heart as hard as her face. She dons a beautiful mask so that she may appear to have that "soft, sweet look that men seem to admire." She then sets out to attract Cummings, a man she has loved from afar. Episode two, by far the best and most noir-like of the three, is about an American lawyer (Robinson) in England, convinced that palm reader Mitchell's prediction that he will murder someone is going to come true. So, to get it over with, he begins searching for a victim from among (what he deems are) the old and useless members of society. There are some terrific sequences in this episode where the haunted attorney carries on conversations with his reflection and shadow. In the final vignette, Boyer plays a circus tightrope walker who dreams that he falls from the high wire during a performance. He meets Stanwyck, an audience member in his nightmare, and romances her, fully aware that he may be inviting his dream to come true. Good performances, especially by Robinson and Mitchell, make this an enjoyable change of pace choice for noir fans. *Destiny* (1944) was originally intended to be a fourth segment of *Flesh and Fantasy*, but was released as a longer, stand-alone film.

Familiar Faces from Television:
❑ Future "Rat Pack" member Peter Lawford (Nick Charles in *The Thin Man*) as a Mardi Gras clown peering down at a body.
❑ Marjorie Lord (Kathy Williams in *The Danny Thomas Show*) as a seamstress' unhappy customer.

Memorable Noir Moments:
❑ When Robinson expresses mild astonishment over a British dowager's interest in things supernatural, the woman explains, "Well, my liver won't permit me to drink, I'm too old for romance and we English are so beastly dull."
❑ Robinson offers an elderly woman a poison-spiked candy and tells her that it's a new cure for her liver problems. The grateful lady asks, "Can I get any more if it works?" Robinson replies honestly, "If it works, you won't need any more."

Fly by Night (1942) 74 min. Nancy Kelly, Richard Carlson, Albert Basserman, Walter Kingsford, Edward Gargan, Adrian Morris. **Screenplay by:** F. Hugh Herbert and Jay Dratler. **Directed by:** Robert Siodmak. **Noir Type:** Asylum. **Noir Themes:** Victim of fate, obsession. ★★½

Pathologist Carlson finds himself a suspect in the murder of a man who's just escaped from an insane asylum. Hoping to prove his innocence, Carlson flees the cops but finds himself in a hotbed of spies led by an evil psychiatrist (Basserman). Along the way, he takes a friendly hostage (Kelly), who helps him infiltrate the asylum to find the inventor of a weapon that the spies want to get their hands on. (The invention subplot is an interesting predecessor to the "great whatsit" in **Kiss Me Deadly**.) It all sounds wonderfully noirish, but what famed director Siodmak has really made is a film noir parody that sometimes resorts to slapstick, with Gargan and Morris as a couple of bumbling Keystone Cops. (The comedic highlight of the film: Carlson trying to buy a pair of panties for Kelly.) Carlson's charisma and some exciting car chases help the sluggish plot. At least Carlson got the opportunity to prepare for his future role as an undercover inmate at La Siesta Sanitarium in the superior **Behind Locked Doors** (1948).

Memorable Noir Moment:
❑ Carlson assuages a gun-wielding mental patient who is trying to convince him that he's not insane. "There's no such thing as insanity," Carlson says soothingly. "It's just like a nightmare, only you have it in the waking hours."

Follow Me Quietly (1949) 59 min. William Lundigan, Dorothy Patrick, Jeff Corey, Edwin Max. **Screenplay by:** Lillie Hayward. **Directed by:** Richard Fleischer. **Noir Type:** Police Procedural. **Noir Themes:** Delusion, paranoia. ★★★

"I have been ordained to destroy all evil. Beware! The Judge." This foreboding note is one of many clues to the identity of a psychopathic, self-righteous serial killer (Max). In a silly piece of police work, homicide detectives Lundigan and Corey construct a faceless mannequin based on the many vague descriptions provided by witnesses and begin showing photographs of it around town. Despite the absurd premise, this low-budget noir works well thanks to a well-developed script and solid performances by Lundigan as the frustrated cop and Patrick as the eager reporter.

Familiar Face from Television:
❑ Frank Ferguson (Gus the ranch hand in *My Friend Flicka*) as victim number seven.

Memorable Noir Moment:
❑ When detective Corey finds Lundigan talking to the mannequin, he remarks, "If you want to talk to a dummy, why don't you talk to me?"

Footsteps in the Night (1957) 62 min. Bill Elliott, Don Haggerty, Douglas Dick, James Flavin. **Screenplay by:** Albert Band and Elwood Ullman. **Directed by:** Jean Yarbrough. **Noir Type:** Police Procedural. **Noir Themes:** Victim of fate, greed. ★★

Elliott and Haggerty star as LA. Sheriff's Department detectives investigating the case of a man strangled during a friendly poker game with his friend (Dick), who swears he was in the kitchen when the murder took place. Elliott believes the man but Haggerty is suspicious. Using a wealthy businessman (Flavin) as bait, Elliott attempts to flush out the real killer. This is the last in a series of "Lt. Doyle" crime dramas. (See *Calling Homicide* and *Sudden Danger*. Another Lt. Doyle film, *Chain of Evidence*, was not available for review by the author at the time of writing.) "Wild Bill" Elliott starred in a number of B westerns in the 1940s and '50s, and Dick was a regular in the syndicated TV series *Waterfront* from 1954 to 1956.

Familiar Face from Television:
❑ Robert Shayne (Inspector Henderson in *The Adventures of Superman*) as the miserly murder victim.

Forbidden (1953) 84 min. Tony Curtis, Joanne Dru, Lyle Bettger, Marvin Miller, Victor Sen Yung. **Screenplay by:** Gil Doud and William Sackheim. **Directed by:** Rudolph Maté. **Noir Type:** Far East. **Noir Themes:** Betrayal, jealousy. ★★

Newspaper reporter Curtis travels to the Asia to find former girlfriend Dru, who's wanted by a gangster back home because she has evidence that can send him to the big house. Bright boy Curtis thinks he's supposed to bring her back for a business transaction. Catching up with her in Macao, he learns that she's engaged to a shady American gambler (Bettger) whose life he recently saved. The grateful Bettger gives Curtis a job in his casino; Curtis repays him by picking up where he left off with Dru. Just when you think you're viewing a remake of *Gilda*, the plot shifts gears and turns into a mediocre action film. Marvin plays the American gangster's henchman who follows Curtis to ensure that he does his job, and Sen Yung (Hop Sing in TV's *Bonanza*) is a sagacious piano player. This minor film noir is interesting only because it was an early starring vehicle for the baby-faced Curtis. Dru, the sister of Peter Marshall, the host of TV's original *Hollywood Squares*, starred in the short-lived TV comedy *Guestward Ho*. Look for Mamie Van Doren (often called "the poor man's Lana Turner") in a bit role as a casino singer.

Familiar Face from Television:
❑ Harry Lauter (Jim Herrick in *Waterfront*) as an American agent receiving a telegram.

Force of Evil (1948) 78 min. John Garfield, Beatrice Pearson, Thomas Gomez, Roy Roberts, Marie Windsor. **Screenplay by**: Abraham Polonsky and Ira Wolfert. **Directed by**: Abraham Polonsky. **Noir Type**: Gambling. **Noir Themes**: Economic repression, corruption, greed. ★★★½

This noir, despite the social commentary about the evils of capitalism (disguised as organized crime), is a pretty good crime story about greed, conscience and the love-hate relationship between two estranged brothers (Garfield and Gomez). Garfield is excellent as a well-paid lawyer for gambling czar Roberts, who wants to legalize and thus monopolize the numbers rackets. They concoct a plan that will pay off the thousands of small-time gamblers who superstitiously play the number 776 on July the 4th. This will bankrupt all the little gambling "banks," including the one run by Garfield's brother. Garfield tries to help Gomez survive the coming devastation by getting him involved in Roberts' big-time plan, but the "honest and respectable" numbers man wants nothing to do with the mob's dirty money. Pearson is Garfield's young love interest, and noir icon Windsor is Roberts' femme fatale wife. Director Polonsky, who wrote the screenplay for **Body and Soul**, also co-wrote this enjoyable (but overrated) film noir. During the 1950s Red scare, Polonsky was blacklisted and didn't direct another film in this country until 1969 (*Tell Them Willie Boy Is Here*).

A gambling czar (Roy Roberts, left) isn't happy with his attorney (John Garfield) in *Force of Evil* (MGM, 1948).

Familiar Face from Television:

❏ Paul Fix (Marshal Micah Torrance in TV's *The Rifleman*) as a gangster named Fico.

Memorable Noir Moment:

❏ A bookkeeper for a small-time numbers operation wants to quit after the business is taken over by the syndicate. "If I go now and walk out of here, how're you going to stop me?" he asks nervously. "How, if I say I won't stay and walk out of here, how're you going to stop me?" A syndicate enforcer responds calmly, "The Combination will stop you … stop you dead — in your tracks."

Four Boys and a Gun (1957) 74 min. Frank Sutton, Larry Green, James Franciscus, William Hinnant, Robert Dryden. **Screenplay by:** Philip Yordan and Leo Townsend. **Directed by:** William Berke. **Noir Type:** Troubled Youth. **Noir Themes:** Character deterioration, fatalism. ★★½

Four young men, not "boys," decide to hold up a boxing arena on a whim, and one of them winds up killing the cop who stumbles upon the robbery. They are eventually rounded up by homicide detectives and taken downtown, where the D.A. gives them a choice — three of them can face life or they can all fry if they don't turn over the guy who pulled the trigger. We learn about their lives via flashbacks. Sutton, who works as a runner for a bookie (Dryden), has been skimming off the top to impress a girl and needs dough to pay back his angry boss; Green, a truck driver, just got dumped by his girl because she prefers men with money; amateur boxer Franciscus has to pay for his wife's Caesarean section; nerdy Hinnant, who lives with his parents, just kind of hangs around, idol-worshipping his buddies. This is an interesting low-budget noir with decent performances by a then-unknown cast. Sutton went on to play Private Pyle's Marine sergeant nemesis in TV's *Gomer Pyle USMC*, and Franciscus starred in several TV dramas, including *Naked City*, *Mr. Novak* and *Longstreet*.

Familiar Faces from Television:

❏ Anne Seymour (Lucia Garret in *Empire*) as Green's mother.
❏ J. Pat O'Malley (Sgt. Lou Bacus in *Staccato* and Bert Beasley in *Maude*) as a boxing manager with disappointing news for Franciscus.
❏ Ned Glass (Sgt. Andy Pendleton on *The Phil Silvers Show*) as the owner of the boys' hangout.

Memorable Noir Moment:

❏ One of Dryden's thugs has a word of advice for Sutton, who's been spending the bookie's dough on a dame. "On your salary, you can't afford to go out with girls you like," he says. "You gotta go out with girls that like *you*."

Fourteen Hours (1951) 92 min. Paul Douglas, Richard Basehart, Barbara Bel Geddes, Debra Paget, Agnes Moorehead, Martin Gabel, Jeffrey Hunter. **Screenplay by:** John Paxton. **Directed by:** Henry Hathaway. **Noir Type:** Troubled Youth. **Noir Themes:** Fatalism, paranoia, distrust. ★★★★

A jumper (Basehart) is perched on the fifteenth floor of a Manhattan hotel, and one of New York's Finest (Douglas), a traffic cop, is trying to talk him down. Within minutes, a crowd of thousands appears, seemingly out of nowhere, to watch the spectacle. Then the media arrive with their news-hungry reporters and television cameras. Smaller dramas are taking place in the buildings around the hotel and in the streets below — a young couple (Paget and Hunter) meet and sparks fly, a woman (Grace Kelly in her film debut) begins having second thoughts about her divorce as she watches events unfold, and five angry cab drivers, unable to get out of the traffic jam, start a pool as to the time Basehart will jump. Meanwhile, a frustrated police psychiatrist (Gabel) convinces Douglas to continue talking with the agitated jumper, and Basehart's shrewish mother (Moorehead) arrives to spook her already jittery son. Basehart's former fiancée (Bel Geddes) also shows up wondering why he broke off their engagement, and a crazed evangelist manages to sneak up to the hotel room, ready to save everyone. It all adds up to a suspenseful and fascinating film, with Douglas and Basehart outstanding as the two men thrown together by fate for fourteen hours on St. Patrick's Day.

Familiar Faces from Television:

❑ Ossie Davis (Oz Jackson in *B.L. Stryker*, Ponder Blue in *Evening Shade*, and Judge Harry Roosevelt in *John Grisham's The Client*) as a cabbie.
❑ Harvey Lembeck (Cpl. Barbella in *The Phil Silvers Show*) as a cabbie.
❑ Willard Waterman (Throckmorton P. Gildersleeve in *The Great Gildersleeve*) as a hotel clerk.
❑ Frank Faylen (Herbert T. Gillis in *The Many Loves of Dobie Gillis*) as a hotel waiter.
❑ Joyce Van Patten (Claudia Gramus in *The Good Guys* and Maureen Slattery in *Unhappily Ever After*), in her film debut, as a spectator wanting to get back to the office.

Memorable Noir Moments:

❑ When Basehart refuses to speak with anyone but Douglas, the reluctant officer asks the psychiatrist what he should talk about. "Anything to sublimate his drive," Gabel responds. "Easy, doc," the bewildered cop pleads. "I took a little French but I didn't keep up with it."
❑ A statement at the end of the film thanks the Rescue Squad of the New York Police Department for its expert advice, stating that the squad "has developed techniques to deal with problems of this nature quietly, quickly, and efficiently." One of its "efficient" techniques includes seating a middle-aged patrolman on a wooden plank tied between two ropes and lowering the brave soul several stories so he can lasso(!) the terrified leaper.

Framed (1947) 82 min. Glenn Ford, Janis Carter, Barry Sullivan, Edgar Buchanan. **Screenplay by:** Ben Maddow. **Directed by:** Richard Wallace. **Noir Type:** Femme Fatale. **Noir Themes:** Greed, lust, betrayal. ★★½

Ford plays an unemployed mining engineer who becomes the patsy for would-be embezzlers Carter and Sullivan. Their scheme is to steal 250 Gs from the bank where Sullivan, the bank president's opportunist son-in-law, is an executive. They then plan to murder Ford in a contrived auto accident, hoping the authorities will believe the body is Sullivan's. The usually reliable Ford is uninteresting here, but Carter is sensational as the wicked femme fatale with a heart of ice that, disastrously for her, Ford begins to melt. Veteran character actor Buchanan (Uncle Joe in TV's *Petticoat Junction*) plays Ford's potential employer, unwittingly enmeshed in the murder plot.

Memorable Noir Moments:

❏ Ford, about to be arrested, asks the pre–Miranda cops, "What's the trouble?" "We'll let the judge tell you," one of them replies, adding, "I wouldn't have the time to read all the charges against you."
❏ After Carter releases the emergency brake, and the car and its unfortunate passenger wind up at the bottom of a steep embankment, the look on her face can only be described as one of sexual excitement. See *Night Editor* for more of naughty girl Carter's carnal theatrics.

The Furies (1950) 109 min. Barbara Stanwyck, Wendell Corey, Walter Huston, Judith Anderson, Gilbert Roland, Thomas Gomez. **Screenplay by:** Charles Schnee. **Directed by:** Anthony Mann. **Noir Type:** Horse Opera. **Noir Themes:** Betrayal, greed, revenge, jealousy. ★★★

Tyrannical cattle rancher Huston plans to turn over the operation of his vast land holdings, called "The Furies," to his headstrong but business-savvy daughter (Stanwyck). But then along comes Anderson, a wealthy widow with a yen to catch herself a husband, causing friction between father and daughter and spoiling Stanwyck's dream of inheriting the cattle business. When daddy hangs Stanwyck's best friend for being a squatter, she vows revenge. With a little help from Corey, the lover who spurned her, she sets out to ruin her once beloved father and gain control of the Furies. Roland plays the Mexican homesteader in love with Stanwyck, and Gomez is "El Tigre," Huston's enforcer. Stanwyck is always good as a femme fatale, this time with an Old West backdrop, and Huston, in his final role, is at his unrestrained best as the crotchety and treacherous cattle baron. An above average psychological Western, *The Furies* is (with the exception of Corey smacking a seemingly appreciative Stanwyck around) short on action and long on talk.

Familiar Faces from Television:

❏ John Bromfield (Frank Morgan in *The Sheriff of Cochise*) as Stanwyck's brother.
❏ Frank Ferguson (Gus the ranch hand in *My Friend Flicka*) as a doctor.

Memorable Noir Moments:

❏ Sensitivity Training Required: After being reproached by Stanwyck, Gomez tells a companion, "Women were created so that man might enjoy his food and sleep, not to give orders."
❏ Fearing that Huston is going to leave her, Anderson rejects his request for a loan. "Money is the only thing that makes loneliness bearable," she explains.
❏ A scantily clad saloon girl who has taken up with Stanwyck's former flame introduces herself to the competition: "I'm new in town, honey." Without missing a beat, Stanwyck replies, "Honey, you wouldn't be new any place."

The Gambler and the Lady (1952-British) 74 min. Dane Clark, Kathleen Byron, Naomi Chance. **Screenplay by:** Sam Newfield. **Directed by:** Patrick Jenkins. **Noir Type:** Gambling. **Noir Themes:** Obsession, betrayal, jealousy, revenge. ★½

Clark plays a social-climbing London gambler ("I just want to be where the best people are") taking etiquette lessons so he'll fit in with the upper class. The crass American falls for a pretty English aristocrat (Chance), dumps his possessive girlfriend (Byron) and tries to avoid a takeover of his gambling operations by the syndicate. Once again, the acting talents of noir veteran Clark are wasted in a tepid British noir. (See *Blackout*, *The Man Is Armed* and *Paid to Kill* for more Clark disappointments.)

Gambling House (1950) 80 min. Victor Mature, Terry Moore, William Bendix. **Screenplay by**: Marvin Borowsky and Allen Rivkin. **Directed by**: Ted Tetzlaff. **Noir Type**: Payback. **Noir Themes**: Fatalism, betrayal, social reform. ★★½

Mature is a small-time hood who, for 50 Gs, takes the rap for a murder committed by gangster Bendix. He pleads self-defense and is found not guilty, but Bendix welshes on the dough and sics Immigration on Mature, who is threatened with deportation as an undesirable. The poor guy never knew he had to file for citizenship (his parents, who died before becoming naturalized, brought him over from Italy at age five). The judge gives him several days to come up with a reason why he should be allowed to remain in America. One reason he finds is Moore, a pretty employee of an organization that helps refugees. In addition to discovering love, he also learns a valuable lesson about patriotism before taking vengeance on Bendix. It's worth a look.

Familiar Face from Television:
❏ Jack Kruschen (Tully in *Hong Kong* and Sam Markowitz in *Busting Loose*) as an Italian immigrant at Ellis Island.

Memorable Noir Moments:
❏ Mature wonders if Moore majored in psychology. She confirms that it was Abnormal Psychology 101 and that "we covered you in the first semester."
❏ Mature calls Bendix's attorney a shyster and suggests that "you'd pick up his spit if he told you to."

Gang Busters (1955) 75 min. Myron Healey, Don Harvey, Sam Edwards, Frank Gerstle, Frank Richards. **Screenplay by**: Phillips H. Lord. **Directed by**: Bill Karn. **Noir Type**: Prison. **Noir Themes**: Law breaking for kicks. ★

Healey plays "Public Enemy Number Four," a master criminal and prison breakout artist. He keeps escaping after being put on cushy work assignments as rewards for good behavior (even after killing a cop!). Detectives Harvey and Gerstle keep arresting him, and the State of Oregon keeps putting him back on those work details that he appreciates so much. Edwards is Healey's gangster groupie who, when released from prison, murders an elderly man in an attempt to impress his idol. Richards is the goon Healey takes with him on his final breakout. This low-budget crime flick is for the hardcore enthusiast only.

Familiar Face from Television:
❏ Ed Hinton (Special Agent Henderson in *I Led Three Lives*) as a prison guard.

The Gangster (1947) 84 min. Barry Sullivan, Belita, Joan Lorring, Akim Tamiroff, Henry (Harry) Morgan, John Ireland, Sheldon Leonard. **Screenplay by**: Daniel Fuchs. **Directed by**: Gordon Wiles. **Noir Type**: Gangster. **Noir Themes**: Paranoia, jealousy, obsession, fatalism. ★★★

A gangster (Barry Sullivan) is behind the eight ball with his former hoodlum buddies in *The Gangster* (Allied Artists, 1947).

Sullivan plays a neurotic hood who had to fight his way out of the gutter to get where he is. But now he spends all of his time worrying about whether his showgirl lover (Belita) is cheating on him. Despite warnings from his high-strung associate (Tamiroff) that a rival (Leonard) is trying to take over the business, Sullivan continues to wander around in a paranoid daze, feeling ugly and unloved because of a facial scar, and seeking acceptance from Tamiroff's cashier (Lorring), who despises him. Morgan is cast against type as a soda jerk who sees himself as quite the ladies' man, and Ireland is a pathetic gambler always just on the verge of hitting it big (sez he). It's overly melodramatic at times, but if you hang in long enough, murder will rear its ugly head. Sullivan gives a strong performance as the insecure hood who finds himself losing the little empire he's built. Look for some familiar noir faces in bit roles: Shelley Winters (Tamiroff's new cashier), Charles McGraw (a hood, of course) and Elisha Cook, Jr. (ditto).

Familiar Faces from Television:

❑ Billy Gray (Bud in *Father Knows Best*) as a little kid.
❑ Sid Melton (Ichabod Mudd, assistant to *Captain Midnight*, and Charlie Halper, owner of the Copa Club in *Make Room for Daddy* a.k.a. *The Danny Thomas Show*) as a stage manager.

Memorable Noir Moment:

❑ Morgan brags about his romantic techniques to the disinterested Sullivan. "Treat 'em like a queen," he says. "Chop suey for dinner, see a show. Oh, sure, psychology. Puts 'em in a frame of mind where they naturally feel obligated, don'tcha know."

The Garment Jungle (1957) 88 min. Lee J. Cobb, Kerwin Mathews, Gia Scala, Richard Boone, Robert Loggia, Valerie French. **Screenplay by:** Harry Kleiner. **Directed by:** Vincent Sherman and Robert Aldrich (uncredited). **Noir Type:** Union. **Noir Themes:** Corruption social reform, betrayal. ★★½

A returning Korean War veteran (Mathews) starts working at a dressmaking business owned by his father (Cobb) in New York City's garment district, where he learns that Cobb's partner, a pro-union advocate, has died in an elevator "accident." Union organizer Loggia swears that thugs working for Boone, head of a union-busting syndicate, tampered with the elevator. Cobb, who keeps Boone on his payroll to discourage union activity, refuses to believe it. After Loggia is beaten up by Boone's thugs at a union meeting, Mathews defies his father and sides with the union. It takes another murder before Cobb finally removes his blinders. Scala plays Loggia's wife and French is Cobb's girlfriend. Boone (TV's Paladin in *Have Gun Will Travel*) is plenty sinister as the ruthless union buster, and Loggia (*T.H.E. Cat* and *Mancuso, F.B.I.*) does a good job as the dedicated union organizer.

Familiar Faces from Television:

❑ Harold J. Stone (Sam Steinberg in *Bridget Loves Bernie* and Hamilton Greeley in *My World and Welcome to It*) as Cobb's plant manager.
❑ Joseph Wiseman (Manny Weisbord in *Crime Story*) as a union organizer.

Gaslight (1944) 114 min. Charles Boyer, Ingrid Bergman, Joseph Cotten, Dame May Whitty, Angela Lansbury. **Screenplay by:** John Balderson, Walter Reisch and John Van Druten. **Directed by:** George Cukor. **Noir Type:** Newlywed. **Noir Themes:** Woman in jeopardy, betrayal. ★★★★

Ten years after her aunt was found strangled in their Victorian London home, newlywed Bergman returns to live there with her groom, a Czech pianist (Boyer) whom she married after a whirlwind romance. Before long, it becomes obvious that Boyer is trying to drive his bride insane. But to what purpose? Scotland Yard inspector Cotten, who hasn't forgotten the decade-old murder, is determined to find out. Lansbury plays a Cockney maid and Whitty is the couple's busybody neighbor. A remake of a 1940 British film of the same title, *Gaslight* no longer seems as chilling, but the performances are outstanding, especially those of Boyer and 18-year-old Lansbury (from TV's *Murder, She Wrote*), in her film debut. Nominated for seven Academy Awards, including Best Actress (Bergman won), Best Actor (Boyer), Best Supporting Actress (Lansbury) and Best Screenplay.

Familiar Face from Television:

❑ You'll have to look hard for this one — in the beginning of the film, Terry Moore (Constance Garret in *Empire*), portraying Bergman's character as a teenager, is seen leaving the house with a man and entering a carriage.

Memorable Noir Moment:

❏ After only a few minutes inside the house where her aunt was murdered, a jittery Bergman utters, "It's all dead in here. It all seems to smell of death."

Gilda (1946) 110 min. Rita Hayworth, Glenn Ford, George Macready, Joseph Calleia, Steven Geray. **Screenplay by:** Marion Parsonnet. **Directed by:** Charles Vidor. **Noir Type:** Triangle. **Noir Themes:** Jealousy, obsession, lust, sexual hostility. ★★★

When a casino owner (Macready) saves the life of a down-and-out gambler (Ford) and gives him a job, an almost unbreakable bond is formed. But not long afterwards, Ford's new boss returns from a business trip with a gorgeous bride (Hayworth) who was once Ford's lover. Feeling betrayed by the man who informed him that "gambling and women do not mix," Ford now must share Macready, whom he obviously cares for, with a woman he considers a tramp. Feeling a responsibility to protect his friend, Ford takes it upon himself to shadow Hayworth but keeps her many romantic trysts to himself. Hayworth, who cares nothing for her middle-aged husband, keeps throwing herself at Ford, but he stubbornly resists her advances. Mean-while, a snooping casino patron (Calleia) and a couple of gun-toting Nazis are making pests of themselves around the gaming tables. Geray is an annoying but philosophical casino janitor, who has a big surprise for the boss. Ford turns in an excellent performance, but all eyes will be on the love goddess, whose rendition of "Put the Blame on Mame" (and not her acting) is the highlight of this interesting melodrama, which tiptoes guardedly around the homosexual attraction between the two men.

A nightclub singer (Rita Hayworth) is escorted from the stage by a bouncer (Joe Sawyer) in *Gilda* (Columbia, 1946).

Familiar Faces from Television:

❏ Joe Sawyer (Sgt. Biff O'Hara in *The Adventures of Rin Tin Tin*) as a casino bouncer.
❏ Gerald Mohr (Christopher Storm in *Foreign Intrigue*) as an Argentine police captain.

Memorable Noir Moments:

❏ Ford lets his misogynism show when he tells Hayworth, "Statistics show that there are more women in the world than anything else — except insects."
❏ Trying his best to be romantic, Macready whispers scarily in Hayworth's ear, "Hate is the only thing that has ever warmed me." See *Witness to Murder* and *Female on the Beach* for more smooth talkers.

The Girl on the Bridge (1951) 76 min. Hugo Haas, Beverly Michaels, Robert Dane, John Close. **Screenplay by:** Hugo Haas and Arnold Phillips. **Directed by:** Hugo Haas. **Noir Type:** Blackmail. **Noir Themes:** Guilt, character deterioration. ★★

A kindly, middle-aged jeweler, whose wife and sons were killed by the Nazis during the war, takes in a young unwed mother (Michaels) and her infant daughter after convincing the former showgirl not to jump off a bridge. He eventually marries her and she becomes pregnant with his child. But just when it looks like they are about to live happily ever after, Dane, the father of Michaels' daughter, shows up. The out-of-work musician is surprisingly decent about the situation, but his greedy business manager (Close) decides to blackmail Haas. Somebody winds up getting murdered, and an innocent man is accused of the crime. Typical Haas twaddle, but Haas the actor, as always, has a charming way about him.

The Glass Alibi (1946) 63 min. Douglas Fowley, Paul Kelly, Anne Gwynne, Maris Wrixon, Cy Kendall, Jack Conrad. **Screenplay by:** Mindret Lord. **Directed by:** W. Lee Wilder. **Noir Type:** Newlywed. **Noir Themes:** Woman in jeopardy, greed, betrayal, lust. ★★★½

Fowley, a miscreant newspaper reporter, meets a rich woman (Wrixon) with only six months to live. Their whirlwind romance leads to marriage, to the chagrin of his girlfriend (Gwynne), who becomes more understanding after she learns about the millions he believes he will inherit after Wrixon dies. The uncooperative Wrixon, however, seems to have developed a new lease on life since the wedding, and her health improves even after the scoundrel replaces her medicine with plain aspirin. Meanwhile, Gwynne's mobster lover (Kendall), who's serving time after being turned in by Fowley, has his slimy henchman (Conrad) keeping an eye on his unfaithful moll. Kelly plays the tough cop who correctly suspects that best friend Fowley's intentions aren't noble. Gwynne is top-notch as the femme fatale, almost rivaling Ann Savage's performance in *Detour*. A mere sixty-three minutes long, this gritty, low-budget noir whizzes through to a terrific ending. Director Wilder tried his luck again in 1955 with an inferior remake (*The Big Bluff*).

Memorable Noir Moment:

❏ Detective Kelly angrily rips into Fowley's "glass alibi": "I can see right through it and break it without half-trying. You built it as strong as you could but it's still glass and I'll break it. I'll smash it."

The Glass Cage *see* The Glass Tomb

The Glass Key (1942) 85 min. Brian Donlevy, Alan Ladd, Veronica Lake, Bonita Granville, Joseph Calleia, William Bendix, Richard Denning, Moroni Olsen. **Screenplay by:** Jonathan

A politician (Brian Donlevy) and a gubernatorial candidate's daughter (Veronica Lake) visit a hospitalized bodyguard (Alan Ladd) under the watchful eye of a nurse (Frances Gifford) in *The Glass Key* (Paramount, 1942).

Latimer. **Directed by:** Stuart Heisler. **Noir Type:** Whodunit. **Noir Themes:** Corruption, conspiracy. ★★★★

Donlevy plays an unethical but powerful political boss, the head of the Voter's League in an unnamed city. Ladd is his two-fisted, loyal aide (i.e., his bodyguard), and Lake, the daughter of a gubernatorial nominee (Olsen), is the beautiful woman who comes between them. When Lake's hellraising brother (Denning) is murdered, suspicion falls on Donlevy because he was furious over Denning's involvement with his sister (Granville). Ladd investigates, hoping to find the real murderer. Between clues, he's beaten viciously by Bendix, the psychopathic henchman of a gambling czar (Calleia) whose operations Donlevy wants to shut down. The chemistry between Ladd and Lake is entertainingly provocative, but it's Bendix, not able to decide whether he wants to kiss Ladd or kill him, who steals the film. A remake of a 1935 film that starred George Raft, *The Glass Key* is a convoluted but thoroughly enjoyable film, based on a novel by mystery writer Dashiell Hammett. Look for Dane Clark (going by his real name, Bernard Zanville) as one of Donlevy's henchmen.

Familiar Face from Television:

❏ Billy Benedict (Whitey in the Bowery Boys movies, Skinny in the East Side Kids movies and Toby in *The Blue Knight*) as the D.A.'s assistant.

Memorable Noir Moments:

❏ Calleia doesn't care for Donlevy's threats to shut down his gambling operations. "I'm too big to take the boot from you now," he says. "You may be too big to take it laying down," Donlevy snaps, "but you're gonna take it."
❏ Sensitivity Training Required: When Ladd chastises Granville for seeing a gambler behind her brother's back, she replies, "I'm free, white…." "And eighteen," Ladd interrupts. See *The City That Never Sleeps*, *Fall Guy* and *Out of the Fog* for more of the same.
❏ Sensitivity Training Required: When Ladd suggests that Donlevy patch things up with Italian-American mobster Calleia, the political boss remarks, "I'll patch up nothing with that pop-eyed spaghetti vendor."
❏ Unhappy about having to back Donlevy's candidate, a political hack complains, "I can't make my boys vote the Reform ticket." "Why not?" punster Donlevy asks. "Most of them come from reform *school*."

The Glass Tomb (1955-British) 60 min. John Ireland, Honor Blackman, Geoffrey Keen, Eric Pohlmann, Sidney James, Liam Redmond. **Screenplay by:** Richard Landau. **Directed by:** Montgomery Tully. **Noir Type:** Cover-Up. **Noir Themes:** Lust, greed, paranoia. ★½

A London carnival owner (Ireland) borrows money for his latest attraction, "The Starving Man," from bookie James, who is being blackmailed by a carnival performer. When the performer is strangled by a talent agent (Keen), Scotland Yard inspector Redmond suspects Ireland. Meanwhile, the show must go on. The murderer discovers that the Starving Man (Pohlmann), who has been locked in a "glass tomb" on a seventy-day fast for the amusement of the curiosity-seeking public, may have been a witness to the killing. Blackman (Pussy Galore in the James Bond film *Goldfinger*) plays Ireland's wife. Boring, dumb and questionably noir, this British film was also released as *The Glass Cage*.

The Glass Web (1953) 81 min. Edward G. Robinson, John Forsythe, Richard Denning, Marcia Henderson, Kathleen Hughes, Hugh Sanders, John Verros. **Screenplay by:** Robert Blees and Leonard Lee. **Directed by:** Jack Arnold. **Noir Type:** Triangle. **Noir Themes:** Betrayal, revenge, jealousy. ★★★

Forsythe, a scriptwriter for a weekly true crime TV series, is being blackmailed by his femme fatale lover (Hughes). Fearful that he'll lose his wife (Henderson) and kids, Forsythe withdraws his family's life savings from the bank and shows up at the starlet's apartment to pay her off. Hearing her arguing with someone, he waits in the stairwell until her visitor leaves. When he enters Hughes' apartment, he finds that she's been strangled. He removes the incriminating evidence of his affair, then takes off. What he doesn't know is that the man arguing with Hughes had been his co-worker, the show's persnickety researcher (Robinson), who also was romantically involved with the actress. When Hughes' estranged husband (Verros) is picked up for the murder, Robinson pushes the show's director (Denning) to do a reenactment of the crime, and Forsythe finds himself having to write the script under the watchful eye of a suspicious homicide detective (Sanders). An interesting look at early live television, *The Glass Web* is a fast-paced suspenser.

Familiar Faces from Television:

❏ Brett Halsey (Paul Templin in *Follow the Sun*) as a studio desk clerk.
❏ Kathleen Freeman (Katie the maid in *Topper* and Flo Shafer in *The Beverly Hillbillies*) as Hughes' maid.
❏ Beverly Garland (Casey Jones in *Decoy*, Barbara Harper Douglas in *My Three Sons* and Dotty West in *Scarecrow and Mrs. King*) as an inebriated partygoer.
❏ Jack Kelly (Brother Bart in *Maverick*) as a studio engineer.

Memorable Noir Moment:

❏ Forsythe describes one of Hughes' provocative outfits as a "barbed wire dress—one she said protected the property but didn't hide the view."

Glory Alley (1952) 79 min. Ralph Meeker, Leslie Caron, Kurt Kasznar, Gilbert Roland, John McIntire, Louis Armstrong. **Screenplay by**: Art Cohn. **Directed by**: Raoul Walsh. **Noir Type**: Boxing. **Noir Themes**: Paranoia, betrayal, character deterioration. ★★

A sports columnist (McIntire) tells his replacement the story of a New Orleans boxing great (Meeker) and how he overcame his reputation as a coward to win the world heavyweight championship. Via flashback, we see the undefeated Meeker enter the ring to take on a well-known contender and then, before the bell for Round 1 even sounds, flee the arena to quit the fight game for a reason known only to himself. His seeming act of cowardice disappoints his manager (Roland), his corner man–trainer (Armstrong), his dancer girlfriend (Caron) and her blind father (Kasznar), not to mention his friends and fans in Glory Alley, a stretch along New Orleans' famous Bourbon Street. After a drunken binge, Meeker joins the Army and gets sent to Korea, where he wins the Congressional Medal of Honor. When he returns to the Alley, he's treated as a hero by everyone except the unforgiving Kasznar. Great jazz sounds from trumpeter Armstrong and trombonist Jack Teagarden spice up this bland boxing tale that contains only about thirty seconds of ring action. The many clichés, the Pollyanna ending and the revelation of Meeker's silly phobia add up to a big letdown. Fight fans, you're better off with **Body and Soul**, **The Set-up** or **Champion**.

Familiar Face from Television:

❏ King Donovan (Bob Cummings' Air Force buddy Harvey Helm in *Love That Bob* and lawyer Herb Thornton in *Please Don't Eat the Daisies*) as a telephone repairman.

Memorable Noir Moment:

❏ Newspaper man McIntire brags that Bourbon Street has "more grifters, grafters, guzzlers and guts than any other street in the world" and more "has-beens, never wases and champions."

The Great Flamarion (1945) 78 min. Erich von Stroheim, Mary Beth Hughes, Dan Duryea, Stephen Barclay. **Screenplay by**: Anne Wigton, Heinz Harold and Richard Weill. **Directed by**: Anthony Mann. **Noir Type**: Femme Fatale. **Noir Themes**: Obsession, betrayal, sexual hostility, revenge, fatalism. ★★★½

This early Mann noir stars von Stroheim as a star of a sharpshooting act who murders his ex-lover (Hughes). After being shot while trying to escape, the dying killer tells his pathetic tale to the clown who finds him. "It all started in Pittsburgh," he begins. Via flashback we learn that von Stroheim has turned sour on women because of a failed romantic relationship. At first, he's unmoved by the persistent advances of his lovely assistant (Hughes), but he eventually succumbs to her abundant charms. Hughes lets it be known that her alcoholic husband (noir icon Duryea), who plays a moving target in von Stroheim's act, is the only thing that stands in the way of their happiness, and wouldn't it be wonderful if the drunken Duryea accidentally staggered in front of a bullet? Later, Hughes double-crosses von Stroheim and runs off to Central America to join her true love (Barclay) and his bicycle act. Von Stroheim, determined to even the score, catches up with her in Mexico City. This is an enjoyable little film, with former silent film star von Stroheim giving a surprisingly laid-back performance (for him, that is). Duryea is excellent as the unfortunate cuckold, and Hughes is terrific as the femme fatale.

Memorable Noir Moment:
❏ After discovering Hughes' body, a stagehand utters a common, but not always accurate, noir complaint: "Them that least deserves it, gets it."

The Great Mystic *see* The Strange Mr. Gregory

The Great Sinner (1949) 110 min. Gregory Peck, Ava Gardner, Melvyn Douglas, Walter Huston, Ethel Barrymore. **Screenplay by:** Ladislas Fodor and Christopher Isherwood. **Directed by:** Robert Siodmak. **Noir Type:** Gambling. **Noir Themes:** Character deterioration, guilt, fatalism. ★★★½

Set in mid-nineteenth century Wiesbaden, Germany, this morbid film traces the downfall of a successful Russian writer (Peck) after he's introduced to gambling by a beautiful woman (Gardner). An inveterate gambler herself, Gardner and her equally addicted father (Huston) are deeply in debt to the casino owner (Douglas). If they're fortunate, Gardner's wealthy grandmother (Barrymore), who has one foot in the grave, will obligingly jump in, leaving them her fortune. However, Granny always seems to bounce back. When Douglas agrees to cancel the debt if Gardner marries him, the lovesick Peck decides to try to win enough money at the roulette table to pay off their debt. Amazingly, he breaks the bank and tries to quit while he's ahead. Unfortunately, he begins seeing his lucky numbers everywhere and gambling fever drives him back to the wheel, where the inevitable happens. The Peck-Gardner chemistry works well; the film's religious tone doesn't.

Familiar Face from Television:
❏ Agnes Moorehead (Endora in *Bewitched*) as a no-nonsense pawnbroker.

Memorable Noir Moment:
❏ A casino owner complains about the growing number of suicides in his establishment. "If we can't prevent suicides, at least we can see they don't happen at the tables," he remarks, adding, "There must be some way to catch them." An observant employee replies, "They often smile before they kill themselves."

The Green Glove (1952) 88 min. Glenn Ford, Geraldine Brooks, Cedric Hardwicke, George Macready. **Screenplay by:** Charles Bennett. **Directed by:** Rudolph Maté. **Noir Type:** On the Run. **Noir Themes:** Greed, guilt. ★★

Veteran Ford and his new girlfriend (Brooks) are on the run from French police, who suspect them of murder. A crooked art dealer (Macready) wants what Ford is searching for — a valuable religious artifact called "the Green Glove." Hardwicke plays the pastor of the small French church where the artifact once rested. Extremely slow moving, it has a few exciting moments (notably a fistfight between Ford and an ex-boxer called Pépe the Crab). Unfortunately, the film contains too much light romantic comedy, namely when Ford and Brooks pretend they're shy newlyweds to get a room in a French inn.

Guest in the House (1944) 117 min. Anne Baxter, Ralph Bellamy, Aline MacMahon, Ruth Warrick, Scott McKay, Marie McDonald. **Screenplay by:** Ketti Frings. **Directed by:** John Brahm. **Noir Type:** Femme Fatale. **Noir Themes:** Paranoia, betrayal, jealousy. ★★★½

Happily married Warrick and Bellamy invite Baxter, the emotionally disturbed fiancée of Bellamy's kid brother (McKay), into their home, hoping her health will improve. She spends her time writing madly in her diary and playing the same song over and over on the phonograph. She even fancies that she's fallen in love with commercial artist Bellamy. Seeing his beautiful live-in model (McDonald) as a potential rival, Baxter schemes to run her off by spreading rumors that McDonald and the artist are having a torrid affair. Then she turns her attention to Warrick and her young daughter. The happy-go-lucky Bellamy, who doesn't have a clue as to what's going on, is shocked to learn that his marriage is beginning to crumble. Baxter is enjoyable as the crazed guest from Hell with an insatiable need to control, and Bellamy is perfect as the jovial, loving husband, whose touchy-feely innocence gets him into big trouble.

Memorable Noir Moment:
❑ Bellamy, who's been hitting the bottle heavily, complains, "This house used to be fun. I was a guy who liked life."

The Guilty (1947) 70 min. Bonita Granville, Don Castle, Wally Cassell, Regis Toomey, John Litel. **Screenplay by:** Robert Presnell, Sr. **Directed by:** John Reinhardt. **Noir Type:** Good Twin, Bad Twin. **Noir Themes:** Jealousy, lust. ★½

Granville plays twins, one a "tramp" and the other a "good girl." When the good twin is murdered, homicide detective Toomey investigates. The twins' boyfriends (Cassell and Castle) and the girls' boarder (Litel) are suspects. A mediocre mystery adapted from a short story by hard-boiled mystery writer Cornell Woolrich.

Guilty Assignment *see* **The Big Town**

Guilty Bystander (1950) 92 min. Zachary Scott, Faye Emerson, Mary Boland, Sam Levene, J. Edward Bromberg, Kay Medford. **Screenplay by:** Don Ettlinger. **Directed by:** Joseph Lerner. **Noir Type:** Boozer. **Noir Themes:** Child in jeopardy, betrayal. ★★

Scott stars as an alcoholic ex-cop eking out a living as the house dick at a seedy hotel owned by Boland. After his ex-wife (Emerson) comes to him for help in finding their missing child, Scott searches for his son, while struggling to stay on the wagon. His investigation leads him to a floozy (Medford) and a murderous gang of jewel thieves led by a hypochondriac gangster (Bromberg). Levene plays Scott's former boss at the department. Noir veteran Scott is disappointing as the rum-dum ex-cop, and Boland, who was known for her comedic roles in the 1930s, is miscast as Scott's spunky boss.

Familiar Face from Television:
❑ Jesse White (Jesse Leeds, one of Danny Thomas' agents on *The Danny Thomas Show*, and the bored Maytag repairman in TV commercials) as a flirtatious bar patron.

Memorable Noir Moments:
❑ Scott plants a big wet one on Medford, and she nearly swoons. "Oh, I've got such a yen for you," she gasps, "it hurts like a toothache."
❑ A wounded Scott shows up at Emerson's doorstep. "You're hurt," she cries. "It's okay," he answers, "it's just a flesh wound." (See *Accused of Murder*, *The Enforcer*, *Jail Bait*, *New York Confidential*, *Riot In Cell Block 11* and *Sleep, My Love*.)

Gun Crazy (1950) 87 min. Peggy Cummins, John Dall, Berry Kroeger, Anabel Shaw, Morris Carnovsky. **Screenplay by:** MacKinlay Kantor and Millard Kaufman. **Directed by:** Joseph H. Lewis. **Noir Type:** On the Run. **Noir Themes:** Obsession, lust, character deterioration, lawbreaking for kicks, guilt. ★★★★½

Dall plays a young man whose fascination with guns has always gotten him into trouble. As a youth, he's caught stealing a gun and is sent to reform school by an understanding, but firm, judge (Carnovsky). Dall later serves as a rifle instructor in the Army and eventually returns to his home town and the sister (Shaw) he hasn't seen in years. While attending a traveling carnival, he participates in a shooting contest with the sexy Cummins, the star of a sharpshooting act, and wins. Sparks fly for the two gun nuts, and Dall eagerly accepts carnival manager Kroeger's job offer. When his star performer and lover dumps him for the younger man, Kroeger realizes he's made a big mistake and fires both of them. The couple go on the road, making a short stop at the justice of the peace. When they run out of dough, Cummins, who's already wanted for murder, suggests that they start pulling hold-ups. The weak-kneed Dall reluctantly agrees but only after she threatens to leave him ("I want a guy with spirit and guts"). Non-violent by nature, Dall adjusts surprisingly well to his new career but insists that they don't hurt anyone. (He learns later that shooting people is a big turn-on for his bride.) Certain that their luck is about to run out, the doomed lovers decide to end their crime spree after one last job, after which, in typical noir fashion, they find themselves fleeing from the F.B.I. and half the cops in the country. A strange and, at times, beautiful film, *Gun Crazy* is director Lewis' masterpiece. Like his later hit **The Big Combo**, this cult classic oozes with sex and violence (1950s style, of course) and is the film that its two young stars are most remembered for. Loosely remade in 1992 as *Guncrazy* with Drew Barrymore.

Familiar Faces from Television:

Husband-and-wife robbers (Peggy Cummins and John Dall) stick up a meat plant in *Gun Crazy* (United Artists, 1950).

❏ Russ Tamblyn, billed as Rusty Tamblyn (Dr. Lawrence Jacoby in *Twin Peaks*), portrays Dall as a youngster.
❏ Ray Teal (Sheriff Roy Coffee in *Bonanza*) as a border guard at the California state line.

Memorable Noir Moments:
❏ He can't say he wasn't warned! A carnival clown gives Dall the lowdown on Cummins, adding, "She ain't the type to make a happy home."
❏ When he reads about their last heist, a guilt-stricken Dall faces reality with refreshing honesty, commenting sadly, "Two people dead just so we can live without working."

The Gunfighter (1950) 84 min. Gregory Peck, Helen Westcott, Millard Mitchell, Jean Parker, Karl Malden, Skip Homeier. **Screenplay by:** William Bowers and William Sellers. **Directed by:** Henry King. **Noir Type:** Horse Opera. **Noir Themes:** Fatalism, revenge. ★★★★½

Peck stars as a disillusioned gunslinger seeking redemption and peace of mind. On the run from three brothers who want to avenge the killing of their kid brother, who drew first, Peck shows up in the town where his best friend (Mitchell) is sheriff. Wanting only to visit with his estranged wife (Westcott) and the eight-year-old son who doesn't know him, the gunfighter refuses to leave until Westcott agrees to meet with him. Despite her love for him, the schoolmarm refuses, fearing what might happen if their son finds out that his father is a notorious killer. Meanwhile the three angry brothers are riding fast, and a wannabe gunslinger (Homeier) is seeking to make a name for himself at Peck's expense. Malden is the bartender whose business has picked up considerably since the famous gunfighter arrived in town, and Parker plays an outlaw's widow. Peck is impressive as the reform-minded gunfighter seeking to atone for the lifestyle that has kept him from the family he loves. One of the best Westerns ever made.

Familiar Faces from Television:
❑ Richard Jaeckel (Lt. Martin Quirk in *Spenser: For Hire* and Lt. Ben Edwards in *Baywatch*) as a tough but stupid cowboy who tests Peck's speed.
❑ Alan Hale, Jr. (the Skipper in *Gilligan's Island*) as Jaeckel's vengeance-minded brother.
❑ Ellen Corby (Grandma Walton in *The Waltons*) as a town busybody.

Memorable Noir Moment:
❑ A poker-playing cowboy makes the mistake of underestimating Peck. "He don't look so tough to me," he remarks to his companions. "Well, if he ain't so tough, there's been an awful lot of sudden deaths in his vicinity," replies his more astute friend.

Gunman in the Streets (1950-U.S.–French) 86 min. Dane Clark, Simone Signoret, Robert Duke, Fernand Gravet. **Screenplay by:** Jacques Companéez and Victor Pahlen. **Directed by:** Frank Tuttle. **Noir Type:** On the Run. **Noir Themes:** Obsession, revenge, betrayal. ★★½

Clark plays a U.S. Army deserter-turned-gangster in post–World War II Paris. After a daring escape while being transported to prison, the sadistic killer goes on the lam, and a French homicide inspector (Gravet) tries to track him down. Wounded during his escape, Clark turns to his former moll (Signoret) for the dough he needs to get out of the city. Her new boyfriend (Duke), an American newspaper reporter, provides the money but insists on tagging along with Clark and Signoret, hoping she'll wise up and drop the loser. Clark gives a convincing performance as the desperate gangster, and Signoret does a good job as the woman torn between two lovers. This U.S.–French co-production was released in France as *The Hunt*, in Canada as *Gangster at Bay* and in Great Britain as *Gunman in the Streets*. It was never shown in U.S. theaters but did show up on American television in 1963 as *Time Running Out*.

The Halliday Brand (1957) 79 min. Joseph Cotten, Viveca Lindfors, Betsy Blair, Ward Bond, Bill Williams, Jay C. Flippen. **Screenplay by:** George W. George and George F. Slavin. **Directed by:** Joseph H. Lewis. **Noir Type:** Horse Opera. **Noir Themes:** Family dysfunction, bigotry, obsession, revenge. ★★½

Bigoted rancher Bond, who doubles as the town sheriff, allows his daughter's half–Indian lover to be lynched by an angry mob for a murder he didn't commit. Bond's grieving daughter (Blair) stays on at the ranch, but his older son (Cotten) is so enraged at the injustice that he leaves home. He meets and falls in love with Lindfors, the sister of the hanged man and the daughter of a storekeeper (Flippen) whom Bond later kills in a gunfight. Cotten's brother (Williams) also falls for Lindfors, while the prodigal son, now an outlaw, tries to force the citizens into firing the sheriff by committing spectacular property crimes. Cotten's outlaw days seem numbered, though, when he learns that his father is terminally ill and wants to see him before he dies. The good cast makes up for the mundane script, but it takes a fair stretch of the imagination to accept noir icon Cotten, only two years younger than Bond, as his son.

Familiar Face from Television:

❑ Jeanette Nolan (Annette Devereaux of the *Hotel de Paree* and Holly Grainger in *The Virginian*) as Lindfors' Indian grandmother.

Hangmen Also Die! (1943) 131 min. Brian Donlevy, Anna Lee, Walter Brennan, Gene Lockhart, Dennis O'Keefe, Alexander Granach. **Screenplay by**: John Wexley. **Directed by**: Fritz Lang. **Noir Type**: Nazi. **Noir Themes**: Betrayal, paranoia, guilt, woman in jeopardy, victim of fate, jealousy. ★★★½

Donlevy plays a Czechoslovakian surgeon, a member of the anti–Nazi underground, who assassinates Gestapo chief Richard Heydrich, the "Hangman of Prague." With no place to hide and the Gestapo combing the streets for him, Donlevy is taken in by a professor (Brennan) and his daughter (Lee). The Nazis take hostages, including Brennan, and promise to execute a few score of them each day until the assassin gives up or is turned in. Ridden with guilt about the inevitable slaughter, Donlevy wants to confess and then kill himself but is talked out of it by his underground superiors. Lee, however, decides to inform on him to save her father. Her fiancé (O'Keefe), meanwhile, believes she's having an affair with Donlevy. Granach is the Gestapo inspector investigating the assassination, and Lockhart (in a top-notch performance) plays a cowardly traitor. Swarming with the usual Nazi villains, patriotic rebels and yellow-bellied quislings, *Hangmen* is more than just a World War II propaganda film thanks to noir icon James Wong Howe's sensational cinematography. Although it's an unusually long film noir at more than two hours, the climax is worth the wait.

Familiar Faces from Television:

❑ Lionel Stander (Max, the chauffeur, in *Hart to Hart*) as a cab driver.
❑ Billy Benedict (Whitey in the Bowery Boys movies, Skinny in the East Side Kids movies and Toby in *The Blue Knight*) as one of the hostages.

Memorable Noir Moment:

❑ A Czechoslovakian traitor, who forgets he's not supposed to understand German, betrays himself by laughing at a Hitler joke — told in German by a suspicious underground colleague.

Hangover Square (1945) 77 min. Laird Cregar, Linda Darnell, George Sanders, Faye Marlowe. **Screenplay by**: Barré Lyndon. **Directed by**: John Brahm. **Noir Type**: Period. **Noir Themes**: Character deterioration, obsession. ★★★★

Cregar, a turn-of-the-century London composer, goes into a Jekyll and Hyde–like murderous rage when he hears loud, discordant sounds, but has no recollection of his crimes afterwards. Darnell is the scheming saloon singer who seduces him into writing hit songs for her, and Marlowe is his adoring fiancée. Sanders plays the Scotland Yard psychiatrist who's been keeping a wary eye on Cregar since he walked into his office expressing concern about his with bouts with amnesia. The Victorian gaslight torches, dark, foggy streets and the haunting musical score give this film a delicious noir flavor. Darnell is enjoyable as the femme fatale, and Cregar is sensational as the tortured composer. Twentieth Century–Fox wisely capitalized on Cregar's success in 1944's *The Lodger* by starring him in this similar role. Unfortunately, Cregar died shortly before *Hangover Square* was released, as a result of complications from excessive dieting. He was only 28. Compare Cregar at his normal weight in *This Gun for Hire*.

Familiar Face from Television:
❑ Alan Napier (Alfred the butler in *Batman*) as Marlowe's father.

Memorable Noir Moment:
❑ Marlowe wisely predicts that Cregar's infatuation with the malignant saloon entertainer will ruin him, warning, "To waste your talents on someone with no real talent and even less reputation — you'll kill your inspiration and be left flat."

The Harder They Fall (1956) 109 min. Humphrey Bogart, Rod Steiger, Jan Sterling, Mike Lane, Max Baer, Jersey Joe Walcott. **Screenplay by:** Philip Yordan. **Directed by:** Mark Robson. **Noir Type:** Boxing. **Noir Themes:** Corruption, greed, betrayal, character deterioration, guilt. ★★★★½

Bogart, a down-and-out sportswriter, takes a job as a P.R. man for a crooked fight promoter (Steiger) who has discovered a new boxing sensation in Argentina. When Steiger realizes that the 275–pound gentle giant (Lane) has a "powder puff punch and a glass jaw," he sends the "Wild Man of the Andes" on a promotional tour of fixed prizefights, with the ultimate aim of pitting him against the heavyweight champion (Baer). Then, of course, Steiger will bet against Lane, who by now believes he's invincible. Meanwhile, Bogey begins having guilt pangs, especially after his wife (Sterling) leaves him as a result of his moral descent. When a boxer dies in the ring while fighting Lane, the grief-stricken Argentine wants to give up fighting. Bogey, who knows that the fighter died as a result of injuries sustained in a previous bout with Baer, convinces Lane to go ahead with his fight against the champ, who is in no mood to go easy on his overrated opponent. *The Harder They Fall* is a brutal and unglamorous exposé of the fight game, with Bogart (in his final role before succumbing to cancer in 1957) outstanding as the writer with a serious moral dilemma. Steiger is excellent as the heartless promoter, and former heavyweight champion Jersey Joe Walcott gives a surprisingly good showing as Lane's compassionate trainer.

Familiar Faces from Television:
❑ Edward Andrews (Commander Rogers Adrian in *Broadside*) as a crooked fight manager who thinks boxers aren't humans.
❑ Harold J. Stone (David Birney's dad, Sam Steinberg, in *Bridget Loves Bernie* and William Windom's publisher, Hamilton Greeley, in *My World and Welcome to It*) as a TV reporter.
❑ Herbie Faye (Private Fender in *The Phil Silvers Show*) as one of Steiger's stooges.
❑ Abel Fernandez (Agent Youngfellow in *The Untouchables*) as a proud Indian boxer who's hesitant to throw a fight in front of his tribe.

❏ Jack Albertson (Ed Brown, the Man, in *Chico and the Man*) as the manager of the boxer killed in the ring.
❏ Peter Leeds (George Colton in *Pete and Gladys*) as the announcer in the championship fight.

Memorable Noir Moments:

❏ Bogey finally levels with the over-confident boxer, telling him, "You don't punch hard enough to bust an egg."
❏ From the Some-Things-Never-Change Department: After it's discovered that the behemoth Lane can neither punch nor take a punch, he's sent to California because "they like freak attractions out there."
❏ Heavyweight champ Baer is angry that Lane has received the "credit" for killing the fighter who died as a result of being pummeled by Baer in a previous bout. "When I butcher a guy, I want the whole world to know it," he complains.

A Hatful of Rain

(1957) 109 min. Don Murray, Eva Marie Saint, Anthony Franciosa, Lloyd Nolan, Henry Silva, Gerald S. O'Loughlin, William Hickey. **Screenplay by:** Michael Vincente Gazzo, Alfred Hayes and Carl Foreman. **Directed by:** Fred Zinnemann. **Noir Type:** Narcotics. **Noir Themes:** Character deterioration, fatalism, betrayal. ★★★½

A Korean War hero (Murray) who became addicted to drugs in a military hospital and eventually kicked the habit, has the monkey on his back once again. His pregnant wife (Saint), unaware of his addiction, thinks his mysterious behavior is due to infidelity and considers dumping him for his brother (Franciosa). The men's father (Nolan), who had placed them in an orphanage during their childhood, arrives in town looking to borrow the $2500 that Franciosa promised to lend him so he could start his own business. The money, however, has gone to support Murray's drug habit. Meanwhile, the cops are cracking down on the city's pushers, drying up Murray's supply, and the only dealer he can find is the vicious Silva, who is serious about collecting the dough Murray already owes him. O'Loughlin (from TV's *The Rookies*) and Hickey play Silva's goons. This well-acted film is a grim, realistic portrayal of the agonies that dope addicts bring upon themselves and their families. Franciosa, reprising his stage role, received an Oscar nomination for Best Actor. He later found success on TV, starring in such series as *Finder of Lost Loves, Valentine's Day, The Name of the Game, Matt Helm* and *Search*. Murray also migrated to the small screen and is best known for his role in the prime time soap opera *Knots Landing*.

Familiar Face from Television:

❏ Art Fleming (the original host of *Jeopardy*) as a mounted police officer.

Memorable Noir Moment:

❏ In the saloon where Franciosa works as a bouncer, Nolan seems determined to embarrass his son, commenting loudly, "What are all these bimbos doing hanging on the bar?"

He Ran All the Way

(1951) 77 min. John Garfield, Shelley Winters, Wallace Ford, Selena Royle, Gladys George, Bobby Hyatt, Norman Lloyd. **Screenplay by:** Guy Endore and Hugo Butler. **Directed by:** John Berry. **Noir Type:** Hostage. **Noir Themes:** Paranoia, child in jeopardy, victim of fate. ★★★★

Fate deals a bad hand to a "plain Jane" bakery worker (Winters) when she meets a good-looking stranger (Garfield) in a public swimming pool. He's actually a cop killer on the lam after a heist gone terribly wrong, and he's using her to avoid a police dragnet. She allows him to escort her home to the tenement apartment she shares with her parents (Ford and Royle) and her kid brother (Hyatt). Soon Garfield is holding the terrified family captive while he tries to figure out how to get out of town. Ford, meanwhile, is wondering why his daughter seems to be taking a shine to the killer. George plays Garfield's beer guzzling, not-so-loving mother, and Lloyd is his unfortunate partner, the "brains" behind the heist. It's a terrific film, with Garfield giving a great performance that marked the end of his all-too-short career. He died of a heart attack a year later at the age of 39. The entire cast is wonderful, with special kudos going to Winters and the young Hyatt.

Memorable Noir Moments:

❑ "If you were a man, you'd be out looking for a job," Garfield's nagging mother complains. Her loving son snaps back, "If *you* were a man, I'd kick your teeth in."

❑ When his hostages refuse to eat the turkey he's purchased for them, Garfield threatens to shoot one of them unless they join him in the meal. "Funny thing," says the hurt cop killer, pushing his plate away in disgust. "All I ever asked you people was just for a place to hole up for a couple of days. That's all. Something you'd give an alley cat."

He Walked by Night (1948) 79 min. Richard Basehart, Scott Brady, Roy Roberts, Whit Bissell, Jimmy Cardwell, Jack Webb. **Screenplay by**: John C. Higgins and Crane Wilbur. **Directed by**: Alfred L. Werker and Anthony Mann (uncredited). **Noir Type**: Police Procedural. **Noir Themes**: Fatalism, paranoia, greed. ★★★★

This Werker-Mann thriller, the film that reportedly inspired Jack Webb's hit TV series *Dragnet*, boasts of an intense performance by Basehart as a psychopathic killer on the run. He's an electronics wizard who steals spare parts from radio stores and builds devices that a local businessman (Bissell) happily, but innocently, leases to his customers. While attempting to break into a shop one evening to add to his hardware collection, Basehart is stopped and questioned by an off-duty police officer, whom he callously shoots and kills. This results in an exhaustive manhunt, led by police captain Roberts, detectives Brady and Cardwell and police scientist Webb. Monitoring their radio transmissions, Basehart stays one step ahead of the cops, changing his *modus operandi* from burglary to armed robbery and altering his appearance for each heist. From its brutal beginning to its exciting climax in the Los Angeles storm drain system (a location used extensively in 1954's science fiction classic *Them!*), *He Walked by Night* is an attention-grabber.

Familiar Faces from Television:

❑ John Dehner (reporter Duke Williams in *The Roaring Twenties*) as a cop at the Bureau of Record and Identification.

❑ Jack Bailey (the host of *Queen for a Day* and Bob Barker's predecessor on *Truth or Consequences*) as a bathrobe-clad witness.

❑ Frank Cady (Doc Williams on *The Adventures of Ozzie and Harriet* and Sam Drucker on *Petticoat Junction* and *Green Acres*) as a suspect at police headquarters.

Memorable Noir Moment:

❑ A policeman asks Basehart to show him some form of identification. "How about my Army

A panicky killer (Richard Basehart) seeks shelter in a Los Angeles storm drain in *He Walked by Night* (Eagle-Lion, 1948).

discharge? I have it right here," he says as he pulls a gun from his jacket pocket and cold-bloodedly shoots the cop.

Heartaches (1947) 71 min. Sheila Ryan, Edward Norris, Chill Wills, Kenneth Farrell, James Seay. **Screenplay by:** George Bricker. **Directed by:** Basil Wrangell. **Noir Type:** Show Biz. **Noir Themes:** Betrayal, jealousy, revenge. ★★½

When somebody starts sending death threats to crooner Farrell, and a couple of his associates are murdered, newspaper reporter Norris searches for the killer with help from girlfriend Ryan, who's also Farrell's press agent. Homicide detective Seay helps out. The interesting hook in this B film is that the handsome Farrell can't hold a note to save his life. His burgeoning Hollywood career is a sham because his voice has to be dubbed by his homely, more talented friend (Wills). There's some great music in this one, including the famous title song by songwriters John Klenner and Al Hoffman. The intentional humor works nicely at times.

Familiar Face from Television:
❑ Frank Orth (Inspector Faraday in *Boston Blackie*) as Farrell's agent.

Memorable Noir Moments:
❑ When Norris asks Wills, the sensational voice behind the phony crooner, about his apparent lack of pride, the self-deprecating singer responds, "Who ever heard of a stooge being proud?" (Moe, Larry and Curly might disagree with him on that.)
❑ When the murderer tells Norris that things would have worked out differently "if that girl of yours hadn't shot off her big mouth," the indignant reporter exclaims, "My girl's mouth is *not* big."

Heat Wave (1954-British) 69 min. Alex Nicol, Hillary Brooke, Sidney James, Paul Carpenter, Alan Wheatley. **Screenplay by:** Ken Hughes. **Directed by:** Ken Hughes. **Noir Type:** Femme Fatale. **Noir Themes:** Betrayal, jealousy. ★★

Nicol stars as a struggling American novelist in England who gets involved with Brooke, the adulterous wife of a wealthy businessman (James). James, who has taken a liking to the young writer, confides in him that that he has less than a year to live and is planning to alter his will, leaving his wife with next to nothing. Brooke, meanwhile, drops her pianist boyfriend (Carpenter) and makes a play for Nicol, who breaks the bad news to her. Told in flashback by Nicol to Scotland Yard inspector Wheatley, the investigator looking into James' suspicious death, this British noir, released in England as *The House Across the Lake*, is slow-moving and without much punch, but Brooke helps liven things up as the greedy femme fatale.

Memorable Noir Moment:
❑ When Nicol is slow to respond to Brooke's advances, the surprised temptress remarks, "Don't tell me I'm not your type." "You're a woman, aren'tcha?" responds the writer.

Hell Bound (1957) 69 min. John Russell, June Blair, Stuart Whitman, Margo Woode, George Mather, Stanley Adams, Frank Fenton. **Screenplay by:** Richard Landau. **Directed by:** William J. Hole, Jr. **Noir Type:** Heist. **Noir Themes:** Betrayal, greed, sexual hostility, corruption. ★★½

Russell (TV's *The Lawman*) portrays a particularly vile criminal mastermind who plots the theft of a ship's supply of war surplus narcotics, which he hopes grateful drug suppliers will turn into "big, white, fluffy, happy clouds." His convoluted scheme involves his lover (Woode), a fake shipwreck victim (Mather), a diabetic public health officer (Adams), a phony nurse (Woode), and an innocent intern/ambulance driver (Whitman). Hoping to obtain funding for his outrageous plan, Russell films a documentary explaining how it will be played out and presents it to a mobster (Fenton), who agrees to back him. Unknown to Russell, Mather is a hopelessly addicted druggie, and Adams experiences a drastic improvement in his diabetic condition, a necessary ingredient for the success of the plan. Even worse, Blair, who's also Fenton's moll, falls for Whitman while accompanying him on his ambulance calls. Needless to say, this well-thought heist turns into a film noir nightmare.

Familiar Faces from Television:

❏ Sammee Tong (Peter in *Bachelor Father*) as the unlucky seaman who finds himself in front of Whitman's speeding car.
❏ Dehl Berti (John Taylor in the western *Paradise*) as a blind drug pusher "watching" a striptease act.
❏ Frank McGrath (Charlie Wooster in *Wagon Train*) as a police detective arriving at the docks.

Memorable Noir Moments:

❏ When she doesn't get the reaction she hoped for after throwing herself at Russell, Blair comments, "You better see a doctor, Jordan. You've got a low blood count." Russell replies, "You're wrong, Paula. I've got *no* blood."
❏ Ambulance driver Whitman tries his best line on "nurse" Blair: "How come something like you picked something like this for a career?"
❏ When Whitman finds Blair crying over the death of a little boy, he ask, "What are you? A nurse or a woman?" "Because I wear a starched uniform, does that make me any less a woman?" the phony nurse responds.

Hell's Half Acre (1954) 91 min. Wendell Corey, Evelyn Keyes, Keye Luke, Philip Ahn, Elsa Lanchester, Marie Windsor, Nancy Gates. **Screenplay by:** Steve Fisher. **Directed by:** John H. Auer. **Noir Type:** On the Run. **Noir Themes:** Betrayal, greed, revenge. ★½

When a songwriting gangster (Corey) is blackmailed by one of his former hoods, his moll (Gates) takes matters into her own hands, shooting the extortionist in the head. The appreciative Corey volunteers to take the rap, figuring he can get off by claiming self-defense. While he is in a Honolulu jail, his greedy partner (Ahn), during one of his many temper tantrums, accidentally kills Gates. After identifying her body at the morgue, Corey escapes and hides out in Hell's Half Acre, a high-crime slum district, hoping to find his girl's killer. Meanwhile, back in the States, Keyes hears Corey's latest song on the radio and, after recognizing some key words, realizes that the writer might be her long-lost husband, a sailor who was reported missing during the Japanese attack on Pearl Harbor. She says goodbye to her fiancé and travels to Hawaii, where she meets up with a wacky cab driver (Lanchester) and a police lieutenant (Luke) who is also searching for Corey. After learning that her husband might be holed up in Hell's Half Acre, Keyes goes undercover as a taxi dancer in a club there, confronting the dangerous Ahn. The Hawaiian setting is pleasant enough, but the script is confusing, unexciting and downright silly. Noir icon Windsor is wasted as the adulterous wife of one of Ahn's goons.

Familiar Faces from Television:

❏ Jesse White (Jesse Leeds, one of Danny Thomas' agents on *The Danny Thomas Show* and the bored Maytag repairman in TV commercials) as Windsor's cuckolded husband.

Hell's Island (1955) 83 min. John Payne, Mary Murphy, Eduardo Noriega, Francis L. Sullivan, Arnold Moss, Walter Reed. **Screenplay by**: Maxwell Shane. **Directed by**: Phil Karlson. **Noir Type**: Femme Fatale. **Noir Themes**: Betrayal, greed. ★★

   Payne, an $87.50–a-week special security officer (i.e., bouncer) for a Las Vegas casino, is approached by wheelchair-bound Sullivan and his goon (Reed), who want to hire him to find a missing ruby. Reluctant at first, the former assistant D.A., who lost his job because he started boozing heavily when his fiancée (Murphy) married another guy, jumps at the opportunity after learning that Murphy might be involved. After arriving on the Latin American island where Murphy lives, Payne runs into a number of obstacles—a determined policeman (Noriega), a shady antique dealer (Moss), a convention of annoying jukebox salesmen and some hungry alligators— before discovering that Murphy isn't the sweet girl he once loved. Payne overdoes the tough-guy role, but otherwise this standard adventure yarn is mildly enjoyable.

Familiar Face from Television:
❑ Paul Picerni (Agent Lee Hobson in *The Untouchables*) as Murphy's imprisoned husband.

Her Kind of Man (1946) 80 min. Dane Clark, Janis Paige, Zachary Scott, Faye Emerson, George Tobias, Harry Lewis, Howard Smith, Sheldon Leonard. **Screenplay by**: Leopold Atlas and Gordon Kahn. **Directed by**: Frederick de Cordova. **Noir Type**: Gangster. **Noir Themes**: Fatalism, jealousy, betrayal, revenge. ★★

   When Prohibition is repealed, a sociopathic bootlegger (Scott) takes up gambling, kills a crooked gambler (Leonard) in self-defense, goes into the casino business with his brother-in-law (Tobias) and dukes it out with Clark, his romantic rival for the affection of his fiancée (nightclub singer Paige). Emerson plays Scott's sister, Smith is the homicide detective out to prove that Scott is a murderer, and Lewis is Scott's sycophantic goon, who gets slapped one too many times by his abusive boss. With flashbacks that run four deep, this familiar rise-and-fall tale is interesting only because of the fine cast (especially Lewis). Janis Paige went on to star in the short-lived TV situation comedy *It's Always Jan* and had a small role in the drama series *Trapper John, M.D.*

Familiar Faces from Television:
❑ James Flavin (Lt. Donovan in *Man with a Camera*) as a poker player.
❑ John Dehner (reporter Duke Williams in *The Roaring Twenties*) as a guest at the grand opening of Scott's casino.

Memorable Noir Moments:
❑ Sensitivity Training Required: After slapping his right-hand man (Lewis), Scott is chastised by Tobias and Emerson. "Some guys are like women," Scott responds defensively. "Slap 'em down — they love you more."
❑ A detective asks a fatally wounded murder suspect if he knows who shot him. The man replies, "Did I deserve it?" "You did," answers the cop. "Then what's the difference?" the man asks before taking his last breath.

Hidden Fear (1957-U.S./Danish) 83 min. John Payne, Alexander Knox, Conrad Nagel, Natalie Norwick, Anne Neyland. **Screenplay by**: André De Toth. **Directed by**: André De Toth and John Ward Hawkins. **Noir Type:** Wrong Woman. **Noir Themes:** Greed, woman in jeopardy. ★½

A two-fisted American cop (Payne) travels to Copenhagen, where his kid sister (Norwick) has been wrongly imprisoned for murdering her fiancé. While trying to find the real killer, he becomes involved with a counterfeit ring led by Knox and Nagel, and even manages to find time to romance his sister's friend (Neyland). This joint American-Danish production is unentertaining and tedious, with Payne overdoing the tough guy routine, as was his wont at times. There are some nice on-location shots of Copenhagen.

Memorable Noir Moment:
❏ Norwick swears she's innocent of her fiancé's murder but isn't exactly sorry he's dead. "Tony was a busy boy," she tells Payne. "A woman in every town and there were a lot of towns."

The Hidden Room (1949-British) 98 min. Robert Newton, Sally Gray, Phil Brown, Naunton Wayne. **Screenplay by:** Alec Coppel. **Directed by:** Edward Dmytryk. **Noir Type:** Payback. **Noir Themes:** Betrayal, jealousy, paranoia. ★★★

Anglo-American relations are put to the test when an American (Brown) becomes romantically involved with the wife of a British psychiatrist (Newton). Fed up with his straying wife's indiscretions, Newton decides to murder her newest lover. He kidnaps the unlucky Brown and for months keeps him chained to a bed in the cellar of a bombed-out building, waiting for just the right time, when he can be sure that Scotland Yard does not suspect him. In the meantime, he prepares an acid bath to dispose of the body. The perfect crime. Or is it? Newton's wife (Gray) suspects that he's murdered Brown, but the fear of scandal keeps her from reporting her suspicions to the police. An annoyingly persistent Scotland Yard superintendent (Wayne) is on the case and, if that's not enough to delay Newton's murderous intentions, there's also a surprise nemesis in Gray's little dog (see *The Man with My Face*, *The Killing* and *Lady Gangster* for other doggie spoilers). Also known as *Obsession*, this is an enjoyable and effective British suspensor with Newton (TV's *Long John Silver*) quite good as the cuckolded psychiatrist, and Brown equally competent as his likable prisoner.

Memorable Noir Moment:
❏ When Brown suggests that his affair with Newton's wife was just a "harmless flirtation," the gun-wielding psychiatrist responds, "You've heard of 'the last straw,' haven't you, Bill? Well, you're it."

High Sierra (1941) 100 min. Ida Lupino, Humphrey Bogart, Alan Curtis, Arthur Kennedy, Joan Leslie, Barton MacLane, Cornel Wilde. **Screenplay by:** John Huston and W.R. Burnett. **Directed by:** Raoul Walsh. **Noir Type:** Gangster. **Noir Themes:** Obsession, betrayal, paranoia, greed. ★★★★

Bogey's a gangster who's been paroled after eight years in prison thanks to the influence of his aging crime boss, who needs him to pull a heist at a swanky California resort. While driving to the West Coast, the sensitive killer admires the gorgeous scenery, visits the farm where he grew up, and comes to the aid of a young club-footed girl (Leslie) and her family. He eventually arrives at the hideout of his inexperienced accomplices (Curtis and Kennedy), who have been fighting over Curtis' moll (Lupino). MacLane plays the ex-cop who has taken Bogey's place in the crime ring's hierarchy, and Wilde is the squeamish resort hotel clerk who's in on the heist. Bogart was billed beneath Lupino in this outstanding, seminal gangster noir, but his performance was so exceptional that he received top billing in every film afterward. He was the fourth choice for the role of "Mad Dog" Roy Earle, after James Cagney, George Raft and Paul Muni, who all turned it down. Screenwriter Huston would make his directorial debut that year with *The Maltese Falcon*, and he asked Bogey to play Sam Spade after Raft rejected the role. It was Bogey's biggest break yet. Director Walsh remade *High Sierra* as a western, *Colorado Territory* (1949), and Stuart Heisler tried his hand at it with *I Died a Thousand Times* (1955).

Familiar Face from Television:
❑ Willie Best (Willie Slocum in *Waterfront* and Charlie, the elevator operator, in *My Little Margie*) as Algernon.

Memorable Noir Moments:
❑ Sensitivity Training Required: After Lupino decides to get off the bus to go back where she came from, the driver remarks, "Just like all dames, she don't know whether she's comin' or goin'."
❑ Bogey describes Leslie as "mighty pretty." "Is she?" Lupino asks. "Yeah, and decent," Bogey replies undiplomatically, never noticing the hurt in her eyes.
❑ Bogey encourages Lupino to take his gun and use it to mark the face of her abusive boyfriend. When she can't bring herself to do it, the obliging gangster does it for her.

High Tide (1947) 70 min. Lee Tracy, Don Castle, Julie Bishop, Anabel Shaw, Regis Toomey, Douglas Walton, Anthony Warde. **Screenplay by:** Peter Milne and Robert Presnell, Sr. **Directed by:** John Reinhardt. **Noir Type:** P.I. **Noir Themes:** Betrayal, corruption, jealousy. ★★½

The incoming tide threatens to drown the trapped occupants of a crashed vehicle (newspaper editor Tracy and P.I. Castle). A flashback explains how the two friends found themselves in this predicament: Castle is hired to protect former boss Tracy from a local hood (Warde). When Walton, the owner of Tracy's newspaper, is found murdered, homicide detective Toomey suspect Castle because the P.I. was once involved romantically with Walton's wife (Bishop). Castle and Walton's pretty secretary (Shaw) try to prove his innocence. Sounds confusing, but it's a pretty fair low-budget noir with snappy dialogue and a surprise ending. Tracy and Castle turn in good performances.

Memorable Noir Moments:
❑ From the Some-Things-Never-Change Department: When Tracy asks a retired reporter if he likes reading the newspaper he once worked for, the old-timer replies disgustedly, "Murder, cheesecake, rotten politics, scum dredged up to offend the senses." "Circulation, Pop," explains the editor.
❑ The flirtatious Castle strikes out with Shaw. "How about dinner some night?" he asks. "Second Thursday of next week," she replies.

High Wall (1947) 100 min. Robert Taylor, Audrey Totter, Herbert Marshall, Dorothy Patrick. **Screenplay by:** Sydney Boehm and Lester Cole. **Directed by:** Curtis Bernhardt. **Noir Type:** Amnesia. **Noir Themes:** Fatalism, paranoia, betrayal. ★★★½

Former war hero Taylor returns home to his wife and six-year-old boy after two years in a civilian job in Burma. During one of his frequent blackouts, Taylor awakens to find himself behind the wheel of his car, his wife's dead body alongside him, and the cops chasing him. He drives off the road hoping to commit suicide, but instead winds up an amnesiac in a mental institution, where a psychiatrist (Totter) convinces him to undergo brain surgery to recover his memory. With his memory only partially restored as a result of the operation, he remains convinced that that he killed his wife. When a stranger shows up claiming to have knowledge of a third party (Marshall) at the murder scene, Taylor agrees to undergo narcosynthesis treatment to help him recall the events that led to his wife's death. *High Wall* is a tense psychological thriller with Taylor excellent as the disturbed murder suspect, and noir veteran Totter enjoyable as the prim psychiatrist, whose interest in her patient seems to be more than professional.

Familiar Face from Television:
❏ Ray Teal (Sheriff Roy Coffee in *Bonanza*) as a police lieutenant in charge of the manhunt for escaped mental patient Taylor.

Memorable Noir Moment:
❏ A blackmailing janitor foolishly negotiates with an intended victim while standing on a ladder near an open elevator shaft. While the janitor is bickering about the price, the man casually hooks his cane around one of the ladder's legs and yanks.

Highway Dragnet (1954) 70 min. Richard Conte, Joan Bennett, Wanda Hendrix, Reed Hadley, Mary Beth Hughes. **Screenplay by:** Herb Meadow and Jerome Odlum. **Directed by:** Nathan Juran. **Noir Type:** Wrong Man. **Noir Themes:** Victim of fate, paranoia. ★½

Korean War hero Conte stops for a drink in Las Vegas on his way home and has a minor tussle with an intoxicated former model (Hughes). While hitchhiking the next morning, he's picked up by the Vegas police and accused of strangling her. His only alibi is an Army buddy, who now is nowhere to be found. Naturally, Conte escapes so he can prove his innocence, managing to elude a police lieutenant (Hadley) intent on tracking him down. Along the way Conte becomes involved with a fashion photographer (Bennett) and her model (Hendrix). Poor acting, even by the usually dependable Conte and Bennett, and a muddled script make passing up this low-budget noir an easy decision.

Memorable Noir Moment:
❏ A highway patrolman mistakes an off-duty Marine for murder suspect Conte. When the Marine claims that he was with a lady friend all night, the cop asks, "Was your lady friend alive when you left her?" "She wasn't even alive when I was *with* her," replies the G.I.

Highway 301 (1950) 83 min. Steve Cochran, Virginia Grey, Gaby Andre, Edmon Ryan, Robert Webber, Wally Cassell, Richard Egan, Edward Norris, Aline Towne. **Screenplay by:** Andrew L. Stone. **Directed by:** Andrew L. Stone. **Noir Type:** Gangster. **Noir Themes:** Greed, woman in jeopardy, sexual hostility. ★★★★

Despite the hokey opening statements by the governors of Virginia, Maryland and North Carolina ("This picture may save the life of someone in the audience") and the equally hokey closing remarks by the narrator ("You can't be kind to congenital criminals like these"), this underrated little gem really delivers. The brazen "Tri-State Outfit" (Cochran, Cassell, Webber, Egan and Norris) has been pulling bank jobs in broad daylight, and law enforcement officials from three states and the District of Columbia can't come up with a clue as to their identities. Accompanying the gang are Grey and Towne (Cochran's and Cassell's molls) and Webber's latest girlfriend (Andre), who naively believes he's a traveling salesman. Led by vicious killer Cochran, the gang pulls off an armored car heist, the fabled "biggest haul of all time," which turns out to be one of film noir's darkest ironies. Breathing down their necks is the shrewd cop (Ryan), whose extensive manhunt forces the desperate thugs to scatter to their many hideouts. This is an exciting, fast moving, and exceptionally violent film. While the entire cast is excellent, it's Cochran who shines as the despicable, psychopathic gang leader, who will shoot a dame in the back without blinking an eye. Crime may not pay, but it sure is entertaining.

Memorable Noir Moment:
❑ Cassell, assigned by Cochran to watch over an attractive prisoner, tells his moll, "I gotta make like a watchdog tonight." "Well, make sure you stay in your own kennel," she advises.

Highway West (1941) 61 min. Brenda Marshall Arthur Kennedy, Olympe Bradna, William Lundigan, Slim Summerville, Willie Best. **Screenplay by:** Kenneth Gamet and Charles Kenyon. **Directed by:** William McGann. **Noir Type:** Newlywed. **Noir Themes:** Woman in jeopardy, betrayal. ★½

Bank robber Kennedy is on the run, and his unsuspecting bride (Marshall), who thinks he's a traveling salesman (see *Highway 301* for another naive dame), doesn't find out the truth about him until it's too late. After Kennedy is wounded, she abandons him at a doctor's office, where the cops catch up to him. Sentenced to life imprisonment at Folsom Prison, Kennedy serves only three years before escaping. He heads straight for Marshall, who has made a new life for herself and her teenage sister (Bradna) as the owner of a combination motel–diner–gas station. Lundigan plays Marshall's boyfriend, a fish and game warden. Summerville (one of Max Sennett's original Keystone Cops in the 1920s) and Best provide the "comedy" relief. (Best's embarrassing performance was typical of Hollywood's insensitive portrayals of African-Americans in the 1940s.) Even though Kennedy is good as the vicious killer, *Highway West* is a waste of time.

Familiar Faces from Television:
❑ Frank Wilcox (John Brewster in *The Beverly Hillbillies*) as a motorcycle cop.
❑ James Westerfield (John Murrel in *The Travels of Jaimie McPheeters*) as a truck driver at Marshall's diner.

His Kind of Woman (1951) 120 min. Robert Mitchum, Jane Russell, Vincent Price, Tim Holt, Charles McGraw, Raymond Burr, Jim Backus. **Screenplay by:** Frank Fenton and Jack Leonard. **Directed by:** John Farrow. **Noir Type:** South of the Border. **Noir Themes:** Paranoia, distrust. ★★★½

Just when you're ready to give up on this as too slow-moving, the snappy dialogue and camp humor draw you back in. It may take a while, but once you're hooked you'll stayed hooked. Mitchum, sleepy-eyed and disinterested as usual, is a gambler who's offered fifty Gs by hoods to go to Mexico and await further instructions. Broke and in debt to an angry bookie, he accepts the offer. At a Mexican resort, Mitchum meets singer Russell and easily convinces her that she's "his kind of woman." While there, he runs into an odd assortment of characters—an ex–Nazi doctor, a hammy actor (Price), a card shark (Backus), a gambling-crazy honeymooner and his bride, an immigration agent (Holt) and a gangster (McGraw). Eventually, he discovers that he's there to participate in a plan that will allow a deported mobster (Burr) to re-enter the U.S. *His Kind of Woman* certainly deserves its status as a camp classic, thanks to terrific performances, especially by Burr, who's just sensational as the wild-eyed, sadistic gangster, and Price in a hilarious self-parody. (If you're tempted to give up before Price arrives on the scene, give it a little more time. He's worth the wait.)

Familiar Face from Television:
❏ Marjorie Reynolds (Riley's wife Peg in *The Life of Riley*) as Price's soon-to-be ex-wife.

Memorable Noir Moments:
❏ Not used to handing out compliments, Mitchum tells songbird Russell, "I've heard better, but you sing like you do it for a living."
❏ Sensitivity Training Required: Russell volunteers to help rescue Mitchum from Burr's clutches, but Price informs her, "This is a man's work. Women are for weeping."
❏ Russell walks in on Mitchum while he's ironing his money. "What do you do when you have no money?" she asks. "I iron my pants," he replies.
❏ While Mitchum is taking a savage beating from Burr and his henchman aboard a yacht, a wounded Price, enjoying every minute of the adventure, rushes to his rescue. After rounding up a number of armed hotel guests and some Mexican Keystone Cops, the actor promises them that "survivors will get a part in my next picture." He then piles them into a motorboat, ignoring protests that there are too many hombres onboard, and valiantly takes his place, *à la* George Washington crossing the Delaware. The boat sinks like a rock.

Hit and Run (1957) 84 min. Hugo Haas, Cleo Moore, Vince Edwards. **Screenplay by**: Hugo Haas. **Directed by**: Hugo Haas. **Noir Type**: Good Twin, Bad Twin. **Noir Themes**: Lust, jealousy. ✶

A typical Haas mess: a half-hearted femme fatale (Moore), a jovial cuckold (Haas) and his ex-con twin brother (Haas again), a horny mechanic (Edwards) all involved in an inane murder plot. Throw in a sexy lion tamer and you have another turkey written, produced and directed by (did I mention starring?) Hugo Haas. Worth viewing only for laughs. Vince Edwards went on to play the lead role in the TV series *Ben Casey*, and Cleo Moore, who starred in six other Haas films, retired and eventually ran for governor of Louisiana. She lost.

The Hitch-Hiker (1953) 71 min. Edmund O'Brien, Frank Lovejoy, William Talman. **Screenplay by**: Collier Young and Ida Lupino. **Directed by**: Ida Lupino. **Noir Type**: Hostage. **Noir Themes**: Victim of fate, paranoia. ✶✶✶

Two buddies (O'Brien and Lovejoy) heading north to the mountains for a fishing

A killer (William Talman) keeps his one good eye on the map and on his hostages (Frank Lovejoy, left, and Edmond O'Brien) in *The Hitch-Hiker* (RKO, 1953).

trip impulsively decide to drive south toward Mexico instead. Along the way they pick up a hitchhiker (Talman), an escaped convict who has been robbing and killing motorists. The unlucky friends are forced to drive the killer five hundred miles across the desert to the Mexican town of Santa Rosalia, where the killer hopes to find a boat to take him to California. One of the hostages cracks under the strain; the other remains calm and hopeful. Talman is terrific as the sadistic psycho with a paralyzed eyelid that never closes, even when he sleeps. Based on the true story of a real-life spree killer, *The Hitch-Hiker* is a bit dated but definitely worth a viewing.

Memorable Noir Moment:
❑ Talman traces his emotional problems back to childhood. "When I was born," he tells his hostages, "they took one look at this puss and told me to get lost."

Hitler's Children (1942) 80 min. Tim Holt, Bonita Granville, Kent Smith, Otto Kruger, H.B. Warner, Lloyd Corrigan. **Screenplay by:** Emmet Lavery. **Directed by:** Edward Dmytryk. **Noir Type:** Nazi. **Noir Themes:** Woman in jeopardy, betrayal, fatalism. ★★★½

Narrated by a Smith, a teacher at an American school in Berlin, the film involves a German youth (Holt) and an American girl (Granville), who fall in love despite their disparate moral and political views. Holt grows up to be a Gestapo officer and Granville, who was born in Germany and thus considered a German citizen, is sent to a labor camp for re-education and impregnation to produce offspring for the Fuehrer. Smith, Granville's employer and former teacher, attempts to find her and get her out of the country. Meanwhile, Holt seems determined to protect Granville from his Gestapo superior (Kruger), who fears her American values and spunk and wants to have her sterilized along with other societal "misfits." Warner plays a courageous Catholic bishop, and Corrigan is a less-than-heroic German reporter. Surprisingly well-done and thought provoking, this early anti–Nazi propaganda film was a big sensation with the American public, who would soon have first-hand contact with Hitler's dedicated children on the battlefield. Holt and Granville do well as the ill-fated lovers, and Warner is terrific as the intrepid cleric.

Familiar Face from Television:
- ❑ Hans Conried (Uncle Tonoose in *The Danny Thomas Show* and the voice of Snidley Whiplash in *The Bullwinkle Show*) as the education minister.

Memorable Noir Moment:
- ❑ A frightened journalist responds feebly to Smith's request for help. "I wouldn't make a very good hero," he says honestly, adding, "I don't even make a good Nazi."

Hollow Triumph (1948) 83 min. Paul Henreid, Joan Bennett, John Qualen. **Screenplay by:** Daniel Fuchs. **Directed by:** Steve Sekely. **Noir Type:** Impersonator. **Noir Themes:** Obsession, paranoia. ★★★★

Henreid plays a criminal just released from jail and already in deep trouble. He and his gang rob a gambling joint owned by Qualen, but only Henreid survives the heist. Knowing that he's being hunted by the vengeful mobster, he goes into hiding, taking on menial jobs and eventually concocting a plan to assume the identity of a psychiatrist who's his exact look-alike (except for that scar on his cheek). But the plan has some major flaws, which result in a wonderfully ironic twist ending. Bennett, the psychiatrist's secretary and mistress, falls in love with his impersonator. Also known as *The Scar*.

Familiar Face from Television:
- ❑ Jack Webb (Sgt. Friday in *Dragnet*), in his film debut, as a hit man nicknamed Bulls-eye.

Memorable Noir Moment:
- ❑ Henreid, at his new job, nervously pumps gas for two hit men on his trail. (Gas is an amazing 25 cents a gallon, and the cheapskate killers order a buck's worth.)

Hollywood Story (1951) 76 min. Richard Conte, Julie Adams, Richard Egan, Henry Hull, Jim Backus. **Screenplay by:** Fred Brady and Frederick Kohner. **Directed by:** William Castle. **Noir Type:** Show Biz. **Noir Themes:** Jealousy, betrayal. ★★

Loosely based on a true murder mystery, this tediously slow film stars Conte as a neophyte producer who decides to make a film about the 20-year-old murder of a silent film director. Before long, someone's taking potshots at Conte and trying to frame him for murder. Adams plays the daughter of a famous silent film star, and

Hull is an out-of-work screenwriter employed by Conte. Egan is the cop investigating the still-open case, and Backus, in an irrelevant role, plays Conte's agent and the film's narrator. Boring stuff despite the presence of noir veteran Conte. Several famous silent film stars, including Elmo Lincoln, the screen's first Tarzan, and Francis X. Bushman, the original Ben Hur, make cameo appearances.

Familiar Face from Television:
❑ Joel McCrea (Marshal Mike Dunbar in *Wichita Town*) as himself.

Memorable Noir Moment:
❑ Conte enters a funeral parlor to obtain information on the murder case he's been researching and is greeted by a stuffed-shirt undertaker. "We are sorry for your loss," the man recites. Amused, Conte replies, "I was just browsing."

The Hoodlum (1951) 61 min. Lawrence Tierney, Edward Tierney, Allene Roberts, Lisa Golm. **Screenplay by:** Sam Neuman and Nat Tanchuk. **Directed by:** Max Nosseck. **Noir Type:** Jailbird. **Noir Themes:** Lawbreaking for kicks. ★★

Tierney plays a sociopathic con who is granted an early release from prison because his Ma (Golm) sobs before the Parole Board. Tierney's good-guy brother (played by Tierney's real life sibling, Edward) reluctantly takes him on at the family-owned gas station. The jailbird promptly repays his brother's kindness by stealing his girl (Roberts) and getting her pregnant. The nine-to-five world doesn't hold much interest for the ex-con, especially after he notices an armored car pull up in front of the bank across the street from the station. This is pretty lame stuff, but the ingeniously planned heist saves the film. While Edward Tierney's career went nowhere after this movie, big brother Lawrence had an impressive Hollywood career that continued into the late 1990s. The middle Tierney brother, Scott Brady, played in a number of B films, gaining minor fame on TV as *Shotgun Slade*.

Memorable Noir Moment:
❑ Tierney's Ma, on her deathbed, finally wises up and tells her bad boy, who's always hated the smell of the nearby dump, "You *are* the smell. You *are* the stink."

Hoodlum Empire (1952) 98 min. Brian Donlevy, John Russell, Claire Trevor, Forrest Tucker, Vera Ralston, Luther Adler. **Screenplay by:** Bob Considine and Bruce Manning. **Directed by:** Joseph Kane. **Noir Type:** Gangster. **Noir Themes:** Betrayal, corruption. ★★

Gangster Russell (TV's *The Lawman*) returns from the war with a French bride (Ralston) and attempts to go straight. He breaks up with his former moll (Trevor), distances himself from the crime syndicate headed by his uncle (Adler) and opens a small-town gas station with his GI buddies. His former superior officer (Donlevy), now a U.S. Senator, is heading up a crime commission to investigate Adler and his psychopathic henchman (Tucker), who implicate the innocent Russell by laundering illegal gambling money in his name. A routine crime drama with lots of familiar noir and TV faces. Tucker went on to star in the popular 1960s TV comedy Western *F Troop*.

Familiar Faces from Television:

A war hero (John Russell) gets the best of a hood trying to install slot machines in his diner in *Hoodlum Empire* (Republic, 1952).

- ❏ William Schallert (Patti's dad in *The Patty Duke Show*) as the Senate committee inquiry clerk.
- ❏ Roy Roberts (Captain Huxley in *Oh Susanna*) as a police chief.
- ❏ Richard Jaeckel (Lt. Martin Quirk in *Spenser: For Hire* and Lt. Ben Edwards in *Baywatch*) as one of Russell's GI buddies.
- ❏ Whit Bissell (Gen. Heywood Kirk in *The Time Tunnel*) as a pickpocket.

House by the River (1950) 88 min. Louis Hayward, Lee Bowman, Jane Wyatt, Dorothy Patrick. **Screenplay by:** Mel Dinelli. **Directed by:** Fritz Lang. **Noir Type:** Period. **Noir Themes:** Betrayal, guilt. ★★★

A struggling writer (Hayward) makes a pass at his new servant (Patrick) and accidentally strangles her when she screams. When his brother (Bowman) discovers the body, Hayward begs him to help dispose of it. A sucker for his whining kid brother and in love with Hayward's wife (Wyatt), Bowman helps him toss the body into a nearby-polluted river. The publicity surrounding the case of the missing girl gives Hayward's writing career the boost it needed, and before long he's signing autographed copies of his latest book and penning a new novel based on Patrick's murder. Meanwhile, a worried Bowman learns that the burlap bag containing the body had his name stenciled on the inside of it. This is an atmospheric little gem with Hayward giving a good performance as the reprehensible murderer.

Familiar Face from Television:
❏ Kathleen Freeman (Katie the maid in *Topper* and Flo Shafer in *The Beverly Hillbillies*) as a chunky square dancer.

Memorable Noir Moment:
❏ When a neighbor complains about the putrid river, the ecology-minded Bowman observes, "It's people who should be blamed for the filth, not the river."

House of Bamboo (1955) 105 min. Robert Ryan, Robert Stack, Shirley Yamaguchi, Cameron Mitchell, Sessue Hayakawa. **Screenplay by:** Harry Kleiner. **Directed by:** Samuel Fuller. **Noir Type:** Far East. **Noir Themes:** Betrayal, corruption, sexual hostility. ★★★

Stack, an American Army cop in Tokyo, infiltrates Ryan's gang of veterans, who are suspected of having killed an American soldier and several Japanese during a recent military train heist. Yamaguchi, the widow of one of the robbers, moves in with Stack in an undercover role herself—a "kimono girl" (a hooker who caters to

An undercover cop (Robert Stack) enjoys a bath, Japanese style, with a little help from a kimono girl (Shirley Yamaguchi) in *House of Bamboo* (20th Century–Fox, 1955).

foreigners)—to help him find her husband's killer. Mitchell is Ryan's *ichi-ban*, his "number one boy," who's jealous of Stack's growing stature in the gang and of Ryan's strange attraction to the newcomer. Hayakawa has a small role as a Tokyo detective. Essentially a remake of *The Street with No Name*, *House of Bamboo* is fast-moving (despite the slow-to-blossom romance between Stack and Yamaguchi) and beautifully photographed, but the poor editing job during the film's climax (a flub that has Ryan fleeing from the same stairwell twice) hurts the otherwise technically appealing production.

Familiar Face from Television:

❏ DeForest Kelley (Dr. Bones McCoy in *Star Trek*) as a gang member.

Memorable Noir Moments:

❏ Ryan plans to have the Japanese police kill Stack during a staged robbery. "How do you like that for top-level strategy?" he asks. "A straitjacket would fit you just right," Stack replies.
❏ When a bank job is blown because of undercover man Stack's intervention, Ryan thinks another gang member squealed. Bursting in on the unfortunate gangster while he's bathing, Ryan empties his gun. With water pouring out of the holes in the wooden tub, he carries on a one-way conversation with the dead man, expressing his disappointment in him.

House of Horrors (1946) 65 min. Robert Lowery, Virginia Grey, Bill Goodwin, Rondo Hatton, Martin Kosleck. **Screenplay by:** George Bricker **Directed by:** Jean Yarbrough. **Noir Type:** Horror. **Noir Themes:** Revenge, paranoia, betrayal. ★★½

Hatton, who needed no makeup to play his monster parts (he suffered from a disfiguring disease of the pituitary gland called acromegaly), reprises his role of "The Creeper," first introduced to audiences in the Sherlock Holmes movie *The Pearl of Death*. Pulled from the river by suicidal artist Kosleck, the grateful psychopath begins killing his rescuer's enemies, the New York art critics who Kosleck believes are persecuting him. Along the way, the Creeper knocks off a couple of women because they scream when he chases them (who wouldn't?). Goodwin is the homicide detective investigating the killings, Lowery plays a commercial artist suspected by Goodwin, and Grey is Lowery's art critic girlfriend. Dark and shadowy, *House of Horrors* is mostly laughable, but there are worse ways to spend an hour. The actors do a good job, except for poor Hatton, who played the Creeper one last time in *The Brute Man* (also released in 1946) before dying of a heart attack the same year.

Familiar Faces from Television:

❏ Virginia Christine (the widow Ovie in *Tales of Wells Fargo*) as a streetwalker.
❏ Byron Foulger (Wendell Gibbs in *Petticoat Junction*) as an easily swayed art customer.
❏ Alan Napier (Alfred the butler in *Batman*) as an arrogant art critic.
❏ Syd Saylor (Wally in *Waterfront*) as the morgue attendant.

House of Numbers (1957) 90 min. Jack Palance, Barbara Lang, Harold J. Stone, Edward Platt. **Screenplay by:** Don Mankiewicz. **Directed by:** Russell Rouse. **Noir Type:** Prison. **Noir Themes:** Jealousy, paranoia, fatalism. ★★½

Palance (in a dual role) plays brothers in this prison break-in, breakout flick.

The younger brother, an ex-boxer, is serving a life sentence in San Quentin for beating a man to death for talking to his wife (Lang) at a bar. After the prisoner pushes a guard over the railing of his third-tier cellblock, Palance, fearing his brother will be sentenced to death if the guard dies, plans to break into prison to trade places with him — temporarily. The meticulous plan, however, is jeopardized by an observant, but corrupt, prison guard (Stone). Complicating things, the elder Palance is beginning to fall for his brother's wife. Despite its ingenious premise and competent acting, this prison noir (which co-stars the real-life inmates of San Quentin) falls short of its potential because of gaping holes in the script and a cop-out ending. Platt, who plays the warden, later played the "Chief" in the hit 1960s TV spy comedy *Get Smart*.

Memorable Noir Moment:
❑ Political correctness in the 1950s? Stone explains to Palance that cons should now be referred to as "inmates" and prison guards should called "correctional officers."

House of Strangers (1949) 101 min. Edward G. Robinson, Susan Hayward, Richard Conte, Luther Adler, Efrem Zimbalist, Jr., Paul Valentine, Debra Paget. **Screenplay by:** Philip Yordan. **Directed by:** Joseph L. Mankiewicz. **Noir Type:** Soap Opera. **Noir Themes:** Family dysfunction, betrayal, greed, lust. ★★½

Robinson, barber turned successful banker, reigns over his Italian-American family like a feudal lord. While sons Adler, Zimbalist, and Valentine work at menial jobs in his bank, his favorite son (Conte) is a successful attorney. When Robinson is brought up on charges of violating banking laws, it's Conte who winds up serving a seven-year prison stretch. Things fall apart for Robinson when his other sons betray him by putting him out to pasture and taking over the bank. Beautiful Hayward is the classy dame Conte has fallen for despite his engagement to Paget. The dialogue between Conte and Hayward is meant to be sexy and cute, but comes off as silly. Only an excellent performance by Robinson, despite his exaggerated Italian accent, saves this boring film. Zimbalist went on to star in the highly successful TV series *77 Sunset Strip* and *The F.B.I.*

Memorable Noir Moments:
❑ When the government shuts down Robinson's bank on a technicality, Conte asks him, "Have you read the new Banking Act?" The old man replies, "I don't even read-a the old one."
❑ During an argument over traditional values, Paget's prudish mother tells Robinson, "I'll have you know my husband died happy." The old banker replies, "Your husband was *happy to die*. That's-a different."

The House on 92nd Street (1945) 88 min. William Eythe, Lloyd Nolan, Signe Hasso, Gene Lockhart, Leo G. Carroll, Harry Bellaver. **Screenplay by:** Barré Lyndon, Jack Moffit and John Monks, Jr. **Directed by:** Henry Hathaway. **Noir Type:** Nazi. **Noir Themes:** Conspiracy, distrust. ★★★★

This exciting espionage thriller, based on actual events, stars Eythe as a patriotic college student who is approached by pre–World War II Nazi spies and invited to visit Germany. He immediately reports the incident to G-man Nolan, who recruits

An undercover F.B.I. agent (William Eythe, left) watches as a suspicious Nazi spy (Leo G. Carroll) inspects a crate in *The House on 92nd Street* (20th Century–Fox, 1945).

him as a double agent. After graduating from a spy school in Hamburg, Eythe reports to his Nazi contacts (Hasso, Carroll and Bellaver) in New York. The spies are suspicious of Eythe but have no choice except to trust him with stolen American secrets, which he then turns over to Nolan. The story also involves the Nazis' plan to steal America's A-bomb secrets and how dedicated F.B.I. personnel, using painstaking, pre-computer age techniques, foil the plot. A forerunner of future police procedurals such as *T-Men* and *The Naked City*, the film's semi-documentary style works well, giving the story an enjoyable sense of realism. With the exception of the leading actors, all of the F.B.I. personnel portrayed in the film were real-life Bureau employees.

Familiar Faces from Television:
- ❑ E.G. Marshall (Lawrence Preston in *The Defenders*), in his film debut, as a morgue attendant.
- ❑ Vincent Gardenia (Frank Lorenzo in *All in the Family*) as a student learning to make bombs at a Nazi spy-training school.
- ❑ Paul Ford (Colonel Hall in *The Phil Silvers Show*) as a police desk sergeant.

The House on Telegraph Hill (1951) 93 min. Richard Basehart, Valentina Cortese, William Lundigan, Fay Baker. **Screenplay by:** Elick Moll and Frank Partos. **Directed by:** Robert Wise. **Noir Type:** Impersonator. **Noir Themes:** Woman in jeopardy, greed, betrayal. ★★½

Nazi concentration camp prisoner Cortese gets more than she bargained for when she steals the identity of her best friend, who died in the camp. After the war, she travels to the U.S. pretending to be the mother of her friend's little boy, who stands to inherit the fortune of the deceased aunt he had been living with since he was born. Cortese falls in love with and marries the boy's guardian (Basehart) and moves into a stately mansion overlooking San Francisco. It isn't long before she begins to suspect that Basehart and the boy's governess (Baker) are a couple. When she's almost killed in a suspicious car accident, the desperate woman seeks out a former Army officer (Lundigan) whom she met in Poland. It's a long haul to the end of this slow-moving film, but the climactic payoff, a wonderful bit of film noir irony, is worth the wait. Italian actress Cortese and Basehart were real-life husband and wife for many years. Lundigan went on to host the long-running dramatic anthology series *Climax* and the monthly musical variety series *Shower of Stars* (both ran from 1954 to 1958 on CBS).

The Houston Story (1956) 79 min. Gene Barry, Barbara Hale, Edward Arnold, Paul Richards, John Zaremba, Frank Jenks, Jeanne Cooper. **Screenplay by:** James B. Gordon. **Directed by:** William Castle. **Noir Type:** Gangster. **Noir Themes:** Greed, betrayal, lust, obsession. ★★½

Barry is a greedy "working stiff" oil driller with a brilliant plan to tap into the oil lines belonging to the big companies and sell the siphoned oil to foreign governments—to the tune of five million dollars a year. The local crime lord (Arnold) and his boss (Zaremba) think Barry has a pretty good idea and back his scheme. For a while, Barry is sitting pretty, putting his best friend (Jenks), an honest cab driver, in charge of his dummy corporation. But it all starts crumbling when Arnold's jealous second-in-command (Richards) tries to double-cross Barry. Cooper plays Barry's waitress girlfriend, whom he drops for a nightclub singer (Hale, cast way against type as a treacherous femme fatale). It's a bit slow at times but Hale, who performs a sexy rendition of "Put the Blame on Mame," is exciting. Barry later gained fame in TV's *Bat Masterson* and *Burke's Law*, while Richards went on to star in the series *Breaking Point* and Zaremba played in *I Led Three Lives* and *The Time Tunnel*.

Memorable Noir Moments:

❑ Barry discourages his marriage-minded girlfriend, saying, "Three's a crowd, honey. I don't like the idea of a mortgage sitting down with us every time we eat."
❑ A police inspector, offering a new definition for a familiar term, says, "A flunky is a hood with a Social Security number."

Human Desire (1954) 90 min. Glenn Ford, Gloria Grahame, Broderick Crawford, Edgar Buchanan. **Screenplay by:** Alfred Hayes. **Directed by:** Fritz Lang. **Noir Type:** Femme Fatale. **Noir Themes:** Obsession, lust, sexual hostility, character deterioration, betrayal, jealousy. ★★½

A jealous railroad employee (Broderick Crawford) discusses a romantic rival with his wife (Gloria Grahame) in *Human Desire* (Columbia, 1954).

Ford is a Korean War veteran who returns to his stateside job as a train engineer. He becomes involved with Grahame, the wife of the railroad company's assistant train master (Crawford), after her jealous husband commits a vicious murder. Desperate to retrieve from Crawford an incriminating letter that can connect her to the killing, Grahame tries to convince Ford to murder him. Buchanan (TV's *Judge Roy Bean*) plays Ford's friend and co-worker. A tawdry remake of Jean Renoir's provocative *La Bete Humaine*, which starred Simone Signoret, *Human Desire* is notable mainly for Grahame's solid performance as the abused wife.

Familiar Face from Television:
❏ John Zaremba (Special Agent Jerry Dressler in *I Led Three Lives* and Dr. Raymond Swain in *The Time Tunnel*) as a train conductor named Russell.

Memorable Noir Moment:
❏ Grahame's blonde pal responds to Crawford's remark that dames think an awful lot about dressing up. "Much better to have good looks than brains," she says, "because most of the men *I* know can see much better than they can think." Later, she theorizes that "all women are alike. They've just got different faces so the men can tell them apart."

The Human Jungle (1954) 82 min. Gary Merrill, Jan Sterling, Paula Raymond, Chuck Connors, Regis Toomey, Emile Meyer. **Screenplay by:** William Sackheim and Daniel Fuchs. **Directed by:** Joseph M. Newman. **Noir Type:** Police Procedural. **Noir Themes:** Corruption, paranoia, woman in jeopardy. ★★½

Thanks to a pretty good correspondence course, a cop (Merrill) passes the bar exam and tells his superior (Meyer) that he wants to quit and go to work for a well-known law firm. Meyer, however, convinces him to replace the kindly, but inept, captain of the city's worst precinct. Facing resentment from his new men, the ambitious Merrill begins a crackdown on crime, rounding up every two-bit hood and juvenile delinquent in his jurisdiction, while investigating the brutal murder of a local call girl. Raymond is his understanding wife, Toomey is his trusted lieutenant and Sterling plays a singing stripper, who acts as an alibi for a vicious killer (Connors). This low budget noir is nicely done. Connors, who went on to star in TV's *The Rifleman* a few years later, gives a good performance as the cocky killer.

Familiar Faces from Television:
❏ Claude Akins (Sheriff Elroy Lobo in two series—*B.J. and the Bear* and *Lobo*) as a hood.
❏ James Westerfield (John Murrel in *The Travels of Jaimie McPheeters*) as an incompetent police captain.
❏ Henry Kulky (Otto Schmidlap in *The Life of Riley*) as a bartender.

Memorable Noir Moments:
❏ A cop reflects sadly on the body of a murdered call girl, saying, "When are these floozies gonna learn?"
❏ Connors, while chasing the terrified Sterling through a bottling plant, resorts to name calling. "You rotten dame!" he screams in frustration.

Humoresque (1946) 123 min. Joan Crawford, John Garfield, Oscar Levant, J. Carrol Naish, Joan Chandler, Ruth Nelson, Paul Cavanagh. **Screenplay by:** Clifford Odets and Zachary

Gold. **Directed by:** Jean Negulescu. **Noir Type:** Ambition. **Noir Themes:** Obsession, fatalism. ★★★

The heavy-drinking wife (Crawford) of a liberal-minded older man (Cavanagh) has a stable of paramours at her beck and call but takes a special interest in a young, ambitious violinist (Garfield). After jumpstarting Garfield's struggling career by getting him an audition with a famous conductor and signing him up with a well-known manager, Crawford falls in love with the seemingly unimpressed musician. Garfield, whose poor working class parents (Naish and Nelson) own a New York neighborhood grocery store, gains fame, loses interest in his childhood girlfriend (Chandler) and eventually falls for Crawford. Nelson turns thumbs down on her son's affair with the twice-married socialite, who she feels will destroy his career, but Garfield defies his devoted mother and makes plans to marry Crawford when her divorce is finalized. Unfortunately, his first love, music, drives a wedge between them, leading to tragedy and Garfield's plaintive lament, "Nothing comes free. One way or another, you pay for what you are." Originally intended as a starring vehicle for Garfield after his tremendous success in **The Postman Always Rings Twice**, this "woman's melodrama" became all Crawford's after she won an Oscar for her performance in **Mildred Pierce**. The entire cast is excellent, but Levant, as Garfield's wisecracking accompanist, has the best lines.

Familiar Faces from Television:
❑ Tom D'Andrea (Gillis in *The Life of Riley*) as Garfield's brother.
❑ Craig Stevens (Peter Gunn) as one of Crawford's idolizing young men.

Memorable Noir Moments:
❑ Levant levels with Garfield, who is becoming impatient while waiting for his big break. "You're suffering from the old American itch," he tells him. "You wanna get there fast, and you don't wanna pay for the ride."
❑ "I enjoy people who drink," Levant remarks while Garfield attempts to sober up Crawford. "At least they know what to blame everything on."

Hunt the Man Down (1950) 68 min. Gig Young, Lynne Roberts, James Anderson, Harry Shannon, Gerald Mohr, Cleo Moore. **Screenplay by:** DaVallon Scott. **Directed by:** George Archainbaud. **Noir Type:** Whodunit. **Noir Themes:** Victim of the law, betrayal. ★★

Stock whodunit with Anderson as a con who escaped after being wrongly convicted of a murder twelve years earlier. He's back in jail now because of the publicity he received for stopping a stickup man in the bar where he (Anderson) worked. Young, the dedicated public defender convinced of Anderson's innocence, gets on the trail of the real killer. Shannon plays Young's father, a one-armed ex-cop who comes out of retirement to help his son. Somebody is out to stop the investigation and doesn't care who gets killed in the process. Well-acted but slow moving, this low budget noir isn't one of Young's best.

The Hunted (1948) 88 min. Preston Foster, Belita, Pierre Watkin, Frank Ferguson, Larry Blake. **Screenplay by:** Steve Fisher. **Directed by:** Jack Bernhard. **Noir Type:** Jailbird. **Noir Themes:** Betrayal, paranoia. ★★

Former English ice skater Belita plays, as she did in *Suspense* two years earlier, an ice skater! This being a film noir, she's also an ex-con, paroled after four years in prison for participating in a jewelry heist with her brother and his accomplice (Blake). Still maintaining her innocence, she looks up her old flame (Foster), the cop who arrested her. Foster, however, is a bit nervous because after the trial she threatened to kill him. But he finds her a place to live and a job working as a figure skater for a local hockey arena managed by Ferguson. Foster, of course, falls in love all over again. But just when he convinces himself of Belita's innocence, her former lawyer (Watkin), whom she also had threatened, is found murdered. When Belita takes it on the lam, Foster, unhappy about being played for a sucker again, vows to hunt her down. It's not as good as it sounds.

Memorable Noir Moment:
❑ Belita asks homicide detective Foster the $64,000 question: "What happens to a guy's heart when he becomes a cop?" He has no answer.

I Confess (1953) 95 min. Montgomery Clift, Anne Baxter, Karl Malden, Brian Aherne, O.E. Hasse, Dolly Haas. **Screenplay by:** George Tabori and William Archibald. **Directed by:** Alfred Hitchcock. **Noir Type:** Religion. **Noir Themes:** Fatalism, paranoia, guilt, betrayal. ★★★

After rectory employee Hasse, disguised as a Catholic priest, kills a shady attorney while robbing the man's Quebec home, he confesses his crime to priest Clift. Bound by the seal of the confessional, Clift cannot reveal the killer to police investigator Malden. Malden, who has found witnesses who saw a priest leave the attorney's house on the night of the murder, begins to suspect that Clift may be the killer. When the cop discovers that the deceased attorney had been blackmailing Clift's former girlfriend (Baxter), now married to an important politician, he charges the priest with the murder. Meanwhile, Hasse, worried that Clift might crack under the strain and break the confessional seal, plants evidence implicating him. Aherne is the prosecutor, and Haas is Hasse's conscience-stricken wife. This minor Hitchcock film isn't one of The Master's best efforts, but Clift gives a nicely subdued performance, and Baxter is good as the woman in love with a memory.

Memorable Noir Moment:
❑ Before he's arrested, Clift wanders the streets of Quebec trying to decide whether to give up the priesthood and go on the lam. At one point he stops at a movie theater and stares at an advertisement of the current attraction — the 1951 Bogart film noir *The Enforcer*.

I Died a Thousand Times (1955) 109 min. Jack Palance, Shelley Winters, Lori Nelson, Lee Marvin, Earl Holliman, Lon Chaney, Jr. **Screenplay by:** W.R. Burnett. **Directed by:** Stuart Heisler. **Noir Type:** Gangster. **Noir Themes:** Betrayal, paranoia, greed. ★★½

A faithful, but inferior, remake of the classic *High Sierra*, this film stars Palance as the sympathetic (but dangerous) ex-con involved in a jewel caper. On his way to join his inexperienced partners (Marvin and Holliman) at a mountain lodge, Palance meets a poor family traveling west, and is attracted to the pretty granddaughter (Nelson), who needs an operation to cure her clubfoot. He falls in love with her and pays

An ex-con (Jack Palance) and his new moll (Shelley Winters) in *I Died a Thousand Times* (Warner Bros., 1955).

for the ungrateful girl's surgery, but it's his new moll (Winters) who winds up sticking by him through the botched-up heist. Chaney plays the seriously ill crime boss, who bought Palance a pardon from his life sentence. Palance gives it his best effort but is unable to duplicate Bogey's sensational performance. Entertaining, but see the original first. Nelson went on to co-star in the TV comedy *How to Marry a Millionaire*, and yes, that's Dennis Hopper getting a mambo lesson from Winters.

Familiar Face from Television:
❑ Nick Adams (Johnny Yuma in *The Rebel*) as a nervous bellboy.

Memorable Noir Moment:
❑ A cliché-spouting crook gets the drop on Palance: "Give me any trouble and I'll fill ya full of lead."

I, Jane Doe (1948) 85 min. Ruth Hussey, Vera Ralston, John Carroll, Gene Lockhart, John Howard, Benay Venuta. **Screenplay by**: Decla Dunning and Lawrence Kimble. **Directed by**: John H. Auer. **Noir Type**: Trial. **Noir Themes**: Betrayal, revenge. ★½

Ludicrous tale of an illegal French immigrant (Ralston) brought to trial for the murder of an ex–G.I. (Carroll). She refuses to talk and won't even give her real name, hence the Jane Doe tag given her by the media. After she's found guilty and sentenced to death, she receives a stay of execution when it's discovered that she's pregnant. Motherhood also brings a change of heart, and she decides she wants to talk after all. She's granted a new trial and gets herself a new lawyer — the victim's wife (Hussey). Via flashbacks, the jury finally gets to hear her pathetic tale — how she fell in love with and married fighter pilot Carroll after he was shot down in France, how she followed him to America after he abandoned her, and how she discovered that he was already married. Lockhart and Howard play the prosecutors, and Venuta is a lawyer on Hussey's staff (which, interestingly for the 1940s, seems to be composed entirely of women).

Familiar Face from Television:
❑ Myron Healey (Doc Holliday in *The Life and Legend of Wyatt Earp*) as a hospital intern.

I Love Trouble (1947) 93 min. Franchot Tone, Janet Blair, Janis Carter, Adele Jergens, Steven Geray, Tom Powers, Glenda Farrell, Lynn Merrick. **Screenplay by:** Roy Huggins. **Directed by:** S. Sylvan Simon. **Noir Type:** P.I. **Noir Themes:** Betrayal, jealousy. ★★

Tone plays a jaunty gumshoe hired by a politician (Powers) to find out about his wife's past (she turns out to have been a bubble dancer). During his investigation, the private eye is beaten up several times, flirted with by just about every woman in the film except his faithful secretary (Farrell), and arrested for murder by homicide detective Powers. Keeping track of the female characters (Blair, Carter, Jergens and Merrick) is the key to following this confusing noir. Geray plays a shady nightclub owner. Interesting primarily for a peek at two relative newcomers to film, Raymond Burr and John Ireland, who play Geray's hoods.

Memorable Noir Moment:
❑ A tough chauffeur warns Tone him about continuing his investigation. "There ain't nothin' in it for you but a Chicago overcoat," he says.

I Married a Communist (1950) 73 min. Robert Ryan, Laraine Day, Janis Carter, John Agar, Thomas Gomez, William Talman. **Screenplay by:** Robert Hardy Andrews and Charles Grayson. **Directed by:** Robert Stevenson. **Noir Type:** Commie. **Noir Themes:** Conspiracy, lust, betrayal. ★★½

Ryan, the newly married vice-president of a shipping company, has a secret past: As a young member of the Communist Party, he killed a man during a Party-agitated riot. Unfortunately for him, Commies Gomez and Carter (Ryan's former lover) want him back now that he holds such an influential position. They blackmail him into sabotaging labor negotiations with the longshoreman's union, forcing a strike. Ryan's bride (Day) is in the dark about his tainted past and is justifiably confused by his violent mood swings. Her impressionable brother (Agar) falls in love with Commie temptress Carter and begins spouting Party propaganda at union meetings. Carnival worker Talman doubles as a contract killer for the Party. Also known as *The Woman on Pier 13*, this standard Red hysteria film was produced by billionaire Howard Hughes (see Hughes' other Red films *I Was a Communist for the F.B.I.* and *The Whip Hand*). Carter is enjoyable as the Party's femme fatale.

A commie bad guy (Thomas Gomez, left) blackmails a former Party member (Robert Ryan, right), now a successful capitalist, in *I Married a Communist* (RKO, 1950).

I, the Jury (1953) 87 min. Biff Elliot, Preston Foster, Peggie Castle, Margaret Sheridan, Elisha Cook, Jr. **Screenplay by:** Harry Essex. **Directed by:** Harry Essex. **Noir Type:** P.I. **Noir Themes:** Revenge, sexual hostility. ★★

A one-armed man sits at his desk looking over photographs. The front door opens slowly and a hand appears, holding a gun wrapped in a towel. The startled man gets up, but a shot rings out and he falls to the floor, seriously wounded. Crawling to the telephone, he dies just as he reaches it. It's the Christmas season, and "Hark the Herald Angels Sing" is playing in the background, scarcely heard over an electrifying jazz score. *I, the Jury* begins *and* ends with a bang, but everything in between is wearisome. Elliot plays Mike Hammer, Mickey Spillane's famous detective, and he's out to avenge the murder of his best friend. Sheridan is his secretary, who, along with every other woman in the film, can't seem to resist the manly P.I. Foster plays the homicide detective who tries to keep Elliot in line, and Castle is the sexy psychiatrist who has more on her mind than psychoanalyzing the cute private eye. Noir veteran Cook plays a dimwitted bee collector and part-time Santa Claus. There are a few exciting fight scenes, but the slow-moving plot is much too confusing, and Elliot is just not believable as Spillane's brutal, virile, misogynistic, homophobic detective. Ralph Meeker was the definitive Mike Hammer in 1955's ***Kiss Me Deadly***.

A psychiatrist (Peggie Castle) tries to seduce private eye Mike Hammer (Biff Elliot) in *I, the Jury* (United Artists, 1953).

Familiar Face from Television:

❏ Joe Besser ("Stinky" on *The Abbott and Costello Show*) as an elevator operator.

Memorable Noir Moments:

❏ Elliot warns a guy to keep his mouth shut. "Act like a clam," he tells him, "or I'll open you up like one."

❏ The girlfriend of a murdered man, over her period of mourning and out on the town, swears, "From now on, no one cuts me so deep that I can't close the wound."
❏ In the arms of a gorgeous femme fatale, the well-prepared detective pulls the trigger as she reaches for a gun. "Mike, how *could* you?" she gasps in surprise. "It was easy," answers the P.I., as she slumps to the floor.

I Wake Up Screaming (1941) 82 min. Betty Grable, Victor Mature, Carole Landis, Laird Cregar, Elisha Cook, Jr., Alan Mowbray, Allyn Joslyn. **Screenplay by:** Dwight Taylor. **Directed by:** H. Bruce Humberstone. **Noir Type:** Whodunit. **Noir Themes:** Obsession, lust, corruption, jealousy. ★★★½

In this film noir take-off of *Pygmalion*, Mature plays a sports promoter who, for kicks, turns waitress Landis into a celebrity. Has-been actor Mowbray and columnist Joslyn, who are both involved in Mature's plan to make Landis famous, fall head over heels for her. Unfortunately, someone murders her just as she's about to travel to Hollywood to star in her first movie. Landis' sister (Grable) is hoping the killer's not Mature, but homicide detective Cregar goes after the promoter with a vengeance. Veteran character actor Cook plays a weirdo desk clerk in the sisters' apartment

An angry sports promoter (Victor Mature) roughs up a hotel desk clerk (Elisha Cook, Jr.) in *I Wake Up Screaming* (20th Century–Fox, 1941).

building. This is an entertaining film (if you can ignore the constant playing of *Over the Rainbow*), with moments of genuine dread thanks to Cregar's remarkable performance. Mature and Grable, in her first major non-musical role, are excellent together. The dark city streets, dense shadows and unusual camera angles sometimes clash with the film's humorous moments, but somehow the suspense is maintained. Two of the stars died several years later — Cregar, at 28, in 1944 due to complications associated with a crash diet, and Landis, at 29, in 1948 from an overdose of sleeping pills. Remade as *Vicki* in 1953.

Familiar Face from Television:
❑ Chick Chandler (Toubo Smith in *Soldiers of Fortune*) as a reporter.

Memorable Noir Moments:
❑ When Mowbray complains that women are all alike, Joslyn counters, "For Pete's sake, what difference does that make? You've got to have them. They're standard equipment."
❑ Mature wakes up to find the huge, menacing Cregar sitting beside his bed. "Someday you're going to talk in your sleep," Cregar says, "and when that day comes I want to be around."

I Walk Alone (1948) 98 min. Burt Lancaster, Lizabeth Scott, Kirk Douglas, Wendell Corey, Mike Mazurki, Kristine Miller, Marc Lawrence. **Screenplay by:** Charles Schnee. **Directed by:** Byron Haskin. **Noir Type:** Payback. **Noir Themes:** Betrayal, revenge, greed. ★★★

A cynical ex-con (Lancaster) is paroled after serving fourteen years on a murder charge. Because of a prior agreement with his former bootlegging partner (Douglas), Lancaster expects to return home as co-owner of a successful nightspot, The Regent Club. But double-crossing Douglas has other plans. Lancaster's pal (Corey), a bookkeeper for Douglas, is guilt-stricken over his part in the double cross, and a sultry nightclub singer (Scott) falls for Lancaster after she learns what a heel boyfriend Douglas really is. Miller is the society widow Douglas is planning to marry for "business reasons," noir veteran Mazurki is the club's tough doorman and bouncer, and Lawrence is a bootlegger turned used car salesman. The excellent cast turns this average crime story into a fast-moving, entertaining noir. Corey is especially good as the morose bookkeeper.

Memorable Noir Moments:
❑ Lancaster and Miller aren't discussing baseball at the bar. "You're a very attractive man," she says. "Keep going," he says. "How far do you want me to go?" she asks. Lancaster smiles. "I'm at the plate. You're doing the pitching."
❑ After performing, Scott asks the audience if there are any requests. Her romantic rival Miller asks for *I Lost My Man*. "I'm sorry," Scott says, "but I don't think I know the words to that." "You ought to learn them," Miller meows.
❑ Lancaster, accustomed to dealing with double-crossers the old-fashioned way, storms into Douglas' office with four goons and tries to coerce him into writing a contract confirming their 50–50 partnership in the club. The unconcerned Douglas has Corey explain to the bewildered Lancaster how the club is really three different corporations and that Lancaster can't come up with anything less than eight and a half percent, *after* stockholder approval. It's a riot.

A nightclub bookkeeper (Wendell Corey, seated) explains corporate law to an angry ex-part-ner (Lancaster) and his thugs, while the club's owner (Kirk Douglas, front right) looks on in *I Walk Alone* (Paramount, 1948).

I Walked with a Zombie (1943) 69 min. Tom Conway, Frances Dee, James Ellison, Edith Barrett, James Bell, Christine Gordon, Darby Jones. **Screenplay by**: Curt Siodmak and Ardel Wray. **Directed by**: Jacques Tourneur. **Noir Type**: Horror. **Noir Themes**: Woman in jeopardy, betrayal, fatalism, guilt. ★★★★½

Nurse Dee is hired by a sugar cane plantation owner (Conway) to care for his catatonic wife (Gordon) in the West Indies. Dee quickly falls for her charming boss and, out of love for him, tries desperately to awaken Gordon from her trance-like state. When medical treatment fails, she resorts to voodoo. Ellison, Conway's half-brother, thinks that Conway deliberately drove his wife insane; the family doctor (Bell) feels that Gordon needs insulin shock treatment, which could kill her; and the natives believe she's a zombie. Barrett plays the stepbrothers' mother, a medical missionary, who blames herself for Gordon's condition, and Jones is the wide-eyed zombie with marching orders from the witch doctor. A short, eerily beautiful film, the horror is ingeniously suggestive, making it all the more frightening. The cast's low-key performances, the haunting cinematography and the creepy, drum-dominated soundtrack help make this an unforgettable horror classic.

Memorable Noir Moment:

❑ Conway conducts a less-than-upbeat new employee orientation. "There's no beauty here, only death and decay," he tells Dee. Conway's depressing attitude must be contagious because Dee later informs him, "Your wife isn't living. She's in a world that's empty of joy and meaning."

I Want to Live! (1958) 120 min. Susan Hayward, Simon Oakland, Virginia Vincent, Theodore Bikel, Wesley Lau, Philip Coolidge, Lou Krugman, James Philbrook, Joe De Santis. **Screenplay by:** Don Mankiewicz and Nelson Gidding. **Directed by:** Robert Wise. **Noir Type:** Wrong Woman. **Noir Themes:** Woman in jeopardy, victim of fate, betrayal, guilt. ★★★★

Based on the true story of good-time party girl and convicted murderess Barbara Graham, the premise of this melodrama is that Graham (Hayward) was innocent of beating an elderly woman to death during a robbery and was unjustly sentenced to die in California's gas chamber. The film traces the prostitute's many run-ins with the law and her temporary rehabilitation after marrying a bartender (Lau) who becomes an abusive drug addict. To support her baby, she joins up with petty crooks Coolidge, Krugman and Philbrook, until all are arrested for the murder. Philbrook, who turns state's evidence, claims that Hayward, who had spurned his advances earlier, did the actual killing. Coolidge and Krugman, supposedly the real murderers, keep quiet, hoping all the publicity that "Bloody Babs" is getting will somehow help their case. When all three are convicted and sentenced to die, a guilt-stricken newspaperman (Oakland) tries to undo the damage done by the media and their spectacular news coverage of the trial. Along with Hayward's attorney (De Santis) and a kind-hearted psychologist (Bikel), Oakland crusades relentlessly for a new trial. Vincent plays Hayward's more sensible prostitute girlfriend, who goes straight. While Hayward's character is far from sympathetic and the film assumes her innocence despite an abundance of evidence to the contrary, *I Want to Live!* is guaranteed to provoke strong feelings about the death penalty. The script is powerful and thought provoking in its presentation of the mental and emotional agonies of prisoners on Death Row, and Hayward's intense performance earned her, finally, a Best Actress Oscar. The film was up for five other Academy Awards, including a Best Director nomination for Wise, who actually witnessed an execution at San Quentin in preparation for the film.

Familiar Faces from Television:
- ❏ Gage Clark (Superintendent Bascom in *Mr. Peepers*) as Hayward's first lawyer.
- ❏ Dabbs Greer (Mr. Jonus in *Gunsmoke* and the Reverend Robert Alden in *Little House on the Prairie*) as a captain at San Quentin.
- ❏ Raymond Bailey (banker Milburn Drysdale in *The Beverly Hillbillies*) as the warden.
- ❏ Gavin MacLeod (Murray Slaughter in *The Mary Tyler Moore Show* and Captain Merrill Stubing in *The Love Boat*) as an angry cop during Hayward's interrogation.
- ❏ Peter Breck (Nick Barkley in *The Big Valley* and Clay Culhane in *Black Saddle*) as Hayward's phony alibi.
- ❏ Jack Weston (Chick Adams in *My Sister Eileen* and Walter Hathaway in *The Hathaways*) as a drunken G.I. at a party.
- ❏ Brett Halsey (Paul Templin in *Follow the Sun*) as a sailor at a party.

Memorable Noir Moments:

❑ When Hayward throws a cup of water into an interrogator's face, the cop fumes, "Lousy hop-headed slut. I'd like to spread you out and stamp you into the ground."
❑ "Whom do you wish to be notified in case of death or serious illness?" asks a prison matron. "Marlon Brando," cracks Hayward.

I Was a Communist for the F.B.I. (1951) 83 min. Frank Lovejoy, Dorothy Hart, Philip Carey, Richard Webb, Ron Hagerthy, James Millican, Paul Picerni. **Screenplay by:** Crane Wilbur. **Directed by:** Gordon Douglas. **Noir Type:** Commie. **Noir Themes:** Conspiracy, betrayal, paranoia. ★★★½

Unable to tell anyone that he's working undercover for the F.B.I. and has only been *posing* as a faithful Communist Party member for the past nine years, Lovejoy unjustly suffers the alienation of his friends and family and especially his son (Hagerthy) and brother (Picerni). F.B.I. agents Webb and Carey monitor his activities and collect information in preparation for a final showdown with the Commies, who want to "incite riots, discontent and open warfare among the people." Millican is Lovejoy's wary party superior, and Hart is a disillusioned schoolteacher who learns that Communism isn't quite what she expected it to be. Detractors of this film have

An angry American (Paul Picerni) lets his brother (Frank Lovejoy) know what he thinks about Communism in *I Was a Communist for the F.B.I.* (Warner Bros., 1951). Lovejoy's other brother (Russ Conway) and Communist girlfriend (Dorothy Hart) look on.

panned it as a "reprehensible," self-serving propaganda piece, designed to pacify Sen. Joseph McCarthy and the Red hunters of the House Un-American Activities Committee (described in the film by comrade Millican as made up of "fat-headed politicians whose only aim is to crash the headlines"). Politics aside, this tense and suspenseful noir works well, mainly because Lovejoy does such a good job as the beleaguered patriot. Based on a true story, the film takes an interesting peek at the paranoia and fear that permeated American society in the 1950s. In 1953, Red hysteria hit American television in the form of a weekly dramatic series—*I Led Three Lives*, starring Richard Carlson as the undercover man. Its plot was almost identical to *I Was a Communist for the F.B.I.*

Familiar Face from Television:

❑ Russ Conway (Lt. Pete Kile in *Richard Diamond, Private Detective*) as one of Lovejoy's brothers.

Memorable Noir Moment:

❑ When a little boy in Lovejoy's apartment building asks him for some batting advice, the undercover man gladly obliges. The boy's father rushes out of his apartment and tells Lovejoy to stay away from his son. When Lovejoy complains that he was simply teaching him baseball, the man responds coldly, "Baseball is for Americans."

I'll Get You (1952-British) 78 min. George Raft, Sally Gray, Clifford Evans, Reginald Tate. **Screenplay by:** John Baines. **Directed by:** Seymour Friedman. **Noir Type:** Undercover. **Noir Themes:** Conspiracy. ★★

F.B.I. agent Raft, posing as a production designer for a large aircraft corporation, sneaks into London to search for Evans, the head of a ring that's kidnapping American scientists and selling them to the Russians. The G-man and a spunky British intelligence agent (Gray) scour the British underworld for the bad guys and wind up falling in love. How could the young, attractive secret agent resist the 60-year-old charmer? Tate plays Gray's boss, and Piper is the Scotland Yard inspector assigned to find illegal immigrant Raft. Okay British programmer (originally titled *Escape Route*), worth viewing just to see tough guy Raft walk around while wearing a dainty apron.

Memorable Noir Moment:

❑ From the Some-Things-Never-Change Department: After Raft casually sneaks away from the airport, avoiding immigration officials, a Scotland Yard official remarks, "What are they running down there? Immigration control or a game of hunt the missing alien?"

Illegal (1955) 88 min. Edward G. Robinson, Nina Foch, Hugh Marlowe, Albert Dekker, Ellen Corby, Jan Merlin, Jayne Mansfield. **Screenplay by:** W.R. Burnett and James R. Webb. **Directed by:** Lewis Allen. **Noir Type:** Boozer. **Noir Themes:** Character deterioration, corruption, betrayal. ★★★

A flamboyant D.A. (Robinson) with political ambitions convicts an innocent man of murder. When the real murderer confesses, Robinson is too late to stop the poor guy from frying. Guilt-ridden ("I'd rather see 100 guilty men go free than execute another innocent man"), he quits his job and hits the bottle hard, ending his budding romance with his former assistant (Foch), who marries co-worker Marlowe on the rebound. When Robinson finally sobers up, he starts his own practice, attracting the attention of crime lord Dekker, who hires him as a mouthpiece for the mob. His grandstanding (including drinking a bottle of poison to prove it was harmless) makes him a favorite with the grateful mobsters. Merlin is Dekker's nasty henchman; Corby, in a step up from her usual maid roles, plays Robinson's faithful secretary; and Mansfield has a small part as a sexy piano player. This fast-paced film is entertaining thanks in large part to Robinson's hard-boiled performance.

Familiar Faces from Television:
❏ Edward Platt (Maxwell Smart's Chief in *Get Smart*) as the new D.A.
❏ Henry Kulky (Otto Schmidlap in *The Life of Riley*) as a witness to a murder.
❏ DeForest Kelley (Bones McCoy in *Star Trek*) as the innocent man convicted of murder.

Memorable Noir Moment:
❏ When a murder suspect is advised to seek legal help, he responds disgustedly, "I'm through with mouthpieces. They take the fee, I take the rap."

Illegal Entry (1949) 84 min. Howard Duff, Marta Toren, George Brent, Tom Tully, Paul Stewart, Richard Rober. **Screenplay by:** Art Cohen and Joel Malone. **Directed by:** Frederick de Cordova. **Noir Type:** Undercover. **Noir Themes:** Paranoia, lust. ★★½

Immigration and Naturalization Service agent Brent recruits a pilot (Duff) to infiltrate a ring that's smuggling illegal European aliens into the U.S. by way of Mexico. Headed by Rober, Tully and Brent, the ring ("vicious and rotten and trading in on peoples' miseries") has been tossing illegals out of airplanes whenever INS agents get too close. Duff falls for his Army buddy's widow (Toren) even though she seems to be involved with the bad guys. Good performances by Duff and Stewart highlight this above average B movie.

Familiar Face from Television:
❏ Kenneth Tobey (Chuck Martin in *The Whirlybirds*) as a pilot.

Memorable Noir Moment:
❏ From the Some-Things-Never-Change Department: the film opens with statements by two real-life INS officials who confirm that "our greatest single problem is illegal entry."

Impact (1949) 111 min. Brian Donlevy, Ella Raines, Helen Walker, Charles Coburn, Anna May Wong. **Screenplay by:** Dorothy Reid and Jay Dratler. **Directed by:** Arthur Lubin. **Noir Type:** Triangle. **Noir Themes:** Betrayal. ★★★

This is an interesting yarn about a ruthless businessman (Donlevy), the *Double Indemnity*–type victim of his scheming wife (Walker) and her lover (Kolb). The tables are turned, however, when Donlevy survives but is believed to have been killed. Starting a new life in a small Idaho town, he meets gas station owner and war widow Raines, who hires him as an auto mechanic. The fresh Idaho air soon has Donlevy falling in love and trying to forget his former life. Meanwhile, Walker is in a heap of trouble as the prime suspect in his "murder." Will he do the right thing and reveal that the reports of his death were greatly exaggerated? The acting is good and the plot intriguing, but the ending is a big letdown. Donlevy is terrific, as is Walker, who gives Barbara Stanwyck a run for her money in the femme fatale department. Coburn, who should have spent more time perfecting his Irish brogue, plays the elderly cop who breaks the case, and Wong is Donlevy's frightened housekeeper. Gossip queen Sheilah Graham makes a cameo appearance as herself.

Familiar Face from Television:
❑ Clarence Kolb, (Vernon Albright's boss, Mr. Honeywell, in *My Little Margie*) as Donlevy's boss.

Memorable Noir Moment:
❑ Sensitivity Training Required: Former grease monkey Donlevy offers to take over for Raines under the hood, adding, "That's no job for a girl."

Impulse (1955) 80 min. Arthur Kennedy, Constance Smith, Joy Shelton, Jack Allen, James Carney. **Screenplay by:** Cy Endfield and Lawrence Huntington. **Directed by:** Charles De la Tour and Cy Endfield (uncredited). **Noir Type:** Femme Fatale. **Noir Themes:** Betrayal, greed, victim of fate. ★★

Kennedy, an American real estate agent in England, finds himself becoming increasingly bored — with his job, his wife and his life in general. While the missus (Shelton) is visiting her mother in London, Kennedy comes to the aid of a beautiful cabaret singer (Smith) with car trouble, and ends up having a brief fling with her. Unfortunately, Smith turns out to be the partner of a jewel thief (Allen) who is being hunted by an angry mobster (Carney) determined to get his share of the loot. Kennedy soon finds himself on the run as a murder suspect and pining for the good old, unexciting days. This British "thriller" is boring, but the usually dependable Kennedy gives it his best shot.

In a Lonely Place (1950) 94 min. Humphrey Bogart, Gloria Grahame, Frank Lovejoy, Carl Benton Reid, Art Smith, Martha Stewart. **Screenplay by:** Andrew Solt. **Directed by:** Nicholas Ray. **Noir Type:** Show Biz. **Noir Themes:** Paranoia, distrust, jealousy, sexual hostility. ★★★★

When a hatcheck girl at a Hollywood restaurant (Stewart) is strangled, a violence-prone screenwriter (Bogart), the last person the girl was seen with, becomes the number one suspect. Bogey's next-door neighbor (Grahame) provides him with an alibi, and detectives Reid and Lovejoy are forced to release him. Bogey and Grahame fall in love, giving his writing a much-needed boost, to the delight of his agent (Smith). Grahame, however, discovers Bogey's violent side after she witnesses him pummel a driver during an episode of road rage. She begins to suspect that perhaps he murdered Stewart after all. Meanwhile, Bogey has been walking around whistling "The Wedding March." Noir icons Bogart and Grahame are wonderful as the lovers doomed by their mutual paranoia and suspicions.

Familiar Faces from Television:
❑ Billy Gray (Bud on *Father Knows Best*) as a kid seeking autographs outside a Hollywood restaurant.
❑ Myron Healey (Doc Holliday in *The Life and Legend of Wyatt Earp*) as a post office clerk.

Memorable Noir Moments:

❑ Having said that she liked Bogey's face, Grahame fends off the screenwriter's advances. "I said I liked it," she tells him. "I didn't say I wanted to kiss it."
❑ A former girlfriend, who has been unsuccessful in contacting him by telephone, asks Bogey, "Don't you like to talk any more?" "Not to people who have my number," replies Mr. Cool.

Inner Sanctum (1948) 62 min. Charles Russell, Mary Beth Hughes, Lee Patrick. **Screenplay by:** Jerome Todd Gollard. **Directed by:** Lew Landers. **Noir Type:** Cover-Up. **Noir Themes:** Child in jeopardy, fatalism, betrayal. ★★½

Russell kills his wife during a struggle on a train station platform and tosses her body onto a departing freight train. A young boy sees him disposing of the body but thinks it's just a package. When heavy rains and an overflowing river wash out the roads, Russell is stranded at the boarding house where the kid and his annoyingly overprotective mother (Patrick) live. When word about the murder gets around, Russell decides to cover up his crime by killing the boy, who he fears will eventually make the connection. Hughes plays the lonely boarder who doesn't care that Russell's a killer. This entertaining little noir had no connection to the famous radio series of the same title.

Memorable Noir Moments:

❑ Old sod Willie (Roscoe Ates), making conversation at the dinner table, remarks, "When you tell a woman over 40 she's beautiful, you're not a liar, you're a philanthropist."
❑ When Hughes discovers the boy tied up in Russell's room, she tells the killer, "You're even too bad for me."
❑ When Hughes hints that she knows Russell killed his wife, he tells her, "You're very pretty, when you're lips aren't moving."

Inside Job (1946) 65 min. Preston Foster, Alan Curtis, Ann Rutherford, Jimmy Moss, Milburn Stone. **Screenplay by:** George Bricker and Jerry Warner. **Directed by:** Jean Yarbrough. **Noir Type:** Jailbird. **Noir Themes:** Guilt, betrayal. ★★

An ex-con (Curtis), working as a mime in a department store window, is blackmailed by his ex-partner (Foster) into stealing the store's Christmas receipts. Curtis decides that if he's going to get involved in a heist, he might as well keep all of the dough. He enlists his pretty wife (Rutherford) in his scheme, and together they walk away with more than 250 Gs. On the lam, the two hide out from the cops, the D.A. (Stone) and the enraged Foster, who wants his share of the take. In their tenement hideout, the couple befriends a little boy; Rutherford starts falling for the kid, with disastrous results. This slow and insipid crime-doesn't-pay tale was adapted from a story co-written by Tod Browning, director of the original (1931) *Dracula*.

Familiar Faces from Television:

❑ Joe Sawyer (Sgt. Biff O'Hara in *The Adventures of Rin Tin Tin*) as Todd's police officer dad.
❑ Ruby Dandridge (Oriole in *Beulah* and Delilah in *Father of the Bride*) as Todd's nanny.

Invasion of the Body Snatchers (1956) 80 min. Kevin McCarthy, Dana Wynter, Larry Gates, King Donovan, Carolyn Jones. **Screenplay by:** Daniel Mainwaring [as Geoffrey Homes]. **Directed by:** Don Siegel. **Noir Type:** Impersonator. **Noir Themes:** Paranoia, betrayal, distrust. ★★★★

A doctor (McCarthy) and an old flame (Wynter) find themselves on the run from weird alien organisms that have taken over the bodies of nearly everyone in their small California town. The film opens with a hysterical McCarthy relating his fantastic story to two disbelieving physicians at a San Francisco hospital. Via flashback, the film follows McCarthy as he returns home from a medical convention to find that "something evil had taken possession of the town." A number of his patients and friends seem to be experiencing (as psychiatrist Gates describes it) "an epidemic of mass hysteria," claiming that their loved ones aren't the same people they used to be … literally. That's because, as McCarthy, Wynter and their friends (Donovan and Jones) discover, family members are being replaced in their sleep by clones growing out of enormous pods which somebody is placing near their beds. The sleep-deprived quartet dare not close their eyes for a moment lest they too awaken as emotionless creatures in "an untroubled world where everyone is the same." Realizing that they can trust no one in town, they frantically try to contact federal and state authorities in the hope that somebody will believe them before it's too late. Meanwhile, trucks filled with the grotesque pods are hitting the highways and traveling in every direction. *Invasion* has gained a reputation over the decades as a science fiction cult classic, and deservedly so, thanks to an intelligent script by the blacklisted Daniel Mainwaring (writing as Geoffrey Homes) and solid performances by McCarthy and Wynter. Based on the Jack Finney novel *The Body Snatchers*, the film spawned (pardon the pun) a number of imitations and a more special effects-oriented remake in 1978. McCarthy made a cameo appearance in that film, reprising his role of the panic-stricken doctor.

Familiar Faces from Television:
- ❑ Tom Fadden (Duffield in *Broken Arrow* and Silas Perry in *Cimarron City*) as a lawn-mowing victim of the pod people.
- ❑ Virginia Christine (the widow Ovie in *Tales of Wells Fargo*) as Fadden's suspicious niece.
- ❑ Dabbs Greer (Mr. Jonus in *Gunsmoke* and the Reverend Robert Alden in *Little House on the Prairie*) as an alien gas station attendant.
- ❑ Richard Deacon (Mel Cooley in *The Dick Van Dyke Show*) as a hospital doctor.
- ❑ Whit Bissell (Gen. Heywood Kirk in *The Time Tunnel*) as a hospital psychiatrist.

Memorable Noir Moment:
- ❑ "Keep your eyes wide and blank. Show no interest or excitement," McCarthy warns Wynter as they try to fool the emotionless aliens into believing they too have been changed. Ten seconds later, the forgetful Wynter screams at the sight of a dog running in front of a bus.

The Iron Curtain (1948) 87 min. Dana Andrews, Gene Tierney, June Havoc, Berry Kroeger, Stefan Schnabel, Eduard Franz. **Screenplay by:** Milton Krims. **Directed by:** William A. Wellman. **Noir Type:** Commie. **Noir Themes:** Conspiracy, paranoia, betrayal. ★★★

Based on a true story, *The Iron Curtain* is about a code clerk (Andrews) at the Russian Embassy in Canada, who becomes disillusioned with the Soviet Union's preparation for a war of conquest. Taking top secret embassy documents to prove the Soviets are stealing atomic secrets, Andrews and his wife (Tierney) attempt to defect. It's not as easy as he expected, though, when busy Canadian officials don't

A defector wannabe (Dana Andrews, seated right) is intimidated by Russian secret police in *The Iron Curtain* (20th Century–Fox, 1948).

have time to meet with him, and the newspapers think he's a crackpot. Meanwhile, back at the embassy, boss man Schnabel and his comrades are in panic mode, trying to figure out how to save their own hides after Party headquarters in Moscow learns that its intricate spy network is in danger of collapsing. Kroeger plays a Commie spy who's infiltrated Canadian politics, and Franz is a rum-dum Russian major, whose disappointment with the Party and his Marxist hero father may lead him to a firing squad. Havoc plays the femme fatale embassy secretary who uses her charms to test the loyalty of newly arrived Party members. This is a well-done, early Red menace noir, with Andrews giving a solid, low-key performance.

Memorable Noir Moment:

❑ Andrews, aware that turning over classified papers to Canadian authorities could mean a death sentence for him and his family, decides to take a stand. "We must all die sooner or later, so it doesn't really matter," he says. "It's how we die and why we die that's important."

Iron Man (1951) 81 min. Jeff Chandler, Evelyn Keyes, Stephen McNally, Rock Hudson, Jim Backus. **Screenplay by:** George Zuckerman and Borden Chase. **Directed by:** Joseph Pevney. **Noir Type:** Boxing. **Noir Themes:** Paranoia, betrayal. ★★★½

Coal miners Chandler and Hudson make a career switch and try their hands at boxing. Managed by his ambitious brother (McNally), the normally meek Chandler becomes the ring's "Iron Man," a ferocious, if clumsy, fighter. Hated by the crowd for his dirty tactics, he eventually wins the heavyweight title. His wife (Keyes), who at first sees only dollar signs, eventually realizes that the fight game isn't for her man, and pushes him to open the radio repair store they've always dreamed of owning. Backus plays a sportswriter–boxing manager. Good acting and exciting fight scenes make this a humdinger of a boxing film. The Chandler-Hudson boxing match alone is worth the price of admission.

Familiar Face from Television:
❑ James Arness (Matt Dillon in *Gunsmoke*) as a coal miner.

Memorable Noir Moment:
❑ During one of Chandler's more ruthless fights, a concerned McNally comments, "Blood's thicker than water, especially when it's all over your brother's face."

Isle of the Dead (1945) 72 min. Boris Karloff, Ellen Drew, Marc Cramer, Katherine Emery, Jason Robards, Sr., Helene Thimig. **Screenplay by:** Ardel Wray. **Directed by:** Mark Robson. **Noir Type:** Plague. **Noir Themes:** Fatalism, paranoia, distrust. ★★★

During the Balkan War of 1912, a Greek general (Karloff) and an American war correspondent (Cramer) leave the battleground to visit an island cemetery where Karloff's wife is buried. While on the island, they discover that bodies are missing. At a nearby cottage, an archaeologist (Robards) explains that years ago the villagers began robbing the graves for valuable artifacts and burned the bodies. Robards' superstitious servant (Thimig) tells them that the villagers were destroying legendary demons, called vyrkolakas, and that a servant girl (Drew) is one of these monsters, sucking the life out of her sickly mistress (Emery). At first, Karloff scoffs at Thimig's fears, but when a windborne plague hits the island, and the cottage guests begin dying, he begins to suspect that Drew may be a vyrkolaka after all. This antagonizes Cramer, who's fallen in love with the servant girl. While the group waits for the wind to shift, the paranoid Karloff swears he will protect them from Drew and any other vyrkolakas that happen to show up. This entertaining B horror film from producer Val Lewton and director Mark Robson, who also teamed to do **Bedlam** and **The Seventh Victim**, provides some genuine chills (especially the disturbing mausoleum scene).

Familiar Face from Television:
❑ Alan Napier (Alfred the butler in *Batman*) as Emery's husband.

Memorable Noir Moment:
❑ When Karloff ridicules Thimig's superstitious beliefs, the servant points to Emery. "Look there, there is one who is pale and weak," she says. "And upstairs? There is one who is rosy and red and full of blood."

Ivy (1947) 98 min. Joan Fontaine, Patric Knowles, Herbert Marshall, Richard Ney, Cedric Hardwicke. **Screenplay by:** Charles Bennett. **Directed by:** Sam Wood. **Noir Type:** Femme Fatale. **Noir Themes:** Betrayal, greed. ★★½

Fontaine plays a turn-of-the-century femme fatale attempting to juggle three men — her devoted, unemployed husband (Ney), a lovesick doctor (Knowles) and a wealthy older man (Marshall). Being left alone in Knowles' surgery room with a cabinet full of poisons is just too big a temptation for Fontaine, and it isn't long before she dispatches poor Ney, allowing Knowles to take the blame and freeing her to pursue Marshall. Fontaine is deliciously sociopathic in the title role and has excellent support from the rest of the cast, including her real-life mother, Lillian Fontaine, who has a small part. Now if the film were only twenty minutes shorter....

Jail Bait (1954) 70 min. Lyle Talbot, Herbert Rawlinson, Dolores Fuller, Steve Reeves, Timothy Farrell, Clancy Malone, Theodora Thurman. **Screenplay by**: Edward D. Wood, Jr. **Directed by**: Edward D. Wood, Jr. **Noir Type**: Plastic Surgery. **Noir Themes**: Betrayal, sexual hostility, corruption, law breaking for kicks. ✷

The late Ed Wood, Jr., has the reputation of being the worst director of all time. The questionably noir *Jail Bait*, supposedly his "first legitimate film" and his tribute to the classic TV series *Dragnet*, may not be as bad as his better-known, lower budget films (*Glen or Glenda?*, *Bride of the Monster* and *Plan 9 from Outer Space*), but it's still atrocious. Talbot and Reeves are Los Angeles detectives investigating an

Left to right, a plastic surgeon (Herbert Rawlinson), a cop (John Robert Martin), the surgeon's daughter (Dolores Fuller), a homicide detective (Lyle Talbot) and an eyewitness (Mona McKinnon) view a killer's new face in *Jail Bait* (Howco, 1954).

armed robbery and murder committed by small-time hoods Farrell and Malone. Fuller plays Malone's sister, Rawlinson is their plastic surgeon father, and Thurman is Farrell's abused moll. The "jail bait" in the title has nothing to do with alluring teenyboppers but refers to Malone's gun, which is the instrument of his downfall. The acting is par for an Ed Wood film — pathetic but enjoyably so. Old pros Talbot and Rawlinson deliver their lines woodenly (pardon the pun), but even they aren't as bad as Fuller (Ed Wood's girlfriend, who got equal billing with veteran character actor Talbot, probably Wood's biggest "name" actor in Wood's stable after Bela Lugosi). This was Thurman's film debut, and as best as can be determined, her last acting job. It's obvious from Rawlinson's performance that the former silent film actor was very ill and was experiencing breathing difficulties during filming. He died of cancer the day after shooting ended. On the bright side, he never had to view the finished product. Talbot migrated to television, where he was a semi-regular in *The Adventures of Ozzie and Harriet* for ten years. Former Mr. America, Mr. World and Mr. Universe, Steve Reeves later starred as Hercules and other mythological characters in a slew of Italian-made cheapies. Ed Wood went on to direct a number of softcore porn flicks before dying in 1978 at the age of 54. To understand Wood's filmmaking philosophy (e.g., the one-take scene), the reader is referred to the excellent 1994 film *Ed Wood* starring Johnny Depp.

Memorable Noir Moments:
- ❏ It's "just a flesh wound," a doctor tells Talbot, referring to a woman who was shot in the back by Farrell. (For more variations of the cliché, see *Guilty Bystander*, *The Enforcer*, *New York Confidential*, *Riot in Cell Block 11*, *Accused of Murder* and *Sleep, My Love*.)
- ❏ Plastic surgeon Rawlinson somberly ponders his profession: "Plastic surgery at times seems to me to be very, very complicated."
- ❏ From the Ed Wood School of Screenwriting: Referring to Talbot, Rawlinson tells Fuller, "This afternoon we had a long telephone conversation earlier in the day."
- ❏ From the Ed Wood School of Editing: The killer flees with Talbot in pursuit. The clean-shaven cop, who was wearing a light colored suit when he began his chase in the living room, has mysteriously grown a mustache and changed into a dark suit by the time he gets to the front porch.

Jealousy (1945) 71 min. Jane Randolph, John Loder, Karen Morley, Nils Asther, Hugo Haas. **Screenplay by:** Arnold Phillips and Gustav Machaty. **Directed by:** Gustav Machaty. **Noir Type:** Triangle. **Noir Themes:** Jealousy, paranoia, betrayal. ★★

This somewhat enjoyable B movie has cab driver Randolph suffering emotional and verbal abuse from her suicidal husband (Asther), a has-been writer. She meets Loder, a successful doctor, and they quickly fall in love. Asther, suspecting that she's cheating, begins following her. To complicate matters, Loder's medical associate (Morley) has been secretly in love with the good doctor for seven years and isn't at all happy about his new relationship with Randolph. Before long somebody commits murder and somebody else gets framed. A mildly entertaining whodunit with some nice photography but no big surprises. Haas, who went on to direct bleak, low-budget melodramas in the 1950s, has a small role as Asther's Czech immigrant friend.

Jennifer (1953) 73 min. Ida Lupino, Howard Duff, Robert Nichols, Mary Shipp. **Screenplay by**: Virginia Myers. **Directed by**: Joel Newton. **Noir Type**: Missing Person. **Noir Themes**: Obsession, paranoia, woman in jeopardy. ★½

Real-life husband and wife Duff and Lupino star in this tedious film about a neurotic woman (Lupino) hired by Shipp to be the new caretaker of her vacant mansion. Lupino becomes obsessed with discovering what happened to the previous caretaker, who mysteriously disappeared, leaving behind her clothes and diary. Duff, the manager of a general store, has an eye for the new girl in town, and Nichols, his creepy employee, has an interesting theory or two about the missing girl. Noir icon Lupino is wasted in a role that has her doing little except skulking nervously around the old house while Halloween music plays in the background. Famed cinematographer James Wong Howe provides the atmospheric cinematography.

Familiar Faces from Television:
❑ Ned Glass (Sgt. Andy Pendleton on *The Phil Silvers Show*) as Dr. Levy.
❑ Russ Conway (Lt. Pete Kile in *Richard Diamond, Private Detective*) as the gardener.

Jeopardy (1953) 69 min. Barbara Stanwyck, Barry Sullivan, Ralph Meeker, Lee Aaker. **Screenplay by**: Mel Dinelli. **Directed by**: John Sturges. **Noir Type**: South of the Border. **Noir Themes**: Victim of fate, woman in jeopardy. ★★★½

Stanwyck, Sullivan's wife and Aaker's mom, narrates this "what I did on my summer vacation" film noir. Sullivan can't wait to introduce his family to an out-of-the-way beach in Baja, Mexico, that he used to visit when he was single. When little Aaker wanders onto a deteriorating jetty, Sullivan rescues him but falls into the water as the pier crumbles. His foot gets stuck under one of the heavy timbers, which Stanwyck and Aaker cannot budge. With the tide slowly coming in, Sullivan realizes that he will drown in about four hours, so he sends Stanwyck off to find a rope at an empty filling station they had passed earlier. Unbeknownst to the family, Mexican police are on the lookout for a dangerous escaped prisoner (Meeker), who happens upon the desperate Stanwyck. Needless to say, the killer's not in the mood to help. When he takes her hostage, she must use her feminine charms to persuade him to do the right thing. There's a lot of suspense packed into this short film, and the acting is first-rate. Young Aaker went on to play Rusty in TV's *The Adventures of Rin Tin Tin*.

Memorable Noir Moments:
❑ Meeker sniffs Stanwyck's neck and is disappointed. "I like *cheap* perfume," he says. "It doesn't last as long but it hits harder."
❑ The family gets stopped at a roadblock by Mexican police. Later, Aaker asks his father what they were looking for and Sullivan, evidently not impressed with *la policía*, replies, "Somebody lost a goat or a cow or something."

Jigsaw (1949) 70 min. Franchot Tone, Jean Wallace, Myron McCormick, Marc Lawrence, Betty Harper. **Screenplay by**: Fletcher Markle and Vincent McConnor. **Directed by**: Fletcher Markle. **Noir Type**: Racist. **Noir Themes**: Bigotry, corruption, conspiracy, bigotry. ★½

What starts out as an interesting murder mystery ends up a confusing yawn.

Tone is an assistant D.A. looking into the murder of his columnist friend (McCormick), who was investigating a racist hate group. Wallace is the group's femme fatale assigned to seduce Tone, and Harper is the columnist's widow. Even Lawrence, that old reliable baddie, can't salvage this mess. Henry Fonda, Marlene Dietrich, Burgess Meredith, John Garfield and Marsha Hunt (all real-life friends of Franchot Tone, who financed the film) appear in uncredited cameos.

Johnny Angel (1945) 76 min. George Raft, Claire Trevor, Signe Hasso, Hoagy Carmichael, Marvin Miller, Margaret Wycherly. **Screenplay by:** Steve Fisher. **Directed by:** Edwin L. Marin. **Noir Type:** High Seas. **Noir Themes:** Betrayal, greed, revenge. ★★

A two-fisted sea captain (Raft) tries to unravel the mystery of his father's murder. The only witness to the crime is a beautiful French girl (Hasso), who was a passenger aboard his father's ship. But she's making herself scarce in New Orleans. With some help from a friendly cab driver (Carmichael), Raft tracks her down and convinces her to help. Meanwhile, Raft must fight off the advances of his boss' wife (femme fatale Trevor), who's disgusted with her weak husband (Miller) and his overly protective ex-nanny (Wycherly). There's too much talk between fistfights and too many women throwing themselves at Raft, who gives a stiff performance. Hasso is bland, but Miller (from TV's *The Millionaire*) is enjoyable as the spineless cuckold.

Familiar Face from Television:
❑ John Hamilton (Perry White in *The Adventures of Superman*) as the harbormaster.

Memorable Noir Moments:
❑ One of the girls at a New Orleans nightspot comes on a little too strong for Raft, who comments, "You've been eating vitamins again."
❑ "There are only two things I've never had enough of in my life," Trevor tells Raft. "Money and you, Johnny."

Johnny Eager (1942) 102 min. Robert Taylor, Lana Turner, Van Heflin, Edward Arnold, Robert Sterling, Henry O'Neill. **Screenplay by:** John Lee Mahin and James Edward Grant. **Directed by:** Mervyn LeRoy. **Noir Type:** Gangster. **Noir Themes:** Betrayal, greed, guilt. ★★★★

A seemingly reformed ex-con (Taylor) has taken a job driving a cab, but it's all an act to fool his gullible parole officer (O'Neill). In reality, he's still the number one hood in town and is desperately trying to open a dog-racing track. But that's not going to happen on the watch of the incorruptible D.A. (Arnold). Luckily for Taylor, Arnold's stepdaughter (Turner), falls hard for him. After tricking the girl into plugging one of his own men in the back, Taylor blackmails Arnold into laying off his gambling operation. Meanwhile, the guilt-stricken girl is in a near catatonic state, prompting her former boyfriend (Sterling) to make the gangster an offer he can't refuse. The alcoholic Heflin is the closest thing to a conscience that Taylor has, but even Heflin continues to be amazed at the sociopathic behavior of his friend. A thoroughly enjoyable study of a morally bankrupt heel who learns a noirish lesson about love and friendship, *Johnny Eager* is a showcase for Taylor, cast against his usual good guy image. Heflin almost steals the film in an Academy Award–winning performance. Sterling later starred in the 1950s TV comedy series *Topper*, along with his wife Anne Jeffreys.

Familiar Face from Television:
❏ Barry Nelson (Bart Adams in *The Hunter* and George Cooper in *My Favorite Husband*) as a double-dealing hood.

Memorable Noir Moment:
❏ Taylor's jealous moll can't help but admire his charm. "Is there any dame you haven't got in your pocket?" she asks. "You don't feel crowded, do you, sugar?" answers the confident hood.

Johnny Guitar (1954) 110 min.
Joan Crawford, Sterling Hayden, Mercedes McCambridge, Scott Brady, Ward Bond, Ben Cooper, Ernest Borgnine, Royal Dano, Frank Ferguson. **Screenplay by:** Philip Yordan. **Directed by:** Nicholas Ray. **Noir Type:** Horse Opera. **Noir Themes:** Jealousy, obsession. revenge, betrayal. ★★★★

One of the oddest Westerns ever made, *Johnny Guitar* stars the 50-year-old Crawford as the gun-toting owner of an Arizona saloon, who has two younger men, Hayden (in the title role) and Brady (the "Dancin' Kid"), competing for her love. McCambridge plays a sexually frustrated rancher who has a hankering for Brady but wants to see him killed because "he makes her feel like a woman and that frightens her." Jealous of Crawford, she incites the marshal (Ferguson) and a prominent community leader (Bond) into running the saloonkeeper out of town and arresting Brady and his gang (Cooper, Borgnine and Dano) for a stagecoach robbery they didn't commit. Expecting to make a fortune when the railroad passes through town, Crawford holds her ground and refuses to leave. Meanwhile, Brady and his gang decide that as long as they're getting the blame for the stagecoach robbery, they might as well hold up the bank before they take a powder. The tension mounts between Crawford and McCambridge, leading to a lynching by a creepy-looking posse dressed in their funeral duds and an exciting shootout between the two ladies as the menfolk look on in awe and fascination. Crawford and McCambridge are nothing short of amazing as two strong-willed women who take no guff from the men around them. Hayden is terrific as the "gun crazy" guitar player, and Brady does a fine job as the silver miner turned bank robber. A Western noir classic.

Familiar Faces from Television:
❏ Paul Fix (Marshal Micah Torrance in TV's *The Rifleman*) as a roulette wheel operator.
❏ Denver Pyle (Uncle Jessie in *The Dukes of Hazzard*) as a member of the posse.

Memorable Noir Moment:
❏ One of Crawford's casino employees complains bitterly to the bartender about the boss. "Never seen a woman who was more a man," he says. "She thinks like one, acts like one, and sometimes makes me feel like I'm not."

Johnny O'Clock (1947) 95 min.
Dick Powell, Evelyn Keyes, Lee J. Cobb, Thomas Gomez, Jim Bannon, Nina Foch, Ellen Drew. **Screenplay by:** Robert Rossen. **Directed by:** Robert Rossen. **Noir Type:** Gangster. **Noir Themes:** Betrayal, jealousy, lust. ★★★½

A gambler (Dick Powell, right) has a difference of opinion with a hood (John Kellogg) in *Johnny O'Clock* (Columbia, 1947).

Powell, a partner in Gomez's casino, is pursued by the older man's sexy young wife (Drew) but rebuffs her advances. When the casino hat check girl (Foch), depressed about her failed romance with a crooked cop (Bannon), is found dead in her apartment, an apparent suicide, a police inspector (Cobb) investigates her death. Because the missing Bannon was connected to the casino, Cobb centers his investigation around Powell. Meanwhile, Foch's sister (Keyes) arrives in town and falls hard for the suave gambler, who is frantically searching for a lost item that, if found by the jealous Gomez, could threaten his job and possibly his life. The convoluted plot is offset by the excellent acting and clever dialogue. Look for a poker-playing Jeff Chandler (*sans* his trademark white hair) in his screen debut.

Memorable Noir Moments:

❏ Powell and Keyes share a romantic moment. "You're a strange kid," he says. "I'm a mixed-up kid," she admits.
❏ Detective Cobb makes Powell a proposition: "In return for certain information ... I'll give you a break." The distrustful gambler replies: "My arms or my legs?"

Johnny Rocco (1958) 84 min. Richard Eyer, Stephen McNally, Coleen Gray, Russ Conway, Leslie Bradley, James Flavin, Frank Wilcox. **Screenplay by:** James O'Hanlon and Sam

Roeca. **Directed by**: Paul Landres. **Noir Type**: Religion. **Noir Themes**: Child in jeopardy, family dysfunction, fatalism, guilt, paranoia. ★★½

Gangster McNally's young son (Eyer) witnesses his father's partner (Flavin) kill a motorcycle cop. As a result, the kid develops a severe stutter. His teacher (Gray) and a neighborhood priest (Bradley) try to help him by encouraging him to sing in the church choir, something the anti-clergy McNally is dead set against. Meanwhile, Flavin and his boss (Wilcox) think that the kid may have made a confession to the priest, and homicide detective Conway, obsessed with solving the crime, tries to get Eyer to squeal on his dad. McNally does a competent job as the abusive father with a conscience, and Eyer is good as his traumatized son.

Memorable Noir Moments:

❑ Schoolteacher Gray objects to McNally addressing her as "Jack." "Sorry," he says. "I call all dames Jack."
❑ McNally explains to Gray how his wife died giving birth to Eyer. "She went out when he came in," explains Mr. Sensitivity.

Johnny Stool Pigeon (1949) 76 min. Howard Duff, Shelley Winters, Dan Duryea, Tony Curtis, John McIntire, Barry Kelley. **Screenplay by**: Robert L. Richards. **Directed by**: William Castle. **Noir Type**: Narcotics. **Noir Themes**: Greed, social reform. ★★★

Duff, a Treasury Department narcotics agent, is assigned to bust a dope smuggling ring in Canada. He recruits a prisoner (Duryea), a cop hater from way back, to go undercover with him as potential customers for a large drug buy. Winters plays the femme fatale assigned by Canadian-based drug lord Kelley to keep an eye on the two. She falls hard for Duff but, because he's all business, she sets her sights on Duryea. McIntire is the manager of a dude ranch that's a front for drug traffickers, and Curtis (billed as Anthony Curtis) is his sinister, mute trigger man. It's a fast-moving and fun noir with a talented cast and a great special effects climax.

Familiar Face from Television:

❑ Leif Erickson (Big John Cannon in *High Chaparral*) as Pringle, a customs agent at the Mexican border.

Memorable Noir Moment:

❑ Convict Duryea responds to Duff's offer of a possible early release from Alcatraz if he'll help him bust a narcotics ring. "I'll rot in this place forever," he says, "before I'll be a stool pigeon for a copper."

Journey into Fear (1942) 71 min. Joseph Cotten, Dolores Del Rio, Ruth Warrick, Orson Welles, Agnes Moorehead, Everett Sloane, Jack Moss. **Screenplay by**: Joseph Cotten and Orson Welles (uncredited). **Directed by**: Norman Foster and Orson Welles. **Noir Type**: Nazi. **Noir Themes**: Paranoia, victim of fate. ★★★★

An American ballistics specialist (Cotten) and his wife (Warrick) are about to leave Turkey for the States, unaware that Nazi spies are itching to assassinate him because he has information that might impede Germany's war effort. The Turkish chief of police (Welles), hoping to throw the Nazis off Cotten's trail, places him on a steamship without letting him say goodbye to his wife. In addition to the cattle and other livestock, there are enough spies and counterspies onboard to worry a James Bond, never mind a mild-mannered and terribly confused American scientist. Fellow passengers include a sexy dancer (Del Rio), the nagging French wife (Moorehead) of an American Communist, and a number of other oddball characters. Cotten is wonderful as the bumbling newlywed, who can't believe he's actually a pawn in a dangerous game of international intrigue and has no clue as to how to protect himself from an obese and dangerous assassin (Moss), who's waiting for just the right moment. This one has it all, including some delightful humor and a suspenseful Hitchcockian climax.

Familiar Face from Television:
❏ Hans Conried (Uncle Tonoose in *The Danny Thomas Show* and the voice of Snidley Whiplash in *The Bullwinkle Show*) as a stage magician.

Memorable Noir Moment:
❏ When Cotten is forced by Nazi spies to leave the ship, a helpful passenger hands him an umbrella with a sharpened point. The clumsy Cotten accidentally pokes one of the spies in the butt with the umbrella tip and shrugs sheepishly as the Nazi disarms him.

The Judge (1949) 69 min. Milburn Stone, Katherine DeMille, Paul Guilfoyle, Stanley Waxman, Jonathan Hale, Norman Budd. **Screenplay by:** Samuel Newman, Elmer Clifton and Anson Bond. **Directed by:** Elmer Clifton. **Noir Type:** Triangle. **Noir Themes:** Betrayal, corruption, revenge. ★★½

Stone plays a shrewd lawyer who specializes in getting murderers off the hook. The story, narrated by "the Judge" (Hale), begins with the shocking murder of a crippled 11-year-old boy by one of Stone's former psychopathic clients (Budd). The lawyer then discovers that his wife (DeMille, director Cecil B. DeMille's adopted daughter) has been having an affair with the psychiatrist (Waxman) who's working on the child killing case. A vengeful Stone pressures his latest client (Guilfoyle), a cop killer he helped get off on a technicality, to participate in an outrageous revenge scheme. Stone (Doc in TV's *Gunsmoke*), in a rare starring role, is good as the cunning attorney, and DeMille does a competent job as his "vicious, scheming little tramp" of a wife. Not a bad little suspense programmer, but the background music has got to go.

Familiar Faces from Television:
❏ John Hamilton (Perry White in *Superman*) as a police inspector.
❏ Barney Phillips (Sgt. Ed Jacobs in *Dragnet*, Capt. Franks in *Felony Squad* and Maj. Kaiser in *Twelve O'Clock High*) as a newspaper reporter.

Julie (1956) 99 min. Doris Day, Louis Jourdan, Barry Sullivan, Frank Lovejoy. **Screenplay by:** Andrew L. Stone. **Directed by:** Andrew L. Stone. **Noir Type:** Psycho. **Noir Themes:** Woman in jeopardy, obsession. ★½

This disaster starts with Day gaily singing the title song. You might think you're about to enjoy one of her many light romantic comedies so you keep looking for Rock Hudson's name among the credits. But, alas, it's nowhere to be found. Instead, you see Louis Jourdan and Barry Sullivan, and it soon dawns on you that you're watching a "suspense" film. Jourdan plays a nutcase who killed Day's first husband so he

Under sodium pentathol, a child killer (Norman Budd, seated) relives a murder for, left to right, his lawyer (Milburn Stone), a homicide detective (John Hamilton), a patrolman and a psychiatrist (Stanley Waxman) in *The Judge* (Film Classics, 1949).

could marry her. She's discovered his secret, and now he wants to kill *her*. Sullivan plays a friend who helps her hide from her stalker husband, and noir veteran Lovejoy is an ineffective cop. Will Jourdan succeed in killing Day? Day is narrating, so you figure it out. What starts out as a lame suspense thriller takes a sudden turn approximately an hour into the film and becomes *Airport*, with Day at the controls of a runaway airliner. Yawn.

Familiar Face from Television:

❑ Jack Kelly (Brother Bart in *Maverick*) as a pilot.

Memorable Noir Moment:

❑ Day, in bed with Jourdan, tests him to find out if he killed her first husband. He admits it and asks if she suspected. When she says yes, he asks, "And you married me anyway?" She replies, fingers crossed, "Maybe my love for you is just as violent as your love for me." Such a fibber, Doris.

Kansas City Confidential (1952) 98 min. John Payne, Preston Foster, Coleen Gray, Jack Elam, Neville Brand, Lee Van Cleef. **Screenplay by:** George Bruce and Harry Essex. **Directed by:** Phil Karlson. **Noir Type:** Heist. **Noir Themes:** Victim of fate, greed, betrayal. ★★★½

Armored car robbers (Neville Brand, left and Lee Van Cleef) work over their fall guy (John Payne) in *Kansas City Confidential* (United Artists, 1952).

Foster, an embittered ex-cop, recruits Elam, Brand and Van Cleef for an armored car heist. Foster is the only one who knows the identity of the others. Anonymous himself, he makes the gang "cop proof" and "stool pigeon proof" by having everyone wear masks from day one. Immediately after the robbery, an unfortunate war hero and ex-con (Payne) gets picked up because he's driving the same kind of commercial van as the robbers. After being worked over by some disagreeable cops, he's released and begins searching for the crooks. He finds himself in a small Mexican resort, where the gang is meeting to split the dough. Foster, however, is planning an ingenious double-cross. Gray plays Foster's daughter, who shows up at the resort unexpectedly and falls in love with Payne. This is a brutal and fast-paced noir with excellent performances by Payne, Foster and those three great character actors, Elam, Brand and Van Cleef.

Memorable Noir Moments:

❏ During interrogation, the cops mention Payne's Army decorations—a Bronze Star and a Purple Heart—and he angrily responds, "Try and buy a cup of coffee with them."

❏ Guns seem to change hands every few minutes in this film: Preston takes one away from Elam; Payne also disarms Elam; Payne later takes Van Cleef's gun away from *him* and forces Brand to drop *his* down a well; Van Cleef soon returns the favor, taking *Payne's* gun away (the one Payne took away from *Elam*). Confusing, but fun to watch.

Keeper of the Flame (1942) 100 min. Spencer Tracy, Katharine Hepburn, Richard Whorf, Margaret Wycherly, Howard da Silva, Darryl Hickman. **Screenplay by**: Donald Ogden Stewart. **Directed by**: George Cukor. **Noir Type**: Whodunit. **Noir Themes**: Betrayal, guilt. ★★

When a famous and much-loved American hero, the founder of the patriotic "American Union Movement," dies after driving his car off of a washed-out bridge, the nation mourns. Reporter Tracy, back from covering the war in Europe, decides to write a book about the man's life. He manages to win the confidence of the man's reclusive and secretive widow (Hepburn) and soon begins to suspect foul play. Hickman, the young son of the estate's gatekeeper (da Silva), tells Tracy that on the night of the accident he warned somebody in the house that the bridge was out. Was the man murdered? Hepburn's not talking, her loony mother-in-law (Wycherly) *is* but nobody's listening, and her late husband's private secretary (Whorf) seems eager to burn the dead man's papers. Hepburn and Tracy hold the tedious film together.

Familiar Face from Television:
❑ Forrest Tucker (Sgt. O'Rourke in *F Troop*) as Hepburn's cousin.

Key Largo (1948) 101 min. Humphrey Bogart, Edward G. Robinson, Lauren Bacall, Lionel Barrymore, Claire Trevor, Thomas Gomez, Harry Lewis, John Rodney, Dan Seymour, Marc Lawrence. **Screenplay by**: Richard Brooks and John Huston. **Directed by**: John Huston. **Noir Type**: Gangster. **Noir Themes**: Fatalism, greed, paranoia, betrayal. ★★★★

When war hero Bogart stops in the Florida Keys to visit hotel owners Barrymore and Bacall, the father and widow of one of his men, he winds up a hostage in the middle of a hurricane. Deported gangster Robinson and his gang (Gomez, Lewis, Rodney and Seymour) have taken over the empty hotel while waiting for another mobster (Lawrence) to arrive to buy their counterfeit dough. They then plan to head for Cuba by boat. Unfortunately for them, a hurricane delays their departure. They entertain themselves by terrorizing their captives, depriving Robinson's alcoholic moll (Trevor) of her booze, knocking off a deputy sheriff, and refusing to allow local Seminole families to take shelter from the hurricane inside the hotel. Bogey, after risking his life on the battlefield against German soldiers, is in no mood to take any chances with gangsters, even if it means looking like a coward in front of the lovely Bacall and wheelchair-bound Barrymore, who unrealistically expect him to stand up to the vicious thugs. Trevor won the Academy Award for Best Supporting Actress for her performance as the star nightclub singer turned lush. Bogey is entertainingly low-key as the cynical war hero, but the movie belongs primarily to that other film noir icon, Robinson, who reprises his famous gangster roles with a delicious exhibition of viciousness and lewdness.

Familiar Faces from Television:
❑ Jay Silverheels (Tonto in *The Lone Ranger*) as a Seminole on the run from the law.
❑ Monte Blue (Sheriff Hollister in *Sky King*) as the sheriff.

Memorable Noir Moments:
❑ After Bogey refuses to be goaded into a shootout with Robinson, the sympathetic Trevor tells him, "It's better to be a live coward than a dead hero."

A gangster (Edward G. Robinson, left) and his hostages (Humphrey Bogart, Lionel Barrymore [seated], and Lauren Bacall) in *Key Largo* (Warner Bros., 1948).

❑ A deputy sheriff tells the hostages that when he was knocked unconscious, the lights went out. Gangster Lewis is happy to take credit. "I'm the electrician," he brags.

Key Man *see* A Life at Stake

Key Witness (1947) 67 min. John Beal, Trudy Marshall, Jimmy Lloyd, Helen Mowery, Barbara Read, Douglas Fowley. **Screenplay by:** Edward Bock and Raymond L. Schrock. **Directed by:** D. Ross Lederman. **Noir Type:** Impersonator. **Noir Themes:** Victim of fate. ✫

Beal is a draftsman and amateur inventor married to a nagging wife (Read). While she's out of town, his co-worker (Lloyd) takes him to the racetrack and tries to fix him up with Mowery, a dame with a jealous husband (Fowley), who kills her in a fit of rage. Of course, Beal gets the blame and goes on the lam. During his travels as a hobo, he discovers a body and assumes the dead man's identity. He later learns that the dead man's wealthy father, who hasn't seen him since he was two years old, desperately wants a reunion. He obliges. An ultra-cheapie B noir, this *Detour* wannabe has all of the cult favorite's flaws, but none of its charm.

Familiar Face from Television:
❑ John Hamilton (Perry White in *The Adventures of Superman*) as the coroner.

Kill Me Tomorrow (1957-British) 80 min. Pat O'Brien, Lois Maxwell, George Coulouris, Wensley Pithey, Freddie Mills, Ronald Adam, Claude Kingston. **Screenplay by:** Robert Falconer, Paddy Manning O'Brine. **Directed by:** Terence Fisher. **Noir Type:** Newspaper. **Noir Themes:** Child in jeopardy, fatalism, greed. ★★½

O'Brien, a heavy-drinking American reporter on a London newspaper, quits his job after a dispute with the editor (Adam), and then finds out that his young son (Kingston) needs an expensive life-saving operation. During a late night visit to his former boss to ask for a loan, O'Brien witnesses the man's murder by diamond smugglers Coulouris and Mills. He decides to blackmail the killers, but in a kindly way — he volunteers to take the murder rap for the price of his son's surgery. The bad guys agree, but when O'Brien's confession is rejected by Scotland Yard inspector Pithey, they decide to kidnap young Kingston as insurance. Naturally, this makes O'Brien's blood boil, and he and fellow reporter Maxwell try to rescue the boy. At 58, the chunky O'Brien was a little long in the tooth to be playing the tough, two-fisted hero, and it's a bit of stretch to believe that the pretty, twenty-something Maxwell (Miss Moneypenny in the James Bond films) finds him irresistible. Still, it's a fair British crime drama that seems shorter than its eighty minutes.

Killer Bait *see* **Too Late for Tears**

The Killer Is Loose (1956) 79 min. Joseph Cotten, Rhonda Fleming, Wendell Corey, Alan Hale, Jr. **Screenplay by:** Harold Medford. **Directed by:** Budd Boetticher. **Noir Type:** Payback. **Noir Themes:** Revenge. ★½

Detective Cotten accidentally kills the wife of a psychopathic bank robber (Corey), who promises to get even. When he escapes from prison, Corey targets Cotten's pregnant wife (Fleming). Hale plays a clumsy cop, a part that prepared him for his best known role — that of a clumsy sea captain in TV's *Gilligan's Island*. The acting is terrible, and the usually reliable Cotten and Corey are disappointing.

The Killer That Stalked New York (1951) 79 min. Evelyn Keyes, Charles Korvin, William Bishop, Barry Kelley. **Screenplay by:** Harry Essex. **Directed by:** Earl McEvoy. **Noir Type:** Plague. **Noir Themes:** Victim of fate, betrayal, greed, social reform, revenge. ★★★½

The killer that's stalking New York City isn't the mad-dog kind you might have thought. It's actually smallpox being carried by a nightclub singer and part-time jewel thief (Keyes), who picked up the dreaded disease while in Cuba stealing diamonds for her husband (Korvin). Bishop is the doctor who misdiagnoses her condition and sends her on her way to infect millions of New Yorkers. When health officials become aware of the disease, Bishop is appointed the head of an investigating team to find the unknown carrier. Unknown to him, T-man Kelley also is hunting

Opposite, top: An escaped killer (Wendell Corey) buys a change of wardrobe in *The Killer Is Loose* (United Artists, 1956). *Bottom:* A modern day Typhoid Mary (Evelyn Keyes) gets the drop on a doctor (William Bishop) in *The Killer That Stalked New York* (Columbia, 1951).

for Keyes, who's becoming progressively sicker as she wanders the city searching for her cheating husband (he's taken off with the diamonds). Broadcasting the motto "Be Safe, Be Sure, Be Vaccinated!," the city begins the almost impossible task of vaccinating all New Yorkers, some of whom, in cynical Big Apple fashion, are dead set against it, believing it all to be hype. But when the vaccine runs out, city officials are faced with a possible panic. This effective little suspense noir, with Keyes doing a fine job as a modern-day Typhoid Mary, was made the same year as the similar *Panic in the Streets*. When *Panic* hit the theaters first, *Killer* was held by the studio and not released until the following year.

Familiar Faces from Television:
- ❑ Dorothy Malone (Constance Mackenzie in *Peyton Place*) as Keyes' two-timing sister.
- ❑ Richard Egan (Jim Redigo in *Empire*) as a Fed.
- ❑ Arthur Space (Doc Weaver on *Lassie* and Velvet's dad in *National Velvet*) as a doctor on the smallpox investigating team.
- ❑ Paul Picerni (Agent Lee Hobson in *The Untouchables*) as a member of the investigating team.
- ❑ Connie Gilchrist (Purity, pub proprietress and girlfriend of *Long John Silver*) as Korvin's landlady.
- ❑ Jim Backus (Thurston Howell III of *Gilligan's Island*) as a lecherous nightclub owner.
- ❑ Roy Roberts (Captain Huxley in *Oh Susanna*) as the mayor.

Memorable Noir Moment:
- ❑ When Keyes remarks that she had asked her sister to keep an eye on her husband while she was away, Backus gleefully replies, "She did better — she *gave* him the eye."

The Killers (1946) 105 min. Edmund O'Brien, Ava Gardner, Burt Lancaster, Albert Dekker, Sam Levene, William Conrad, Charles McGraw, Jack Lambert, Jeff Corey, Charles D. Brown. **Screenplay by:** Anthony Veiller. **Directed by:** Robert Siodmak. **Noir Type:** Femme Fatale. **Noir Themes:** Betrayal, fatalism, obsession, lust. ★★★★★

Two brazen hit men (McGraw and Conrad, in his film debut) show up one evening in an unlikely film noir locale (Brentwood, New Jersey) and put eight slugs into a filling station attendant (Lancaster), who had waited passively for them in his cheap hotel room. (When asked by a friend why the killers are after him, Lancaster replied simply, "I did something wrong once.") An insurance investigator (O'Brien), obsessed with discovering the reason for the killing, seeks out Lancaster's friends and enemies — his beautiful but scheming girlfriend (Gardner), his prison cellmate (Brown), his partners in a big heist (crime boss Dekker and goons Lambert and Corey) and a police detective (Levene). What the investigator uncovers turns out to be the "double-cross to end all double-crosses." Lancaster, in his film debut, gives a sensational performance as the depressed loser. Gardner distinguishes herself in the femme fatale role, proving that she was not just a gorgeous sex symbol but a genuinely talented actress. This classic noir, based loosely on an Ernest Hemingway short story of the same title, was remade in 1964 with John Cassavetes in the Lancaster role, Angie Dickinson as the femme fatale, Lee Marvin and Clu Gulager as the killers and Ronald Reagan (in his final film before turning to politics) as the crime boss. The classic TV show *Dragnet* borrowed Miklos Rozsa's compelling score (dum da dum dum) and made it famous.

A double-crossing robber (Burt Lancaster) gets the drop on his partners (Jeff Corey and Charles Middleton, rear, and Albert Dekker) while another partner (Jack Lambert) lies unconscious. From *The Killers* (Universal, 1946).

Familiar Face from Television:
❑ Virginia Christine (the widow Ovie in *Tales of Wells Fargo*) as Levene's wife.

Memorable Noir Moments:
❑ Gardner makes a noirish confession to Lancaster. "I'm poison, Swede," she admits, "to myself and everybody around me."
❑ When O'Brien asks if a delirious patient can answer any more questions, a hospital intern shakes his head and replies, "He's dead now, except he's breathing."
❑ Dekker reveals the number one item on his hate list, saying, "If there's anything in the world I hate, it's a double-crossing dame."

Killer's Kiss (1955) 67 min. Frank Silvera, Jamie Smith, Irene Kane. **Screenplay by:** Stanley Kubrick. **Directed by:** Stanley Kubrick. **Noir Type:** Triangle. **Noir Themes:** Obsession, lust, revenge. ★★

Produced, directed, edited, photographed and written by the legendary Stanley Kubrick, *Killer's Kiss* doesn't have much of a plot. A down-and-out boxer (Smith) wants to marry a taxi dancer (Kane) after knowing her for only two days, but a lecherous small-time hood (Silvera) doesn't appreciate being horned in on and sends some goons to work the boxer over. His bungling henchmen, however, mistake an

An unlucky boxing manager (Jerry Jarrett) is assaulted by two hoods in a case of mistaken identity in *Killer's Kiss* (United Artists, 1955).

innocent bystander for Smith and wind up killing the unfortunate man. Trying another ploy, they grab Kane and wait for Smith to show up looking for her. The acting is so-so, but the photography is excellent (especially during the boxing match, which is shot from every imaginable angle), and the enjoyable Latin jazz score fools you into believing that something's really happening.

Memorable Noir Moments:

❑ When Silvera pushes himself on Kane, she tells him, "Can't you get it, Vinnie? You're just an old man. You smell bad." Evidently incapable of taking a hint, Silvera replies, "I'm mad about you."

❑ During a bizarre mannequin factory climax, Smith and Silvera (in what must be the clumsiest brawl ever filmed) assault one another with plastic torsos and legs.

The Killing (1956) 83 min. Sterling Hayden, Coleen Gray, Jay C. Flippen, Marie Windsor, Elisha Cook, Jr., Ted de Corsia, Joe Sawyer, Vince Edwards, Timothy Carey, Kola Kwariani, Jay Adler. **Screenplay by:** Stanley Kubrick. **Directed by:** Stanley Kubrick. **Noir Type:** Heist. **Noir Themes:** Greed, betrayal, fatalism, obsession, paranoia, jealousy. ★★★★½

Hayden plays an ex-con who masterminds a racetrack heist that is expected to earn him and his men a cool two million bucks. His gang includes an odd assortment of characters—Flippen, a paternal alcoholic who supplies the up-front dough;

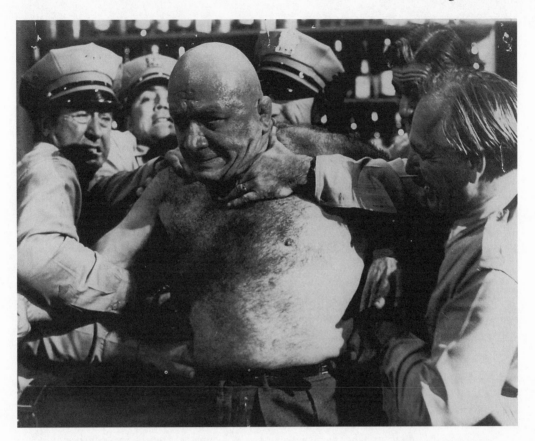

An ex-wrestler (Kola Kwarian) does a good job of distracting cops during a racetrack heist in *The Killing* (United Artists, 1956).

crooked cop de Corsia, who owes a tidy gambling debt to an impatient mobster (Adler); Sawyer, a track bartender who needs dough to care for his sickly wife; and Cook, a track teller, whose shrewish and greedy wife (Windsor) is in cahoots with her lover (Edwards) to rob the robbers. Hayden hires Kwariani and Carey to cause distractions at the track — Kwariani, a chess-playing ex-wrestler, to pick a fight, and Carey, a psychotic marksman, to shoot a racehorse. Gray is Hayden's childhood sweetheart, who waited for him while he served a five-year stretch in the pen. Of course, this being one of the darkest and most ironic of films noirs, nothing turns out the way anyone expects. Shot on a shoestring budget, *The Killing* gets the most for its money with awesome camera angles, a *Dragnet*–type narration that jumps back and forth in time, and top-notch acting by the entire cast. Noir veterans Cook and Windsor are outstanding, and Carey, with his perpetually frozen grin and weird acting style, is amazing. Hayden gives one of his best performances as the master criminal wannabe. A close second to *the* classic heist film, ***The Asphalt Jungle***, Kubrick's *The Killing* is an eloquent masterpiece that cries out for multiple viewings.

Memorable Noir Moments:

❑ Hayden tries to wipe the smirk off Windsor's face. "I know you like a book," he says. "You're a no-good, nosy little tramp. You'd sell your own mother for a piece of fudge."
❑ A little French poodle and its annoying, baby-talking owner spoil a lifetime of dreams at the airport. See *The Hidden Room*, *The Man with My Face* and *Lady Gangster* for other spoiler mutts, and *Armored Car Robbery* for another entertaining airport mishap.

A Kiss Before Dying (1956) 94 min. Robert Wagner, Jeffrey Hunter, Virginia Leith, Joanne Woodward, Mary Astor, George Macready. **Screenplay by**: Lawrence Roman. **Directed by**: Gerd Oswald. **Noir Type**: Psycho. **Noir Themes**: Betrayal, woman in jeopardy, greed. ★★★½

A Korean War veteran (Wagner), now a college student, gets his girlfriend (Woodward) pregnant. Knowing that her wealthy daddy (Macready) would disown her if he found out, Wagner decides that the only way to marry into her rich family is to get rid of Woodward and romance her sister (Leith). After making Woodward's death look like a suicide, Wagner ingratiates himself with Macready and Leith but worries when Leith comes to the conclusion that Woodward was murdered. Hunter plays a homicide detective convinced that Leith is on the right track. Astor plays Wagner's mother. The tension-filled script, a horrifying rooftop scene and good performances, especially by Wagner (cast way against type as the handsome psychopath) make this Technicolor noir a real nail-biter. Remade in 1991 with Matt Dillon and Sean Young.

Memorable Noir Moments:

❑ From the Some-Things-Never-Change Department: Woodward goes on a guilt trip because of her pregnancy. "It's all my fault," she tells Wagner. "It's always the girl's fault."
❑ Like Zachary Scott in *Danger Signal* and Claude Rains in *The Unsuspected*, Wagner tricks Woodward into writing her own suicide note (by having her translate a Spanish sentence into English).

Kiss Me Deadly (1955) 105 min. Ralph Meeker, Maxine Cooper, Paul Stewart, Gaby Rodgers, Wesley Addy, Jack Elam, Jack Lambert, Albert Dekker. **Screenplay by**: A.I. Bezzerides. **Directed by**: Robert Aldrich. **Noir Type**: P.I. **Noir Themes**: Obsession, fatalism, betrayal, greed. ★★★★½

Hard-boiled author Mickey Spillane's macho private eye, Mike Hammer (Meeker), picks up a nearly naked female hitchhiker who has just escaped from a mental institution. They're kidnapped by bad guys Dekker, Elam, Lambert and Stewart, who believe the girl is carrying the key to a mysterious object ("the great whatsit") they're desperately searching for. After torturing the girl, they put her and Meeker back in their car and push it over an embankment, leaving them for dead. The girl dies but Meeker recovers and becomes obsessed with the dead woman and her secret. Cooper plays the P.I.'s secretary and lover, Rodgers is the hitchhiker's strange roommate, and Addy is the police detective who warns Spillane to mind his own business. Meeker is sensational as the shady bedroom dick, whose specialty is the "big squeeze" (playing husbands and wives against each other in divorce cases). He makes no bones about what he is—a remorseless opportunist seemingly unable to think before acting (perhaps as a result of all those knocks on the head). Rodgers is excellent as the shorthaired, whiny-voiced sexpot, whose curiosity is her downfall.

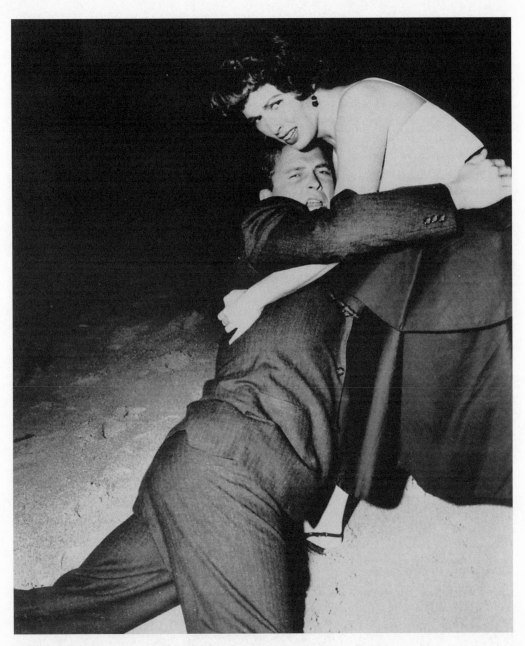

P.I. Mike Hammer (Ralph Meeker) and secretary Velda (Maxine Cooper) finally find the "great whatsit" in *Kiss Me Deadly* (United Artists, 1955).

Despite its dated plot, the ultra-violent *Kiss Me Deadly* has gained a cult following over the years. It's a wild roller coaster ride that can be enjoyed over and over. In fact, a second viewing might be necessary to follow the complicated storyline. The original, ambiguous ending has been slightly altered in the restored version, settling some, but not all, questions. See *I, the Jury* and *My Gun Is Quick* for more Mike Hammer noir.

Familiar Faces from Television:

❑ Cloris Leachman (Phyllis in *The Mary Tyler Moore Show* and *Phyllis*) as the hitchhiker.
❑ Percy Helton (Homer Cratchit in *The Beverly Hillbillies*) as a weasely morgue attendant.

Memorable Noir Moments:

❑ When Meeker wakes up in the hospital, he finds Cooper standing over his bed. "You're never around when I need you," he chides. "You never need me when I'm around," she answers.
❑ After his second attempt on Meeker's life fails, Stewart tries to make a deal. "What's it worth to you," he asks Meeker, "to turn your considerable talents back to the gutter you crawled out of?"
❑ After blackjacking Meeker, thugs Elam and Lambert address him as "Mr. Hammer." "For a couple of cannons, you guys sure are polite," Meeker says. The philosophical Lambert replies, "We're on this earth for such a brief span, we might as well be."

Kiss of Death (1947) 98 min. Victor Mature, Brian Donlevy, Coleen Gray, Richard Widmark, Taylor Holmes. **Screenplay by:** Ben Hecht and Charles Lederer. **Directed by:** Henry Hathaway. **Noir Type:** Gangster. **Noir Themes:** Betrayal, law breaking for kicks, fatalism, child in jeopardy. ★★★★

An assistant D.A. (Brian Donlevy) visits with a psycho (Richard Widmark, center) and a squealer (Victor Mature) in *Kiss of Death* (20th Century–Fox, 1947).

Mature, a hood who gets nabbed after pulling a jewelry store heist, is offered a deal by assistant D.A. Donlevy if he'll squeal on his partners. Mature refuses even though it means facing a twenty-year stretch and leaving his wife and two kids alone. The mob's lawyer (Holmes) promises Mature that his family will be taken care of and that he'll see to it that he's paroled. While in prison, Mature hears that his wife has committed suicide and that his kids have been placed in an orphanage. So he contacts Donlevy and sings like a canary. Released on parole, he marries his daughters' former babysitter (Gray) and tries to live a normal life. The D.A., however, has other plans for him — he wants him to help trap psychopathic killer Widmark. Filmed on location in and around New York City and in upstate New York, *Kiss of Death* is a violent, action-packed film. Mature gives one of his best performances as the "good" crook turned squealer, and Donlevy is good as the persistent D.A. who makes Mature earn his freedom. But it's Widmark, in his film debut, who steals the film with his impressive portrayal of the giggling psychopath.

Familiar Face from Television:

❑ Karl Malden (*The Streets of San Francisco*) as a police sergeant working with the assistant D.A.

Memorable Noir Moments:

❑ Widmark tells an informant's mom how he deals with squealers. "I let 'em have it in the belly," he says gleefully, "so they can roll around for a long time thinking it over."

❑ In one of the most famous scenes in film noir, the giggling Widmark straps a hood's mother to her wheelchair and rolls her down a flight of stairs. See *The Beast with Five Fingers*, *The Lineup* and *Whiplash* for more wheelchair mishaps.

Kiss the Blood Off My Hands (1948) 80 min. Joan Fontaine, Burt Lancaster, Robert Newton. **Screenplay by:** Leonardo Bercovici. **Directed by:** Norman Foster. **Noir Type:** Troubled Veteran. **Noir Themes:** Paranoia, woman in jeopardy, fatalism. ★★

Despite the gruesome title, this is merely a slow-moving romantic melodrama about a love destined to fail. Lancaster is a disturbed American war veteran in England, who has a serious temper problem. After accidentally killing a pub owner, he breaks into nurse Fontaine's apartment while hiding from pursuing bobbies. Fontaine, surprisingly sympathetic, doesn't report him. Romance blossoms, but Lancaster must spend six months in prison for violent attacks against a police officer and a train passenger who wouldn't fall for one of his con games. When Lancaster is released, Fontaine gets him a job as a truck driver at her clinic. He attempts to go straight, hoping the police will never suspect him in the pub killing, but a witness (Newton) blackmails him into helping him hijack the clinic's drug shipment. Noir icon Lancaster, the lovely Fontaine and Newton (terrific as the detestable small-time hood) do their best, but they can't overcome the trite script. Newton went on to star in the syndicated TV series *Long John Silver*.

Kiss Tomorrow Goodbye (1950) 102 min. James Cagney, Barbara Payton, Ward Bond, Helena Carter, Luther Adler, Barton MacLane, Steve Brodie, Neville Brand. **Screenplay by:** Harry Brown. **Directed by:** Gordon Douglas. **Noir Type:** Gangster. **Noir Themes:** Betrayal, greed, corruption. ★★★½

Cagney is a violent convict who recently escaped from a prison farm. He hooks up with Payton, the sister of an inmate (Brand) whom he viciously murdered during the breakout. Believing that guards shot her brother, Payton falls in love with the brutal killer following a brief noirish romance (she throws herself into his arms after he slaps her around with a towel because she nearly sliced off his ear with a kitchen knife). Teaming up with petty thief Brodie, Cagney begins a crime wave that attracts the attention of crooked cops Bond and MacLane, who make the mistake of trying to shake them down. Between heists, Cagney romances and marries a wealthy industrialist's kooky daughter (Carter), hires a shady attorney (Adler) and kills and maims a few people. This is a brutal film with Cagney giving an enjoyable, but hammy, performance.

Familiar Faces from Television:
❑ William Frawley (Fred Mertz on *I Love Lucy* and Uncle Bub on *My Three Sons*) as a prison farm guard.
❑ Kenneth Tobey (Chuck Martin in *The Whirlybirds*) as a plainclothes detective.
❑ King Donovan (Bob Cummings' Air Force buddy Harvey Helm in *Love That Bob* and lawyer Herb Thornton in *Please Don't Eat the Daisies*) as the driver for two gangsters.
❑ Frank Wilcox (John Brewster in *The Beverly Hillbillies*) as a doctor.
❑ Ann Tyrrell (Vi in *Private Secretary* and Olive in *The Ann Sothern Show*) as a holdup victim.

Memorable Noir Moments:
❑ After a run-in with a pair of crooked cops, Cagney warns his moll, "Any cop that'll shake you down is a cop that'll kill you. And just for the fun of it, too."
❑ Even a squealer finds Cagney offensive. "I wouldn't cut you down if you were hanging," he tells him.
❑ Cagney, filling in a form for a gun permit, asks, "Here, where it says 'Reason for Permit.' What do I put?" A not-so-helpful cop replies sarcastically, "That's where you put the reason for requesting the permit."

Knock on Any Door (1949) 100 min. Humphrey Bogart, John Derek, George Macready, Allene Roberts. **Screenplay by**: Daniel Taradash and John Monks, Jr. **Directed by**: Nicholas Ray. **Noir Type**: Trial. **Noir Themes**: Social reform, betrayal. ★★★

Civil attorney Bogart returns to criminal practice to defend a young felon (Derek) accused of viciously murdering a cop during a robbery attempt. In what must be one of the longest opening statements in film history, Bogart laments to the jury about Derek's miserable life, from his youth in Hell's Kitchen and a stretch in a brutal reform school to his feeble attempt at going straight after marrying a nice girl (Roberts). And who's to blame for Derek's rapid descent into crime? Why, *we* are, of course. Society. But because D.A. Macready has no such goody-two-shoes feelings about the baby-faced criminal, Bogart has to rely on Derek's friends, who testify that

Opposite, top: A small-time hood (Burt Lancaster) mugs a victim in a London alley in *Kiss the Blood Off My Hands* (Universal-International, 1948). *Bottom:* A gangster (James Cagney, center), his attorney (Luther Adler, second from left), his moll (Barbara Payton) and his partner (Steve Brodie, at phonograph) blackmail two crooked cops (Ward Bond, left and Barton MacLane, rear) in *Kiss Tomorrow Goodbye* (Warner Bros., 1950).

he was with them when somebody emptied a revolver into the unfortunate patrolman. Bogart turns in a solid performance as the guilt-stricken lawyer trying to assuage his conscience after bumbling a case that caused Derek's immigrant father to be imprisoned and, eventually, to commit suicide. Derek does a good job as the kid whose noir philosophy ("Live fast, die young, have a good-looking corpse") leads to inevitable tragedy. Despite its preachiness, this is a fine film, but the courtroom finale is disappointing.

Familiar Faces from Television:

❑ Sid Melton (Ichabod Mudd in *Captain Midnight* and Charlie Halper in *Make Room for Daddy* a.k.a. *The Danny Thomas Show*) as a squinty-eyed pool player.
❑ Cara Williams (Gladys Porter in *Pete and Gladys*) as a neighborhood girl with the hots for Derek.
❑ Myron Healey (Doc Holliday in *The Life and Legend of Wyatt Earp*) as an assistant D.A.

Memorable Noir Moments:

❑ From the Stupid Criminal Department: A stickup man slips after robbing a subway cashier and slides beneath a guard rail, falling to his death on the platform below. See *Raw Deal, Sealed Lips, The Long Wait* and *Escape in the Fog* for more dumb criminals.
❑ Two wide-eyed young girls in the courtroom are obviously smitten with the handsome defendant as he testifies in his own defense. "He's wouldn't kill anybody," one remarks. The other, in a near-swoon, replies, "He kills *me!*"

Ladies in Retirement (1941) 91 min. Ida Lupino, Louis Hayward, Evelyn Keyes, Elsa Lanchester, Edith Barrett, Isobel Elsom. **Screenplay by:** Reginald Denham and Garrett Fort. **Directed by:** Charles Vidor. **Noir Type:** Period. **Noir Themes:** Betrayal, paranoia, guilt. ★★★

Lupino plays the housekeeping companion of ex-actress Elsom in late nineteenth century England. When Lupino's balmy sisters (Lanchester and Barrett) are evicted from their London home and faced with asylum commitment, Lupino convinces her employer to allow them to visit her for a couple of days. Two days turn into six weeks, and the long-suffering Elsom can stand them no longer — especially the junk-collecting Lanchester, who feels she "must tidy up the river banks," bringing the debris home with her. Lupino, who has sworn that she would never allow her siblings to be committed, sees only one solution to her dilemma — murder. Hayward (Lupino's real-life husband at the time) plays her scheming nephew, and Keyes is the servant girl with an eye for the dashing Hayward. Lupino, 23 at the time, has difficulty passing as a forty-ish spinster, but she gives an excellent performance as the desperate woman whose mission in life is to protect her demented sisters. Barrett and Lanchester, who seems to have been typecast as an eccentric oddball in most of her films, do well as the harmlessly mad sisters.

Memorable Noir Moments:

❑ Barrett, terrified of thunder and lightning, hugs Lupino tightly during a particularly nasty storm. A visiting nun asks her, "Don't you believe we're being watched over?" "Oh yes," the paranoid Barrett replies, "but I'm never quite sure *who's* watching us."
❑ After hearing a hellfire and brimstone sermon at church, Barrett asks Lupino where Hell is located. The murderess replies somberly, "Hell is like the kingdom of Heaven. It's within."

A nephew (Louis Hayward) greets his loony aunts (Edith Barrett, left, and Elsa Lanchester) in *Ladies in Retirement* (Columbia, 1941).

The Lady Confesses (1945) 64 min. Hugh Beaumont, Mary Beth Hughes, Edmund MacDonald, Emmett Vogan. **Screenplay by:** Helen Martin. **Directed by:** Sam Newfield. **Noir Type:** Whodunit. **Noir Themes:** Woman in jeopardy, betrayal. ★★

Hughes is engaged to Beaumont, whose wife disappeared almost seven years ago. Before they can marry, however, Beaumont's wife shows up on Hughes' doorstep to inform her that she'll never give up her husband. A few hours later, the wife's strangled body is found. Homicide detective Vogan has two suspects— Beaumont, who has an alibi that seems almost too pat, and nightclub owner MacDonald. Hughes goes undercover as a photographer at MacDonald's club to clear her man's name. Pretty boring, but at least it's short.

The Lady from Shanghai (1948) 87 min. Rita Hayworth, Orson Welles, Everett Sloane, Glenn Anders, Ted de Corsia. **Screenplay by:** Orson Welles. **Directed by:** Orson Welles. **Noir Type:** Femme Fatale. **Noir Themes:** Betrayal, greed, victim of fate. ★★★★

Irish sailor Welles hires on as a boatswain aboard a yacht sailing from New York to San Francisco via Acapulco and becomes embroiled in a bogus murder plot involving Hayworth, her crippled husband (Sloane), Sloane's wacko law partner (Anders)

Orson Welles in the famous Mirror Maze scene in *The Lady from Shanghai* (Columbia, 1948).

and a sleazy private investigator (de Corsia). The convoluted plot is painful to follow, but the film is so stylishly done that you might not care. The famous climax in a funhouse hall of mirrors is the highlight of this weird movie, which bombed at the box office. The breathtaking Hayworth, the real-life Mrs. Welles at the time, does a good job with her part, as does Welles, despite his wearisome brogue, as the hapless Irishman.

Memorable Noir Moment:

❏ Before first meeting the beautiful Hayworth in New York's Central Park, narrator Wells comments, "Some people can smell danger. Not me."

The Lady Gambles (1949) 98 min. Barbara Stanwyck, Robert Preston, Stephen McNally, Edith Barrett, John Hoyt. **Screenplay by:** Roy Huggins and Halsted Welles. **Directed by:** Michael Gordon. **Noir Type:** Gambling. **Noir Themes:** Obsession, character deterioration, betrayal, guilt, social reform. ★★★

During her first visit to Las Vegas, a desert oasis of "quick marriages, quick divorces and quick money," a freelance magazine writer (Stanwyck) becomes addicted to gambling. Her patient husband (Preston) finally gives up on her after she loses their entire savings, leaving her with an open invitation to return to him when she kicks the habit. Her compulsion drives her from the Vegas poker tables to a job at a mob-owned racetrack and a degrading stint as a B-girl in a seedy beer hall. She ends up with a hustler named Frenchie in back alley dice games. It's all quite melodramatic, of course, and Stanwyck plays it to the hilt, especially during her orgasmic dice-tossing scenes. McNally plays the crooked casino manager who takes her in after Preston leaves her. Hoyt is a doctor at the emergency room where she ends up, and Barrett is her neurotic sister. Look for Tony Curtis in a bit role as a bellboy.

Familiar Faces from Television:
❑ Leif Erickson (Big John Cannon in *High Chaparral*) as a poker-playing hood.
❑ Peter Leeds (George Colton in *Pete and Gladys*) as a Vegas hotel clerk.

Memorable Noir Moment:
❑ Poker-playing hoods discuss Stanwyck and her gambling habit. "She's worse than a lush," one says. "I'd rather have a lush around any time," says another, adding, "At least a lush'll pass out once in a while."

Lady Gangster (1942) 62 min. Faye Emerson, Frank Wilcox, Julie Bishop, Roland Drew, Ruth Ford, Dorothy Adams. **Screenplay by:** Anthony Coldeway. **Directed by:** Robert Florey. **Noir Type:** Gangster. **Noir Themes:** Betrayal, greed. ✦

A gangster's moll (Emerson) gets nabbed for bank robbery, while boyfriend Drew and his boys escape. Thanks to old friend Wilcox, Emerson gets out on bail and double-crosses her cohorts, stashing the forty Gs with her landlady. While in jail, she remains on her best behavior, hoping for parole and a chance to get to the dough, but a squealer (Ford) and a lip-reading mute (Adams) have different plans for her. This is a real stinker, but the Three-Stooges-meet-the-Keystone-Cops climax is good for a few chuckles. Emerson became a regular panelist on TV's *I've Got a Secret*, Bishop later co-starred with Bob Cummings in *My Hero*, and Wilcox had a recurring role in the hit comedy series *The Beverly Hillbillies*.

Familiar Face from Television:
❑ Jackie Gleason (Ralph Kramden of *The Honeymooners*) as a rotund getaway driver.

Memorable Noir Moment:
❑ Emerson is foiled at the bank by a little dog. See *The Hidden Room*, *The Man with My Face* and *The Killing* for other crime-busting mutts.

Lady in the Death House (1944) 56 min. Jean Parker, Lionel Atwill, Douglas Fowley, Marcia Mae Jones. **Screenplay by:** Harry O. Hoyt. **Directed by:** Steve Sekely. **Noir Type:** Wrong Woman. **Noir Themes:** Woman in jeopardy, betrayal, guilt. ✦

Parker is a secretary wrongly sentenced to die in the electric chair for killing a blackmailer. Boyfriend Fowley (the electrocutioner!) and a famed criminologist (Atwill) frantically try to prove her innocence. Jones plays Parker's rebellious sister. Silly but short.

Familiar Face from Television:

❏ Byron Foulger (Wendell Gibbs in *Petticoat Junction*) as an eyewitness to the murder.

Memorable Noir Moment:

❏ Sensitivity Training Required: When Atwill tells a group of reporters that convicted killer Parker doesn't blame her executioner boyfriend for the job he must do, one of them replies, "She's right, but who'd expect a woman to be *that* logical?"

Lady in the Lake (1947) 105 min. Robert Montgomery, Audrey Totter, Lloyd Nolan, Leon Ames, Jayne Meadows. **Screenplay by:** Steve Fisher and Raymond Chandler. **Directed by:** Robert Montgomery. **Noir Type:** P.I. **Noir Themes:** Corruption, betrayal. ✭✭

Montgomery is Raymond Chandler's famous private eye, Philip Marlowe, in this slow-moving and hard-to-follow mystery. He's hired by a magazine editor (Totter) to find the missing wife of her boss (Ames). A woman's body is soon discovered in a country lake, and Montgomery finds himself mixed up with a shady cop (Nolan) and a mystery lady (Meadows). Along the way, he suffers a few beatings, gets framed for drunk driving (twice) and, of course, falls in love with Totter. The film's biggest attraction is Montgomery's innovative use of the camera, allowing the viewer to see

Cops (Tom Tully, left, and Lloyd Nolan, center) question P.I. Philip Marlowe (Robert Montgomery) in *Lady in the Lake* (MGM, 1947).

things through his eyes. But even that gets annoying, especially with the excessive number of mirror shots, the only purpose of which seems to be to provide Montgomery with ample screen time. This strange film does have its good points, however—namely, Totter as the femme fatale and Nolan as the tough, two-fisted cop. Meadows does a fine job of overacting. Although it's been said that Montgomery was the screen's closest counterpart to Chandler's fictional private investigator, Chandler himself did not appreciate Montgomery's portrayal, preferring instead Dick Powell's in *Murder, My Sweet*.

Memorable Noir Moment:
❑ "Do you fall in love with *all* your clients?" Totter asks Montgomery. "Only the ones in skirts," he replies.

Lady on a Train (1945) 94 min. Deanna Durbin, Ralph Bellamy, Edward Everett Horton, Dan Duryea, George Coulouris, David Bruce, Allen Jenkins. **Screenplay by:** Edmund Beloin and Robert O'Brien. **Directed by:** Charles David. **Noir Type:** Comedy. **Noir Themes:** Woman in jeopardy, greed. ★★★½

A train passenger (Durbin) witnesses a murder committed in a building across from a train station. When she reports it to the police, they see the mystery book she's been reading and write her off as a kook. So she seeks help from a mystery writer (Bruce), who falls in love with her after reluctantly joining her investigation. When she discovers that the victim, a rich businessman, has been reported killed in a freak accident, she sneaks onto his estate, where she's mistaken for the dead man's fiancée. Invited to sit through a reading of the will, she learns that the fiancé has inherited everything and that the man's nephews (Bellamy and Duryea) have been left nothing. Jenkins and Coulouris are the killer's henchmen, who try to prevent Durbin from getting too close to the truth. Horton is an employee of Durbin's father, assigned by his boss to look after her while she's in New York. An intelligent and, at times, very funny film. Look for Al LaRue, who later became B western star Lash LaRue, playing a waiter.

Familiar Faces from Television:
❑ William Frawley (Fred Mertz in *I Love Lucy* and Uncle Bub in *My Three Sons*) as a desk sergeant at a police station.
❑ Thurston Hall (Mr. Schuyler, Topper's boss, in *Topper*) as the murder victim.
❑ George Chandler (Uncle Petrie Martin in *Lassie* and Ichabod Adams in *Ichabod and Me*) as a nightclub customer admiring himself in a two-way mirror.

A Lady Without Passport (1950) 72 min. Hedy Lamarr, John Hodiak, James Craig, George Macready. **Screenplay by:** Howard Dimsdale. **Directed by:** Joseph H. Lewis. **Noir Type:** South of the Border. **Noir Themes:** Obsession, social reform. ★★

Hodiak is an undercover immigration agent posing as a Hungarian refugee in Cuba in order to infiltrate Macready's gang, which smuggles illegal aliens into the U.S. The beautiful Lamarr, a former concentration camp prisoner trying to make her way to America, falls in love with Hodiak. But before the G-man can tell her the truth about himself, the jealous Macready spills the beans and convinces Lamarr that the

Hodiak is interested only in arresting her. Lamarr's beauty and the unique aerial photography keep this from being too tedious to watch.

Familiar Faces from Television:

❑ Steven Hill (Daniel Briggs in *Mission Impossible* and D.A. Adam Schiff in *Law & Order*) as an immigration cop named Jack.

❑ King Donovan (Bob Cummings' Air Force buddy Harvey Helm in *Love That Bob* and lawyer Herb Thornton in *Please Don't Eat the Daisies*) as a doctor at the coroner's office.

Memorable Noir Moment:

❑ When Macready lets on that he knows Hodiak's real identity, the G-man drops his phony Hungarian accent. "It's out in the open," Hodiak admits. "Where the stench can reach any nostril," adds Macready.

Larceny (1948) 89 min. John Payne, Joan Caulfield, Dan Duryea, Shelley Winters, Richard Rober, Dan O'Herlihy. **Screenplay by:** William Bowers, Herbert Margolis and Lou Morheim. **Directed by:** George Sherman. **Noir Type:** Con Artist. **Noir Themes:** Betrayal, lust, greed, jealousy. ★★★½

A gang of smooth con men (Payne, Duryea, Rober and O'Herlihy) prey on a war hero's widow (Caulfield). Payne romances Caufield after pretending to be her late husband's war buddy and convinces her to invest a hundred grand to set up a center for orphaned kids, supposedly her late husband's last request. Duryea's moll (Winters) threatens to blow the whole scam when she arrives in town seeking to continue her affair with Payne, who's beginning to fall for his pretty victim. This programmer has many plusses—a fast-moving plot, witty dialogue and good performances by Payne and Duryea as the con men at odds with each other over the gorgeous Winters.

Familiar Face from Television:

❑ Don Wilson (Jack Benny's announcer on *The Jack Benny Show*) as the emcee of a post–Rose Bowl charity auction.

Memorable Noir Moments:

❑ With the gang between jobs, Winters remarks that Duryea "doesn't believe in unemployment … it's the root of all evil." "Funny," Payne says. "I thought that women were."

❑ When Payne gets a little too rough with the bothersome Winters, she complains, "Stop twisting my arm. People will think we're married."

The Las Vegas Story (1952) 88 min. Jane Russell, Victor Mature, Vincent Price, Hoagy Carmichael, Jay C. Flippen. **Screenplay by:** Paul Jarrico, Earl Felton and Harry Essex. **Directed by:** Robert Stevenson. **Noir Type:** Gambling. **Noir Themes:** Fatalism, obsession. ★½

This is an unmemorable murder yarn about a former nightclub singer (Russell), her gambling-addicted, embezzler husband (Price), her ex-lover (Mature) and a $150,000 necklace that changes hands more often than an insecure rummy player. A big disappointment, but voluptuous Russell is nice to look at.

Memorable Noir Moment:

❑ A new bride, having just received a congratulatory kiss from Mature, grudgingly admits

Victor Mature and Jane Russell in *The Las Vegas Story* (RKO, 1952).

that it would only be fair for Russell to kiss Bill, the groom. Russell brags, "If I kissed Bill, there wouldn't be anything fair about it."

The Last Mile (1959) 81 min. Mickey Rooney, Frank Overton, Don Barry, Clifford David, Leon Janney. **Screenplay by:** Milton Subotsky and Seton I. Miller. **Directed by:** Howard W. Koch. **Noir Type:** Prison. **Noir Themes:** Fatalism, corruption, social reform. ★★★

Rooney plays a half-pint killer on Death Row who, along with David and other inmates, are waiting their turn to walk that last mile. Overton is the chaplain who tries to comfort the men, and Barry and Janney are two of the prison's sadistic screws. While the first half of the film is tediously slow, espousing an anti-capital punishment sentiment ("I hope I'm the last guy who ever sits in this rotten chair"), action fans won't want to miss the second half, when Rooney gets fed up with Barry's cruelty and attempts a daring escape. Rooney is good as the remorseless convict, although he overdoes it at times, and Overton is enjoyable as the fearless priest. Don "Red" Barry, who starred in a number of B westerns in the 1940s and '50s, including the *Red Ryder* series, is entertaining as the cruel guard who incurs Rooney's wrath.

Familiar Face from Television:

❑ Michael Constantine (Principal Seymour Kaufman in *Room 222*) as the crazy inmate in Cell No. 1.

Memorable Noir Moments:

❑ A nervous convict on his way to the chair tells his pals, "You know, it's funny. I never had much to do with electricity before."
❑ Rooney reacts to a priest's unsolicited spiritual advice. "I've got two lousy weeks left," he complains, "and you're asking me to have faith?"

Laura (1944) 88 min. Gene Tierney, Dana Andrews, Clifton Webb, Vincent Price, Judith Anderson, Dorothy Adams. **Screenplay by:** Jay Dratler, Samuel Hoffenstein and Betty Reinhardt. **Directed by:** Otto Preminger. **Noir Type:** Whodunit. **Noir Themes:** Obsession, jealousy, betrayal. ★★★★★

A hard-boiled hero cop (Andrews), investigating the apparent shotgun murder of an advertising executive (Tierney), becomes obsessed with the victim's portrait as he tries to smoke out the murderer from a handful of suspects: the arrogant, eccentric (and most likely gay) columnist (Webb) who helped advance the lowly clerk's career and transformed her into a noted socialite; Tierney's fiancé (Price), "a male beauty in distress"; Tierney's middle-aged aunt (Anderson), who's been sleeping with Price; and, finally, Tierney's fiercely loyal maid (Adams), who has an obvious distaste for cops in general and for Andrews in particular. *The* classic mystery film, *Laura* is as much fun to watch as it was more than a half century ago. The entire cast

Dana Andrews and Gene Tierney in *Laura* (20th Century–Fox, 1944).

is fabulous, especially Webb, who was nominated for an Academy Award for Best Supporting Actor. Andrews, whose performance is wonderfully low-key, somehow manages to remain believable even as he questions suspects with a lit cigarette dangling from his lips.

Familiar Faces from Television:

❑ Cara Williams (Gladys Porter in *Pete and Gladys*) as one of Tierney's co-workers.

❑ James Flavin (Lt. Donovan in *Man with a Camera*) as a plainclothes cop standing guard at Tierney's apartment.

Memorable Noir Moments:

❑ When Andrews informs Webb that he's a suspect in Tierney's murder, the fey columnist glances into a mirror and remarks, "How singularly innocent I look this morning."

❑ Asked by Webb if he has ever been in love, Andrews replies, "A doll in Washington Heights once got a fox fur out of me."

❑ When Tierney tries to convince society columnist Webb to endorse a pen in a magazine ad, he candidly admits, "I don't use a pen. I write with a goose quill dipped in venom."

❑ Tierney's feisty maid tells Andrews, "I ain't afraid of cops. I was brought up to spit whenever I saw one."

The Lawless (1950) 83 min. Macdonald Carey, Gail Russell, Lee Patrick, John Hoyt, Lalo Rios, Johnny Sands. **Screenplay by:** Daniel Mainwaring [as Geoffrey Homes]. **Directed by:** Joseph Losey. **Noir Type:** Racist. **Noir Themes:** Bigotry, paranoia, social reform. ★★★

Carey stars as a crusading newspaper editor in a small California town ("Santa Marta, the Friendly City"), where poor Mexican farm workers are struggling to coexist peacefully with their middle-class white neighbors. When a young farm worker (Rios) becomes involved in a brawl with local Anglo toughs, he accidentally slugs a cop. In a panic, he flees the scene, stealing an ice cream truck and then a parked car. A series of misfortunate incidents (a cop dies in the chase and a teenage girl claims Rios assaulted her) enlarges the manhunt and causes the white community to riot, egged on by the irresponsible reporting of an out-of-town reporter (Patrick). Carey, who becomes romantically involved with a beautiful Mexican-American journalist (Russell), goes out on a limb to defend Rios in an editorial, asking for donations for the boy's defense. Hoyt, cast way against type, plays an idealistic businessman trying to teach his bigoted son (Sands) to be more open-minded. Look for Martha Hyer in a small role as a reporter's girlfriend. Carey went on to star in TV's *Lock Up* and is best remembered for his long-running role (1965 to his death in 1994) as Dr. Tom Horton in *Days of Our Lives*.

Familiar Faces from Television:

❑ Future heartthrob Tab Hunter in his film debut (Paul Morgan in *The Tab Hunter Show* and George Shumway in *Mary Hartman, Mary Hartman*) as a local tough.

❑ Willard Waterman (*The Great Gildersleeve*) as the parent of one of the boys involved in a fight at a dance.

Memorable Noir Moments:

❑ Sensitivity Training Required: Russell overhears reporter Patrick commenting on the town's Mexican citizenry: "They all look alike to me."

❑ From the Some-Things-Never-Change Department: Patrick wonders aloud about her fellow journalists, "What gets into newspapermen? Why can't they act like people?"

Leave Her to Heaven (1945) 110 min. Gene Tierney, Cornel Wilde, Jeanne Crain, Vincent Price, Mary Phillips, Darryl Hickman. **Screenplay by:** Jo Swerling. **Directed by:** John M. Stahl. **Noir Type:** Femme Fatale. **Noir Themes:** Jealousy, paranoia, revenge. ★★★★

When author Wilde meets the ravishing Tierney, who happens to be reading his latest book, he has no idea what fate has in store for him. After a whirlwind three-day romance with the writer, Tierney breaks her engagement to Price, a politician running for district attorney, and announces to her family, to Wilde's surprise, that they are getting married. Her mother (Phillips) and adopted sister (Crain) seem happy for her, but they also know something dark and sinister about her that Wilde doesn't. The couple's honeymoon ends abruptly when Wilde's crippled brother (Hickman) innocently comes between them, and Tierney's insane jealousy drives her to solve *that* problem in no time. Hoping to make Wilde happy, she decides to get pregnant but soon has some pretty ugly second thoughts. Finally, suspecting that something is going on between Wilde and Crain, Tierney plans one of film noir's sickest revenge schemes. Tierney's performance is perfect—she's truly evil and so easy to despise—earning her an Oscar nomination for Best Actress, which was won that year by Joan Crawford for **Mildred Pierce**. The low-key Wilde and Crain are the perfect foils for Tierney.

Familiar Faces from Television:
❑ Reed Hadley (Capt. John Braddock in *Racket Squad*) as Hickman's doctor.
❑ Ray Collins (Lieutenant Tragg in *Perry Mason*) as Crain's mediocre defense attorney.

Memorable Noir Moments:
❑ Wilde's future mother-in-law tries to explain Tierney's strange behavior to him. "There's nothing wrong with Ellen [Tierney]," she lies. "It's just that she loves too much."
❑ Viewing herself in the mirror, the pregnant Tierney remarks, "Look at me. I hate the little beast. I wish it would die."

The Leopard Man (1943) 66 min. Dennis O'Keefe, Margo, Jean Brooks, Isabel Jewell, James Bell. **Screenplay by:** Ardel Wray. **Directed by:** Jacques Tourneur. **Noir Type:** Horror. **Noir Themes:** Woman in danger, paranoia, guilt. ★★★½

More of a mystery than a genuine horror film, *The Leopard Man* is, nevertheless, a hauntingly eerie thriller from producer Val Lewton. Based on the novel, *Black Alibi*, by pulp writer Cornell Woolrich, it's about a series of killings, supposedly by an escaped leopard, in a small New Mexico town. (The leopard had been part of a selfish publicity stunt by nightclub dancer Brooks and her agent [O'Keefe] to overshadow a performance by rival performer Margo. When Margo frightened the leopard with her castanets, it escaped into the night, killing a teenage girl.) But O'Keefe and Brooks are convinced that the next two victims have been torn apart by a more dangerous predator—a psychopathic killer. Unable to persuade the local police department and its civilian adviser (Bell), the two investigate on their own. Beautifully photographed and succinctly written, *The Leopard Man* is horrifyingly (but never obscenely) violent.

Memorable Noir Moment:

❑ An Anglo cigarette girl complains to dancer Brooks about the *Latina* competition. "When dudes come out to New Mexico, they want to wallow in Latin glamour," she says, adding, "This is a tough town for blondes."

The Letter (1940) 95 min. Bette Davis, Herbert Marshall, James Stephenson, Gale Sondergaard, Sen Yung. **Screenplay by:** Howard Koch. **Directed by:** William Wyler. **Noir Type:** Triangle. **Noir Themes:** Betrayal, jealousy, guilt, revenge. ★★★★

Davis shines as the adulterous wife of a rubber plantation manager (Marshall). The film opens with her emptying a gun into a man who she later says tried to sexually assault her. The police don't buy her explanation, though, and they charge her with murder. A lawyer–family friend (Stephenson) takes on her case and is soon contacted by blackmailers claiming they have a letter written by Davis contradicting her. Stepping over moral and legal lines, the reluctant Stephenson purchases the letter from the victim's mysterious Eurasian wife (Sondergaard), and things start looking up for Davis. While this early film noir opens with startling ferocity (the ultra-violent shooting), it soon evolves into a fascinating mystery that emphasizes character development. Davis fans will be thrilled with her performance, but the film's most intriguing characters are Stephenson as the tormented attorney and (Victor) Sen Yung (Hop Sing in TV's *Bonanza*) as his wily assistant. Remade in 1947 as *The Unfaithful*, with Ann Sheridan.

Memorable Noir Moment:

❑ After shooting her lover six times, Davis calmly orders a servant to send someone to the district officer and "tell him there's been an accident and Mr. Hammond's dead."

A Life at Stake (1954) 78 min. Angela Lansbury, Keith Andes, Douglass Dumbrille, Claudia Barrett, Charles Maxwell. **Screenplay by:** Russ Bender. **Directed by:** Paul Guilfoyle. **Noir Type:** Femme Fatale. **Noir Themes:** Obsession, betrayal, greed, lust, paranoia. ★★½

A bankrupt home builder (Andes) is offered a real estate partnership by a sexy housewife (Lansbury) and her husband (Dumbrille) ... if, as collateral, he'll make them his beneficiaries in a $175,000 life insurance policy. Hesitant at first, Andes is easily persuaded by Lansbury's ample charms. After the papers are signed, Lansbury's kid sister (Barrett) lets it slip that Lansbury was once married to another of Dumbrille's business partners, who died in a mysterious auto crash, leaving Dumbrille to collect on a hefty insurance policy. Already paranoid, Andes starts worrying that the two entrepreneurs are planning to kill him, especially after a couple of near-fatal "accidents." That doesn't stop him from continuing his affair with Lansbury, but it does have him looking over his shoulder everywhere he goes. Meanwhile, the cops think he's loony, the insurance company won't cancel his policy, and Barrett is beginning to think he's kind of cute. Also known as *Key Man*, this is a nicely acted suspense noir with Lansbury (from TV's *Murder, She Wrote*) quite the surprise as a scheming seductress.

Memorable Noir Moment:

❑ When Lansbury brings up the insurance policy as a condition of their business agreement,

Andes balks. "Nobody's getting rich when I shove off," he informs her. "Not even if they give me that last push themselves."

Lightning Strikes Twice (1951) 91 min. Richard Todd, Ruth Roman, Mercedes McCambridge, Zachary Scott. **Screenplay by:** Lenore Coffee. **Directed by:** King Vidor. **Noir Type:** Triangle. **Noir Themes:** Distrust, jealousy, betrayal. ★★½

Todd, about to be executed for his wife's murder, gets a break and receives a new trial. Luckily for him, the lone female juror (McCambridge) has been in love with him since childhood and deliberately causes a hung jury, which results in a mistrial and Todd's eventual release. Returning home, he finds that his friends and neighbors still think he's guilty. He meets a new girl in town (Roman), who believes in his innocence, and eventually they fall in love. Pretty soon, though, even Roman begins to have doubts. Scott plays Todd's best friend, a rich playboy who is spurned by Roman. Irish-born actor Todd is a bit stiff as the ex-con, but Roman and McCambridge are fun to watch.

Familiar Face from Television:
❑ Darryl Hickman (Dobie's brother, Darvey, in *The Many Loves of Dobie Gillis* and Ben Canfield in the short-lived Civil War drama series *The Americans*) as McCambridge's crippled brother.

Memorable Noir Moments:
❑ Sensitivity Training Required: A bus passenger comments on the photo of a front-page murder victim. "It's always the good lookers that get into trouble," he says. "Nobody ever bothers to kill the dogs."
❑ McCambridge responds to Roman's declaration of love for suspected wife killer Todd. "You don't love him," she says. "You're fascinated by the smell of murder."

The Limping Man (1953-British) 76 min. Lloyd Bridges, Moira Lister, Alan Wheatley, Leslie Phillips, Helene Cordet, Andre Van Gyseghem. **Screenplay by:** Ian Stuart Black and Reginald Long. **Directed by:** Charles De la Tour and Cy Endfield (uncredited). **Noir Type:** Whodunit. **Noir Themes:** Victim of fate, greed. ★★

A former American G.I. (Bridges) returns to London, hoping to rekindle his wartime romance with an actress (Lister). As he gets off the plane, he witnesses a fellow passenger being gunned down by a sniper. The killer, who carries a cane (hence, *The Limping Man*), drives off, leaving Bridges to face Wheatley and Phillips, the Scotland Yard inspectors investigating the shooting. If witnessing a murder two minutes after setting foot in a foreign country isn't trouble enough, the unlucky American discovers that his former girlfriend may be implicated in the crime and must try to prove her innocence. Nightclub singer Cordet is the victim's wife, and Van Gyseghem plays a stage doorman who happens to walk with a cane. There's a ridiculous surprise ending that the directors probably thought would compensate for the tedious plot. This British noir might be a big disappointment for fans of the usually reliable Bridges.

The Lineup (1958) 85 min. Eli Wallach, Robert Keith, Warner Anderson, Richard Jaeckel, Emile Meyer. **Screenplay by:** Stirling Silliphant. **Directed by:** Don Siegel. **Noir Type:** Narcotics. **Noir Themes:** Greed, fatalism, paranoia, sexual hostility. ★★★½

Unsuspecting travelers are being used by the mob to smuggle heroin into the country. Even worse, they're being killed by a psychopathic hit man (Wallach), whose job it is to retrieve the drugs. After a cop is killed trying to stop a taxi driver from fleeing with a satchel full of heroin, San Francisco detectives Anderson and Meyer take on the case. They attempt to track down the bad guys—Wallach; his misogynistic associate (Keith), who's writing a book containing the last words of Wallach's victims; and their dipso getaway driver (Jaeckel). It's not the cops, however, that the bad guys need to worry about, but a little girl and her dolly. This effective, ultra-violent film (director Siegel later gave us *Dirty Harry*) is entertaining thanks to fascinating performances by Wallach and Keith, perhaps the oddest pair of villains in film noir. Warner Anderson, who plays Lt. Guthrie here, also played the same character in the 1954–60 TV series of the same name.

Familiar Face from Television:
❏ Raymond Bailey (banker Milburn Drysdale in *The Beverly Hillbillies*) as an unwitting heroin smuggler.

Memorable Noir Moments:
❏ Keith and Jaeckel discuss their hit man boss. "Dancer's an addict, an addict with a real big habit," Keith observes. "H like in heroin?" asks Jaeckel. "H like in hate," responds Keith.
❏ A long-time member of the Women Hater's Club, Keith reacts to the tears of a frightened mother. "See. You cry," he says. "That's why women have no place in society."
❏ "The Man," an arrogant, wheelchair-bound drug kingpin, makes the foolish mistake of threatening Wallach. (For other interesting wheelchair mishaps, see *The Beast with Five Fingers*, *Kiss of Death* and *Whiplash*.)

Loan Shark (1952) 74 min. George Raft, Dorothy Hart, Paul Stewart, John Hoyt. **Screenplay by**: Eugene Ling and Martin Rackin. **Directed by**: Seymour Friedman. **Noir Type**: Payback. **Noir Themes**: Revenge, economic repression. ✶✶

A low-budget crime drama, *Loan Shark* never gets off the ground, despite the presence of noir veterans Raft, Stewart and Hoyt. Raft, playing his usual tough guy character, is an ex-con out to avenge the murder of his brother-in-law at the hands of loan sharks (Stewart and Hoyt). Unfortunately, there's not much left of the legendary Raft charisma to salvage the film. Fifty-seven at the time, George just couldn't play those two-fisted tough guys and lover boys like he used to. But the former hoofer still looked pretty good in his obligatory dancing scene with Hart, his romantic interest.

Memorable Noir Moment:
❏ In an obvious tribute to his most famous character, Guido Rinaldo in *Scarface*, Raft once again gives us his trademark coin toss routine.

The Locket (1946) 86 min. Laraine Day, Brian Aherne, Robert Mitchum, Gene Raymond, Reginald Denny. **Screenplay by**: Sheridan Gibney. **Directed by**: John Brahm. **Noir Type**: Femme Fatale. **Noir Themes**: Paranoia, distrust. ✶✶

On the day he's supposed to marry his fiancée (Day), Aherne is visited by a psychiatrist (Raymond) who claims to be Day's ex-husband. Raymond warns him that

An ex-con (**George Raft**, left) visits a couple of tough money lenders (**John Hoyt** and **Lawrence Dobkin**) in *Loan Shark* (Lippert, 1952).

Day is a kleptomaniac and, possibly, a murderess. He tells him the strange tale of how he met her and how he was similarly warned by Day's former fiancé (Mitchum), who believed that Day killed her boss (Cortez) while trying to steal his jewels. Raymond, to his regret, didn't believe Mitchum, and, of course, Aherne doesn't believe Raymond. Confusing? At one point, there's a flashback that goes three deep. The excellent cast can't redeem the convoluted script.

Familiar Face from Television:
❑ Ellen Corby (Grandma Walton in *The Waltons*) as a kitchen worker.

The Lodger (1944) 84 min. Merle Oberon, George Sanders, Laird Cregar, Cedric Hardwicke, Sara Allgood. **Screenplay by:** Barré Lyndon. **Directed by:** John Brahm. **Noir Type:** Period. **Noir Themes:** Sexual hostility, woman in jeopardy, paranoia. ★★★★

Cregar plays a mysterious pathologist who rents a room in the London house owned by Hardwicke and his wife (Allgood). While London's Whitechapel area is being terrorized almost nightly by Jack the Ripper, Cregar's weird behavior attracts the justifiable suspicions of his landlords and of Scotland Yard inspector Sanders. Oberon is the couple's niece, the star attraction of a burlesque-type show, who takes a friendly interest in the creepy new lodger. A remake of Hitchcock's classic silent film of the same name, this definitive Jack the Ripper movie spawned a faithful, but inferior, remake (1953's **Man in the Attic**) with Jack Palance, who fails to equal Cregar's *tour de force* performance.

Memorable Noir Moment:

❑ Cregar rants about his "genius" brother to showgirl Oberon. "It was the beauty of women that led him to his destruction," he tells her, adding, "Yours is a beauty that could destroy a man." A visibly shaken Oberon responds, "Is that a compliment?" Ignoring her, Cregar goes on, "Or it could destroy *you*. Have you ever thought of *that*?"

Lonelyhearts (1958) 108 min. Montgomery Clift, Robert Ryan, Myrna Loy, Dolores Hart, Maureen Stapleton, Frank Maxwell. **Screenplay by:** Dore Schary. **Directed by:** Vincent J. Donehue. **Noir Type:** Newspaper. **Noir Themes:** Fatalism, betrayal, guilt, jealousy. ★★★½

Wannabe writer Clift lands a job on a newspaper and is assigned by the cynical publisher (Ryan) to the lovelorn column. At first, the column is a joke to Clift, but eventually the sensitive reporter begins to empathize with the troubled folks who seek his advice. When he asks his boss to assign him to another job, Ryan challenges him to meet with one of his fans, who he believes are all self-serving fakes. Clift agrees but makes the mistake of choosing a lonely married woman (Stapleton), who falsely wrote that her husband (Maxwell) is a cripple who can't perform sexually. Stapleton, it seems, has more on her mind than talking about her problems, and this only seems to validate Ryan's negative opinion of humanity. Hart plays Clift's girlfriend and Loy is Ryan's long-suffering wife, whose brief affair ten years earlier he won't let her forget. Ryan is the perfect louse, and Clift is fascinating as the sympathetic writer who, though he can barely deal with his own emotional problems, tries to solve the public's. Stapleton, in her film debut, was nominated for an Oscar for Best Supporting Actress. A depressing but interesting soap opera.

Familiar Faces from Television:

❑ Jackie Coogan (Uncle Fester in *The Addams Family*) as the reporter who lost the lovelorn column to Clift.
❑ Mike Kellin (Chief Petty Officer Willie Miller in *The Wackiest Ship in the Army*) as a reporter who gets socked by an inebriated Clift.

Memorable Noirs Moments:

❑ Publisher Ryan, who has a low opinion of everyone, shares his impression of Clift with Loy. "He's a fake," he says. "A scribbling punk trying to play the part of goody two shoes. He'll steal my fillings when I lie dead on the street."
❑ After Stapleton seduces Clift, the guilt-stricken columnist makes it clear he doesn't want to see her again. "Listen," she shouts. "You wanted a sad story, you heard a sad story. You also wanted some action and so did I."

The Long Night (1947) 101 min. Henry Fonda, Barbara Bel Geddes, Vincent Price, Ann Dvorak. **Screenplay by:** John Wexley. **Directed by:** Anatole Litvak. **Noir Type:** Troubled Veteran. **Noir Themes:** Obsession, fatalism, jealousy. ★★

Litvak pulls all the tricks out of his noir hat, but only Sol Polito's expressionist photography and Dimitri Tiomkin's haunting score raise this disappointing film above mediocrity. Fonda is wasted as a World War II vet whose jealousy causes him to explode in one insane moment and become a murderer. Flashbacks and double flashbacks tell Fonda's story as he holes up in his hotel room trying to avoid police bullets. Price, as a second-rate magician, spends the entire film trying to seduce Bel Geddes, whom the jealous, marriage-minded Fonda has known for all of six weeks. Dvorak, Price's assistant, plays the girl who falls for Fonda, even though he won't give her a tumble. It's depressingly slow, but trying to identify all of the film's familiar character actors helps to pass the time.

Familiar Faces from Television:
❏ Ellen Corby (Grandma Walton from *The Waltons*) as a face in the crowd.
❏ Byron Foulger (Wendell Gibbs in *Petticoat Junction*) as a man with a bicycle.

The Long Wait (1954) 93 min. Anthony Quinn, Charles Coburn, Gene Evans, Peggie Castle, Mary Ellen Kay, Shawn Smith, Dolores Donlon, Barry Kelley, James Millican. **Screenplay by:** Alan Green and Lesser Samuels. **Directed by:** Victor Saville. **Noir Type:** Amnesia. **Noir Themes:** Paranoia, greed, corruption. ★★

After losing his memory in a car crash, ex–G.I. Quinn has almost given up hope of discovering who he is when he gets a lead that brings him back to his hometown. There he discovers that he was a bank teller suspected of stealing 250 Gs and that he's wanted for murdering the D.A. Homicide detectives (Kelley and Millican) are delighted when Quinn shows up, but their bubble bursts when they discover that, in addition to his memory, Quinn lost his fingerprints in the fiery crash, making the only evidence against him useless. Determined to discover the truth about himself, Quinn must first find his former girlfriend. Unfortunately, she has had plastic surgery, leaving him an amnesiac trying to find a person whose face he has never seen. He narrows his list down to four beautiful women — Kay, who works at a casino owned by a racketeer (Evans); Castle, the manager of a clothing store also owned by Evans; Donlon, Evans' moll; and Smith, Evans' secretary. It doesn't take a genius to find the common denominator here. Coburn plays Quinn's former boss, apparently an understanding and forgiving bank president. Adapted from a Mickey Spillane novel, *The Long Wait* is unexciting and predictable. Macho man Quinn, a typical Spillane hero, starts fights at the slightest provocation and violently romances every dame he meets. However, the exquisitely filmed warehouse scene, where Quinn awaits his fate at the hands of a maniacal killer, is the viewer's reward for staying awake. Donlon became *Playboy* magazine's August 1957 Playmate of the Month.

Memorable Noir Moment:
❏ From the Stupid Criminal Department: Three of Evans' witless goons attempt to kill Quinn by tossing him off a 200–foot cliff. One of them turns off a lantern so they can work in darkness. When Quinn, who's bound hand and foot, makes his getaway move, hood number one mistakes hood number two for their intended victim and shoots him. Number One then promptly falls off the cliff after jumping over hood number three, who's already been killed by their prisoner. (See *Raw Deal, Sealed Lips, Knock on Any Door* and *Escape in the Fog* for further examples of faulty hiring practices by gangster management.)

Loophole (1954) 79 min. Barry Sullivan, Charles McGraw, Dorothy Malone, Don Haggerty, Mary Beth Hughes, Don Beddoe. **Screenplay by:** Warren Douglas. **Directed by:** Harold Schuster. **Noir Type:** Wrong Man. **Noir Themes:** Victim of fate, greed, betrayal. ★★½

A mild-mannered teller (Beddoe), masquerading as a member of an auditing team, enters a bank where Sullivan works and calmly walks out with nearly fifty thousand dollars, leaving Sullivan to take the rap. Haggerty, the cop investigating the robbery, believes that the ex–G.I. is innocent, but a hard-boiled insurance investigator (McGraw) doesn't buy Sullivan's story. When Sullivan loses his position at the bank, McGraw doggedly hounds him, causing him to be fired from each lowly job he finds. Malone plays Sullivan's devoted wife, and femme fatale Hughes is Beddoe's greedy girlfriend. Fairly entertaining, but the ending is puzzling.

Lost, Lonely and Vicious (1958) 73 min. Ken Clayton, Barbara Wilson, Lilyan Chauvin, Richard Gilden. **Screenplay by:** Norman Graham. **Directed by:** Frank Myers. **Noir Type:** Troubled Youth. **Noir Themes:** Fatalism, jealousy. ★

This is a deservedly obscure, low-budget movie with a mostly unknown cast. Clayton plays a fast-driving, self-pitying actor with a Thunderbird and a death wish, and Wilson is the pretty drug store clerk who makes him want to live again. Chauvin plays his worried drama coach and lover, and Gilden is an untalented actor wannabe, whose jealousy and antagonism fuel Clayton's depression. Loosely based (and the keyword here is "loosely") on the short career of Hollywood idol James Dean, who was killed in a car crash in 1955, this is a boring and forgettable film. James Dean lookalike Clayton's second (and last) film was a small role in the 1959 science fiction movie *The Cosmic Man*, making his Hollywood career even shorter than James Dean's. Wilson played a teenage gang member in 1957's **Teenage Doll**.

Memorable Noir Moment:
❏ An aspiring actress noirishly bemoans her taste in men. "Why did I get mixed up with a bum like you?" she cries.

The Lost Moment (1947) 89 min. Robert Cummings, Susan Hayward, Agnes Moorehead, Joan Lorring, Eduardo Ciannelli. **Screenplay by:** Leonardo Bercovici. **Directed by:** Martin Gabel. **Noir Type:** Period. **Noir Themes:** Greed, betrayal, guilt. ★★

In the late nineteenth century, publisher Cummings travels to Venice to find out if a famous poet's love letters still exist and, if so, to obtain them by any means possible. Amazingly, the poet's lover (Moorehead, unrecognizable in a terrific makeup job) is still alive. She's a blind, 105-year-old woman who lives with her schizophrenic great grandniece (Hayward). It seems that whenever Hayward puts on Moorehead's ring, she assumes her identity as well. When Cummings is fortunate enough to walk in on her during her hallucinatory state, she thinks he's her poet lover. Ciannelli plays the local parish priest, and Lorring is the young maid with a crush on the American publisher. Highly melodramatic and, at times, downright boring, the film does have its enjoyable moments— and the gorgeous Hayward is usually right there in the middle of them.

Familiar Face from Television:

❑ Minerva Urecal (Annie in *The Adventures of Tugboat Annie* and "Mother" in *Peter Gunn*) as Lorring's mother.

Memorable Noir Moment:

❑ When Cummings expresses doubt that Hayward is capable of murder, Moorehead scoffs. "It's the gentle souls," she says, "who seem sweet and loving to the world, with the innocence of children, and then out of nowhere, something happens, and you have murder."

The Lost Weekend

The Lost Weekend (1945) 101 min. Ray Milland, Jane Wyman, Phillip Terry, Howard da Silva, Doris Dowling, Frank Faylen. **Screenplay by:** Charles Brackett and Billy Wilder. **Directed by:** Billy Wilder. **Noir Type:** Boozer. **Noir Themes:** Obsession, fatalism, betrayal. ★★★★★

Milland is outstanding in this intense story of a man, his girl and his bottle. The novelist wannabe is suffering from writer's block and alcoholism. A binge drinker, he tries to conceal his dependence from those who love him — his understanding girl (Wyman) and his long-suffering brother (Terry). To pay for his booze, Milland, who's being financially supported by his brother, steals money from his cleaning lady, hocks his typewriter and snatches a pocketbook. When he can't come up with any money, he resorts to begging his local bartender (da Silva) for "just one more." He hides bottles in his apartment — in the vacuum cleaner bag, the ceiling light fixture, and even at the end of a string outside the window — but can't remember where they are. Swearing off the stuff once again, he makes a valiant effort to start his novel but can't get past the title and dedication page before ransacking his apartment in a frenzied search for a bottle he had hidden (and finished) during a previous bender. When a spiteful male nurse (Faylen) in the alcoholic ward promises him he'll soon be suffering from delirium tremens and seeing little animals, Milland scoffs — until he watches in horror as an imaginary bat bites off a mouse's head. Dowling plays a barfly whore who's attracted to Milland. Unfortunately for her, he has only one love — his hooch. Milland won a Best Actor Oscar for his amazing performance as the nice guy on the path to self-destruction. The film also won for Best Director, Best Picture and Best Screenplay. Many of the "problem films" of the 1940s and 1950s have lost much of their punch by now, but *The Lost Weekend* certainly isn't one of them.

Memorable Noir Moment:

❑ A bitchy male nurse in the hospital's alcoholic ward "Hangover Square" gleefully warns Milland that he'll be visited by the DTs after bedtime. "Delirium is a disease of the night," the nurse says.

The Louisiana Hussy

The Louisiana Hussy (1959) 66 min. Nan Peterson, Robert Richards, Peter Coe, Betty Lynn, Harry Lauter. **Screenplay by:** Charles Lang. **Directed by:** Lee Sholem. **Noir Type:** Femme Fatale. **Noir Themes:** Obsession, lust, jealousy, revenge. ★

"She's a tramp, a nymphomaniac," Richards warns his lovesick Cajun brother (Coe). He left out "bad actress." Peterson plays a voluptuous femme fatale who cheerfully destroys the lives of the men around her. Richards almost falls for her trap on his wedding night, but his love for his bride (Lynn) causes him to exercise restraint. So the temptress moves on to big brother Coe, who's not yet over losing Lynn to

Richards. Also known as *The Secret of Nina Duprez*, the film begins promisingly with Peterson making a getaway on horseback while being chased by her angry, gun-waving lover (veteran character actor Lauter), whose wife she drove to suicide. But it's all downhill from there (except for some nice location shots of Louisiana's bayou country). Peterson's other "big" film was another bomb, *The Hideous Sun Demon*, released the same year. Lynn is better known for her role of Thelma Lou, Barney Fife's girlfriend, on TV's *The Andy Griffith Show*.

Love from a Stranger (1947) 81 min. Sylvia Sidney, John Hodiak, Ann Richards, John Howard. **Screenplay by:** Philip MacDonald. **Directed by:** Richard Whorf. **Noir Type:** Period. **Noir Themes:** Woman in jeopardy, greed, paranoia. ★★★

Wife killer Hodiak leaves American authorities thinking he's dead when he flees to Victorian England, where he knocks off a spouse or two before meeting a pretty lottery winner (Sidney). Sidney jilts her fiancé (Howard) and marries the debonair strangler. They move to a cottage in a secret (at Hodiak's insistence) location, where Hodiak spends a lot of time in the basement supposedly conducting experiments with dangerous chemicals. Actually, he's busy down there digging a hole in the concrete floor. Meanwhile, Howard and Richards, Sidney's best friend, become worried when they discover that she has given Hodiak power of attorney over her affairs and that he has already started transferring funds from her bank. They contact Scotland Yard and the race is on to find the honeymooning couple before Hodiak can follow through with his murderous plan. A suspenseful tale with Hodiak convincing as the Bluebeard-like killer.

Memorable Noir Moment:
❏ An English bobby, reading about Hodiak on a wanted poster, figures Britain's got enough criminals of its own without importing them. "South American extraction, eh?" he comments. "Why don't he stay home and do his dirty work?"

Love Letters (1945) 101 min. Jennifer Jones, Joseph Cotten, Ann Richards, Cecil Kellaway, Robert Sully. **Screenplay by:** Ayn Rand. **Directed by:** William Dieterle. **Noir Type:** Amnesia. **Noir Themes:** Betrayal, paranoia. ★★

Maudlin soap opera with Cotten as an English soldier in Italy playing Cyrano de Bergerac for his buddy (Sully) by writing love letters to Jones. By the time Sully returns to England, Jones is madly in love with him, believing him to be the sensitive author of all those beautiful letters. When the wounded Cotten comes home, he finds that Sully has been murdered and that Jones, now an amnesiac, has spent a year in a prison hospital following her manslaughter conviction. Cotten falls in love with her but spends most of his time worrying that she'll regain her memory and come to hate him when she discovers that he wrote the letters. Richards plays Jones' best friend. It's a boring film but the acting is good, with Jones receiving a Best Actress Oscar nomination.

Memorable Noir Moment:
❏ Amnesia victim Jones expresses a positive mental attitude about her malady. "Since I have no past, I have no future," she says. "Only the moment. Only now."

The Lucky Stiff (1949) 99 min. Dorothy Lamour, Brian Donlevy, Claire Trevor, Irene Hervey, Robert Armstrong. **Screenplay by:** Lewis R. Foster. **Directed by:** Lewis R. Foster. **Noir Type:** Whodunit. **Noir Themes:** Betrayal, greed. ★½

Attorney Donlevy takes on a protection racket using the "ghost" of a nightclub singer (Lamour), supposedly executed for killing Hervey's husband. Trevor is Donlevy's lovesick secretary, and Armstrong is a police detective. The talented cast is wasted in this intolerably long, questionably noir slapstick, which was produced by comedian Jack Benny.

Familiar Faces from Television:
❑ Warner Anderson (Lt. Ben Guthrie in *The Lineup* and Matthew Swain in *Peyton Place*) as a nightclub manager.
❑ Joe Sawyer (Sgt. Biff O'Hara in *The Adventures of Rin Tin Tin*) as a hood.

Lured (1947) 102 min. Lucille Ball, George Sanders, Charles Coburn, Cedric Hardwicke, Boris Karloff. **Screenplay by:** Leo Rosten. **Directed by:** Douglas Sirk. **Noir Type:** Missing Person. **Noir Themes:** Woman in jeopardy, obsession. ★★½

Ball is an American taxi dancer in London who agrees to act as a decoy for Scotland Yard after her friend falls victim to a serial killer. She meets a number of oddballs through her police-sponsored personal column ads, and her zany misadventures will have you half expecting Desi to pop up at any moment to scold her. Coburn is the police inspector trying to find out what happened to all of the missing girls, and Karloff, in a too-small role, is a crackpot, has-been designer. Sanders plays a rich playboy attracted to the beautiful redhead, and Hardwicke is his stiff, humorless secretary. Who's the killer? Who cares? Sit back and enjoy the acting.

Lust for Gold (1949) 90 min. Ida Lupino, Glenn Ford, Gig Young, William Prince, Edgar Buchanan, Will Geer, Paul Ford. **Screenplay by:** Ted Sherdeman and Richard English. **Directed by:** S. Sylvan Simon. **Noir Type:** Gold Fever. **Noir Themes:** Greed, paranoia, jealousy, revenge. ★★★

"This is the story of Superstition Mountain — the biography of a death trap." These are the foreboding words of narrator Prince, who is searching for the Lost Dutchman's gold mine in the Arizona mountains. He stumbles across a body and reports it to local cops (Paul Ford, Geer and Silverheels), who don't seem too interested. Prince investigates on his own and learns that his grandfather, German immigrant Glenn Ford, the so-called "Dutchman," murdered his partner (Buchanan) and the two men who found the mine first. Returning to town with five thousand dollars worth of gold and the prospect of untold wealth, Ford finds he must fend off the many "well-wishers" who are trying to ingratiate themselves with him. Lupino, the beautiful femme fatale owner of the town's bakery, schemes with her husband (Young) to take Ford for every cent he has. But the wily prospector is no easy mark. This combination of Western, adventure and murder mystery is enjoyable thanks mostly to the presence of noir icons Lupino and Glenn Ford, cast as a heavy for a change, and the many familiar faces that keep popping up. There's also an exciting, well-staged battle scene between Spanish gold thieves and Apaches, who are perturbed that the Spaniards have violated the home of their thunder gods.

Familiar Faces from Television:

❑ Percy Helton (Homer Cratchit in *The Beverly Hillbillies*) as a barber.
❑ Billy Gray (Bud in *Father Knows Best*) as a little boy in Helton's barber shop.
❑ John Doucette (Jim Weston in *Lock Up* and Captain Andrews in *The Partners*) as a customer in the barbershop.
❑ Hayden Rorke (Dr. Bellows in *I Dream of Jeannie*) as a greedy, ill-fated gold hunter. (In **Rope of Sand**, Rorke plays a greedy, ill-fated *diamond* hunter.)

Memorable Noir Moment:

❑ After Ford signs his mine claim with an "X," a woman in the crowd remarks, "A stupid foreigner that can't even read or write finds a million dollar gold mine," and adds, to the embarrassment of her milquetoast husband, "And you get eleven dollars a week clerking in a hardware store. You and your high school diploma."

M (1951) 88 min. David Wayne, Howard da Silva, Martin Gabel, Luther Adler, Steve Brodie, Raymond Burr, Walter Burke, Norman Lloyd. **Screenplay by:** Norman Reilly Raine and Leo Katcher. **Directed by:** Joseph Losey. **Noir Type:** Psycho. **Noir Themes:** Child in jeopardy, sexual hostility, revenge. ★★★

Wayne plays a psychopathic child killer with a shoe fetish, hunted by both the police and the mob. Released from a mental institution, Wayne wanders the streets

A child killer (David Wayne) practices his strangulation technique on a doll in *M* (Columbia, 1951).

of Los Angeles like a depraved Pied Piper attracting little girls with his flute. Da Silva and Brodie are the cops in charge of the investigation, and Gabel is the mobster concerned about the increased police activity, which is adversely affecting his illegal operations. He and his underlings (Burr, Burke and Lloyd) plan a city-wide search for the killer in the hopes that the good publicity will put an end to the police raids. Wayne gives a fine performance as the pathetic pedophile, literally marked with an "M" for murderer, and Adler is excellent as Gabel's alcoholic mouthpiece, who must defend the killer before a jury of his peers— thieves, cutthroats and racketeers. This is a good remake of the superior Fritz Lang 1931 film, which starred Peter Lorre as the child murderer.

Familiar Face from Television:

❑ Jim Backus (Thurston Howell III of *Gilligan's Island*) as the Mayor of Los Angeles.

Memorable Noir Moment:

❑ Burke, who appears to be in charge of narcotics distribution for the mob, isn't happy about the increased police presence. "You can't even show your face around high schools these days," he complains.

Macao (1952) 81 min. Robert Mitchum, Jane Russell, William Bendix, Thomas Gomez, Gloria Grahame, Brad Dexter. **Screenplay by:** Bernard C. Schoenfeld and Stanley Rubin. **Directed by:** Josef von Sternberg and Nicholas Ray (uncredited). **Noir Type:** Far East. **Noir Themes:** Victim of fate, corruption, betrayal. ★★★

When an undercover officer of the International Police is murdered by a gang of jewel smugglers in Macao, the "Monte Carlo of the Orient," the cops send in another agent to take his place. On the run from the law, Mitchum arrives in Macao on the same boat as a sexy nightclub singer (Russell) and a traveling salesman (Bendix). Casino owner Dexter, the gang's ringleader, believes that Mitchum is the undercover cop sent to lure him beyond the three-mile limit so the international cops can apprehend him. After hiring Russell to sing at his casino, Dexter bribes Mitchum to leave Macao. Mitchum refuses because he's fallen for man-hater Russell, who in turn is getting the evil eye from Dexter's jealous moll (Grahame), a croupier at the club. A little confusing, but interesting nevertheless thanks to the witty dialogue and the chemistry between sex symbols Russell and Mitchum. Gomez is terrific as the corrupt Portuguese police lieutenant, but noir icon Grahame has a too-small part.

Familiar Face from Television:

❑ Philip Ahn (Master Kan in *Kung Fu*) as one of Dexter's knife-wielding henchmen.

Memorable Noir Moments:

❑ Looking up from the bottom of a staircase, Mitchum catches a glimpse of Russell changing nylons. "Enjoy the view?" she asks. "Well, it's not the Taj Mahal or the Hanging Gardens of Babylon," he replies nonchalantly. "But it's not bad."
❑ When Grahame tries on the diamond bracelet that a casino loser has cashed in, Dexter remarks, "You don't want that junk. Diamonds would only cheapen you." "Yeah," she agrees. "But what a way to be cheap."
❑ Bendix assumes that his female barber understands only pidgin English. "Me wantchee

shavey ... chop, chop," he barks. "Who do you like this year?" she asks as she applies the lather. "The Giants or the Dodgers?"

The Macomber Affair (1947) 89 min. Gregory Peck, Robert Preston, Joan Bennett, Reginald Denny. **Screenplay by:** Frank Arnold, Seymour Bennett and Casey Robinson. **Directed by:** Zoltan Korda. **Noir Type:** Femme Fatale. **Noir Themes:** Betrayal, fatalism. ★★★

Ernest Hemingway's story "The Short Happy Life of Francis Macomber" gets the noir treatment, with Peck playing a great white hunter hired to take a husband and wife (Preston and Bennett) on safari. The film opens with Preston's body being flown to Nairobi, where a police captain (Denny) begins an investigation. Denny learns that Preston turned coward during a lion hunt and that his shrewish wife wouldn't let him live it down, cruelly throwing herself at the interested, but self-restrained, hunter. Ashamed of his cowardice, the brooding Preston eventually managed to regain his self-respect during another hunt but paid a steep price for it — a bullet in the back. Peck does a fine job as the laid-back hunter, and Preston and Bennett are perfect as the married couple who have gone a few rounds over the years.

Memorable Noir Moment:
❏ Sensitivity Training Required: When Bennett insists on accompanying the men on a hunt, Peck asks Preston, "Why don't you order her to stay?"

Mad at the World (1955) 76 min. Frank Lovejoy, Keefe Brasselle, Cathy O'Donnell, Karen Sharpe, Stanley Clements, Paul Dubov. **Screenplay by:** Harry Essex. **Directed by:** Harry Essex. **Noir Type:** Payback. **Noir Themes:** Revenge, child in jeopardy, law breaking for kicks. ★★

Members of a Chicago teen gang "borrow" a car from a parking lot and go looking for trouble. When Korean war hero Brasselle and his wife (O'Donnell) cross their path, the drunken gang leader (Dubov) tosses a whiskey bottle at them, striking their infant. With his baby in critical condition, Brasselle goes looking for revenge, while tough cop Lovejoy tries to dissuade him. Clements plays a gang members, and Sharpe is a neighborhood "bad girl." TV producer Aaron Spelling (Tori's dad) has a small part as the hapless owner of the stolen automobile. In the film's prologue, Senator Estes Kefauver (see *The Captive City*), chairman of the Senate Crime Investigating Committee, informs the viewer of the dangers of juvenile delinquency and "how one great American city fought to bring this destructive human fire under control." Another forgettable delinquent noir, in which actors in their thirties portray "teenage" gang members.

Familiar Face from Television:
❏ Joe Besser ("Stinky" on *The Abbott and Costello Show*) as a gas station attendant.

Memorable Noir Moment:
❏ Waitress Sharpe makes small talk with the disinterested Brasselle. "I've got a trade," she brags. "I'm a manicurist. Cuticles and everything. Only I'm real lousy at it."

Make Haste to Live (1954) 90 min. Dorothy McGuire, Stephen McNally, Mary Murphy, Edgar Buchanan, John Howard. **Screenplay by:** Warren Duff. **Directed by:** William A. Seiter. **Noir Type:** Payback. **Noir Themes:** Revenge, woman in jeopardy. ★★

A former gangster and cop killer (McNally), who has spent the past eighteen years wrongly imprisoned for murdering his wife (McGuire), shows up in the little New Mexico town where McGuire, very much alive and the owner of the local newspaper, has been hiding out with their daughter (Murphy), whom McNally has never seen. He's back for vengeance because she let him go to prison instead of coming forward to prove his innocence. Everyone in town, including Murphy and McGuire's archaeologist boyfriend (Howard), thinks that McNally is McGuire's brother, but the suspicious sheriff (Buchanan) does a background check. Tedious and slow until the exciting climax in a labyrinthine Indian cliff dwelling.

Familiar Faces from Television:
❑ Ron Hagerthy (Clipper in *Sky King*) as Murphy's boyfriend.
❑ Carolyn Jones (Morticia in *The Addams Family*) as McGuire's best friend.

Memorable Noir Moment:
❑ McGuire seems relieved when McNally tells her he prayed while in prison. Her hopes are dashed, however, when he explains, "I prayed you were dying slowly of some disease."

The Maltese Falcon (1941) 100 min. Humphrey Bogart, Mary Astor, Peter Lorre, Sydney Greenstreet, Gladys George, Barton MacLane, Ward Bond, Jerome Cowan, Lee Patrick, Elisha Cook, Jr. **Screenplay by:** John Huston. **Directed by:** John Huston. **Noir Type:** P.I. **Noir Themes:** Obsession, greed, betrayal, fatalism. ★★★★★

Bogey is Sam Spade, pulp writer Dashiel Hammett's tough private eye. Business is slow until a gorgeous dame (Astor) shows up at the office he shares with his partner (Cowan), and hires them to tail the guy who ran off with her little sister. The shamuses know she's lying but two hundred bucks is two hundred bucks. Unfortunately for Cowan, somebody plugs him while he's following the alleged Romeo, and then somebody plugs the Romeo. While cops MacLane and Bond are busy trying to pin the murders on Bogey, the P.I. meets three quirky characters searching for a valuable statuette of a black bird they call the Maltese Falcon, "the stuff dreams are made of." Greenstreet is the Fat Man, who's been obsessed with the bird for the past seventeen years. Cook is his neurotic gunsel, and Lorre is the effeminate squirt who attempts to bribe Bogey into disclosing the bird's whereabouts. The P.I., who knows nothing about the Falcon, sees an opportunity to make some dough and plays along. Meanwhile, he begins falling for the untrustworthy Astor, who's also in on the treasure hunt. George plays Cowan's cheating wife, and Patrick is Bogey's secretary. This classic film noir (some says it was the first) improves with age and multiple viewings. The entire cast is wonderful, with top kudos going to Bogey, Lorre and Greenstreet (who made his film debut here at the age of 61 and was nominated for a Best Supporting Actor Oscar). Two previous versions of the film, *The Maltese Falcon* (1931) and *Satan Met a Lady* (1936), are entertaining but pale by comparison. This outstanding film noir was nominated for an Academy Award for Best Picture and is rated number 23 on the American Film Institute's List of America's 100 Greatest Movies. For his directorial debut, Huston (who received an Oscar nomination for Best Screenplay for this film) wanted George Raft to play Sam Spade, but the star turned it down. Raft also turned down three other films that Bogey gladly accepted —

Dead End, **High Sierra** (the film that made Humphrey Bogart a household name) and **Casablanca**.

Memorable Noir Moments:
- ❑ Psychotic gunman Cook, fed up with Bogey's lack of respect, warns him, "Keep on ridin' me, they're gonna be picking lead out of your liver."
- ❑ Bogey, who had been having an affair with his partner's wife, lets Astor in on his otherwise admirable code of ethics: "When a man's partner is killed, he's supposed to do something about it." Bogey reaffirmed this creed in 1947's **Dead Reckoning** ("When a guy's buddy is killed, he ought to do something about it").
- ❑ Prissy Lorre isn't happy about getting slapped around by Bogey, who advises him, "When you're slapped, you'll take it and like it."

Man Bait (1952-British) 78 min. George Brent, Marguerite Chapman, Peter Reynolds, Diana Dors. **Screenplay by:** Frederick Knott. **Directed by:** Terence Fisher. **Noir Type:** Blackmail. **Noir Themes:** Victim of fate, greed. ★★½

The manager of a London bookstore (Brent) has come into a little money, which he intends to spend on an operation for his invalid wife. One evening while working late with a sexy employee (Dors), the middle-aged man gives in to temptation and kisses the willing younger girl. When Dors informs her ex-con boyfriend (Reynolds) about the incident, he pressures her into blackmailing her boss. Brent ignores Dors' threats and warns her that he'll report her to the police if she persists in her extortion attempts. Reynolds convinces her to write a letter to Brent's wife, hoping that Brent will take their threats more seriously. This proves disastrous for Brent, and the extortion game turns into a murder case, with Brent the number one suspect. Chapman plays Brent's former wartime nurse and now loyal assistant, who has kept her love for him a secret. Originally released as *The Last Page*, this is a pretty fair British noir with good performances by Brent and 21-year-old starlet Dors (who was touted as the "English Marilyn Monroe") playing the initially reluctant femme fatale.

The Man from Laramie (1955) 104 min. James Stewart, Arthur Kennedy, Donald Crisp, Cathy O'Donnell, Alex Nicol, Aline MacMahon, Wallace Ford. **Screenplay by:** Philip Yordan and Frank Burt. **Directed by:** Anthony Mann. **Noir Type:** Horse Opera. **Noir Themes:** Revenge, paranoia, greed. ★★★★

Stewart rides into the town of Coronado, New Mexico, with three mule teams loaded with supplies for the town's general store, which is owned by O'Donnell. His real reason for making the thousand-mile trek from Laramie, Wyoming, however, is to find the men selling repeating rifles to the Apaches, who used the weapons to massacre his kid brother and other Army cavalrymen. Suspects include a tyrannical rancher (Crisp); Crisp's psychopathic son (Nicol); and their ambitious ranch foreman (Kennedy), who's also O'Donnell's fiancé. After being falsely arrested for murder, Stewart is released thanks to Crisp's rival, a tough old rancher (MacMahon) who hires Stewart as her foreman. Nicol, believing that Stewart is a hired gun, sets out to get rid of him. Meanwhile, the impatient Apaches are looking for the next shipment of rifles, which they've already paid for. This is another fine Anthony Mann noir western, with an excellent cast, beautiful outdoor photography and lots of action.

❑ Jack Elam (George Taggert in *Temple Houston*) as the town drunk with all the secrets.
❑ Frank de Kova (Chief Wild Eagle on *F Troop*) as a priest.

Memorable Noir Moment:
❑ Stewart responds to MacMahon's offer to get him out of jail if he agrees to work for her. "You're just a hard, scheming old woman, aren't you?" he says. "And ugly, too," she adds.

The Man I Love (1946) 96 min. Ida Lupino, Robert Alda, Andrea King, Bruce Bennett, Warren Douglas, Martha Vickers, Don McGuire. **Screenplay by:** Jo Pagano. **Directed by:** Raoul Walsh. **Noir Type:** Soap Opera. **Noir Themes:** Obsession, betrayal, fatalism. ★★½

Nightclub singer Lupino goes home for Christmas and finds herself falling in love with a has-been pianist (Bennett). Complicating things is tough nightclub owner Alda, who has the unrequited hots for Lupino. King is Lupino's sister, whose delusional husband is suffering from shell shock in a veteran's hospital, leaving her to work as a waitress and care for her young son. Douglas is Lupino's wayward brother. Vickers, her lovesick younger sister, has a crush on McGuire, the married man next door. Lupino is always a pleasure to watch, but this atmospheric soap opera might be too soppy for the hard-core crime fan.

Familiar Face from Television:
❑ Craig Stevens (*Peter Gunn*) as a bandleader.

Memorable Noir Moment:
❑ Before taking Lupino in his arms and kissing her, Bennett whispers sweet nothings in her ear: "You crazy little dame, you." (A big improvement over George Macready, George Sanders and Jeff Chandler in **Gilda**, **Witness to Murder** and **Female on the Beach**, respectively.)

Man in the Attic (1953) 82 min. Jack Palance, Constance Smith, Byron Palmer, Frances Bavier, Rhys Williams. **Screenplay by:** Robert Presnell, Jr., and Barre Lyndon. **Directed by:** Hugo Fregonese. **Noir Type:** Period. **Noir Themes:** Sexual hostility, woman in jeopardy, paranoia. ★★½

This inferior remake of **The Lodger** stars Palance as a London pathologist who takes a room in the home of Williams and Bavier. While Palance is conducting secret experiments in the attic, Bavier suspects that he might be Jack the Ripper, the serial killer terrorizing London. The couple's showgirl niece (Smith), meanwhile, has developed a fascination with Palance, who takes her interest much too seriously. Palmer, a Scotland Yard detective, also has a yen for the sexy dancer. Palance is good as the strange lodger, but the film is too slow-moving, and Bavier, in her pre–Mayberry days, looks and acts too much like Aunt Bea fussing around Andy's house.

Familiar Face from Television:
❑ Sean McClory (Jack McGivern in *The Californians* and Miles Delaney in *Bring 'Em Back Alive*) as an Irish constable.

Man in the Dark (1953) 70 min. Edmond O'Brien, Audrey Totter, Ted de Corsia, Horace McMahon, Nick Dennis. **Screenplay by:** George Bricker and Jack Leonard. **Directed by:** Lew Landers. **Noir Type:** Amnesia. **Noir Themes:** Greed, distrust. ★★

O'Brien plays an imprisoned mobster who undergoes experimental surgery to remove his criminal instincts. The operation is a success, but one of its side effects is amnesia. O'Brien's former gang (de Corsia, Dennis and McMahon) kidnap him from the hospital, hoping he'll lead them to the 130 Gs he hid after their last armored car heist. At first, they suspect that he's holding out and try beating the information out of him. When he doesn't talk, even after they threaten to kill him, they begin taking him to familiar haunts to help him remember. Totter is the loyal moll who's starting to fall in love all over again — this time with the new O'Brien. Filmed in 3-D, this remake of *The Man Who Lived Twice* (1936) doesn't have much going for it except its exciting amusement park finale.

Memorable Noir Moment:
❑ O'Brien, nervous about his upcoming surgery, says, "I was born on a Monday. I might as well go out on a Monday. Like dirty laundry."

The Man in the Net (1959) 97 min. Alan Ladd, Carolyn Jones, Diane Brewster, John Lupton, Charles McGraw. **Screenplay by:** Reginald Rose. **Directed by:** Michael Curtiz. **Noir Type:** Wrong Man. **Noir Themes:** Betrayal, lust. ★½

Ladd, nearing the end of his career (he died at 50 in 1964 of an overdose of sedatives mixed with alcohol), plays a painter married to an emotionally disturbed alcoholic (Jones). Jones wants him to give up suburban life and his painting to return to his commercial artist job in New York City. After a visit to New York, where he declines a $30,000-a-year job offer (to the amazement of more than a couple of cops), Ladd finds his home ransacked, his paintings destroyed and his wife missing. Before authorities can arrest Ladd for murder, the local sheriff (McGraw), who has been having an affair with Jones, and an angry vigilante group send him fleeing into the woods, where he's hidden by a group of children. Desperate to prove his innocence, Ladd enlists the kids to help him find the real murderer. Lupton plays the spoiled son of a wealthy businessman, and Brewster is Lupton's wife. This tale of adultery, blackmail and murder is a big disappointment considering director Curtiz's and Ladd's past noir successes. Jones went on to star in the hit TV comedy series *The Addams Family*, and Brewster played Beaver's schoolteacher in *Leave It to Beaver*.

Familiar Faces from Television:
❑ Michael McGreevey (cabin boy Chip in *Riverboat*) as the sheriff's son.
❑ Alvin Childress (Amos in *Amos and Andy*) as a servant.

Man in the Shadow (1957) 80 min. Jeff Chandler, Orson Welles, Colleen Miller, Ben Alexander, Barbara Lawrence, John Larch, Leo Gordon, Martin Garralaga, Royal Dano. **Screenplay by:** Gene L. Coon. **Directed by:** Jack Arnold. **Noir Type:** Cover-Up. **Noir Themes:** Corruption, bigotry, betrayal. ★★½

This modern-day Western has Chandler, the newly elected sheriff of a small town, going up against a powerful rancher (Welles) while investigating the vicious murder of a migrant Mexican worker. The worker, it seems, had been just a little too friendly with Welles' young daughter (Miller). Despite the eyewitness report by a Mexican field hand (Garralaga) that two of Welles' ranch hands (Larch and Gordon) cold-bloodedly murdered the *bracero*, the townsfolk, fearful that a vindictive Welles will ruin their economy, actively oppose Chandler's investigation, preferring to believe that the victim was involved in a fatal auto accident. But the sheriff's determination grows, especially when his wife (Lawrence) begins receiving threatening telephone calls and Larch attempts to kill him by disabling his car brakes. With even his deputy (Alexander) failing him, Chandler and a brave farmer (Dano) must face Welles and his men alone. An action-packed film with Welles giving a strong performance, but the storyline is hard to swallow.

Familiar Faces from Television:

❑ Paul Fix (Marshal Micah Torrance in TV's *The Rifleman*) as a town council member.
❑ Mort Mills (Marshal Frank Tallman in *Man Without a Gun*) as the ranch's gateman.
❑ William Schallert (Patty's dad in *The Patty Duke Show*) as a town council member.
❑ Harry Harvey (Mayor George Dixon in *Man Without a Gun*) as the town doctor.

Memorable Noir Moments:

❑ From the Some-Things-Never-Change Department: Discussing the influx of migrant workers and illegal immigrants, a town council members remarks, "Nobody knows how many of them are here and nobody cares."
❑ Disgusted with the lack of support he's receiving from the townspeople, Sheriff Chandler complains, "There isn't a yard of guts in this whole town. This isn't a town. It's a trained dog act."

Man in the Vault (1956) 73 min. William Campbell, Karen Sharpe, Anita Ekberg, Berry Kroeger, James Seay, Mike Mazurki. **Screenplay by:** Burt Kennedy. **Directed by:** Andrew V. McLaglen. **Noir Type:** Heist. **Noir Themes:** Greed, lust. ★½

Campbell stars as a locksmith who's offered five grand by bad guy Kroeger to make a key to a safety deposit box owned by a rival gangster (Seay). When Campbell refuses, Kroeger convinces the locksmith to reconsider by threatening his girl (Sharpe). Sex kitten Ekberg plays Seay's unfaithful moll, and noir heavy Mazurki is Kroeger's goon. Latino actor Pedro Gonzalez-Gonzalez, who later played in a number of John Wayne Westerns, has a bit role as Campbell's friend, who's about to go on a TV show called *You Bet Your Life*— an inside joke because the actor actually had appeared on Groucho Marx's popular quiz show as a contestant. Noir veterans Mazurki and Kroeger, who plays one of the worst-dressed criminals in film noir, help make this low-budget film more bearable. *Man in the Vault* was made by John Wayne's Batjac Productions and directed by actor Victor McLaglen's son.

Familiar Face from Television:

❑ Paul Fix (Marshal Micah Torrance in TV's *The Rifleman*) as one of Kroeger's hoods.

Memorable Noir Moment:

❑ Gangster Seay is feeling superior to his rival, Kroeger. "I'm far from an honest man," Seay tells him. "But I worked my way up to the curb. You've never been able to get out of the gutter."

The Man Is Armed (1956) 70 min. Dane Clark, William Talman, May Wynn, Robert Horton, Barton MacLane. **Screenplay by:** Richard Landau, Robert C. Dennis and Don Mar-

A girl (Karen Sharpe) is startled outside her home by a drunken lawyer (Robert Keys) in *Man in the Vault* (RKO, 1956).

tin. **Directed by:** Franklin Adreon. **Noir Type:** Heist. **Noir Themes:** Betrayal, obsession, paranoia, revenge. ★½

Truck driver and frustrated composer Clark, just released from San Quentin after being railroaded by his boss (Talman), starts out looking for revenge and ends up being hunted by police detective MacLane after participating in a poorly planned half-million-dollar heist. Out of the joint a mere two weeks, the psychotic Clark kills three men, kidnaps his former girlfriend (Wynn), assaults her new boyfriend (Horton) twice, robs a payroll company and tricks a little old lady into handing over her car. Noir veterans Clark, Talman and MacLane are wasted in this low-budget, amateurish production. Horton overcame this disaster and went on to co-star in the hit TV western *Wagon Train*.

Memorable Noir Moment:

❑ A murder victim's sexy girlfriend swears to detective MacLane that her boyfriend was alive the last time she saw him. "Are you sure?" he asks. "There's one thing I do know," she replies with a smile. "That's the difference between a live one and a dead one."

Man of the West (1958) 100 min. Gary Cooper, Julie London, Lee J. Cobb, Arthur O'Connell, Jack Lord, John Dehner, Royal Dano, Bob Wilke. **Screenplay by:** Reginald Rose. **Directed by:** Anthony Mann. **Noir Type:** Horse Opera. **Noir Themes:** Greed, lust, sexual hostility, guilt. ★★★★

A reformed outlaw (Cooper), on his way to find a schoolteacher for his town, is aboard a train when it's held up by his old gang. He and his traveling companions (gambler O'Connell and singer London) are left stranded in the mountainous countryside but make their way to the outlaws' hideout, where Cooper's uncle (gang leader Cobb) welcomes him with open arms. The other gang members (Wilke, Dano and Lord), aren't that hospitable, but they're so excited about the sexy London that Cooper must pretend she's his woman to protect her from their sexual advances. After another of Cooper's cousins (Dehner) shows up, the gang heads out to Lassoo City to rob the bank. A violent saga, *Man of the West* is another of director Mann's famous thinking man's oaters. Cooper is excellent as the reformed outlaw who's forced to revert to the brutal behavior he so long ago renounced. Cobb does a fine job as the crazed, but sentimental, gang leader. London later co-starred in TV's *Emergency*, and Lord went on to star in *Stoney Burke* and the super-successful *Hawaii Five-O*.

Familiar Face from Television:
❑ Frank Ferguson (Gus the ranch hand in *My Friend Flicka*) as the sheriff.

Memorable Noir Moments:
❑ After a sexual assault by gang members, London complains that "men I meet all think they have a right to get their hands on me, like it comes with the introduction."
❑ A determined Cooper shouts a warning to Cobb, who's hiding in the mountains, "You've outlived your kind and you've outlived your time, and I'm coming to get you."

The Man on the Eiffel Tower (1949) 97 min. Charles Laughton, Franchot Tone, Burgess Meredith, Robert Hutton, Jean Wallace, Patricia Roc, Belita. **Screenplay by:** Harry Brown. **Directed by:** Burgess Meredith. **Noir Type:** Wrong Man. **Noir Themes:** Lawbreaking for kicks, greed, betrayal. ★★★½

An unemployed ne'er-do-well (Hutton) hires a psychopathic hit man (Tone) to kill his wealthy aunt. Hutton expects to inherit her fortune and have enough money to pay off his wife (Roc) in a divorce settlement, freeing him to marry his lover (Wallace). Coincidentally, a slow-witted street vendor (Meredith), fed up with being nagged by his wife (Belita) about their financial problems, chooses the evening of the murder to burglarize the victim's mansion. Unfortunately for him, he stumbles over the body, runs into Tone and leaves his bloodstained fingerprints all over the room. Tone, feeling playful, agrees to help the bungling thief to escape from prison once he's arrested, if he'll keep his mouth shut. Realizing that the police will never believe his story, Meredith agrees and is soon captured by Inspector Maigret (Laughton), who knows the man is innocent and arranges for him to escape, hoping he'll lead him to the real murderer. This is the start of a strange cat-and-mouse game between Laughton and Tone, who seems to be getting a big kick out of helping the detective build a case against him. Laughton is delightful as mystery writer Georges Simenon's famous Parisian sleuth, but Tone is uninteresting as the manic-depressive psychopath. The Eiffel Tower climax is exciting and well staged (except for that falling mannequin).

Memorable Noir Moment:
❑ Laughton is astonished by a handwriting expert's precise analysis of a letter written by a

killer. "Tell me, what do you do when a girl writes you a love letter?" he asks. "Oh, I never would read it," the analyst replies. "It would tell me far too much about her."

The Man Who Cheated Himself (1950) 81 min. Lee J. Cobb, John Dall, Jane Wyatt. **Screenplay by:** Phillip MacDonald and Seton I. Miller. **Directed by:** Felix E. Feist. **Noir Type:** Cover-Up. **Noir Themes:** Obsession, corruption. ★★★

The Man Who Cheated Himself presents a familiar film noir plot — a good cop who goes bad because of a dame. San Francisco homicide detective Cobb is having an affair with a married woman (Wyatt, cast against type as a femme fatale), who thinks her estranged husband is out to kill her. When the man shows up unexpectedly one night, she panics and shoots him. Now Cobb must cover up the crime. His younger brother (Dall) has just started working the homicide detail, and the two of them are assigned to the case. Wearing matching trenchcoats and hats, the cops investigate, Dall for real and Cobb trying to throw him off the scent. Cobb, not normally cast in a romantic role, is surprisingly good in his love scenes with Wyatt of *Father Knows Best* fame.

Memorable Noir Moment:
❏ When invited by the wealthy Wyatt to quit his poor paying job and marry her, Cobb declines, asking, "What's a million or two between friends?"

The Man Who Died Twice (1958) 70 min. Rod Cameron, Vera Ralston, Mike Mazurki, Gerald Milton, Richard Karlan, Louis Jean Heydt, John Maxwell, Bob Anderson, Don Megowan. **Screenplay by:** Richard C. Sarafian. **Directed by:** Joseph Kane. **Noir Type:** Narcotics. **Noir Themes:** Greed, betrayal, lust. ★½

A Kansas City police officer (Cameron) arrives in the big city after the car his brother (Megowan) was driving crashes into an embankment, leaving only a charred body. He's immediately recruited by local cops (Heydt, Maxwell and Anderson) to go undercover at his brother's nightclub, which is a front for a narcotics operation. Cameron's sister-in-law (Ralston) is a singer at the club, and bartender Mazurki is a drug pusher with romantic designs on the widow. Meanwhile, a couple of Chicago hit men (Milton and Karlan) are looking for the dope that Megowan stashed in Ralston's apartment. No surprises here, especially with the giveaway title. The matronly Ralston, a former professional ice skater, gives her final, and worst, performance before retiring from the screen. Despite the promising opening (three killings in the first two minutes), this is a mediocre crime noir. The square-jawed Cameron starred in several popular TV detective shows in the 1950s (*City Detective*, *State Trooper* and *Coronado 9*). Noir veteran Mazurki was typecast in two short-lived comedies, *The Chicago Teddy Bears* (as a gangster) and *It's About Time* (as a caveman). Maxwell and Anderson both had roles in the crime drama *The Court of Last Resort*, and Heydt played in the adventure series, *Waterfront*.

Familiar Faces from Television:
❏ Jesslyn Fax (Angela in *Our Miss Brooks* and Wilma Fritter in *Many Happy Returns*) as an elderly police informant.
❏ Paul Picerni (Agent Lee Hobson on *The Untouchables*) as a detective.

❑ Don Haggerty (Jeffrey Jones in *The Files of Jeffrey Jones* and Marsh Murdock in *The Life and Legend of Wyatt Earp*) as Picerni's partner.

The Man with My Face (1951) 86 min. Barry Nelson, Lynn Ainley, Carole Mathews, John Harvey. **Screenplay by**: Vin Bogert, Tom McGowan, Edward Montagne and Samuel W. Taylor. **Directed by**: Edward Montagne. **Noir Type**: Wrong Man. **Noir Themes**: Victim of fate, betrayal. ★★½

Nelson, in a dual role, plays an innocent man who gets involved in a million-dollar heist because he's the spitting image of the real crook. Ainley is his femme fatale wife, and Mathews is his former girlfriend. The real star of the film, though, is a Doberman Pinscher called King (played by himself). This is an interesting, but slow-moving movie, containing some terrific Puerto Rican location shots. Nelson went on to star in the TV spy series *The Hunter* and the comedy show *My Favorite Husband*, and was a regular guest panelist on *To Tell the Truth* from 1962 to 1965.

Familiar Face from Television:

❑ Jack Warden (Detective Lieutenant Mike Haines in *N.Y.P.D.*) as Mathews' brother.

Memorable Noir Moments:

❑ When Nelson thinks about getting away from the Doberman that's guarding him, the dog's trainer advises him, "He'll stick closer to you than a guy you owe five bucks to."
❑ In the film's exciting finale, Nelson and the Doberman dogfight to the finish. (See *The Hidden Room*, *Lady Gangster* and *The Killing* for other doggie crime fighters.)

The Man with the Golden Arm (1955) 119 min. Frank Sinatra, Kim Novak, Eleanor Parker, Arnold Stang, Darren McGavin, Robert Strauss. **Screenplay by**: Lewis Meltzer and Walter Newman. **Directed by**: Otto Preminger. **Noir Type**: Narcotics. **Noir Themes**: Obsession, fatalism, betrayal, guilt, fatalism. ★★★★

Confident of his newfound talent as a drummer, an optimistic junkie (Sinatra) returns to his Chicago neighborhood after spending six months in the hospital for heroin addiction. His only desire now is to stay clean and become a musician, but it's an uphill battle. His wife (Parker), a psychotic malingerer, holds together their loveless marriage by pretending to be crippled, and deprecates his musical ambition; his former boss (Strauss) forces him to return to his job as a dealer in an illegal poker game; and the neighborhood pusher (McGavin) is eager to get him hooked again. Before long, that "forty pound monkey" is on Sinatra's back once again, and the only ones who care are his former lover (Novak), who still carries a torch for him, and his street-smart derelict friend (Stang). A dated, but powerful, look at the plight of a wretched heroin addict, this is one of Sinatra's best films. McGavin is terrific as the repulsive dope peddler, and Parker and Novak are good as the women in Sinatra's life. But the big surprise is veteran comic Stang, perhaps best known for a TV commercial ("What a chunk a' chocolate"), who does a fine job as Sinatra's devoted pal.

Familiar Face from Television:

❑ Leonid Kinskey (Pierre in *The People's Choice*) as the quack who is treating Parker.

Memorable Noir Moment:

❑ Pusher McGavin taunts reformed junkie Sinatra. "The monkey is never dead, dealer," he claims. "The monkey never dies. When you kill him off, he just hides in the corner, waiting his turn."

Manhandled (1949) 97 min. Dorothy Lamour, Dan Duryea, Sterling Hayden, Irene Hervey, Alan Napier, Art Smith, Harold Vermilyea. **Screenplay by**: Whitman Chambers and Lewis R. Foster. **Directed by**: Lewis R. Foster. **Noir Type**: Nightmare. **Noir Themes**: Woman in jeopardy, victim of the law, betrayal, greed. ★½

Not even noir icons Duryea and Hayden can salvage this muddled film about a man (Napier) whose faithless wife (Hervey) is murdered. Napier had confided earlier to a psychiatrist (Vermilyea) that he had been having nightmares about killing Hervey. So, naturally, he's the number one suspect. Vermilyea's secretary (Lamour) unethically tells her neighbor, repulsive P.I. Duryea, about Napier's dream, and Duryea tries to capitalize on the situation. Smith is the detective in charge of the bungling cops, and Hayden is the insurance investigator out to recover some missing jewels.

Familiar Faces from Television:
❏ Keye Luke (Master Po in *Kung Fu*) as a dry cleaning proprietor.

Memorable Noir Moments:
❏ Napier tells Hervey, who's planning a night on the town, "Go ahead, deck yourself out like some cheap little carnival biddy."
❏ When Duryea calls her boss' patients "crackpots," Lamour scolds him, "They're not crackpots. They're mental cases."

Mark of the Whistler (1944) 60 min. Richard Dix, Janis Carter, John Calvert, Matt Willis, Paul Guilfoyle. **Screenplay by**: George Bricker. **Directed by**: William Castle. **Noir Type**: Impersonator. **Noir Themes**: Greed, paranoia, revenge. ★★½

Dix plays a hobo who decides to claim the dormant bank account of a missing man whose name is the same as his. He investigates the man's background, assumes his identity and manages to convince the bank that he's the legal owner of the account. Expecting only a small amount, he's elated when they hand him nearly thirty grand in cash. But his elation is short-lived when an eager beaver newspaper reporter (Carter) takes his picture as he's leaving the bank and splashes it on the front page. Two brothers (Calvert and Willis), who are out for revenge against the real owner of the bank account, see the story and plot to hunt Dix down and murder him. Guilfoyle plays the crippled peddler who befriends the former hobo. Dix is believable as the likable transient who turns to fraud to alleviate his economic situation. Based on a script from the radio program *The Whistler*, by pulp fiction writer Cornell Woolrich, this is the second of four Whistler films that were directed by Castle. (For more in the Whistler series, see *The Whistler*, *Power of the Whistler*, *Voice of the Whistler*, *Mysterious Intruder*, *The Return of the Whistler*, *Secret of the Whistler* and *The Thirteenth Hour*.)

Memorable Noir Moment:
❏ When reporter Carter offers to exchange her nightclub beat with a colleague, he responds, "No thanks. I meet a better class of heels in night court."

The Mask of Diijon (1946) 73 min. Erich von Stroheim, Jeanne Bates, William Wright, Edward Van Sloan. **Screenplay by:** Griffin Jay. **Directed by:** Lew Landers. **Noir Type:** Payback. **Noir Themes:** Jealousy, character deterioration, revenge. ★

A maddened magician's jealousy drives him over the edge. Because the magician (von Stroheim) sullenly walks around with only one screen face — stolid — it's difficult to determine when he actually arrives at the edge. Bates is the magician's wife and stage assistant, and Wright is the young man from her past who offers to assist the down-and-out magician by getting him a gig at a nightclub. Von Stroheim, whose only interest of late is reading occult books about hypnotism, reluctantly accepts the job to stop his wife's nagging. After the act flops, the depressed magician discovers that he does indeed have hypnotic powers when, in an unintentionally hilarious scene, he prevents a stick-up man from robbing a coffee shop. Convinced that Bates is having an affair, von Stroheim concocts a ridiculous plan for revenge, despite warnings in his books about using hypnotism for evil purposes. Somebody must have hypnotized the producers into making this terrible film.

The Mask of Dimitrios (1944) 95 min. Sydney Greenstreet, Peter Lorre, Faye Emerson, Zachary Scott, Steven Geray, Kurt Katch, Victor Francen. **Screenplay by:** Frank Gruber. **Directed by:** Jean Negulesco. **Noir Type:** Blackmail. **Noir Themes:** Greed, betrayal. ★★★★½

While vacationing in Istanbul in 1938, a Dutch mystery writer (Lorre) becomes embroiled in a real-life mystery. When a Turkish chief of police (Katch), a wannabe mystery writer, brags to Lorre that an archcriminal has been found floating in the Bospherus, the intrigued writer asks to see the body. At the morgue, Katch tells the writer about how the criminal (Scott, in his film debut) viciously murdered a merchant fifteen years earlier and fled Turkey, leaving his partner to face the hangman. Fascinated, Lorre decides to investigate and travels to Scott's old haunts (Athens, Sofia, Geneva and Paris), learning about Scott's involvement in extortion, murder, espionage and political assassination. Along the way, Lorre encounters a mysterious fat man (Greenstreet), who involves him in a daring blackmail scheme. Emerson plays the woman who makes the mistake of falling in love with Scott; Geray is a Yugoslav government employee, suckered by Scott into spying against his country; and Francen is the retired "employer of spy labor." This has it all — fine acting, a droll script, an impressive visual style and a satisfying ending. Don't miss it.

Memorable Noir Moment:

❑ Before shooting a terrified blackmailer several times, Scott comments that, while the man had always been ingenious, "Ingenuity is never a substitute for intelligence."

Miami Exposé (1956) 73 min. Lee J. Cobb, Patricia Medina, Alan Napier, Edward Arnold, Michael Granger, Harry Lauter. **Screenplay by:** James B. Gordon. **Directed by:** Fred. F. Sears. **Noir Type:** Gambling. **Noir Themes:** Corruption, woman in jeopardy, greed, revenge, obsession. ★★½

Homicide detective Cobb investigates after his boss and a two-bit hood are stabbed to death in a hotel room. The hood's widow (Medina), fearing that she's next, flees to Havana, where an American gangster (Granger) promises to protect her.

Meanwhile, a rival mobster (Napier), the man responsible for the two murders, has paid a corrupt lobbyist (Arnold) a million dollars to gain support from prominent citizens, using blackmail if necessary, for legalized gambling in Florida. Cobb tracks Medina to Havana and brings her back to Florida to use her as bait to trap Napier. Naturally, Granger isn't pleased with this turn of events, and shows up in Miami looking for Cobb. It all leads to a violent showdown outside a cabin in the Everglades, where Cobb has assigned a lucky detective (noir veteran Lauter) the job of watching over the sexy Medina. A subplot has Cobb yearning for retirement so he can marry the widow of a murdered cop, who won't say "I do" until he says "I quit." Cobb turns in a good performance, getting another opportunity to play the romantic lead as he did in 1950's *The Man Who Cheated Himself.* This was veteran character actor Arnold's final film; he died of a cerebral hemorrhage during production. This standard crime yarn opens with a hokey statement by the Governor of Florida, who reminds viewers that the events they are about to witness "could happen in *your* state."

Memorable Noir Moments:

❑ Lecherous mobster Granger, who isn't exactly mourning the death of Medina's husband, wants to discuss her "future." When Medina complains that her husband isn't even cold yet, Granger backs off. "Yeah, sure, I know. I'm jumpin' the gun," he tells her. "When a guy gets a little older he likes to make every day count."
❑ Optimist Granger assures Medina that she's perfectly safe. "You have nothing to worry about," he says, "except maybe some nut with a gun."
❑ Medina comments on the "two-bit heels" in her life. "The world is full of them," she complains. "My father was one, the first guy I ever loved was one, and the shmoe I married was one."

The Midnight Story (1957) 89 min. Tony Curtis, Marisa Pavan, Gilbert Roland, Jay C. Flippen, Argentina Brunetti, Ted de Corsia, Richard Monda. **Screenplay by:** John Robinson and Edwin Blum. **Directed by:** Joseph Pevney. **Noir Type:** Whodunit. **Noir Themes:** Obsession, guilt, betrayal. ★★★½

When a neighborhood priest is murdered in a San Francisco alley, motorcycle cop Curtis, a friend of the priest, resigns from the force to pursue leads on his own. His investigation leads him to a local fish store owner (Roland). After ingratiating himself with the suspect, Curtis accepts Roland's job offer and an invitation to move into his house, where he becomes emotionally involved with Roland's mother Brunetti, his kid brother Monda, and, especially, his pretty cousin Pavan. Torn between his desire to find the priest's killer and his feelings for this generous Italian-American family, Curtis finds himself hoping that Roland's alibi proves true. But homicide lieutenant de Corsia and police sergeant Flippen are beginning to think that the former cop is on to something big. Curtis does a good job as the cop obsessed with finding his friend's murderer, but Roland's performance is the highlight of this solid, well-scripted mystery.

Familiar Faces from Television:

❑ Kathleen Freeman (Katie, the maid, in *Topper* and Flo Shafer in *The Beverly Hillbillies*) as an adulterous pool player's "ball and chain."

A murder victim's associate (John Cliff, seated) listens as police brass (from left, Ted de Corsia, Jay C. Flippen, and Russ Conway) refuse to allow a traffic cop (Tony Curtis) to transfer to homicide to investigate a priest killing in *The Midnight Story* (Universal, 1957).

❏ Russ Conway (Lt. Pete Kile in *Richard Diamond, Private Detective*) as a homicide detective.

Memorable Noir Moment:
❏ An over-the-hill stripper being questioned in a roomful of cops comments, "If I'd have known it was going to be this big an audience I'd have brought my bubbles."

Mildred Pierce (1945) 112 min. Joan Crawford, Zachary Scott, Jack Carson, Eve Arden, Ann Blyth, Bruce Bennett. Moroni Olsen, Jo Ann Marlowe. **Screenplay by:** Ranald Mac-Dougall. **Directed by:** Michael Curtiz. **Noir Type:** Ambition. **Noir Themes:** Betrayal, obsession, greed. ★★★★½

This brilliantly directed noir opens with someone emptying a revolver into restaurateur Crawford's second husband (Scott) and Crawford trying to set up her business partner (Carson) as the fall guy. After all of the suspects are summoned downtown, homicide inspector Olsen drags the sordid tale out of the businesswoman by informing her that he has charged her first husband (Bennett) with the murder. Crawford is sensational (winning a Best Actress Oscar for her performance, beating out Gene Tierney for another great film noir, *Leave Her to Heaven*) as the dedicated mom determined to provide for her children (Blyth and Marlowe). After Bennett

An entrepreneur (Joan Crawford) keeps a wary eye on her boyfriend (Zachary Scott) and her femme fatale daughter (Ann Blyth) in *Mildred Pierce* (Warner Bros., 1945).

leaves her for a wealthy woman, Crawford takes a job as a waitress, despite the embarrassment it causes Blyth, her spoiled older daughter. Crawford's ambition, however, drives her to open a chain of restaurants; in the process, she falls in love with professional loafer Scott, who's dollar poor and real estate rich. At last, Crawford reaches a position where, she thinks, Blyth should be content and proud of her workaholic mother. But things quickly deteriorate after Crawford, again catering to Blyth's social climbing obsession, reluctantly marries playboy Scott, leading to the scoundrel's untimely death. Blyth is wonderfully bitchy as Crawford's femme fatale daughter, and Arden is entertaining in her usual wisecracking sidekick role. Both received Oscar nominations for Best Supporting Actress. The film also garnered nominations for Best Picture (losing out to **The Lost Weekend**), Best Screenplay and Best Black and White Cinematography.

Familiar Face from Television:
❏ Lee Patrick (Cosmo's wife, Henrietta in *Topper*) as Bennett's sugar mommy.

Memorable Noir Moments:
❏ A Los Angeles homicide inspector explains his job description to a murder suspect. "Being

a detective's like … well, like making an automobile," he explains. "You just put them together one by one and the first thing you know, you've got an automobile, or a murderer."

❑ Arden, adjusting her nylons, tells ogler Carson, "Leave something on me, I might catch cold."

❑ Crawford tells the flirtatious Carson, "Friendship's a lot more lasting than love." He responds, "Yeah, but not as entertaining."

Ministry of Fear (1944) 86 min. Ray Milland, Marjorie Reynolds, Carl Esmond, Dan Duryea, Hillary Brooke, Percy Waram. **Screenplay by:** Seton I. Miller. **Directed by:** Fritz Lang. **Noir Type:** Nazi. **Noir Themes:** Victim of fate, betrayal, paranoia. ★★★★

Immediately after being released from an English asylum, former inmate Milland (who was imprisoned for the mercy killing of his wife) stumbles onto a Nazi spy ring that has stolen classified information about British mine fields. Innocently uttering a secret password to a carnival fortune teller, Milland is mistaken for a Nazi spy and allowed to win a cake that contains stolen microfilm. After the real spy (Duryea) shows up, a phony blind man steals the cake from Milland and is killed by German bombs during a blitzkrieg. Certain that the police wouldn't believe a former asylum inmate, Milland tries to uncover the spy ring with some help from an Austrian immigrant (Reynolds) and her brother (Esmond), who operate a suspicious charitable organization called "Mothers of Free Nations." Femme fatale Brooke plays a psychic medium, and Waram is the Scotland Yard inspector seeking to charge Milland with murder. This dark and compelling espionage film hooks the viewer in the first ten minutes and manages to maintain the suspense until its exciting rooftop climax.

Memorable Noir Moment:

❑ A grinning spy regrets not killing Milland when he had the opportunity. "The trouble with me is," the gun-wielding Nazi says, "I like people too much."

The Missing Juror (1944) 66 min. Jim Bannon, Janis Carter, George Macready, Joseph Crehan, Cliff Clark. **Screenplay by:** Charles O'Neal. **Directed by:** Oscar "Budd" Boetticher. **Noir Type:** Payback. **Noir Themes:** Revenge, victim of the law. ★★½

When an innocent man (Macready) is convicted of murder and sentenced to be hanged, a newspaper reporter (Bannon) investigates and helps capture the real killer. Macready is pardoned but by now, after having imagined himself being hanged hundreds of times, he's mentally deranged and must be sent to an asylum for psychiatric treatment. Before long, members of the jury that convicted Macready are being bumped off one by one. Juror Carter is Bannon's love interest, Clark is the homicide detective on the case, and Crehan provides the comedy relief as Bannon's editor. Cheaply made with no big surprises, but fast-paced and entertaining.

Familiar Faces from Television:

❑ Mike Mazurki (Clon in *It's About Time*) as a masseur at a steam bath.
❑ Ray Teal (Sheriff Roy Coffee in *Bonanza*) as a detective conducting a lineup.

Memorable Noir Moment:

❑ From the Some-Things-Never-Change Department: Reporter Bannon is shocked when a detective suggests that his reporting may have spawned a copycat killer, and replies, "It's ridiculous to think that a newspaper story would inspire someone to go out and start to kill an entire jury."

Missing Women (1951) 60 min. Penny Edwards, James Millican, John Gallaudet, John Alvin, James Brown, Robert Shayne. **Screenplay by:** John K. Butler. **Directed by:** Philip Ford. **Noir Type:** Missing Person. **Noir Themes:** Victim of fate, woman in jeopardy. ★½

Newlywed Edwards loses her groom on her wedding day when he's murdered by two car thieves (Millican and Alvin) in Lover's Lane, where the happy couple stopped to remove the cans and the "Just Married" sign from their car. Too impatient to wait for the cops to find the killers, Edwards goes undercover and infiltrates a hot-car ring led by Shayne. Meanwhile, the amateur detective has been reported missing by her parents, and Missing Persons detective Brown teams up with homicide detective Gallaudet to find her. There's only one woman missing in this low-budget noir so the reason for the plural in the title is anybody's guess. The best thing that can be said about this is that it's mercifully brief.

Memorable Noir Moment:

❑ Having shown Edwards' photo around all the restaurants and beauty salons in town, a cop explains the department's theory to a store owner. "If she's alive, she has to eat," he says, "and, being a woman, she probably goes to beauty parlors now and then."

Mr. Arkadin (1955) 100 min. Orson Welles, Paola Mori, Robert Arden, Akim Tamiroff, Michael Redgrave, Patricia Medina. **Screenplay by:** Orson Welles. **Directed by:** Orson Welles. **Noir Type:** Cover-Up. **Noir Themes:** Corruption, betrayal, greed. ★★

A wealthy financier (Welles), claiming he can't remember events before 1927, hires a blackmailer (Arden) to find out his real identity. Arden, who's been romancing the millionaire's daughter (Mori), travels around postwar Europe and Mexico, interviewing former underworld characters (the proprietor of a flea circus, an effeminate antiques dealer [Redgrave], a baroness who works as a sales clerk, a dying ex-con [Tamiroff], a heroin addict and his bigamist wife). Arden soon discovers that everyone he talks with about Welles ends up murdered, and he begins to worry about his own safety. Medina plays Arden's accomplice. *Mr. Arkadin* was backed financially by Spanish and Swiss investors and released in Great Britain as *Confidential Report.* Welles was hoping for another *Citizen Kane* but wound up with a cheap parody instead. Arden, who seems to shout all of his lines, is terrible as the self-described "world's prize sucker," but the bearded Welles is intriguing as the multi-millionaire whose relationship with his daughter might be considered just a tad unhealthy. Look for German actor Gert Frobe, who played James Bond's nemesis Goldfinger, as a plainclothes detective with an English grammar problem.

Memorable Noir Moments:

❑ During a religious ceremony in Spain, cross-carrying *Penitentes* parade barefoot through the cobblestone streets. Medina wants to know what they're doing. "They're making penance," someone explains. "It means they're sorry for their sins." "They must be *awful* sorry," she observes.

A dying man (Gregoire Aslan) passes on a secret to a con man's girlfriend (Patricia Medina) in *Mr. Arkadin* **(Warner Bros., 1955).**

❑ "Crooks aren't the worst people in the world," claims a former criminal. "They're just the stupidest."

The Mob (1951) 87 min. Broderick Crawford, Betty Buehler, Richard Kiley, Neville Brand, Ernest Borgnine. **Screenplay by:** William Bowers. **Directed by:** Robert Parrish. **Noir Type:** Undercover. **Noir Themes:** Corruption, paranoia. ★★★½

Tough cop Crawford happens on the scene when a witness against the mob is shot to death on a dark street. After the killer fools him by flashing a badge, Crawford allows him to get away. To make matters worse, it was too dark to get a look at the man's face. His unhappy superiors send him undercover to flush out the killer, whom they suspect is the unknown boss of the mob's waterfront activities. Posing as a longshoreman, Crawford tries unsuccessfully to ingratiate himself with low-level hoods Borgnine and Brand, and befriends a mysterious co-worker (Kiley, in his film debut). Buehler plays Crawford's fiancée, who becomes a pawn in the undercover game. This brutal noir is populated by seedy characters—hoods and cops alike—and, as in many films noirs, it's difficult to distinguish the good guys from the bad guys. Crawford is excellent as the unlucky cop attempting to atone for the biggest screw-up of his career. You'll see a lot of familiar noir faces here, including Emile Meyer, Jay Adler, Harry Lauter and Robert Foulk, in small roles.

Familiar Faces from Television:

❑ Frank de Kova (Chief Wild Eagle on *F Troop*) as a stevedore decked by Crawford.
❑ Charles Bronson, billed as Charles Buchinsky (Mike Kovac in *Man with a Camera*, Paul Moreno in *Empire* and Linc Murdock in *The Travels of Jaime McPheeters*) as a longshoreman.

Memorable Noir Moments:

❑ Sensitivity Training Required: When asked by Kiley why a smart guy like him wants to work on the docks, Crawford replies, "Maybe I like hard work." Kiley wisecracks, "I thought you said you were Irish."
❑ Crawford disarms a hook-wielding dock worker and knocks him to the ground. He then tells the man's surprised buddies, "You better take your sorority sister home, boys. I think she's had a very hard day."

Money Madness (1948) 73 min. Hugh Beaumont, Frances Rafferty, Harlan Warde, Cecil Weston. **Screenplay by:** Al Martin. **Directed by:** Sam Newfield. **Noir Type:** Psycho. **Noir Themes:** Woman in jeopardy, betrayal, jealousy. ★½

Before gaining fame as the Beaver's dad on TV's *Leave It to Beaver*, Hugh Beaumont played in a number B movies, some of them pretty awful. This is one of them. He plays a psychopathic killer who's unable to spend the two hundred Gs he's stolen because the dough's too hot. He takes a job as a cab driver and meets a pretty waitress (Rafferty). When she introduces him to her sickly aunt (Weston), Beaumont comes up with a plan to marry the waitress, kill the old woman and plant the stolen money in her house so that Rafferty can inherit it. Needless to say, Rafferty isn't too happy when her groom coldly confesses to poisoning her aunt, but she feels she can't go to the cops because they might think she's an accomplice. Complicating things, Rafferty's lawyer (Warde) falls in love with her, and one of Beaumont's angry partners shows up looking for his cut of the loot.

Memorable Noir Moment:

❑ Sensitivity Training Required: Trying to get the reticent waitress to open up a little, suave lawyer Warde tells her, "You don't talk much for a woman."

Monsieur Verdoux (1947) 102 min. Charles Chaplin, Martha Raye, Mady Correll, Charles Evans. **Screenplay by:** Charles Chaplin. **Directed by:** Charles Chaplin. **Noir Type:** Comedy. **Noir Themes:** Betrayal, sexual hostility, woman in jeopardy. ★★★½

When a French bank cashier (Chaplin) loses his job during the Great Depression, he finds another way to support his invalid wife (Correll) and little boy. He becomes a modern-day Bluebeard, marrying wealthy women and murdering them for their money, which he promptly invests in the stock market. Raye plays one of his more fortunate wives, a down-to-earth lottery winner whose luck seems to protect her from Chaplin's absurd murder schemes. Evans is the police inspector on his trail. Despite the preachy anti-war message and silly slapstick, this black comedy works well. Producer-director-screenwriter Chaplin is terrific as the oddball serial killer, whose love for his family drives him to kill.

Familiar Face from Television:

❏ William Frawley (Fred Mertz on *I Love Lucy* and Uncle Bub on *My Three Sons*) as the owner of the house where one of Chaplin's weddings is to take place.

Memorable Noir Moment:

❏ A down-and-out Chaplin faces a noir reality. "Despair is a narcotic," he says. "It allows the mind into indifference."

Moonrise (1948) 90 min. Dane Clark, Gail Russell, Ethel Barrymore, Henry (Harry) Morgan, Allyn Joslyn, Lloyd Bridges. **Screenplay by:** Charles Haas. **Directed by:** Frank Borzage. **Noir Type:** Cover-Up. **Noir Themes:** Paranoia, guilt. ★★★

Growing up in the South, Clark had been mercilessly teased and beaten by the other kids because his father was hanged for murder. As an adult, jobless and nearly friendless, he finds himself still fighting the same old battles. During a brawl with Bridges, one of his childhood tormentors, Clark grabs the rock that Bridges is wielding and fractures his skull with it. He hides the body in the swamp and picks up where he left off—romancing Bridges' fiancée (Russell). The only evidence that can link Clark to the crime is a knife he lost during the fight. When a slow-witted deaf-mute (Morgan) finds it, Clark becomes concerned that the sheriff (Joslyn) will put two and two together. Agitated and paranoid, he finds himself faced with a noirish dilemma — if he can't retrieve the knife, he'll have to go on the lam or turn himself in. Barrymore plays his backwoods grandmother, who helps him understand himself and his murderer father. A somber and dark film, *Moonrise* gave Dane Clark a chance to prove what a truly talented actor he was.

Familiar Face from Television:

❏ Harry Lauter (Jim Herrick in *Waterfront*) as the guy who's dancing with Russell when Clark cuts in.

Memorable Noir Moment:

❏ Country sheriff Joslyn offers some backwoods wisdom. "Sometimes murder is like love," he says. "It takes two to commit it."

Moontide (1942) 94 min. Jean Gabin, Ida Lupino, Thomas Mitchell, Claude Rains, Jerome Cowan. **Screenplay by:** John O'Hara. **Directed by:** Archie Mayo. **Noir Type:** Blackmail. **Noir Themes:** Betrayal, revenge, woman in jeopardy. ★★

French actor Gabin made his American screen debut in this story about a tough, independent-minded sailor, and how he's tamed by the gentle hash slinger (Lupino) he saved from committing suicide. While Gabin and Lupino are busy setting up house on a live-bait barge, police are searching for the strangler of a local old salt. The couple's friend (Rains) thinks that Gabon may be the killer. Blackmailer Mitchell, whom Gabin has been supporting financially because of a previous crime, isn't happy about Lupino showing up and threatening his meal ticket. Cowan plays a surgeon whose boat keeps breaking down near Gabin's barge. Gabin gives an interesting performance, making this weak film noir entry a bit easier to swallow. He made another American film (1944's *The Imposter*) before heading back to France, where his career flourished. Noir icon Fritz Lang directed for a few days before Mayo took over the directorial chores.

Familiar Face from Television:
❑ Victor Sen Yung (Hop Sing in *Bonanza*) as a bait supplier.

Moss Rose (1947) 82 min. Victor Mature, Peggy Cummins, Ethel Barrymore, Vincent Price, Patricia Medina, Margo Woode, Rhys Williams. **Screenplay by:** Jules Furthman and Tom Reed. **Directed by:** Gregory Ratoff. **Noir Type:** Period. **Noir Themes:** Woman in jeopardy, jealousy. ★★½

In Victorian England, a Cockney chorus girl (Cummins) finds the body of fellow showgirl (Woods), who was smothered after being administered a sleeping potion. The murderer has left behind an out-of-season moss rose placed inside a bible. Moments before finding the body, Cummins witnessed Woods' lover (Mature) rushing from the building. She later attempts to blackmail him, threatening to squeal to Scotland Yard inspectors Price and Williams. Mature is surprised to discover that Cummins doesn't want money — she merely wants to spend the next two weeks at his palatial estate, where she can pretend to be a "lady." "Preposterous," declares Mature, as if reading the viewer's mind. But, considering the trouble the chorus girl can cause him (he's engaged to be married to fellow blue blood Medina), Mature relents. At the estate, she meets Mature's adoring mother (Barrymore) and his jealous fiancée. Before long, Cummins finds herself falling for the murder suspect and discovering yet another deadly moss rose hidden in a Bible. Cummins is delightful as the wannabe lady, and Price gives a less hammy performance than usual.

Memorable Noir Moment:
❑ "Being a lady in a place like this ought to be no bloomin' trouble at all," Cummins remarks while looking around the mansion.

Murder by Contract (1958) 81 min. Vince Edwards, Herschel Bernardi, Philip Pine, Caprice Toriel. **Screenplay by:** Ben Simcoe. **Directed by:** Irving Lerner. **Noir Type:** Hit Man. **Noir Themes:** Paranoia, sexual hostility, woman in jeopardy. ★★½

The film that is said to have influenced director Martin Scorsese the most, *Murder by Contract* is the story of a polite, misogynistic hit man (Edwards) who got involved in the murder business to finance the house of his dreams. He's hired to kill a witness (Toriel) due to testify against his boss, and spends most of the film making his two contacts (Bernardi and Pine) nervous about his laid-back attitude (he'd rather see the sights and go fishing than plan the hit). When Edwards finds out that the mark is a woman, he balks, not because he's sentimental or chivalrous but because he feels he should be paid extra for killing a dame. Tempers flare after Edwards botches the job twice, causing everyone to have second thoughts. This is an interesting little film that emphasizes character development over plot, allowing us to learn more about the hit man than we really want to know. Edwards, who's really good here, later played TV's hunky doctor, *Ben Casey*. Bernardi later starred in *Arnie*, and Pine co-starred in *The Blue Knight*.

Memorable Noir Moment:

❑ When Edwards finds out that his mark is a female, he says, "I don't like women. They move around too much."

Murder Is My Beat (1955) 77 min. Paul Langton, Barbara Payton, Robert Shayne. **Screenplay by:** Aubrey Wisberg. **Directed by:** Edgar G. Ulmer. **Noir Type:** Bad Cop. **Noir Themes:** Woman in jeopardy, betrayal. ★★★

Tough cop Langton proves to be an old softie after arresting nightclub singer Payton for murdering her boyfriend. While transporting Payton to prison, Langton decides that she deserves a chance to prove her innocence and runs off with her to find the murderer. His superior (Shayne) tracks them to a cheap motel, where he finds only the depressed Langton, a victim of "the oldest pitch a dame can make." Langton shares the whole sordid story with him and the viewer. Shayne (Inspector Henderson on TV's *The Adventures of Superman*) does a fine job, and Payton is reasonably good as the ambiguous femme fatale, but Langton's performance as the hard-boiled cop is painfully reminiscent of William Marshall's acting in **Blackmail**. Skillfully directed by noir veteran Ulmer, this B movie is enjoyable despite its muddled plot. This was Payton's last film after a series of scandals damaged her career. She died of heart and liver failure in 1967 at the age of 40.

A good cop (Paul Langton) goes bad over a femme fatale (Barbara Payton) in *Murder Is My Beat* (Allied Artists, 1955).

Memorable Noir Moments:

❑ How tough is Langton? He's so tough that he walks four miles in a raging blizzard to arrest a murder suspect because, as he says, "I hate the wanton destruction of human life." (When he arrives at the cabin hideout after the long, perilous trek, the murder suspect asks him, "Do you want me to come with you now?" "No rush," the chilly cop replies.

❑ Payton wins the award for film noir's most ungraceful leap from a moving vehicle. Langton tells Payton that she's to jump as the train slows down to ten miles an hour, when he'll yell, "Now!" At the moment of truth, however, he violently shoves her and she lands unceremoniously on her face. The humor appears to have been unintentional.

Murder, My Sweet (1944) 95 min. Dick Powell, Claire Trevor, Anne Shirley, Otto Kruger, Mike Mazurki, Miles Mander, Don Douglas, Ralf Harolde, Douglas Walton. **Screenplay by:** John Paxton. **Directed by:** Edward Dmytryk. **Noir Type:** P.I. **Noir Themes:** Paranoia, greed, betrayal, sexual hostility, jealousy. ★★★★★

Powell stars as Raymond Chandler's hard-boiled sleuth, Philip Marlowe, on a case involving a missing dame and a jade necklace worth a hundred grand. He's hired by a huge, slow-witted ex-con (Mazurki) to find a former girlfriend but soon finds himself suspected of murdering another client, a foppish ladies' man (Watson). While trying to find the real killer, Powell becomes involved with a dangerous blackmailer (Kruger), a suspicious cop (Douglas), a narcotics dispensing doctor (Harolde) and an elderly tycoon (Mander), his pretty daughter (Shirley) and his femme fatale wife (Trevor). Despite a number of blows to the head, which render him unconscious for a good portion of his investigation, and a three-day bout with a mind-altering drug, Powell somehow manages to keep track of the clues and maintain his biting sense of humor. This is a classic film noir that boasts of innovative photography, snappy dialogue and a wonderfully dark and dreary setting. It was director Dmytryk's first A-film and Powell's first dramatic role. After aggressively seeking the lead role in *Double Indemnity* and losing it to Fred MacMurray, Powell finally found what he had been looking for in *Murder, My Sweet*. While the famous literary detective has been played by other actors, including Humphrey Bogart (*The Big Sleep*), Robert Montgomery (*Lady in the Lake*) and George Montgomery (*The Brasher Doubloon*), Powell's interpretation of the tough P.I. is said to have been author Chandler's favorite. The film's original title, *Farewell, My Lovely*, was changed because the studio feared that audiences would assume that this was just another of song-and-dance man Powell's musicals. A test showing in New England proved these fears to be correct when audiences stayed away by the hundreds. Once the title was changed to spark the fans' interest, history was made. The public loved Powell's new image so much that he never returned to musicals. A correctly entitled (but disappointing) version was released in 1975 with aging noir icon Robert Mitchum as Marlowe.

Memorable Noir Moments:

❑ During an intense police interrogation, Powell is asked why he was at his office so late. "I'm a homing pigeon," he replies. "I always come back to the stinking coop no matter how late it is."

❑ Not an admirer of private investigators, a police lieutenant lambastes Powell. "You're not a detective," he says. "You're a slot machine. You'd slit your own throat for six bucks plus tax."

❏ A gun-wielding dame tells Powell, "This will be the first time I've killed anyone I know so little and liked so much."
❏ When Trevor asks him to kill a blackmailer for her, Powell asks, "Why me? Because I'm hard and know how to use a gun? Or just because I wear pants?"

Murder Without Tears (1953) 65 min. Craig Stevens, Joyce Holden, Richard Benedict, Eddie Norris, Tom Hubbard, Clair Regis. **Screenplay by**: Joe Pagano and William Raynor. **Directed by**: William Beaudine. **Noir Type**: Police Procedural. **Noir Themes**: Jealousy, betrayal, revenge. ✯

Somebody kills Norris' cheating wife (Regis) and all the evidence points to the jealous husband, who claims he's suffering from alcoholic-related amnesia. His homicide detective friend (Stevens) investigates and is forced to charge Norris with murder. During the trial, a bank clerk (Holden) reads about the case and provides an airtight alibi for Norris. With the charges dropped, Stevens and his partner (Hubbard) reopen the investigation, hoping to find the real murderer. Benedict plays a vicious killer who loves his dog, Mr. Snuffy. This boring mess is interesting in that the cops' interrogation styles (short, curt questions, delivered in monotone) are almost identical to those of Sgt. Joe Friday (Jack Webb) and his partner on the TV series *Dragnet*, one of the most popular shows on television the year this film was made.

My Favorite Brunette (1947) 87 min. Bob Hope, Dorothy Lamour, Peter Lorre, Lon Chaney, Jr., Charles Dingle, John Hoyt. **Screenplay by**: Edmund Beloin and Jack Rose. **Directed by**: Elliott Nugent. **Noir Type**: Comedy. **Noir Themes**: Conspiracy, woman in jeopardy. ✯✯✯

Hope, a Chinatown baby photographer, is minding the office of the vacationing P.I. next door. Wannabe detective Hope is playing P.I. when the beautiful Lamour arrives at the office seeking help. She hires the impersonator to break up an espionage ring (Dingle, Lorre, Hoyt and Chaney) that is looking to steal a map that shows the location of a uranium-rich mine. Narrated by Hope while on San Quentin's Death Row, this dated private eye spoof still manages a few good laughs in the form of a non-stop barrage of one-liners ("I get airsick when I step on a thick carpet," "Oh, oh, the schizo's about to phrenia"). Lorre, in an amusing self-parody, is enjoyable as a diminutive killer studying to become an American citizen, and Chaney is good as Dingle's dimwitted, muscle-bound henchman, who takes a liking to Hope. Look for a couple of famous actors in surprise cameos as the real P.I. and the prison executioner.

Familiar Faces from Television:
❏ Ray Teal (Sheriff Coffee in *Bonanza*) a state trooper.
❏ James Flavin (Lt. Donovan in *Man with a Camera*) as a cop at a detective convention.

Memorable Noir Moments:
❏ Phony psychiatrist Hoyt tells phony P.I. Hope that Lamour is "suffering from an acute form of schizophrenia accompanied by visual aberrations and increasingly severe paranoid delusions." "And how is she mentally?" asks Hope.
❏ Hope gets the drop on Lorre and gang and, playing the tough guy, warns, "I'll fill ya so full of holes you'll look like a fat clarinet."

My Gun Is Quick (1957) 88 min. Robert Bray, Whitney Blake, Patricia Donahue, Donald Randolph, Pamela Duncan. **Screenplay by**: Richard Collins and Richard Powell. **Directed by**: Phil Victor and George A. White. **Noir Type**: P.I. **Noir Themes**: Greed, betrayal, fatalism. ★½

Mickey Spillane's two-fisted private eye Mike Hammer (Bray) is determined to find out who murdered a sweet stripper from Nebraska. His investigation leads him to a former Army colonel (Randolph) who served ten years in prison for smuggling Nazi jewels out of Germany. Randolph offers to cut Bray in for a cool 250 Gs if he'll help him find the missing ice. When Bray isn't seducing the dames (Blake, Donahue and Duncan), he's spending the remainder of his time trying to regain consciousness after being beat up by three French sailors who are also after the loot. This atmospheric, but boring, movie was the third in a series of 1950s Mike Hammer films noirs (see *Kiss Me Deadly* and *I, the Jury*). Bray became a regular in TV's *Lassie*, Blake co-starred in the popular situation comedy *Hazel*, and Donahue played in the detective series *Michael Shayne*.

Familiar Faces from Television:
❑ Terence De Marney (Case Thomas in *Johnny Ringo*) as a grieving mute.
❑ Leon Askin (Pierre in *The Charlie Farrell Show*) as a fence.

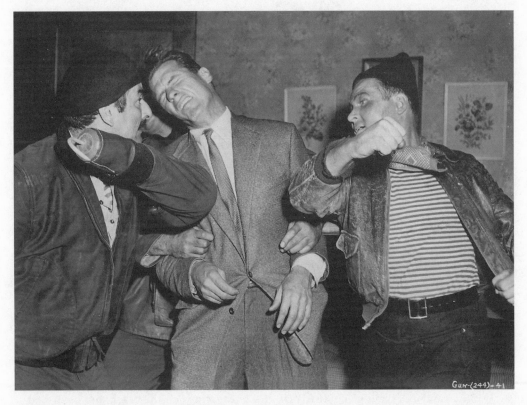

Private eye Mike Hammer (Robert Bray) gets worked over by French seamen looking for stolen Nazi jewels in *My Gun Is Quick* (United Artists, 1957).

Memorable Noir Moment:

❑ Bray, enjoying a film noir pity party, laments to his loyal secretary, "I just crawled out of a sewer. Not a decent person left in the world."

My Name Is Julia Ross (1945) 65 min. Nina Foch, Dame May Whitty, George Macready, Roland Varno. **Screenplay by:** Muriel Roy Bolton. **Directed by:** Joseph H. Lewis. **Noir Type:** Impersonator. **Noir Themes:** Woman in jeopardy, paranoia, victim of fate. ★★★★

Foch, an unemployed American in London, is grateful for her new live-in position — that of private secretary to a wealthy dowager (Whitty) — but, fortunately for the viewer, the mundane job turns into a film noir nightmare. On her first day at her new job, Foch is drugged by Whitty's psychopathic, middle-aged son (Macready) and taken to a mansion outside London, where she's passed off as his ill wife, recently released from a mental institution. It's obvious to Foch that Whitty and Macready are covering up something, but she can't get the servants or the townspeople to believe her because they all think she's balmy. Trapped inside the estate by a high wall and a locked gate, the spunky captive tries every trick up her sleeve to escape or contact

While a captive servant girl (Nina Foch) lies unconscious on the beach, her boyfriend (Roland Varno) attempts to stop a rock-wielding maniac (George Macready) from pummeling her in *My Name Is Julia Ross* (Columbia, 1945).

her boyfriend (Varno) in London, but Whitty and Macready always seem one step ahead of her. A frightening and compelling suspenser, this was director Lewis' first noir, the film he considered the impetus for his successful career. Foch is perfect as the victim caught up in a seemingly hopeless situation, and Macready is excellent as the mama's boy with a penchant for pocket knives. This classic film noir inspired the excellent *Dead of Winter* (1987) with Mary Steenburgen.

Memorable Noir Moment:
❏ An English copper, unlike many of his film noir American counterparts, actually yells a warning to a fleeing suspect before plugging him in the back. (See *The Crimson Kimono* and *The Red House* for other thoughtful American cops.)

My Son John (1952) 122 min. Helen Hayes, Robert Walker, Van Heflin, Dean Jagger, Frank McHugh. **Screenplay by:** Myles Connolly, John Lee Mahin and Leo McCarey. **Directed by:** Leo McCarey. **Noir Type:** Commie. **Noir Themes:** Conspiracy, betrayal, paranoia, guilt. ★★

Hayes and Jagger are the proud parents of two high school football heroes who have enlisted in the Army to fight the creeping Red menace in Korea. And, oh yeah, there's also another son (Walker), who happens to be a Communist. Hayes, his loving mother, is relieved when the atheistic Walker swears on the family Bible that he's not a Commie. Schoolteacher Jagger, however, suspects differently and, in a frustrated rage, beans his son over the head with the Good Book, hoping to knock some sense into him. And that's about as exciting as this melodrama gets. McHugh provides minimal comic relief as the family's parish priest, and Hayes, the "First Lady of the American Theater," horribly overacts as the all–American mom who's forced by F.B.I. agent Heflin to choose between her country and her son. Walker, unfortunately, doesn't match his sensational performance in *Strangers on a Train*, and Jagger seems to be along just for the ride. Indicative of the era, this propaganda film earned an Oscar nomination for Best Motion Picture Story. During filming, Walker died of respiratory failure due to an adverse reaction to a prescribed sedative. Stand-ins and footage from *Strangers on a Train* had to be used to complete the final scenes, contributing to the cheap look of the film.

Familiar Face from Television:
❏ Richard Jaeckel (Lt. Martin Quirk in *Spenser: For Hire* and Lt. Ben Edwards in *Baywatch*) as one of the sons of Hayes and Jagger.

Memorable Noir Moments:
❏ Concerned about her boy's well-being, Hayes asks Walker if he has a girlfriend. The unemotional party hack responds, "Sentimentalizing over the biological urge isn't really a guarantee of human happiness."
❏ Bible believer Hayes falls for Walker's protestations that he's not a Communist but simply a liberal. "I love the downtrodden, the helpless minorities," he explains.

Mysterious Intruder (1946) 61 min. Richard Dix, Barton MacLane, Helen Mowery, Mike Mazurki, Paul E. Burns, Pamela Blake. **Screenplay by:** Eric Taylor. **Directed by:** William Castle. **Noir Type:** Missing Person. **Noir Themes:** Greed, betrayal. ★★★

This fifth entry in *The Whistler* series stars Dix as an unethical, hard-boiled private eye hired by Burns, elderly proprietor of a used phonograph shop, to find a missing woman (Blake). The old man doesn't have enough money to pay Dix's rate, but promises him that if he finds Blake, she'll make him a wealthy man. Of course, Dix sees dollar signs and agrees to take the case. Because the old man hasn't seen the missing woman since she was a young girl and wouldn't be able to recognize her, Dix hires Mowery to impersonate her and find out how much dough is involved. Believing her to be Blake, the old man tells Mowery that he has something of hers that's worth $200,000. Before he can explain, he's stabbed to death by Mazurki, who's also looking for the treasure. Dix is pretty good as a private eye with some major character flaws, and Mowery does well as the femme fatale. The film, narrated occasionally by the shadowy Whistler, moves briskly to an exciting and ironic conclusion. (See also *The Whistler, Mark of the Whistler, Power of the Whistler, Voice of the Whistler, Secret of the Whistler, The Thirteenth Hour* and *The Return of the Whistler*.)

Memorable Noir Moment:

❑ All in a day's work: Clumsy P.I. Dix breaks into Mazurki's house and carefully removes his shoes, placing one in each suit pocket. He quietly tiptoes down a corridor and stumbles over some empty bottles. Luckily for him, Mazurki is dead drunk on the floor. When the police arrive, Dix escapes through the window, knocks over a couple of garbage cans, loses a shoe and gets shot at by the cops and a gun-toting neighbor.

Mystery in Mexico (1948) 66 min. William Lundigan, Jacqueline White, Ricardo Cortez, Tony Barrett, Walter Reed. **Screenplay by:** Lawrence Kimble. **Directed by:** Robert Wise. **Noir Type:** South of the Border. **Noir Themes:** Greed, jealousy. ★★½

An insurance investigator (Lundigan) travels to Mexico City to search for a missing colleague (Reed), who he suspects has stolen a valuable necklace. Along the way, Lundigan ingratiates himself with nightclub singer White, Reed's sister, suspecting that she may have something to do with the missing jewelry. Once in Mexico, they run across some bad guys (Cortez and Barrett), who are also looking for the stolen necklace and the missing agent. Competently acted, with Lundigan and White engaging in a lot of enjoyable romantic banter.

Mystery Street (1950) 93 min. Ricardo Montalban, Sally Forrest, Bruce Bennett, Elsa Lanchester, Marshall Thompson, Jan Sterling, Edmon Ryan. **Screenplay by:** Sydney Boehm and Richard Brooks. **Directed by:** John Sturges. **Noir Type:** Police Procedural. **Noir Themes:** Victim of fate, greed, lust. ★★★

Montalban is a Massachusetts detective investigating the case of a murdered bar girl (Sterling). Thompson is charged with the murder, but he's an innocent man who happened to be in the wrong place at the wrong time. Forrest, Thompson's loyal wife, believes in her husband's innocence but thinks he may have cheated on her with Sterling. Bennett is the Harvard forensics scientist who helps Montalban find the real murderer (Ryan), a married man from one of Boston's oldest families, who killed Sterling because she was pregnant with his child. Lanchester, Sterling's greedy, alcoholic landlady, makes the mistake of trying to blackmail Ryan. This is a fast-mover,

Detectives (Ricardo Montalban, left, and Wally Maher) discuss a murder scene with a suspect's wife (Sally Forrest, right) and her waitress friend (Betsy Blair) in *Mystery Street* (MGM, 1950).

peppered with fascinating 1950s forensics information. The cast is first rate, especially Montalban as the Latino cop who locks horns with a killer WASP.

Familiar Faces from Television:
- ❑ Willard Waterman (*The Great Gildersleeve*) as a mortician.
- ❑ King Donovan (Bob Cummings' Air Force buddy Harvey Helm in *Love That Bob* and lawyer Herb Thornton in *Please Don't Eat the Daisies*) as a reporter.
- ❑ Ned Glass (Sgt. Andy Pendleton on *The Phil Silvers Show*) as Dr. Levy.

Memorable Noir Moment:
- ❑ At the Grass Skirt Bar, Sterling tells the inebriated Thompson that he could use some fresh air. When he suggests that somebody open a window, she replies, "Fresh air couldn't get in here with a permit."

Naked Alibi (1954) 85 min. Sterling Hayden, Gloria Grahame, Gene Barry, Marcia Henderson, Don Haggerty. **Screenplay by:** Lawrence Roman. **Directed by:** Jerry Hopper. **Noir Type:** Psycho. **Noir Themes:** Paranoia, betrayal, revenge, woman in jeopardy. ★★½

Somebody has killed three detectives, and police chief Hayden suspects a baker (Barry) who threatened one of the cops after they had arrested him for being drunk and disorderly. Determined to prove Barry's guilt, Hayden gets rough with the baker and is later fired for police brutality. Hayden and a former colleague (Haggerty) begin following the suspect, hoping he will lead them to the murder weapon. Unable to take the pressure, Barry leaves his wife (Henderson) and baby and flees to a Mexican border town, where a sexy cantina singer (noir icon Grahame) has been waiting for him. Guilty of adultery, yes, but is Barry the vicious cop killer? Despite Barry's tendency to overact, the film works well.

Familiar Face from Television:
❑ Chuck Connors (Lukas McCain, *The Rifleman*) as a police captain.

The Naked City (1948) 96 min. Barry Fitzgerald, Howard Duff, Dorothy Hart, Don Taylor, Ted de Corsia. **Screenplay by**: Alvin Maltz and Marvin Wald. **Directed by**: Jules Dassin. **Noir Type**: Police Procedural. **Noir Themes**: Greed, betrayal. ★★★★

Fitzgerald is excellent as a crusty homicide detective investigating the murder of a model, who was chloroformed and drowned in her bathtub. Veteran bad guy de

New York City detectives (Don Taylor, left and Barry Fitzgerald) console the grieving parents (Adelaide Klein and Grover Burgess) of a murdered girl in *The Naked City* (Universal-International, 1948).

Corsia is the harmonica-playing ex-wrestler who murdered the girl and, later, his own accomplice. Taylor plays Fitzgerald's inexperienced partner, and Duff, a habitual liar and small-time thief, is their number one suspect. The film follows the detectives as they hit the streets and painstakingly go about the mundane work of solving the crimes. Fitzgerald gives an enjoyable, tongue-in-cheek performance as the aging Irish-American cop, and veteran character actor de Corsia is sensational as the vicious killer. Cinematographer William Daniels' innovative on-location photography earned him an Oscar. Despite the sometimes tedious narration by producer Mark Hellinger, who utters the film's most famous line ("There are eight million stories in the Naked City. This has been one of them"), this classic has lost none of its charm and excitement. The film that spawned a successful TV series, *The Naked City* is a must-see for all noir fans. (Those film historians and reviewers who insist that the exciting climax takes place on the *Brooklyn* Bridge are referred to the engraved sign that clearly reads "*Williamsburg* Bridge.")

Familiar Faces from Television:
❏ Kathleen Freeman (Katie, the maid in *Topper* and Flo Shafer in *The Beverly Hillbillies*) as a subway rider discussing the recent murder.
❏ James Gregory (Inspector Frank Luger on *Barney Miller*) as a police officer on the beat.
❏ Paul Ford (Sgt. Bilko's boss, Colonel Hall, on *The Phil Silvers Show*) as a homicide detective.

Memorable Noir Moment:
❏ The grieving mother of the murdered model cries, "My God, why wasn't she born ugly?"

The Naked Spur (1953) 91 min. James Stewart, Janet Leigh, Robert Ryan, Ralph Meeker, Millard Mitchell. **Screenplay by:** Sam Rolfe and Harold Jack Bloom. **Directed by:** Anthony Mann. **Noir Type:** Horse Opera. **Noir Themes:** Greed, fatalism, betrayal, distrust. ★★★★

A bounty hunter (Stewart) hopes to collect the reward on murderer Ryan's head and buy back the land that his faithless wife sold while he was off fighting in the Civil War. While trekking through the mountainous countryside, Stewart meets a gold prospector (Mitchell) and pays him twenty dollars to help him find Ryan. After cornering the killer, Stewart and Mitchell are joined by a dishonorably discharged soldier (Meeker), and the three capture Ryan and Leigh, the girl accompanying him. When Mitchell and Meeker discover that there's a five thousand dollar reward for Ryan's capture, they insist on an equal share, which doesn't sit well with Stewart because a one-third share wouldn't be enough to buy back his land. Capitalizing on the situation, the devious Ryan begins to play the men against each other and even uses Leigh as sexual bait in his desperate efforts to escape. Complicating things, a band of normally friendly Blackfeet Indians show up looking for Meeker, who raped one of their women. A fine cast, some spectacular outdoor scenery and an action-packed script make this film a winner, worthy of its reputation as one of the finest Westerns ever made. Ryan stands out as the jovial, but psychotic, killer, and Meeker is excellent as the "morally unstable" ex-soldier. The 53-year-old Mitchell died of lung cancer the year the film was released.

A killer's girl (Janet Leigh) protects her man against a bounty hunter (Ralph Meeker) in *The Naked Spur* (MGM, 1953).

Memorable Noir Moment:

❑ Stewart and Ryan enjoy a campsite chat. "It's your choice," Stewart offers. "A bullet right here on the trail or a rope in Abilene." "Choosin' the way to die, what's the difference?" the philosophical Ryan answers. "Choosin' the way to live. That's the hard part."

The Naked Street (1955) 84 min. Anthony Quinn, Farley Granger, Anne Bancroft, Peter Graves, Else Neft. **Screenplay by**: Maxwell Shane. **Directed by**: Maxwell Shane. **Noir Type**: Gangster. **Noir Themes**: Betrayal, revenge. ★★½

Quinn plays a brutal New York crime chieftain who, between murders, pays a weekly visit to his elderly mother (Neft) and sister (Bancroft) for dinner at their Brooklyn apartment. When he learns that Bancroft is pregnant and that the father (Granger) is in prison awaiting execution for killing a liquor store owner during a robbery, Quinn quickly makes arrangements to get the father-to-be released. After hiring a prominent attorney, Quinn has his goons torture two eyewitnesses until they agree to change their testimony. Granger, feeling pretty lucky to have escaped the chair, is more than happy to make an honest woman out of Bancroft, especially since it means marrying into the big time. But Quinn, who doesn't like the punk, hires him to drive one of his trucks at an insulting 80 bucks a week. The conflict between the two men reaches the danger point when Granger, pushing his luck, starts cheating on Bancroft. Told in flashback by a reporter (Graves), *The Naked Street* is an average crime drama with Quinn and Bancroft giving top-notch performances.

Familiar Faces from Television:

❏ Sid Melton (Ichabod Mudd, assistant to *Captain Midnight*, and Charlie Halper, owner of the Copa Club, in *Make Room for Daddy* a.k.a. *The Danny Thomas Show*) as a wedding reception guest.

❏ Lee Van Cleef (Ninja master John Peter McCallister in *The Master*) as a poker-playing jewelry fence.

Memorable Noir Moment:

❏ Graves, delivering an epithet for a street hood about to be executed, notes, "Just another victim of the slum, the gangs and himself."

The Narrow Margin (1952) 70 min. Charles McGraw, Marie Windsor, Jacqueline White, Don Beddoe, Paul Maxey. **Screenplay by:** Earl Felton. **Directed by:** Richard Fleischer. **Noir Type:** Impersonator. **Noir Themes:** Woman in jeopardy. ✭✭✭✭

McGraw plays a tough detective assigned to protect a mobster's widow who's traveling by train to testify against her late husband's cohorts. Noir icon Windsor is the woman McGraw is assigned to watch. Beddoe is his careless partner, and White is the classy lady who McGraw fears might be mistaken for Windsor. In a setting that's

Charles McGraw and Marie Windsor in *The Narrow Margin* (RKO, 1952).

already claustrophobic, a corpulent passenger (Maxey) wanders suspiciously about the train, making corridor passage tricky. The hard-boiled McGraw and the sarcastic Windsor are believable in their obvious distaste for each other, and the suspense works well thanks to the appropriately menacing bad guys and the fast-paced plot filled with surprising twists. Remade in 1990 as *Narrow Margin*, with Gene Hackman and Anne Archer.

Memorable Noir Moments:
- ❑ Beddoe and McGraw bet five dollars on what Windsor will be like. McGraw, who says she'll be a "sixty cent special, cheap, flashy, strictly poison under the gravy," wins the bet.
- ❑ When McGraw tries to squeeze by Maxey in the train's passageway, the fat man comments jovially, "Nobody loves a fat man except his grocer and his tailor."

Never Trust a Gambler (1951) 79 min. Dane Clark, Cathy O'Donnell, Tom Drake, Jeff Corey, Rhys Williams. **Screenplay by:** Jesse Lasky, Jr., and Jerome Odlum. **Directed by:** Ralph Murphy. **Noir Type:** Cover-Up. **Noir Themes:** Woman in jeopardy, betrayal. ★★

Gambler Clark, wanted as a key witness in a murder trial, shows up at his ex-wife's home pleading for a place to hide. He's on the run, he tells his ex (O'Donnell), because he's scheduled to be a witness against his best friend in a murder trial, and his testimony is certain to convict the innocent man. O'Donnell is determined to kick him out, but when he shows her his bank book, which lists monthly deposits of six hundred dollars, she relents and lets him stay, believing he's a changed man and has a real job. While shopping, she runs into one of her former roommate's boyfriends, an intoxicated cop (Williams), who follows her home and tries to force himself on her. Clark, while trying to protect O'Donnell, accidentally kills the cop, and the big cover-up begins. Homicide detectives Drake and Corey, investigating Williams' death, find their way to O'Donnell. Of course, Drake falls in love with her. It's all pretty standard stuff, with Clark and Corey giving lackluster performances.

Familiar Face from Television:
- ❑ Percy Helton (Homer Cratchit in *The Beverly Hillbillies*) as a liquor salesman.

Memorable Noir Moments:
- ❑ Three street-wise ladies wait outside the detectives' office, while a fourth is being questioned. One wonders if "they're giving her the third degree." Her gum-chewing companion answers, "I don't know. I didn't get *my* degree at this college."
- ❑ A film noir first? O'Donnell pays for her gas with a credit card.
- ❑ Referring to his deceased former partner, detective Corey answers Drake's question about whether or not the cop was off duty when he was killed: "On or off, he only had one thing on his mind — a skirt."

New York Confidential (1955) 87 min. Broderick Crawford, Richard Conte, Marilyn Maxwell, Anne Bancroft, J. Carrol Naish, Onslow Stevens. **Screenplay by:** Clarence Greene and Russell Rouse. **Directed by:** Russell Rouse. **Noir Type:** Hit Man. **Noir Themes:** Corruption, betrayal, social reform. ★★★

When an underling makes an unauthorized hit in his territory, the New York syndicate boss (Crawford) borrows a hit man (Conte) from his Chicago counterpart

(Stevens) to take care of the upstart. The vicious Conte does such a good job that Crawford arranges a "transfer" for him and hires him as his bodyguard. Eventually, Conte climbs the ladder to take over the number two spot previously held by Naish, who's facing deportation to Italy. Conte is so loyal to his new boss that he even rejects advances by Crawford's lover (Maxwell) and independent-minded daughter (Bancroft). However, his loyalty is put to the ultimate test when a hit against a corrupt political figure goes bad, and a crime commission gets closer to putting the syndicate out of business. Conte gives a chillingly realistic performance as the expert hit man, and Crawford is excellent as the organized crime lord who, like his modern-day TV counterpart, Tony Soprano, has his share of personal family problems, including caring for his elderly mother.

Familiar Faces from Television:
- ❑ John Doucette (Jim Weston in *Lock Up* and Captain Andrews in *The Partners*) as a gangster who bites the dust in a syndicate-operated bar.
- ❑ Frank Ferguson (Gus the ranch hand in *My Friend Flicka*) as the doctor who patches up Crawford after an attempted hit.
- ❑ Henry Kulky (Otto Schmidlap in *The Life of Riley*) as a lookout for a couple of hit men in a hotel.

Memorable Noir Moments:
- ❑ Syndicate chieftain Crawford expresses admiration for Conte's devotion to his Chicago boss. "Loyalty—that's something you can't buy," he says. "Half the pigs that work for us can't even spell it."
- ❑ A doctor, in typical noir fashion, dismisses Crawford's gunshot wound as "just a little flesh wound." (See also *Accused of Murder, Jail Bait, Guilty Bystander, The Enforcer, Riot in Cell Block 11* and *Sleep, My Love.*)
- ❑ Bancroft compliments Conte at the breakfast table: "You're not like the rest of Papa's hoodlums." "I like the term 'employee,'" he tells her.

New York Photographer *see* Violated

Niagara (1953) 92 min. Marilyn Monroe, Joseph Cotten, Jean Peters, Casey Adams, Richard Allan. **Screenplay by:** Charles Brackett, Walter Reisch and Richard Breen. **Directed by:** Henry Hathaway. **Noir Type:** Troubled Veteran. **Noir Themes:** Betrayal, jealousy, paranoia, revenge, woman in jeopardy. ★★★★

A couple (Peters and Adams) on a delayed honeymoon to Niagara Falls reluctantly become involved in the lives of an emotionally unbalanced Korean war veteran (Cotten) and his voluptuous wife (Monroe), who are staying at the same motel. Peters soon discovers that Monroe is cheating on her husband with Allan but doesn't learn until it's too late that the lovers have concocted a plan to murder Cotten and run off together. After the former beer hall waitress reports that her husband is missing, police discover a man's body floating in the river, evidently a suicide, and ask Monroe to identify it. Fully expecting it to be Cotten, Monroe goes into shock and is hospitalized when she realizes that it's the body of her lover. Meanwhile, Peters notices Cotten lurking around the motel and begins to fear for Monroe's life. Cotten's performance as the cuckolded neurotic is impeccable, but the film belongs to Monroe, oozing sexuality, as his unfaithful wife.

Familiar Faces from Television:

❑ Don Wilson (Jack Benny's announcer on *The Jack Benny Show*) as Adams' annoyingly jolly boss.
❑ Minerva Urecal (Annie in *The Adventures of Tugboat Annie* and "Mother" in *Peter Gunn*) as Allan's landlady.

Memorable Noir Moments:

❑ When Monroe sashays across the motel courtyard wearing a clinging, low-cut red dress, a grinning Adams asks his wife, "Why don't you ever get a dress like that?" Peters good-naturedly replies, "Listen, for a dress like that you've got to start laying plans when you're about 13."
❑ An enraged Cotten, not as thrilled as Adams about Monroe's red dress, angrily describes it as being "cut down so low in the front, you can see her kneecaps."

Night and the City (1950) 95 min. Richard Widmark, Gene Tierney, Googie Withers, Herbert Lom, Francis L. Sullivan, Hugh Marlowe, Stanislaus Zbyszko, Mike Mazurki, Ken Richmond. **Screenplay by:** Jo Eisinger. **Directed by:** Jules Dassin. **Noir Type:** Ambition. **Noir Themes:** Betrayal, paranoia, greed. ★★★★½

Widmark, a small-time hustler ("an artist without an art") with high ambitions ("I just want to *be* somebody"), is excited about his latest get-rich-quick scheme — controlling the wrestling game in London. Underworld chieftain Lom has the sport in his back pocket and would normally eliminate any competitor who tried to weasel his way into the business. But Widmark has an ace in the hole — Lom's beloved father (Zbyszko), a famous Greco-Roman wrestler, who's horrified to find his son promoting fake wrestling matches. Widmark has conned the old man into believing that he wants to bring back the true art of wrestling to London audiences. Zbyszko and his young wrestling prodigy (Richmond) sign up with the street-smart loser, paralyzing Lom, who doesn't dare take out Widmark for fear of further antagonizing Daddy. The only thing Widmark lacks to pull off this venture is dough. He tries hitting up his employer, corpulent nightclub owner Sullivan, who gets a big chuckle out of the scheme. However, Sullivan's treacherous wife (Withers), Widmark's former lover, foolishly gives him some money with the understanding that he'll use it to get her a coveted liquor license so she can open her own club and leave her husband. Tierney plays Widmark's girlfriend, a nightclub singer, who, while fed up with his lies and lame-brained schemes, still loves him. Marlowe is her romance-minded neighbor. Veteran noir actor Mazurki plays "The Strangler," a phony wrestler, the epitome of everything Zbyszko hates about the fraudulent "sport." While Mazurki and Zbyszko angrily take on each other in a thrilling, impromptu wrestling match, Widmark watches helplessly as his latest dream goes down the drain once again. A dark, depressing film, *Night and the City* is a now considered a classic, a must-see for every noir fan. Widmark, who brought not only his terrific talents to the role but also his famous giggle from **Kiss of Death**, is in great form as one of film noir's biggest losers. British-born character actor Sullivan also turns in a top-notch performance as the masochistic nightclub owner, who despises himself for tolerating his faithless wife and their loveless marriage. *Night and the City* was Dassin's first film while in European exile after being identified as a Communist by fellow director Edward

A phony wrestling promoter (Richard Widmark, right) isn't having any luck putting the touch on a vindictive nightclub owner (Francis L. Sullivan) in *Night and the City* (20th Century–Fox, 1950).

Dmytryk during the House Un-American Activities Committee hearings. Remade in 1992 with Robert DeNiro and Jessica Lange as the ill-fated lovers.

Memorable Noir Moments:
- ❏ Obviously a good judge of character, Lom makes a prediction about Widmark's future: "Born a hustler, you'll die a hustler."
- ❏ The long-suffering Tierney has heard it all before, but Widmark just can't help himself. "This is different, Mary," he says, referring to his latest scheme. "This can't lose."

Night Editor (1946) 65 min. William Gargan, Janis Carter, Jeff Donnell, Paul E. Burns. **Screenplay by:** Hal Smith. **Directed by:** Henry Levin. **Noir Type:** Bad Cop. **Noir Themes:** Lust, obsession, betrayal, character deterioration. ★★★½

Despite the devotion of his wife and young son, homicide detective Gargan is having an affair with the beautiful Carter, who's married to a wealthy older man. While Gargan and Carter are parked in a secluded spot near the ocean, another car parks nearby. They watch in horror as the driver viciously beats his female companion to death with a tire iron. Instinctively, Gargan begins to give chase but stops when Carter reminds him about the scandal that would surely follow. Guilt-ridden and fearful, Gargan begins a cover-up. An innocent man is arrested and convicted of the murder, and when Gargan recognizes a local banker as the killer, he faces a tough moral dilemma — arrest him and end up in jail himself or let the patsy go to the chair. Narrated by a New York newspaper editor, this is a suspenseful and intriguing film, with Gargan nicely underplaying his role, and Carter deliciously wicked as the femme fatale. The surprise ending will be hated by some, loved by others. Gargan, brother of veteran character actor Ed Gargan, starred in the early TV series *Martin Kane, Private Eye*.

Familiar Face from Television:
❑ Frank Wilcox (John Brewster in *The Beverly Hillbillies*) as the murderer.

Memorable Noir Moments:
❑ In an state of obvious sexual excitement, Carter demands to see the body of the girl brutally beaten to death with a tire iron. (See Carter in *Framed* for more of the same.)
❑ Gargan, upset with Carter's callousness about the murder and the fact that an innocent man is going to the chair, tells her, "You're rotten. Pure, no good, first-rate, high-grade, A-number-one rotten."

Night Has a Thousand Eyes (1948) 80 min. Edward G. Robinson, Gail Russell, John Lund, Virginia Bruce, Jerome Cowan, William Demarest. **Screenplay by:** Barré Lyndon and Jonathan Latimer. **Directed by:** John Farrow. **Noir Type:** Fantasy. **Noir Themes:** Fatalism, paranoia, woman in jeopardy, victim of fate. ★★★½

Robinson, a stage clairvoyant who experiences real visions and premonitions, tells his story to the suicidal Russell and her boyfriend Lund. Via flashback, we see him on stage performing his phony act with his assistants (Bruce and Cowan). Suddenly, he warns a member of the audience to hurry home because her child is in danger. She returns later to thank him and to confirm that her son, who was playing with matches, had set the bed on fire. The visions begin to come more often, and soon Robinson and his stage partners are rolling in dough from his racetrack and stock market predictions. The premonitions, however, turn ominous, and Robinson, frightened and depressed about this "gift" he never wanted, runs off and becomes a hermit for the next twenty years. But now he's back, and his sixth sense is warning him about Russell's imminent death. Lund, believing that Robinson is a con artist, calls in policeman Demarest to investigate. The plot of this very eerie noir is hard to swallow, but Robinson is so good that he pulls it off.

Familiar Face from Television:
❑ Richard Webb (*Captain Midnight*) as Cowan's business associate.

Memorable Noir Moment:
❑ A cop warns the unarmed Robinson, who has left the room he was ordered to stay in, not to continue down the stairs. "One more step and I'll wing ya," he warns. Robinson ignores him and the trigger-happy, typical noir cop aims and pulls the trigger — twice.

A mentalist (Edward G. Robinson) and his assistant (Virginia Bruce) amaze the audience in *Night Has a Thousand Eyes* (Paramount, 1948).

The Night Holds Terror (1955) 86 min. Jack Kelly, Hildy Parks, Vince Edwards, John Cassavetes, David Gross. **Screenplay by:** Andrew L. Stone. **Directed by:** Andrew L. Stone. **Noir Type:** Hostage. **Noir Themes:** Victim of fate, greed, betrayal. ★★★

Kelly, a businessman on his way home after a hard day at work, is kidnapped by a hitchhiker (Edwards) and his two cohorts (Cassavetes and Gross). Just when it seems that the psychos are going to kill him after finding only 10 bucks on him, Kelly talks them out of it by promising to sell his car and giving them the two grand he expects to get for it. The car salesman, however, is unable to come up with the entire amount in cash so the thugs decide to hole up at Kelly's house until the bank opens the next morning. At the house, ladies' man Edwards tries to force himself on Kelly's attractive wife (Parks), while Kelly seethes and his two terrified kids huddle in their room. When the hoods discover that his father is a wealthy businessman, they get the bright idea of holding Kelly for ransom. Based on a true story, this is a taut, dramatic thriller, with Kelly, Cassavetes and Edwards, early in their careers, giving solid performances.

Familiar Faces from Television:
❑ Barney Phillips (Sgt. Ed Jacobs in *Dragnet,* Capt. Franks in *Felony Squad* and Maj. Kaiser in *Twelve O'Clock High*) as the car dealer.
❑ Jack Kruschen (Tully in *Hong Kong* and Sam Markowitz in *Busting Loose*) as a police detective.

Memorable Noir Moment:
❑ From the Some-Things-Never-Change Department: An unsympathetic journalist complains angrily because the cops have killed his scoop on Kelly's kidnapping and are asking reporters to sit on the story to protect the victim. "You gyp me out of my exclusive. Now you want me to twirl my thumbs while one of these double-crossing cutthroats makes a sucker out of me," he says, referring to his colleagues.

Night into Morning (1951) 86 min. Ray Milland, John Hodiak, Nancy Davis, Lewis Stone. **Screenplay by:** Leonard Spigelgass and Karl Tunberg. **Directed by:** Fletcher Markle. **Noir Type:** Boozer. **Noir Themes:** Victim of fate, character deterioration, fatalism. ★★★

While teaching his English class, college professor Milland hears an explosion and the sound of fire engines. What he doesn't realize is that the trucks are racing to his home, where a gas explosion has taken the lives of his wife and ten-year-old son. Devastated, he holes up at a three-dollar-a-night fleabag hotel and begins drinking heavily. Colleagues Stone, Hodiak and Davis, who lost her husband in the war, reach out to him, but are rebuffed. Bent on self-destruction, he contemplates suicide. A strong performance by Milland, who had an Oscar-winning bout with the bottle in 1945's **The Lost Moment**, greatly helps the weepy plot.

Familiar Faces from Television:
❑ Rosemary DeCamp (Bob's sister Margaret MacDonald in *The Bob Cummings Show*) as Milland's wife.
❑ Jean Hagen (Margaret Williams in *Make Room for Daddy*) as the lonely girl who makes a play for the uninterested Milland.
❑ Whit Bissell (Gen. Heywood Kirk in *The Time Tunnel*) as the owner of a gravestone company.

The Night of the Hunter (1955) 93 min. Robert Mitchum, Shelley Winters, Lillian Gish, Peter Graves, Billy Chapin, Sally Jane Bruce. **Screenplay by:** James Agee. **Directed by:** Charles Laughton. **Noir Type:** Psycho. **Noir Themes:** Sexual hostility, child in jeopardy, greed, paranoia, sexual hostility. ★★★★½

Mitchum, in what many believe to be his greatest performance, plays a psychopathic, self-ordained preacher who terrorizes two children (Chapin and Bruce). After marrying their slow-witted mother (Winters), the switchblade-wielding misogynist discovers that his stepchildren know where their recently hanged father (Graves) hid the ten thousand dollars he stole. Determined to lay his hands on the loot, Mitchum chases the petrified youngsters down river, setting the stage for a showdown with a feisty spinster (silent film star Gish), who makes a habit of taking in the littlest victims of the Great Depression — orphans and abandoned children. This brilliantly directed and stunningly photographed allegory of good versus evil was actor Laughton's only directorial attempt. It failed at the box office but today is considered a masterpiece. Hard core noir fans might be disappointed by the weak ending, and churchgoers who view this film may never again be able to sing the words to "Leaning on the Everlasting Arms" without thinking of Mitchum's evil preacher.

Familiar Face from Television:
❑ John Hamilton (Perry White in *The Adventures of Superman*) as a passerby in the street greeting Gish. Don't blink.

Memorable Noir Moments:
❑ Using his hands (with the words LOVE and HATE tattooed across his fingers as a visual aid), Mitchum gives a raving mini-sermon explaining the eternal battle of good and evil to his dumbfounded admirers.
❑ Spinster Gish comments on the romantic and sexual inclinations of her species: "Women is fools. All of them."

The Night Runner (1957) 79 min. Ray Danton, Colleen Miller, Willis Bouchey, Robert Anderson. **Screenplay by:** Gene Levitt. **Directed by:** Abner Biberman. **Noir Type:** Psycho. **Noir Themes:** Paranoia, guilt. ★★★

Against the recommendation of his psychiatrist, a potentially violent inmate (Danton) at Woodale State Hospital is released because of overcrowding at the facility. Danton, hoping to keep his background a secret as he tries to readjust to society in a peaceful ocean community, falls in love with the pretty daughter (Miller) of a motel owner (Bouchey) and attempts to dodge the questions of a suspicious cop (Anderson). Things begin looking up for Danton when he lands a job as a draftsman and Miller responds favorably to his romantic overtures. Then someone discovers his secret and makes the fatal mistake of calling him a lunatic and threatening to expose him. Danton gives a strong performance as the psycho whose problems seem to stem from a childhood incident when "a mean old man" (his father) shot and killed one of his favorite seagulls.

Familiar Face from Television:
❑ Merry Anders ("Mike" McCall in *How to Marry a Millionaire*) as an auto mechanic's pregnant wife.

Memorable Noir Moment:

❏ Danton's worried psychiatrist gives him some last-minute advice. "No stress, no strain!" he shouts as the human time bomb boards a bus headed to freedom and an unsuspecting community. Wishful thinking, doc.

Night Unto Night (1949) 84 min. Ronald Reagan, Viveca Lindfors, Broderick Crawford, Rosemary DeCamp, Osa Massen, Art Baker. **Screenplay by:** Kathryn Scola. **Directed by:** Don Siegel. **Noir Type:** Soap Opera. **Noir Themes:** Fatalism, obsession, jealousy, family dysfunction. ★★

Biochemist Reagan, diagnosed with incurable epilepsy, rents an old Florida Keys beach house from a troubled widow (Lindfors), who's been hearing her dead husband's voice lately. Lindfors' spiteful sister (Massen) makes a play for Reagan, but Ron only has eyes for his landlady. And vice versa. When the scientist's epilepsy becomes more frequent and more severe, he takes to lingering around an ominous gun rack. Crawford, in a departure from his usual tough guy roles, plays a friendly artist; DeCamp is Crawford's wife; and Baker is Reagan's doctor. The cast is good, but the film is a tepid, uneventful melodrama, with all of the interesting stuff happening after the film was made — Lindfors and director Siegel married (1949), they divorced (1953), Crawford became a big TV star (*Highway Patrol*, 1955–59), Siegel directed Reagan's last film (1964's neo-noir, *The Killers*), and in 1980, Reagan ... well, you know the rest.

Familiar Faces from Television:

❏ Craig Stevens (*Peter Gunn*) as Massen's boyfriend.
❏ Joe Devlin (Sam Catchem in *Dick Tracy*) as a moving man.

Memorable Noir Moments:

❏ The flirtatious Massen asks Reagan why he's all alone in such a big house. "I came here to be by myself," he answers. "Oh, a misogynist," she says, adding, "I read a book once."
❏ Reagan gets philosophical with his doctor, saying, "Death isn't the worst thing in a man's life. Only the last." (More than thirty years later, President Reagan quipped to doctors removing a would-be assassin's bullet from his side, "I hope you guys are Republicans.")

Night Without Sleep (1952) 77 min. Gary Merrill, Linda Darnell, June Vincent, Hildegarde Neff. **Screenplay by:** Elick Moll and Frank Partos. **Directed by:** Roy Ward Baker. **Noir Type:** Boozer. **Noir Themes:** Character deterioration, betrayal. ★½

Merrill, an alcoholic songwriter, has been experiencing blackouts and is told by his analyst that he's potentially violent. Awakening after a night of heavy drinking, Merrill has the disturbing feeling that he has killed someone. During flashbacks, we meet his possible victims — his shrewish wife (Vincent), his jealous girlfriend (Neff) and the beautiful actress (Darnell) who is infatuated with him. Dark, brooding and boring.

Familiar Face from Television:

❏ Hugh Beaumont (Beaver's dad, Ward Cleaver, in *Leave It to Beaver*) as Merrill's friend and party host.

Nightfall (1956) 80 min. Aldo Ray, Brian Keith, Anne Bancroft, James Gregory, Rudy Bond. **Screenplay by:** Sterling Silliphant. **Directed by:** Jacques Tourneur. **Noir Type:** On the Run. **Noir Themes:** Victim of fate, paranoia. ★★★½

Artist Ray is being pursued by cops, who think he's a murderer, and by two bank robbers (Keith and Bond), who believe he has their loot. Gregory (Inspector Frank Luger in TV's *Barney Miller*) is the insurance investigator trailing Ray, hoping to find the money. Bancroft, a model, falls for the artist and tries to help clear him. This is a fast-moving and enjoyable film, but Ray is unexciting in the lead role. Bond, however, is excellent as the psychopathic bank robber who's just itching to knock off Ray.

Memorable Noir Moment:

❑ In a scene reminiscent of *Border Incident*, a bad guy gets his comeuppance beneath a snow plow.

Nightmare (1956) 89 min. Edward G. Robinson, Kevin McCarthy, Virginia Christine, Connie Russell. **Screenplay by:** Maxwell Shane. **Directed by:** Maxwell Shane. **Noir Type:** Nightmare. **Noir Themes:** Victim of fate, paranoia. ★★★

McCarthy does a good job with the DeForest Kelley role in this faithful remake of 1947's *Fear in the Night*. He plays, instead of Kelley's bank teller, a hip jazz musician whose nightmare of murder turns out to have really happened. He goes to his square brother-in-law (Robinson), a New Orleans homicide detective, to help him unravel the strange events that caused him to kill a stranger in a mirrored room of an eerie mansion. Christine plays Robinson's pregnant wife, and Russell is McCarthy's babe, a nightclub singer. The creative jazz score and the terrific expressionistic photography help move things along nicely.

Familiar Face from Television:

❑ Gage Clark (Superintendent Bascom in *Mr. Peepers*) as McCarthy's weird next-door neighbor.

Nightmare Alley (1947) 111 min. Tyrone Power, Joan Blondell, Coleen Gray, Mike Mazurki, Helen Walker. **Screenplay by:** Jules Furthman. **Directed by:** Edmund Goulding. **Noir Type:** Con Artist. **Noir Themes:** Character deterioration, greed, betrayal, obsession, guilt. ★★★★

This fascinatingly morbid film details the rise and fall of a fast-talking, sociopathic con artist (Power) who works at a traveling carnival. The ambitious roustabout and barker romances a kindly mentalist (Blondell) to obtain her secret mind-reading code after accidentally killing her dipso partner (Keith) by plying him with wood alcohol. After seducing Gray, the young girlfriend of the carnival's strongman (Mazurki), Power is forced into a shotgun wedding. Shortly thereafter, he and his bride leave the sleazy carnie life to become a successful nightclub mentalist team, using the secret code he weaseled out of Blondell. Not content with his newfound fame, Power teams up with Walker, a corrupt "consulting psychologist," who feeds him confidential information, which he uses to bilk her trusting patients out of their fortunes. The "spook racket" is highly profitable for Power, but his spiritualist empire

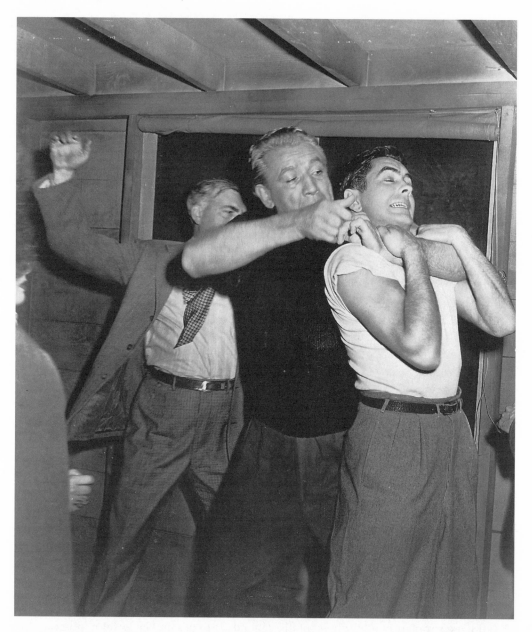

A carnival owner (James Flavin) tries to stop the strongman (Mike Mazurki, center) from shortening the career of an aspiring mentalist (Tyrone Power) in *Nightmare Alley* (20th Century–Fox, 1947).

is threatened by Gray's basic sense of decency and Walker's greed. Matinee idol Power, cast way against type here, gives a strong performance. Blondell is terrific, too, as is Walker as the calculating femme fatale. The film's best scenes are early on at the carnival, where the star attraction is the "geek," a pathetic rum-dum who bites off the heads of chickens for a bottle of booze and a place to sleep. Nearly forgotten and rarely seen, *Nightmare Alley,* despite its cop-out ending, is a memorable experience.

Familiar Faces from Television:

❑ Roy Roberts (Captain Huxley in *Oh Susanna*) as a carnie boss.
❑ George Chandler (Uncle Petrie Martin in *Lassie* and Ichabod Adams in *Ichabod and Me*) as a hobo enthralled by Power's spiel.

Memorable Noir Moments:

❑ Powell gets an earful when he tries to con an outraged Gray. "You're not talking to one of your chumps," she tells him. "You're talking to your wife. You're talking to somebody who knows you red, white, and blue."
❑ A carnie worker, after witnessing the "geek" run amuck with the D.T.'s asks his boss, "How can a guy get so low?" "He reached too high," is the man's noirish response.

99 River Street (1953) 83 min. John Payne, Evelyn Keyes, Brad Dexter, Frank Faylen, Peggie Castle, Jay Adler, Jack Lambert. **Screenplay by**: Robert Smith. **Directed by**: Phil Karlson. **Noir Type**: Wrong Man. **Noir Themes**: Betrayal, victim of fate. ★★★½

Payne is a washed-up heavyweight contender who's forced to drive a cab after

A gangster (Jack Lambert) manhandles an adulterous housewife (Peggie Castle) in *99 River Street* (United Artists, 1953).

being sidelined by an eye injury. He's married to a fickle ex-showgirl (Castle) who, disillusioned with their marriage, constantly berates him about his inability to shower her with luxuries. Payne discovers that she has been cheating on him with a diamond thief and murderer (Dexter) and that they plan to run off to South America. Adler is the pet store owner and diamond fence who refuses to pay Dexter because he brought a dame in on the job. So Dexter kills Castle and plants her body in her husband's cab. Before long, the cops are searching for Payne, who's being helped by Keyes, a struggling actress, and Faylen, his dispatcher and former trainer. Lambert plays Adler's vicious henchman. Payne is excellent as the pug who likes using his fists to settle scores, and Castle is perfect as his femme fatale wife. Be prepared for a knock-out climax.

Memorable Noir Moments:
❑ Payne tries to discourage Keyes from hanging around. "Any time you get hooked up with a dame," he says, "you're bound to end up in trouble."
❑ An already beaten Lambert gets a word of advice from an angry Payne. "Spill, punk, or I'll splash your brains out," he warns.

No Man of Her Own (1950) 98 min. Barbara Stanwyck, John Lund, Jane Cowl, Henry O'Neill, Lyle Bettger, Phyllis Thaxter, Richard Denning. **Screenplay by:** Sally Benson and Catherine Turney. **Directed by:** Mitchell Leisen. **Noir Type:** Impersonator. **Noir Themes:** Guilt, paranoia, betrayal, fatalism. ★★½

Stanwyck (43 at the time) plays a young woman expecting a child out of wedlock (gasp!). The father (Bettger, in his screen debut), a real louse, slides a ticket to San Francisco and a five-dollar bill under his locked door as Stanwyck stands outside his apartment sobbing hysterically. On the train she meets a young married couple (Denning and Thaxter), who take a shine to her. Unfortunately, there's a terrible wreck and Denning and Thaxter are killed. In the hospital, after giving birth to a boy, Stanwyck realizes that she's been mistaken for Thaxter, who was seven months pregnant, and that Denning's wealthy parents (Cowl and O'Neill), who have never met their daughter-in-law, want her to come live with them. Penniless, she goes along with the impersonation for the sake of her baby. Denning's brother (Lund) suspects that she's not really his sister-in-law but falls in love with her anyway, making her guilt even more unbearable. Things heat up when she receives an anonymous telegram ("Who are you? Where did you come from? What are you doing there?"). Based on the Cornell Woolrich novel *I Married a Dead Man*, this soap opera noir is entertaining but dragged-out. Denning went on to star in TV's *Mr. and Mrs. North* and *Michael Shayne* and played the Governor in *Hawaii Five-O*. In 1996, *No Man of Her Own* was remade as a comedy (*Mrs. Winterbourne*) starring talk show host Ricki Lake.

Familiar Faces from Television:
❑ Kathleen Freeman (Katie the maid in *Topper* and Flo Shafer in *The Beverly Hillbillies*) as a guest at the country club dance.
❑ Willard Waterman (*The Great Gildersleeve*) also as a guest at the country club dance.

No Man's Woman (1955) 70 min. Marie Windsor, John Archer, Patric Knowles, Nancy Gates, Jil Jarmyn, Richard Crane. **Screenplay by:** John K. Butler. **Directed by:** Franklin Adreon. **Noir Type:** Femme Fatale. **Noir Themes:** Greed, betrayal, revenge. ★½

Somebody knocks off a shrewish art dealer (Windsor), and cops wind up with a handful of suspects, all with pretty good motives. Unfortunately, there's no motive for the viewer to continue with this dribble once the very watchable Windsor gets her comeuppance.

Memorable Noir Moment:

❑ When Windsor's father-in-law offers to add thirty grand to the settlement pot if she agrees to give his son a divorce, she quips, "Thirty thousand dollars? That's not a settlement, pop. That's a tip."
❑ Windsor's irate father-in-law comments that "any way you look at it, that woman is a witch." Her equally irate husband agrees, adding, "And no matter how you spell it."

No Questions Asked (1951) 81 min. Barry Sullivan, Arlene Dahl, George Murphy, Jean Hagen, Richard Simmons. **Screenplay by:** Sidney Sheldon. **Directed by:** Harold F. Kress. **Noir Type:** Bad Cop. **Noir Themes:** Character deterioration, obsession, greed, betrayal. ★★★

After his gold-digging fiancée (Dahl) dumps him for a wealthy man (Simmons), insurance investigator Sullivan decides to climb the ladder of success the easy way. He becomes, in effect, a legal fence, working with fur and jewel thieves to return stolen merchandise for a price so his insurance company doesn't have to pay up. While he makes a nice little commission on each deal, he soon learns an expensive lesson about walking on the dark side. Hagen is the girl who loves him, and Murphy is the cop who's trying to put him away. An effective little twist on the good cop gone bad, this noir supports the old adage, "there's one born every minute."

Familiar Faces from Television:

❑ Madge Blake (Dick Grayson's Aunt Harriet in *Batman* and Flora MacMichael in *The Real McCoys*) as Dahl's nosy neighbor.
❑ Richard Anderson (Oscar Goldman in *The Six Million Dollar Man*) as a detective.

Memorable Noir Moments:

❑ Sensitivity Training Required: When asked by a detective if he would recognize the man who asked him to deliver a package, a delivery boy replies, "He was Chinese. They all kinda look alike."
❑ Two female impersonators hold up the ladies room at a concert, getting away with almost a million dollars worth of jewels. They are described by their victims as being pretty.

No Time to Be Young (1957) 82 min. Robert Vaughn, Roger Smith, Tom Pittman, Dorothy Green, Merry Anders, Kathleen Nolan. **Screenplay by:** John McPartland and Raphael Hayes. **Directed by:** David Lowell Rich. **Noir Type:** Troubled Youth. **Noir Themes:** Paranoia, bigotry, revenge. ★★

Egomaniac and violent sociopath Vaughn is drafted after being kicked out of college. Not eager to put on a "monkey suit," he decides to buy a schooner and sail to Central America with his buddies (Smith and Pittman). Being broke doesn't bother Vaughn because he has this great idea of knocking over the supermarket where Smith works. He and his two reluctant accomplices plan for about thirty minutes before diving headfirst into the heist. Naturally, things go awry and the stickup tyros find themselves on the run. Before the film gets around to the actual heist, however, viewers are subjected to three dull subplots involving the boys' love lives. Green plays Vaughn's middle-aged English teacher and lover; Anders, a hell kitten who works in a drive-in diner, is the girl Smith wants to marry; and Nolan is Pittman's young bride, who thinks the writer wannabe has already sold his first novel. Vaughn, TV's *The Man from U.N.C.L.E.*, isn't too bad in his film debut as a punk who seems determined to prove that crime doesn't pay. Smith later starred in the hit private eye series *77 Sunset Strip*; Nolan went on to play in *The Real McCoys*; Anders co-starred in *How to Marry a Millionaire*; and Green played Jennifer Brooks from 1973 to 1977 in *The Young and the Restless*. Although the film is mostly boring, the climax is exciting, and the noirish manner in which Vaughn loses the stick-up dough is humorous and original.

Familiar Face from Television:

❑ Sara Selby (Ma Smalley, owner of the boarding house, in *Gunsmoke*) as Vaughn's workaholic mom.

Memorable Noir Moment:

❑ Vaughn gets tough with a liquor store clerk after the man calls him a "smart punk." "That's a word a fat guy your age never oughta use," Vaughn warns the man before leaving without paying for his bottle of vodka.

No Way Out (1950) 106 min. Richard Widmark, Linda Darnell, Stephen McNally, Sidney Poitier, Mildred Joanne Smith, Harry Bellaver. **Screenplay by**: Joseph L. Mankiewicz and Lesser Samuels. **Directed by**: Joseph L. Mankiewicz. **Noir Type**: Racist. **Noir Themes**: Bigotry, revenge, paranoia. ★★★★

After Widmark and his kid brother are shot during a robbery attempt, they're treated by the hospital's first black doctor (Poitier). Poitier suspects that there's something more seriously wrong with Widmark's brother than his minor gunshot wound, and administers a spinal tap. The man dies under Poitier's care, and Widmark later claims that Poitier murdered his brother. When Widmark refuses to give his permission for an autopsy, Poitier and his boss (McNally) visit the dead man's ex-wife (Darnell), hoping she will intervene with her former brother-in-law. She does, but the bigot convinces her to alert his friends in their poor white neighborhood (where "the stink gets in your skin") to arm themselves for a race war. Meanwhile, the residents of the nearby black community decide that the best defense is a good offense and plan a surprise raid, ensuring a busy night for the hospital's emergency room staff. Bellaver plays Widmark's deaf-mute brother, and Smith is Poitier's wife. *No Way Out* take an honest look at racial turmoil in a late 1940s American city. Poitier, in his Hollywood debut (his first film was an Army documentary), is excellent as the idealistic young doctor. Widmark, portraying yet another psychopath (see *Kiss of Death*, *Road House* and *The Street with No Name*), gives a dynamic performance, and Darnell does well in a seedy, unglamorous role, said to be her favorite.

Familiar Faces from Television:

❑ Ossie Davis (Oz Jackson in *B.L. Stryker*, Ponder Blue in *Evening Shade* and Judge Harry

A racist (Richard Widmark) gets medical aid from his sister-in-law (Linda Darnell) and a doctor (Sidney Poitier) in *No Way Out* (20th Century–Fox, 1950).

Roosevelt in *John Grisham's The Client*), in his film debut, as Poitier's brother. (Davis' real-life wife, Ruby Dee, also in her film debut, appears as his wife.)
❑ Amanda Randolph (Ramona Smith, Kingfish's mother-in-law in *Amos and Andy*) as McNally's housekeeper.
❑ Ray Teal (Sheriff Roy Coffee in *Bonanza*) as a guard in the hospital's prison ward.
❑ Ann Tyrrell (Vi in *Private Secretary* and Olive in *The Ann Sothern Show*) as a hospital nurse.
❑ Harry Lauter (Jim Herrick in *Waterfront*) as a hospital orderly.

Memorable Noir Moments:
❑ Darnell suggests that McNally and Poitier offer money to Widmark's family for their permission to conduct an autopsy, adding, "For two bits, they'll sell his eyeballs."
❑ One of Widmark's lewd buddies tells Darnell, "You're a big girl now, ain'tcha?" "I even smoke," she says, disinterested. "I'll bet," he replies.

Nobody Lives Forever (1946) 100 min. John Garfield, Geraldine Fitzgerald, Walter Brennan, Faye Emerson, George Tobias, George Coulouris. **Screenplay by:** W.R. Burnett. **Directed by:** Jean Negulesco. **Noir Type:** Con Artist. **Noir Themes:** Greed, woman in jeopardy, betrayal. ★★★

Recently discharged from the Army because of wounds sustained in combat, con man Garfield returns to New York expecting to find his torch singer girlfriend

(Emerson) waiting for him and his money earning interest. He discovers instead that Emerson has found herself a new man and has given him Garfield's dough to start a business. After "persuading" the man to return his fifty Gs plus interest, Garfield kisses Emerson goodbye, slaps her hard across the face and heads for California with his henchman (Tobias) for rest and recuperation. Once there, he looks up his old mentor (Brennan), who's selling peeks at the moon through a telescope for ten cents and lifting wallets from drunks. Coulouris, Garfield's archrival in the confidence game, convinces him to finance his latest sting — ripping off a rich widow (Fitzgerald). But when Garfield meets the gorgeous mark, he begins having second thoughts. Garfield is terrific, as usual, and Emerson is first-rate as the blonde femme fatale.

Familiar Faces from Television:
❏ Robert Shayne (Inspector Henderson in *Superman*) as Fitzgerald's new lover.
❏ James Flavin (Lt. Donovan in *Man with a Camera*) as one of Coulouris' goons.
❏ Richard Erdman (Peter Fairfield III in *The Tab Hunter Show*) as a bellboy.

Memorable Noir Moments:
❏ Garfield, looking uncomfortable doing the rhumba with Fitzgerald, remarks, "A man looks kind of silly doing this. It's all right for a woman."
❏ Gaines asks Tobias, who slept through an entire concert, "Don't you simply adore Bach?" "Bock?" asks the bewildered Tobias. "Oh, yeah. Ice cold with a nice big head on it."

Nocturne (1946) 88 min. George Raft, Lynn Bari, Virginia Huston, Joseph Pevney, Edward Ashley, Mabel Paige. **Screenplay by:** Jonathan Latimer. **Directed by:** Edwin L. Marin. **Noir Type:** Whodunit. **Noir Themes:** Jealousy, revenge. ★★★

A songwriter (Ashley) writes his final tune, "Nocturne," while simultaneously breaking up with one of his numerous girlfriends. A shot rings out, and the composer falls to the floor dead — his masterpiece left unfinished. Despite the official verdict that Ashley committed suicide, homicide detective Raft becomes obsessed with proving murder even after he's suspended from the force. Using photographs that hung like trophies on the songwriter's wall, Raft tracks down ten beautiful girls, all of whom Ashley had called "Dolores." The investigation seems to point to Bari as the prime suspect, but Raft doesn't rule out her nightclub singer sister (Huston), Huston's pianist husband (Pevney) or an oafish brute (Hoffman), whose job it is to push Pevney's piano from table to table for customer requests. Raft nicely underplays his role as the soft-spoken, two-fisted detective, who lives with his elderly mom (Paige), an amateur sleuth herself.

Memorable Noir Moments:
❏ A sexy live-in maid gives the cops her two cents about her late boss, whose body is on the living room floor. "He was a lady killer," she says, "but don't get no ideas. I'm no lady."
❏ A frustrated photographer, annoyed with his difficult model, utters a common noir complaint. "Women!" he exclaims. "I can't tell you how sick I am of women."

Nora Prentiss (1947) 111 min. Ann Sheridan, Kent Smith, Bruce Bennett, Robert Alda, Rosemary DeCamp. **Screenplay by:** N. Richard Nash. **Directed by:** Vincent Sherman. **Noir Type:** Impersonator. **Noir Themes:** Obsession, lust, paranoia, betrayal, fatalism, character deterioration. ★★★½

A doctor (Kent Smith) realizes he should have left the office on time when a patient (John Ridgely) makes an after-hours visit and has a coronary in *Nora Prentiss* (Warner Bros., 1947).

This is an appealing tale about a successful doctor (Smith) who falls for a night-club singer (Sheridan) but can't get up the nerve to ask his wife for a divorce. What he eventually does about the situation takes a lot more nerve than simply 'fessing up to his old lady. Bennett is Smith's partner, a playboy doctor whose lifestyle Smith frowns upon until he finds himself in the proverbial glass house. Alda is the night-club owner smitten with Sheridan, his star performer, and DeCamp is Smith's overly secure wife, whose hectic schedule contributes to her husband's straying. Sheridan is terrific as the facetious, worldly dame, a role she played so well in an earlier film noir, *They Drive by Night*, and would do once again a few years later in *Woman on the Run*. James Wong Howe's expressionistic photography and Nash's fine script make this "woman's picture" a real winner.

Familiar Face from Television:

❏ John Newland (host of *One Step Beyond*) as a reporter.

Memorable Noir Moments:

❏ After being treated for injuries she sustained in an accident, Sheridan asks her doctor for a drink. "I keep a little for medicinal purposes," he tells her. "That's my brand," she replies.

❏ Smith wonders if his critically ill patient can stay with friends or family instead of at the YMCA, just in case.... "It's a big city and there's nobody to know whether you're alive or dead," the man observes sadly but with the hint of a smile. "And very few people that care."

❏ Sheridan, her skirt hiked well above the knee, chastises a couple of oglers in the doctor's office. "I've been examined already," she says.

Notorious (1946) 101 min. Cary Grant, Ingrid Bergman, Claude Rains, Louis Calhern, Leopoldine Konstantin. **Screenplay by**: Ben Hecht. **Directed by**: Alfred Hitchcock. **Noir Type**: Undercover. **Noir Themes**: Betrayal, jealousy, woman in jeopardy. ★★★★★

F.B.I. agent Grant convinces Bergman, the playgirl daughter of a convicted Nazi spy, to go undercover to infiltrate a den of postwar Nazis in Rio de Janeiro. Of course, the two fall madly in love, but then one of the Nazis (Rains) asks Bergman to marry him, and Grant's boss (Calhern) gives her the go-ahead, which doesn't sit well with the jealous Grant. After the marriage, Grant discovers that Rains, his domineering mother (Konstantin) and their band of spies are involved in obtaining a relatively obscure substance (uranium), which they're sure will help the future master race to win the next war. Grant, whose character is far from sympathetic, gives a wonderfully subdued performance; Bergman is terrific as the woman spurned by her jealous lover; and Rains has never been better. Hitchcock and Hecht scored big with this one.

Familiar Face from Television:

❏ Frank Wilcox (John Brewster in *The Beverly Hillbillies*) as an F.B.I. agent outside a courtroom.

Memorable Noir Moment:

❏ After Rains learns that his wife is an American agent, he worries about the punishment he and his mother might receive at the hands of his Nazi pals. Mama reassures him, saying, "We are protected by the enormity of your stupidity."

Nowhere to Go (1958-British) 88 min. George Nader, Bernard Lee, Bessie Love, Maggie Smith, Geoffrey Keen. **Screenplay by**: Seth Holt and Kenneth Tynan. **Directed by**: Seth Holt. **Noir Type**: On the Run. **Noir Themes**: Greed, betrayal, paranoia. ★★½

Nader, a Canadian con man in England, steals a valuable coin collection from a middle-aged hockey fan (Love), sells it and puts the money in a safety deposit box, expecting to retrieve it after serving a three- to five-year jail term. A small price to pay, he figures, to be set for life. However, a no-nonsense judge sentences him to ten years, upsetting his plans. The impatient Nader breaks out of prison with a helping hand from his partner (Lee) and attempts to retrieve the money. But the poor sap has a run of bad luck after Lee tries to double-cross him. He winds up being chased by a Scotland Yard inspector (Keen) determined to nab him on a murder charge. Smith, in her first major role, plays a helpful lass who goes out on a limb for the escaped con. Although difficult to follow at times, this is an entertaining British noir, with American actor Nader, his career on the decline, starring in the first of a number of cheap European productions. Nader also starred in TV's *The Adventures of Ellery Queen, Man and the Challenge* and *Shannon*. Lee later played "M" in James

Bond films, and Smith went on to win two Academy Awards (Best Actress for *The Prime of Miss Jean Brodie* and Best Supporting Actress for *California Suite*).

Memorable Noir Moment:
❑ Nader is asked why he wears a special shoe that causes him to limp whenever he visits the bank where his stolen loot is stashed. "Nobody ever looks a cripple in the eye," he answers.

Obsession *see* The Hidden Room

Odd Man Out (1947) 116 min. James Mason, Robert Newton, Kathleen Sullivan, Cyril Cusack, F.J. McCormick, Denis O'Dea, W.G. Fay, Dan O'Herlihy, Roy Irving, Joseph Tomelty. **Screenplay by:** F.L. Green and R.C. Sherriff. **Directed by:** Carol Reed. **Noir Type:** Heist. **Noir Themes:** Fatalism, guilt, obsession. ★★★★½

James Mason (in one of the best performances of his career) is the local Irish Republican Army (IRA) leader in Belfast, who has been hiding out in the home of the woman (Sullivan) who loves him ever since his escape from prison six months ago. He and three comrades—Cusack, O'Herlihy, and Irving—stick up a local mill to obtain funds for the "cause." The heist, which they expected to be a no-brainer, goes horribly wrong, and Mason, after being shot in the shoulder, kills a mill employee. After falling off the running board of their speeding getaway car and being abandoned by his panicky cohorts, the seriously wounded gunman tries to elude a police dragnet led by a determined police inspector (O'Dea). In terrible pain and often delirious, the killer runs into a number of Belfast residents, who, fearing both the IRA and the police, want nothing to do with the fugitive and nervously send him on his way. A frightened cabbie (Tomelty), unceremoniously dumps him in a junkyard bathtub, asking that he remember his name if the IRA finds him and forget it if the cops pick him up. A street person (McCormick) with a passion for budgies, and his neurotic painter friend (Newton, in a frenzied performance), try to capitalize on Mason's predicament—McCormick hoping to get a reward from Fay, a local parish priest eager to hear Mason's confession, and the crazed Newton wanting desperately to paint the dying man's portrait. Meanwhile, Sullivan, who has convinced a seaman to smuggle her dying lover aboard a freighter, rushes to Fay's church hoping that Mason will somehow manage to make his way there. When he doesn't, she goes looking for him. Following the credits and during a spectacular aerial shot of the city, British director Reed's premise scrolls the screen: "This story is told against a background of political unrest in a city of Northern Ireland. It is not concerned with the struggle between the law and an illegal organisation, but only with the conflict in the hearts of the people when they become unexpectedly involved." Reed, however, was not successful in his avowed attempt to underplay the film's political connotations. Politicos on both sides of the often violent struggle have accused the director of favoritism in filming this urban nightmare about the downfall of an IRA chief. Politics aside, many consider Reed's breakthrough film a masterpiece of film noir and wonder, rightfully so, why it never earned a place on the American Film Institute's List of America's 100 Greatest Movies.

Memorable Noir Moment:

❑ When a priest asks a by-the-book police inspector if his experience has shown that all men and women are bad, the constable replies in typical noir fashion, "In my profession, Father, there is neither good nor bad. There is innocence or guilt. That's all."

❑ When a subordinate expresses concern about Mason's recent non-violent mindset, the IRA chief muses sadly, "If only we *could* throw the guns away, make our cause in the parliaments instead of the back streets."

Odds Against Tomorrow (1959) 95 min. Harry Belafonte, Robert Ryan, Ed Begley, Gloria Grahame, Shelley Winters, Will Kuluva. **Screenplay by:** Abe Polonsky (as John O. Killens) and Nelson Gidding. **Directed by:** Robert Wise. **Noir Type:** Heist. **Noir Themes:** Bigotry, greed, distrust, lust. ★★★½

Begley, an ex–New York cop who was kicked off the force for criminal activity, recruits musician Belafonte and ex-con Ryan to pull a bank job in a small upstate New York town. Complicating the well-planned caper is the small matter of color — Belafonte's. Ryan is a white bigot. Not the jovial Archie Bunker type either — he's the potentially violent kind. Initially reluctant to participate in the caper, Belafonte is forced to sign on when loan sharks threaten his ex-wife and kid if he can't come up with the dough to pay his substantial gambling debts. The penniless Ryan is quick

A jazz musician and gambling addict (Harry Belafonte, left) confronts his loan shark's goon (Lew Gallo) in *Odds Against Tomorrow* (United Artists, 1959).

to join in because his injured pride won't allow his girlfriend (Winters) to continuing supporting him. Of course, like most heist noirs, nothing goes according to plan. Noir icon Grahame has a minor role as Winters' lusty neighbor with an eye for Ryan. Filmed on location in New York, this top-notch crime film has great acting, a terrific jazz score, an important social message and a fiery climax reminiscent of **White Heat**. Look for Cicely Tyson (*The Autobiography of Miss Jane Pittman* and *Roots*) as a bartender in a jazz joint. (Some film historians cite *Odds Against Tomorrow* as the final film of the classic noir cycle. Others believe it was Orson Welles' **Touch of Evil** released a year earlier.)

Familiar Face from Television:
❑ Wayne Rogers (Trapper John in *M*A*S*H*) in his film debut as a soldier showing off in a neighborhood bar.

Memorable Noir Moments:
❑ When Begley asks him to join the heist, Belafonte, feeling like a small-timer, declines and explains, "I'm just a bone picker in a four-man graveyard."
❑ Loan shark Kuluva wants the money that Belafonte owes him "tonight at eight or I'll kill you and everything you own."
❑ Winters assures boyfriend Ryan that money isn't important to her. "There's only one thing I care about," she tells him. "I know," he replies cynically, "but what happens when I get old?"

On Dangerous Ground (1951) 82 min. Ida Lupino, Robert Ryan, Ward Bond, Ed Begley, Sumner Williams. **Screenplay by:** A.I. Bezzerides and Nicholas Ray. **Directed by:** Nicholas Ray. **Noir Type:** Payback. **Noir Themes:** Fatalism, revenge. ★★★★

When a neurotic New York City cop (Ryan), on the verge of a nervous breakdown, brutalizes yet another suspect, his boss (Begley) sends him to cool off in upstate New York, where he immediately becomes involved in a manhunt for a young girl's killer (Williams). Along with the girl's shotgun-toting father (Bond), Ryan chases the fugitive into the mountains, tracking him to the cabin where the killer's blind sister (Lupino) lives. Fearful of Bond, who's hellbent on vengeance, Lupino decides to trust Ryan with the whereabouts of her brother, hoping he'll be able to bring the boy back to civilization where he can be institutionalized. Does she realize she's putting her faith in Dirty Harry's role model? Will Ryan change his opinion that "cops have no friends"? Ryan is sensational as the disillusioned detective, who faces the toughest decision of his career, and Lupino is excellent as the sweet blind girl forced to place her trust in a brutal stranger.

Familiar Faces from Television:
❑ Nita Talbot (Beatrice Dane in *The Thin Man*) as an underage barfly.
❑ Olive Carey (Macdonald Carey's secretary in *Lock Up* and Elsie in *Mr. Adams and Eve*) as Bond's wife.
❑ Joe Devlin (Sam Catchem in *Dick Tracy*) as a bartender.

Memorable Noir Moments:
❑ After Ryan ruptures a thug's bladder during an "interrogation," and the city's faces another

lawsuit, his boss warns him to be more careful in the future. "You don't get information being careful," Ryan replies.
❑ During one of his frequent bouts with self-pity, Ryan reflects on his sports trophies from an earlier, more promising era. "Who cares?" he wonders. (See *The Killing* for Sterling Hayden's fatalistic film noir musing, "What's the difference?")

On the Waterfront (1954) 108 min. Marlon Brando, Karl Malden, Lee J. Cobb, Rod Steiger, Eva Marie Saint, Leif Erickson. **Screenplay by:** Budd Schulberg. **Directed by:** Elia Kazan. **Noir Type:** Union. **Noir Themes:** Corruption, fatalism, betrayal, revenge, guilt, economic repression. ★★★★★

Brando stars as a slow-witted longshoreman who keeps pigeons and runs errands for union boss Cobb. An ex-pug with a "one-way ticket to Palookaville," Brando meets and falls for the sister of the man he lured to a tenement rooftop to be roughed up by Cobb's hoods. Instead, the man, who was scheduled to testify against Cobb for the city's crime commission, was thrown from the roof to his death. The guilt-stricken Brando now faces a dilemma—turn canary and cooperate with a crime commission investigator (Erickson), which would help Saint to gain closure in her brother's murder, or keep his mouth shut, protecting himself and his brother (Steiger), one of Cobb's men. Helping him with that tough decision is an idealistic Catholic priest (Malden), whose church is the docks and whose parishioners are the fearful stevedores, who are forced to pay Cobb a percentage of their earnings and who are bound by their self-imposed D&D (deaf and dumb) code. Look for Pat Hingle, in his film debut, as a bartender and Nehemiah Persoff as a taxi driver. Brando is unforgettable as the ex-boxer who threw away his shot at the title because his brother decided that it wasn't his time, and Saint, in her film debut, is excellent as the college girl who falls for Brando's tender side. Cobb almost steals the film as the vicious "butcher with a camel hair's coat," whose goons terrorize the dock workers. Nominated for twelve Academy Awards, *On the Waterfront* received eight—Best Picture, Best Director, Best Actor (Brando), Best Supporting Actress (Saint), Best Black and White Cinematography (Boris Kaufman), Best Film Editing, Best Art Direction/Set Direction and Best Writing (Story and Screenplay). Malden, Cobb and Steiger all were nominated for Best Supporting Actor. The film was rated Number 8 on the American Film Institute's List of America's 100 Greatest Movies.

Familiar Faces from Television:
❑ Fred Gwynne (Officer Muldoon in *Car 54, Where Are You?* and Herman Munster in *The Munsters*), in his film debut, as Cobb's tall, lanky henchman.
❑ Martin Balsam (Murray Klein in *Archie Bunker's Place*), in his film debut, as a crime commission investigator.

Memorable Noir Moments:
❑ After a "canary" is thrown from a roof, one of Cobb's goons jokes, "Maybe he could sing, but he couldn't fly."
❑ A loan shark tells his reluctant customers, "When I'm dead and gone, you'll know what a friend I was." "Why don't you drop dead now," one of them suggests, "so we can test your theory."
❑ In the famous taxi scene, Brando complains to Steiger about having been forced to throw

a fight that could have led to a championship match. "I coulda had class," he moans. "I coulda been a contender. I coulda *been* somebody. Instead of a bum, which I am."

Once a Thief (1950) 89 min. June Havoc, Cesar Romero, Marie McDonald, Lon Chaney, Jr., Iris Adrian. **Screenplay by:** Richard S. Conway and W. Lee Wilder. **Directed by:** W. Lee Wilder. **Noir Type:** Payback. **Noir Themes:** Betrayal, revenge. ★★½

An unemployed factory worker (Havoc) meets a savvy shoplifter (Adrian) who teaches her the tricks of the trade but abandons her when a heist goes wrong. While on the run for stealing an expensive wristwatch, Havoc takes a job as a waitress. After a two-bit bookie (Romero) sneaks a peak at her meager savings account, he romances her and then takes her for every buck she has before turning her in to the cops. While Havoc is serving a year in the pen, Romero starts cozying up to her best friend (McDonald), causing Havoc to start thinking about murder. This is a pretty good low-budget film, with Havoc excellent as the femme fatale. There are many future TV actors in this B film. Havoc starred in a mid–1950s TV situation comedy called *Willy*, while Latin lover Romero appeared in *Passport to Danger*, *Batman* (where he played The Joker) and *Falcon Crest*. Even veteran character actor Chaney, who plays Romero's underling here, wound up on TV (as an Indian chief!) in the situation comedy *Pistols 'n Petticoats*. Adrian had a role in the short-lived series *The Ted Knight Show*. Marie "The Body" McDonald wasn't so fortunate, dying at 41 of an accidental drug overdose in 1965, after seven marriages and a singing and acting career that never got off the ground.

Familiar Faces from Television:
❑ Ann Tyrrell (Vi in *Private Secretary* and Olive in *The Ann Sothern Show*) as a prison dentist.
❑ Kathleen Freeman (Katie the maid in *Topper* and Flo Shafer in *The Beverly Hillbillies*) as a waitress.

Memorable Noir Moment:
❑ Havoc's first mistake is listening to petty thief Adrian, who tells her, "Life is a merry-go-round and someday you're gonna latch on to the ring. You've got nothin' to worry about. Just stick around me."

One Way Street (1950) 79 min. James Mason, Marta Toren, Dan Duryea, William Conrad. **Screenplay by:** Lawrence Kimble. **Directed by:** Hugo Fregonese. **Noir Type:** South of the Border. **Noir Themes:** Fatalism, betrayal, revenge. ★½

A doctor (Mason), working for a gang of thieves, double-crosses his employers and takes off with the boss' moll (Toren) and the loot from a recent heist. On their way to Mexico City, Mason and Toren are sidetracked when mechanical difficulties force their small plane to land near a tiny Mexican village, where Mason, unable to save a sick child, uses his medical skills to cure a horse. The couple, suddenly turning humanitarian, decide to stay on and build a hospital for the grateful *campesinos*. Meanwhile, the betrayed gang leader (Duryea), vowing revenge, sends his right hand man (Conrad) to find the couple. What starts out promisingly enough turns into a stodgy melodrama that even noir icon Duryea can't save.

Familiar Faces from Television:

❑ Rock Hudson (Commissioner McMillan in *McMillan and Wife*) as a truck driver involved in an collision.
❑ King Donovan (Bob Cummings' Air Force buddy Harvey Helm in *Love That Bob* and lawyer Herb Thornton in *Please Don't Eat the Daisies*) as a gang member.
❑ Jack Elam (George Taggert in *Temple Huston*) as a gang member.

Open Secret (1948) 70 min. John Ireland, Jane Randolph, Sheldon Leonard, George Tyne. **Screenplay by**: Henry Blankfort, Max Wilk and John Bright. **Directed by**: John Reinhardt. **Noir Type**: Racist. **Noir Themes**: Bigotry. ★★

Honeymooners Ireland and Randolph decide to visit with Ireland's Army buddy while passing through town. They discover that the buddy, who was involved with an anti–Semitic group, has been murdered. Ireland interrupts his honeymoon to investigate. Leonard is the police detective on the case, and Tyne is a Jewish store owner, a victim of the hate group. This is a well-intentioned but boring B film.

Familiar Faces from Television:

❑ King Donovan (Bob Cummings' Air Force buddy Harvey Helm in *Love that Bob* and lawyer Herb Thornton in *Please Don't Eat the Daisies*) as a member of the hate group.
❑ Arthur O'Connell (Mr. Hansen in *Mr. Peepers* and Edwin Carpenter in *The Second Hundred Years*) as the hate group's second-in-command.

Ossessione ("Obsession") (1942-Italian) 140 min. Clara Calamai, Massimo Girotti, Juan De Landa, Dhia Cristiani. **Screenplay by**: Luchino Visconti, Mario Alicata, Giuseppe De Santis and Gianni Puccini. **Directed by**: Luchino Visconti. **Noir Type**: Femme Fatale. **Noir Themes**: Obsession, betrayal, guilt, jealousy, distrust. ★★★★

Girotti plays a penniless drifter who does some handyman work at a tavern owned by the portly, middle-aged De Landa and his young wife, Calamai. He stays long enough to have a short affair with Calamai, who has long been revolted by her husband's touch. She won't run away with her new lover, however, because she has grown accustomed to the security of a home and business. Girotti leaves on his own but runs into the couple in another town, where De Landa invites him to return to the tavern to do some more work for him. On the road, Girotti and Calamai kill the drunken tavern keeper, making it look like an auto accident. They think they've gotten away with murder, but the cops continue their investigation. A nervous Girotti tries to convince Calamai to leave town with him, especially since the suspicious neighbors are beginning to gossip, but she's quite happy to operate her dead husband's lucrative tavern. And then there's the matter of De Landa's large insurance policy. Depressed and conscience-stricken, Girotti becomes involved with a kindly prostitute (Cristiani), causing Calamai to threaten to turn him in to the police. This was Italian director Visconti's first film, a neo-realistic, film noir version of the James Cain novel *The Postman Always Rings Twice*. While Tay Garnett's 1946 classic noir, which retained Cain's title, is far superior in its production values, Visconti's is much more suggestive and earthy.

Memorable Noir Moment:

❑ When a fussbudget landlady warns new tenant Girotti not to sleep in bed with his shoes on, the offended drifter replies, "Only the dead wear shoes in bed."

The Other Woman (1954) 81 min. Hugo Haas, Cleo Moore, Lance Fuller, Lucille Barkley, Jack Macy, John Qualen. **Screenplay by:** Hugo Haas. **Directed by:** Hugo Haas. **Noir Type:** Show Biz. **Noir Themes:** Revenge, paranoia. ★★

Haas plays a middle-aged Hollywood director victimized by a no-talent, aspiring actress (Moore), who was humiliated when Haas fired her from his latest film. Moore and her lover (Fuller) concoct a get-even scheme, which includes slipping Haas a mickey and making him believe that he had sex with her. Then, a couple of months later, she tells him she's pregnant and demands fifty grand to keep her mouth shut. Haas, worried about his career and his marriage to the boss' daughter (Barkley), can't come up with the dough, so he develops a plan of his own. Macy plays Haas' suspicious father-in-law, and veteran character actor Qualen is a hapless street vendor. As usual, Haas wrote, produced, directed and starred in this mildly enjoyable cheapie noir. In the final scene, Haas addresses the audience and asks, "How did it happen?" The same question could be asked about most of his films.

Out of the Fog (1941) 93 min. Ida Lupino, John Garfield, Thomas Mitchell, Eddie Albert, John Qualen. **Screenplay by:** Robert Rossen, Jerry Wald and Richard Macaulay. **Directed by:** Anatole Litvak. **Noir Type:** Ambition. **Noir Themes:** Economic repression, greed, revenge. ★★★★

Garfield is sensational as an ambitious New York hood, a sociopath with no redeeming qualities, operating a small protection racket along the piers of Brooklyn. Switchboard operator Lupino, tired of being "ordinary," falls for the flashy hood and plans to run off to Cuba with him even though she knows he's been terrorizing her tailor father (Mitchell) and his fishing partner (Qualen). Albert is Lupino's uninteresting boyfriend, whom she drops when Garfield shows up flashing his smile and his wallet. Mitchell and Qualen bring charges against Garfield but plot their own unique revenge after losing in court. The acting is exceptional, with Garfield taking top honors in this early noir entry. Leo Gorcey (Slip Mahoney of the *Bowery Boys* films) plays a bartender, and Bernard Gorcey (Leo's real-life pop, who played Louie Dumbrowski in the same series) is a card-playing customer.

Memorable Noir Moments:
❑ Short order cook Qualen's aging boss has been pressuring him to marry her. Mitchell advises him to tell her that he only likes chorus girls with sweaters. "Then she'll fire me," Qualen says. "Or worse, she'll put on a sweater."
❑ Sensitivity Training Required: Garfield tells Mitchell and Albert that Lupino is "free, white and 21, and makes her own decisions." (See *The City That Never Sleeps, Fall Guy* and *The Glass Key*.)

Out of the Past (1947) 97 min. Robert Mitchum, Jane Greer, Kirk Douglas, Rhonda Fleming, Steve Brodie, Virginia Huston, Paul Valentine. **Screenplay by:** Daniel Mainwaring (as Geoffrey Homes). **Directed by:** Jacques Tourneur. **Noir Type:** Femme Fatale. **Noir Themes:** Obsession, betrayal, fatalism, greed, lust. ★★★★★

A small-town gas station owner (Mitchum) has a dark past, which he has kept from the woman he loves (Huston). But when a hood (Valentine) from his previous life accidentally stumbles into his establishment, the former P.I. decides to come clean

Gangsters Kirk Douglas (center) and Paul Valentine have a chat with an ex–P.I. (Robert Mitchum, right) in *Out of the Past* (RKO, 1947).

with his girl. Years earlier, he tells her, he was hired by a gangster (Douglas) to find his moll (Greer), who shot him and ran off with forty grand of his dough. Mitchum caught up with her in Acapulco and fell madly in love with her, buying into her story that, yes, she shot the abusive Douglas but didn't steal his money. They ran off together, always keeping one step ahead of Douglas' new P.I. (Brodie), Mitchum's former partner. Eventually, Brodie caught up with them and everything hit the fan, with Greer ditching Mitchum and leaving him to face a murder rap. Thus, his new identity and life. Huston decides to stick by her man as he's about to meet with Douglas and Greer, who's back with the gangster. Mitchum is sensational as the classic noir protagonist, doomed because he has stumbled into the web of a lethal femme fatale, convincingly played by the beautiful Greer. Douglas is terrific as the vicious, but lovesick, gangster who will forgive Greer anything, including shooting him four times. Despite its convoluted plot, *Out of the Past* really delivers and is worthy of its reputation as *the* quintessential film noir.

Familiar Face from Television:

❏ Richard Webb (*Captain Midnight*) as Mitchum's romantic rival.

Memorable Noir Moments:

❏ Private eye Brodie expresses his old-fashioned opinion about gun-toting women. "A dame with a rod is like a guy with a knitting needle," he says.
❏ Mitchum, finally wise to Greer, tells her straight: "You're like a leaf that the wind blows from one gutter to another."
❏ Greer informs the defeated and broken Mitchum, "You're no good. Neither am I. That's why we deserve each other."

The Outcasts of Poker Flat (1952) 80 min. Anne Baxter, Dale Robertson, Cameron Mitchell, Miriam Hopkins, Craig Hill, Barbara Bates, Billy Lynn. **Screenplay by:** Edmund H. North. **Directed by:** Joseph M. Newman. **Noir Type:** Horse Opera. **Noir Themes:** Betrayal, greed, sexual hostility, paranoia, jealousy. ★★½

After Mitchell robs the bank in the small mining town of Poker Flat, double-crossing his two partners, he leaves the loot with his frightened wife (Baxter) and hightails it out of town. The citizens of Poker Flat, disgusted with the rampant crime and immorality, decide to run some of its undesirables out of town, including Baxter, a gambler (Robertson), an over-the-hill saloon girl (Hopkins) and the town drunk (Lynn). The four come across Hill and Bates, an unmarried couple expecting a baby, and they all hole up in a mountain cabin during a blizzard, with only a day's supply of food. Guess who shows up shortly thereafter looking for his money and his wife? But by now, Baxter, fed up with the abusive Mitchell, has fallen in love with Robertson and schemes against her husband, who's holding them hostage and eating all of the food. *Outcasts* tries hard to deliver a suspenseful, action-packed Western but is only partially successful and that's thanks to good performances by Baxter and Mitchell. Robertson and Mitchell went on to star in two of TV's more successful westerns, *Tales of Wells Fargo* and *High Chaparral*, respectively.

Memorable Noir Moments:

❏ Driven out of town by the good citizens of Poker Flat, Hopkins comments dryly, "If there's one thing that turns my stomach, it's respectability."
❏ Town drunk Lynn tells Hopkins that he's grateful that the townsfolk gave him a horse before sending him on his way. "A fellow told me once, he said, 'Jake, if you get hold of a good horse or a good woman, don't let go.' I got myself a good horse," he says, hopefully. "You better quit while you're ahead," the aging saloon girl advises.

Outside the Law (1956) 81 min. Ray Danton, Leigh Snowden, Grant Williams, Onslow Stevens, Raymond Bailey. **Screenplay by:** Danny Arnold. **Directed by:** Jack Arnold. **Noir Type:** Undercover. **Noir Themes:** Betrayal, obsession, jealousy. ★★½

Danton, a convict paroled into the Army during World War II, is recruited by his estranged Secret Service father (Stevens) to go undercover to help bust an international counterfeiting ring led by Bailey and Williams. Waving the carrot stick of a complete expunging of his criminal record, Stevens convinces the reluctant Danton to ingratiate himself with Snowden, the widow of a G.I. who was involved with the counterfeiters. Danton falls in love with Snowden and soon finds that the dangerous Williams doesn't like the competition. This is a standard crime drama with an interesting subplot involving the strained relationship between Danton and his straight-arrow father over the ex-con's drunk-driving accident, in which an elderly woman was severely injured. Stevens is particularly good as the guilt-ridden father seeking to redeem himself with his unforgiving son. Stevens starred in the early TV religious drama *This Is the Life*, and Bailey later played the scheming banker in the hit comedy series *The Beverly Hillbillies*. Williams, who would eventually land a part as a detective in the TV series *Hawaiian Eye*, is probably best known for his starring role in the classic science fiction movie *The Incredible Shrinking Man*. Danton went on to co-star in the short-lived TV adventure series *The Alaskans*, and in the 1970s tried his hand at directing low-budget horror films.

Familiar Face from Television:
❑ Jack Kruschen (Tully in *Hong Kong* and Sam Markowitz in *Busting Loose*) as a T-man with a stomach ailment.

Outside the Wall (1950) 80 min. Richard Basehart, Marilyn Maxwell, Signe Hasso, Dorothy Hart, John Hoyt. **Screenplay by:** Crane Wilbur. **Directed by:** Crane Wilbur. **Noir Type:** Jailbird. **Noir Themes:** Greed, betrayal. ★★½

A solid cast helps this mundane tale of a pardoned ex-con and his struggle to keep his nose clean. Basehart plays the troubled con, behind bars since he was 14 years old for the accidental killing of a reformatory guard. Released after serving fifteen years, he's totally unprepared for life outside the wall. He lands a job as a lab assistant in a small-town sanatorium that cares for tuberculosis patients. There he meets two nurses—a money-hungry femme fatale (Maxwell) and Hart, the kind of girl you'd like to bring home to meet Mom. Of course, our naive hero falls for the flashy Maxwell. A dying former prison pal (Hoyt) is brought to the sanatorium and tries to enlist Basehart to help him protect the dough he has stashed away from an armored car heist. Reluctant at first, Basehart finally agrees, seeing a way to make a few bucks to impress nurse Maxwell. Unfortunately, he becomes involved with Hoyt's deceitful wife (Hasso) and his gang, who are eager to find the stolen money. Basehart does a good job as the shy, 30-year-old jailbird, who's never kissed a girl but is trying make up for lost time.

Familiar Face from Television:
❑ Joe Besser ("Stinky" on *The Abbott and Costello Show*) as a sympathetic short-order cook.
❑ Harry Morgan (Col. Potter in *M*A*S*H*) as the sadistic gang leader with a dandy nail file collection.

Memorable Noir Moments:
❑ Just before his release from prison, Basehart listens as an elderly con reminisces. "There ain't nothin' in all the world like a dame," the old man recalls. "They can be sweet and wonderful, and they can tear your heart out."
❑ An intoxicated Basehart remembers what he learned about dames when he catches a barfly trying to snatch his wallet. "The only thing I know about women is what I learned from thieves, kidnappers and murderers," he informs her. "They told me about your kind but I didn't want to believe them."

The Ox-Bow Incident (1943) 75 min. Henry Fonda, Dana Andrews, Mary Beth Hughes, Anthony Quinn, William Eythe, Henry (Harry) Morgan, Harry Davenport, Frank Conroy,

Marc Lawrence, Francis Ford, Jane Darwell. **Screenplay by:** Lamar Trotti. **Directed by:** William A. Wellman. **Noir Type:** Horse Opera. **Noir Themes:** Revenge, victims of fate, fatalism, guilt. ★★★★★

Two thirsty cowhands (Fonda and Morgan) arrive in town just in time to be pressured into joining a vigilante mob being organized to track down and lynch the cattle thieves who reportedly murdered a local rancher. Led by an arrogant ex–Confederate officer (Conroy), who's determined to make a man out of his sensitive son (Eythe), and an irate friend of the victim (Lawrence), the vigilantes take on the semblance of legality when they are formed into a posse by a deputy sheriff acting outside his authority. A courageous storekeeper (Davenport) tries vainly to dissuade the mob and even rides along in the hope that he can stall them while somebody tries to find the sheriff. In the middle of the night, the group comes upon the campsite of three men (Andrews, Quinn and Ford), who protest their innocence even though they are traveling with cattle that bear the murdered man's brand. With no bill of sale to back up their story that they purchased the animals from the victim, the situation seems hopeless for them. Then a few of the vigilantes begin to have second thoughts. Hughes, doing her best Mae West impersonation, has a minor role as a saloon girl run out of town by the married women ("not that she did anything, but they just couldn't get over being afraid she might"). Darwell plays "Ma," the elderly cattle rancher who's eager to see a hanging. Among the many other familiar faces, look for former East Side kid Billy Benedict as the bearer of bad tidings, Rondo Hatton (the "Creeper" in *The Brute Man* and *House of Horrors*) as a vigilante, and Margaret Hamilton (the Wicked Witch in *The Wizard of Oz*) as the judge's housekeeper. Fonda does a terrific job as one of the few sensible voices among the lyncher wannabes, and Quinn is excellent as the multilingual Mexican desperado who knows when to keep his mouth shut. *The Ox-Bow Incident*, which was nominated for an Academy Award for Best Picture, is a suspenseful, depressing allegory about the terror of mob "justice" and the descent into brutality by otherwise decent citizens.

Familiar Faces from Television:
☐ George Chandler (Uncle Petrie Martin in *Lassie* and Ichabod Adams in *Ichabod and Me*) riding shotgun on a stagecoach.
☐ Frank McGrath (Charlie Wooster in *Wagon Train*) as a vigilante.

Memorable Noir Moments:
☐ When the town judge threatens to arrest the vigilantes for impeding the course of justice, one of them shouts, "You can't impede what don't move anyway."
☐ Sensitivity Training Required: When Davenport, hoping to prevent a hanging, shows a vigilante the farewell letter Andrews has written to his wife, the angry letter-writer complains, "I thought there was one white man among you, but I was wrong."
☐ When Eythe balks at participating in the hanging, his macho dad warns him, "I'll have no female boys bearing my name."

Paid in Full (1950) 105 min. Robert Cummings, Lizabeth Scott, Diana Lynn, Eve Arden, Ray Collins. **Screenplay by:** Robert Blees and Charles Schnee. **Directed by:** William Dieterle. **Noir Type:** Soap Opera. **Noir Themes:** Fatalism, jealousy. ★★½

Get the tissues ready, folks. A pregnant Scott shows up at a hospital in a strange city about to give birth. The doctor (Collins) advises her of something she already knows—that he can save either the baby or her, but not the both of them. She insists that he protect the baby at all costs. Before she goes under anesthesia, we learn the whole dismal story via flashback. Scott and Lynn are siblings. Cummings loves Lynn, the selfish, bratty sister; Scott, the sweet one, loves Cummings; and Lynn loves herself. When Cummings proposes, Lynn accepts, and they settle down in what Cummings believes is a happy marriage. Lynn, however, is bored to tears and decides that they should have a baby. After their little girl is born, Lynn becomes jealous of Cummings because, after all, this is *her* baby, not his. Without giving too much away, the lucky Cummings winds up with, believe it or not, both of the sisters (not at the same time, of course), one of whom must spend some time in a sanitarium after tragedy strikes. Arden plays her usual wisecracking best friend role. Definitely not for the hardcore crime fan but Scott's and Lynn's characters are fun to analyze. Look for Carol Channing, in her film debut, as a customer thinking about buying a dress that Lynn is modeling.

Memorable Noir Moment:

❑ Older sibling Scott gives some sisterly advice to Lynn, encouraging her to make sure that her husband-to-be will be happy. Lynn is shocked at the advice, exclaiming, "I thought he was supposed to make *me* happy!"

Paid to Kill (1954-British) 72 min. Dane Clark, Thea Gregory, Paul Carpenter, Cecile Chevreau, Anthony Forwood. **Screenplay by:** Paul Tabori. **Directed by:** Montgomery Tully. **Noir Type:** Hit Man. **Noir Themes:** Fatalism, betrayal. ★★

After the deal of a lifetime goes sour and Clark, the American president of an English company, faces financial ruin, he blackmails his reluctant friend (Carpenter), a small-time hood, into killing him so his wife (Gregory) can collect on his large insurance policy. Later, when the failed deal is revived, Clark attempts to call Carpenter off, but the man can't be found. Desperate after several attempts on his life, Clark and his faithful secretary (Chevreau) team up to find the missing hit man before it's too late. A familiar tale, more stylishly told in 1944's *The Whistler*, this British noir is nothing to brag about.

Memorable Noir Moment:

❑ The British P.I. hired by Gregory to find the missing hit man thinks he's supposed to be looking for a straying husband. When told that there's no "other woman" involved, the disappointed detective remarks, "Oh, it's a pity. It's always easier to find them when there is."

Panic in the Streets (1950) 96 min. Richard Widmark, Paul Douglas, Barbara Bel Geddes, Jack Palance, Zero Mostel, Guy Thomajan. **Screenplay by:** Richard Murphy. **Directed by:** Elia Kazan. **Noir Type:** Plague. **Noir Themes:** Greed, betrayal, paranoia, obsession. ★★★★

After small-time gangster Palance murders an illegal alien in New Orleans, an alert coroner calls in a U.S. Health Service doctor (Widmark) to examine the body.

Widmark confirms the coroner's suspicions that the man had pneumonic plague. The first order of business, Widmark tells the mayor, is to find the murderer quickly, before he can take a powder and spread the disease to the rest of the country. A skeptical police captain (Douglas), who has a personal reason to dislike doctors, has his men bring in all the small-time criminals in town, "pickpockets, sneak thieves, and wife beaters," while Widmark begins scouring the city for clues to the dead man's identity. Meanwhile, Palance and his sniveling underling (Mostel) wonder why the cops are making such a big deal about a dead foreigner and come to the conclusion that the man must have smuggled something valuable into the country. So they begin their own search for the man's cousin (Thomajan), who they suspect is holding out on them and who's beginning to exhibit plague-like symptoms. Widmark and Douglas are fine as the germ-hunting detectives thrown together by fate, but it's the evil Palance and whiny Mostel who make this film so enjoyable, helping it to win an Oscar for Best Motion Picture Story. Bel Geddes has a small role as the doctor's easygoing wife.

Familiar Face from Television:
❑ Tommy Rettig (Jeff Miller, Lassie's original owner, in *Lassie*) as Widmark's son.

Memorable Noir Moment:
❑ Palance can't hide his disdain for Mostel's shrewish wife. "If there's anything I don't like," he says, "it's a smart-cracking dame."

The Paradine Case (1947) 115 min. Gregory Peck, Charles Laughton, Charles Coburn, Ann Todd, Ethel Barrymore, Louis Jourdan, (Alida) Valli, Joan Tetzel. **Screenplay by:** David O. Selznick. **Directed by:** Alfred Hitchcock. **Noir Type:** Whodunit. **Noir Themes:** Obsession, fatalism, betrayal, jealousy, guilt. ★★½

An English barrister (Peck) falls in love with his beautiful client (Valli), who has been accused of poisoning her blind husband. Frantic to see her freed, Peck hopes to prove to the jury that Valli's husband committed suicide with the help of his misogynistic valet (Jourdan). Eventually, Peck comes to believe that Jourdan was in love with Valli and killed his master so he could be with her. Meanwhile, Peck's devoted wife (Todd) tries to deal gracefully with the "other woman" problem. Laughton is the lecherous judge presiding over the case, Coburn is Peck's assistant counsel, and Tetzel is Coburn's law-savvy daughter. Barrymore, who received an Academy Award nomination for Best Supporting Actress, plays Laughton's long-suffering wife. Cut from its original 132 minutes, this talk fest is still overly long and not one of Hitchcock's best.

Familiar Face from Television:
❑ Leo G. Carroll (Cosmo Topper in *Topper* and Mr. Waverly in *The Man from U.N.C.L.E.*) as the prosecutor.

Memorable Noir Moments:
❑ A longtime member of the woman hater's club, Jourdan informs Peck that he worked for the *master* of the house, not the *mistress*. "I would never have served a woman," he states. "It is not in my character to do that."

❑ Commenting on Peck's infatuation with Valli, Tetzel tells Coburn, "Men who have been good too long get a longing for the mud and want to wallow in it."

Parole, Inc. (1949) 71 min. Michael O'Shea, Turhan Bey, Evelyn Ankers, Lyle Talbot. **Screenplay by:** Sherman L. Lowe. **Directed by:** Alfred Zeisler. **Noir Type:** Undercover. **Noir Themes:** Corruption, betrayal. ★½

O'Shea is a smiley-faced undercover agent assigned to break up a ring of gangsters, who have Parole Board members on its payroll. Criminals are being paroled early and sent to work for the gambling syndicate headed by Bey and Ankers. O'Shea, bandaged up like one of the Three Stooges after an explosives factory accident, dictates his tale from a hospital bed. The syndicate's headquarters, the Pastime Club, is a "combination gin mill and cheap cafe," but gangsters hang out there playing the pinball machines and gin rummy. Veteran character actor Talbot is wasted in a role as a city bigwig. This low-budget B film is no better than its 1937 predecessor, *Parole Racket*.

Memorable Noir Moments:

❑ While holding about ten gang members at bay with a revolver, O'Shea is forced to shoot one of them, attracting the attention of another bad guy, who sneaks up behind him and knocks him unconscious. After being congratulated by the boss for doing a good job, the gangster brags, "I heard the shot and I figured *something* was wrong." Unfortunately, this is typical dialogue for *Parole, Inc.*
❑ O'Shea struggles to find a good hiding place for the latest technological advance in listening device, which is bigger than a suitcase. (See *Shoot to Kill* for another troublesome listening device.)

Party Girl (1958) 99 min. Robert Taylor, Cyd Charisse, Lee J. Cobb, John Ireland, Kent Smith, Corey Allen. **Screenplay by:** George Wells. **Directed by:** Nicholas Ray. **Noir Type:** Gangster. **Noir Themes:** Betrayal, woman in jeopardy, fatalism. ★★★½

Taylor stars as a 1930s mouthpiece for the Chicago mob. The crippled attorney, who uses his disability to earn points with gullible jurors, meets a beautiful showgirl (Charisse), and they fall in love. She wants him to quit the rackets and, after he gets his bum leg operated on in Europe, he bravely informs his mobster boss (Cobb) that he's through. Cobb has another job for him, though, and, with a little persuasion in the form of a bottle of acid, convinces him to stay on to defend a psychopathic mobster (Allen) on a murder charge. Ireland plays one of Cobb's thugs, and Smith is the D.A. looking to put the gang away. This film is cruelly slow at times, but Cobb is entertaining as the vicious crime lord who keeps referring to himself in the third person (see *Destination Murder* for another pretentious gangster with the same annoying habit). Charisse's hot dance numbers and the sporadic violence should help sustain the drowsiest viewer's attention. The climax is sensational.

Memorable Noir Moment:

❑ Charisse shares some helpful advice with a beginning showgirl about the men at an upcoming party. "Never get crowded into a corner," she says. "Never let them get too close. After a while, they go away."

The People Against O'Hara (1951) 102 min. Spencer Tracy, Pat O'Brien, Diana Lynn, John Hodiak, Eduardo Ciannelli, James Arness, J.C. Flippen. **Screenplay by:** John Monks, Jr. **Directed by:** John Sturges. **Noir Type:** Wrong Man. **Noir Themes:** Fatalism, corruption. ★★★

A former district attorney (Tracy), now a civil lawyer, takes on a murder case against the wishes of his daughter (Lynn), who is afraid the stress will cause him to start hitting the bottle again. Arness (Matt Dillon of TV's *Gunsmoke*) plays the man framed in the murder of his boss. Determined to get his client off the hook and to beat the pompous D.A. (Hodiak), Tracy, already nipping the booze, resorts to bribing a witness (Flippen). When that fails, he puts his life in danger in an attempt to trap the real killer. O'Brien plays a homicide detective, an old buddy of Tracy, who tries to help his friend by passing on information. Ciannelli is the gangster husband of Arness' girlfriend. Keep a sharp eye out for Charles Bronson (billed as Charles Buchinsky) in a bit role as one of six hoodlum brothers. Tracy and O'Brien, both looking older and more worn than their real ages (early 50s), are excellent in their first film together.

Familiar Faces from Television:
❑ William Schallert (Patty's dad in *The Patty Duke Show*) as an ambulance doctor.
❑ Richard Anderson (Oscar Goldman in *The Six Million Dollar Man*) as Lynn's boyfriend.
❑ Ann Doran (Mrs. Kingston, the blind insurance investigator's housekeeper, in *Longstreet*) as a policewoman.
❑ Ned Glass (Sgt. Andy Pendleton on *The Phil Silvers Show*) as a judge.

Memorable Noir Moment:
❑ Sensitivity Training Required: A murder suspect, when asked by an Italian-American assistant D.A. what his alibi is, says he was pumping air into the eel tank at the fish market because the motor had broken. By way of explanation, he adds, "The eels are for the walyos." He then turns apologetically to the D.A. and says, "Oh, excuse me, Mr. Barra, I forgot that *you* were one."

Phantom Lady (1944) 87 min. Ella Raines, Alan Curtis, Franchot Tone, Thomas Gomez, Elisha Cook, Jr. **Screenplay by:** Bernard C. Schoenfeld. **Directed by:** Robert Siodmak. **Noir Type:** Wrong Man. **Noir Themes:** Betrayal, lust, paranoia, woman in jeopardy. ★★★★

Curtis is accused of murdering his wife, and his only alibi is a stranger he spent the evening with at a show. Strangely, all the witnesses seem to have forgotten that they saw him with the woman, and he's soon convicted and sentenced to die in the electric chair. Raines, his gutsy secretary, and Gomez, the police inspector who arrested him, are the only two who believe his story. With her only clue being a woman's hat, Raines goes undercover and winds up stalking a bartender, playing the tramp for a jazz drummer (Cook), and unknowingly teaming up with the real killer in the search for the phantom lady. Stylishly directed by noir icon Robert Siodmak, and based on pulp fiction writer Cornell Woolrich's novel, this superlative film noir classic is not to be missed.

Familiar Face from Television:
❑ Milburn Stone (Doc on *Gunsmoke*) is the voice of the D.A. in Curtis' murder trial.

Memorable Noir Moment:

❑ Cook, eyes bulging and smiling demonically, performs an incredible, sexually stimulating drum solo for the appreciative Raines.

The Phenix City Story (1955) 100 min. John McIntire, Richard Kiley, Kathryn Grant, Edward Andrews, John Larch, James Edwards. **Screenplay by:** Crane Wilbur and Daniel Mainwaring. **Directed by:** Phil Karlson. **Noir Type:** Politics. **Noir Themes:** Social reform, corruption, greed, betrayal. ★★★

After returning from postwar Germany, a war crimes prosecutor (Kiley) moves his family to his hometown, Phenix City, Alabama, "Sin City of the South," where vice is a $100 million-a-year industry. Gambling, prostitution, dope and murder are rampant in the small town because the local mob boss (Andrews) has the police department and politicians on his payroll. After a childhood friend and a little black girl are viciously murdered by Andrews' brutal goon (Larch), reformer Kiley convinces his hesitant father (McIntire) to run for Attorney General. Grant is a blackjack dealer in one of the mob's casinos, and Edwards plays the father of the slain girl. Kiley narrates this exceptionally violent film, which was based on actual events. Veteran character actor Larch (terrific here as one of film noir's most repugnant villains)

A political reformer (Richard Kiley) gets first aid from his wife (Lenka Peterson) as his shocked father (John McIntire) watches in *The Phenix City Story* (Allied Artists, 1955).

went on to play in TV's *Arrest and Trial* and *Convoy*. Andrews later co-starred in the World War II situation comedy *Broadside*. Reporter Clete Roberts, in a 13-minute introduction, interviews real-life residents of Phenix City about the crime and corruption that occurred there.

Memorable Noir Moments:

❑ While whittling a piece of wood, a real-life citizen of Phenix City talks about how honest elections can help defeat corruption and syndicated crime. "If you turn on a light, a bright light in a rat's face," he says, "he'll run for cover, and it doesn't make any difference if that rat is in the city dump or in the city hall."
❑ Addressing a meeting of the citizens committee, Kiley tries to dissuade them from becoming vigilantes. "I'm naive," he admits. "But I still have faith in that ballot box." An angry committee member isn't so confident. "Next election day," he says, "just watch 'em being stuffed like turkeys."

Philo Vance's Gamble (1947) 62 min. Alan Curtis, Terry Austin, Frank Jenks, Gavin Gordon, Cliff Clark, James Burke. **Screenplay by:** Eugene Conrad and Arthur St. Claire. **Directed by:** Basil Wrangell. **Noir Type:** P.I. **Noir Themes:** Greed, betrayal. ★½

Curtis stars as mystery writer S.S. Van Dine's private detective hero, Philo Vance, on a case involving murder and the theft of a $250,000 emerald. Austin is the wannabe starlet whose career depends on the gem. Gordon is her financial backer, who has put all of his available money into a syndicated pool created especially to profit from the fencing of the emerald. Jenks is Curtis' feeble-minded assistant, and Clark and Burke are the equally dumb cops assigned to the case. Fairly good acting doesn't make up for the silly script, which resorts three times to the familiar gunshot from behind a curtain or door to avoid disclosing the identity of the murderer.

Memorable Noir Moments:

❑ Curtis tells a bad guy who has the drop on him why he wouldn't dare shoot. "The gas chamber's much too smelly for your fastidious taste," he says.
❑ After detective Burke tries on a bit of a dead man's cologne, his partner, Clarke, tells him, "You smell like a chorus girl the day after Christmas."

Pickup (1951) 78 min. Hugo Haas, Beverly Michaels, Allan Nixon, Howland Chamberlin. **Screenplay by:** Hugo Haas and Arnold Phillips. **Directed by:** Hugo Haas. **Noir Type:** Triangle. **Noir Themes:** Greed, betrayal, lust. ★★½

Haas stars as the widowed trainmaster of an isolated railroad station. After his dog dies, the lonely man goes to town to buy a puppy. Instead, he winds up with a gorgeous young bride (Michaels), a gold digger with one eye on Haas' savings account and another on his handsome young co-worker (Nixon). Before their marriage, Haas had been experiencing a strange ringing in his ears, and one day, after an argument with his new wife, he suddenly goes deaf. Michaels and Nixon soon become accustomed to flirting with each as if Haas weren't there. Then, after Haas is struck by a car, he regains his hearing. He rushes home to tell his wife the good news, but wisely decides to keep his recovery a secret after hearing Michaels tell Nixon how she married him for his money. *Pickup* is one of those films you might be embarrassed about liking. The production values are poor and the acting is mediocre. Yet it's strangely fascinating, and Michaels, a tall, leggy beauty, is such fun to watch. Bernard Gorcey, who played Louie Dumbrowski in the *Bowery Boys* films, has a small role as a carnival worker with a puppy for sale. *Pickup* marked Czechoslovakian-born Haas' American directorial debut.

Memorable Noir Moment:

❏ From the Some-Things-Never-Change Department: After a physician explains Haas' deafness to Michaels, Nixon asks her, "What did the doctor say?" "Who can understand them?" she replies, with a shrug.

Pickup on South Street (1953) 81 min. Richard Widmark, Jean Peters, Thelma Ritter, Richard Kiley, Murvyn Vye, Willis Bouchey. **Screenplay by**: Samuel Fuller. **Directed by**: Samuel Fuller. **Noir Type**: Commie. **Noir Themes**: Conspiracy, greed, betrayal, lust. ★★★½

Widmark plays a pickpocket, a three-time loser recently released from prison, who snatches a top secret microfilm from Peters' handbag on a New York City subway. Peters was delivering the information for Communist spy Kiley, her former lover. Unaware of her handbag's contents or of Kiley's true identity, she promises him that she'll try to find the thief. A street vendor and professional snitch (Ritter), who's already sold Widmark's address to police captain Vye and F.B.I. agent Bouchey, also sells it to Peters. (Ritter is saving for a cemetery plot and tombstone so she won't have to be buried in Potter's Field.) Vye and Willis fail in their appeal to Widmark's sense of patriotism ("Are you waving the flag at *me*?"), and Peters tries to seduce him out of the microfilm. But he's so intent on making a profit from it, even that doesn't work. Sparks fly for Peters, however, and she falls in love with the greedy crook. Widmark and Peters are terrific, especially during their torrid love scenes, and veteran character actress Ritter shines in her Oscar-nominated performance.

Familiar Face from Television:

❏ Milburn Stone (Doc in *Gunsmoke*) as an F.B.I. agent.

Memorable Noir Moment:

❏ Vye can't hide his distaste for the grinning Widmark. "You'll always be a two-bit cannon," he tells him, "and when they pick you up in the gutter, dead, your hand'll be in a drunk's pocket."

The Picture of Dorian Gray (1945) 110 min. George Sanders, Hurd Hatfield, Donna Reed, Angela Lansbury, Lowell Gilmore, Peter Lawford. **Screenplay by**: Albert Lewin. **Directed by**: Albert Lewin. **Noir Type**: Fantasy. **Noir Themes**: Character deterioration, fatalism, revenge. ★★★½

When Londoner Hatfield views his portrait, painted by a friend (Gilmore), he wishes that the painting would grow old and that he could stay young forever, swearing that he would sacrifice his soul to make his wish come true. The good news is that he gets his wish and stops aging; the bad news is that being eternally young isn't what it's cracked up to be. After falling in love with a saloon singer (Lansbury), he makes the mistake of listening to a cynical, hedonistic friend (Sanders), who suggests that Hatfield find out if the girl's apparent purity will stand the test. After he beds Lansbury, the disgusted Hatfield drops her, vowing to live only for pleasure for

the rest of his life. Meanwhile, his portrait not only begins to age, it starts deteriorating, as if it were suffering from "moral leprosy." While guiltily aware of his transformation from average Joe to super deviant, Hatfield is seemingly unable to stop
his insatiable desire for pleasure, which eventually leads to blackmail and murder.
His only hopes appears to be Reed, Gilmore's beautiful young daughter, who's desperately in love with him. Not as frightening as it once was, the horrors in this visually striking film are subtle (except for a terrifying scene, which was photographed
in Technicolor as a gimmick, where Hatfield allows a friend to view the painting).
The film, narrated by Cedric Hardwicke, contains fine performances by Hatfield and
Lansbury, who was nominated for an Academy Award for Best Supporting Actress.
Lansbury's real-life mother (Moyna MacGill) has a small part as a duchess.

Memorable Noir Moment:
❑ Sanders, entertaining dinner guests with his misogynistic views about women, observes,
  "Women inspire us with the desire to do masterpieces and always prevent us from carry-
  ing them out."

Pitfall (1948) 84 min. Dick Powell, Lizabeth Scott, Jane Wyatt, Raymond Burr, Byron Barr.
Screenplay by: Karl Kamb. **Directed by:** André De Toth. **Noir Type:** Triangle. **Noir Themes:**
Obsession, lust, betrayal, woman in jeopardy. ★★★
  Powell is a successful insurance agent bored with the American dream — the
wife (Wyatt), the kid, the house in the suburbs. A gorgeous model (Scott) comes along
and helps him relieve his boredom. The affair doesn't last long because when Scott
finds out that Powell is married, she ends it quickly. What should have been just a
once-in-a-lifetime fling turns into Powell's worst nightmare when a shady P.I. (Burr),
who has had designs on Scott for some time, decides to make serious trouble for
Powell's family. Meanwhile, Scott's jealous boyfriend (Barr), a convict whom Burr
has been taunting about his girl's infidelity, is about to be released on parole. Noir
icons Scott, Burr and Powell make this a pleasurable film noir viewing experience.

Memorable Noir Moment:
❑ At the breakfast table, Powell ponders his humdrum existence. "You were voted the pret-
  tiest girl in the class," he tells Wyatt. "I was voted the boy most likely to succeed. Something should happen to people like that." "Something did," Wyatt reminds him. "They got
  married."

A Place in the Sun (1951) 122 min. Montgomery Clift, Elizabeth Taylor, Shelley Win-
ters, Anne Revere, Herbert Heyes, Keefe Brasselle, Shepperd Strudwick. **Screenplay by:** Harry
Brown and Michael Wilson. **Directed by:** George Stevens. **Noir Type:** Triangle. **Noir Themes:**
Betrayal, fatalism, jealousy, guilt, woman in jeopardy. ★★★★
  Clift, the unemployed son of a street missionary (Revere), arrives in town and
lands a job on the assembly line of a bathing suit plant owned by his rich uncle
(Heyes). There he meets co-worker Winters and, violating the company ban on frat-
ernization, begins to date her. When Winters gets pregnant, she begins nagging him
about marrying her, but by now Clift has fallen in love with a beautiful socialite
(Taylor) and sees Winters as an obstacle to his career and social advancement. When

A defendant (Montgomery Clift, seated) explains things to his defense attorney (Walter Sande) during his murder trial in *A Place in the Sun* (Paramount, 1951).

Winters threatens to share their secret with Taylor's family, Clift begins thinking of ways he can be rid of her. Then he remembers ... she doesn't know how to swim. Brasselle plays Clift's snobby cousin, and Strudwick is Taylor's wealthy father. Based on a real-life murder case, *A Place in the Sun* is a showcase for the stunning beauty of the 18-year-old Taylor and the low-key acting style of Clift, which earned him an Academy Award nomination for Best Actor. Winters was nominated for an Oscar for Best Supporting Actress for her role as the dowdy plant worker, who turns understandably nasty when Clift balks at marrying her. Nominated for Best Picture, the film took home six Oscars, including the Best Director and Best Screenplay awards. It also made the number 92 spot on the American Film Institute's List of America's 100 Greatest Movies. Look for veteran noir baddie Ted de Corsia cast against type as the trial judge.

Familiar Faces from Television:
- ❑ Raymond Burr (*Perry Mason* and *Ironside*) as the district attorney.
- ❑ Fred Clark (Harry Morton, George and Gracie's neighbor in *The George Burns and Gracie Allen Show*) as the defense attorney.
- ❑ Kathleen Freeman (Katie the maid in *Topper* and Flo Shafer in *The Beverly Hillbillies*) as an assembly line worker and trial witness.

Memorable Noir Moment:

❏ A Death Row inmate, whose own noir universe will soon end abruptly, shouts to a comrade walking that last mile, "I hope you find a better world than this."

Playgirl (1954) 85 min. Shelley Winters, Barry Sullivan, Colleen Miller, Richard Long. **Screenplay by:** Robert Blees. **Directed by:** Joseph Pevney. **Noir Type:** Triangle. **Noir Themes:** Jealousy, obsession, character deterioration, woman in jeopardy. ★★½

A small-town Nebraska girl (Miller) arrives in New York City, as do thousands of others who "pour in looking for a career, success, love, or something they can't even define," and makes it big as a fashion model. A magazine publisher (Sullivan), who's cheating on his wife with nightclub singer Winters, makes a play for the naive girl, prompting the jealous Winters to steal a gun she finds in the glove compartment of a car belonging to professional loafer Long. Somebody gets killed and a couple of careers are ruined as a result. Entertaining fluff with Winters giving a boisterous performance as the jealous femme fatale.

Familiar Faces from Television:

❏ Kent Taylor (*Boston Blackie*) as a gangster with an eye for Miller.
❏ Barnard Hughes (Max Merlin in *Mr. Merlin*, Buzz Richman in *Blossom*, "Pop" Cavanaugh in *The Cavanaughs* and Dr. Joe Bogert in *Doc*) as the manager of a country club.
❏ Paul Richards (Dr. McKinley Thompson in *Breaking Point*) as a hit man.
❏ Peter Leeds (George Colton in *Pete and Gladys*) as a man at the airport.

Memorable Noir Moments:

❏ At the airport, Winters collides with a rushing passenger. "Sorry, we almost locked bumpers," she says good-naturedly. "If there's any damage to the chassis," the man says, "I'll be glad to pay for repairs." "Buster, you couldn't even pay for the headlights," Winters responds.
❏ When Long assures Winters that she has a great future ahead of her, the depressed showgirl responds, "The only trouble with the future ... is it gets here so much sooner than it used to." (See *Autumn Leaves*, where *Playgirl* screenwriter Blees, who evidently liked this line, has Joan Crawford repeating it.)

Please Murder Me (1956) 78 min. Raymond Burr, Angela Lansbury, Dick Foran, John Dehner. **Screenplay by:** Donald Hyde and Al C. Ward. **Directed by:** Peter Godfrey. **Noir Type:** Trial. **Noir Themes:** Obsession, betrayal, revenge. ★★★

The film opens with attorney Burr purchasing a revolver late one evening and going to his office, where he leaves a tape-recorded message for the district attorney. He tells him that in fifty-five minutes he will be murdered and proceeds to explain the events that led him to this predicament. Via flashback, the viewer learns that Burr has fallen in love with his best friend's wife (Lansbury) and that he has decided to tell his friend (Foran) about the affair. It's a difficult decision because the cuckolded husband saved Burr's life during the war by taking a bullet for him at Iwo Jima. Foran takes the bad news surprisingly well and asks Burr to give him some time to think about things. A few days later, Lansbury, who's claiming self-defense, is arrested for murdering her husband. Burr defends her in court against prosecuting attorney Dehner's premeditated murder charge. Will Dehner have better luck than the worst

D.A. in history, Perry Mason's nemesis, Hamilton Burger, or will Lansbury (from TV's *Murder, She Wrote*) go free? *Perry Mason* fans who miss the beginning of this film might think that they're watching a rerun of the television series that made Raymond Burr a household name. There are some clever plot twists in this tightly scripted film noir, and Burr and Lansbury turn in solid performances.

Familiar Faces from Television:
- ❏ Denver Pyle (Uncle Jessie in *The Dukes of Hazzard*) as a homicide detective.
- ❏ Madge Blake (Dick Grayson's Aunt Harriet in *Batman* and Flora MacMichael in *The Real McCoys*) as a maid.

Memorable Noir Moment:
- ❏ In a letter to Burr, Foran pathetically declares his love for femme fatale Lansbury, even though she hasn't reciprocated. "She isn't a woman," he writes. "Myra's a disease. In a way, she's already destroyed me. I just hope she doesn't end up destroying you."

Plunder Road (1957) 72 min. Gene Raymond, Wayne Morris, Elisha Cook, Jr., Stafford Repp, Steven Ritch, Jeanne Cooper. **Screenplay by:** Steven Ritch. **Directed by:** Hubert Cornfield. **Noir Type:** Heist. **Noir Themes:** Greed. ★★★½

This is a better-than-average heist film about five losers (Raymond, Morris, Cook, Repp and Ritch) who hold up a government train and get away with five million dollars in gold bars. There are no detailed planning scenes here, as in *The Asphalt Jungle* and *The Killing*. Instead, the film's first 12 minutes focus on the daring and ingenious heist, after which the thieves separate into three trucks and head west to split the loot. Or so they think. The tension and suspense is maintained throughout, as we wonder who's going to get caught and how. As a heist film, *Plunder Road* pales in comparison to *The Asphalt Jungle* and *The Killing*; however, Cornfield does an admirable job with his limited budget. Raymond, a 1930s romantic leading man, plays the college-educated mastermind. (Morris seems particularly awed by his boss' educational credentials, at a time when the average person, never mind crooks, barely finished high school.) Cooper is Raymond's girl who is waiting for him to arrive in Los Angeles. (A publicity photograph shows Morris and Nora Hayden menacingly brandishing guns. This is odd because Hayden is on screen only for two minutes as a waitress who has nothing to do with the gang or the heist.) Fine performances, a suspenseful script and a terrific ending contribute to the fun.

Memorable Noir Moment:
- ❏ Raymond, replying to Ritch's suggestion that they head for the tightly guarded border, says, "An *idea* couldn't get past the border right now."

Port of New York (1949) 79 min. Scott Brady, Richard Rober, Yul Brynner, Neville Brand. **Screenplay by:** Eugene Ling. **Directed by:** Laslo Benedek. **Noir Type:** Narcotics. **Noir Themes:** Greed. ★★

This documentary-style noir is reminiscent of Anthony Mann's *T-Men* filmed a year earlier, only it's not nearly as good. A customs man (Brady) and a narcotics agent (Rober) team up to find a drug shipment hijacked by Brynner's gang. Brynner, acting more like Dracula than a vicious gangster, makes a poor showing in his film debut. Brand, after his remarkable Hollywood debut in **D.O.A.**, is wasted here in a bit role as Brynner's henchman. The going is slow and the plot uninteresting, but the realistic New York City locations help to make it bearable.

Portrait of a Sinner (1959-British) 96 min. Nadja Tiller, Tony Britton, William Bendix, Natasha Parry, Norman Wooland, Donald Wolfit, Tony Wright. **Screenplay by:** Audrey Erskine-Lindop and Dudley Leslie. **Directed by:** Robert Siodmak. **Noir Type:** Femme Fatale. **Noir Themes:** Obsession, lust, betrayal, sexual hostility. ★★½

British archaeologist Britton is engaged to perky socialite Parry, whose uncle (Wolfit) is the owner of an influential London newspaper and a potential sponsor of Britton's search for Noah's Ark. Life couldn't be grander for the handsome bachelor, until he falls in love with a sultry fraulein (Tiller). After Tiller tells him that she lives with a girlfriend, Parry discovers that the roommate is really her elderly American "boss" (Bendix), who swears to him that their relationship is platonic. The situation deteriorates when Tilley's abusive, drug-dealing boyfriend (Wright) returns from sea in desperate need of fifteen hundred pounds to replace the stash he was forced to destroy during a police raid. And there's not much that Tilley wouldn't do to help her only true love. Meanwhile, the obsessed Britton doesn't seem to care that he could be losing everything that was once important to him — his fiancé, his long-anticipated archaeological jaunt to Mt. Ararat, and his best friend and fellow archaeologist, Wooland. Originally released as *The Rough and the Smooth*, this interesting film, Siodmak's first British feature, deals frankly with such topics as prostitution, masochism and the psychological damage of sexual child abuse. Bendix, whose long-running TV series, *The Life of Riley*, ended a year earlier, is good as the pathetic American businessman in love with a girl half his age. It's reported that Siodmak wanted film newcomer Peter O'Toole for the role of the wayward archaeologist, but co-producer George Minter nixed that idea, and the part went to Britton, who does a fine job. Austrian starlet Tiller (Miss Austria 1949) doesn't fare as well with her, at times, incomprehensible accent.

Memorable Noir Moment:
❑ From the Some-Things-Never-Change Department: "Are you something in the government?" Tiller asks Britton as they share a taxi. "No, why?" the puzzled archaeologist replies. "You sound a little pompous," she replies.
❑ A playful Britton sweet-talks his giggling lover: "You beautiful, blonde bitch."

Portrait of Jennie (1948) 86 min. Jennifer Jones, Joseph Cotten, Ethel Barrymore, Cecil Kellaway, David Wayne, Lillian Gish. **Screenplay by:** Paul Osborn and Peter Berneis. **Directed by:** William Dieterle. **Noir Type:** Fantasy. **Noir Themes:** Obsession, fatalism. ★★★★

Cotten plays a starving artist "caught by an enchantment beyond time and change." The enchantment is Jones, a child he meets one wintry evening in New York's Central Park after finally selling one of his paintings to two sympathetic art dealers (Barrymore and Kellaway) for $12.50. The mysterious girl bluntly informs him that she'll hurry up and get older so the two of them can be married. But, strangely, Cotten's paintings of the black waters around an old lighthouse off the Cape Cod coast seem to frighten her. Jones visits him several more times during the next few months, each time aging mysteriously. During her absences, he investigates and is mystified to discover that time seems to have no meaning for the girl. He eventually falls in love with her, a young woman by now, and paints her portrait, a masterpiece born out of an obsession that eventually leads to tragedy. Wayne, in his film debut, is a cabbie who gets his artist friend a job painting a controversial mural in an Irish pub. Silent film star Gish plays a nun. This is a terrific little film with an outstanding cast.

Familiar Face from Television:
❑ Anne Francis (*Honey West*) as one of three teenage girls in a museum admiring Jennie's portrait.

Memorable Noir Moment:
❑ Art dealer Barrymore bluntly informs Cotten that there isn't a drop of love in his work, adding, "I'm an old maid and nobody knows more about love than an old maid."

Possessed (1947) 108 min. Joan Crawford, Van Heflin, Raymond Massey, Geraldine Brooks, Stanley Ridges. **Screenplay by:** Silvia Richards and Ranald MacDougall. **Directed by:** Curtis Bernhardt. **Noir Type:** Triangle. **Noir Themes:** Obsession, paranoia, jealousy, betrayal. ★★★★

When a dazed and hallucinating Crawford is found wandering the Los Angeles streets searching for her former lover (Heflin), she's taken to a hospital's psychiatric ward where, under sodium pentathol, she's able to tell the staff psychiatrist (Ridges) her sordid story. Via flashback, we witness the mentally unstable Crawford being dropped by Heflin because she has become overly possessive and marriage-minded. Vowing to wait for Heflin's unlikely change of heart, she continues in her job as a live-in nurse for the equally unstable wife of a rich industrialist (Massey). After Heflin accepts an out-of-state position and her patient drowns in a lake, an apparent suicide, Crawford accepts her stodgy employer's marriage proposal. But threatening their already slim chances for happiness is Massey's daughter (Brooks), who returns from college believing that Crawford and her father have been having an affair which may have prompted her mother to commit suicide. Once the two women iron out their differences, Crawford and Massey marry, but the footloose Heflin returns and becomes romantically involved with Brooks. Seething with jealousy, Crawford's schizophrenia worsens, leading to tragedy. Crawford is outstanding in a role that earned her an Academy Award nomination for Best Actress, and Brooks makes a fine film debut. Heflin is excellent as the jaunty cad.

Memorable Noir Moment:
❑ When Massey proposes to the forlorn Crawford, she sobs with relief, saying, "Something happens to a woman when she isn't wanted. Something dreadful."

The Postman Always Rings Twice (1946) 113 min. Lana Turner, John Garfield, Cecil Kellaway, Hume Cronyn, Leon Ames. **Screenplay by:** Harry Ruskin and Niven Busch. **Directed by:** Tay Garnett. **Noir Type:** Femme Fatale. **Noir Themes:** Betrayal, obsession, lust, greed. ★★★★★

Drifter Garfield's inclination is to heed his itching feet and keep on going after a motorist drops him off at the Twin Oaks diner. But after just one look at Turner, the sexy blonde wife of the diner's owner (Kellaway), the vagabond applies for a job. Narrated by Garfield, the story follows the doomed lovers as they discover their fiery passion for each other and make plans to get rid of the heavy-drinking Kellaway. After bungling an attempt at murdering the oblivious cuckold in his bathtub, they eventually succeed, making it look like an auto accident. But the wily D.A. (Ames), who's not about to let them get away with murder, sets a trap for them, making Turner's corrupt defense attorney (Cronyn) work a little harder to earn his money. Pulp fiction writer James Cain's sizzling novel became a film noir classic thanks to Garnett's ingenious direction and standout performances by Garfield and Turner as the lovers who believe their only chance at happiness lies in getting rid of the amiable Kellaway, who, drunk or sober, is mysteriously blind to the sexual tension around him. (See *Ossessione* for an earlier, Italian version of Cain's novel.) Garfield's role almost went to Cameron Mitchell when the future star of **Body and Soul** was drafted. But when the Army released Garfield because of his heart condition, the unfortunate Mitchell lost a golden opportunity.

Familiar Face from Television:

❑ Audrey Totter (Beth Purcell in *Cimarron City* and Nurse Wilcox in *Medical Center*) as a sexy waitress with car trouble.

Memorable Noir Moment:

❑ Turner's plaintive cry of "I wanna be somebody" is shared by other film noir losers, including a hustler (**Night and the City**), drug pusher (**Stakeout on Dope Street**) and boxer (**Champion**).
❑ Tough guy Garfield romances Turner, saying, "Give me a kiss or I'll sock ya." A little later, whipped and whining, he pleads, "Have you got a little kiss for me?"
❑ As the future murderers prepare to hitchhike their way to happiness, Turner wishes she and Garfield had taken her husband's car. "Stealing a man's wife — that's one thing," Garfield says. "But stealing his car — that's larceny."

Power of the Whistler (1945) 66 min. Richard Dix, Janis Carter, Jeff Donnell, Loren Tindall. **Screenplay by:** Aubrey Wisberg. **Directed by:** Lew Landers. **Noir Type:** Amnesia. **Noir Themes:** Woman in jeopardy. ✶✶

The third, and weakest, in **The Whistler** series, this B noir features Dix as an escaped homicidal maniac, who suffers amnesia after being hit by a car. Carter is the gorgeous department store buyer who tries to help him find his real identity after her fortune-telling cards show that he only has twenty-four hours to live. She eventually falls in love with the charmer but, being none too bright, she fails to connect him to the trail of dead animals he leaves behind, and never even asks him about his favorite reading material — *The Art of Poison*. When Donnell, Carter's younger, smarter sister, joins the search for Dix's identity, she quickly becomes suspicious of the psycho, who finally regains his memory and realizes that he's got some important things to do at a New Jersey mental institution. Dix starred in six Whistler films. (See also *The Whistler, Mark of the Whistler, Voice of the Whistler, Mysterious Intruder, Secret of the Whistler, The Thirteenth Hour* and *The Return of the Whistler*.)

Memorable Noir Moments:

❑ When the warden of a mental institution is asked why he didn't report Dix's escape, he explains that the psycho was almost cured anyway, but that "he certainly fooled us with his madman's cunning."

❑ When two highway patrolmen, who are supposed to be searching for the homicidal maniac, stop Dix and ask for some identification, he shows them the name sewn on the inside label of his stolen suit jacket. Satisfied, the New Jersey cops allow him to continue on his way.

The Pretender (1947) 69 min. Albert Dekker, Catherine Craig, Charles Drake, Alan Carney, Linda Stirling. **Screenplay by**: Don Martin and Doris Miller. **Directed by**: W. Lee Wilder. **Noir Type**: Hit Man. **Noir Themes**: Paranoia, greed. ★★★½

Investment broker Dekker has been playing the stock market with a wealthy client's money and losing big time. Realizing that this could mean prison for him, he pretends to be in love with the client (Craig) and asks her to marry him. Unfortunately for him, she's already engaged and turns him down. Undeterred, he hires gangster Carney to have Craig's fiancé (Drake) bumped off. Having never seen Drake, Dekker tells Carney to keep checking the society pages for a photograph of the two together. When Craig breaks her engagement to Drake, she and the relieved Dekker elope. Dekker's relief is short-lived, though, when he sees his and Craig's photograph in the morning newspaper and it dawns on him that Carney's hit man will think that he's the target. Panicky, he visits Carney and asks that the killer be called off. Carney, thinking it's the funniest thing that has ever happened, jovially agrees, and even tells Dekker that he'll return half his money. But only moments later, Carney is shot and killed by a former girlfriend (Stirling). The increasingly fearful and paranoid Dekker becomes a hermit, resorting to eating canned goods and fruit in his bedroom because he's worried that his wife's new servants might be trying to poison him. When he can't find Carney's successor because of an ironic name mix-up, he starts carrying a gun. The plot isn't unique (see 1944's *The Whistler* and 1954's *Paid to Kill*), but Dekker's enjoyable performance and John Alton's expert cinematography will keep you hooked until the sensational climax.

The Price of Fear (1956) 79 min. Merle Oberon, Lex Barker, Charles Drake, Warren Stevens, Phillip Pine. **Screenplay by**: Robert Tallman. **Directed by**: Abner Biberman. **Noir Type**: Wrong Man. **Noir Themes**: Victim of fate, betrayal. ★★½

Gangster Stevens has just bought out Barker's partner in a dog-racing track, and Barker isn't happy about it. In front of twenty witnesses, he threatens to kill his ex-partner and storms off. Stevens ingeniously has the man knocked off, leaving Barker the main suspect. While trying to avoid being followed by Stevens' henchman (Pine), Barker jumps out of a cab and takes off in Oberon's car, leaving her standing dumbfounded in the street. Oberon, however, isn't upset about having her car stolen because she had just been involved in a hit-and-run accident. Barker is now a suspect in two crimes and is being investigated by his homicide detective pal (Drake). A former Tarzan (1949–53), Barker gives a low-key, but sometimes wooden, performance, and Oberon has seen better days. But the film manages to sustain interest until its predictable ending.

Memorable Noir Moment:

❑ When a hood asks for something to read while he waits, a pawnshop owner hands him a foreign-language paper. "Hey, this is a foreign newspaper," the thug complains. "You think I'm illiterate?"

Private Hell 36 (1954) 81 min. Steve Cochran, Howard Duff, Ida Lupino, Dean Jagger, Dorothy Malone. **Screenplay by:** Collier Young and Ida Lupino. **Directed by:** Don Siegel. **Noir Type:** Bad Cop. **Noir Themes:** Greed, obsession, corruption, betrayal, guilt. ★★★

The offbeat title refers to trailer number 36 at a Los Angeles mobile home park, where sticky-fingered cops Cochran and Duff have stashed the stolen loot they recovered from a thief killed in a car crash while trying to escape. But the real hell can be found in family man Duff's guilty conscience ("I can't look in the mirror without gagging"). Weak-willed, he allowed the amoral Cochran to pocket eighty grand and, worse, accepted half. Cochran, fed up with risking his life for peanuts, sees the dough as his way into nightclub singer Lupino's materialistic heart. Duff, on the other hand, realizes that the stolen money is driving a wedge between him and his family — his wife (Malone) and their little girl. Jagger plays their suspicious boss. Excellent performances by Cochran and Duff more than compensate for the tedious script.

Familiar Faces from Television:

A good-cop-gone-bad (Howard Duff) and his concerned wife (Dorothy Malone) in *Private Hell 36* (Filmmakers, 1954).

❑ Richard Deacon (Mel Cooley in *The Dick Van Dyke Show*) as a pharmacist.
❑ King Donovan (Air Force officer Harvey Helm in *Love That Bob* and lawyer Herb Thornton in *Please Don't Eat the Daisies*) as a holdup man.
❑ Jimmy Hawkins (Tagg Oakley in *Annie Oakley*) as a delivery boy.

Memorable Noir Moment:

❑ In an rare film noir reference to a television show, Lupino, who's being grilled by Cochran, says, "I've seen all this on *Dragnet*." (See **Witness to Murder** for another film noir allusion to the famed TV detective series.)

The Prowler (1951) 92 min. Van Heflin, Evelyn Keyes, John Maxwell. Emerson Treacy. **Screenplay by:** Hugo Butler. **Directed by:** Joseph Losey. **Noir Type:** Bad Cop. **Noir Themes:** Greed, betrayal, corruption, obsession. ★★★½

Heflin stars as a disgruntled cop who becomes obsessed with Keyes, the wife of an all-night disk jockey (Tracy), after she reports sighting a prowler. A high school basketball hero who failed at college, Heflin's dream now is to own a motel in Las Vegas and sleep while the dough rolls in. When he discovers that Tracy has a will that leaves sixty-two thousand dollars to Keyes, he decides to kill the man by shooting him as a prowler, and then marry his widow. Maxwell plays Heflin's boring, rock-collecting partner. Heflin is terrific as the killer cop, and Keyes is enjoyable as

An on-the-run ex-cop (Van Heflin) takes his first look at his newborn son held by the doctor (Wheaton Chambers) outside a desert shack in *The Prowler* (United Artists, 1951).

the woman who fears that she married a murderer. *The Prowler* is an intense film noir study of the American Dream gone sour.

Familiar Face from Television:

❑ Madge Blake (Dick Grayson's aunt in *Batman* and Flora MacMichael in *The Real McCoys*) as Keyes' sister-in-law.

Memorable Noir Moment:

❑ Heflin makes a pass at the unwilling Keyes, who slaps him silly. "You're a real cop," she tells him. "You want everything for free."

Pursued (1947) 105 min. Teresa Wright, Robert Mitchum, Judith Anderson, Dean Jagger, Alan Hale, John Rodney, Harry Carey, Jr. **Screenplay by:** Niven Busch. **Directed by:** Raoul Walsh. **Noir Type:** Horse Opera. **Noir Themes:** Revenge, obsession, victim of fate, betrayal, jealousy. ★★★★

Mitchum plays the victim of a fanatical one-armed man (Jagger), who killed Mitchum's entire family twenty years earlier and now wants to finish the job. Taken in as a child by Jagger's former sister-in-law (Anderson), Mitchum grows up with Anderson's two children (Wright and Rodney). He suffers from amnesia about the murder of his own family and has frightening dreams and visions of an ominous pair of boots and spurs. As grown men, Mitchum and Rodney toss a coin to determine who will go off to fight in the Spanish-American War and who will stay behind to work the family ranch. Mitchum loses the toss but returns with the Congressional Medal of Honor and a hankering to marry Wright. But Rodney, bitter at having to share the proceeds of the family business with Mitchum, whom he's always considered to be an outsider, kicks him out after the unlucky veteran loses another coin toss. Mitchum's pathetic gambling history doesn't stop him from buying into a casino owned by Hale. Meanwhile, the one-armed man has taken to hanging around town, and a proud general store clerk (Carey) has been courting Wright. Considered by some to be the first noir Western, *Pursued* is a dark and intriguing film about a man haunted by a tragic past and victimized by an obsessed killer's irrational hatred.

Memorable Noir Moment:

❑ The determined Mitchum, who has alienated Wright because he had to kill a couple of otherwise sympathetic bushwhackers, tells her, "I'd have to climb across two graves to get to you, but nothing in the world would hold me back."

Pushover (1954) 88 min. Fred MacMurray, Kim Novak, Phil Carey, Dorothy Malone, E.G. Marshall, Paul Richards. **Screenplay by:** Roy Huggins. **Directed by:** Richard Quine. **Noir Type:** Bad Cop. **Noir Themes:** Greed, obsession, lust, corruption. ★★★

MacMurray plays a good cop gone bad over a gorgeous dame and a case full of money. As part of an undercover operation to catch Novak's bank robber boyfriend (Richards), MacMurray romances her while he and partner Carey spy on her with binoculars and tape her phone conversations, hoping that Richards will show up with the 250 Gs from a recent bank heist. Although Novak discovers his deception, she realizes that she loves him anyway and tempts him with a plan to kill Richards and run off with the dough. At first, he's repulsed, but later agrees to her plan, which, of course, immediately goes awry. Watching MacMurray's world crumble around him might arouse some viewer sympathy and a secret hope that he'll get away with it, but this has happened to too many film noir characters too many times to expect a different outcome now (to MacMurray himself in ***Double Indemnity*** and to Charles McGraw in ***Roadblock***, among others). Malone plays Novak's next-door neighbor, a nurse whom the lecherous Carey has been admiring from afar with his binoculars. Marshall, who went on to star in the highly successful 1960s TV series *The Defenders*, has a small role as MacMurray's boss. This is a fast-moving, nicely acted film, a worthy addition to the bad cop theme so prevalent in film noir.

Familiar Faces from Television:
❑ Paul Picerni (Agent Lee Hobson in *The Untouchables*) as a masher who gets fresh with Malone.
❑ Marion Ross (Marion Cunningham, Richie's mom, in *Happy Days*) as a guest at a party thrown by Malone.

Memorable Noir Moment:
❑ Sensitivity Training Required: MacMurray tells Carey about how he swore as a kid that he would have plenty of money when he grew up. Now, as a poor cop, he complains, "I owe the Chinaman $2.30 on last week's laundry bill."
❑ During a conversation about dames, MacMurray notes that Carey doesn't seem to like women much. "What keeps *you* single?" Carey asks. "Maybe I like 'em *too* much," MacMurray answers.

Queen Bee (1955) 95 min. Joan Crawford, Barry Sullivan, Betsy Palmer, John Ireland, Lucy Marlow. **Screenplay by:** Ranald MacDougall. **Directed by:** Ranald MacDougall. **Noir Type:** Femme Fatale. **Noir Themes:** Family dysfunction, jealousy, betrayal. ★★★½

Visiting her older cousin (Crawford) at her Georgia mansion, Marlow finds she's arrived at a vicious bee hive, where Crawford is the "queen bee who stings all her rivals to death." Sullivan, Crawford's browbeaten husband, understandably spends all of his time boozing it up, while his sister (Palmer), engaged to Crawford's former lover (Ireland), spends *her* time dodging the jealous Crawford's verbal assaults. At first, the naive Marlow sees only Crawford's outer beauty, but she eventually comes to realize that the cousin she once admired and respected has, as Sullivan puts it, "the instincts of a headhunter." When Crawford's spitefulness causes a suicide in the family, Sullivan, finally able to tear himself away from the bottle, realizes he must do something about his evil wife, and quickly. Crawford has a field day playing one of her most vile characters. Fay Wray, of *King Kong* fame, plays Sullivan's mentally unbalanced ex-fiancée, whom he jilted for Crawford.

Familiar Face from Television:
❑ Olan Soule (Mr. Pfeiffer in *My Three Sons* and Fred Springer in *Arnie*) as Crawford's psychiatrist.

Memorable Noir Moments:
❑ "You're some fancy kind of disease," Sullivan tells Crawford. "I had it once. Now I'm immune."

Joan Crawford in *Queen Bee* (Columbia, 1955).

❑ Referring to Marlow, Crawford puts on her sweet act and says, "How young and lovely she is." Ireland isn't fooled. "Yeah," he remarks, "and how you hate her for it."

Quicksand (1950) 79 min. Mickey Rooney, Jeanne Cagney, Barbara Bates, Peter Lorre. **Screenplay by:** Robert Smith. **Directed by:** Irving Pichel. **Noir Type:** Cover-Up. **Noir Themes:** Obsession, lust, greed. ★★★

Remember how much mischief Rooney got into as teenager Andy Hardy back in the thirties? That was nothing compared to the trouble he has as a film noir garage mechanic in 1950. In need of some dough for a date with waitress Cagney (actor James Cagney's sister), he swipes twenty bucks from the garage's cash register, intending to replace the money the next day. From there it's all downhill for the unlucky Rooney, who sinks deeper and deeper into the muck, committing a series of crimes, each one worst than the last, in a futile effort to cover up his original foolish act. Bates is the good girl who loves Rooney no matter what but can't seem to get to second base with him because he only has eyes for Cagney. Lorre plays the sleazy arcade owner who blackmails him. Rooney, already a veteran of more than 70 movies at age 30, gives a strong performance, helping this minor noir to hold up despite its disappointing ending.

A grease monkey (Mickey Rooney, left) and his waitress date (Jeanne Cagney) meet with a slimy blackmailer (Peter Lorre) in *Quicksand* (United Artists, 1950).

Familiar Faces from Television:
- ❑ Jack Elam (George Taggert in *Temple Houston*) as a guy in a bar.
- ❑ Jimmy Dodd (the head Mouseketeer in *The Mickey Mouse Club*) as a garage mechanic.
- ❑ Minerva Urecal (Annie in *The Adventures of Tugboat Annie* and "Mother" in *Peter Gunn*) as a the landlady.
- ❑ Ray Teal (Sheriff Roy Coffee in *Bonanza*) as a motorcycle cop.

Memorable Noir Moment:
- ❑ After double-crossing Rooney, Cagney tries to kiss him. "I wouldn't dirty my lips," he tells her.

Race Street (1948) 79 min. George Raft, William Bendix, Marilyn Maxwell, Frank Faylen, Harry Morgan, Gale Robbins. **Screenplay by:** Martin Rackin. **Directed by:** Edwin L. Marin. **Noir Type:** Payback. **Noir Themes:** Revenge, betrayal. ★★½

When his best pal (Morgan) is bumped off by the syndicate, which is trying to weasel in on all the bookmakers in San Francisco, bookie Raft vows revenge. Syndicate chief Faylen decides that Raft is his only obstacle to controlling the city's gambling operations and, with the help of a traitor close to the bookie, plans to rub him out. Bendix is the police lieutenant looking to break up Faylen's gang, with or without assistance from boyhood friend Raft, who's no stoolie. Maxwell plays Raft's girlfriend, and Robbins is his nightclub singer sister. Although the debonair Raft is enjoyable as the nice-guy bookie, and Bendix gives his usual solid performance, *Race Street* is little more than an average crime noir with a few good fight scenes thrown in to keep things interesting.

Familiar Face from Television:
❑ George Chandler (Uncle Petrie Martin in *Lassie* and Ichabod Adams in *Ichabod and Me*) as a waiter.

The Racket (1951) 88 min. Robert Mitchum, Robert Ryan, Lizabeth Scott, William Talman, Ray Collins, William Conrad, Brett King. **Screenplay by:** William Wister Haines and W.R. Burnett. **Directed by:** John Cromwell. **Noir Type:** Gangster. **Noir Themes:** Corruption, paranoia. ★★★★

Ryan gives a seething performance as a hopelessly old-fashioned gangster, a dinosaur who has been ruling his town with an iron fist but who refuses to give in to pressure from the new syndicate boss (known only as the "old man") and his sophisticated henchmen to tone down the rough stuff and get with the times. Mitchum, an honest cop surrounded by crooked superiors and politicians, is out to nab Ryan and his younger brother (King). Scott is the wily torch singer with matrimonial plans for King, despite Ryan's disapproval. Collins plays a wishy-washy assistant D.A., who's supported by the syndicate in his bid to become mayor, and Conrad is one of the many cops on the syndicate's payroll. Mitchum gives too laid-back of a performance, even for him, but Talman, as Mitchum's gung-ho protégé, is excellent.

Familiar Faces from Television:
❑ Don Porter (Peter Sands, Susie's boss, in *Private Secretary* and Professor Lawrence, Gidget's dad, in *Gidget*) as the "old man's" assistant.
❑ Milburn Stone (Doc in *Gunsmoke*) as a member of the Crime Commission.

Memorable Noir Moment:
❑ Ryan has a few choice words for nightclub singer Scott. "Why, you cheap, little, clip-joint canary," he fumes.

Rage in Heaven (1941) 82 min. Robert Montgomery, Ingrid Bergman, George Sanders, Oscar Homolka. **Screenplay by:** Christopher Isherwood and Robert Thoeren. **Directed by:** W.S. Van Dyke II. **Noir Type:** Psycho. **Noir Themes:** Character deterioration, paranoia, woman in jeopardy, jealousy. ★★★

Montgomery, the insane heir to a British iron works factory, marries Bergman, his mother's assistant and companion. His best friend (Sanders) also loves Bergman but never makes his feelings known once she chooses Montgomery. As the plot progresses, so does Montgomery's insanity. In an attempt to prove his manliness to Bergman, he accepts the role as head of the family business, a position vacated by his father's death. Montgomery's pitiful decisions cause the factory workers to riot, and he narrowly escapes being killed by the angry mob. His jealousy over the imagined affair between Sanders and Bergman brings him to the brink of murder. After driving away Bergman, he concocts a sinister plot, in which he hopes to destroy himself and the two people who love him the most. Homolka plays an eccentric French psychiatrist ("nervous cases are apt to be influenced by the moon"), whom Bergman turns to for help. Although it's hard to swallow that his insanity wouldn't be noticed by those closest to him, Montgomery skillfully manages to remain believable as the nutcase.

Memorable Noir Moment:

❑ "Evidence! Evidence! I spit on evidence," Homolka shouts when told by Bergman that the evidence looks bad for Sanders, who is facing the death penalty.

The Raging Tide (1951) 93 min. Richard Conte, Shelley Winters, Stephen McNally, Charles Bickford, Alex Nicol, John McIntire. **Screenplay by:** Ernest K. Gann. **Directed by:** George Sherman. **Noir Type:** High Seas. **Noir Themes:** Betrayal, revenge. ★★½

Conte plays a San Francisco hood who stows away aboard a fishing boat owned by an old Swede (Bickford) after knocking off a rival. The kindly fisherman buys Conte's story about boarding the boat to sleep off a drunken binge and allows him to stay on and earn his keep. The killer begins to see Bickford as a father figure and starts enjoying the rugged fisherman's life, more so than Bickford's ungrateful son (Nicol), whom the hood hires to collect his payoffs while the ship is in dock. Nicol seems to think that his duties include romancing Conte's girl (Winters). McNally is the patient cop waiting for Conte to show his face, and McIntire is an old sea-dog who witnessed Conte fleeing from the murder scene but can't quite place him. Somewhat sentimental, the film and its unexpected ending still pack a mild punch.

Memorable Noir Moments:

❑ Winters feels that the police department should hire smaller cops. "Little men are smarter," she claims. "There's not so much space between their ears."
❑ Expertly fending off Nicol's unwanted advances, Winters tells him, "I've met enough wolves in my time to overrun Siberia."

Railroaded (1947) 71 min. John Ireland, Sheila Ryan, Hugh Beaumont, Jane Randolph. **Screenplay by:** John C. Higgins. **Directed by:** Anthony Mann. **Noir Type:** Psycho. **Noir Themes:** Greed, sexual hostility, betrayal. ★★★

Beaumont is a detective whose love for a suspected cop killer's sister (Ryan) prompts him to work during his free time to help prove the kid's innocence. We know the identity of the real murder from the beginning, but that doesn't detract from the film's suspense. Ireland's performance as the sadistic killer, who perfumes his bullets and sensuously massages his gun, is reason enough to view this taut crime thriller—that plus a terrific cat fight between Ireland's boozing girlfriend (Randolph), and Ryan.

Memorable Noir Moment:

❑ When Randolph expresses remorse about a cop's murder, Ireland consoles her. "Don't think about it," he advises. "Cops ain't people."

Ramrod (1947) 94 min. Joel McCrea, Veronica Lake, Don DeFore, Donald Crisp, Preston Foster, Arleen Whelan, Charles Ruggles, Ian MacDonald. **Screenplay by:** John C. Moffitt, Graham Baker and Cecile Kramer. **Directed by:** André De Toth. **Noir Type:** Horse Opera. **Noir Themes:** Greed, obsession, betrayal, revenge. ★★★

Lake is the conniving daughter of cattle rancher Ruggles, who's trying to force her to marry a fellow cattleman (Foster). But the rebellious Lake has chosen Mac-Donald, a wannabe sheep rancher, who's run out of town by Foster. Lake then decides to turn her ex-fiancé's ranch into a cattle operation, hiring recovering drunk McCrea to be her foreman. Her blind ambition and unscrupulous tactics start a range war that results in a number of killings and a final showdown between McCrea and Foster. Crisp plays the honest sheriff caught in the middle. The petite Lake does a good job as the greedy femme fatale who uses her sexuality to manipulate the men around her, and McCrea is fine as the quiet, but fearless, ramrod. This is a pretty good Western with an excellent supporting cast, especially Don DeFore (from TV's *Hazel*) as McCrea's gunslinger pal and Whelan as a love-smitten seamstress.

Familiar Faces from Television:
❑ Lloyd Bridges (Mike Nelson in *Sea Hunt*) as one of Foster's ranch hands.
❑ Ray Teal (Sheriff Roy Coffee in *Bonanza*) as Foster's ramrod.

Memorable Noir Moment:
❑ When the sheriff questions DeFore about a shootout that ended in his opponent's death, the gunman replies, "While he was shootin' first, I was shootin' careful."

Rancho Notorious (1952) 89 min. Marlene Dietrich, Arthur Kennedy, Mel Ferrer, Lloyd Gough, Gloria Henry. **Screenplay by:** Daniel Taradash. **Directed by:** Fritz Lang. **Noir Type:** Horse Opera. **Noir Themes:** Revenge, sexual hostility, jealousy. ★★★★

Cowhand Kennedy, hell-bent on vengeance, searches for the killer (Gough) who raped and murdered his fiancée (Henry). Along the way, Kennedy meets up with a suave outlaw (Ferrer), who brings him to the "Chuck-a-Luck," a ranch named after a game of chance and owned by Ferrer's lover, former saloon entertainer Dietrich. The ranch serves as a haven for on-the-run outlaws, who pay Dietrich a ten percent cut of their loot for the privilege of hiding out there. When Kennedy notices that Dietrich is wearing the diamond brooch he had given to Henry on the day she was killed, he realizes that the killer, whose face he has never seen, is also at the ranch. But, as he soon learns, asking too many questions in an outlaw's den may get him killed. Dietrich falls for the handsome young cowboy, causing Ferrer, the fastest gun in the West, to seethe with jealousy. This unusual tale of "hate, murder, and revenge" (as the movie's silly theme song reminds us over and over) works well thanks to fine performances by the entire cast and expert direction by noir icon Fritz Lang. Reportedly, the film was supposed to have been called *Chuck-a-Luck*, but because it was feared that Europeans wouldn't understand it, the title was changed to *Rancho Notorious*. Gloria Henry went on to play Dennis' mom on TV's *Dennis the Menace*.

Familiar Faces from Television:
❑ George Reeves (Superman/Clark Kent in *The Adventures of Superman*) as a scar-faced outlaw.
❑ Jack Elam (George Taggert in *Temple Houston*) as an outlaw who'd rather not split his loot with Dietrich.
❑ Frank Ferguson (Gus the ranch hand in *My Friend Flicka*) as an outlaw preacher.

❑ Russell Johnson (the Professor in *Gilligan's Island*) as a wheel spinner in a gambling house owned by William Frawley (Fred Mertz on *I Love Lucy* and Uncle Bub on *My Three Sons*).
❑ John Doucette (Jim Weston in *Lock Up* and Captain Andrews in *The Partners*) as an outlaw with long white hair.

Memorable Noir Moment:

❑ Kennedy sweet-talks the gullible Dietrich into disclosing the information he needs to find his fiancée's killer. "I like a woman that's sometimes cold like ice, sometimes burning like the sun," he tells her, adding, "a pipe dream in blue jeans or in a birthday suit."

Raw Deal (1948) 79 min. Dennis O'Keefe, Claire Trevor, Marsha Hunt, John Ireland, Raymond Burr. **Screenplay by:** Leopold Atlas and John C. Higgins. **Directed by:** Anthony Mann. **Noir Type:** On the Run. **Noir Themes:** Obsession, betrayal, sadism. ★★★½

O'Keefe plays an escaped convict on the run with his moll (Trevor). Along the way they grab a hostage (Hunt) who works for O'Keefe's lawyer. O'Keefe and Hunt eventually fall for each other, leaving the jealous Trevor feeling like a third wheel. Burr is the hood O'Keefe took the rap for, and Ireland is Burr's vicious henchman. The cast in this hard-boiled and fast-paced noir is excellent, especially Trevor as the lovesick tag-a-long.

Memorable Noir Moments:

❑ Burr, annoyed because his girlfriend spilled a drink on him, tosses a burning flambé in her face. (See *The Big Heat* for similar heroics by Lee Marvin and *Abandoned*, where Burr gets his comeuppance.)
❑ From the Stupid Criminal Department: It's such a dark and foggy noir night in Corkscrew Alley that the two dopey hoods lying in wait for O'Keefe wind up plugging each other. (See *Raw Deal, Knock on Any Door, The Long Wait* and *Escape in the Fog* for more dumb thugs.)

Rawhide (1951) 86 min. Tyrone Power, Susan Hayward, Hugh Marlowe, Dean Jagger, Edgar Buchanan, Jack Elam, George Tobias. **Screenplay by:** Dudley Nichols. **Directed by:** Henry Hathaway. **Noir Type:** Horse Opera. **Noir Themes:** Greed, sexual hostility, betrayal, woman in jeopardy, child in jeopardy. ★★★

Power and Buchanan operate the relay station at Rawhide Pass, a stopover for stagecoaches traveling the Overland Trail between San Francisco and St. Louis (a twenty-five-day trip "when the weather and Injuns behave"). When it's reported that escaped killer Marlowe and his gang (Jagger, Elam and Tobias) are in the area, passenger Hayward and her little niece are forced off the stage and stranded at the station because of a company rule that forbids placing children in harm's way. Unfortunately for them, the gang shows up at the station with plans to rob a stagecoach carrying a hundred thousand dollars in gold. After killing Buchanan, the outlaws take Power and Hayward captive, believing them to be husband and wife, and settle back to wait for the stage. Meanwhile, the lecherous Elam has his evil eye on Hayward, jeopardizing Marlowe's daring plan. This is a nicely done suspense Western with acting kudos going to Hayward, Marlowe and the ever-villainous Elam.

Familiar Face from Television:

❑ Kenneth Tobey (Chuck Martin in *The Whirlybirds*) as a cavalry officer.

Memorable Noir Moment:

❑ Marlowe has some noirish advice for his hostage, Power. "When you get a little older and some of the green wears off of you," he says, "you'll learn never to trust anyone with anything."

Rear Window (1954) 112 min. James Stewart, Grace Kelly, Wendell Corey, Thelma Ritter, Raymond Burr. **Screenplay by**: John Michael Hayes. **Directed by**: Alfred Hitchcock. **Noir Type**: Impersonator. **Noir Themes**: Obsession, paranoia. ★★★★★

Stylish, suspenseful and masterfully directed, this Hitchcock classic stars Stewart as a magazine news photographer who, while confined to his apartment with a broken leg, becomes obsessed with spying on his neighbors. Sitting in his wheelchair in front of his apartment's rear window, Stewart watches the occupants of the building across the courtyard as they go about their daily routines—the spinster, whom he's labeled "Miss Lonely Hearts"; "Miss Torso," the sexy ballet dancer; the frustrated songwriter; the newlyweds (the only neighbors who keep their shades drawn most of the time); the couple who sleep on their fire escape because of the sweltering heat; and a costume jewelry salesman (Burr) and his invalid wife, who fight often. During one of Stewart's all night-long vigils, he witnesses some strange happenings in Burr's apartment, leading him to believe that the salesman has murdered and dismembered his wife. He shares his suspicions with his beautiful, marriage-minded girlfriend (Kelly), who at first scoffs at his wild imagination. Next, he phones his war buddy (Corey), a New York City cop, who reluctantly investigates. Before long, Stewart converts both Kelly and his private nurse (Ritter) to his addictive voyeurism, and convinces them that Burr is indeed a wife killer. The impatient Kelly and Ritter decide to play amateur detective. Based on a story by pulp writer Cornell Woolrich, *Rear Window* is one of Hitchcock's best. Stewart and Kelly are sensational, and pretty sexy, too, and Burr, although he has only a few lines, is truly menacing. The American Film Institute ranged *Rear Window* as number 42 on its List of America's 100 Greatest Movies.

Familiar Face from Television:

❑ Frank Cady (Doc Williams in *The Adventures of Ozzie and Harriet* and Sam Drucker in *Petticoat Junction* and *Green Acres*) as the man who sleeps on the fire escape.

Memorable Noir Moments:

❑ While Stewart's songwriting neighbor plays his latest composition, Kelly asks, "Where does a man get inspiration to write a song like that?" Ever the romantic, Stewart replies, "He gets it from the landlady, once a month."
❑ Disappointed to learn that Burr may not have murdered his wife, Kelly admits to Stewart that "we're two of the most frightening ghouls I've ever known."

Rebecca (1940) 130 min. Laurence Olivier, Joan Fontaine, Judith Anderson, George Sanders, Nigel Bruce, Florence Bates. **Screenplay by**: Joan Harrison and Robert E. Sherwood. **Directed by**: Alfred Hitchcock. **Noir Type**: Newlywed. **Noir Themes**: Obsession, fatalism, jealousy, woman in jeopardy. ★★★★

Fontaine, the dowdy traveling companion of an American dowager (Bates), meets and marries widower Olivier after a whirlwind romance in Monte Carlo. When they return to his magnificent estate outside of London, the timid Fontaine is unable to assume the role of mistress of the house because the sinister housekeeper (Anderson) already seems to be doing the job quite well, thank you, since the death of her beloved mistress, Rebecca, Olivier's deceased wife. With reminders of Rebecca strewn around the mansion and Olivier endlessly moping about, Fontaine tries gamely but futilely to get her husband's mind off of his first wife and onto her. Sanders plays Rebecca's favorite cousin, and Bruce is the estate's manager. Some hardcore crime fans might have a problem with all of the "old boys" and "my dears," but Anderson's portrayal of the malignant, probably lesbian, housekeeper, obsessed with her dead mistress, is phenomenal and helps make this classic worthy of repeat viewings. Hitchcock scored big with this, his first American film, with Academy Awards for Best Picture and Best Black and White Cinematography. Other nominations included Best Actor (Olivier), Best Actress (Fontaine), Best Supporting Actress (Anderson), and Best Screenplay.

Familiar Face from Television:
- ❏ Leo G. Carroll (Cosmo Topper in *Topper* and Mr. Waverly in *The Man from U.N.C.L.E.*) as a London doctor.

Memorable Noir Moments:
- ❏ Fontaine's dirty-minded employer (Bates) suspects there's a reason for her quick engagement to Olivier. "Tell me, have you been doing anything you shouldn't?" she asks.
- ❏ When Olivier proposes to her, the puzzled Fontaine, showing her need for a good self-esteem course, responds, "I'm not the sort of person men marry."

The Reckless Moment (1949) 83 min. James Mason, Joan Bennett, Geraldine Brooks, Roy Roberts, Shepperd Strudwick. **Screenplay by:** Henry Garson and Robert W. Soderberg. **Directed by:** Max Ophüls. **Noir Type:** Blackmail. **Noir Themes:** Guilt, victim of fate. ★★★½

Bennett is a well-to-do wife and mother, whose 17-year-old daughter (Brooks) is seeing an older man (Strudwick) against her wishes. When she confronts the shady character, he offers to break off the relationship—for a price. Bennett refuses and promptly informs her daughter about Strudwick's proposition. At first, Brooks doesn't believe her, but when she and Strudwick secretly meet outside the family boathouse, he admits his treachery. Brooks strikes him with a flashlight and runs away, and when Strudwick tries to follow, he becomes dizzy and falls over a railing, landing on an anchor in the sand. The next day, Bennett discovers the body and hides it. After the cops find the dead man, Mason, who works for small-time hood Roberts, shows up with Brooks' love letters to Strudwick and blackmails Bennett. Bennett is impressive as the strong-willed woman who, with her husband away on business in Europe, must face a dangerous crisis alone. Mason does a fine job as the sympathetic blackmailer who finds himself strangely attracted to his victim.

Familiar Face from Television:
- ❏ William Schallert (Patty's dad from *The Patty Duke Show*) as a police lieutenant.

Memorable Noir Moments:
- ❏ From the Some-Things-Never-Change Department: When Bennett tells her daughter that she too was once 17, the girl retorts, "When you're 17 today, you know what the score is."

❑ After dragging Strudwick's body into a motorboat and dumping it miles away, Bennett first words out of her motherly mouth are to her unkempt son. "Roll down your pants and button your jacket," she tells him.

The Red House (1947) 100 min. Edward G. Robinson, Lon McCallister, Allene Roberts, Judith Anderson, Rory Calhoun, Julie London. **Screenplay by:** Delmer Daves. **Directed by:** Delmer Daves. **Noir Type:** Cover-Up. **Noir Themes:** Character deterioration, paranoia, guilt. ★★★½

Robinson, a crippled farmer with a dark secret that has driven him mad and paralyzed him with fear, and his devoted sister (Anderson) discourage their ward (Roberts) from venturing into the surrounding woods to locate an ominous red house. Hired hand McCallister can't be stopped, however, and he and Roberts join forces to uncover a 15-year-old mystery. Gorgeous Julie London is McCallister's fickle high school sweetheart, and Calhoun is the armed guardian of the woods. Strong performances, eerie photography, and a haunting musical score do wonders for this otherwise slow-moving noir.

Memorable Noir Moment:
❑ A film noir cop actually fires a warning shot over the head of a fleeing, unarmed suspect rather than unhesitatingly plugging him in the back. (See *The Crimson Kimono* for an equally considerate noir cop.)

Red Light (1949) 83 min. George Raft, Virginia Mayo, Gene Lockhart, Henry (Harry) Morgan, Raymond Burr, Arthur Franz, Barton MacLane. **Screenplay by:** George Callahan. **Directed by:** Roy Del Ruth. **Noir Type:** Religion. **Noir Themes:** Revenge. ★★★

Raft plays a trucking firm owner whose brother (Franz), a Catholic chaplain, returns from the war to pastor his own church. Unfortunately, convict Burr hires his soon-to-be-released cellmate (Morgan) to kill the priest to get even with Raft, who had Burr sent to prison for embezzlement. When Raft shows up at his brother's hotel room, he finds Franz has been seriously wounded and asks him who did it; just before dying, Franz replies that it's written in the Bible. After futilely searching his brother's Bible for a clue, Raft remembers that all hotel rooms contain Gideon Bibles and goes back to retrieve it. When he discovers that the Good Book is gone, he hunts down each hotel guest who occupied the room after his brother's murder. During his search, he meets Mayo and hires her to help him find the missing book. Meanwhile, Burr, who's just been released from prison, starts worrying that he might be implicated in the murder if the Bible is found. Lockhart plays Raft's impatient business partner, and MacLane is the tough homicide detective assigned to the case. Despite its religious overtones and its tendency to be preachy, *Red Light* is a fast-moving tale of murder and revenge, with Burr terrific as usual.

Familiar Face from Television:
❑ William Frawley (Fred Mertz on *I Love Lucy* and Uncle Bub on *My Three Sons*) as a hotel clerk.

Memorable Noir Moment:
❑ When it's suggested to Raft that his murdered brother wouldn't have wanted him to seek revenge, he spits out, "The meek shall inherit the earth. Yeah! Six feet of it."

The Red Menace

The Red Menace (1949) 81 min. Robert Rockwell, Hannelore Axman, Shepard Menken, Barbara Fuller, Betty Lou Gerson, Duke Williams. **Screenplay by**: Albert DeMond and Gerald Geraghty. **Directed by**: R.G. Springsteen. **Noir Type**: Commie. **Noir Themes**: Conspiracy, paranoia, betrayal, social reform. ★★½

Rockwell stars as an angry ex–G.I. who, after being taken in by a real estate scam, is tempted by the Communist Party pitch that only it cares about the anguished cries of neglected veterans. When he meets the lovely Axman, an immigrant Party member and Marxism teacher, Rockwell is reeled in. But he soon becomes aware of the negatives of his new lifestyle — murder, ostracism, and suicide. Together, he and Axman go on the lam, fleeing Commie goon squads and immigration agents, who they fear might deport Axman for lying about her Party membership on a residency application. Fuller plays a lass who, despite pleadings from her elderly mom and parish priest, seduces recruits for the Party. Her poet lover and comrade (Menken) isn't thrilled about her role as a siren, but accepts it manfully. Yet, when his superiors criticize his poetry, he tears up his Party membership card in a patriotic temper tantrum. Femme fatale Gerson, another gorgeous Commie babe, is the true believer in the bunch, and she'll stop at nothing to advance the cause (and her own rise to power). In the 1940s and 1950s, blacks were portrayed stereotypically in films as janitors, porters, servants, and, if they were lucky, musicians. (See **When Strangers Marry** for one of the few interesting exceptions to the rule.) Yet, ironically, one of the more sympathetic and intelligent characters in this film is a black reporter (Williams) for a Communist Party newspaper. This enjoyable propaganda piece about foreign powers infiltrating the good old U.S. of A. in the form of atheistic Communism has been trashed over the years as another badly made Red scare film. However, the plot is intelligently structured, the acting is competent, and, if the Red Scare hoopla isn't taken too seriously, some viewers might actually have a good time watching this unintentionally funny noir. Rockwell went on to play the shy biology teacher, Mr. Boynton, Eve Arden's love interest, in the successful 1950s TV series *Our Miss Brooks*.

Memorable Noir Moment:

❏ The narrator (a member of the Los Angeles City Council) describes Rockwell as "a misguided young man, fallen under the spell of Marxian hatred and revenge, unaware that he's only the tool of men who would destroy his country."
❏ Sensitivity Training Required: Williams' editor, showing his true Commie face, remarks that the comrades have been "wasting our time on those African ingrates."

Reign of Terror

Reign of Terror (1949) 89 min. Robert Cummings, Arlene Dahl, Richard Hart, Arnold Moss, Richard Basehart, Charles McGraw. **Screenplay by**: Philip Yordan and Aeneas MacKenzie. **Directed by**: Anthony Mann. **Noir Type**: Period. **Noir Themes**: Paranoia, corruption. ★★★

Cummings stars as an undercover agent working for the exiled Marquis de Lafayette during the French Revolution. He assumes the identity of an infamous executioner, while seeking to retrieve a black book containing the "hit list" of the power hungry Robespierre (Basehart), "a fanatic with powdered wig and twisted mind." To ensure that Basehart does not become dictator of France, Cummings and his former lover (Dahl) must gain possession of the book without arousing the suspicions of

A French revolutionary (Robert Cummings) and his co-conspirator (Arlene Dahl) in *Reign of Terror* (Walter Wanger, 1949).

Basehart's right-hand man (Hart) and the sadistic chief of the secret police (Moss), who's sitting on both sides of the espionage fence. Noir veteran McGraw plays Basehart's vicious sergeant-at-arms. Beautiful noir photography by cinematographer John Alton, a fast-moving script, and good performances, especially by Moss, all add up to an enjoyable action yarn. Also known as *The Black Book*.

Familiar Faces from Television:
❑ Russ Tamblyn (Dr. Lawrence Jacoby in *Twin Peaks*) as a farmer's son.
❑ John Doucette (Jim Weston in *Lock Up* and Captain Andrews in *The Partners*) as a anti–Robespierre farmer.

Memorable Noir Moments:
❑ When Basehart orders Moss to meet with the infamous executioner, "the terror of Strasbourg," Moss asks how he will be able to identify him. "One snake to the other," Basehart answers. "You'll smell each other out."
❑ Hiding behind locked doors, Basehart and Hart prepare to face an angry mob. The terrified Hart worries that they'll be torn apart. "I made the mob," the overconfident Basehart tells him. "The mob are my children. They won't turn against their father."

Repeat Performance (1947) 91 min. Louis Hayward, Joan Leslie, Richard Basehart, Virginia Field, Tom Conway, Natalie Schafer. **Screenplay by:** Walter Bullock. **Directed by:** Alfred L. Werker. **Noir Type:** Fantasy. **Noir Themes:** Victim of fate, obsession, fatalism, betrayal, character deterioration. ★★★

New Year's Eve, 1947. Broadway actress Leslie shoots and kills her adulterous, alcoholic husband, has-been playwright Hayward. After confiding in her poet friend Basehart (in his film debut), Leslie wishes that she had the year to live over so she could do things differently. Surprisingly, her wish is granted and she discovers that Hayward is still alive. The actress thinks she's tricked destiny, but the same events seem to be reoccurring—Hayward still meets and falls in love with Field, a femme fatale playwright; the neurotic Basehart, despite Leslie's warnings, still hooks up with a wealthy, fickle patron of the arts (Schafer); and Leslie accepts the starring role in a hit Broadway play written by her romantic rival. Meanwhile, the holidays are fast approaching and Leslie can't help but be concerned about Hayward's growing obsession with Field. The intriguing premise suffers from Hayward's overacting and a script filled with holes, but somehow the film manages to fascinate until the surprise ending, which the alert viewer will probably see coming.

Memorable Noir Moments:

❏ Sensitivity Training Required: Leslie wonders why Hayward is questioning her judgment about whether or not to accept a role. The playwright responds sharply, "You're only a woman. You're not expected to have either judgment *or* intelligence."

❏ A tipsy, candid Hayward tells Basehart, "You're the only true friend I've got and that's embarrassing because I don't like you."

❏ On visiting day at the asylum, Leslie asks the recently committed Basehart, "Is it terrible?" "Terrible?" he replies with a grin. "I sort of like it. It's sort of home-like." Shocked, Leslie responds, "Home-like? *This*?" "You didn't know my home," Basehart answers.

The Return of the Whistler (1948) 63 min. Michael Duane, Lenore Aubert, Richard Lane. **Screenplay by:** Edward Bock and Maurice Tombragel. **Directed by:** D. Ross Lederman. **Noir Type:** Missing Person. **Noir Themes:** Woman in jeopardy, greed, family dysfunction. ★★½

Ready to tie the knot after knowing each other for only several weeks, Duane and his fiancée Aubert visit a justice of the peace in a small town. Unfortunately, the civil servant is away on business and the couple decide to spend the night at a local inn. But when the obnoxious desk clerk won't let them share the only available room because they're not married, Duane spends the night at the auto repair shop seeing to a car problem. When he returns to the hotel, to find that Aubert is missing, he hires a private investigator (Lane) to locate her. Based on a Cornell Woolrich story, this last film in the Whistler series is interesting, with Duane and Lane giving good performances. But without Richard Dix (who starred in the other seven Whistler films), there's an obvious void. (See also *The Whistler, Mark of the Whistler, Power of the Whistler, Voice of the Whistler, Mysterious Intruder, Secret of the Whistler* and *The Thirteenth Hour.*) Veteran character actor Dick Lane went on to become a well-known wrestling, roller derby and midget car racing announcer in the Los Angeles area.

Memorable Noir Moment:

❑ While filling in P.I. Lane on how he discovered his fiancée was missing, Duane dreamily wanders off track. "Alice wasn't just a starry-eyed kid," he says. "Life had kicked her around quite a bit." "Stick to the facts, Ted," the bored P.I. says.

Revolt in the Big House (1958) 79 min. Gene Evans, Robert Blake, Timothy Carey, John Qualen, Frank Richards, John Dennis, Walter Barnes. **Screenplay by:** Daniel Hyatt and Eugene Lourie. **Directed by:** R.G. Springsteen. **Noir Type:** Prison. **Noir Themes:** Betrayal, fatalism, paranoia, victim of fate. ★★★

While a ruthless gangster (Evans) lies dying in the hospital after a shoot-out with cops in a New York City subway station, a flashback vividly portrays his short time in the joint and how he engineered a daring escape. After serving only a few months of his twenty-year sentence, Evans teams up with four other cons, oldtimer Qualen, Carey and Carey's flunkies Richards and Dennis. Evans' cellmate, a young Latino (Blake) wrongly convicted of armed robbery, works in the auto shop and would be helpful to Evans' escape plan. But the boy wants to play it straight in the hopes of being paroled after three years. Evans ensures that Blake loses his shot at early release by planting a knife on him and seeing to it that he gets the blame for cutting another prisoner. A bigoted guard (Barnes) is more than happy to rough Blake up a bit and send him to solitary. When he's released from solitary, the disillusioned kid is ready to join in the plan, which involves a prison riot and a surprise that only Evans knows about. This is an entertaining low-budget flick with Carey highly enjoyable in his usual psycho role, and young Blake (TV's *Baretta*) doing a good job as the former gang member who wants to go straight. Evans, as always, is terrific.

Familiar Faces from Television:

❑ Frank Ferguson (Gus the ranch hand in *My Friend Flicka*) as Evans' attorney.
❑ Robert Shayne (Inspector Henderson in *The Adventures of Superman*) as the prison guard in charge of Evans.

Memorable Noir Moment:

❑ Prisoner Carey, who can't understand why the guards won't give him a job in the warehouse, complains, "They're actin' like I was a criminal or somethin'."

Ride Lonesome (1959) 74 min. Randolph Scott, Karen Steele, Pernell Roberts, James Best, Lee Van Cleef, James Coburn. **Screenplay by:** Burt Kennedy. **Directed by:** Budd Boetticher. **Noir Type:** Horse Opera. **Noir Themes:** Revenge, obsession. ★★★

Scott plays a bounty hunter taking a murderer (Best) back to town to hang. Along the way, he meets up with a band of renegade Mescaleros, a sexy widow (Steele), and a couple of outlaws (Roberts and Coburn) who would like to be the ones to turn Best in so they can gain amnesty for their crimes. But the resolute Scott plans to hold on to his prisoner for reasons of his own. Meanwhile, Best's brother (Van Cleef) is riding hard and fast to Best's rescue. Sixty-one-year-old Scott looks terrific and is believable as the secretive bounty hunter with a tragic past. Coburn makes an auspicious film debut as a slow-witted outlaw who'd rather be slopping hogs, and Best (the sheriff from TV's *The Dukes of Hazzard*) is good as the giggling psychopath. The beautiful Steele also gives a good performance and, with her Jayne Mansfield figure, has quite a few profile shots. Roberts went on to star in TV's *Bonanza* and *Trapper John, M.D.*

Memorable Noir Moments:
❑ When Coburn learns that the Indians are planning to attack, he complains that "we ain't done nothin' to 'em." "We're white," Roberts reminds him, adding, "That's good enough."
❑ The lecherous Coburn wonders if widow Steele will ever remarry. Roberts confidently argues that she will because her eyes tell him that "she's the kind that's got a need, a deep, lonely need that only a man can get at."

Ride the Pink Horse (1947) 101 min. Robert Montgomery, Thomas Gomez, Wanda Hendrix, Art Smith, Fred Clark, Andrea King, Richard Gaines. **Screenplay by:** Ben Hecht and Charles Lederer. **Directed by:** Robert Montgomery. **Noir Type:** Blackmail. **Noir Themes:** Revenge, fatalism, betrayal. ★★★★

A tough World War II veteran (Montgomery) seeking the gangster (Clark) responsible for a friend's murder, arrives in a small New Mexico town during the annual festival. When he finds Clark, he picks up where his buddy left off—black-

A wounded Army veteran (Robert Montgomery) and a local Indian girl (Wanda Hendrix) seek help from bartender Martin Garralaga in *Ride the Pink Horse* (Universal-International, 1947).

mailing the hood with a copy of the $100,000 check that Clark used to pay off a politician. With a little help from Gomez, the friendly Mexican owner of a carousel, and a strange Indian girl (Hendrix), Montgomery must elude Clark's knife-wielding thugs, who want to retrieve the check without paying him for it. Meanwhile, a middle-aged G-man (Smith) is tailing the veteran, hoping to get his hands on the evidence that will send Clark to the penitentiary. King plays Clark's scheming moll, and Gaines is his right-hand man. This film is different, exciting, and well-acted, with Gomez giving a standout performance. Montgomery is excellent as the hard-boiled veteran who "fought a war for three years and got nothing out of it but a dangle of ribbons."

Familiar Face from Television:

❏ John Doucette (Jim Weston in *Lock Up* and Captain Andrews in *The Partners*) as one of Clark's thugs.

Memorable Noir Moments:

❏ Carousel operator Gomez shares his questionable success formula with Montgomery. "Some peoples happy when they got money," he says. "Me, I'm only happy when I got nothing."
❏ When Smith appeals to Montgomery's sense of patriotism, the war-weary vet cuts him short. "Look, copper, don't wave any flags at me," he tells him. "I've seen enough flags."
❏ Hendrix is confused when Montgomery refers to women as "babies." "Babies is what you call dames," he explains. "They're dead fish with a lot of perfume on them."

Riff-Raff (1947) 80 min. Pat O'Brien, Anne Jeffreys, Walter Slezak, Jerome Cowan, Marc Krah. **Screenplay by:** Martin Rackin. **Directed by:** Ted Tetzlaff. **Noir Type:** P.I. **Noir Themes:** Greed. ★★★½

O'Brien plays a tough American P.I. in Panama named Hammer (no, not *that* Hammer). He's hired by bad guy Krah (who recently pushed someone out of an airplane to steal an oil field map) as his bodyguard. Not one to worry about conflict of interest, O'Brien takes on another client, oil executive Cowan, who hires him to find Krah and the stolen map. Unfortunately, Krah doesn't last an hour under O'Brien's protection before he's murdered in his bathtub. Slezak and his goons then show up, also seeking the map, which Krah has hidden in plain sight on a bulletin board in O'Brien's office. Distrustful of O'Brien, Cowan sends his girlfriend (nightclub singer Jeffreys) to spy on him, and, of course, she quickly falls in love with the portly, middle-aged private dick. This fast-paced, beautifully photographed noir is witty and entertaining, with O'Brien giving an interesting twist to the hard-boiled private investigator role. Jeffreys later went on to star in the popular TV comedy *Topper* with her husband, Robert Sterling.

Memorable Noir Moment:

❏ When O'Brien won't spill the beans about the location of a map, Slezak has his two brawny hoods work him over, causing the unflinching gumshoe to quip, "I hope you didn't hire these kids by the hour."

Rififi (1955-French) 118 min. Jean Servais, Carl Möhner, Robert Manuel, Jules Dassin (credited as Perlo Vita), Magali Noel, Robert Hossein. **Screenplay by:** Jules Dassin, René Wheeler and Auguste Le Breton. **Directed by:** Jules Dassin. **Noir Type:** Heist. **Noir Themes:** Greed, revenge, betrayal, sexual hostility. ★★★★★

Ex-con Servais, released after serving a five-year prison sentence, masterminds a jewelry store heist in Paris. Servais and his gang (Möhner, Dassin and Manuel) meticulously plan and execute the daring caper, walking away with nearly a quarter of a million francs. Convinced they've gotten away with it, the gang relaxes, but Dassin's weakness for a beautiful nightclub singer (Noel) results in a series of noirish mishaps. A rival gangster (Marcel Lupovici) and his drug addict brother (Hossein) want the stolen jewels and will stop at nothing to get them, including kidnapping and murder. Servais is excellent as the tubercular ex-con, and director Dassin does a surprisingly good job as the Italian safecracker who pays a big price for breaking "the rules." Hailed as the progenitor of all heist films by those who must have forgotten about 1950's *The Asphalt Jungle*, *Rififi* (French gangster slang for "trouble") is known for its ingenious 30-minute-long silent heist — no talking, no background music. American director Dassin's first European film after director Edward Dmytryk identified him as a Communist during the House Un-American Activities Committee hearings was 1949's *Night and the City*. The blacklisted director didn't work again until 1955, when he directed this French noir, also known as *Du Rififi chez les Hommes*.

Memorable Noir Moments:

❏ French gangster Servais nixes the use of guns during the heist. "Get caught with a rod," he tells his partners in the subtitled version of a DVD release, "it's the slammer for life." In the less slangy, dubbed version, it's, "With this, you can get a life term in prison."
❏ When a B-girl approaches Möhner in a nightclub, the hood invites her to join his table. "Sit your moneymaker down," he says (according to the subtitles). In the dubbed version, he puts it a more politely, saying merely, "Sit here. Be my guest."

Du Rififi chez les Hommes *see* Rififi

Riot in Cell Block 11 (1954) 80 min. Neville Brand, Emile Meyer, Frank Faylen, Leo Gordon, Robert Osterloh, Whit Bissell. **Screenplay by:** Richard Collins. **Directed by:** Don Siegel. **Noir Type:** Prison. **Noir Themes:** Social reform, corruption. ★★★★

The film opens, documentary-style, with news reports of nationwide penitentiary riots led by "maddened prisoners" demanding improvement in their conditions. In Folsom Prison's punishment block (Cell Block 11), Brand leads a revolt that soon envelops other areas of the prison. Gordon, Brand's psychotic right-hand man, is a homicidal maniac with a grudge against Bissell, one of the more sadistic screws. Osterloh is the imprisoned ex–military officer who helps Brand draw up a list of demands, which Brand presents to the warden (Meyer) in front of an eager press corps. Meyer, a tough but decent administrator, tries to subdue the riot, but interference by the governor's obstinate emissary (Faylen) makes this impossible. This terrific prison noir still packs a powerful punch, thanks to director Siegel and screenwriter Richard Collins, who didn't sacrifice characterization for action and violence, presenting a fair and rational portrayal of both prisoners and guards. Daring for 1954, the film even touches on unwanted homosexual advances in prison. The actors

Convicts (Leo Gordon and Neville Brand) take charge in *Riot in Cell Block 11* (Allied Artists, 1954).

are first-rate, especially B movie veterans Brand as the brains of the riot and Gordon as his enforcer.

Familiar Face from Television:
❑ William Schallert (Patty's dad from *The Patty Duke Show*) as a reporter.

Memorable Noir Moments:
❑ A religious prisoner expresses misgivings about killing the hostages. "I don't think we should kill them," he says, adding, "I don't think God would approve."
❑ From the Some-Things-Never-Change Department: During Brand's press conference, an impatient reporter yells, "You know what we're interested in." "Yeah, mad dogs running wild," the sneering Brand answers.
❑ The warden offers his medical opinion after Faylen has been stabbed: "Just a flesh wound." (See *Accused of Murder, The Enforcer, Guilty Bystander, Jail Bait, New York Confidential* and *Sleep, My Love.*)

Road House (1948) 95 min. Ida Lupino, Cornel Wilde, Richard Widmark, Celeste Holm. **Screenplay by:** Edward Chodorov. **Directed by:** Jean Negulesco. **Noir Type:** Triangle. **Noir Themes:** Lust, betrayal, victim of the law. ★★

This film has been hailed as everything from "exciting melodrama" to "neglected noir classic." Frankly, "dull bowling noir" is a more apt description. Lupino plays a singer at a combination lounge and bowling alley owned by the psychopathic Widmark and his friend Wilde. Both men fall for the lovely singer, and when she chooses the handsome Wilde, Widmark freaks out. Unfortunately, he doesn't get to perform his patented psycho act until at least 85 minutes into the movie. Holm kind of hangs around, looking forlorn because Wilde doesn't seem to notice her. There is, however, a pretty good fight scene in the lounge between Wilde and a very large customer who has been fresh with Lupino.

Familiar Face from Television:
❑ Ray Teal (Sheriff Roy Coffee in *Bonanza*) as a cop at the railroad station.

Memorable Noir Moment:
❑ When asked how she likes Lupino's singing, Holm replies, "She does more without a voice than anyone I've ever heard."

Roadblock (1951) 73 min. Charles McGraw, Joan Dixon, Lowell Gilmore, Louis Jean Heydt. **Screenplay by:** George Bricker and Steve Fisher. **Directed by:** Harold Daniels. **Noir Type:** Bad Cop. **Noir Themes:** Obsession, greed. ★★★

This short, tightly plotted film is about an honest insurance detective who goes bad over a money-hungry dame. Square-jawed McGraw falls hard for the gorgeous Dixon, but he's only a lousy $340-a-month working stiff and she has bigger plans. So, hoping to win her love, he plans a heist with a shady nightclub owner (Gilmore). The twist is that Dixon reforms and falls for McGraw despite his lower middle-class status, but he's so insecure that he goes ahead with the robbery anyway, beginning his slow descent into corruption and murder. Heydt plays McGraw's detective partner. A solid character actor known for his many small parts in films noirs, McGraw is excellent in one of his few leading roles. Dixon is quite good as the femme fatale with second thoughts. With surprise endings fairly common in films noirs, *Roadblock* contains a very clever "surprise beginning."

Familiar Face from Television:
❑ Milburn Stone ("Doc" in *Gunsmoke*) as a cop investigating the big robbery.

Memorable Noir Moment:
❑ A hood leads McGraw to a mausoleum, where he's hidden $100 Gs from a recent heist. "My uncle's grave," he explains. "He was always good at keeping money, so I thought I'd let him keep mine safe."

Rogue Cop (1954) 87 min. Robert Taylor, Janet Leigh, George Raft, Steve Forrest, Anne Francis, Peter Brocco. **Screenplay by:** Sydney Boehm. **Directed by:** Roy Rowland. **Noir Type:** Bad Cop. **Noir Themes:** Corruption, betrayal, greed. ★★★

Taylor, a cop on the take, is an embarrassment to his fellow officers and to his rookie brother (Forrest). When Forrest witnesses the escape of a small-time hood (Brocco) who has just knifed a rival, he and Taylor team up to track down the killer. Because Brocco has been blackmailing mob boss Raft over a murder he once committed, Raft orders Taylor to make sure his brother doesn't identify Brocco in court. Turning down Raft's substantial bribe, Forrest refuses to cooperate. Fearing that Raft will have his brother killed, Taylor tries to get Forrest's girl (Leigh) to convince him to take the dough. Francis (TV's *Honey West*) plays Raft's alcoholic moll. Taylor's fine performance as a bad cop who thinks that his fellow officers are $75-a-week suckers is what makes this predictable crime drama work so well. Forrest, the real-life younger brother of noir icon Dana Andrews, later starred in the short-lived TV series *The Baron* and *S.W.A.T.*

Familiar Faces from Television:
❑ Vince Edwards (*Ben Casey*) as a hit man.
❑ Ray Teal (Sheriff Coffee in *Bonanza*) as a uniformed cop at an apartment building elevator.
❑ Soon-to-be castaways on *Gilligan's Island*, Alan Hale, Jr. (The Skipper) and Russell Johnson (the Professor) play a mob goon and a patrolman, respectively.
❑ Richard Deacon (Mel Cooley from *The Dick Van Dyke Show*) cast against type as a mob henchman.
❑ Olive Carey (Macdonald Carey's secretary in *Lock Up*) as a newspaper stand vendor and Taylor's street snitch.

Memorable Noir Moments:
❑ Taylor throws her tainted past in Leigh's face. "I know you too well," he says. "We're the same kind of people, the same kind of dirt."
❑ Taylor gets philosophical when arresting hit man Edwards, saying, "We're big and tough. That's why we wind up like this. Little men begging for a break." Insulted, Edwards asks, "*Who's* little?" Handcuffing the killer, Taylor replies, "You're little enough to fit in the chair. That's all that matters."

Rope of Sand (1949) 104 min. Burt Lancaster, Paul Henreid, Claude Rains, Peter Lorre, Corinne Calvet, Sam Jaffe. **Screenplay by:** Walter Doniger and John Paxton. **Directed by:** William Dieterle. **Noir Type:** Adventure. **Noir Themes:** Victim of fate, greed, revenge, obsession. ★★½

A hunter, lured by the promise of easy riches, leaves his guide (Lancaster) and goes into the "forbidden zone," a diamond-rich area of South Africa controlled by the local mining company. When Lancaster finds his client in the desert dying of exposure, he leaves behind the diamonds that the man found and attempts to carry him back to civilization. Eventually they are picked up by the mining company's security police, headed by the villainous Henreid, who, when the hunter dies, tortures Lancaster for the location of the missing diamonds. When Lancaster refuses to talk, Henreid revokes his hunting license and has him deported. Two years later, Lancaster returns, vowing "to get what I already paid for." The mining company manager (Rains) hires a "cheap Cape Town trollop" (Calvet) to play Lancaster and Henreid against each other and to pump the former guide about the location of the diamonds. But, underestimating Lancaster's charms, Calvet falls in love with him. Lorre has a small role as a local hustler, and Jaffe is the company's alcoholic doctor. Rains, Lorre and Henreid co-starred in the classic ***Casablanca*** seven years earlier. They don't fair quite so well here, but, along with Lancaster, they help make this adventure film reasonably entertaining.

Familiar Face from Television:
❑ Hayden Rorke (Dr. Bellows in *I Dream of Jeannie*) as the hunter with diamond fever.

Memorable Noir Moments:

❑ Diamond fever is rampant even among the mining company's security police — a guard (Mike Mazurki) tries to smuggle out a diamond embedded in an open wound. Ouch.

❑ Calvet pleads with Lancaster, who's just been beaten by Henreid's security cops, to give up his plan to retrieve the diamonds. Gritting his teeth in pain, Lancaster tells her that "I'd crawl out of the grave to get what I came after."

The Rough and the Smooth *see* Portrait of a Sinner

Roughshod (1949) 88 min. Robert Sterling, Gloria Grahame, Claude Jarman, Jr., John Ireland, Jeff Donnell, Myrna Dell, Martha Hyer, Jeff Corey. **Screenplay by:** Hugo Butler and Daniel Mainwaring [as Geoffrey Homes]. **Directed by:** Mark Robson. **Noir Type:** Horse Opera. **Noir Themes:** Revenge, paranoia. ★★★

While leading a herd of horses to their ranch, Sterling and his kid brother (Jarman) meet up with four dance hall girls (Grahame, Donnell, Dell and Hyer), who have been run out of town by morally indignant citizens. Sparks fly between Grahame and Sterling, but the cowboy is more than a little hesitant about getting serious with "that kind of woman." Meanwhile, three escaped convicts are headed in their direction and the ringleader (Ireland) is seeking to settle a score with Sterling. This one's short on action but there are plenty of interesting characters, with Grahame turning in a good performance as the saloon girl with a hankering to settle down.

Familiar Face from Television:

❑ Stanley Andrews ("The Old Ranger," host of *Death Valley Days*) as the town blacksmith.

Memorable Noir Moment:

❑ From the Some-Things-Never-Change Department: A wagon driver (Corey) lends a helping hand when Graham's wagon gets stuck on the trail. "Never was a woman who knew how to handle a team," he complains. "Shouldn't let 'em loose on the roads."

Ruby Gentry (1952) 82 min. Jennifer Jones, Charlton Heston, Karl Malden, Barney Phillips, Tom Tully, James Anderson, Josephine Hutchinson. **Screenplay by:** Silvia Richards. **Directed by:** King Vidor. **Noir Type:** Femme Fatale. **Noir Themes:** Obsession, lust, revenge, jealousy, character deterioration. ★★

Jones stars as a coquettish spitfire from the wrong side of the tracks in rural North Carolina. Raised in poverty, at sixteen she moves in with the wealthy Malden to care for his terminally ill wife (Hutchinson). When Jones' boyfriend (Heston) returns from Central America, she determines to land him for a husband. Heston, while not immune to Jones' charms and not above a discreet romantic tryst, has his own idea of a proper wife and marries a wealthy girl with "brains and breeding." When Hutchinson dies, the middle-aged Malden weds Jones, something he's been itching to do for years. But he soon begins to imagine the worst after seeing his new wife dancing in the arms of her former lover and looking like she's enjoying it. Before it's all over, three people are dead, and the whole town is on the verge economic ruin because of Jones, who eventually becomes a fisherman like her father (Tully). This is a boring film with good performances by Jones as the "strange, gaunt woman" and Anderson as her religious fanatic brother, who considers her the "evil spawn of the devil."

Familiar Faces from Television:
❑ Frank Wilcox (John Brewster in *The Beverly Hillbillies*) as a guest at Tully's hunting lodge.
❑ Barney Phillips (Sgt. Ed Jacobs in *Dragnet*, Capt. Franks in *Felony Squad*, and Maj. Kaiser in *Twelve O'Clock High*) as the doctor.

Memorable Noir Moment:
❑ When Jones grabs her brother's guitar and throws it, he snarls, "I oughta kill you for that." "What's stoppin' you?" she taunts. "You ain't suffered enough yet," he answers.

Run of the Arrow (1957) 86 min. Rod Steiger, Sarita Montiel, Brian Keith, Ralph Meeker, Jay C. Flippen, Charles Bronson, H.M. Wynant. **Screenplay by:** Samuel Fuller. **Directed by:** Samuel Fuller. **Noir Type:** Horse Opera. **Noir Themes:** Fatalism, paranoia, revenge, bigotry. ★★★

A disillusioned Confederate infantryman (Steiger), vowing never to recognize the American flag, heads west at the end of the Civil War. Along the way, he meets a dying, alcoholic Indian scout (Flippen), who teaches him the language and customs of the Sioux; becomes an honorary Sioux warrior after proving himself in the harrowing "run of the arrow" trial; marries a beautiful squaw (Montiel); and suffers an identity crisis when called upon to fight against his fellow white men. Keith is the sympathetic Army captain who tries to convince Steiger that Northerners are people, too, and Meeker is the arrogant lieutenant who can't wait to throw a monkey wrench into the peace agreement between the Sioux and the government. Bronson, showing off his amazing physique, plays a wise chief named Blue Buffalo, and Wynant is Crazy Wolf, the renegade Sioux who hates white men. Steiger, despite his lame Irish brogue, is good as the angry Johnny Reb who fired the last bullet of the Civil War at Appomattox. Meeker is appropriately evil as the recipient of that bullet, which is recast and given to Steiger as a souvenir. Writer-producer-director Fuller ingeniously uses the bullet (the film was originally titled "The Last Bullet") as the ironic catalyst that finally ends Steiger's frustrating indecision. Because of her thick accent, Montiel's voice was dubbed by a young actress named Angie Dickinson, who later became TV's *Police Woman*.

Familiar Faces from Television:
❑ Olive Carey (Macdonald Carey's secretary in *Lock Up* and Elsie in *Mr. Adams and Eve*) as Steiger's old Irish mother.
❑ Frank de Kova (Chief Wild Eagle on *F Troop*) as Chief Red Cloud.

Memorable Noir Moment:
❑ After Army scout Flippen brags that he could have become a Sioux chief, Steiger asks him why he never did. "I can't stomach politics," Flippen replies.

Ruthless (1948) 104 min. Zachary Scott, Louis Hayward, Diana Lynn, Martha Vickers, Sydney Greenstreet, Lucille Bremer. **Screenplay by:** S.K. Lauren and Gordon Kahn. **Directed**

by: Edgar G. Ulmer. **Noir Type:** Ambition. **Noir Themes:** Betrayal, character deterioration, jealousy, revenge. ★★★½

Told via numerous flashbacks, *Ruthless* is the story of heartless tycoon Scott and how he rose from an abusive childhood to unparalleled power on Wall Street. Much like George Sanders in **Death of a Scoundrel,** Scott tramples on everyone along the way, even those who care for him the most — his first love (Lynn), whom he drops for socialite Vickers because it will further his career, and his best friend (Hayward). Greenstreet is a Bible-quoting businessman whose life is ruined by his treacherous competitor, and Bremer is Greenstreet's wife, taken in by Scott's charm. Scott, always so believable as a film noir cad, doesn't disappoint here, and Greenstreet's performance as the cuckolded husband is a dandy.

Familiar Face from Television:

❑ Raymond Burr (*Perry Mason* and *Ironside*) as Scott's absentee father.

Memorable Noir Moment:

❑ An astonished Hayward asks Scott the question that's on everybody's mind: "What are you made of, anyway?" "I'm an adding machine," Scott replies.

San Quentin (1946) 66 min. Lawrence Tierney, Barton MacLane, Marian Carr, Harry Shannon, Joe Devlin, Tony Barrett. **Screenplay by:** Lawrence Kimble, Arthur Ross and Howard J. Green. **Directed by:** Gordon Douglas. **Noir Type:** Prison. **Noir Themes:** Social reform, betrayal, revenge. ★★½

Ex-con Tierney, the founder of the Inmate's Welfare League at San Quentin, returns home from the war to his beautiful fiancée (Carr). He's asked by his former warden (Shannon) to make a speech to a group of wary newspaper reporters, informing them of the virtues of the league, a prisoner organization that ensures that cons stay on their best behavior while preparing them for life on the outside. Tierney and his G.I. buddy (Devlin) are proof positive that the idea works and so, the warden mistakenly believes, is prisoner MacLane, a former bank robber who is actually faking rehabilitation. On the way to meet with reporters, MacLane escapes, and he and his partner (Barrett) go on a robbery and murder spree. Tierney feels obligated to the cons at San Quentin, who have lost all their privileges because of the escape, to hunt MacLane down. Short, fast-moving and violent, this low-budget noir is enjoyable thanks to the gritty performances of Tierney and MacLane. Carr and Tierney would team up again in 1947's **The Devil Thumbs a Ride.**

Familiar Face from Television:

❑ Raymond Burr (*Perry Mason* and *Ironside*) as a cheap hood who sells out MacLane for 100 bucks.

Memorable Noir Moment:

❑ Posing as Burr's wife, Carr pumps his jealous moll about his whereabouts. "Is he hot?" she asks. "He ain't even warm," the woman replies. "He's in the cooler."

Scandal Sheet (1952) 82 min. John Derek, Donna Reed, Broderick Crawford, Rosemary DeCamp, Henry (Harry) Morgan. **Screenplay by:** Ted Sherdeman, Eugene Ling and James

Ace reporter John Derek looks over the shoulder of his murderous editor (Broderick Crawford) in *Scandal Sheet* (Columbia, 1952).

Poe. **Directed by:** Phil Karlson. **Noir Type:** Newspaper. **Noir Themes:** Corruption, paranoia, betrayal. ★★★★

Crawford, the new editor of a large New York newspaper, has been increasing circulation by leaps and bounds. But at what cost? He has turned the paper into a trashy tabloid, "pandering to the passions of the base moron," according to an irate board member. Crawford's ace reporter (Derek) and a wisecracking photographer (Morgan) cover sensational murders for the front page, which irks their more conservative colleague (Reed). At a Lonely Hearts Club dance sponsored by the newspaper, Crawford's wife (DeCamp), whom he abandoned years earlier, threatens to make trouble for him. The editor loses his temper and gets a little too rough with her, accidentally killing her. Faced now with losing his lucrative position, he makes it look like she fell in the bathtub and hit her head on the faucet. Derek smells a bigger story and convinces the cops that it was a murder. To avoid being caught, Crawford now finds he must kill again, even as he reluctantly encourages Derek to dig deeper. Based on a novel by director Samuel Fuller, *Scandal Sheet* is a powerful drama that will keep you on the edge of your seat thanks to a well-crafted script and strong performances by Derek and Crawford.

Memorable Noir Moments:

❑ Sensitivity Training Required: Derek describes photographs of a murdered woman as "very unique items—pictures of a dame with her mouth shut."
❑ Crawford tells the shrewish DeCamp, "I made all of my mistakes when I was young and you were the biggest one. I fell for an attractive hunk of flesh."

The Scar *see* Hollow Triumph

The Scarf (1951) 93 min. John Ireland, Mercedes McCambridge, James Barton, Emlyn Williams, Lloyd Gough. **Screenplay by**: E.A. Dupont. **Directed by**: E.A. Dupont. **Noir Type**: Amnesia. **Noir Themes**: Paranoia, betrayal, guilt. ★★½

Ireland escapes from a hospital for the criminally insane, where he had been imprisoned for strangling a woman with a scarf, a crime he doesn't remember committing. After nearly dying in the desert, he's taken in by a turkey farmer (Barton) who believes he's innocent and gives him a job. Later, Ireland meets up with a singing waitress (McCambridge), who must wrestle with her conscience about whether or not to turn him in for the five thousand dollar reward. When Ireland notices that McCambridge's scarf looks like the one that belonged to the woman he was convicted of strangling, his memory begins to return. Only his best friend (Williams), a psychologist, can help him. An interesting but predictable noir, with Ireland giving a good performance.

Familiar Faces from Television:
❑ Lyle Talbot (Joe Randolph in *The Adventures of Ozzie and Harriet*) as a detective.
❑ King Donovan (Bob Cummings' Air Force buddy Harvey Helm in *Love That Bob* and lawyer Herb Thornton in *Please Don't Eat the Daisies*) as a reporter.

Memorable Noir Moment:
❑ The turkey ranch recluse shares his philosophy about dames. "A woman is man's confusion," he tells Ireland.

Scarlet Street (1945) 102 min. Edward G. Robinson, Joan Bennett, Dan Duryea, Rosalind Ivan, Jess Barker. **Screenplay by**: Dudley Nichols. **Directed by**: Fritz Lang. **Noir Type**: Femme Fatale. **Noir Themes**: Obsession, lust, greed, character deterioration, fatalism, guilt. ★★★★★

Robinson plays a henpecked husband (Little Caesar in an apron!), who uses his umbrella to protect a beautiful woman (Bennett) when she is attacked by what appears to be a mugger but is actually her drunken boyfriend (Duryea). Robinson gets lucky, knocking Duryea out cold and accompanying the damsel home. Flattered by Bennett's attention, Robinson eventually becomes her sugar daddy, setting her up in an expensive apartment and paying for it with embezzled funds. Now if he could only figure a way to get rid of his shrewish wife (Ivan), who keeps an enormous portrait of her late husband in their living room. He would then be free to marry Bennett, a masochist who only has eyes for the vicious and scheming Duryea. Forced to paint in the bathroom because his wife can't stand the smell, aspiring artist Robinson moves his equipment and paintings into Bennett's new apartment. When Duryea tries to pawn a couple of the paintings, he's told by an art critic (Barker) that the artist who painted them is a genius. The con man sees dollar signs and manages to convince an

Henpecked artist Edward G. Robinson dries the dishes while the missus (Rosaland Ivan) attends to the bird in *Scarlet Street* (Universal, 1945).

art gallery owner that Bennett is the painter. His get-rich-quick scheme works for a while but is doomed to end in tragedy. Robinson is sensational as the middle-aged patsy who foolishly allows himself to believe, to the ubiquitous strains of "Melancholy Baby," that a gorgeous young woman has fallen for him. Bennett and Duryea are terrific as the dysfunctional lovers. This was the second film for the Lang-Robinson-Bennett-Duryea team after their first joint venture in *The Woman in the Window*.

Familiar Faces from Television:
❑ Syd Saylor (Wally in *Waterfront*) and Joe Devlin (Sam Catchem in *Dick Tracy*) as reporters on the train.
❑ Byron Foulger (Wendell Gibbs in *Petticoat Junction*) as Bennett's landlord.

Memorable Noir Moments:
❑ Bennett complains to boyfriend Duryea that the art critic he's pressuring her to play up to is "getting that look in his eye." "I've been out to dinner with him three times this week," she whines, "and now he's talking about breakfast."
❑ A horrified Robinson finally hears the awful truth from Bennett. "I've wanted to laugh in

your face ever since I first met you," she shrieks. "You're old and ugly and I'm sick of you. Sick, sick sick."

Scene of the Crime (1949) 94 min. Van Johnson, Gloria DeHaven, Tom Drake, Arlene Dahl, Leon Ames, John McIntire, Norman Lloyd. **Screenplay by:** Charles Schnee. **Directed by:** Roy Rowland. **Noir Type:** Police Procedural. **Noir Themes:** Betrayal, lust. ★★½

Johnson plays a homicide detective investigating the murder of his ex-partner, who appears to have been on the take. Dahl, Johnson's worried wife, tries to convince him to quit the force and take a job with her old boyfriend. Drake is the detective's eager young partner, McIntire is the crusty cop who mentored Johnson early in his career, and De Haven is the stripper Johnson is seeing on the side. Ames is Johnson's boss, and Lloyd is a snitch with a sense of humor. *Scene* is a standard crime movie fortified by good performances and a sensational climactic shoot-out.

Familiar Face from Television:
❑ Ray Teal (Sheriff Roy Coffee in *Bonanza*) as a patrolman.

Memorable Noir Moment:
❑ On his death bed, an unrepentant killer is asked if he wants to see his moll before he dies. "That tramp?" he asks. "I hate a tramp. You always gotta tell them, 'I love you.' A waste of time."

Screaming Mimi (1958) 79 min. Anita Ekberg, Philip Carey, Harry Townes, Gypsy Rose Lee. **Screenplay by:** Robert Blees. **Directed by:** Gerd Oswald. **Noir Type:** Psycho. **Noir Themes:** Character deterioration, lust, obsession. ★★★

Ekberg, a dancer, is attacked while showering by a knife-wielding maniac, who's just killed her little dog. Her stepbrother shoots and kills the man, and Ekberg winds up a loony in Highland Sanitarium, the maniac's alma mater. Ekberg's doctor (Townes) falls in love with her and gives up his practice to devote all of his time to finding a cure for her condition. After being released, Ekberg takes a job in a jazz joint owned by Lee. There she meets a crime reporter (Carey) on the trail of a killer called "the Ripper." The only clue left behind by the killer is a statuette of a woman screaming, a copy of which Carey has seen in Ekberg's dressing room. During the course of the investigation, the reporter falls in love with Ekberg, much to Townes' consternation. Things move at a brisk pace and, although there are no big surprises, the film is entertaining. Voluptuous Ekberg, a former Miss Sweden, is enjoyable to watch, especially during her sexy, but silly, rope-and-chain dance.

Memorable Noir Moments:
❑ While flirting with Ekberg, Carey asks, "How tall are you?" "With heels?" she asks. "With anybody, with me for instance," quips the reporter.
❑ Lee, the famous real-life stripper, does a nice rendition of "Put the Blame on Mame." (See *Gilda* and *The Houston Story* for other "Mame" singers.)

Sealed Lips (1941) 62 min. William Gargan, June Clyde, John Litel, Anne Nagel, Ralf Harolde, Mary Gordon. **Screenplay by:** George Waggner. **Directed by:** George Waggner. **Noir Type:** Impersonator. **Noir Themes:** Victim of fate, betrayal. ★★★

John Litel plays dual roles in this early noir — a gangster and a look-alike botanist. The botanist, who has served four years in prison in the mobster's place to protect his wife (Nagel) and mother (Gordon), is about to be released. A cop (Gargan) must prove before the prison term ends that the poor sap is an imposter and that the real gangster is in hiding. A pretty reporter (Clyde) tags alone with Gargan hoping for a scoop. It's not as silly as it sounds. This low-budget noir is quite inventive, making good use of Gargan's deaf, lip-reading assistant (Harolde) and providing the viewer with a thoroughly enjoyable ending, packed with film noir irony.

Memorable Noir Moment:

❑ From the Stupid Criminal Department: A hit man intends to kill Gargan by pushing him in front of a speeding train while his partner distracts him by asking for a light. Gargan drops his lighter and stoops down to pick it up. Moe, who's supposed to shove Curly into the cop, actually pushes him *over* Gargan and onto the tracks, where the unfortunate killer is run over by the train. (See *Raw Deal, Knock on Any Door, The Long Wait* and *Escape in the Fog* for more criminal stupidity.)

Second Chance (1953) 82 min.
Robert Mitchum, Linda Darnell, Jack Palance, Sandro Giglio, Rodolfo Hoyos, Roy Roberts. **Screenplay by**: Oscar Millard and Sydney Boehm. **Directed by**: Rudolph Maté. **Noir Type**: South of the Border. **Noir Themes**: Woman in jeopardy, obsession, betrayal, jealousy. ★★½

American prizefighter Mitchum and his manager (Roberts) are working the Mexican boxing circuit because Mitchum can't face going back to Madison Square Garden, where he killed a man in the ring. His fifteen victories against Mexican fighters have been by decision only, with no knockouts, because he's afraid to use his lethal right hand. In Mexico, he meets and falls in love with a gangster's moll (Darnell), on the run because she's been subpoenaed by a Senate crime commission to testify against her boyfriend. Hit man Palance has been dispatched by the gangster to make sure she doesn't show up at the hearing. The film spends too much time developing the romance between Mitchum and Darnell, but the exciting climax, which takes place on a stalled cable car high in the mountains, is worth waiting for. Mitchum is far too laid-back, almost bored, but Palance is terrific as the libidinous hit man. Giglio plays the brave, by-the-book cable car conductor, and Hoyos is a wife murderer being escorted to jail. Look closely for George Chakiris, future star of *West Side Story*, as an onlooker enjoying a sexy dance. (Hint: he's with a girl and he's wearing a vest.)

Familiar Faces from Television:

❑ Milburn Stone (Doc in *Gunsmoke*) as the unfortunate hotel guest who opens his door expecting to see a bellboy but finds Palance.
❑ Abel Fernandez (Agent Youngfellow in *The Untouchables*) as Palance's boxing opponent.

Memorable Noir Moment:

❑ An ingratiating bartender squeals to Palance about Darnell's whereabouts, adding helpfully that she's with Mitchum, "a very fine prizefighter." Unimpressed, Palance replies, "The cemetery is full of fine prizefighters."

The Second Woman

The Second Woman (1951) 91 min. Robert Young, Betsy Drake, John Sutton. **Screenplay by:** Mort Briskin and Robert Smith. **Directed by:** James V. Kern. **Noir Type:** Whodunit. **Noir Themes:** Fatalism, betrayal. ★★½

The film opens with Young inside a closed garage running his car's motor. Young's current girlfriend (Drake) narrates the events that have brought him to this point. Young's fiancée had been killed in an automobile accident a year earlier, and his recent paranoid behavior has been attributed by the family doctor to the guilt he feels as the driver of the vehicle. But strange, unexplained things have been happening to Young since the accident — an expensive painting has faded, his rosebush has died, his dog has been poisoned, his horse has broken its leg, and his house has burned down. Is it all just bad luck? Is Young unconsciously doing these things to punish himself? Drake tries to help despite Young's efforts to dissuade her from playing detective. Sutton plays a nasty co-worker with an obvious dislike for Young. It's a bit slow, but the scenery is beautiful, and the surprise ending is enjoyable.

Familiar Face from Television:

❑ Jimmy Dodd (the head Mouseketeer in *The Mickey Mouse Club*) as a motorist.

Secret Beyond the Door

Secret Beyond the Door (1948) 98 min. Joan Bennett, Michael Redgrave, Anne Revere, Barbara O'Neil, James Seay, Mark Dennis. **Screenplay by:** Silvia Richards. **Directed by:** Fritz Lang. **Noir Type:** Newlywed. **Noir Themes:** Woman in jeopardy, child in jeopardy, family dysfunction, paranoia. ★½

While on vacation in Mexico, an heiress (Bennett) falls in love with Redgrave, the publisher of a struggling architectural magazine. Despite warnings from her lawyer (Seay) about fortune hunters, she marries Redgrave after knowing him only a few days, moving into his heavily mortgaged mansion, where he lives with his sister (Revere), his mysterious business assistant (O'Neil) and, to Bennett's surprise, his young son (Dennis). It seems that her new hubby forgot to inform her that he was a widower. She also learns about Redgrave's peculiar hobby—creating rooms where murders have been committed and decorating them with the original furniture and even the murder weapons. Eventually, Bennett suspects that Redgrave killed his first wife and that he's planning to do her in also. Well-acted and nicely photographed, *Secret* oozes with film noir atmosphere. But, unfortunately, these things aren't enough to compensate for its muddled and sluggish plot and an ending that's guaranteed to disappoint. For insomniacs only.

Familiar Face from Television:

❑ Natalie Schafer (Mrs. Howell on *Gilligan's Island*) as Bennett's best friend.

Memorable Noir Moment:

❑ Sensitivity Training Required: Redgrave informs his understandably offended bride that "thinking is the prerogative of men."

The Secret Fury

The Secret Fury (1950) 86 min. Claudette Colbert, Robert Ryan, Paul Kelly. **Screenplay by:** Lionel Houser. **Directed by:** Mel Ferrer. **Noir Type:** Asylum. **Noir Themes:** Paranoia, betrayal, woman in jeopardy. ★★

Poor Claudette Colbert — on the verge of madness again (see *Sleep, My Love*). This time it's because somebody speaks up at her wedding and announces that she's already married. That's enough to send any girl to the nuthouse. Ryan, the wannabe groom, stands by his woman through it all. Mostly boring stuff, but you might find it interesting to see 45-year-old Colbert portraying a blushing bride. Keep your eyes open for José Ferrer at a jam session.

Familiar Face from Television:
❏ Paul Picerni (Agent Lee Hobson in *The Untouchables*) as a psychiatrist.

The Secret of Nina Duprez *see* The Louisiana Hussy

Secret of the Whistler (1946) 65 min. Richard Dix, Leslie Brooks, Mary Currier. **Screenplay by:** Raymond L. Schrock. **Directed by:** George Sherman. **Noir Type:** Femme Fatale. **Noir Themes:** Woman in jeopardy, greed, family dysfunction, lust. ★★★

In this sixth film of the Whistler series, Dix stars as a hack artist married to a wealthy woman (Currier) with a heart condition. He's waiting patiently for her to die so he can marry his beautiful model (Brooks). But when Currier actually gets better, he decides to help her along. What he doesn't know is that femme fatale Brooks, who sees him as a pigeon, has her own plans. Dix, as usual, does a good job, and the twist ending is deliciously ironic. (See also *The Whistler, Mark of the Whistler, Power of the Whistler, Voice of the Whistler, Mysterious Intruder, The Thirteenth Hour* and *The Return of the Whistler*.)

Familiar Faces from Television:
❏ Byron Foulger (Wendell Gibbs in *Petticoat Junction*) as a tombstone salesman.
❏ John Hamilton (Perry White in *The Adventures of Superman*) as a newspaper editor.

Memorable Noir Moment:
❏ When a reporter sees slap-and-dab painter Dix returning from a date with his gorgeous model, he comments, "Maybe Harrison ought to be painting barns instead of pictures, but he isn't so dumb at picking a nifty dish."

The Sellout (1951) 83 min. Walter Pidgeon, John Hodiak, Audrey Totter, Paula Raymond, Thomas Gomez, Cameron Mitchell, Karl Malden, Everett Sloane. **Screenplay by:** Charles Palmer. **Directed by:** Gerald Mayer. **Noir Type:** Bad Cop. **Noir Themes:** Corruption, betrayal. ★★★

Newspaper editor Pidgeon is falsely arrested by a despotic county sheriff (Gomez) and tossed into the clink. Rousted and robbed by his cellmates, he swears he'll see to it that Gomez and his deputies are kicked out of office. He begins a series of articles condemning the sheriff's illegal activities and gathers sworn testimony from his victims. A state prosecutor (Hodiak) arrives in town to investigate and teams up with a gung-ho police captain (Malden). They soon run into a seemingly insurmountable obstacle when Pidgeon stops running his stories and refuses to cooperate with them. Has he sold out? Hodiak believes so. Malden swears he hasn't. Totter, a nightclub singer on Gomez's payroll, is out to get something on Hodiak but falls for him instead. Raymond is Pidgeon's daughter, who's married to the D.A. (Mitchell), and Sloane is Gomez's shady attorney. A enjoyable crime drama, with Gomez entertaining as the tyrannical lawman.

Familiar Faces from Television:

❏ Frank Cady (Doc Williams in *The Adventures of Ozzie and Harriet* and Sam Drucker in *Petticoat Junction* and *Green Acres*) as a henpecked bartender.
❏ Ann Tyrrell (Vi in *Private Secretary* and Olive in *The Ann Sothern Show*) as the bartender's bossy wife.
❏ Burt Mustin (Fireman Gus in *Leave It to Beaver* and Mr. Quigley in *All in the Family*) as a judge on the sheriff's payroll.
❏ Roy Engel (the police chief in *My Favorite Martian*, Barney Wingate in *The Virginian* and President Ulysses S. Grant on *The Wild Wild West*) as a gambler ripped off at the sheriff's illegal casino.
❏ Jeff Richards (*Jefferson Drum*, Old West newspaper editor) as a truck driver.
❏ Whit Bissell (Gen. Heywood Kirk in *The Time Tunnel*) as an office snack salesman.

Memorable Noir Moment:

❏ After paying a $14 fine in a dubious court proceeding, a truck driver tells the judge, "I'll take a receipt for this." Sheriff Gomez, eager to get on to the next case, says, "Walking out of here in one piece, that's enough receipt for you. Who's next?"

Serenade (1956) 121 min. Mario Lanza, Joan Fontaine, Sarita Montiel, Vincent Price, Joseph Calleia, Harry Bellaver. **Screenplay by:** Ivan Goff, Ben Roberts and John Twist. **Directed by:** Anthony Mann. **Noir Type:** Show Biz. **Noir Themes:** Obsession, betrayal, jealousy. ★★★

A naive vineyard worker (Lanza) with a beautiful voice is discovered and seduced by a beautiful femme fatale (Fontaine). After jumpstarting his operatic career, she dumps him for an artist. This upsets the lovesick Lanza so much that he develops a fear of singing and runs away to Mexico, where he contracts a mysterious illness and is nursed back to health by Montiel, beautiful daughter of a famous matador. Can this Mexican spitfire make him forget Fontaine? Maybe. Will the tenor ever sing again? You bet. At least a half dozen more times before the film ends. Calleia is Lanza's voice coach, Bellaver is his country cousin and manager, and Price is a stuffed-shirt concert booker. This is a watered-down, Hollywood version of the James M. Cain novel, in which the opera star's voice changes drastically when he discovers that he's attracted to men. Fontaine is terrific as the wicked femme ("I always hurt people; that's *my* talent") but Lanza, who sings like an angel and sports an incredible pompadour, is an unlikely leading man and an even more unlikely noir hero. Unfortunately, the soprano died of a heart attack in 1959 at the age of 38.

Familiar Faces from Television:

❏ Vince Edwards (*Ben Casey*) as Fontaine's prizefighter trophy.
❏ Edward Platt (the Chief in *Get Smart*) as an opera producer.

Memorable Noir Moment:

❏ When Fontaine develops a sudden new interest in newlywed Lanza, Price taunts her. "It's not like you to work over your victims a second time," he says.

The Set-Up (1949) 72 min. Robert Ryan, Audrey Totter, George Tobias, Alan Baxter, Wallace Ford, Percy Helton. **Screenplay by:** Art Cohn. **Directed by:** Robert Wise. **Noir Type:** Boxing. **Noir Themes:** Betrayal, corruption, revenge. ★★★★

Ryan portrays a has-been boxer, old and washed-up at 35, who is so little esteemed that his manager and trainer (Tobias and Helton) don't even bother to tell him that he's supposed to take a dive during his next fight. (This way they don't have to split the 50-buck payoff with him.) In some of the most exciting boxing scenes ever filmed, Ryan (in real life a college heavyweight champion) and his opponent duke it out for four rounds, trading ferocious blows until only one of them is left standing. Before the final round, Ryan's nervous corner men finally tell him to go down. When he doesn't, the slimeballs take off with the dough, leaving Ryan to face the wrath of a gangster (Baxter) who doesn't like welshers. Totter, Ryan's boxing-weary wife, won't even go to the arena to watch her man receive yet another merciless beating. Veteran character actor Ford plays the kindly dressing room attendant who patches up the boxers after their fights. Director Wise and screenwriter Cohn, without being preachy, make a poignant statement about boxing and its sordid world. Despite the pleasant sounding names of the buildings in Wise's world (Par-

Boxers (Robert Ryan, left and James Edwards, center) speak with a dressing room attendant (Wallace Ford) as they wait for their turn in the ring in *The Set-Up* (RKO, 1949).

adise City, Dreamland and the Hotel Cozy), the battered faces, cauliflower ears and hopeless dreams tell the true story. Boxing noir at its best, *The Set-Up* is one of Ryan's finest acting achievements.

Familiar Face from Television:
❑ Darryl Hickman (Ben Canfield in the Civil War drama *The Americans*) as a nervous young high school boxer ready to take on his first professional opponent.

Memorable Noir Moments:
❑ Sensitivity Training Required: All of the white boxers in the dressing room are called by name when their bouts are about to begin. But an African-American boxer (James Edwards) hears instead, "Okay, boy, now let's go."
❑ From the Some-Things-Never-Change Department: The ring announcer reminds the audience that Friday night is wrestling night at the arena and that the wrestlers will take each other on in a ring filled with fish.

711 Ocean Drive (1950) 102 min. Edmond O'Brien, Joanne Dru, Don Porter, Sammy White, Otto Kruger, Howard St. John, Barry Kelley. **Screenplay by**: Richard English and Francis Swann. **Directed by**: Joseph M. Newman. **Noir Type**: Gangster. **Noir Themes**: Character deterioration, greed, lust, betrayal. ★★½

"Because of the disclosures made in this film, powerful underworld interests tried to halt production with threats of violence and reprisal..." The provocative and most likely exaggerated prologue goes on to tell us that it was only thanks to the armed protection of local police departments that the film could be completed. Narrated by St. John, who plays a lieutenant in the police department's "Gangster Squad," the film documents the rise and fall of bookmaker O'Brien (once an honest telephone company employee). Friendly bookie White introduces gambling addict O'Brien to a wire service provider (Kelley). Impressed with O'Brien's technical know-how, Kelley offers him the job of revamping and maintaining the service. O'Brien happily accepts the 150 bucks a week but his greed ("money's the answer to everything") soon has him blackmailing his new boss for a percentage of the business, and eventually he gains control of the operation. Kruger and his henchman (Porter), operators of a national syndicate of wire service providers, convince him to join their plan to charge the bookies for protection (protection from *them*, of course). O'Brien, finally at the top, is missing only one thing — Porter's wife (Dru) — and will stop at nothing, even murder, to get her. A bit long and somewhat dragged out, this film does have its moments, especially the exciting shootout at Boulder Dam. O'Brien is good as the nice guy who never should have left Ma Bell, and Kruger is enjoyably despicable as the evil syndicate chieftain.

Memorable Noir Moment:
❑ On the way to arrest O'Brien for murder, a detective asks his partner how the killer got the way he is. St. John replies, "Too much ambition, maybe. Too many brains working in the wrong direction. Or maybe it's glandular."

The Seventh Victim (1943) 71 min. Tom Conway, Kim Hunter, Jean Brooks, Hugh Beaumont. **Screenplay by**: DeWitt Bodeen and Charles O'Neal. **Directed by**: Mark Robson.

A gangster squad detective (Howard St. John, right) tries to break down a bookmaker (Edmond O'Brien, left) while a colleague looks on in *711 Ocean Drive* (Columbia, 1950).

Noir Type: Missing Person. **Noir Themes:** Conspiracy, paranoia, character deterioration. ★★½

Hunter, in her film debut, plays a boarding school student notified that her sister (Brooks) is missing. She travels to New York City to look for her and soon discovers that Brooks, hopelessly neurotic and suicidal, is on the lam from a coven of Satan worshipers. Beaumont is Hunter's brother-in-law, and Conway is the psychiatrist who's helping Brooks hide out. Although ominous and atmospheric, as one would expect from B horror film producer Val Lewton, this eerily filmed mystery (marking Robson's directing debut) is a bit slow.

Familiar Face from Television:

❑ Barbara Hale (Della Street in *Perry Mason*) as a passenger on a subway car.

Shack Out on 101 (1955) 80 min. Terry Moore, Frank Lovejoy, Lee Marvin, Keenan Wynn, Whit Bissell. **Screenplay by:** Edward Dein and Mildred Dein. **Directed by:** Edward Dein. **Noir Type:** Nuclear. **Noir Themes:** Conspiracy, lust, woman in jeopardy. ★★★½

This is a *very* weird film. All of the action, what little there is of it, takes place in a diner owned by war veteran Wynn. Moore, his sexy waitress, is studying to become a civil servant, and Lovejoy is her lover, a professor at a nearby college, who may or may not be a Commie spy. Marvin is Slob, the short-order cook with "an eight-cylinder body and a two-cylinder mind," who we *know* is a Commie spy. Bissell, one of the diner's few customers, is a traveling jewelry salesman who served in the war with Wynn. The overly familiar plot (the bad guys are recruiting American nuclear physicists, and the good guys are trying to discover the identity of their boss) is more than compensated for by the sidesplitting dialogue. Voluptuous Moore is terrific as the none-too-bright, but feisty, "tomato" everyone seems to have the hots for. But even she can't steal any scenes from Marvin, the film's biggest treat.

Familiar Face from Television:

❑ Len Lesser (Uncle Leo on Seinfeld) as Marvin's spy cohort.

Memorable Noir Moments:

❑ Wynn is demonstrating a new spear gun to war hero Bissell, who's hesitant to use the weapon on a "poor fish." "I told you, fish are cold-blooded," Wynn insists. "This I want to hear straight from the fish's mouth," replies the queasy Bissell.
❑ When Bissell orders a hamburger, cook Marvin implies something that all restaurant customers secretly fear. "A lot of things I could put on that hamburger," he says deviously.

Shadow of a Doubt (1943) 108 min. Joseph Cotten, Teresa Wright, Henry Travers, Patricia Collinge, Hume Cronyn, Macdonald Carey, Wallace Ford. **Screenplay by:** Thornton Wilder, Sally Benson and Alma Reville. **Directed by:** Alfred Hitchcock. **Noir Type:** Psycho. **Noir Themes:** Betrayal, woman in jeopardy, paranoia, sexual hostility. ★★★★★

On the lam, the "Merry Widow" murderer (Cotten) visits his sister and brother-in-law (Collinge and Travers) and their children in peaceful Santa Rosa, California. His philosophical niece (Wright) feels she has a psychic bond with her beloved uncle and is overjoyed at the prospect of Uncle Charlie staying with the family. But her joy is short-lived when a couple of undercover cops (Carey and Ford) show up in town and inform her that they suspect Cotten may be the psycho who has killed several wealthy widows in the past few months. At first she's outraged at the accusation but eventually begins to fear that they may be right. The misogynistic Cotten, meanwhile, has noticed a change in her behavior toward him. A change that worries him. Cronyn makes his film debut as Travers' eccentric mystery buff friend. This was the first time Cotten played a murderer and, according to his autobiography (*Vanity Will Get You Somewhere*) he received personal tutoring from filmdom's number one expert on the subject of murder, Hitchcock himself. He was obviously a good student. Wright and Cotten teamed together again in the 1952 noir, ***The Steel Trap***, this time as husband and wife. *Shadow of a Doubt* was remade in 1958 as the inferior ***Step Down to Terror***.

Familiar Face from Television:

❑ Minerva Urecal (Annie in *The Adventures of Tugboat Annie* and "Mother" in *Peter Gunn*) as a telegraph office employee.

Memorable Noir Moments:

❑ Out of the mouth of babes: When Cotten mentions at the dinner table that he plans to put thirty or forty thousand dollars into the bank, his young nephew advises him, "You won't have it long. The government will get it."

❑ Housewife Collinge, when asked what her brother does for a living, replies, "He's just in business. You know. The way men are."

Shadow of a Woman (1946) 78 min. Andrea King, Helmut Dantine, John Alvin, William Prince, Lisa Golm, Peggy Knudsen. **Screenplay by:** C. Graham Baker and Whitman Chambers. **Directed by:** Joseph Santley. **Noir Type:** Newlywed. **Noir Themes:** Woman in jeopardy, child in jeopardy, greed. ★★½

While on vacation, a lonely and depressed young woman (King) meets an "alternative medicine practitioner" (Dantine) and marries him after a whirlwind romance. Like Joan Bennett in *Secret Beyond the Door*, the new bride receives a few surprises when she moves into her husband's stately old house. She discovers that he lives with his widowed sister (Golm) and her crippled son (Alvin), and that he has a five-year-old son from a former marriage to Knudson, who has hired an attorney (Prince) to help her gain custody of the child. King eventually suspects that the good doctor (author of that best seller, "Are You Eating Your Way to the Grave?") is a quack and, worse, is slowly starving his little boy in order to steal his inheritance. The plot is hard to swallow, but King is enjoyable as the bride with second thoughts.

Familiar Face from Television:

❑ Richard Erdman (Peter Fairfield III in *The Tab Hunter Show*) as a soda jerk.

Memorable Noir Moment:

❑ After telling the cops about the time a huge boulder mysteriously rolled down a hill and nearly killed Dantine, King adds, "I had a premonition that something was wrong."

Shadow on the Wall (1950) 84 min. Ann Sothern, Zachary Scott, Nancy Davis, Gigi Perreau, John McIntire, Kristine Miller, Tom Helmore. **Screenplay by:** William Ludwig. **Directed by:** Pat Jackson. **Noir Type:** Wrong Man. **Noir Themes:** Child in jeopardy, character deterioration, betrayal, jealousy. ★★★

Architect Scott returns from a business trip to discover that his new wife (Miller) is having an affair with her sister's fiancé (Helmore). While unpacking a gun, Scott gets into an argument with Miller and she, fearing he plans to shoot her, knocks him out cold with a mirror. Miller's sister (Sothern) shows up and, in a jealous rage over Helmore, accidentally shoots her with Scott's gun. Scott, who believes that the gun must have gone off when Miller hit him with the mirror, is arrested for the murder. After he's convicted and sentenced to death, the remorseful Sothern pens a confession but, before delivering it to the police, she has a noirish vision of her own electrocution and tears it up. Then she discovers that Scott's six-year-old daughter (Perreau), who's being treated by a psychiatrist (Davis) for shock, witnessed her stepmother's murder, and decides that she must get rid of little girl before her memory of the killing returns. Sothern (TV's *Private Secretary* and the voice of *My Mother the Car*) is terrific as a nice girl who metamorphoses into a vicious femme fatale before our unbelieving eyes. Although we're certain we know the eventual outcome, the suspense still works. Davis does a good job as the dedicated psychiatrist who, ahead of her time, attempts to recreate the crime in Perreau's mind by using dolls. Perreau later acted in two short-lived TV series (*The Betty Hutton Show* and *Follow the Sun*).

Familiar Face from Television:
- ❏ Barbara Billingsley (June Cleaver in *Leave It to Beaver*) as a maid.

Shadow on the Window (1957) 73 min. Philip Carey, Betty Garrett, John Drew Barrymore, Corey Allen, Gerald Sarracini, Jerry Mathers. **Screenplay by:** David P. Harmon and Leo Townsend. **Directed by:** William Asher. **Noir Type:** Hostage. **Noir Themes:** Woman in jeopardy, paranoia. ★★½

A little boy (Mathers) witnesses the kidnapping of his mother (Garrett) and the murder of an elderly man by three crooks (Barrymore, Allen and Sarracini). After wandering onto the highway in a daze, the boy is picked up by a trucker and eventually turned over to the police. In a state of shock, Mathers is unable to communicate and doesn't even recognize his own policeman father (Carey), who must now trace his son's steps to find his estranged wife. Meanwhile, the crooks are beginning to argue over what to do with their hostage. Psycho Barrymore wants to kill her, and the slow-witted Sarracini decides to be her protector. This is a fairly suspenseful noir with lots of familiar TV faces. Mathers, of course, went on to star in *Leave It to Beaver*, and Garrett became a regular on *All in the Family* and *Laverne and Shirley*. Carey starred as TV's *Tales of the 77th Bengal Lancers* and *Philip Marlowe* and later co-starred in *Laredo*.

Familiar Faces from Television:
- ❏ Paul Picerni (Agent Lee Hobson of *The Untouchables*) as a detective.
- ❏ Ainslie Pryor (reporter Joel Smith in *The Adventures of Hiram Holiday*) as a police psychiatrist.
- ❏ Mort Mills (Marshal Frank Tallman in *Man Without a Gun*) as the murder victim's nephew.

Memorable Noir Moment:
- ❏ While a husband is making time with a local barfly, his naive wife wonders why he's late for dinner. "I don't understand it," she tells detectives. "There isn't anything in the world that Jim likes better than corn beef."

Shakedown (1950) 80 min. Howard Duff, Brian Donlevy, Peggy Dow, Lawrence Tierney, Bruce Bennett, Anne Vernon. **Screenplay by:** Alfred Lewis Levitt and Martin Goldsmith. **Directed by:** Joseph Pevney. **Noir Type:** Ambition. **Noir Themes:** Betrayal, greed, corruption, lust. ★★★½

Duff stars as a resourceful, but starving, photographer, itching for a job with a San Francisco newspaper. Hired on probation, he proves so skillful at getting great front-page photos (such as shots of camera-shy gangster Donlevy and of Tierney and his gang pulling a heist) that editor Bennett hires him on full-time. But it isn't long before the morally bankrupt photographer is blackmailing Tierney, double-crossing Donlevy, and cheating on girlfriend Dow with a gangster's widow (Vernon). Duff is first-rate in this disturbing portrait of a ruthless opportunist, who will stop at nothing in his climb to the top. Tierney, as usual, gives a convincing performance as a vicious thug.

Familiar Face from Television:

❏ Rock Hudson (Commissioner McMillan in *McMillan and Wife*) as the doorman of the Bay View Club.

Memorable Noir Moment:

❏ When a speeding car recklessly cuts off the cab that newshound photographer Duff is riding in, the taxi driver remarks, "That's guy's flirtin' with the undertaker." Always on the lookout for a photo opportunity, Duff tells him, "Stay with him for awhile. The romance might be interesting."

The Shanghai Gesture (1941) 106 min. Gene Tierney, Walter Huston, Victor Mature, Ona Munson, Phyllis Brooks. **Screenplay by:** Josef von Sternberg, Geza Herczeg and Jules Furthman. **Directed by:** Josef von Sternberg. **Noir Type:** Far East. **Noir Themes:** Corruption, betrayal, fatalism, revenge, jealousy. ★★★

Tierney is the spoiled daughter of an English businessman (Huston) in Shanghai. Huston uses his influence to try to close down the lucrative gambling casino owned by dragon lady Munson, who goes by the name of "Mother Gin Sling." Not one for sitting still while being attacked, Munson investigates Huston and feels she has enough dirt on him to discourage his plans in her part of the city. Meanwhile, Tierney, who's been losing big at the casino and drinking heavily, has fallen for Mature, a fez-wearing Middle Easterner. Brooks plays a tough-talking Brooklyn girl who has landed a job at the casino and has attracted Mature's roving eye. Veteran noir heavy Mazurki (cast, strangely, as a rickshaw coolie) gets the final line of the film ("You likee Chinee New Year?") after events lead to a tragic holiday showdown. Tierney is good as the beautiful, overindulged daughter who gets the surprise of her young life. Munson, whose comic strip-like appearance must be seen to be believed, gives a puzzling performance, as does the fez-wearing Mature, whose sweet nothings ("my little tulip," "my little broken-footed antelope," "my plucked bird of paradise") seem to be a big hit with the ladies. A weird but fascinating film noir.

Memorable Noir Moments:

❏ Tierney, enraptured by Mother Gin Sling's multinational gambling establishment, remarks to her escort, "The other places are like kindergartens compared to this. It smells so incredibly evil."
❏ When Tierney throws one of her drunken tantrums, Munson gently scolds her, "You're in China and you're white," she says. "It's not good for us to see you like this. You'll bring discredit to your race if you continue."

Shield for Murder (1954) 80 min. Edmond O'Brien, Marla English, John Agar, Emile Meyer, Claude Akins, Carolyn Jones, Hugh Sanders. **Screenplay by:** John C. Higgins and Richard Alan Simmons. **Directed by:** Edmond O'Brien and Howard W. Koch. **Noir Type:** Bad Cop. **Noir Themes:** Greed, corruption, obsession, lust. ★★★

Corrupt detective O'Brien dreams of owning his part of the American dream — a house in the suburbs to share with his girl (English). He wants it so bad that he's willing to kill for it. And he does. He plugs a small-time hood in the back and takes off with the twenty-five Gs belonging to mobster Sanders. O'Brien's protégé (Agar) idolizes him and refuses to believe the worst — until O'Brien kills again, this time to cover up the first murder. Things begin to unravel quickly, of course, and it isn't long before O'Brien takes the short downhill ride that so many other crooked film noir cops have taken. Veteran character actor Meyer plays O'Brien's boss, Akins is a tough P.I. out to get Sanders' money back, and Jones is a barfly who puts the make on O'Brien for a quick spaghetti dinner. Fast-paced and violent, *Shield*'s main attraction is O'Brien's fine performance.

Familiar Faces from Television:

❏ Richard Deacon (Mel Cooley from *The Dick Van Dyke Show*) as a middle-aged night school student, who hides O'Brien for five hundred a day, plus extra for sandwiches.

❏ William Schallert (Patty's dad from *The Patty Duke Show*) as an assistant D.A.

Memorable Noir Moments:

❏ A newspaper reporter explains to his editor why he can't get any information about O'Brien's crime. "Once a cop pulls a trigger," he complains, "it's like a secret society."

❏ English tries to explain O'Brien's psychopathic tendencies. "I think he's lonely," she says. "More than anything else, he wants to be loved, have somebody care for him."

❏ O'Brien pistol-whips two hoods in an Italian restaurant while diners nearly choke on their pasta. "Call the police, call the police," the owner cries. "You *had* the police," replies O'Brien as he casually walks out.

Shock (1946) 70 min. Vincent Price, Lynn Bari, Anabel Shaw, Frank Latimore. **Screenplay by:** Eugene Ling. **Directed by:** Alfred L. Werker. **Noir Type:** Cover-Up. **Noir Themes:** Woman in jeopardy, victim of fate, corruption, lust, betrayal. ★★

While awaiting a reunion with her P.O.W. husband (Latimore) at a hotel, Shaw sees a murder being committed in another room. Already a nervous wreck, she immediately goes into a catatonic state. Psychiatrist Price, whom she saw clubbing his wife to death in full view of a hotel window, is called in by the hotel doctor as a specialist in "these kinds of cases." Price immediately figures out what caused her condition and convinces Latimore to allow him to admit Shaw into his private hospital. There, with the help of his lover, nurse Bari, Price keeps Shaw drugged until they can figure a way out of their predicament, which worsens with each attempted cover-up. A minor noir at best, *Shock* has difficulty maintaining interest despite the presence of the usually sensational Price in one of his first starring roles.

Familiar Face from Television:

❏ Reed Hadley (Capt. John Braddock in *Racket Squad*) as a homicide detective.

Memorable Noir Moment:

❏ Price, who killed his wife so he could be with Bari, wonders aloud, "Was it worth it?" Bari replies with a passionate kiss, but the real answer soon becomes evident to the psychiatrist.

Shockproof (1949) 79 min. Cornel Wilde, Patricia Knight, John Baragrey, Esther Minciotti. **Screenplay by:** Helen Deutsch and Samuel Fuller. **Directed by:** Douglas Sirk. **Noir Type:** Femme Fatale. **Noir Themes:** Paranoia, jealousy, corruption. ★★½

Wilde plays a Los Angeles parole officer who is tempted by his latest parolee (Knight), a woman who murdered her husband. After spending five years in prison,

Knight returns home hoping to continue her romantic relationship with her book-maker boyfriend (Baragrey). Instead, she finds that it would be a violation of her parole to associate with him. When she gets picked up with Baragrey in a police raid on a bookie joint, Wilde gives her a second chance. He moves her into his house to take care of his blind mother (Minciotti) and begins to fall in love with her. They secretly marry, also a violation of her parole. Their marriage and his career are jeopardized when Knight becomes involved in a shooting, and the couple must go on the lam. Wilde and Knight are believable as the love-struck couple, but the otherwise entertaining film is spoiled by its cop-out ending.

Familiar Face from Television:

❏ King Donovan (Air Force officer Harvey Helm in *Love That Bob* and lawyer Herb Thornton in *Please Don't Eat the Daisies*) as a suicidal parolee.

Shoot to Kill (1947) 64 min. Russell Wade, Edmund MacDonald, Vince Barnett, Susan Walters, Douglas Blackley. **Screenplay by:** Edwin V. Westrate. **Directed by:** William Berke. **Noir Type:** Payback. **Noir Themes:** Revenge, lust, betrayal. ✭

This bomb has been described by some reviewers as "not bad" and as an interesting minor B picture. Don't believe it. The plot is so convoluted and confusing and the acting so atrocious that the best thing that can be said about the film is that it's only an hour long. The ambitious Walters, who's telling her story from a hospital bed while in a near-coma state, takes (in flashbacks) a job as a secretary for an up-and-coming assistant D.A. (MacDonald). She eventually marries him, disappointing her boyfriend, newspaper reporter Wade. Blackley is an escaped convict looking to pay back MacDonald, who framed him for murder. Producer and director Berke, the man who gave us the first six *Jungle Jim* films, tries hard with a number of double- and triple-crosses and even a flashback within a flashback. Unfortunately for the film noir fan, he fared better in the jungle than he does in the city.

Memorable Noir Moment:

❏ MacDonald finds a bug planted in his office. This being a 1947 listening device, he has to unravel about 100 feet of wire, frantically moving furniture, rugs and filing cabinets in the process, before finally locating it in a closet. (See *Parole, Inc.* for another impractical bug.)

Short Cut to Hell (1957) 87 min. William Bishop, Robert Ivers, Georgann Johnson, Jacques Aubuchon, Murvyn Vye, Richard Hale. **Screenplay by:** Ted Berkman and Raphael Blau. **Directed by:** James Cagney. **Noir Type:** Hit Man. **Noir Themes:** Revenge, betrayal, woman in jeopardy. ✭✭✭

Actor Cagney tried his hand at directing with this competent remake of *This Gun for Hire*. Ivers is a psycho hit man who's out to get Aubuchon, the client who paid him for his last job in marked bills. Johnson, an aspiring nightclub singer, is taken hostage by Ivers in an effort to elude a police manhunt. After Johnson escapes, the fearful Aubuchon, believing that she's Ivers' girlfriend, orders his sadistic chauffeur (Vye) to persuade her to disclose the killer's whereabouts. Bishop plays the singer's boyfriend, a homicide detective investigating Ivers' last hit, and Hale is Aubuchon's arrogant boss. In the film's prologue, director Cagney introduces "exciting" newcomers Ivers and Johnson, who, although they do well in the lead roles, can't compare to Alan Ladd and Veronica Lake in the original. Cagney never directed another film because, as reported in his biography, *Cagney*, by James McCabe, "I realized I have no interest in telling other people their business." It could also have been because this film was a box office flop. Johnson went on to play in a number of TV shows, including *As the World Turns*, *All My Children*, *The Colbys*, *The Trials of Rosie O'Neill* and *Dr. Quinn, Medicine Woman*; Ivers had minor roles in the short-lived series *Pony Express* and *Mr. Roberts*.

Familiar Face from Television:
❑ Milton Frome (a regular on *The Milton Berle Show* and harried studio boss Lawrence Chapman in *The Beverly Hillbillies*) as a Los Angeles police captain helping Bishop search for his girl.

Memorable Noir Moments:
❑ "Isn't there just one thing about yourself that you like, that you're proud of?" amateur psychologist Johnson asks hit man Ivers. "Yeah," he snarls. "I never miss."
❑ Johnson continues to give unsolicited psychological advice to her kidnapper. "You can't live if you don't respect yourself as a person," she says. "I'm not a person," Ivers replies. "I'm a gun."

Side Street (1950) 83 min. Farley Granger, Cathy O'Donnell, James Craig, Edmon Ryan, Paul Kelly, Jean Hagen. **Screenplay by:** Sydney Boehm. **Directed by:** Anthony Mann. **Noir Type:** On the Run. **Noir Themes:** Guilt, paranoia. ★★★½

A financially strapped part-time mail carrier (Granger), whose wife (O'Donnell) is pregnant, breaks into a filing cabinet in an attorney's office to steal the money he had seen placed there while he was delivering the mail. Expecting to find just a few hundred dollars, he winds up walking away with thirty grand and some documents that could incriminate a ruthless hood (Craig). Understandably fearful, Granger wraps up the money and asks a bartender friend to hold the package for him for a few days. When he finally comes to his senses, he confesses to the attorney (Ryan) and offers to return the dough, which turns out to have been a blackmail payoff. Unfortunately, Granger discovers that the bartender has stolen the dough and is in hiding. On the lam from the cops, who think he's a murderer, and from angry gangsters, Granger seeks a way out of his miserable predicament. Kelly is the homicide detective in charge of the case, and Hagen plays Craig's former girlfriend, an alcoholic nightclub singer. This suspenseful and beautifully photographed noir reunited Granger and O'Donnell after the sensational ***They Live by Night***, and climaxes with an exciting car chase through the narrow streets of lower Manhattan.

Familiar Faces from Television:
❑ King Donovan (Air Force officer Harvey Helm in *Love That Bob* and lawyer Herb Thornton in *Please Don't Eat the Daisies*) as a homicide detective.
❑ Harry Bellaver (Sgt. Arcaro in *Naked City*) as a cab-driving gangster.
❑ James Westerfield (John Murrel in *The Travels of Jaimie McPheeters*) as a retirement-minded patrolman.
❑ Minerva Urecal (Annie in *The Adventures of Tugboat Annie* and "Mother" in *Peter Gunn*) as Craig's nosy neighbor.

Memorable Noir Moments:

❏ After a hood hangs up on his moll, whom he just promised to take to Havana or Miami after she collects a thirty grand blackmail payoff, his partner remarks knowingly, "Havana, Miami, by way of the East River."

❏ When an elderly blackmail victim tries to buy some incriminating photos for only half the agreed-upon price, the callous blonde who's putting the bite on him says, "Take a look at yourself, grandpa. First you sell yourself I'm nuts about you. Crazy for your manly charms. And now you think this is bargain day. Well go on down to Gimbel's Bargain Basement. You're in the wrong department."

The Sign of the Ram (1948) 88 min. Susan Peters, Alexander Knox, Phyllis Thaxter, Peggy Ann Garner, Ron Randell, Allene Roberts, Ross Ford, Diana Douglas. **Screenplay by:** Charles Bennett. **Directed by:** John Sturges. **Noir Type:** Soap Opera. **Noir Themes:** Jealousy, betrayal, paranoia. ★★½

A stepmother (Peters) uses her disability to control her family — husband Knox, adult children Roberts and Ford and teenager Garner. Confined to a wheelchair after saving Roberts and Ford from drowning when they were children, Peters tries to destroy Roberts' romantic relationship with her boyfriend (Randell) and Ford's upcoming marriage to his fiancée (Douglas). The neurotic Garner idolizes her step-mother so much that she tries to kill Peters' new secretary (Thaxter), whom she believes has been trying to seduce Knox. The title refers to Peters' astrological birth sign and fits her to a tee — people born under the sign, according to Randell, are endowed with strong will power and obstinacy of purpose and will stop at nothing to accomplish that purpose. *The Sign of the Ram* is a routine soap opera with good performances by Knox and Peters, who, in real life, was confined to a wheelchair after suffering a spinal injury in a hunting mishap in 1944. This was supposed to be her comeback film, but she retired from the screen soon afterwards and died in 1952 of bronchial pneumonia at the age of 31.

Memorable Noir Moment:

❏ Femme fatale Peters, aware that the sea is "angry because it hadn't quite finished me off," justifies her wicked schemes. "Life's like any other game," she says. "It's not wrong to fight to keep the lead."

Singapore (1947) 79 min. Fred MacMurray, Ava Gardner, Roland Culver, Thomas Gomez, Richard Haydn, George Lloyd. **Screenplay by:** Seton I. Miller and Robert Thoeren. **Directed by:** John Brahm. **Noir Type:** Far East. **Noir Themes:** Greed. ★★

An exotic, but disappointing, noir, *Singapore* is about an American smuggler (MacMurray), who returns to the island after the war to retrieve valuable pearls he hid in his hotel room five years earlier. He runs into his former fiancée (Gardner), who he thought had been killed by Japanese bombs on the day they were to be mar-ried. MacMurray's not as lucky as he sounds, though, because Gardner, who had been captured by the Japanese, is suffering from amnesia and is married to her P.O.W. camp mate (Culver). While MacMurray tries in vain to get Gardner to remember him, two crooks (Gomez and Lloyd) and a police inspector (Haydn) look for the miss-ing pearls. Those who remember MacMurray as the widowed dad in TV's *My Three*

Sons might have a difficult time accepting him as a somewhat scoundrelly adventurer. Remade in 1957 as *Istanbul* with Errol Flynn.

Familiar Faces from Television:
❏ Spring Byington (Lily Ruskin in *December Bride* and Daisy Cooper in *Laramie*) as an American tourist in Singapore.
❏ Philip Ahn (Master Kan in *Kung Fu*) as a bartender.

Memorable Noir Moment:
❏ Discussing the war with MacMurray, hoodlum Gomez remarks, "I like troubled times. They keep the police busy."

Sirocco (1951) 98 min. Humphrey Bogart, Lee J. Cobb, Marta Toren, Everett Sloane, Gerald Mohr, Zero Mostel. **Screenplay by:** A.I. Bezzerides and Hans Jacoby. **Directed by:** Curtis Bernhardt. **Noir Type:** Adventure. **Noir Themes:** Betrayal, obsession, lust, greed. ★★★

Bogart plays a gunrunning profiteer in 1925 Damascus during the war between French occupation troops and Syrian rebels. Cobb is a French colonel who's trying to figure out which one of the city's many food merchants is selling arms to the Syrians. Toren is the colonel's materialistic lover, interested in Bogey because he can help her get out of Damascus and away from the overly possessive Cobb. When a French peace emissary is murdered by the rebels, Cobb decides to meet face to face with the rebel leader and pressures Bogey to help arrange the meeting. Mostel plays an obsequious Syrian businessman, Mohr is Cobb's right-hand man and Sloane is a French commander impatient with the murderous rebels. Bogey does a good job as the gunrunner, and Cobb is terrific as the peace-loving military man with a weakness for scheming dames.

Familiar Face from Television:
❏ Harry Guardino (Hamilton Burger in the revived [1973-74] *Perry Mason*) as the unlucky French lieutenant chosen as a peace emissary.

Memorable Noir Moments:
❏ Toren gives Bogey a backhanded compliment. "You're so ugly," she exclaims. "How can a man so ugly be so handsome?"
❏ When asked if he knows the punishment for selling arms to the Syrian insurgents, Bogey replies, "A slug in the head and a hole in the ground."

Sleep, My Love (1948) 97 min. Claudette Colbert, Robert Cummings, Don Ameche, Raymond Burr, George Coulouris, Hazel Brooks. **Screenplay by:** St. Clair McKelway and Leo Rosten. **Directed by:** Douglas Sirk. **Noir Type:** Triangle. **Noir Themes:** Betrayal, obsession, woman in jeopardy. ★★½

Colbert is the victim of cheating hubby Ameche, who's trying to drive her to madness and suicide so he'll be free to marry femme fatale Brooks. Coulouris plays Ameche's sinister accomplice, and Cummings is Colbert's protector. Burr has a small role as the cop investigating the case. Highlights include an opening scene reminiscent of Pat O'Brien's eerie train ride in **Crack-Up** and a staircase scene that must have seemed like *deja vu* to Burr after his role in 1947's **Desperate**.

Familiar Faces from Television:

❑ Jimmy Dodd (the head Mouseketeer in *The Mickey Mouse Club*) as an elevator operator.
❑ Keye Luke (Master Po in *Kung Fu*) as Cummings' "brother."

Memorable Noir Moment:

❑ When asked about his phony gunshot wound, Ameche replies, "It's only a surface wound." (See *Accused of Murder, The Enforcer, Riot in Cell Block 11, Guilty Bystander* and *Jail Bait* for other variations on the infamous flesh wound cliché.)

The Sleeping City (1950) 85 min. Richard Conte, Coleen Gray, Peggy Dow, Richard Taber. **Screenplay by:** Jo Eisinger. **Directed by:** George Sherman. **Noir Type:** Undercover. **Noir Themes:** Corruption, character deterioration. ★★★½

Somebody is killing interns at City Hospital, and homicide detective Conte, a former medical student, is assigned to go undercover to find the culprit. During the investigation, he falls for Gray, the trauma ward nurse. This grim portrayal of weak-willed, financially strapped doctors, who deprive their patients of proper care to cover their own butts, was filmed at Bellevue Hospital in New York City. Giving in to pressure from the mayor and local politicians, Universal inserted a prologue with Conte explaining that the events in the film did not take place at Bellevue or even in New York. As if anything like this could happen in Fun City! Conte gives his usual reliable performance, but Taber steals the film as a sleazy elevator operator, who also acts as a bookie for the impoverished interns.

Familiar Face from Television:

❑ Jack Lescoule (early TV announcer and sidekick, who appeared with Dave Garroway on *Today* and hosted *The Tonight Show*) as a homicide detective.

Memorable Noir Moment:

❑ When an intern is asked how a patient is doing, he responds, "He's breathing from memory."

The Sleeping Tiger (1954-British) 89 min. Dirk Bogarde, Alexis Smith, Alexander Knox, Hugh Griffith. **Screenplay by:** Harold Buchman and Carl Foreman. **Directed by:** Joseph Losey. **Noir Type:** Triangle. **Noir Themes:** Betrayal, lust, jealousy. ★★½

When a petty criminal (Bogarde) tries to mug a psychiatrist (Knox), he's subdued by the former Army doctor, who then invites him to participate in an experiment on aberrant behavior. Bogarde, preferring the comfort of the doctor's home to a British prison cell, agrees to spend the next six months as Knox's houseguest and guinea pig. The trusting doctor, however, makes the mistake of allowing the sociopath to spend his free time horseback riding with his American wife (Smith), whom he seduces after a "date" at a local beatnik jazz club. While Knox is reveling in the "progress" of his experiment, Bogarde and an accomplice are conducting a mini-crime wave in town, attracting the attention of police inspector Griffith, who has no patience for Knox's unorthodox research. This British noir moves much too slowly before arriving at its enjoyable ending. Bogarde is excellent, though, as the psychologically disturbed thief with a preference for "cheap blondes in cheap dresses" and, of course, doctor's wives.

Memorable Noir Moments:

❑ Smith and Bogarde play "Can You Top this Terrible Childhood Story." Smith wins with, "I came from *two* homes thousands of miles apart and I was a stranger in *both* of them."

❑ When Smith plays hard to get, Bogarde tells her, "You're a tight wire and it wouldn't take very much to break you."

Slightly Scarlet (1956) 99 min. John Payne, Rhonda Fleming, Arlene Dahl, Kent Taylor, Ted de Corsia. **Screenplay by:** Robert Blees. **Directed by:** Allan Dwan. **Noir Type:** Gangster. **Noir Themes:** Corruption, obsession, betrayal. ★★★

A small-time hood (Payne) finagles his way to the top of his gang by betraying his boss (de Corsia) and helping an honest politician (Taylor) get elected. Along the way, he romances Taylor's girlfriend (Fleming), who has her hands full keeping her recently paroled, kleptomaniac sister (Dahl) on the straight and narrow. *Slightly Scarlet* is a dark excursion into organized crime, political corruption and family dysfunction, with Payne and Fleming excellent as the doomed noir lovers. Dahl stands out as the emotionally unstable ex-con.

Familiar Faces from Television:

❑ Ellen Corby (Grandma Walton in *The Waltons*) as Fleming's maid.

❑ Myron Healey (Doc Holliday in *The Life and Legend of Wyatt Earp*) as one of de Corsia's goons.

Memorable Noir Moment:

❑ When Payne reports to de Corsia that he could find no dirt on the mayoral candidate's girlfriend, the chauvinistic gangster replies, "A dame is a dame. There's bound to be something you can nail her on."

Smash-Up, the Story of a Woman (1947) 103 min. Susan Hayward, Lee Bowman, Marsha Hunt, Eddie Albert. **Screenplay by:** John Howard Lawson. **Directed by:** Stuart Heisler. **Noir Type:** Boozer. **Noir Themes:** Obsession, paranoia, jealousy, child in jeopardy. ★★★½

A successful nightclub singer (Hayward), with the beginnings of a serious drinking problem, marries a struggling songwriter (Bowman), has a baby and forgets about the booze ... for a while. When a song co-written by Bowman and his accompanist partner (Albert) tops the charts, Hayward gives up her career to be a stay-at-home mom (with a nanny, of course), while Bowman goes on to be a singing star with too many out-of-town gigs. Hayward's loneliness and understandable jealousy of Bowman's gorgeous secretary (Hunt) drive her to seek solace in the bottle once again, causing a serious rift in her marriage and even placing her little girl's life in danger. Hayward is terrific as Ray Milland's female counterpart (see 1945's *The Lost Weekend*), receiving a Best Actress Oscar nomination for her effort, and Albert does a good job as the couple's sympathetic friend. Warning: Viewing this film may result in your humming or singing its catchy theme song, "Life Can Be Beautiful," for days afterwards.

Familiar Faces from Television:

❑ Noel Neill (Lois Lane in *The Adventures of Superman*) as a partygoer (don't blink — she's carrying a drink, wearing a dark dress and hat, and speaking to party guests as Bowman talks on the telephone).

❑ Robert Shayne (Inspector Henderson in *The Adventures of Superman*) as a proud, new father seated at a bar with Hayward.

Memorable Noir Moment:

❑ Hayward utters the self-justifying words familiar to the loved ones of so many alcoholics: "So I take a drink once in a while. Does that make me a lush or something?"

The Snake Pit (1948) 108 min. Olivia de Havilland, Mark Stevens, Leo Genn, Howard Freeman. **Screenplay by:** Frank Partos and Millen Brand. **Directed by:** Anatole Litvak. **Noir Type:** Asylum. **Noir Themes:** Paranoia, guilt, character deterioration. ★★★½

Newlywed Stevens has no alternative but to institutionalize his bride (de Havilland) when she starts exhibiting some pretty strange behavior. At the state hospital, de Havilland is fortunate enough to be placed under the care of a kindly staff psychiatrist (Genn), who makes her his special case and seeks to restore her to normalcy, using shock treatment, narcosynthesis and psychotherapy to discover the cause of her illness. When Stevens sees slight improvement, he wants to bring his bride home, and another staff member (Freeman) is only too glad to send her on her way to ease the overcrowding. Genn, however, is determined to continue his treatment. The film traces de Havilland's rapid descent into madness as she's transferred from ward to ward, with each neurotic episode worse than the last. While a far cry from the infamous La Siesta Sanitarium in *Behind Locked Doors*, Juniper Hill State Hospital is no Disneyland, with its hundreds of demented inmates forced to abide by the often callous staff's illogical rules and regulations. De Havilland gives a standout performance in Hollywood's sobering first attempt at dealing intelligently with mental illness. Genn's patient, low-key beside manner may cause envious viewers to take a more critical look at their own assembly line medical providers.

Familiar Face from Television:

❑ Jan Clayton (Ellen Miller, Tommy's mom, in *Lassie*) as an inmate vocalist performing at the hospital dance.

Memorable Noir Moments:

❑ During an interview with psychiatrist Genn, Stevens explains why he didn't notice his bride's strange behavior earlier. "When you love somebody," he says, "you're not looking for symptoms."

❑ Genn compliments de Havilland on the kind attention she's given to a potentially violent patient. "Sometimes a sick animal knows better how another sick animal should be treated," she explains.

The Sniper (1952) 87 min. Arthur Franz, Adolphe Menjou, Marie Windsor, Frank Faylen, Richard Kiley. **Screenplay by:** Harry Brown. **Directed by:** Edward Dmytryk. **Noir Type:** Psycho. **Noir Themes:** Sexual hostility, social reform, woman in jeopardy, guilt. ★★★★

The Sniper, we are told in the opening credits, is "the story of a man whose enemy was womankind." Franz, a deranged psychopath with a history of violence against women, is fighting the temptation to take the physical abuse to the next logical step — murder. In desperation, he calls his psychiatrist at the prison psycho ward, but the doctor is on vacation. Even after deliberately burning his shooting hand on a stove, Franz can't get the psychological help he needs at a busy emergency room. Wandering the streets of San Francisco, he seems to run into the city's most annoying women. Finally, unable to restrain himself any longer, he stalks and kills his first victim (Windsor) and sends an ominous note to the police, "Stop me. Find me and stop me. I'm going to do it again." Homicide detective Menjou and police chief Faylen, under intense political pressure, are short on clues after bringing in nearly every sex offender in the city. After police psychiatrist Kiley informs Menjou of the killer's psychological motives, the cop changes the direction of the investigation. Franz, who manages to be both sympathetic and fearsome, is sensational as the baby-faced serial killer, and Menjou does a fine job as the harried detective.

Familiar Face from Television:
❑ Victor Sen Yung (the Cartwright's cook, Hop Sing, in *Bonanza*) as a waiter in a Chinese restaurant.

Memorable Noir Moment:
❑ Sensitivity Training Required: The emergency room doctor bandaging Franz's burned hand tells him, "A man's got no business fooling around with stoves. They're strictly women's business."

So Dark the Night (1946) 71 min. Steven Geray, Micheline Cheirel, Eugene Borden, Ann Codee, Paul Marion. **Screenplay by**: Martin Berkeley and Dwight Babcock. **Directed by**: Joseph H. Lewis. **Noir Type**: Whodunit. **Noir Themes**: Lust, character deterioration. ★★½

Geray is a Parisian detective who vacations in a country village and falls in love with the innkeepers' ambitious daughter (Cheirel). While the girl's father (Borden) is against the relationship, her mother (Codee) encourages her to pursue the policeman, who eventually asks her to marry him. At their engagement party, the girl's fiancé (Marion) threatens to steal her away from the detective. When Marion storms off, Cheirel follows him into the night and never returns. Days later her body is found, and Geray begins a frustrating search to find the murderer, who's been sending notes announcing that "another will die." Czechoslovakian-born Geray does well in a rare starring role.

So Evil My Love (1948) 112 min. Ray Milland, Ann Todd, Geraldine Fitzgerald, Moira Lister, Raymond Huntley. **Screenplay by**: Ronald Millar and Leonard Spigelgass. **Directed by**: Lewis Allen. **Noir Type**: Period. **Noir Themes**: Character deterioration, betrayal, guilt. ★★★★

Todd, a recently widowed missionary to Jamaica, becomes romantically involved with Milland, an artist she met on the long voyage home to Victorian England. Milland, wanted by police on several continents, soon convinces the lovesick Todd to blackmail her best friend (Fitzgerald), who has been cheating on her contemptible husband (Huntley). Meanwhile, unknown to Todd, Milland has been carrying on with an artist's model (Lister) and contemplating a double-cross. The missionary finds herself enjoying this dangerous new lifestyle, but, unfortunately, the extortion plan degenerates into murder. The excellent cast and the delicious ending compensate for the long-winded script.

Familiar Face from Television:

❑ Leo G. Carroll (Cosmo Topper in *Topper* and Mr. Waverly in *The Man from U.N.C.L.E.*) as a private detective.

Memorable Noir Moment:

❑ Sensitivity Training Required: Huntley, advised by Todd that women want to dress up and go out occasionally, informs her that "what women want is one thing; what's good for them is another."

So Well Remembered (1947-British) 114 min. John Mills, Martha Scott, Patricia Roc, Trevor Howard, Richard Carlson, Reginald Tate. **Screenplay by:** John Paxton. **Directed by:** Edward Dmytryk. **Noir Type:** Politics. **Noir Themes:** Betrayal, social reform, economic repression, corruption. ★★★

This British drama stars Mills as a reform-minded small-town politician, and Scott as his ambitious, scheming wife. As the daughter of the man responsible for the existence of the town's slums, Scott has long been considered an outcast by the citizens and, thus, has no empathy for their dismal living conditions. She pushes Mills to run for Parliament, but, when he bows out of the race after realizing that he's being played for a patsy by a corrupt London politician (Tate), she drops him and marries a wealthy Londoner. Her son (Carlson) from her second marriage grows up and returns to his widowed mother's hometown. There he falls in love with Roc, the adopted daughter of an alcoholic doctor (Howard), who knows a terrible secret about Scott. Although enjoyable, *So Well Remembered* is overly long and melodramatic, but Mills' dedicated politician and Scott's predatory femme fatale might give the film noir fan the necessary motivation to view it in one sitting.

Memorable Noir Moment:

❑ Dipso physician Howard drunkenly denounces the booze that he loves so much, claiming, "It's the dire bubonic plague of the soul."

Somewhere in the Night (1946) 110 min. John Hodiak, Nancy Guild, Lloyd Nolan, Richard Conte, Fritz Kortner, Lou Nova, Margo Woode, Houseley Stevenson. **Screenplay by:** Howard Dimsdale, Joseph L. Mankiewicz and Lee Strasberg. **Directed by:** Joseph L. Mankiewicz. **Noir Type:** Amnesia. **Noir Themes:** Paranoia, guilt. ★★½

Suffering from wounds and unable to speak, Marine Hodiak awakens with amnesia in a field hospital. After being transferred to a hospital in Honolulu, he finds a letter from a girl telling him what a louse he is. When he recuperates, he decides not to let on that he's lost his memory so that the military won't investigate him too closely. After being discharged, he moves to a hotel in Los Angeles, his last known address, and begins searching for his true identity. He meets up with a helpful nightclub owner (Conte), a beautiful singer with a "cauliflower heart" (Guild), a sharp homicide detective (Nolan), an insane murder witness (Stevenson), a floozy (Woode) and a mysterious fortuneteller (Kortner) and his goon (Nova). Hodiak soon discovers that almost everyone seems to be interested in a missing suitcase containing two million dollars, which was smuggled out of Germany by a Nazi. Hodiak keeps things moving along nicely, and Woode makes a passable femme fatale.

Sorry, Wrong Number (1948) 89 min. Barbara Stanwyck, Burt Lancaster, Ann Richards, Wendell Corey, Ed Begley, Harold Vermilyea. **Screenplay by**: Lucille Fletcher. **Directed by**: Anatole Litvak. **Noir Type**: Hit Man. **Noir Themes**: Woman in jeopardy, paranoia, greed. ★★★★

Stanwyck plays a "cardiac neurotic," a wealthy hypochondriac whose mental illness has caused her to become, in her words, "a helpless invalid." Lancaster plays her henpecked, but independent-minded, husband. One evening, while Lancaster is out of town, Stanwyck, thanks to a coincidental crossing of telephone wires, overhears a couple of thugs talking about murdering a woman later that night. Frantic, she telephones the police but they dismiss her as a kook. Via flashback, we see how Stanwyck stole Lancaster away from his girl (Richards) and how they eventually married over the objections of her father, pharmaceuticals tycoon Begley. After Lancaster becomes involved with vicious gangsters and industrial espionage, the D.A.'s office starts closing in on him and his reluctant chemist partner (Vermilyea). Between flashbacks, we are treated to Stanwyck's increasingly hysterical outbursts over the telephone, her only means of communication with the outside world, as she comes to believe that *she's* the intended murder victim. Veteran character actor Corey has a small role as Stanwyck's doctor. Stanwyck, who was nominated for an Academy Award for her performance, is outstanding as the neurotic and domineering wife, and Lancaster is brilliantly cast against type as the pathetic milquetoast who seeks to break from his financial dependence on his wife and antagonistic father-in-law. Based on a radio drama starring Agnes Moorehead, *Sorry, Wrong Number* is a classic film noir that shouldn't be missed.

Familiar Faces from Television:
❑ William Conrad (TV's *Cannon*) as Lancaster's gangster partner.
❑ Leif Erickson (Big John Cannon in *High Chaparral*) as Richards' husband, an assistant D.A.
❑ John Bromfield (Frank Morgan in *The Sheriff of Cochise*) as Erickson's partner.

Memorable Noir Moment:
❑ Bachelor Lancaster, still his own man, informs Stanwyck when she asks him to dance, "Where I come from, it's the man who does the picking."
❑ When Stanwyck nixes his idea of moving out of her father's mansion and into an expensive apartment, Lancaster whines, "You've got me sewn up sixteen different ways for three meals a day and pocket money."

The Sound of Fury *see* Try and Get Me

Southside 1-1000 (1950) 73 min. Don DeFore, Andrea King, George Tobias, Morris Ankrum, Robert Osterloh. **Screenplay by**: Leo Townsend and Boris Ingster. **Directed by**: Boris Ingster. **Noir Type**: Undercover. **Noir Themes**: Paranoia, betrayal, greed. ★★★

T-man DeFore goes undercover to break up a counterfeiting ring led by King and his underlings (Tobias and Osterloh). Ankrum plays the gang's master engraver, "a model prisoner whose mainstay is his Bible," who works on counterfeit plates in his San Quentin cell and smuggles them out with an unwitting minister. The overly long (but wonderfully camp) prologue takes the viewer from World War I to the Korean War, before finally making the point that the American dollar is our most important product and that "a counterfeiter is more than a criminal — he's a saboteur." The title refers to the telephone number of the Secret Service ("the watchdogs of the American dollar"). Despite the hokey narration, *Southside* is surprisingly entertaining, thanks in large part to a first-rate performance by King as the icy femme fatale who makes the deadly mistake of falling for a good-looking Fed.

Familiar Face from Television:
❑ Ray Teal (*Bonanza's* Sheriff Roy Coffee) as a plainclothesman at the track.

Memorable Noir Moment:
❑ Two prison guards discuss a Bible-reading counterfeiter. "I think he reads that Bible in his sleep," says one. "When the bad ones get religion, they get it good," replies the other, shaking his head.

Special Agent (1949) 71 min. William Eythe, George Reeves, Laura Elliot [Kasey Rogers], Paul Valentine, Frank Puglia. **Screenplay by:** Lewis R. Foster and Whitman Chambers. **Directed by:** William C. Thomas. **Noir Type:** On the Run. **Noir Themes:** Greed, paranoia, betrayal. ★★

A bored railroad detective (Eythe) becomes involved in the biggest case of his career — a train robbery, in which four railroad employees, including the father of his fiancée (Elliot), were murdered for two mail bags containing a hundred grand in payroll receipts. His investigation leads him to two lumberjack brothers, Reeves and the trigger-happy Valentine, who need the money to buy back the land their grandfather (Puglia) lost years earlier. The killers go on the lam when they find out that the law is closing in on them. Narrated by Truman Bradley, who also hosted TV's *Science Fiction Theater* in the mid–1950s, this low-budget film, "based on material in the official files of American Railroads," contains enough violence and action to keep it mildly interesting.

Familiar Faces from Television:
❑ Frank Cady (Doc Williams in *The Adventures of Ozzie and Harriet* and Sam Drucker in *Petticoat Junction* and *Green Acres*) as the victim of a car theft.
❑ Walter Baldwin (Grandpappy Miller in *Petticoat Junction*) as the train engineer.
❑ Jeff York (Reno McKee in *The Alaskans*) as the train fireman.

Specter of the Rose (1946) 90 min. Judith Anderson, Michael Chekhov, Ivan Kirov, Viola Essen, Charles "Red" Marshall. **Screenplay by:** Ben Hecht. **Directed by:** Ben Hecht. **Noir Type:** Newlywed. **Noir Themes:** Woman in jeopardy, paranoia. ★½

The lead dancer (Kirov) of Anderson's ballet troupe finally seems to have gotten over the passing of his famous ballerina wife, but New York City homicide detective Marshall suspects that Kirov had something to do with her death, even though a doctor concluded that she died of a heart attack. After ballerina newcomer Essen elopes with Kirov, Anderson warns her that her groom has a screw loose. Kirov soon begins calling Essen by his first wife's name and experiencing hallucinations about a knife-wielding alter ego. While this would be enough to scare off most brides, the lovesick Essen keeps hoping for the best. Meanwhile, producer Chekhov, thrilled about the couple's marriage, finds financial backing for a new ballet featuring the almost forgotten star and his new wife. This overrated, low-budget comedy-musical-thriller is guaranteed to cure the most persistent case of insomnia.

Familiar Face from Television:

❑ Lionel Stander (Max, the chauffeur, in *Hart to Hart*) as a poet, of sorts.

Spellbound (1945) 111 min. Ingrid Bergman, Gregory Peck, Leo G. Carroll, Michael Chekhov. **Screenplay by:** Ben Hecht. **Directed by:** Alfred Hitchcock. **Noir Type:** Amnesia. **Noir Themes:** Paranoia, guilt. ★★★★

Peck shows up at a sanitarium claiming to be the replacement for the current director (Carroll), who's being put out to pasture because of his age. A beautiful psychiatrist (Bergman) is immediately attracted to her new boss but soon discovers that he's a paranoid murder suspect and goes on the lam with him so she can help cure his guilt-induced amnesia. Peck, who believes he killed Carroll's real replacement, tries to dissuade Bergman from ruining her career by helping him, but her love for him and her belief in his innocence win him over. Chekhov plays Bergman's mentor, a noted psychoanalyst, who reluctantly agrees to help "the love-smitten analyst playing dream detective" to find the hidden key that will unlock Peck's dark secret. The fine acting, especially by Chekhov, and the ingenious dream sequence (created by artist Salvador Dali) make this Hitchcock thriller worth viewing over and over. The film received Academy Award nominations for Best Picture, Best Supporting Actor (Chekhov), and Best Director, winning an Oscar for Best Score.

Familiar Face from Television:

❑ Dave Willock (Harvey Clayton in *Margie*) as a bellboy.

Memorable Noir Moment:

❑ Psychiatrist Chekhov gives Bergman, his best student, a backhanded compliment. "Women make the best psychoanalysts," he claims. "Until they fall in love. After that they make the best patients."

The Spider (1945) 61 min. Richard Conte, Faye Marlowe, Kurt Kreuger, Martin Kosleck, Mantan Moreland, Ann Savage. **Screenplay by:** Jo Eisinger and W. Scott Darling. **Directed by:** Robert D. Webb. **Noir Type:** P.I. **Noir Themes:** Betrayal, greed. ★★

Marlowe, the assistant in Kreuger's nightclub mind reading act, asks a New Orleans P.I. (Conte) to retrieve an envelope that supposedly contains information proving that Marlowe's sister has been murdered. The murderer is interested in the envelope, too, and strangles Conte's partner (Savage) while trying to obtain it. Conte becomes a suspect in Savage's murder and is later arrested for yet another killing. Moreland is the film's embarrassing African-American comedy relief, and Kosleck plays the mind-reading team's manager. Uninteresting, except for the brief appearance of *Detour*'s Ann Savage in an unusual role for a film noir female — that of a private detective. Of course, she doesn't get a chance to detect anything because she's killed during the first ten minutes. But it's the thought that counts.

Familiar Face from Television:

❏ Cara Williams (Gladys Porter in *Pete and Gladys*) as Savage's roommate.

Spin a Dark Web (1956-British) 76 min. Faith Domergue, Lee Patterson, Rona Anderson, Martin Benson, Robert Arden. **Screenplay by:** Ian Stuart Black. **Directed by:** Vernon Sewell. **Noir Type:** Femme Fatale. **Noir Themes:** Obsession, betrayal, revenge. ★½

After becoming involved in a couple of homicides, Canadian boxer Patterson regrets asking his former Army buddy (Arden) to get him a job with a big-time London gangster (Benson) and tries to quit. Benson's sociopathic sister (Domergue), who has made Patterson her boy-toy, isn't happy about his decision to take a powder and threatens to kill his former girlfriend (Anderson) in retaliation. This is a lame British noir, originally released as *Soho Incident*, with Domergue once again ineffective as a ruthless femme fatale (see *Where Danger Lives*). Patterson went on to co-star in the TV detective series *SurfSide Six*.

The Spiral Staircase (1946) 83 min. Dorothy McGuire, George Brent, Ethel Barrymore, Kent Smith, Rhonda Fleming, Elsa Lanchester, Gordon Oliver, Rhys Williams. **Screenplay by:** Mel Dinelli. **Directed by:** Robert Siodmak. **Noir Type:** Period. **Noir Themes:** Woman in jeopardy. ★★★★

A serial killer has been murdering physically handicapped girls in turn-of-the-century New England because "there's no room in the whole world for imperfection." McGuire, a mute servant girl and perhaps the killer's next victim, works in a mansion belonging to an elderly invalid (Barrymore) and her sons, ladies' man Oliver and the mild-mannered Brent. McGuire is in love with a country doctor (Smith), who's been encouraging her to try to regain the use of her voice, which she lost as a child after witnessing her mother and father perish in a fire. Fleming is Brent's personal secretary and Oliver's most recent romantic conquest, and Lanchester and Williams are husband-and-wife servants. There are plenty of suspects in this highly suspenseful and atmospheric thriller, and first-time viewers will be kept guessing until the end. Barrymore (Drew Barrymore's great aunt) was nominated for an Academy Award for her role as the cantankerous, former big-game hunter.

Familiar Face from Television:

❏ Ellen Corby (Grandma Walton in *The Waltons*) as a murder victim's neighbor.

Memorable Noir Moment:

❏ Barrymore reminisces about her late husband and their days as big-game hunters. "I wasn't as beautiful as his first wife," she says, "but I was a much better shot."

The Spiritualist *see* The Amazing Mr. X

Split Second (1953) 85 min. Stephen McNally, Alexis Smith, Jan Sterling, Keith Andes, Paul Kelly, Robert Paige, Richard Egan, Frank de Kova. **Screenplay by:** William Bowers and Irving Wallace. **Directed by:** Dick Powell. **Noir Type:** Nuclear. **Noir Themes:** Victim of fate, betrayal. ★★★★

Sterling plays a dancer who's hitchhiking to her next gig, and reporter Andes is the guy who gives her a lift. Lovers Smith and Paige are on their way to Las Vegas so Smith can divorce her physician husband (Egan). The unfortunate foursome run into McNally, an escaped killer who, along with partners Kelly and de Kova, takes them hostage. McNally phones Egan and threatens to kill Smith if he doesn't come to an abandoned mining town in the Nevada desert to treat Kelly, who was shot while escaping. To complicate matters, the Army has scheduled an atomic bomb test for the next day, and the ghost town is only a couple of miles from point zero. While the hostages are terrified, McNally isn't at all worried. He figures he'll have plenty of time to get out of there, minus the hostages, of course. McNally, in one of his best roles, is sensational as the trigger-happy gang leader. Sterling is just right as the cynical, street-wise dancer, and Smith is delightfully shameful as the sniveling cheat who'll do anything, including throwing herself at the sadistic killer, to get out of her dangerous predicament. This exciting thriller marked former song-and-dance man and noir icon Powell's directorial debut.

Memorable Noir Moments:
❑ McNally warns Smith's husband not to call the cops. "Play it straight, you get yourself a wife," he tells him. "Get cute, you get yourself a corpse."
❑ Reporter Andes, who's covering the Army's nuclear test, isn't impressed. "When you've seen one atom bomb," he quips, " you've seen them all."

Stakeout on Dope Street (1958) 83 min. Yale Wexler, Jonathan Haze, Morris Miller, Abby Dalton, Allen Kramer, Herman Rudin. **Screenplay by:** Andrew J. Fenady, Irvin Kershner and Irwin Schwartz. **Directed by:** Irvin Kershner. **Noir Type:** Narcotics. **Noir Themes:** Greed, victim of fate, guilt, social reform. ★★½

Three youths (Wexter, Haze and Miller) find an attaché case filled with pure, uncut heroin after a cop killer (Rudin) drops it while fleeing from the law. After five minutes of struggling with the dilemma of whether or not to turn the dope over to the cops, the working class kids decide to sell it on the streets. They recruit a pathetic junkie (Kramer) to help them jump-start their sales, and start thinking about the goodies (sports cars, clothes, bongo drums) they're going to buy with the dough. Wannabe artist Wexler begins having conscience pangs when his girlfriend (Dalton) gives him grief about his new career in pharmaceuticals. Meanwhile, the cops and a couple of angry hoods are scouring the city for the missing mooch. This is a very low-budget film with an unknown cast, but, in addition to the fascinating title, the *Dragnet*-style narration and the hyperactive musical score, there's something weirdly entertaining about it. Kramer gives a camp, almost ten-minute-long discourse on what it's like to go through heroin withdrawal. Dalton later had a successful TV career playing in such hit shows as *Hennesey*, *The Joey Bishop Show* and *Falcon Crest*.

Familiar Face from Television:
❑ Herschel Bernardi (*Arnie*) as Mr. Big.

Memorable Noir Moments:
❑ Tyro drug pusher Miller, who wants "to *be* somebody," complains bitterly that he's "livin' in a hole that may be sixty years long."

❑ Describing his stay in jail, where he needed a fix "to keep the monkey quiet," a junkie laments, "In here, you don't get a fix. You get a bed and you get a basin."

Station West (1948) 92 min. Dick Powell, Jane Greer, Agnes Moorehead, Burl Ives, Tom Powers, Raymond Burr, Gordon Oliver, Guinn Williams. **Screenplay by**: Winston Miller and Frank Fenton. **Directed by**: Sidney Lanfield. **Noir Type**: Horse Opera. **Noir Themes**: Greed, betrayal. ★★★

Undercover federal agent Powell tries to find out who robbed and murdered two soldiers who were guarding a gold shipment. His investigation leads him to a saloon and gambling joint run by Greer and her lover, Oliver. After impressing Greer and the citizenry by taking on the toughest guy in town (Williams) in a fistfight, Powell sets a trap for the murderers. Burr plays a cowardly lawyer with a substantial gambling debt, Moorehead is a wealthy widow, Powers is an uncooperative Army captain and Ives is a guitar-strumming hotel desk clerk. Powell, playing a Western version of his hardboiled detective, Philip Marlowe (see *Murder, My Sweet*), is enjoyable as the wisecracking undercover agent, and the lovely Greer, fresh from *Out of the Past*, is once again delightful as a femme fatale. B western veteran Guinn "Big Boy" Williams later played a roustabout in TV's *Circus Boy*.

Familiar Faces from Television:

❑ John Doucette (Jim Weston in *Lock Up* and Captain Andrews in *The Partners*) as the bartender.

Memorable Noir Moments:

❑ The brawny Williams, after being sucker-punched by Powell, comments menacingly, "You're too small to make that big of a mistake."
❑ Powell gives Burr, who has double-crossed the gold thieves, some good advice. "Get on that horse and ride him until he dies," he says. "Then run until you have to crawl, and you might be lucky."

The Steel Helmet (1951) 84 min. Gene Evans, Robert Hutton, Richard Loo, Steve Brodie, James Edwards, Richard Monahan, William Chun, Harold Fong. **Screenplay by**: Samuel Fuller. **Directed by**: Samuel Fuller. **Noir Type**: Combat. **Noir Themes**: Fatalism, revenge. ★★★★

Evans stars as a tough Korean War infantryman who holes up in a Buddhist temple with a squad of mostly raw recruits while seeking a North Korean prisoner to bring back for interrogation. Conveniently, hiding inside the temple there's already a sneaky Red major (Fong), who has plans to kill the Americans one by one. Brodie is the green lieutenant in charge of the squad; Hutton is a "conchie" (conscientious objector); Loo is a veteran Japanese-American soldier; Edwards plays an African-American medic; and Monahan is a young G.I. with a baldness problem. A South Korean orphan (Chun) has attached himself to Evans and is in the habit of writing prayers of safety for the gruff sergeant. Surprisingly for the era, the film deals with some controversial issues—race, religion, conscientious objection and the interment of Japanese-American citizens during World War II. No glamorous John Wayne vehicle, *The Steel Helmet*, a precursor of the more realistic Vietnam films to come, is a violent, disquieting film noir study of the realities of an unpopular war and the psychological problems faced by the G.I.s who fought it. Character actor Evans gives a strong performance in one of his rare starring roles and Loo, often typecast as a Japanese villain (see *The Clay Pigeon*), is excellent as the heroic, American-as-apple-pie G.I.

Familiar Face from Television:

❑ Sid Melton (Ichabod Mudd, assistant to *Captain Midnight*, and Charlie Halper, owner of the Copa Club, in *Make Room for Daddy* a.k.a. *The Danny Thomas Show*) as a tight-lipped soldier.

Memorable Noir Moments:

❑ Hutton is concerned that the good guys and the bad guys all look alike. Combat veteran Evans gives him some helpful hints on how to distinguish between them "He's a South Korean when he's runnin' *with* ya," he says. "He's a North Korean when he's runnin' *after* ya."

❑ When Brodie orders one of his men to risk his life to retrieve the dog tags of a dead American soldier, the cynical, but practical, Evans tells him, "A dead man is nothing but a corpse. Nobody cares who he is now."

The Steel Jungle (1956) 86 min. Perry Lopez, Beverly Garland, Walter Abel, Ted de Corsia, Kenneth Tobey, Leo Gordon. **Screenplay by:** Walter Doniger. **Directed by:** Walter Doniger. **Noir Type:** Prison. **Noir Themes:** Betrayal, corruption, paranoia, woman in jeopardy. ✭✭

A small-time bookie (Lopez) goes to prison rather than cooperate with authorities, who offered him a deal if he would turn state's evidence against his gambling syndicate employers, "The Combination." Sentenced to one year, he leaves behind his pregnant wife (Garland), who had been begging him to go straight for the sake of his unborn child. Inside, he meets up with his boss (de Corsia), who's doing time for tax evasion. After Lopez witnesses de Corsia's goons kill a guard, he refuses to identify the killers for the no-nonsense warden (Abel) and sympathetic prison psychiatrist (Tobey). Not appreciative of Lopez's loyalty, de Corsia and his henchman (Gordon) try to make sure he remains quiet by threatening Garland, who's having pregnancy problems at home. Unexciting.

Familiar Faces from Television:

❑ Joe Flynn (Captain Binghamton in *McHale's Navy*) as a bespectacled convict.
❑ Kay E. Kuter (Newt Kiley in *Petticoat Junction* and *Green Acres*) as a con named "Stringbean."
❑ Edward Platt (the Chief in *Get Smart*) as the judge in Lopez's trial.
❑ Jack Kruschen (Tully in *Hong Kong* and Sam Markowitz in *Busting Loose*) as a good citizen truck driver.

Memorable Noir Moments:

❑ When the yard period bell rings, Lopez asks an elderly con if he's going outside. "Out there you're either the pushers or the pushed," the man says. "I'm too old to be either."
❑ When Lopez demands to know where his missing wife is, tough guy de Corsia answers, "Couple of days, look for her at the bottom of the river. She'll be the dame wearin' the cement shoes."

The Steel Trap (1952) 85 min. Joseph Cotten, Teresa Wright, Eddie Marr, Aline Towne. **Screenplay by:** Andrew L. Stone. **Directed by:** Andrew L. Stone. **Noir Type:** On the Run. **Noir Themes:** Paranoia, guilt, greed. ✭✭✭✭

Nine years after appearing together in Hitchcock's masterful thriller, *Shadow of a Doubt*, Cotten and Wright reunite in this thoroughly enjoyable noir about a bank teller (Cotten) who, in a hastily planned heist, steals a million dollars from his employer. Because of its lack of an extradition treaty with the U.S., Cotten decides to flee to Brazil, telling his unsuspecting wife (Wright) that they're going there on bank business. Proving the old adage that if something can go wrong it will, the hapless Cotten runs into more difficulties and bad luck than most film noir bank robbers combined. This suspenseful, sometimes humorous, tale succeeds because of Cotten's delightful performance and Stone's imaginative script.

Familiar Face from Television:

❑ Ed Nelson (Dr. Michael Rossi in *Peyton Place*) as an airline passenger waiting in line and (don't blink) as an extra dancing in a nightclub.

Memorable Noir Moment:

❑ When Wright discovers that Cotten is a thief, he noirishly justifies his actions. "We've only so many days, so many hours, so many minutes to live," he explains, "and we're suckers if we don't cram into them all the happiness we can get away with regardless of how we do it."

Step Down to Terror (1958) 75 min. Charles Drake, Colleen Miller, Rod Taylor, Josephine Hutchinson. **Screenplay by:** Mel Dinelli, Czenzi Ormonde and Chris Cooper. **Directed by:** Harry Keller. **Noir Type:** Psycho. **Noir Themes:** Women in danger, betrayal, family dysfunction. ★★

There are some movies that just don't need remaking. Hitchcock's *Shadow of a Doubt* is one of them. Why Universal felt it necessary to even try is a mystery. Prodigal son Drake, in the Joseph Cotten role, returns home to mom (Hutchinson) to hide out from the cops. Taylor, an undercover detective posing as a newspaper man, falls in love with Drake's widowed sister-in-law (Miller) and tries to arrest the killer without causing the sickly Hutchinson to suffer a heart attack. Dreary and uninteresting. Taylor went to star in a number of TV series, the most successful being *Hong Kong* in the early 1960s.

Memorable Noir Moment:

❑ "Cops have harder heads than anybody," Drake assures Miller after beaning Taylor with a bedpost knob. (This isn't the first use of a bedpost knob as a film noir weapon. See also *C-Man*.)

A Stolen Face (1952-British) 72 min. Paul Henreid, Lizabeth Scott, André Morell, Mary MacKenzie. **Screenplay by:** Martin Berkeley and Richard Landau. **Directed by:** Terence Fisher. **Noir Type:** Plastic Surgery. **Noir Themes:** Obsession, betrayal. ★★★

While vacationing in the English countryside, a plastic surgeon (Henreid) meets a beautiful concert pianist (Scott) and falls in love with her. Scott reciprocates but feels obligated to her marriage-minded manager (Morell), who's been responsible for her tremendous success. When she leaves Henreid without warning and returns home to wed Morell, the despondent surgeon throws himself into his work. His next case is a horribly scarred female inmate at the prison hospital, where he's been doing charity work and trying to prove his theory that convicts who received plastic surgery are rarely repeat offenders. He gives his new patient Scott's face and, after the operation, marries the little sociopath, hoping to turn her into a clone of his lost love. Not only can't his bride (Scott in a dual role) play the piano, she's a clumsy kleptomaniac, an alcoholic and, quite possibly, a nymphomaniac. Meanwhile, when Morell decides that he can't marry Scott because she's in love with Henreid, the excited pianist rushes back to London to tell Henreid the good news. This British noir is a bit far-fetched, but it works well because of Scott's smooth portrayal of the soft-spoken American beauty and the heavy drinking Cockney jailbird.

Memorable Noir Moment:
❑ From the Some-Things-Never-Change Department: Before leaving the doctor's office with her young son, who had surgery performed to regain the use of his fingers, a mother promises the surgeon that she'll pay him someday. "Why is it," the doctor asks a colleague, "that the poor always worry about paying their bills and the rich have to be reminded?"

Stolen Identity (1953) 81 min. Donald Buka, Joan Camden, Francis Lederer. **Screenplay by**: Robert Hill. **Directed by**: Gunther von Fritsch. **Noir Type**: Impersonator. **Noir Themes**: Paranoia, betrayal, jealousy. ★★★

Buka, a cab driver in Austria, has neither a residency permit nor working papers because of his minor criminal record. On New Year's eve, his luck changes when a visiting American is shot in the back seat of his taxi by a jealous husband. Desperate to return to the U.S., Buka hides the man's body, steals his passport, and attempts to pick up an airline ticket to New York being held at the man's hotel. There he runs into Camden, who's running away from her husband (Lederer), who killed her American lover. When she confronts Buka about his impersonation, he spills the beans, and they try to leave the country together, hoping to evade both the police and Lederer. Well-done and atmospheric, this minor noir entry was produced by actor Turhan Bey (***The Amazing Mr. X***).

A Stolen Life (1946) 107 min. Bette Davis, Glenn Ford, Dane Clark, Walter Brennan, Charles Ruggles, Bruce Bennett. **Screenplay by**: Catherine Turney. **Directed by**: Curtis Bernhardt. **Noir Type**: Good Twin, Bad Twin. **Noir Themes**: Betrayal, jealousy, obsession. ★★

Davis has a field day playing twins who are interested in the same man (Ford). The sweet sister (Davis #1) loses the young lighthouse engineer to her more devious sibling (Davis #2), who can't stay faithful to the patsy once she marries him. Fate intervenes, giving Davis #1 another chance at happiness, but at what cost? Ruggles is the sisters' guardian, Brennan plays a cantankerous lighthouse keeper, Bennett is the bad sister's lover, and Clark is an egotistical artist ("a Rasputin of the paint pots"). This tedious remake of the 1939 British film of the same title was produced by Davis, who in 1964 again played twins in the more enjoyable *Dead Ringer*.

Familiar Faces from Television:
❑ Tom Fadden (Duffield in *Broken Arrow* and Silas Perry in *Cimarron City*) as a fisherman.
❑ James Flavin (Lt. Donovan in *Man with a Camera*) as a detective investigating an accidental drowning.

Storm Fear (1956) 88 min. Cornel Wilde, Jean Wallace, Dan Duryea, David Stollery, Lee Grant, Steven Hill, Dennis Weaver. **Screenplay by**: Horton Foote. **Directed by**: Cornel Wilde. **Noir Type**: Hostage. **Noir Themes**: Betrayal, guilt, greed. ★★★

A wounded bank robber (Wilde), on the lam with what's left of his gang (Hill and Grant), holes up at the isolated farmhouse of his sickly brother (Duryea) and sister-in-law (Wallace). Has-been writer Duryea isn't at all happy to see his younger brother, the black sheep of the family who used to be Wallace's lover. Twelve-year-old Stollery believes that Duryea is his dad and that Wilde is his uncle, but it's really vice versa. Weaver (TV's *McCloud*), a hired hand with a yen for Wallace, is more of a dad to Stollery than Duryea *or* Wilde. While Wilde tries to make up for lost time with Wallace, psycho Hill, who does a fine job as an unstable gang member with a greedy eye on the loot, spends *his* time beating up the sickly Duryea, threatening Stollery and trading insults with dipso Grant. Hill is better known for his roles on TV's *Mission Impossible* and *Law & Order*. This suspenseful noir, an amalgam of *The Desperate Hours* and *Key Largo*, was also produced by Wilde.

Memorable Noir Moment:
❑ Duryea has a few brotherly, noirish, words for Wilde. "You're nothing but a bum, Charlie. You'll end up in the gutter just like Papa," he shouts. "A thieving, murdering bum. You'll end up just like I told Mama you would."

Storm Warning (1950) 93 min. Ginger Rogers, Ronald Reagan, Doris Day, Steve Cochran. **Screenplay by**: Richard Brooks and Daniel Fuchs. **Directed by**: Stuart Heisler. **Noir Type**: Racist. **Noir Themes**: Bigotry, woman in jeopardy, victim of fate, family dysfunction. ★★★½

While visiting her sister (Day) in a small southern town, fashion model Rogers witnesses the murder of a newspaper reporter by the Ku Klux Klan. One of the two unhooded faces she sees belongs to her brother-in-law (Cochran), whom she meets for the first time later that evening. Reagan, the crusading D.A., enlists Rogers as a witness against the Klan, causing a serious dilemma for the model. Should she do the right thing and testify, or should she protect her sister? Rogers and Day, two actresses noted for their musicals, are excellent. Seeing the usually smooth and debonair Cochran portray a none-too-bright hayseed may be a shock to the system, but he does it well. The film, however, suffers from a lack of realism — race is never mentioned; no one speaks with a southern accent; Klan members are portrayed as naive dupes of the imperial wizard, whose only motive for organizing them is financial gain; and the only black faces on screen are the ones in the crowd scenes. Despite these shortcomings, the tightly woven script and solid acting make this an enjoyable film.

Familiar Faces from Television:
❑ Ned Glass (Sgt. Andy Pendleton in *The Phil Silvers Show* and Doc in the film *West Side Story*) as the proprietor of a recreation center and bowling alley.
❑ King Donovan (Bob Cummings' Air Force buddy Harvey Helm in *Love That Bob* and lawyer Herb Thornton in *Please Don't Eat the Daisies*) as an ambulance attendant.

Memorable Noir Moment:
❑ The imperial wizard gives a pretty accurate description of his followers. "You know the

boys," he says. "Without those white hoods to hide in, they're no heroes. That's why they need the hoods in the first place."

The Story of Molly X (1949) 82 min. June Havoc, John Russell, Dorothy Hart, Elliot Lewis, Charles McGraw. **Screenplay by:** Crane Wilbur. **Directed by:** Crane Wilbur. **Noir Type:** Prison. **Noir Themes:** Revenge, jealousy, betrayal, guilt. ★★★½

The brains behind a gang of thieves (Havoc) is determined to find and kill the man who murdered her gangster husband. After a jewelry heist goes wrong, she learns that one of the gang (Lewis) is the killer and shoots him. Russell helps her load the body onto the refrigeration car of an eastbound train before the two go on the lam. When they arrive at their hideout, the cops are waiting for them, thanks to two captured gang members who sang like canaries. When Lewis' body is found, homicide detective McGraw suspects that either Russell or Havoc committed the murder, but he can't do a ballistics test until their 38s have been found. Both are convicted of the jewelry store robbery, and Russell is sent to the state pen while Havoc goes to a California woman's institution that specializes in rehabilitation instead of punishment. Once there, tough gal Havoc gets into trouble breaking rules and refusing to work. When an inmate is transferred to San Quentin for execution, Havoc begins to worry that the cops will find the gun she hid and that she'll soon be facing the gas chamber herself. So she becomes a model prisoner, hoping for an early parole so she can retrieve the gun. Meanwhile, Lewis' revenge-minded moll (Hart), who's been cooperating with McGraw, shows up as an inmate at the institution, threatening Havoc's plans. This low-budget B noir is a pleasant surprise, with an intelligent script that even ventures into sexual abuse of children as a reason for a criminal's antisocial behavior. The occasional snappy dialogue ("The coppers couldn't find a pair of pajamas in a bowl of soup" admittedly isn't a good example), good acting, terrific surprise ending and enjoyable action scenes (especially the amazingly realistic fistfight between Havoc and Hart, where the two go at it like a couple of professional middleweights) all add up to an entertaining and unforgettable film noir experience.

Familiar Faces from Television:

❑ Connie Gilchrist (Purity, pub proprietress and girlfriend of *Long John Silver*) as an inmate saying grace before a meal.
❑ Kathleen Freeman (Katie the maid in *Topper* and Flo Shafer in *The Beverly Hillbillies*) as an inmate in the tailor shop.

Memorable Noir Moments:

❑ Gangster Lewis appreciates the way recently widowed Havoc is looking these days. "You should always wear black, baby," he says. "Yeah," interrupts his jealous moll, "grief becomes her, doesn't it?"
❑ When Hart goes too far in her sarcasm toward Havoc, the impatient Lewis gives her a valuable geography lesson. "That's San Francisco Bay out there," he says. "The water's deep and it's cold and sometimes they don't come back."
❑ When the prosecutor asks a member of Havoc's gang if it's unusual for a woman to be in charge of a criminal ring, the witness replies, "It used to be. It's not any more. First thing you know, the dames'll take over the whole racket."
❑ The feisty Havoc warns Hart to "keep out of my way. If I have to slap you down, you'll stay down." And she means it, too.

The Strange Affair of Uncle Harry (1945) 80 min. George Sanders, Geraldine Fitzgerald, Ella Raines, Moyna MacGill. **Screenplay by:** Steven Longstreet. **Directed by:** Robert Siodmak. **Noir Type:** Triangle. **Noir Themes:** Family dysfunction, lust. ★★★½

Sanders, known as Uncle Harry to the town's children, is a mild-mannered bachelor who lives with his two unmarried sisters (Fitzgerald and McGill). Fitzgerald has an unnatural attachment to her brother and isn't pleased when Raines shows up in their small town and sets her sights on him. When Sanders and Rains decide to get married, the sisters find themselves searching for a new place to live. McGill is genuinely happy for her brother, but Fitzgerald is hell bent on destroying the relationship so she'll have Sanders all to herself again. Sanders nicely underplays his role as the quiet, unassuming brother, but Fitzgerald is too stiff as his pompous, overbearing sister. Raines and McGill are fine in supporting roles, but what keeps the viewer engrossed is the perverse thought that at any moment we'll see Fitzgerald try to seduce her brother. Sanders comes off as Mr. Innocence in this scandalous scenario, but it's strange that the girl he finally picks to fall in love with bears a resemblance to his sister that's too close for comfort. Also known as *Uncle Harry*, the film con-

Eligible bachelor George Sanders tries to make time with the new girl in town (Ella Raines) in *The Strange Affair of Uncle Harry* (Universal, 1945).

tains such a cop-out ending, thanks to the friendly 1940s thought police, that it reportedly caused the producer (Joan Harrison) to quit Universal in disgust.

Familiar Face from Television:
❑ Harry von Zell (announcer of *The George Burns and Gracie Allen Show*) as a pharmacist and member of a barber shop quartet.

Memorable Noir Moments:
❑ A pharmacist tells the inquisitive Sanders about a special poison mixture. "One pinch and you wake up being measured for a harp," he boasts.
❑ The loves of Sanders' life (sister Fitzgerald and fiancée Raines) go toe-to-toe over the old bachelor.

Strange Bargain (1949) 68 min. Jeffrey Lynn, Martha Scott, Harry (Henry) Morgan, Richard Gaines, Katherine Emery, Henry O'Neill. **Screenplay by:** Lillie Hayward. **Directed by:** Will Price. **Noir Type:** Cover-Up. **Noir Themes:** Victim of fate, fatalism. ★★★

Lynn plays one of the most sympathetic characters in all of film noir. In the hole financially every month, with a wife (Scott), two kids and a mortgage, the assistant bookkeeper approaches his boss (Gaines) for a raise only to be told that business is so bad that he'll have to be let go. Lynn is shocked when Gaines tells him that he's planning to commit suicide and needs his help to make his death look like a murder so his wife and son can collect the insurance money. Lynn refuses but the persistent Gaines calls him later that evening and tells him to hurry over. When he gets to Gaines' house, he finds an envelope addressed to him containing ten grand, a gun and the man's body. Inside the envelope is a note begging him to do the right thing. Lynn, acting according to Gaines' instructions, goes outside with the gun, shoots two bullets through the window and then disposes of the weapon. Homicide detective Morgan investigates and decides that Lynn's new boss (O'Neill) is the logical suspect, leaving Lynn in a serious moral dilemma — tell what he knows to protect O'Neill or keep quiet so Gaines' family can collect the insurance. *Strange Bargain* is a low budget, but gripping, suspense film with an enjoyable surprise ending.

Familiar Face from Television:
❑ John Hamilton (Perry White in *The Adventures of Superman*) as an employee of Gaines' firm.

Memorable Noir Moments:
❑ Sensitivity Training Required: Scott chides Lynn when he says he won't make any more mistakes, "You're a man and men are *always* making mistakes."
❑ When a secretary worries that a police officer might think she's the killer, the cop replies, "You know policemen don't think, miss."

Strange Fascination (1952) 80 min. Hugo Haas, Cleo Moore, Mona Barrie, Rick Vallin. **Screenplay by:** Hugo Haas. **Directed by:** Hugo Haas. **Noir Type:** Newlywed. **Noir Themes:** Obsession, lust, character deterioration, jealousy. ★★

Haas plays a Viennese concert pianist who lucks on to his very own angel (Barrie), a middle-aged American widow, who brings him to the U.S. and finances his career. While on the concert circuit, he meets a star-struck young dancer (Moore), whom he romances and eventually marries. A bit of bad luck puts the newlyweds in dire financial straits, and his usual source of funds dries up when Barrie turns her back on him. Moore takes up modeling to help pay the bills, but jealousy infects Haas so badly that he forbids her to work, fearing she'll meet someone. Soon Moore's old dancing partner (Vallin) returns, looking to pick up where they left off, causing Haas to hit the bottle. Before long, the $100,000 accidental insurance policy he took out on his hands begins to look mighty tempting. There's nothing fascinating about *Strange Fascination* except how Haas (who, as usual, wrote, produced, directed and starred) was able to finance this odd film.

Strange Illusion (1945) 84 min. James (Jimmy) Lydon, Warren William, Sally Eilers, Regis Toomey, Charles Arnt. **Screenplay by:** Adele Comandini. **Directed by:** Edgar G. Ulmer. **Noir Type:** Asylum. **Noir Themes:** Corruption, paranoia, lust. ★★½

Lydon plays a young man whose strange dreams leads him to investigate William, the man who wants to marry Lydon's recently widowed mother (Eilers). Lydon voluntarily commits himself to an insane asylum operated by William's cohort (Arnt) to gather evidence against the crooks. Toomey, Lydon's family doctor, teams up with his young patient to get the goods on Arnt and William. William is splendid as the murderous rake whose downfall, like that of mastermind criminal Doc Riedenschneider in *The Asphalt Jungle*, is his "problem" with young girls. This weird and often slow-moving film, director Ulmer's low-budget update of *Hamlet*, is enjoyable at times. Lydon, former star of the "Henry Aldrich" film series, later played Biffen Cardoza from the planet Herculon in the 1950s TV series *Rocky Jones, Space Ranger*.

Familiar Face from Television:

❏ John Hamilton (Perry White in *The Adventures of Superman*) as a banker friend of the family.

Memorable Noir Moment:

❏ Sensitivity Training Required: When told by Arnt that he would be considered a guest, not a patient, at the insane asylum, Lydon replies, "A guest? Well, that's white of you." (See *Detour*, *The Devil and Daniel Webster* and *The Blue Dahlia*.)

Strange Impersonation (1946) 68 min. Brenda Marshall, William Gargan, Hillary Brooke, Ruth Ford. **Screenplay by:** Mindret Lord. **Directed by:** Anthony Mann. **Noir Type:** Plastic Surgery. **Noir Themes:** Woman in jeopardy, jealousy, betrayal, greed. ★★★

An impatient laboratory chemist (Marshall) tests her new anesthesia formula on herself with a little help from her assistant, femme fatale Brooke. While Marshall is semi-conscious, Brooke deliberately tampers with the mixture and causes an explosion, which disfigures the chemist's face. Marshall's fiancé (Gargan) wants to marry her immediately, but the devious Brooke, whose aim all along was to grab Gargan for herself, drives a wedge between the lovers. Marshall assumes the identity of a recently deceased blackmailer (Ford), skips town to get plastic surgery and returns to find that Gargan has married Brooke. While not everyone will applaud the surprise ending, this low-budget noir is still likable, with everyone giving enjoyable performances. Brooke went on to become a regular in the TV comedy series *My Little Margie* and *The Abbott and Costello Show*, and, later, the hit private eye drama, *Richard Diamond, Private Detective*.

Familiar Faces from Television:
- ❏ Lyle Talbot (Joe Randolph in *The Adventures of Ozzie and Harriet*) as a detective.
- ❏ Mary Treen (Hilda, the maid, on *The Joey Bishop Show*) as a nurse.

Strange Intruder (1956) 82 min. Edmund Purdom, Ida Lupino, Ann Harding, Carl Benton Reid, Gloria Talbott, Jacques Bergerac. **Screenplay by:** David Evans and Warren Douglas. **Directed by:** Irving Rapper. **Noir Type:** Troubled Veteran. **Noir Themes:** Child in jeopardy, betrayal, paranoia, jealousy. ★★

Purdom, a disturbed, former P.O.W., returns home from Korea with a mission — to kill his buddy's two little children. He believes he made a promise to his dying friend, who callously remarked that he thought the kids would be better off dead than living with their mother (Lupino) and her lover (Bergerac). Released for the weekend from the psychiatric ward of the veteran's hospital, Purdom visits his friend's family — mom and dad (Harding and Reid), sis (Talbott) and, of course, cheating spouse Lupino and her kids. Hearing his dead buddy's voice encouraging him to keep his promise, the troubled Purdom determines to do just that, even though he's beginning to feel like one of the family. While the P.O.W. camp sequence is interesting, the remainder of the film may be too tedious to sit through unless you're a rabid fan of noir icon Lupino. British actor Purdom's Hollywood career went downhill after *Strange Intruder*, and he took to starring in European action epics.

The Strange Love of Martha Ivers (1946) 115 min. Barbara Stanwyck, Van Heflin, Lizabeth Scott, Kirk Douglas, Judith Anderson. **Screenplay by:** Robert Rossen. **Directed by:** Lewis Milestone. **Noir Type:** Cover-Up. **Noir Themes:** Paranoia, guilt, betrayal, lust. ★★★★

On his way to California, war hero Heflin gets stranded in his hometown. There he meets the lovely Scott, who's on parole for a trumped-up theft charge. When she's picked up for parole violation, he goes to the D.A. (Douglas), a childhood friend, for help. Douglas isn't happy about seeing Heflin, his former romantic rival, because he thinks that Heflin witnessed his wife (Stanwyck) murdering her wealthy aunt (Anderson) seventeen years earlier and that he's back in town to blackmail them. Threatening Scott with a prison term, Douglas forces her to betray Heflin, who soon discovers that an innocent man had been prosecuted by Douglas and hanged for the murder committed by Stanwyck. Douglas, in his film debut, gives an electrifying performance as the weak-kneed boozer with political ambitions, and Stanwyck is excellent as the murderous femme fatale. Heflin and Scott also stand out in this classic film noir. Look for future director Blake Edwards (*Breakfast at Tiffany's, The Pink Panther*) in a bit role as a hitchhiking sailor.

Familiar Faces from Television:
- ❏ Darryl Hickman (Dobie's brother, Darvey, in *The Many Loves of Dobie Gillis* and Ben Canfield in *The Americans*) as Heflin's character as a teenager.
- ❏ James Flavin (Lt. Donovan in *Man with a Camera*) as a police detective.

Memorable Noir Moment:

❑ When a detective flashes his badge, cop hater Heflin comments, "You don't have to show me who you are. I can tell by the smell."

The Strange Mr. Gregory (1945) 63 min. Edmund Lowe, Jean Rogers, Don Douglas, Marjorie Hoshelle. **Screenplay by:** Charles Belden. **Directed by:** Phil Rosen. **Noir Type:** Impersonator. **Noir Themes:** Obsession, lust, jealousy. ★½

Lowe, a sleight-of hand-performer, hypnotist and necromancer, falls hard for Rogers, the wife of a businessman and amateur magician (Douglas). When she refuses his advances, Lowe concocts a diabolical plot to get rid of his competition. Using the old reliable "Kalamudra Death Trance," a state of suspended animation, Lowe fakes his own murder and sees to it that Douglas gets charged with the crime. Returning as his own twin brother, he makes his move on the vulnerable Rogers but doesn't count on interference from her savvy friend (Hoshelle). Also known as *The Great Mystic*, this film's outrageous plot is reminiscent of two later bombs, **The Mask of Diijon** (1946) and **Hit and Run** (1957).

Memorable Noir Moment:

❑ When Lowe is asked at to saw a woman in half at a party, he replies that he left his saw at home. The flirtatious Hoshelle tells him, "I'll bet you don't need a saw to saw a woman in half. You can do it just with your eyes."

Strange Triangle (1946) 65 min. Signe Hasso, Preston Foster, Anabel Shaw, Shepperd Strudwick, Roy Roberts. **Screenplay by:** Charles G. Booth and Mortimer Braus. **Directed by:** Ray McCarey. **Noir Type:** Femme Fatale. **Noir Themes:** Betrayal, lust, greed. ★★½

War veteran Foster returns home to a new job as district supervisor of bank examiners at Roberts' bank. His first assignment is to audit a branch being managed by Roberts' younger brother (Strudwick). Before beginning the task, Foster has a fling with a mysterious woman (Hasso), who unceremoniously dumps him afterwards. He later discovers that the woman was Strudwick's wife, a con artist from way back, who has the pitiable Strudwick embezzling funds from the bank to support her luxurious lifestyle. Strudwick's loyal assistant (Shaw) convinces Foster to help get her boss out of his predicament, but the devious Hasso has other plans, which lead to murder. Nicely done, with Hasso doing a good job as the femme fatale.

Memorable Noir Moment:

❑ Unaware that Foster is describing his brother's wife, Roberts listens attentively as his employee describes his recent one-night stand. "No dame ever hit me so hard or so fast," Foster tells his appreciative boss.

The Strange Woman (1946) 100 min. Hedy Lamarr, George Sanders, Louis Hayward, Gene Lockhart, Hillary Brooke. **Screenplay by:** Herb Meadow. **Directed by:** Edgar G. Ulmer. **Noir Type:** Femme Fatale. **Noir Themes:** Betrayal, greed, obsession, lust, guilt. ★★★

An impoverished girl (Lamarr) in rugged eighteenth century Maine knows exactly what she wants to be when she grows up — a rich man's wife. After she blossoms into a luscious beauty, Lockhart, the middle-aged owner of the town's lumber mill, pursues her and makes her his wife. For a while, she's satisfied being married to the richest man in town and enjoying her reputation as a lady of charitable works, but eventually she seduces her weak-willed stepson (Hayward), who's been away at school spending his father's money "on hard drink and easy women." Lamarr convinces the reluctant Hayward to commit a murder that she claims will ensure their happiness. But soon afterwards, she drops the poor sap, causing him to become a suicidal drunkard. She then turns her attention to Sanders, best friend Brooke's fiancé. All seems to be going well for Lamarr until she hears a fire-and-brimstone preacher's sermon entitled, "The Strange Woman," which she believes is directed at her. Lamarr is fascinating as the conniving siren hell-bent on living the good life, even if it means destroying those who love her. Hayward is good as her faint-hearted fall guy, but the aristocratic Sanders is miscast as the rugged lumberman.

Familiar Face from Television:

❏ Ray Teal (Sheriff Roy Coffee in *Bonanza*) as a lumberjack.

Memorable Noir Moment:

❏ When a friend remarks that Lamarr could have her pick of the youngest and best-looking sailors in port, the mercenary beauty replies, "I don't want the youngest. I want the richest."

The Stranger (1946) 95 min. Edward G. Robinson, Loretta Young, Orson Welles, Philip Merivale, Richard Long, Konstantin Shayne. **Screenplay by:** Anthony Veiller. **Directed by:** Orson Welles. **Noir Type:** Nazi. **Noir Themes:** Woman in jeopardy, betrayal, paranoia. ★★★★½

Robinson, a member of the Allied War Crimes Commission, is eager to find a notorious war criminal. After allowing a Nazi-turned-religious fanatic (Shayne) to escape from prison, Robinson follows the man to Harper, a small Connecticut town, where he hopes Shayne will lead him to his former superior officer (Welles). Needless to say, Welles, who has assumed a new identity as a college professor, isn't happy to see Shayne show up on the day he's to be married to Young, the daughter of a Supreme Court Justice (Merivale). He strangles his former comrade as they kneel in prayer and buries the body in the woods. Because there are no known photographs of the wanted Nazi, Robinson now must rely on Welles' bride to supply the evidence he needs to arrest the college professor. But Young, blinded by love and loyalty, is having none of this nonsense about her groom being a war criminal. Meanwhile, the panicky Welles is beginning to worry that she might crack under the pressure and begins plotting her demise. *The Stranger* is a wonderfully suspenseful film noir, with Robinson and Welles outstanding as the two sworn enemies determined to outwit each other. Young is believable as the bride who can't accept that "she could ever have given her love to such a creature." Nineteen-year-old Richard Long (later the star of TV's *Bourbon Street Beat*, *Nanny and the Professor* and *The Big Valley*) plays Young's kid brother.

Memorable Noir Moments:

❏ How wrong can you be? On a dark night, Young turns down Robinson's offer to accompany her home, adding, "In Harper, there's nothing to be afraid of."

❑ Nazi hunter Robinson responds to a that's-funny-he-doesn't-look-like-a-Nazi observation. "They look like other people and act like other people," he says, adding, "When it's to their benefit."

A Stranger Came Home *see* The Unholy Four

Stranger on the Prowl (1952-Italian) 82 min. Paul Muni, Joan Lorring, Vittorio Manunta, Luisa Rossi. **Screenplay by:** Ben Barzman. **Directed by:** Joseph Losey (as Andrea Forzano). **Noir Type:** On the Run. **Noir Themes:** Victim of fate, paranoia. ★★

This low-budget Italian noir stars Muni as a tramp being hunted by police for murdering a shopkeeper. He crosses paths with an impoverished eight-year-old boy (Manunta), who imagines he's also being pursued — for stealing a bottle of milk from the murdered woman. Muni sees the kid as his chance to get away and accompanies the boy through the dark alleys of the war-ravaged Italian town, eluding the cops. Rossi is Manunta's mother, and Lorring plays a bicycle racer's abused girlfriend, who's also sexually harassed by her boss. Muni, with a lustful look in his eyes, takes the unlucky working girl hostage. The predictable plot isn't helped by the actors' hard-to-understand accents, especially young Manunta's. In order to get the film shown in the U.S., Losey, who was experiencing big problems with the Commie hunters in the House Un-American Activities Committee, had to direct under an Italian pseudonym.

Stranger on the Third Floor (1940) 64 min. John McGuire, Margaret Tallichet, Peter Lorre, Elisha Cook, Jr., Charles Halton. **Screenplay by:** Frank Partos. **Directed by:** Boris Ingster. **Noir Type:** Wrong Man. **Noir Themes:** Victim of the law, paranoia. ★★★★

Hailed by some film historians as the first film noir, *Stranger* is the suspenseful story of a newspaper reporter (McGuire), whose testimony helps convict a taxi driver (Cook) of murder. Although he didn't actually witness the murder, McGuire saw Cook fleeing from the scene, and this is enough for the indifferent jury to come back with a guilty verdict. Tallichet is the reporter's fiancée, who's disturbed that McGuire may be responsible for sending an innocent man to the chair. When McGuire sees a man (Lorre) fleeing from a neighbor's apartment, he investigates and finds the neighbor (Halton) with his throat cut — the same way the restaurant owner was murdered. Because he and Halton didn't get along, McGuire becomes a suspect, causing him to realize that Cook may have been innocent after all. With her boyfriend under investigation, Tallichet begins searching for the man seen fleeing Halton's apartment. Director Ingster and director of photography Nicholas Musuraca provide a visually appealing film that speeds toward an exciting climax. Lorre's role is brief but exceptional, and McGuire's unusually lengthy nightmare sequence is intense.

Memorable Noir Moments:

❑ McGuire, testifying against Cook, gives his eyewitness account. "It wasn't very nice," he says. "His throat was cut. Blood was still dripping into the open drawer of the cash register."

❑ McGuire coaxes a shy Tallichet into his apartment and manages to get her to remove her wet shoes and stockings before the morality police (his landlady and next door neighbor) barge in to upset his plans.

Strangers on a Train (1951) 101 min. Farley Granger, Robert Walker, Ruth Roman, Leo G. Carroll, Patricia Hitchcock, Laura Elliott [Kasey Rogers], Jonathan Hale. **Screenplay by:** Raymond Chandler and Czenzi Ormonde. **Directed by:** Alfred Hitchcock. **Noir Type:** Psycho. **Noir Themes:** Fatalism, guilt, paranoia. ★★★★★

En route to finalize his divorce from Elliott, tennis pro Granger meets a man on the train who seems to know all about him — even that he plans to marry Roman, the beautiful daughter of U.S. Senator Carroll. The stranger (Walker), after some small talk, makes Granger a proposition — he suggests that they swap murders—"you do my murder; I do yours." Granger, convinced that Walker is a harmless nut, brushes it off as a "good idea" and quickly dismisses him. When Walker learns that Elliott, who's pregnant by another man, has refused to divorce Granger, he goes ahead with his side of the "bargain," fully expecting the tennis pro to reciprocate by killing Hale, Walker's hated father. When the flabbergasted Granger refuses, Walker relentlessly stalks him, hoping to spur him to action. Meanwhile, the police have assigned two detectives to follow Granger day and night, and his fiancée is becoming increasingly

A killer (Robert Walker, left) tells his unwitting accomplice (Farley Granger) about a recent murder in *Strangers on a Train* (Warner Bros., 1951).

suspicious. Hitchcock (the director's daughter) plays Roman's perky sister, whose resemblance to the murdered Elliot is beginning to unnerve Walker. Don't be surprised if you find yourself sympathizing more with the psychopathic killer than with the self-centered tennis pro, who handles his predicament with an astounding lack of good judgment. From its ordinary beginning (two strangers breaking the boredom of a long train trip by chatting) and the sensationally photographed murder (through a pair of eyeglasses) to the thrilling climax (a runaway merry-go-round caused by an idiot noir cop), *Strangers on a Train* is first-rate entertainment. Walker, who gives a remarkably chilling performance, died of respiratory failure at age 32 shortly after *Strangers'* release and while he was filming **My Son John**.

Familiar Face from Television:
❑ Marion Lorne (Aunt Clara on *Bewitched*) as Walker's slightly daffy mother.

Memorable Noir Moment:
❑ When Hitchcock calls Granger's late wife "a tramp," she's scolded by her father, who reminds her that everybody's entitled to the pursuit of happiness. "From what I hear," Hitchcock says, "she pursued it in all directions."
❑ Psychopathic murderer Walker is dismayed to discover that curiosity seekers have made the boat ride, where he killed Elliot, the longest line in the amusement park. "I don't think that's a very nice way to make money," he remarks critically to the ride's operator.

Stray Dog (1949-Japanese) 122 min. Toshiro Mifune, Takashi Shimura, Ko Kimura, Keiko Awaji. **Screenplay by:** Akira Kurosawa and Ryuzo Kikushima. **Directed by:** Akira Kurosawa. **Noir Type:** Far East. **Noir Themes:** Victim of fate, guilt. ★★★★½

Mifune, a rookie homicide detective riding a crowded Tokyo bus, loses his service revolver to a "public conveyance pickpocket." Embarrassed, he offers his resignation but is instead assigned by his superior to find the pickpocket and the gun. While the desperate cop wanders Tokyo's seedy neighborhoods and slums looking for leads, the gun, a valuable rarity in postwar Tokyo, finds its way to a disaffected war veteran (Kimura), who uses it in a series of robberies to impress his girlfriend (Awaji), a chorus dancer at the Blue Bird Club. After Kimura wounds a woman during his first robbery attempt, the guilt-stricken Mifune teams up with an older and more experienced cop (Shimura), and the two resort to old-fashioned leg work in the midst of a sweltering heat wave hoping to track down the robber before he can use the gun again. But during another robbery, Kimura kills a Tokyo housewife, adding to the rookie's grief and self-reproach. Will the determined cops find the killer before he uses the four remaining bullets? This riveting police procedural, released in Japan in 1949 as *Nora Inu* and in the U.S. in 1963 as *Stray Dog*, was one of director Kurosawa's (*Rashomon* and *The Seven Samurai*) most important early works. Stylistically impressive, beautifully photographed and intensely suspenseful, this classic Japanese film noir offers an interesting look at postwar Japan, including an entertaining manhunt during a real-life baseball game.

Memorable Noir Moments:
❑ From the Some-Things-Never-Change Department: A female pickpocket, feeling harassed by Mifune and Shimura's questioning, warns them, "It's against human rights. I'll sue."

❑ Shimura warns Mifune against acting rashly when they spot an armed suspect at the baseball game. Reminding him of the threat to the crowd, he remarks, "Bullets aren't fouled balls."

❑ Sensitivity Training Required: An unsympathetic design man at the Blue Bird Club explains to detectives the reason for chorus girl Awaji's absence. "Those monthly things," he says. "She always makes trouble then."

❑ Leaving an uncooperative witness to face her angry mother, Shimura tells his partner, "Mothers make good prosecutors."

Street of Chance (1942) 74 min. Burgess Meredith, Claire Trevor, Louise Platt, Sheldon Leonard, Jerome Cowan. **Screenplay by:** Garrett Fort. **Directed by:** Jack Hively. **Noir Type:** Amnesia. **Noir Themes:** Victim of fate, betrayal. ★★½

Meredith gets hit on the head by falling debris at a construction site and regains the memory he previously lost as a result of a similar head injury a year earlier. The gimmick here is that since the first accident he's been living a new life and now he doesn't remember anything about it (double amnesia noir!). Confusing? It gets more complicated. He returns to his wife (Platt) thinking he had just left her that morning, gets his old job back, gets chased by a mysterious stranger (Leonard) and finds that he has a girlfriend (Trevor). And if all that isn't enough, the mild-mannered businessman is wanted for murder! What starts out as an intriguing premise, soon declines into a pretty standard whodunit, with Meredith playing amateur detective and wearing an outlandishly oversized fedora. However, thanks to fine performances by Meredith and Trevor, this early film noir, based on the novel "The Black Curtain" by pulp fiction writer Cornell Woolrich, is still a fun ride.

Memorable Noir Moments:

❑ When amnesiac breadwinner Meredith returns home, his wife informs him that he's been gone an entire year. Flabbergasted that's she's doing so well, he asks, "How did you manage to get along?"

❑ Uttering a common film noir complaint, Trevor tells amnesia victim Meredith, who doesn't even recognize her, "Why do I love you like this? You're no good and you never will be."

The Street with No Name (1948) 91 min. Mark Stevens, Richard Widmark, Lloyd Nolan, Barbara Lawrence, Ed Begley, John McIntire, Donald Buka. **Screenplay by:** Harry Kleiner. **Directed by:** William Keighley. **Noir Type:** Undercover. **Noir Themes:** Betrayal, corruption, sexual hostility. ★★★½

Stevens plays an F.B.I. agent who goes undercover to get the goods on a gang of robbers led by Widmark and his second-in-command (Buka). Nolan is in charge of the operation, and McIntire is Stevens' undercover F.B.I. contact. Begley plays the local police chief, and Lawrence is Widmark's feisty wife. This was Widmark's first film after his tremendous success as a psycho killer in 1947's *Kiss of Death*. His performance here is a bit more subdued; he's just slightly less psychopathic. Buka gives a pretty good showing as Widmark's menacing henchman. Interestingly, Nolan played the same character in *House on 92nd Street*, and both films make use of real-life F.B.I. employees. *Street* was remade with an Oriental flavor in 1955 as *House of Bamboo*.

Memorable Noir Moment:

❏ Widmark hands a poorly dressed Stevens a wad of dough and tells him, "Buy yourself a closet full of clothes. I like my boys to look sharp."

The Strip (1951) 85 min. Mickey Rooney, Sally Forrest, William Demarest, James Craig, Kay Brown, Tom Powers. **Screenplay by:** Allen Rivkin. **Directed by:** Leslie Kardos. **Noir Type:** Show Biz. **Noir Themes:** Obsession, betrayal, jealousy. ★★½

When his girlfriend (Forrest) is found shot and his ex-boss (Craig) is murdered, jazz drummer Rooney is questioned by homicide detective Powers and, via flashback, we hear his side of the sordid tale. Wounded in Korea, Rooney leaves the hospital with a new set of drums and heads for Hollywood and, he hopes, a career in music. Along the way he meets bookie Craig, who gives him a job as a phone man in a horse-betting parlor. Rooney, while escaping a police raid, runs into Forrest, a pretty wannabe actress, who works as a cigarette girl and dancer in a Sunset Strip jazz joint owned by Demarest (Uncle Charlie in TV's *My Three Sons*). Rooney falls hard for her and signs on as a drummer at the club just so he can be close to her. Trying to make an impression, the little drummer makes the mistake of introducing her to Craig, hoping he'll be able to help her break into the movies. But the suave bookie has more on his mind than being helpful, and Forrest doesn't seem to mind the attention. Fearing he's losing his girl, the obsessed Rooney begins following them around. This standard crime drama works well thanks to a good performance by Rooney, who did his own drumming, and some terrific jazz from Louis Armstrong and His Band. Crooner Vic Damone appears as himself.

Familiar Faces from Television:

❏ Tommy Rettig (Jeff Miller, Lassie's original owner, in *Lassie*) as a bratty kid.
❏ Jeff Richards (*Jefferson Drum*, Old West newspaper editor) as a patient at a military hospital.

Memorable Noir Moment:

❏ Former numbers man Rooney confesses to his new employer that his last job wasn't as an insurance salesman. "I couldn't sell a dollar bill for eighty-eight cents," he admits.

Sudden Danger (1955) 85 min. Bill Elliott, Tom Drake, Beverly Garland. **Screenplay by:** Dan Ullman and Elwood Ullman. **Directed by:** Hubert Cornfield. **Noir Type:** Police Procedural. **Noir Themes:** Greed, betrayal. ★★

The first of the "Lt. Doyle" crime dramas starring former B western star "Wild Bill" Elliott finds the Los Angeles detective investigating the suspicious death of a blind man's mother. Elliott suspects that the son (Drake) did away with his mother, who was responsible for the accident that caused his blindness, so he could collect the insurance money and get an operation to restore his sight. Garland plays Drake's girlfriend, whom he refuses to marry until he can see again. While slightly better than the other films in the low-budget series, *Sudden Danger* is still a confusing whodunit with little action and even less suspense. (See *Calling Homicide* and *Footsteps in the Night*. Another Lt. Doyle film, *Chain of Evidence*, was not available for review by the author at the time of writing.)

Familiar Faces from Television:

- ❏ Minerva Urecal (Annie in *The Adventures of Tugboat Annie* and "Mother" in *Peter Gunn*) as Drake's landlady.
- ❏ Lyle Talbot (Joe Randolph in *The Adventures of Ozzie and Harriet*) as an out-of-town businessman.

Sudden Fear (1952) 110 min. Joan Crawford, Jack Palance, Gloria Grahame, Bruce Bennett. **Screenplay by:** Lenore Coffee and Robert Smith. **Directed by:** David Miller. **Noir Type:** Triangle. **Noir Themes:** Woman in danger, betrayal, greed. ★★★★

Playwright Crawford believes that Palance isn't good-looking enough to play the lead in her new Broadway play and has him replaced with a more appealing actor. Letting bygones be bygones, Palance romances her on a train trip to San Francisco and settles the question once and for all—he's romantic all right, romantic enough to bed and wed her in record time. Crawford is deliriously happy, but Palance, when

he's not counting his bride's money, is committing adultery with his old flame (femme fatale Grahame), who's arrived in town to share in his good fortune. When Palance discovers that Crawford is updating her will, he mistakenly believes that he is going to be short-changed and decides to kill her before her attorney (Bennett) returns from a business trip to finalize things. While Palance discusses his plans with Grahame, their conversation is accidentally recorded on Crawford's newfangled dictating machine. The next day, with the proof of their criminal intent in her fidgety little hands, Crawford drops the record, shattering it. She's then forced to come up with her own plan to turn the tables on the scheming couple. And does she! Downright

Jack Palance plays an actor with murder on his mind in *Sudden Fear* (RKO, 1952).

lethargic for the first 60 minutes, the film eventually gains momentum before finally exploding in one of film noir's most suspenseful climaxes. Crawford and Palance received Oscar nominations for their performances.

Familiar Face from Television:

❏ Mike Connors billed as "Touch" Connors (*Mannix*), in his film debut, as Bennett's younger brother and Grahame's patsy.

Memorable Noir Moment:

❏ Crawford listens in shock as her dictating machine plays back Palance and Grahame's love-making. "Kiss me. Kiss me. Harder. Harder," Grahame begs. Palance responds passionately, "I'm crazy about you. I could break your bones."

Suddenly (1954) 77 min. Frank Sinatra, Sterling Hayden, James Gleason, Nancy Gates. **Screenplay by:** Richard Sale. **Directed by:** Lewis Allen. **Noir Type:** Hostage. **Noir Themes:** Conspiracy, child in jeopardy, paranoia. ★★★★

A deputy sheriff jokingly explains to a passing motorist that, despite the town's name ("Suddenly"), things are so slow nowadays that the town council is thinking of changing the name to "Gradually." What the deputy doesn't know is that assassin

A fellow hostage (James Gleason, upper left) restrains a captive sheriff (Sterling Hayden) while a wannabe assassin (Frank Sinatra) straightens his broken arm in *Suddenly* (United Artists, 1954). Other hostages (Nancy Gates, center, and Kim Charney) look on.

Sinatra is coming to town with his two accomplices to kill the President of the United States at a non-scheduled train stop in town. The trio invades a house overlooking the train station and holds a family and the town's sheriff (Hayden) hostage. Sinatra is wonderfully despicable as the psycho, who enjoys bragging about the twenty-seven Germans he killed during the war. Hayden and the boy's grandfather (Gleason), a retired Secret Serviceman, must figure out a way to stop the killers. Gates is the pacifist war widow who won't let her son play with toy guns. Super acting, a believable plot and a slam-bang climax make this a classic not to be missed.

Memorable Noir Moments:

❑ Sinatra tells his gunman to keep an eye on the hostages. "Anybody gets brave, kill 'em all," he says, adding, "You can only hang once."

❑ From the Some-Things-Never-Change Department: During his guns-don't-kill-people-do sermon, Hayden tells the unconvinced Gates, "Guns aren't necessarily bad. It depends on who's using them."

❑ When Sinatra mentions that he won the Silver Star in the war, his eight-year-old hostage pipes up, "Aw, you stole it," earning himself a vicious slap in the face.

The Sun Sets at Dawn (1950) 71 min. Phillip Shawn, Sally Parr, Walter Reed, Lee Frederick, Howard St. John, Raymond Bramley. **Screenplay by:** Paul Sloane. **Directed by:** Paul Sloane. **Noir Type:** Wrong Man. **Noir Themes:** Victim of the law, fatalism, social reform. ★½

Shawn stars as a youth scheduled to die in the electric chair for a murder he didn't commit, while his girlfriend (Parr) mourns, and everyone from the prison guards to the warden (St. John) frets about her unhappiness. While newspaper reporters wait for the scheduled electrocution, the unnamed state's first, the deputy warden (Bramley) has his hands full trying to get the newfangled electric chair to work properly. In the meantime, Chaplain Reed attempts to comfort Shawn, who contemplates his meaningless life. Frederick, a gangster with a new identity, turns out to be a key figure in the drama. Tedious.

Familiar Face from Television:

❑ King Donovan (Air Force officer Harvey Helm in *Love That Bob* and lawyer Herb Thornton in *Please Don't Eat the Daisies*) as a reporter.

Memorable Noir Moment:

❑ With his electrocution imminent, Death Row inmate Shawn wonders aloud why he didn't make any sports teams in high school. "Lots of us have to sit in the grandstands," replies the chaplain, trying to console him. "But why? Why?" the prisoner asks. "We can't all be players," notes the clergyman. "No," Shawn, answers. "We can't all sit in the grandstands either. Some of us always have to sit in the bleachers. I could never figure it out." Neither will the viewer.

Sunset Blvd. (1950) 110 min. William Holden, Gloria Swanson, Erich von Stroheim, Nancy Olson, Jack Webb. **Screenplay by:** Charles Brackett, Billy Wilder and D.M. Marshman, Jr. **Directed by:** Billy Wilder. **Noir Type:** Show Biz. **Noir Themes:** Obsession, paranoia, jealousy. ★★★★½

Pursued by a couple of automobile repo men, a down-and-out screenwriter (Holden) pulls into the driveway of what appears to be an abandoned estate. He soon learns that it's owned by an aging, silent film queen (Swanson). She mistakes him for the undertaker who's supposed to deliver a casket for her recently deceased pet monkey. When he informs her that he's a highly successful screenwriter, a stretch of the imagination to say the least, she offers him the job of editing the comeback script she hopes will propel her into the limelight once again. Penniless and with his own recent screenplay rejected by the studios, Holden accepts the job. At his new boss' insistence, he moves into the mansion, which is occupied only by Swanson and her strange, fiercely loyal butler (von Stroheim). Holden soon becomes Swanson's lover, the reluctant recipient of her lavish gifts. When he meets wannabe screenwriter Olson (a studio script reader and fiancée of his friend, Webb), he begins sneaking out of the house to collaborate with her on a screenplay. It isn't long before Webb and Holden fall in love, alienating his jealous sugar mommy, who claims she has a gun and knows how to use it. Number 12 on the American Film Institute's List of America's 100 Greatest Movies, *Sunset Blvd.* is a sensational Hollywood self-parody. Swanson's *tour de force* performance as the self-deluded, has-been star earned her an Oscar nomination. The film was nominated for ten other Academy Awards, including Best Picture, Best Director, Best Actor (Holden), Best Supporting Actor (von Stroheim) and Best Supporting Actress (Olson), winning three Oscars (Best Story and Screenplay, Best Art Direction and Set Decoration, and Best Score of a Drama or Comedy). Look for cameos by famed director Cecil B. DeMille and gossip columnist Hedda Hopper as themselves, and silent screen stars Buster Keaton, Anna Nilsson and H.B. Warner as Swanson's weekly bridge partners.

Familiar Face from Television:
❑ Fred Clark (Harry Morton, George and Gracie's neighbor in *The George Burns and Gracie Allen Show*) as the studio executive who rejects Holden's script.

Memorable Noir Moments:
❑ Viewing one of her silent films, Swanson boasts, "We didn't need *dialogue*. We had *faces*."
❑ Holden paints a picture of his relationship with Swanson: "An older woman who's well-to-do. A younger man who's not doing too well."
❑ When Swanson threatens suicide, bragging that a hundred thousand fans will mourn her loss, Holden callously retorts, "You'd be killing yourself to an empty house. The audience left twenty years ago."

The Suspect (1944) 85 min. Charles Laughton, Ella Raines, Stanley Ridges, Rosalind Ivan, Henry Daniell. **Screenplay by:** Bertram Millhauser and Arthur T. Horman. **Directed by:** Robert Siodmak. **Noir Type:** Period. **Noir Themes:** Character deterioration, paranoia, guilt. ★★★★

A Victorian London tobacco shop manager (Laughton) has had enough of his shrewish wife (Ivan). The day after moving out of their bedroom and into his son's vacant room, Laughton meets a lonely young secretary (Raines), and they become close friends. But when they both realize that the friendship is heading in a romantic direction, Laughton breaks it off because his wife won't give him a divorce. When the evil-tempered Ivan learns about them, she makes the mistake of threatening to expose Raines as a tramp, causing the normally mild-mannered shopkeeper to decide to shut her up—for good. Ivan's demise leaves him free to marry his true love, until a persistent Scotland Yard inspector (Ridges) and a blackmailing neighbor (Daniell) get too close to discovering the truth. Laughton is perfect as the cold-blooded, but sympathetic, killer, and Ivan is equally impressive as his hateful spouse.

Memorable Noir Moment:

❑ When Laughton moves out of their bedroom, his despicable wife says, "I'd like to know what's going on in your head." Laughton replies coldly but truthfully, "It's much better that you shouldn't Cora. It might frighten you."

Suspense (1946) 101 min. Barry Sullivan, Belita, Albert Dekker, Bonita Granville. **Screenplay by**: Philip Yordan. **Directed by**: Frank Tuttle. **Noir Type**: Ambition. **Noir Themes**: Obsession, lust, jealousy. ★½

Sullivan plays an ambitious drifter who gets a job selling peanuts at an Ice Capades–type show. He's soon promoted by the producer (Dekker), whom he thanks for the career advancement by seducing his wife (Belita), the star of the show. Enter former girlfriend Granville. An avalanche and two murders do nothing to advance the lame plot, and several lengthy ice-skating numbers (designed especially for former ice skating star Belita) only slow things down even more. Contrary to the title, the suspense is non-existent.

Familiar Face from Television:

❑ Billy Gray (Bud in *Father Knows Best*) as a little boy at the zoo.

Suspicion (1941) 99 min. Cary Grant, Joan Fontaine, Cedric Hardwicke, Nigel Bruce, Dame May Whitty. **Screenplay by**: Joan Harrison, Samson Raphaelson and Alma Reville. **Directed by**: Alfred Hitchcock. **Noir Type**: Newlywed. **Noir Themes**: Paranoia, woman in jeopardy. ★★

Exceptionally well-acted but generally boring suspenser about Fontaine and a charming, but good-for-nothing, playboy (Grant), who saves her from spinsterhood. The honeymoon ends quickly when Fontaine discovers that the unemployed Grant has taken it for granted that they would be living on her income. After Grant discovers that she receives only a paltry annual allowance from her wealthy parents (Hardwicke and Whitty), Fontaine gets the idea that he wants to kill her for the insurance. While Grant, Fontaine and Grant's wealthy and eccentric best friend (Bruce) are enjoyable, this is a disappointing Hitchcock offering, with an unsatisfying ending. Fontaine won a Best Actress Oscar for her performance.

Familiar Face from Television:

❑ Leo G. Carroll (Cosmo Topper in *Topper* and Mr. Waverly in *The Man from U.N.C.L.E.*) as Grant's cousin and former boss.

Swamp Fire (1946) 69 min. Johnny Weissmuller, Virginia Grey, Buster Crabbe, Carol Thurston. **Screenplay by**: Daniel Mainwaring (as Geoffrey Homes). **Directed by**: William H. Pine. **Noir Type**: Troubled Veteran. **Noir Themes**: Guilt, jealousy, revenge, obsession, economic repression. ★½

Weissmuller takes a break from his "Tarzan" and "Jungle Jim" roles to play a troubled ex–Coast Guard officer whose ship was sunk by a German U-boat. After returning home to Louisiana's bayou country and his girlfriend (Thurston), he reluctantly takes back his old job as a bar pilot with the Coast Guard Reserves, guiding vessels to safety during bad weather. Lacking self-confidence and struggling with guilt over losing his ship and so many of his crew, Weissmuller allows himself to be goaded into piloting a boat in a dense fog, with tragic results. Grey is a rich femme fatale who decides she wants Weissmuller all to herself and schemes to take him away from Thurston. Although the film is packed with such exciting diversions as boat collisions, a fiery marsh blaze, a dandy cat fight between Thurston and Grey, and a toe-to-toe between the big guy and another former screen Tarzan (Crabbe), somebody still felt it was necessary to have Weissmuller mix it up with a swamp alligator. While Weissmuller, in his only non-jungle leading role, gives a mediocre performance, Crabbe isn't too bad, even with that bogus Cajun accent.

Familiar Face from Television:

❑ Barely recognizable, but the ears give it away — David Janssen (Richard Diamond in *Richard Diamond, Private Detective* and Richard Kimble in *The Fugitive*) as the teenager announcing Weissmuller's return.

Sweet Smell of Success (1957) 96 min. Burt Lancaster, Tony Curtis, Susan Harrison, Martin Milner, Sam Levene, Barbara Nichols, Jeff Donnell, Emile Meyer. **Screenplay by:** Clifford Odets and Ernest Lehman. **Directed by:** Alexander Mackendrick. **Noir Type:** Ambition. **Noir Themes:** Obsession, jealousy, corruption, betrayal, revenge. ★★★★★

Curtis, an unethical press agent, will do *anything* to curry favor with an important New York columnist (Lancaster), who's even more repulsive than Curtis. When Lancaster's sister (Harrison) starts seeing jazz guitarist Milner (star of TV's *Route 66* and *Adam 12*), the perversely jealous Lancaster convinces Curtis to break up the relationship by refusing to give Curtis' clients any space in his all-important column, "The Eyes of Broadway." With his bread and butter at stake, Curtis invents a slanderous story about Milner and entices a libidinous columnist to run it by fixing him up with his girlfriend, the unwilling Nichols. When the obstinate young musician refuses to buckle under Lancaster's sadistic attempts to ruin his career and his relationship with Harrison, the unholy alliance comes up with yet another plan, only this time they go too far. Levene plays Milner's loyal manager, Donnell is Curtis' secretary, and Meyer is a vicious cop who owes Lancaster a big favor. Lancaster is terrific as the arrogant columnist who makes and breaks careers on a whim, and Curtis is equally good as the press agent "immersed in the theology of making a fast buck." This is a sordid but highly entertaining film. James Wong Howe's outstanding cinematography and the hot jazz score by the Chico Hamilton Quartet are the icing on this delicious noir cake.

Familiar Faces from Television:

❑ David White (*Larry Tate* in Bewitched) as a libidinous columnist.
❑ Edith Atwater (Phyllis Hammon in *Love on a Rooftop* and Aunt Gertrude in *The Hardy Boys Mysteries*) as Lancaster's secretary.

Memorable Noir Moments:

❑ Even the vile Lancaster can't stomach his shady hireling. "I'd hate to take a bite out of you," he tells Curtis. "You're a cookie full of arsenic."

❑ When Nichols says she accompanied a columnist to his apartment the evening before, Curtis asks her where the man's wife was. "I don't know," the blonde replies. "It was a big apartment."

❑ After watching a drunk being thrown out of a nightclub into the cold New York night, Lancaster takes a look around and remarks, "I love this dirty town."

The System (1953) 90 min. Frank Lovejoy, Joan Weldon, Don Beddoe, Jerome Cowan, Fay Roope, Paul Picerni. **Screenplay by**: Jo Eisinger. **Directed by**: Lewis Seiler. **Noir Type**: Gangster. **Noir Themes**: Social reform, corruption. ★★

The "System" is a big-city gambling syndicate, headed by good-guy bookie Lovejoy. It's also the title of a series of exposés written by Lovejoy's long-time friend, newspaperman Beddoe. City officials have been closing their eyes to Lovejoy's illegal activities, causing Beddoe to become an anti-gambling crusader. Beddoe's editor (Roope) tries to make a deal with Lovejoy — he'll stop the articles if Lovejoy will stop seeing his daughter (Weldon). No dice, says Lovejoy, who's in love with Weldon. Lovejoy's out-of-town associates, unhappy with all of the negative publicity, advise Lovejoy to "drop the dame," but they have no more luck than Roope. Soon there's a murder, a suicide, and a state hearing presided over by a hotshot special prosecutor (Picerni). It sounds pretty exciting, but even reliable Lovejoy, whose character is probably the nicest film noir criminal ever, looks bored.

Memorable Noir Moment:

❑ When asked why he borrowed a large sum of money from Lovejoy, one of the syndicate's bookies gets a big laugh at the crime hearing when he replies, "No bank'll borrow me money on *my* reputation."

T-Men (1948) 92 min. Dennis O'Keefe, Alfred Ryder, Mary Meade, Wallace Ford, Charles McGraw, Herbert Heyes. **Screenplay by**: John C. Higgins. **Directed by**: Anthony Mann. **Noir Type**: Undercover. **Noir Themes**: Greed, paranoia. ★★★½

This is typical Anthony Mann noir — slow moving and methodical before finally building to a slam-bang ending. And, as usual, it's worth the wait. A documentary style police thriller, *T-Men* follows the undercover activities of two treasury agents, O'Keefe and Ryder, as they infiltrate a counterfeiting ring and try to keep their cover from being blown. They run across some very dangerous hoods, in particular McGraw, whose ruthlessness is demonstrated early on and who, thankfully, has a good amount of screen time. He shines at being evil. Once you get past the prologue warning that reproducing U.S. currency is frowned upon by the government and the opening statement by the "former chief coordinator of the law enforcement agencies of the Treasury Department," things slowly, but surely, start to improve.

Familiar Face from Television:

❑ June Lockhart (Ruth Martin in *Lassie* and Maureen Robinson in *Lost in Space*) as a newlywed married to a T-man.

Memorable Noir Moment:

❏ During a vicious interrogation, a stalwart undercover agent refuses to answer questions, commenting bravely that he can't hear a thing. McGraw viciously slaps the T-Man's ears. "You hear any better now?" he asks.

Take One False Step (1949) 94 min. William Powell, Shelley Winters, Marsha Hunt, Dorothy Hart, James Gleason, Sheldon Leonard. **Screenplay by:** Chester Erskine and Irwin Shaw. **Directed by:** Chester Erskine. **Noir Type:** Whodunit. **Noir Themes:** Victim of fate. ★★

Powell, a college professor seeking funds for a pet project, runs into an old flame (Winters), who's interested in picking up where they left off. Happily married to Hart, Powell does his best to discourage Winters, but the dipso is persistent. To shut her up, he accepts her invitation to a party that turns out to be a party for two. The next day the newspapers report that Winters is missing and believed dead and that the police are looking for a mystery man. Seeking to clear himself before his potential donor gets wind of the scandal, he investigates with the help of a friend (Hunt), gets bit by a German Shepherd, and spends considerable time trying to find a doctor in Los Angeles who hasn't been notified by the police to be on the lookout for a rabies victim. Gleason and Leonard play the homicide detectives on Powell's trail. It's all pretty tedious, although Powell is still very smooth fifteen years after his best-known role, that of Nick Charles, the suave private detective in *The Thin Man*.

Familiar Face from Television:

❏ Minerva Urecal (Annie in *The Adventures of Tugboat Annie* and "Mother" in *Peter Gunn*) as a gas station attendant.

Talk About a Stranger (1952) 65 min. George Murphy, Nancy Davis, Billy Gray, Lewis Stone, Kurt Kasznar. **Screenplay by:** Margaret Fitts. **Directed by:** David Bradley. **Noir Type:** Payback. **Noir Themes:** Paranoia, revenge. ★★★

A boy and his dog, a mysterious stranger, a murder case ... you'll find all of the elements of a good story in this underrated little gem. Murphy and his wife (Davis) are expecting a baby, and when they ask their adolescent son (Gray) whether he'd prefer a brother or a sister, he answers, "a dog!" When Gray finds a stray mutt, he's the happiest kid in the world ... until somebody poisons his new pet. He suspects Kasznar, a mysterious stranger who has taken over the old house near Murphy's orange orchard. Acting on the advice of newspaper editor Stone, Gray tries to gather evidence against Kasznar and soon finds himself involved in a murder investigation. This is a disquieting film, in which the lead character, a young boy, is so deeply disturbed by what he perceives to be a terrible injustice that he seeks an adult-like vengeance on the perpetrator. Visually striking, thanks to veteran cinematographer John Alton, *Talk About a Stranger* merits a viewing by all noir fans. While the ending is somewhat disappointing, there are some scenes that might startle even the hardened horror fan. Murphy eventually became a U.S. senator from California; Davis became Nancy Reagan, wife of President Ronald Reagan; and Gray later played "Bud" (his nickname in this film also) in TV's *Father Knows Best*.

Familiar Faces from Television:

❏ Kathleen Freeman (Katie the maid in *Topper* and Flo Shafer in *The Beverly Hillbillies*) as a grocery store clerk.
❏ Burt Mustin (Fireman Gus in *Leave It to Beaver* and Mr. Quigley in *All in the Family*) as a watch repairman.

Memorable Noir Moment:

❏ After Gray finds the body of his dog, the camera zooms in on his face, with Kasznar's eerie Victorian house in the background. His childlike countenance gradually changes to one of pure hatred, even evil.

The Tall Target (1951) 78 min. Dick Powell, Paula Raymond, Adolphe Menjou, Marshall Thompson, Ruby Dee, Will Geer, Will Wright, Katherine Warren. **Screenplay by:** George Worthing Yates and Art Cohn. **Directed by:** Anthony Mann. **Noir Type:** Period. **Noir Themes:** Conspiracy, betrayal. ★★★

A New York City police inspector (Powell) suspects that President-elect Abraham Lincoln will be assassinated while making a pre-inaugural address in Baltimore. When his report is dismissed by his superiors, Powell resigns and hops aboard a southbound train headed for Baltimore, where he plans to warn Lincoln personally. Onboard, he discovers the body of a fellow police officer and, after he himself is attacked, comes to the conclusion that the assassins are on the train. There are no shortage of suspects: a mysterious woman (Warren) and her sick husband; an irate businessman (Wright), who feels that Lincoln will ruin the economy; a heavy-drinking Army Reserve colonel (Menjou); a West Point cadet (Thompson) from the South; and the cadet's sister (Raymond) and their slave (Dee). Powell, without badge, gun or good sense, must find the assassins and convince the authorities of the reality of the plot before the train pulls into Baltimore. Geer plays the ill-tempered conductor. While the outcome of this historical thriller is known from the start, this doesn't detract from the overall enjoyment of watching Powell, a bumbling cop, come to the rescue of the Great Emancipator. There are a few scenes that defy believability, though — in particular, when an assassin shoots at Powell's head, which is covered by a newspaper, and the blank cartridge burns a huge hole in the paper but leaves nary a mark on the fearless cop's face.

Familiar Faces from Television:

❏ Barbara Billingsley (June Cleaver in *Leave It to Beaver*) as the mother of a pesky child.
❏ Jeff Richards (*Jefferson Drum*, Old West newspaper editor) as a Philadelphia police officer.
❏ Leif Erickson (Big John Cannon in *High Chaparral*) as an assassin impersonating Powell.
❏ Percy Helton (Homer Cratchit in *The Beverly Hillbillies*) as a train passenger.

Memorable Noir Moments:

❏ When a gun-wielding assassin offers Powell a cigar, the cop asks, "You hand out cigars to all your victims?" "Gives them something to do with their hands," the killer replies.
❏ From the Some-Things-Never-Change Department: Southern belle Raymond resorts to stereotyping Powell when the New York City cop tries to confiscate her train ticket. "Must all you New Yorkers be so insufferably boorish?" she asks.

The Tattered Dress (1957) 93 min. Jeff Chandler, Jeanne Crain, Jack Carson, Gail Russell, George Tobias, Elaine Stewart, Philip Reed. **Screenplay by:** George Zuckerman. **Directed by:** Jack Arnold. **Noir Type:** Trial. **Noir Themes:** Revenge, corruption. ★★

When a rich, jealous husband (Reed) plugs the guy who made a play for his adulterous wife (Stewart), a shady lawyer (Chandler), who specializes in getting guilty people off, takes on his case. Chandler humiliates the local sheriff (Carson) during cross-examination and, despite being an undesirable "New York lawyer" in a small California town, wins over the jury. The killer walks, and the angry Carson, who was a friend of the murdered man, frames Chandler by making it appear that a member of the jury, Carson's lover (Russell), was bribed by the lawyer. Now Chandler must defend himself in a trial that could end his career and send him to the big house. His estranged wife (Crain) and a Las Vegas comedian (Tobias) rush to his side to give him moral support. This boring trial drama can boast of a good performance by Carter and an exciting, surprise finale on the steps of the courthouse. Arnold (who also directed *The Glass Web*) was better known for his 1950s science fiction classics, such as *It Came from Outer Space, Tarantula, the Creature from the Black Lagoon* and *The Incredible Shrinking Man.*

Familiar Faces from Television:
❏ William Schallert (Patty's dad in *The Patty Duke Show*) as the court clerk.
❏ Edward Andrews (Commander Rogers Adrian in *Broadside*) as a pompous attorney called in to defend Chandler.
❏ Edward Platt (the Chief in *Get Smart*) as a reporter covering the trial.

Memorable Noir Moment:
❏ When all else fails, try honesty. A desperate Chandler admits to the jury that he became "the mouthpiece for racketeers, murderers, dope peddlers and panderers."

The Tattooed Stranger (1950) 64 min. John Miles, Patricia Barry, Walter Kinsella, Frank Tweddell. **Screenplay by:** Phil Reisman, Jr. **Directed by:** Edward J. Montagne. **Noir Type:** Police Procedural. **Noir Themes:** Greed, paranoia. ★★★

A rookie homicide detective (Miles), his experienced partner (Kinsella) and their boss (Tweddell) investigate the shotgun murder of a Jane Doe, whose body was found in Central Park. With the help of a pretty botanist (White), the detectives uncover crimes in which the woman had been involved — bigamy, insurance fraud and blackmail. In addition to some great location shots of Manhattan and the Bronx, this noir is perfect if you like your crime movies seedy, speedy and short. This top-notch, low-budget quickie pulls no punches and the relatively unknown cast does a fine job. It's an entertaining look at New York City police professionals tracking down a killer in a pre-computer, pre–DNA era.

Familiar Face from Television:
❏ Jack Lord (Steve McGarrett in *Hawaii Five-O*) as a crime lab technician.

Memorable Noir Moment:
❏ When his supervisor assigns a crusty veteran to work with a new homicide cop, the

self-conscious detective complains, "I've never worked with a college boy cop before. I might use bad grammar."

Teenage Doll (1957) 68 min. Fay Spain, June Kenney, John Brinkley, Ziva Rodann, Dorothy Neumann, Sandy Smith, Barbara Wilson. **Screenplay by**: Charles B. Griffith. **Directed by**: Roger Corman. **Noir Type**: Troubled Youth. **Noir Themes**: Lawbreaking for kicks, paranoia, social reform, child in jeopardy. ★★★

This schlock noir from producer-director Corman stars Spain as the teenage gang leader of the Black Widows, the female branch of the all-guy gang, the Tarantulas. Kenney is a middle-class juvenile delinquent wannabe, who accidentally kills a Black Widow in a brawl over a boy (Brinkley). Out for revenge, Spain's gang, one of them packing a rod, goes looking for the terrified Kenney, who's hiding out with the Vandals and the Vandalettes. Corman surprises us with nice character development and an intelligent look into the dysfunctional family lives of these "hellcats in tight pants"— Spain, whose father has young girls over while his wife works the night shift; Smith, who lives in a run-down shack and is abusive to her little sister; a Latina (Israeli actress Rodann), who steals from her immigrant family's cash register; and Wilson, a good cop's wayward daughter, who thinks nothing of lifting her old man's gun while he's sleeping. But the most interesting character is Kenney's mother (Neumann), a bony, middle-aged cartoon caricature with pigtails and large hair bows, who, while trapped in a loveless marriage, pines for lost opportunities and for the bootlegger she once loved. Some hip viewers might really dig this B movie, which climaxes with a disappointing four-gang rumble in an auto junkyard.

Familiar Face from Television:

❑ Ed Nelson (Dr. Michael Rossi in *Peyton Place*) as a uniformed cop.

Memorable Noir Moments:

❑ Parents will believe anything! When Neumann asks her daughter where the blood on her blouse came from, the inventive teenager replies, "A meat truck full of meat went right by me doing about ninety. A side of beef fell off and knocked me down." The concerned mother's reply to this lame story? "A sixteen-year-old girl shouldn't be out where a truck might hit her."
❑ Kenney listens patiently while Mom reminisces about an old flame. "Someday you'll meet a man like that," Neumann says. "You'll know he's cheap and worthless and treacherous, but you won't care."

Temptation (1946) 92 min. Merle Oberon, George Brent, Charles Korvin, Paul Lukas. **Screenplay by**: Robert Thoeren. **Directed by**: Irving Pichel. **Noir Type**: Femme Fatale. **Noir Themes**: Greed, lust, guilt, fatalism. ★½

Egyptologist Brent takes time out from his search for the mummy of Ramses V to marry scheming femme fatale Oberon, despite warnings from his trusted doctor (Lukas). Oberon falls hard for a double-dealing rake (Korvin) and together they plot Brent's murder. Decent acting, boring plot.

Tension (1949) 95 min. Richard Basehart, Audrey Totter, Cyd Charisse, Barry Sullivan, William Conrad. **Screenplay by**: Allen Rivkin. **Directed by**: John Berry. **Noir Type**: Femme Fatale. **Noir Themes**: Lust, betrayal, jealousy, revenge. ★★★

Homicide detective Sullivan opens the film using a rubber band as a visual aid to demonstrate how applying tension eventually will cause a suspect to snap. The suspect in his most recent case is a timid, "four-eyed pill pusher" (pharmacist Basehart), whose wife (Totter) has been cheating on him. The unfortunate working stiff has been slaving day and night to buy his ungrateful wife a house in the suburbs, but Totter cares nothing for the American dream. Furs and fast cars are her thing. When she runs off with her rich new lover, Basehart confronts the man and is humiliated in a fistfight with him. That's when he starts thinking about murder. After assuming a new identity as part of his plan, he meets the lovely Charisse and falls hard for her. Will her love be enough to restrain his murderous urge? Sullivan and his partner (Conrad) don't think so after Totter's boyfriend is found murdered. Totter has a field day portraying the tawdry and calculating femme fatale in this enjoyable B movie. (Sullivan and Conrad also pull double duty as extras crossing the street during an evening scene outside the all-night drug store where Basehart works.)

Familiar Face from Television:
❑ Tom D'Andrea (Riley's best pal, Gillis, in *The Life of Riley*) as the drugstore counterman.

Memorable Noir Moment:
❑ Basehart realizes he's wasting his breath pleading with Totter as she packs her bags to run off with her boyfriend. "It was different in San Diego," she tells him. "You were cute in your uniform. You were full of laughs then. Well, you're all laughed out now."

Terror at Midnight (1956) 70 min. Scott Brady, Joan Vohs, Frank Faylen, John Dehner, Virginia Gregg, Percy Helton. **Screenplay by:** John K. Butler. **Directed by:** Franklin Adreon. **Noir Type:** Wrong Woman. **Noir Themes:** Victim of fate, jealousy, sexual hostility. ★★

Brady plays a rookie homicide detective whose fiancé (Vohs) stupidly becomes involved in a hit-and-run accident while driving his car, which leads to her entanglement with car thieves Faylen and Dehner. Her bad luck continues and she eventually becomes a suspect in two murders, while (yawn) Brady frantically tries to clear her. Gregg plays Faylen's dipso wife, and Helton is a slimy bond bailsman, who encourages Vohs to flee the accident scene so he can blackmail her.

Familiar Face from Television:
❑ Kem Dibbs (Captain Geral in *Captain Video and His Video Rangers* and TV's original *Buck Rogers*) as Dehner's partner.

Terror in a Texas Town (1958) 80 min. Sterling Hayden, Sebastian Cabot, Carol Kelly, Ned Young, Victor Millan, Frank Ferguson, Ted Stanhope. **Screenplay by:** Ben L. Perry. **Directed by:** Joseph H. Lewis. **Noir Type:** Horse Opera. **Noir Themes:** Revenge, greed, corruption, sexual hostility. ★★★

A Swedish whaler (Hayden) returns home to his Texas ranch after years at sea only to find that his father (Stanhope) has been murdered. The killer is a vicious, one-armed gunslinger (Young) working for the owner of the town's hotel (Cabot), who has been trying to force reluctant farmers to sell their oil-rich land. The only witness to the killing is a Mexican farmer (Millan), who's not talking because he has two kids and another on the way. Meanwhile, Hayden is forced to investigate on his own when he discovers that the sheriff is on Cabot's payroll. Kelly is Young's long-suffering, alcoholic girlfriend, and Ferguson plays a fearful rancher who suddenly finds his courage when told that there's oil on his land. This offbeat Western, director Lewis' last film, boasts of a fine performance by the always reliable Hayden and an incredible showdown between the one-armed killer and the harpoon-wielding seaman. Cabot later gained fame playing Mr. French in TV's long-running situation comedy *Family Affair*. Ben L. Perry was a front for the film's real screenwriter, blacklisted Dalton Trumbo.

Familiar Faces from Television:
- ❑ Eugene Martin (Joey Drum in *Jefferson Drum*) as Millan's son.
- ❑ Byron Foulger (Wendell Gibbs in *Petticoat Junction*) as the town's minister.
- ❑ Sheb Wooley (Pete Nolan in *Rawhide*) as one of Cabot's goons.

Memorable Noir Moments:
- ❑ A sloshed Kelly explains why she's so attached to her murderous lover: "I stay with him because, as low as I am, I can turn around and see him and remember there's somebody lower."
- ❑ When Kelly tells Young that Hayden doesn't look like he might be so easy to handle, the gunman replies, "Nothing looks easy to you. You know why? It's because *you're* so easy."

Terror Street (1953-British) 83 min. Dan Duryea, Eisle Albiin, Ann Gudrun, John Chandos. **Screenplay by:** Steve Fisher. **Directed by:** Montgomery Tully. **Noir Type:** Wrong Man. **Noir Themes:** Paranoia, revenge. ★½

Noir icon Duryea is wasted in this tedious film about an American Air Force pilot who has gone AWOL in London to look for his missing English wife (Albiin). When he finally finds her living in an expensive apartment, he figures that she has found herself a lover. Later, a British customs agent (Chandos), who's paying Albiin's rent, murders her and frames the hapless Duryea. On the lam, Duryea meets a kindhearted charity worker (Gudrun) and together they face blackmailers and diamond smugglers in an attempt to unravel the mystery behind his wife's death. Not one of Duryea's best.

Memorable Noir Moment:
- ❑ Albiin's friend and next-door neighbor, who believes that Duryea killed Albiin, wants to know why. After all, "she wasn't *that* bad. She only liked a good time."

They Drive by Night (1940) 93 min. George Raft, Ann Sheridan, Humphrey Bogart, Ida Lupino, Gale Page, Alan Hale. **Screenplay by:** Jerry Wald and Richard Macaulay. **Directed by:** Raoul Walsh. **Noir Type:** Triangle. **Noir Themes:** Obsession, economic repression. ★★★★

Trucking brothers Raft and Bogart haul produce, evade a loan shark out to repossess their truck, and fight drowsiness at the wheel. Page is Bogart's devoted wife, who hates the trucking business because it keeps them apart, and Sheridan is the wisecracking waitress who falls for Raft. When the brothers lose their truck, Raft takes a job as the plant manager for a happy-go-lucky trucking tycoon (Hale). Hale's femme fatale wife (Lupino) tries desperately to seduce Raft, who is loyal to his boss and wants nothing to do with her. His scornful rejections provoke a latent madness in Lupino, which leads to tragedy. A fast-moving script, excellent performances and witty dialogue help make this a winner. Lupino's amazing courtroom scene and overall dazzling performance makes one wonder why she was often referred to at the time as a "poor man's Bette Davis."

Familiar Faces from Television:
❑ Frank Faylen (Herbert T. Gillis in *The Many Loves of Dobie Gillis*) as a truck driver.
❑ John Hamilton (Perry White in *The Adventures of Superman*) as a defense attorney.

Memorable Noir Moments:
❑ A frightened loan shark, about to repossess Raft and Bogart's truck, says, "If you touch me, I'll call a policeman." "If *I* touch you," Bogey replies, "you'll call an *ambulance.*"
❑ When Raft suggests they stop at Mandel's Diner for a bite to eat, Bogey complains that he wants to get home to his wife. Raft remarks that "Pearl can't cook a steak like Billy Mandel." The smiling Bogey replies, "I ain't interested in *steaks.*"

They Live by Night (1949) 95 min. Farley Granger, Cathy O'Donnell, Howard da Silva, Jay C. Flippen, Helen Craig, Will Wright. **Screenplay by:** Charles Schnee. **Directed by:** Nicholas Ray. **Noir Type:** On the Run. **Noir Themes:** Lust, greed. ★★★★

This is director Ray's first film and it's a terrific one. During the Great Depression, hardened convicts da Silva and Flippen escape from jail, taking young Granger with them so they can use him as a getaway driver for their planned bank jobs. The cons hole up at a garage belonging to da Silva's brother (Wright), whose tomboyish daughter (O'Donnell) soon falls in love with the young escapee. Granger, who went to prison at age 16 and is now an inexperienced 23, falls hard for O'Donnell, and they eventually marry. However, the couple's plan to set up house like "real people" seems doomed to fail as they always must stay one step ahead of the law. Granger and O'Donnell are wonderful as the hopeless lovers, seemingly blind to their predicament, and da Silva is terrific as the self-conscious, one-eyed gangster.

Memorable Noir Moments:
❑ Da Silva's ogling of niece O'Donnell might be a figment of one's dirty imagination, but he seems to settle the matter decisively when his hand lingers just a little too long after inserting money into her blouse pocket.
❑ When an inebriated Wright calls provocatively to daughter O'Donnell, she looks *very* uncomfortable and admits to Granger that she doesn't like her old man much. What's with this family anyway?

They Made Me a Killer (1946) 64 min. Robert Lowery, Barbara Britton, Lola Lane, James Bush, Edmund MacDonald. **Screenplay by:** Daniel Mainwaring (as Geoffrey Homes), Winston Miller and Kae Salkow. **Directed by:** William C. Thomas. **Noir Type:** On the Run. **Noir Themes:** Victim of fate. ★½

Auto mechanic Lowery is on his way to San Francisco to start a new life after his brother's accidental death. Stopping in a small town to sell his car, he meets Lane, who says her boyfriend (Bush) will buy it for her if it's fast. During the test drive, Bush and his brother (MacDonald) stick up a bank and force Lowery to be their getaway driver, leaving him to take the rap after the car crashes. The police nab Lowery and, of course, don't believe his story. So he escapes and searches for the gang, teaming up with Britton, the pretty sister of a bank employee killed during the holdup. This is wearisome stuff with too many poorly staged fistfights and shootouts. Lowery went on to play Big Jim Champion in TV's *Circus Boy*, and Britton later starred in the series *Mr. & Mrs. North*.

They Won't Believe Me (1947) 95 min. Robert Young, Susan Hayward, Jane Greer, Rita Johnson, Tom Powers. **Screenplay by**: Jonathan Latimer. **Directed by**: Irving Pichel. **Noir Type**: Wrong Man. **Noir Themes**: Betrayal, victim of fate, fatalism. ★★★★

This is an intriguing tale of a reprehensible cad (Young), the three women in his life — his wife (Johnson) and his two girlfriends (Hayward and Greer) — and how fate deals them all a dirty hand. Young, a lecherous stockbroker who can't seem to keep away from the ladies, always seems to wind up back with his wealthy and forgiving wife. He drops newspaper reporter Greer when Johnson finds out about them and becomes involved with a self-described gold digger (Hayward). Unfortunately, his philandering leads to tragedy for two of the women and a murder charge against him. Young (TV's *Marcus Welby, M.D.*) is wonderfully cast against type as a loathsome husband who gets his noirish comeuppance when he tries to capitalize on an unfortunate accident.

Familiar Face from Television:
❑ Frank Ferguson (Gus the ranch hand in *My Friend Flicka*) as Young's defense attorney.

Memorable Noir Moment:
❑ Defendant Young, who isn't as encouraged as his attorney about the length of time the jury has been deliberating, quips, "Maybe they like the free meals."

The Thief (1952) 85 min. Ray Milland, Martin Gabel, Rita Gam. **Screenplay by**: Clarence Greene and Russell Rouse. **Directed by**: Russell Rouse. **Noir Type**: Nuclear. **Noir Themes**: Betrayal, paranoia, guilt. ★★½

Milland, a distinguished nuclear physicist working for the Atomic Energy Commission in Washington, has been turning over secret information to a spy (Gabel). When one of Gabel's operatives is accidentally killed in New York and the stolen classified information is found on him, the F.B.I. begins tailing AEC employees, including Milland, who flees to New York hoping to board a ship bound for Cairo. Why this film is called *The Thief* instead of *The Traitor* or *The Spy* is as big a mystery as why it was filmed with no dialogue. That's right, the actors have no lines at all, and 85 minutes of just music (even if the film did receive an Oscar nomination for Best Score) can become pretty monotonous. But the versatile Milland manages to pull it off with an excellent performance. Gam makes her film debut as Milland's sexy neighbor.

Thieves' Highway (1949) 94 min. Richard Conte, Valentina Cortese, Lee J. Cobb, Jack Oakie, Millard Mitchell, Barbara Lawrence. **Screenplay by**: A.I. Bezzerides. **Directed by**: Jules Dassin. **Noir Type**: Payback. **Noir Themes**: Revenge, corruption. ★★★½

Conte is a veteran who returns from the war to find that his truck driver father has lost both his legs in an "accident" deliberately caused by a crooked produce wholesaler (Cobb) to avoid paying the old man for his load. Vowing revenge, Conte teams up with Mitchell to deliver two truckloads of apples to Cobb who, aided by a seductive hooker (Cortese), proceeds to cheat Conte out of his money. Reminiscent of *They Drive by Night*, *Thieves' Highway* has a convincing, fast-moving plot, and the actors are excellent, especially Cobb as the shady wholesaler and Cortese as the femme fatale with second thoughts. Soon after he made *Thieves' Highway*, Director Dassin (*Brute Force*, *The Naked City*, *Night and the City* and *Two Smart People*) was identified as a Communist by fellow director Edward Dmytryk during House Un-American Activities Committee hearings.

Memorable Noir Moment:
❑ Conte cautions the scheming Mitchell to be on the up and up. "I worked like a dog for that dough," he says. "Gyp me and I'll cut your throat."

The Third Man (1949-British) 104 min. Joseph Cotten, Orson Welles, Alida Valli, Trevor Howard, Bernard Lee. **Screenplay by:** Graham Greene. **Directed by:** Carol Reed. **Noir Type:** Gangster. **Noir Themes:** Betrayal, greed, woman in jeopardy. ★★★★★

An American Western writer (Cotten) arrives in postwar Vienna, "happy as a lark and without a cent," expecting to get a job with his best friend (Welles). Unfortunately, he arrives just in time for Welles' funeral. Cotten is told that Welles was struck by a car while crossing the street, but, because of conflicting stories and too many coincidences, Cotten suspects that his childhood friend may have been murdered. Cotten meets Welles' Czechoslovakian lover (Valli), in Vienna on a forged passport, and convinces her to help him investigate. A British military police officer (Howard) and his subordinate (Lee), eager to send the nosy American packing, inform him that Welles had been a small-time gangster specializing in the black market sale of watered-down penicillin, which was being administered to sick civilians, including children. Shocked and disgusted, Cotten agrees to give up his investigation and leave the country. But after Cotten sees Welles hiding in a darkened alley outside Valli's apartment building, his loyalty and friendship are put to the ultimate test. The exciting climax in the labyrinthine Vienna sewer system is reminiscent of the Los Angeles storm drain manhunt in the 1948 film noir *He Walked by Night*. *The Third Man*, which has been rated number 57 on the American Film Institute's List of America's 100 Greatest Movies, is one of the best suspense films ever made. Cotten, Welles and Valli are just sensational; Reed was nominated for an Academy Award for Best Director, while Robert Krasker won an Oscar for Best Cinematography (black-and-white). The Third Man Theme, with its perky zither music, almost seems inappropriate considering the film's dark content, but, strangely, it works like a charm. Don't miss this outstanding classic.

Memorable Noir Moment:
❑ Valli reminisces about her lover. "He never grew up," she tells Cotten. "The world grew up around him, that's all."

Third Party Risk *see* **The Deadly Game**

The Thirteenth Hour (1947) 65 min. Richard Dix, Karen Morley, Regis Toomey. **Screenplay by:** Edward Bock and Raymond L. Schrock. **Directed by:** William Clemens. **Noir Type:** Wrong Man. **Noir Themes:** Betrayal, greed. ★★

In this seventh *Whistler* film, Dix plays the owner of a trucking firm who gets himself into a big jam. He has an accident while trying to avoid a car speeding down the wrong side of the highway and temporarily loses his license on an undeserved DUI charge. The cop who ticketed him also happens to be his romantic rival for the affections of a pretty cafe owner (Morley). In an argument outside the courthouse, Dix stupidly threatens the cop in front of witnesses. When the cop is found murdered, guess who gets the blame. Dix goes on the lam and tries to find the real killer, a man he believes is missing his right thumb. Toomey plays the detective who's after Dix. It's pretty standard stuff, and, unfortunately, it was the last film for Dix, who died of a heart attack at 55 in 1949, ending a long film career which included six other films in *The Whistler* series. (See also *The Whistler, Mark of the Whistler, Power of the Whistler, Voice of the Whistler, Mysterious Intruder, Secret of the Whistler,* and *The Return of the Whistler.*)

The 13th Letter (1951) 85 min. Charles Boyer, Michael Rennie, Linda Darnell, Constance Smith. **Screenplay by:** Howard Koch. **Directed by:** Otto Preminger. **Noir Type:** Whodunit. **Noir Themes:** Paranoia, betrayal, revenge. ★★★½

A new doctor (Rennie) in a small Canadian town begins receiving poison pen letters accusing him of having an affair with Smith, the young wife of his colleague (Boyer), and advising him to leave town ... or else. Other townsfolk start receiving similar letters, denouncing Rennie and Smith at first and later accusing other citizens of such crimes as embezzlement and child molestation. Paranoia sets in as folks start suspecting each other of being the slanderer, whose signature is simply a hand-drawn feather. This is an intriguing drama that focuses on the horrible consequences of slander and libel — wrongful imprisonment, suicide and even murder. Boyer, in a comeback of sorts, gives a fine performance as the aging doctor trying to keep his beautiful young wife in line. Darnell portrays a lame girl trying to seduce Rennie.

This Gun for Hire (1942) 80 min. Alan Ladd, Veronica Lake, Robert Preston, Laird Cregar, Marc Lawrence. **Screenplay by:** Albert Maltz and W.R. Burnett. **Directed by:** Frank Tuttle. **Noir Type:** Hit Man. **Noir Themes:** Revenge, betrayal, woman in jeopardy, corruption. ★★★★½

Ladd is a cat-loving hit man who's out to get the client who betrayed him by paying him in marked bills. Cregar, delightfully despicable as Ladd's double-crossing client, works for a chemical company that's selling secrets to the Japanese. Veteran baddy Lawrence plays his goon. Because of her connection to Cregar, nightclub performer Lake is approached by a U.S. senator, who convinces her to work undercover to help prove that Cregar and his boss are traitors. Her mission is so top secret that she can't even tell her detective boyfriend (Preston) about it. On the train to Los Angeles, she's taken hostage by Ladd and soon discovers that there's a dark, Freudian reason for his descent into murder and self-destruction. *This Gun for Hire*, the film that made Alan Ladd a star, was the first of seven films starring the fabulous Ladd-Lake team (including two other films noirs, **The Glass Key** and **The Blue Dahlia**). Actor James Cagney directed a 1957 remake entitled **Short Cut to Hell**.

Familiar Face from Television:
❑ Yvonne De Carlo (*The Munsters*) in a non-speaking bit part as a nightclub showgirl.

Memorable Noir Moments:
❑ Sensitivity Training Required: Preston proposes to Lake, a professional singer, by asking her what it will take to get her to "darn my socks and cook my corn beef and cabbage."
❑ When Creger pays off Ladd, the distrustful hit man warns him that the money had better be clean. Creger jokes that Ladd couldn't very well go to the police about it, causing Ladd to remark menacingly, "I'm my own police."

This Woman Is Dangerous (1952) 100 min. Joan Crawford, Dennis Morgan, David Brian, Richard Webb, Philip Carey, Mari Aldon. **Screenplay by:** Daniel Mainwaring (as Geoffrey Homes) and George Worthing Yates. **Directed by:** Felix E. Feist. **Noir Type:** Triangle. **Noir Themes:** Lust, jealousy, paranoia. ★★

Ex-con Crawford is the brains behind a gang of thieves. Together with her cop killer lover (Brian) and his brother and sister-in-law (Carey and Aldon), they hit an illegal gambling casino and get away with ninety grand. Crawford takes her share of the loot and gets the eye operation she desperately needs to save her sight. She falls in love with her doctor (Morgan) but keeps her past a dark secret. Insanely jealous, Brian hires a private detective to find out if there's anything between them. Mostly boring except for Brian's scenes, this lame melodrama will probably appeal to Crawford fans.

Familiar Face from Television:
❑ Sherry Jackson (Danny Thomas' first TV daughter in *Make Room for Daddy* a.k.a. *The Danny Thomas Show*) as Morgan's daughter.

Memorable Noir Moment:
❑ Morgan, unaware of Crawford's past, extols the fact that prisoners can learn an honest trade in the pen. Crawford replies sarcastically, "They put you in the laundry and steam you soft as a potato."

The Threat (1949) 65 min. Charles McGraw, Michael O'Shea, Virginia Grey, Anthony Caruso, Frank Richards, Frank Conroy, Don McGuire. **Screenplay by:** Dick Irving Hyland and Hugh King. **Directed by:** Felix E. Feist. **Noir Type:** Payback. **Noir Themes:** Revenge, betrayal, sadism. ★★★★½

McGraw, a brutal psychopath who has escaped from Folsom Prison, intends to keep his promise about getting even with the cop (Shea) who arrested him, the D.A. (Conroy) who convicted him, and the showgirl (Grey) who he believes betrayed him. Along with his goons (Caruso and Richards), McGraw kidnaps his three victims and a furniture mover (McGuire), whose van he needs for a getaway. Gravel-voiced McGraw is brilliant as the sadistic killer, a role similar to one he played in 1948's

T-Men—only this time around you'll get to see even more of him, perhaps more than you can stand if you're the queasy type. The tension never lets up.

Memorable Noir Moment:
❑ McGraw sweet-talks a hostage into turning over his gun and then rewards the sucker by plugging him.

Three Steps North (1951-U.S./Italian) 85 min. Lloyd Bridges, Lea Padovani, Aldo Fabrizi, William Tubbs. **Screenplay by:** Lester Fuller. **Directed by:** W. Lee Wilder. **Noir Type:** Troubled Veteran. **Noir Themes:** Corruption, greed. ★½

An ex–G.I. (Bridges) returns to Italy after having spent four years in an Army stockade for small-time black marketeering. "I found out quick that a guy with half a brain could make himself a fast buck" selling cigarettes, canned milk and chocolate, he recalls. He reunites with his former Italian girlfriend (Padovani), but he's really trying to retrieve the four million lire (about six thousand bucks) he buried "three steps north" of a tree before being arrested by the military police. He winds up being suspected by Italian cops of murder. Fabrizi is the caretaker of an American military cemetery, and Tubbs is an American gangster hiding out from the IRS. Unsuspenseful and tedious, this Italian-American co-production is a big disappointment for Bridges fans.

Memorable Noir Moment:
❑ An American gangster, hiding out from the IRS because he "forgot" the date his taxes were due, complains, "Why should a right guy get slapped in the can because he ain't got a calendar?"

Three Strangers (1946) 92 min. Sydney Greenstreet, Geraldine Fitzgerald, Peter Lorre, Alan Napier, Rosalind Ivan. **Screenplay by:** John Huston and Howard Koch. **Directed by:** Jean Negulesco. **Noir Type:** Fantasy. **Noir Themes:** Jealousy, greed, betrayal. ★★★½

Fitzgerald, a worshipper of Kwan Yin, the Chinese goddess of "fortune and destiny, of life and death," convinces two men (Lorre and Greenstreet) to join her in a ceremony in front of a statue of the goddess at midnight on the Chinese New Year, when, according to legend, the goddess will grant a wish to three strangers. After they make their collective wish (that Lorre's sweepstakes ticket will win), the three go their separate ways. Alcoholic Lorre is later arrested and charged with a bobby's murder; barrister Greenstreet misappropriates a client's funds, loses it all, and contemplates suicide; and Fitzgerald ruthlessly schemes to win back her straying husband. The cast is perfect, with the usually sinister Lorre playing a sympathetic character for a change, and the ending is wonderfully ironic. Screenwriter Huston reportedly based this unusual and entertaining story on his real-life experience with a lottery ticket and a mysterious Burmese statue.

Tight Spot (1955) 97 min. Ginger Rogers, Edward G. Robinson, Brian Keith, Lorne Greene. **Screenplay by:** William Bowers. **Directed by:** Phil Karlson. **Noir Type:** Gangster. **Noir Themes:** Woman in jeopardy, victim of the law. ★★★

Rogers is terrific as a wrongly imprisoned model who's being pressured by D.A.

A stranger (Sidney Greenstreet) tips his hat to a future partner (Geraldine Fitzgerald) in *Three Strangers* (Warner Bros., 1946).

Robinson to testify against a vicious mobster (Greene). Keith is the cop assigned to protect her. Before long, the cop and the con find themselves falling in love, while the nervous Greene is eager to make his move. Good acting (especially by Rogers as the wisecracking witness) and a clever plot twist add to this gritty film noir's enjoyment. Greene went on to star as the wealthy patriarch in one of TV's most successful Westerns, *Bonanza*.

Memorable Noir Moments:
- ❑ Rogers, in a remark aimed at Keith, can't hide her disdain. "Men!" she exclaims. "They oughta trade themselves in for something a girl really needs."
- ❑ A prison matron asks Rogers what she likes about Keith. "That he's here, I guess," replies the con, who hasn't been with a man in years.

Time Without Pity (1957-British) 88 min. Michael Redgrave, Ann Todd, Leo McKern, Peter Cushing, Alec McCowen. **Screenplay by:** Ben Barzman. **Directed by:** Joseph Losey. **Noir Type:** Boozer. **Noir Themes:** Fatalism, guilt, social reform. ★★★

Released from rehab only 24 hours before his son (McCowen) is to be executed for murdering a girlfriend, an alcoholic writer (Redgrave) rushes to prove the young man's innocence. His drunken investigation leads him to the guilty party, an automobile manufacturer (McKern), and his unfaithful wife (Todd). Will Redgrave be able to prove that McKern is the killer before his son is hanged? Will he even be able to function with all that booze in him? Redgrave is excellent as the conscience-stricken father trying desperately to atone for his absence during his son's trial. McKern does a good job as the despicable industrialist given to explosive temper tantrums. Cushing, best known for his horror roles, plays McCowen's attorney. This British noir is a bit slow at times, but the sensational ending is worth waiting for. *Time Without Pity*, with more mirrors than a funhouse, contains some interesting film noir cinematography.

Memorable Noir Moment:
❑ After Redgrave suggests that McKern and Todd are hiding something, attorney Cushing asks him if the couple look like the type who would have such secrets. "Everyone has a secret," Redgrave replies. "It's not always written in the face."

Timetable (1956) 79 min. Mark Stevens, King Calder, Felicia Farr, Marianne Stewart, Wesley Addy. **Screenplay by:** Aben Kandel. **Directed by:** Mark Stevens. **Noir Type:** Bad Cop. **Noir Themes:** Greed, betrayal, lust. ★★★

Stevens plays an insurance investigator gone bad over a dame (Farr), and Stewart is the loving wife he betrays. With Farr and her alcoholic husband (Addy) as his accomplices, Stevens' concocts a heist plan with a "foolproof" timetable that turns out to be very fallible, crumbling under the heavy hand of fate. Calder is Stevens' long-time friend, the railroad cop assigned to the case. Stevens, who also produced and directed this **Roadblock**-like noir, is first-rate as the unlucky neophyte criminal.

Familiar Faces from Television:
❑ Jack Klugman (Oscar Madison in *The Odd Couple* and medical examiner *Quincy*), in his film debut, as a small-time crook.

Memorable Noir Moment:
❑ After Stevens comments that a recent heist has all the makings of a perfect crime, a colleague tells him, "I've been a cop for a long time. I've seen some good jobs and some bad jobs, but I've never seen a perfect one." "Well," replies Stevens, "there's always a first time." "There's no such thing as a perfect crime," his buddy says. "Just a lucky one."

To Have and Have Not (1944) 100 min. Humphrey Bogart, Walter Brennan, Lauren Bacall, Dolores Moran, Hoagy Carmichael, Sheldon Leonard, Walter Szurovy, Dan Seymour. **Screenplay by:** Jules Furthman and William Faulkner. **Directed by:** Howard Hawks. **Noir Type:** Adventure. **Noir Themes:** Conspiracy, victim of fate. ★★★★

Bogart and Bacall's first film together is a dandy. He's the American skipper of a fishing boat in French-controlled Martinique, and she's an American stranded there. Sparks begin to fly early on, but complicating the budding romance are Nazi-sympathizing French cops (Seymour and Leonard), who are looking to ferret out of members of the resistance. Bogey reluctantly agrees to smuggle one of the resistance leaders (Szurovy) and his wife (Moran) into Martinique but has his hands full trying to keep his rum-dum first mate (Brennan) out of trouble. Based loosely on the Ernest Hemingway novel, *To Have and Have Not* is an entertaining, well-acted film with snappy, suggestive dialogue, but it's probably most famous for the off-camera romance between the 45-year-old Bogart and the 18-year-old Bacall, which resulted in Bogey's divorce from actress Mayo Methot. Bogey and Bacall were married in 1945 and were together until his death from esophageal cancer in 1957.

Memorable Noir Moment:

❑ In what is now a classic line of dialogue, Bacall seductively invites a grinning Bogey to just whistle if he needs her. "You know how to whistle, don't you Steve?" she asks. "You just put your lips together and blow."

To the Ends of the Earth (1948) 109 min. Dick Powell, Signe Hasso, Ludwig Donath, Vladimir Sokoloff, John Hoyt. **Screenplay by:** Jay Richard Kennedy. **Directed by:** Robert Stevenson. **Noir Type:** Narcotics. **Noir Themes:** Greed, betrayal. ★★★

Powell stars as an agent of the Federal Bureau of Narcotics, a branch of the U.S. Treasury Department, in search of an opium smuggling ring. The trail, which takes him to Shanghai, Cairo and Havana, eventually leads to murder, slavery and multiple suicides. Hasso, a young Chinese girl's governess, is Powell's prime suspect. Sokoloff plays a Chinese narcotics agent, and Hoyt has a small part as a drug smuggler fronting as a tour guide operator. Heavily narrated by Powell, this is a fast-paced and suspenseful thriller with a shocking climax.

Memorable Noir Moment:

❑ Powell convinces a Coast Guard skipper to chase a suspected drug-smuggling ship past the twelve-mile legal limit, hoping the bluff will force the ship's captain to surrender. But instead, the ship's panicky crew decides to destroy all of its illegal cargo, which isn't drugs after all. Instead, Powell watches helplessly as several scores of screaming Chinese slaves are tossed overboard and, chained together, quickly sink to the bottom of the ocean.

Tokyo File 212 (1951) 84 min. Florence Marly, Robert Peyton, Katsu Kaika Haida, Satoshi Nakamura, Suisei Matsui. **Screenplay by:** Dorrell and Stuart McGowan. **Directed by:** Dorrell and Stuart McGowan. **Noir Type:** Far East. **Noir Themes:** Conspiracy, fatalism, betrayal. ★★½

A disappointed kamikaze pilot (Haida), whose training was interrupted because of Japan's surrender, learns the hard way that Communism isn't all that it's cracked up to be. American undercover agent Peyton travels to Tokyo to search for Haida, an old college chum. He's not interested in talking about football games or favorite professors, either. He hopes that Haida will lead him to the number one comrade in Japan (Nakamura), who's been smuggling secret military information to the North Koreans. Peyton teams up with the sultry Marly, whose sister is being held hostage in North Korea. If you speak Japanese (there's an awful lot of it without subtitles), you might really enjoy this obscure, low-budget flick. Who knows? The dialogue might be great. The on-location photography, which includes Tokyo's exotic night spots and its surrounding countryside, is nicely done. The exciting climax isn't bad either.

Tomorrow Is Another Day (1951) 90 min. Ruth Roman, Steve Cochran, Ray Teal, Lurene Tuttle, Hugh Sanders. **Screenplay by:** Art Cohn and Guy Endore. **Directed by:** Felix E. Feist. **Noir Type:** Jailbird. **Noir Themes:** Paranoia, victim of fate. ★★★

An ex-con (Cochran), imprisoned when he was thirteen for murdering his father because he "slapped my mother around once too often," can't seem to stay out of trouble. On the day of his release, after serving eighteen years, he's almost arrested for beating up a reporter who befriended him simply to get a scoop. Cochran travels to New York, where he falls for a beautiful, but hardened, dime-a-minute taxi dancer (Roman). When Roman's lover (Sanders), a jealous cop, shows up at her apartment and starts slapping her around, Cochran tries to protect her. When the cop pulls his gun, Cochran disarms him, but Sanders knocks him cold. While Cochran is unconscious, the panicky Roman shoots the cop as he approaches her, ready to administer another of his frequent beatings. When Roman realizes that Cochran doesn't know what happened, she manages to convince him that he killed Sanders. They go on the lam, fall in love, get married and, amazingly, become lettuce pickers. All seems well until Cochran's photo appears in a pulp magazine offering a thousand dollar reward for information leading to his capture, which causes their new friends (Teal and Tuttle) to start thinking about how much they could use the reward money. Cochran is terrific as the recently released ex-con, and Roman is enjoyable as the repentant femme fatale. The ending, however, is disappointing.

Familiar Face from Television:

❏ Lee Patrick (Cosmo's wife, Henrietta in *Topper*) as Roman's sister in law.

Memorable Noir Moment:

❏ With his official release only minutes away, Cochran swears to the warden, "Nobody will ever put me in a stinking cage again."

Too Late for Tears (1949) 99 min. Lizabeth Scott, Dan Duryea, Don DeFore, Arthur Kennedy, Kristine Miller. **Screenplay by:** Roy Huggins. **Directed by:** Byron Haskin. **Noir Type:** Femme Fatale. **Noir Themes:** Greed, betrayal. ★★★

Scott and Kennedy are unlucky enough to have a bag containing sixty thousand dollars thrown into their convertible by mistake. The dough, which was intended for Duryea, causes big marital problems because the greedy Scott wants to keep it and Kennedy wants to turn it in to the police. Scott is excellent as the femme fatale who'll do anything to keep her newfound wealth. Duryea plays his usual bad-guy role with gusto, this time as a crooked P.I., who's adept at slapping women around but who's no match for Scott in the guts department. DeFore is the mysterious stranger who comes to the aid of Kennedy's sister (Miller), who's trying to figure out why her brother has suddenly disappeared. Also known as *Killer Bait*, this is a fast-moving and enjoyable crime drama.

Familiar Faces from Television:

❏ Denver Pyle (Uncle Jessy in *The Dukes of Hazzard*) as a train station flirt.
❏ Jimmy Dodd (the head Mouseketeer in *The Mickey Mouse Club*) as a car thief.

Memorable Noir Moment:

❏ Looking at the bundles of cash she has just emptied onto her bed, Scott tells hubby Kennedy, "You could make it work for us for the rest of our lives." Unenthused, Kennedy replies,

A greedy wife (Lizabeth Scott) tries to convince her reluctant husband (Arthur Kennedy) that they should keep the 60 Gs somebody tossed into their car by mistake in *Too Late for Tears* (United Artists, 1949).

> "If we don't report this, it's a felony. It's the same as stealing it. It's a blind alley, with a big barred gate at the end."

Touch of Evil (1958) 111 min. Charlton Heston, Janet Leigh, Orson Welles, Joseph Calleia, Akim Tamiroff, Marlene Dietrich. **Screenplay by:** Orson Welles. **Directed by:** Orson Welles. **Noir Type:** Bad Cop. **Noir Themes:** Corruption, betrayal, bigotry. ★★★★★

The honeymoon of a Mexican detective (Heston) and his American bride (Leigh) gets cut short when a bomb planted in a car on the Mexican side of the border explodes on the American side, killing a wealthy American and his stripper girlfriend. A legendary gringo detective (Welles) takes charge of the investigation, quickly fingering a Mexican national for the crime. Heston hangs around long enough to learn that Welles' investigation tactics are somewhat shady if not downright illegal. The corrupt American cop must resort to extreme measures to keep his Mexican counterpart quiet. Meanwhile, Tamiroff, the American brother of a Mexican crime lord, attempts to blackmail Heston into dropping the charges against his brother by photographing Leigh in a compromising situation. Dietrich plays a Mexican gypsy, Welles' former girlfriend. Look for cameos by Joseph Cotten as a police doctor, Zsa Zsa Gabor as the owner of a strip club, and Mercedes McCambridge as a butch biker.

Orson Welles in *Touch of Evil* (Universal-International, 1958).

While Heston may seem miscast as a Mexican cop, he actually turns in a fine performance, avoiding the use of a phony accent. Calleia is excellent as Welles' loyal partner, who is so blinded by his devotion to the man who once took a bullet for him that he's oblivious to Welles' crimes. But it's Welles, at his biggest and grubbiest, who deserves top honors, playing an egocentric, obese, racist, alcoholic cop, who long ago learned to rationalize his phony arrests. Forty years after the film was made, a reconstructed director's cut was released that incorporated soundtrack and editing changes that were requested by Welles in his now famous 58-page memo to Universal Studios, written after the studio shot additional scenes and re-edited the film. Unfortunately, studio execs ignored Welles' impassioned pleas. The 1998 director's cut, with its subtle changes, improves the already near perfect film. Some film historians point to *Touch of Evil* as the last film of the classic noir period.

Familiar Faces from Television:
❏ Dennis Weaver (Chester in *Gunsmoke* and Marshal Sam McCloud in *McCloud*) as a loony motel clerk.
❏ Joi Lansing (Shirley Swanson in *The Bob Cummings Show* and Goldie in *Klondike*) as the blonde in the exploding car.

Memorable Noir Moments:
❏ A frightened murder suspect, suspecting that a frame-up is in the works, asks Welles,

"What are you trying to do?" "We're trying to strap you to the electric chair, boy," the cop replies truthfully.
❑ "Have you forgotten your old friend?" asks Welles. "I didn't recognize you," responds Dietrich, looking him up and down. "You should lay off those candy bars."

A Tragedy at Midnight (1942) 69 min. John Howard, Margaret Lindsay, Roscoe Karns, Keye Luke. **Screenplay by:** Isabel Dawn. **Directed by:** Joseph Santley. **Noir Type:** Whodunit. **Noir Themes:** Betrayal, paranoia. ★½

Howard plays a radio detective who taunts murderers and embarrasses the inept police department with his crime solving skills. Detective Karns and the other "dopes in blue" have been trying to figure out how to shut him up, with one Keystone Cop actually suggesting that the department boycott the show's sponsor, Roastie Toasties breakfast cereal. But the cops get lucky when a beautiful woman is found dead in Howard's bedroom. Howard and his wacky wife (Lindsay) go on the run, desperate to find the real murderer so he won't have to miss his weekly show. Played strictly for laughs, with Luke as the couple's stereotyped "smart China boy" servant, this poor man's Nick and Nora Charles mystery has a few comical moments, but, for the most part, it's a waste of time.

Familiar Faces from Television:
❑ Minerva Urecal (Annie in *The Adventures of Tugboat Annie* and "Mother" in *Peter Gunn*) as a cabin housekeeper.

Memorable Noir Moments:
❑ Luke ponders the dead woman in his boss' bed. "Too bad kill beautiful lady," he remarks, "when so many ugly ones in world."
❑ From the Some-Things-Never-Change Department: Lindsay's old-fashioned aunt complains, "You so-called moderns. You marry so quickly you don't even known your married name until you look at your divorce."

The Trap (1959) 84 min. Richard Widmark, Lee J. Cobb, Tina Louise, Earl Holliman, Carl Benton Reid. **Screenplay by:** Richard Alan Simmons and Norman Panama. **Directed by:** Norman Panama. **Noir Type:** Gangster. **Noir Themes:** Betrayal, jealousy, family dysfunction, greed. ★★

Widmark, a syndicate lawyer, is forced to pressure his father, a small-town sheriff (Reid), into abandoning an airport stakeout so that a fleeing mobster (Cobb) can make his getaway. Not even on speaking terms with Reid because of a stint in the reformatory as a juvenile, Widmark somehow manages to convince the old man to turn his back on the law. But the deputy (Holliman), Widmark's jealous younger brother, now married to the lawyer's old flame (Louise), has his eye on the fifteen grand reward that's being offered for Cobb's capture. The talented cast is wasted in this lame action noir. Louise's faltering career was given a boost five years later when she was chosen to play Ginger in the hit TV series *Gilligan's Island*.

Familiar Face from Television:
❑ Lorne Greene (Ben Cartwright in *Bonanza*) as Cobb's loyal henchman.

Trapped (1949) 78 min. Lloyd Bridges, John Hoyt, Barbara Payton, James Todd. **Screenplay by:** Earl Fenton and George Zuckerman. **Directed by:** Richard Fleischer. **Noir Type:** Undercover. **Noir Themes:** Greed, betrayal. ★★★

Convict Bridges, serving time for counterfeiting, is set free to help the Secret Service find the gang that's using his old counterfeit plates. Bridges escapes the T-Men, foolishly thinking he's pulled a fast one, but it's all part of the agents' plan, as is their surveillance of his girlfriend (Payton). Hoyt, who usually was typecast as a gangster or an evil Nazi, is the Treasury agent who goes undercover to gain Bridges' trust and to nab Todd, the head of the ring. Bridges was always terrific as a bad guy, and, though he's not quite as despicable here as in *Try and Get Me*, he still elicits his share of hisses. Despite its similarities to **T-Men**, *Trapped* stands on its own as a suspenseful and well-plotted noir.

Memorable Noir Moment:
❑ A federal marshal escorting the handcuffed Bridges is having problems catching forty winks on a bus. "No rest for the *wicked*," he comments. "*I'm* doin' all right," responds his prisoner.

The Treasure of the Sierra Madre (1948) 126 min. Humphrey Bogart, Walter Huston, Tim Holt, Bruce Bennett, Alfonso Bedoya. **Screenplay by:** John Huston. **Directed by:** John Huston. **Noir Type:** Gold Fever. **Noir Themes:** Greed, paranoia, distrust, character deterioration, betrayal. ★★★★★

Bogart, an American down on his luck in Mexico and taken to panhandling, wins a small lottery and uses the prize money to help finance a gold prospecting expedition with two of his countrymen (Huston and Holt). With the elderly, but experienced, Huston in the lead, the three trek through the rugged Mexican terrain dreaming of riches. Eventually, they find a mother lode and start mining, each man hiding his share of the gold dust. Before long, the increasingly paranoid Bogey becomes suspicious that his partners are planning to double-cross him, causing a dangerous rift in the once trusting team. And, if that's not bad enough, an intruder (Bennett) arrives and attempts to blackmail them into giving him a share. While the partners decide the fate of the unwelcome guest, a gang of bandits led by the vicious Bedoya rides in their direction. This powerful film, which is rated number 30 on the American Film Institute's List of America's 100 Greatest Movies, is one of director Huston's best, earning him Oscars for Best Director and Best Screenplay. Bogey turns in an astonishing performance as a seemingly average guy who falls prey to gold fever and greed, driving him to the brink of madness and murder. Huston's father, Walter, won the Oscar for Best Supporting Actor for his role of the savvy gold prospector responsible for the trio's "success." Bedoya is wonderfully camp as the grinning, but treacherous, bandit, and B western veteran Holt gives the most impressive performance of his career as Bogey's once easygoing partner. Holt's actor father, Jack Holt, has a bit role as an old man in a flophouse, and noir veteran Ann Sheridan has a cameo as a streetwalker.

Familiar Face from Television:
❑ Robert Blake (Detective Tony Baretta in *Baretta*) as a young seller of lottery tickets.

Memorable Noir Moments:

❑ When Holt and Huston decide to send a portion of the gold to a man's widow back in the States, the unmoved Bogey ridicules them, saying "You two guys must have been born in a revival meeting."

❑ Holt comes to a un-noir-like conclusion about events. "The worst ain't so bad when it finally happens," he says. "Not half as bad as you figure it'll be before it happens."

❑ When Bedoya claims he and his men are *federales*, Bogey demands to see their badges. The bandit retorts with his now famous line, "Badges? We ain't got no badges. We don't need no badges. I don't have to show you no stinking badges."

Try and Get Me (1950) 90 min. Frank Lovejoy, Lloyd Bridges, Kathleen Ryan, Richard Carlson. **Screenplay by:** Jo Pagano. **Directed by:** Cy Endfield. **Noir Type:** Troubled Veteran. **Noir Themes:** Guilt, paranoia, greed, character deterioration. ★★★★

Lovejoy gives his best performance ever as a war veteran whose desperation drives him to team up with a sociopathic petty crook (Bridges). While his pregnant wife and small child think he's working the night shift at the factory, Lovejoy is really Bridges' getaway driver in a series of small-time hold-ups. The money helps his family get back on their feet but Lovejoy, way over his head, begins experiencing conscience pangs. He wants out — but only after one last job, the fabled "big one" that will set his family up for life. Naturally, the job turns sour and ends with a murder.

A petty crook-turned-murderer (Lloyd Bridges) and his reluctant partner (Frank Lovejoy) in *Try and Get Me* (United Artists, 1950).

The community is soon in an uproar about the partners' latest crime, thanks to irresponsible reporting by an opportunistic journalist (Carlson). Eventually, Lovejoy's nagging guilt wears him down and results in the pair's capture. The exciting and thought-provoking climax is one of the best of its kind. A terrified Lovejoy (no heroics here) and a crazed Bridges ... well, see for yourself. Also known as *The Sound of Fury*, *Try and Get Me* delivers it all — an exciting story, fine acting, top-notch photography, and a social message you won't soon forget.

Memorable Noir Moment:
❑ Psycho Bridges shows his romantic side when he blows heavily into a dame's ear from a good six inches away, causing her to chide, "You big baboon."

The Turning Point (1952) 85 min. William Holden, Edmond O'Brien, Alexis Smith, Tom Tully, Ed Begley, Ted de Corsia. Screenplay by: Warren Duff. Directed by: William Dieterle. Noir Type: Gangster. Noir Themes: Betrayal, corruption. ★★½

Crusading reporter Holden, covering the crime commission headed by his friend (O'Brien), discovers that O'Brien's policeman father (Tully) has ties to a vicious crime lord (Begley). Holden confronts Tully, giving him the opportunity to make amends by turning state's evidence. But the worried Begley has the cop gunned down during a staged robbery. Smith plays the socialite who helps the love-smitten O'Brien gather the evidence that will bring Begley to justice. Begley does a fine job as the brutal syndicate chieftain, and veteran character actor de Corsia is enjoyable as Begley's Irish henchman, brogue and all, in this otherwise standard crime drama.

Familiar Faces from Television:
❑ Carolyn Jones (Morticia of *The Addams Family*) as a mobster's moll.
❑ Neville Brand (Al Capone in *The Untouchables* and Reese Bennett in *Laredo*) as a hit man named Red.
❑ Robert Rockwell (Mr. Boynton in *Our Miss Brooks*) as a reporter covering O'Brien's press conference.
❑ Ray Teal (Sheriff Roy Coffee in *Bonanza*) as a uniformed police captain.

Memorable Noir Moment:
❑ Even de Corsia is shocked when Begley suggests burning down an office building to destroy incriminating evidence. "But there are apartments above the place," de Corsia protests. "A dozen people live there." Begley smiles and asks, "You wouldn't believe we'd do it?" "No," replies de Corsia. "That's what makes it good," Begley says, adding, "I don't think a jury would believe it either."

Twist of Fate (1954-British) 88 min. Ginger Rogers, Stanley Baker, Herbert Lom, Jacques Bergerac. Screenplay by: Robert Westerby and Carl Nystrom. Directed by: David Miller. Noir Type: Triangle. Noir Themes: Betrayal, jealousy, greed. ★½

Rogers is having an affair with a married businessman (Baker) who has promised her that he will divorce his wife. When she finds out he's been fibbing, she hooks up with a handsome clay potter (Bergerac, Rogers' real-life husband number four at the time). Meanwhile, penniless gambler Lom, who's also a fence for Baker's illegal enterprise (minting gold coins), gleefully discovers his boss' hidden safe, which is full of goodies. Eventually, there are several killings to keep viewers interested (if their alarm clocks are set to go off about seventy-five minutes into the film). This British noir was originally released as *Beautiful Stranger*.

The Two Mrs. Carrolls (1947) 99 min. Humphrey Bogart, Barbara Stanwyck, Alexis Smith, Nigel Bruce, Patrick O'Moore, Ann Carter, Barry Bernard. **Screenplay by:** Thomas Job. **Directed by:** Peter Godfrey. **Noir Type:** Psycho. **Noir Themes:** Woman in danger, betrayal, obsession, paranoia. ★★

Bogart is a psychopathic artist who paints his wife as the angel of death and, when she no longer inspires him, poisons her so he'll be free to marry his new inspiration (Stanwyck). After less than two years of marriage, Bogart finds his creativity once again heading south. Then he meets the beautiful and wealthy Smith and starts making plans to get rid of the second Mrs. Carroll. But complicating his scheme are Stanwyck's former fiancé (O'Moore), who's still in love with her, and a greedy, blackmailing chemist (Bernard). Bruce plays Stanwyck's bungling doctor, and Carter is the killer's precocious daughter from his first marriage. Overly melodramatic and lacking suspense, this disappointing Bogart vehicle, at best, prepared him for his future role as the paranoid Captain Queeg in 1954's *The Caine Mutiny*, and Stanwyck for her portrayal as another wife in distress in 1948's ***Sorry, Wrong Number***.

Two O'Clock Courage (1945) 66 min. Tom Conway, Ann Rutherford, Richard Lane, Lester Matthews, Emory Parnell, Jane Greer. **Screenplay by:** Robert E. Kent. **Directed by:** Anthony Mann. **Noir Type:** Amnesia. **Noir Themes:** Victim of fate, paranoia. ★½

Conway plays an amnesiac who may or may not have killed a noted Broadway producer. He teams up with a helpful cabbie (Rutherford) in an effort to discover his real identity and to find out if he's the killer the cops are hunting. Matthews is Conway's playwright friend, Lane plays an idiotic reporter, and Parnell is an equally idiotic homicide detective. The film's feeble attempts at humor fail miserably. The only thing noteworthy about this remake of 1936's *Two in the Dark* is that it marked the screen debut of Jane Greer, who was billed under her real name, Bettejane Greer.

Two of a Kind (1951) 75 min. Edmond O'Brien, Lizabeth Scott. Alexander Knox, Terry Moore, Griff Barnett, Virginia Brissac, Robert Anderson. **Screenplay by:** James Gunn and Lawrence Kimble. **Directed by:** Henry Levin. **Noir Type:** Con Artist. **Noir Themes:** Greed, guilt, betrayal. ★★

Con artist Scott recruits a small-time gambler (O'Brien), currently employed at a bingo parlor, in a scheme to convince an elderly couple (Barnett and Brissac) that their long-lost son has been found. But Scott informs him that before he can pass for the couple's son and become heir to their $10 million fortune, he has to lose the tip of his left pinky—in a car door, which she volunteers to slam. Knox plays Scott's lover, the mastermind behind the scheme that, of course, turns noirishly sour, and Moore is the wealthy couple's daffy niece. Terribly slow but the presence of noir icons O'Brien and Scott, although an unlikely romantic pair, make the film bearable.

Familiar Face from Television:
❑ Claire Carleton (Mrs. Mulligan in *The Mickey Rooney Show* and Alice Purdy in *Cimarron City*) as a fortuneteller.

Memorable Noir Moment:
❑ When asked by O'Brien if her mystery partner is a male, Scott replies, "I don't trust women any more than you do."

Two Smart People (1946) 93 min. Lucille Ball, John Hodiak, Lloyd Nolan, Elisha Cook, Jr. **Screenplay by:** Ethel Hill, Ralph Wheelwright and Leslie Charteris. **Directed by:** Jules Dassin. **Noir Type:** Con Artist. **Noir Themes:** Greed, betrayal. ★★

Nolan is a cop who wants to take con artist Hodiak back to New York to stand trial for stealing bonds. Hodiak, who's already negotiated a plea bargain for a short sentence, suggests a last fling for the both of them — traveling to Mexico and then New Orleans for the Mardi Gras. Nolan, who's near retirement and actually likes Hodiak, jumps at the opportunity but worries the whole trip that his prisoner will try to escape. Ball, hoping to find the bonds that Hodiak stole, tags along, as does the scary-looking Cook, who wants his share, too. Along the way, Hodiak and Ball discover that they have "larceny in common" and fall in love. It's a silly mess and much too long, but Ball, filmdom's most stunning redhead, is a pleasure to watch.

Memorable Noir Moment:
❑ While south of the border, Ball asks Cook not to hurt the handsome Hodiak. "Snap out of it, beautiful," Cook advises. "Get that Mexican moonlight out of your eyes."

Uncle Harry *see* The Strange Affair of Uncle Harry

Under the Gun (1951) 84 min. Richard Conte, Audrey Totter, John McIntire, Sam Jaffe, Royal Dano. **Screenplay by:** George Zuckerman. **Directed by:** Ted Tetzlaff. **Noir Type:** Prison. **Noir Themes:** Betrayal, woman in jeopardy, revenge. ★★½

When a New York gangster (Conte) murders a man in Florida, he makes the mistake of doing it in front of a beautiful, down-home nightclub singer (Totter) who can't be bought off. After she betrays him on the witness stand, the shocked gangster is sent to a state prison farm, where he vows to escape. But he faces a major obstacle in the prison's unusual trusty system, in which fellow prisoners called "shooters," hoping to earn pardons, stand guard over the chain gangs and wait for the opportunity to gun down wannabe escapees. And Dano, a trusty with an itchy trigger finger, is just waiting for Conte to make his move. McIntire plays the county sheriff who's determined to keep Conte in prison for twenty years, and Jaffe is a philosophical convict who accepts a dangerous proposition that could cost him his life. Conte is good as the detestable hood who chooses a unique way to "escape" from prison.

Familiar Face from Television:
❑ Phillip Pine (Sgt. Newman in *The Blue Knight*) as one of Conte's henchmen.

Memorable Noir Moment:
❑ After a trusty earns his pardon by plugging an escaping prisoner in the back, the warden

looks to the chain gang for his new "shooter." When no one volunteers, the puzzled warden remarks, "I don't know why you men hate the shooters." Duh.

The Undercover Man (1949) 85 min. Glenn Ford, Nina Foch, James Whitmore, Barry Kelley, Anthony Caruso. **Screenplay by:** Sydney Boehm. **Directed by:** Joseph H. Lewis. **Noir Type:** Police Procedural. **Noir Themes:** Greed, betrayal, corruption. ★★★

Despite the film's misleading title, nobody goes undercover in this one. Ford plays a Treasury agent out to bust a mobster referred to only as "the Big Fellow," but who obviously is supposed to be real-life gangster Al Capone. Foch is Ford's long-suffering wife, and Whitmore, in his film debut, plays a hotheaded agent eager for some action. Kelley is appropriately despicable as the mob's attorney, and noir veteran Caruso is good as the deadbeat dad and mob bookkeeper who tries to make a deal with Ford. Witnesses are rubbed out, juries bribed, and agents' families threatened, but in the end, as we all know, the Big Fellow goes up on income tax evasion charges. Director Lewis does a fine job with this suspenseful drama, also known as *The Chicago Story*.

Memorable Noir Moment:
❑ When asked why he bothered to come to Kelley's mansion if not to take a bribe, Ford hands the crooked lawyer a subpoena and says, "I came here to borrow some books. Here's my library card."

Undercurrent (1946) 114 min. Katharine Hepburn, Robert Taylor, Robert Mitchum, Edmund Gwenn. **Screenplay by:** Edward Chorodov, George Oppenheimer and Marguerite Roberts. **Directed by:** Vincente Minnelli. **Noir Type:** Newlywed. **Noir Themes:** Paranoia, jealousy, family dysfunction, woman in jeopardy. ★★

Hepburn, the dowdy daughter of a scientist (Gwenn), marries an airplane manufacturer (Taylor). She soon learns that Taylor has a dark secret concerning the mysterious disappearance of his brother (Mitchum), who Hepburn suspects may have been killed by her husband. She noses around, asking too many questions to suit Taylor, and the marriage begins to show signs of strain. So will the viewer despite the excellent cast.

Familiar Face from Television:
❑ Barbara Billingsley (June Cleaver, Beaver's mom, in *Leave It to Beaver*) as a dinner guest. Don't blink.

Undertow (1949) 70 min. Scott Brady, John Russell, Dorothy Hart, Bruce Bennett, Peggy Dow. **Screenplay by:** Arthur T. Horman and Lee Loeb. **Directed by:** William Castle. **Noir Type:** On the Run. **Noir Themes:** Victim of the law, betrayal. ★★½

Somebody has framed ex–G.I. Brady for the murder of a local crime lord. School-teacher Dow, while helping the on-the-run war veteran to find the real killer, falls in love with him. Russell is his friend, a casino boss who worked for the murdered racketeer; homicide detective Bennett is Brady's childhood buddy; and Hart, the murdered man's niece, is the femme fatale whom Brady wants to marry. While it's not difficult to figure out who the killer is, Brady is entertaining enough to make this a good view. In the 1950s, Brady went on to star in TV's *Shotgun Slade*, and Russell became *The Lawman*.

Familiar Face from Television:

❑ Rock Hudson, billed as "Roc Hudson" (Commissioner McMillan in *McMillan and Wife*), as a detective. (This was his second film, after debuting in *Fighter Squadron* a year earlier.)

The Underworld Story (1950) 89 min. Dan Duryea, Herbert Marshall, Gale Storm, Howard da Silva, Michael O'Shea, Mary Anderson, Gar Moore. **Screenplay by:** Henry Blankfort. **Directed by:** Cy Endfield. **Noir Type:** Newspaper. **Noir Themes:** Betrayal, guilt, bigotry, greed. ★★½

After Moore, the son of wealthy newspaper publisher Marshall, kills his wife, he and his father conspire to frame their black maid (Anderson). Unethical reporter Duryea, fired from his previous job and now half-owner of a small-town newspaper, sees the murder case an opportunity to make headlines and a few bucks. His partner (Storm), who went to school with Anderson, is more concerned with her friend's fate than with selling newspapers, much to Duryea's annoyance. While D.A. O'Shea is building his case against the innocent maid, Marshall and Moore approach a notorious gangster (da Silva) for help in disposing of the nosy reporter. Except for the presence of noir icon Duryea as the likable scoundrel, *The Underworld Story* (a.k.a. *The Whipped*) is a pretty standard crime drama.

Familiar Face from Television:

❑ Alan Hale, Jr. (the Skipper in *Gilligan's Island*) as one of da Silva's goons.

Memorable Noir Moment:

❑ After spoiling Duryea's treacherous plan to betray a trusting murder suspect for the twenty-five thousand dollar reward, O'Shea comments in front of the reporter's colleagues, "Things are tough all over. Pretty soon a man won't be able to sell his own mother." Duryea's response to losing the reward is a common noir complaint: "When will I learn never to trust a cop?"

The Unfaithful (1947) 109 min. Ann Sheridan, Lew Ayres, Zachary Scott, Eve Arden, Steven Geray, John Hoyt, Marta Mitrovich. **Screenplay by:** David Goodis and James Gunn. **Directed by:** Vincent Sherman. **Noir Type:** Triangle. **Noir Themes:** Betrayal, jealousy, guilt. ★★★

Sheridan plays a wife who was unfaithful to her G.I. husband (Scott) while he was fighting overseas. But before Scott returned from the war, she broke up with her artist lover, who soon began stalking her. One evening, while being assaulted by her ex-lover, Sheridan stabs him to death. She concocts a story about an attempted burglary, which Scott unhesitatingly buys. But the investigating homicide detective (Hoyt) has doubts about her tale. When a family friend and divorce lawyer (Ayres) is contacted by a blackmailing art dealer (Geray), who has a bust of Sheridan that was created by her boyfriend, Sheridan begs him to retrieve it. But by then, the greedy extortionist has already sold it to the dead man's widow (Mitrovich), who's more interested in revenge than money. A loose remake of 1940's **The Letter**, *The Unfaithful*, while overly preachy about cheating wives, is enjoyable thanks to strong performances by Sheridan and Ayres.

Memorable Noir Moment:

❑ Judging by his reaction, you'd think Sheridan was cheating on her lawyer and not her husband. "You're no different than all the other cheating, conniving women who parade through my office," Ayres scolds, "except that you're more of a hypocrite."

Unfaithfully Yours (1948) 105 min. Rex Harrison, Linda Darnell, Barbara Lawrence, Rudy Vallee, Kurt Kreuger, Edgar Kennedy. **Screenplay by:** Preston Sturges. **Directed by:** Preston Sturges. **Noir Type:** Comedy. **Noir Themes:** Jealousy, revenge, distrust. ★★★½

When famous British conductor Harrison returns from a concert tour, he has a big surprise waiting for him. It seems that his stodgy brother-in-law (Vallee) took him a bit too literally when he asked him to keep an eye on his wife (Darnell) during his absence. Vallee, who's married to Darnell's kid sister (Lawrence), informs Harrison that he hired a private eye (Kennedy) to follow Darnell around. After angrily destroying the P.I.'s report without bothering to read it, jealousy and curiosity finally get the best of the conductor, especially since Vallee has already informed him that the P.I. witnessed a scantily clad Darnell visiting the apartment of Harrison's good-looking secretary (Kreuger) late one night. During a concert performance, the maniacal Harrison visualizes three possible responses to his wife's infidelity—murder, magnanimity and Russian Roulette. Later, he attempts to bring imagination to reality with unexpected results. Thankfully, this enjoyable farce doesn't take itself too seriously, resorting often to some hilarious Three Stooges–like slapstick. Especially funny is Harrison's battle of wits with a modern "Disc Recorder," which is "so simple, it operates itself." Harrison is excellent as the obsessed conductor, and veteran comic actor Kennedy is entertaining as the private eye who's also Harrison's biggest fan. Remade in 1984 with Dudley Moore and Nastassia Kinski.

Familiar Face from Television:

❑ Lionel Stander (Max in *Hart to Hart*) as Harrison's manager.

Memorable Noir Moment:

❑ While Harrison and Darnell engage in love talk at the airport, an envious Lawrence tells her husband that "some men naturally make you think of Brut champagne," adding, "with others you think of prune juice." When Vallee chuckles, Lawrence tells him, "You have nothing to laugh at."

The Unholy Four (1953-British) 78 min. Paulette Goddard, William Sylvester, Patrick Holt, Paul Carpenter, Alvys Mahen, Russell Napier. **Screenplay by:** Michael Carreras. **Directed by:** Terence Fisher. **Noir Type:** Whodunit. **Noir Themes:** Revenge, obsession, jealousy. ★½

A muddled and, at times, incomprehensible plot ruins this tale of a former amnesiac (Sylvester), who returns to London after four years of wandering. He tries to figure out which of his three friends fed him a mickey while on a fishing trip in Portugal and conked him over the head, leaving him to die. On his first night home, somebody kills one of the three men, leaving Scotland Yard inspector Napier with no shortage of suspects—there's Sylvester and his wife (Goddard); Sylvester's two remaining friends (Holt and Carpenter), both of whom are in love with Goddard; and Goddard's social secretary (Mahen), who blames Sylvester for her father's death. Three bodies later, Napier figures it all out. This British noir, released in England as *A Stranger Came Home*, was former Paramount star Goddard's penultimate film, her last one being a 1964 Italian production, *Time of Indifference*.

Memorable Noir Moment:

❏ Sensitivity Training Required: When asked if a woman could have bludgeoned the victim, the coroner replies editorially, "Women. They're getting too capable for their own good these days."

The Unholy Wife (1957) 94 min. Diana Dors, Rod Steiger, Tom Tryon, Arthur Franz, Marie Windsor. **Screenplay by:** William Durkee and Jonathan Latimer. **Directed by:** John Farrow. **Noir Type:** Femme Fatale. **Noir Themes:** Betrayal. ★★

This film easily could have been subtitled *The Wife from Hell*. British actress Dors, in her first U.S. film, is a bar girl who enters into a loveless marriage with a rich wine grower (Steiger), who has his own strange reason for marrying Dors. After their marriage, Dors begins an affair with a rodeo cowboy (Tryon), and the lovers starting planning Steiger's demise. Their first "perfect crime" goes awry, and Dors is forced to come with up yet *another* perfect crime, which doesn't succeed either thanks to Steiger's brother, buttinsky priest Franz. Steiger is hopelessly miscast and Dors, while she's pleasant enough to look at, doesn't put enough oomph into her performance. Noir icon Marie Windsor appears in a cameo as a bar girl. Tryon went on to became a writer of horror fiction.

Memorable Noir Moment:

❏ Dors and Tryon whisper sweet nothings to each other before passionately embracing. "Having your cake and eating it, too?" Tryon asks "Such a handsome cake," she replies. "Oh, you!" says Tryon.

Union Station (1950) 80 min. William Holden, Nancy Olson, Barry Fitzgerald, Lyle Bettger, Allene Roberts, Jan Sterling. **Screenplay by:** Sydney Boehm. **Directed by:** Rudolph Maté. **Noir Type:** Police Procedural. **Noir Themes:** Women in danger, greed. ★★★½

Holden, the chief of security at Chicago's Union Station, gets a tip from a train passenger (Olson) about two men who were carrying guns aboard a train. The tip pays off when Holden discovers that the men are involved in the kidnapping of a blind girl (Roberts). Police detective Fitzgerald is called in to help the private security cop, and together they manage to bungle things so badly that civilian Olson must bail them out. Bettger is the leader of the three-man kidnapping ring, and blonde bombshell Sterling is his moll, who learns the hard way that her man's no gentleman. This is a fast-paced and well-acted noir from the director of *D.O.A.*

Memorable Noir Moments:

❏ The Union Station security force and the Chicago cops play musical chairs on the subway while tailing a suspect who's much smarter than his pursuers.
❏ During an unusual interrogation procedure, private security cops hold a suspect's head in the path of an oncoming train until he talks.
❏ A bad guy meets his untimely demise in, of all things, a Chicago cattle stampede.

The Unknown Man (1951) 86 min. Walter Pidgeon, Ann Harding, Barry Sullivan, Keefe Brasselle, Lewis Stone, Eduard Franz. **Screenplay by:** George Froeschel and Ronald Millar. **Directed by:** Richard Thorpe. **Noir Type:** Payback. **Noir Themes:** Guilt, fatalism, corruption. ★★

A lawyer (Pidgeon) is eaten up with guilt when he realizes he may have unwittingly helped to free a murderer (Brasselle). He investigates further and finds that his suspicions were correct but that Brasselle was just a goon for the corrupt head of the Crime Commission (Franz). His aggrieved sense of justice eventually leads him to defend Brasselle once again, this time for a murder that he himself committed. Sullivan plays the D.A, who doesn't care which murder Brasselle is convicted of, as long as he fries. Harding is Pidgeon's concerned wife, and Stone is the judge trying the case. Well-acted, but overly long and improbable, this one isn't for the sleepy.

Familiar Faces from Television:
❑ Richard Anderson (Oscar Goldman in *The Six Million Dollar Man*) as Pidgeon's son.
❑ Jimmy Dodd (the head Mouseketeer in *The Mickey Mouse Club*) as a photographer.
❑ Jeff York (Reno McKee in *The Alaskans*) as a guard.

Memorable Noir Moment:
❑ From the Some-Things-Never-Change Department: A grieving father gives his opinion of the criminal justice system after his son's murderer is freed. "What a dirty, filthy, rotten business," he complains. "And they call it justice."

Unmasked (1950) 60 min. Raymond Burr, Robert Rockwell, Barbara Fuller, Hillary Brooke, Paul Harvey. **Screenplay by:** Albert DeMond and Norman S. Hall. **Directed by:** George Blair. **Noir Type:** Wrong Man. **Noir Themes:** Betrayal, victim of fate. ★★½

On the spur of the moment, Burr, the publisher of a struggling newspaper, decides to strangle his showgirl lover (Brooke) to avoid paying back the fifty Gs he owes her. He ingeniously manages to frame Brooke's husband (Harvey), causing the old cuckold to go on the lam. Homicide detective Rockwell tails Harvey's daughter (Fuller), hoping she'll lead him to her father, who's holed up in a cheap motel with a hundred grand of his wife's jewelry, his supposed motive for the murder. As usual, Burr is an excellent heavy ("a blackmailing, unprincipled leech" to be exact). Rockwell and Fuller are reunited after co-starring in their unintentionally funny *The Red Menace.*

Familiar Face from Television:
❑ John Eldredge (Harry Archer in *Meet Corliss Archer*) as a mobster.

Memorable Noir Moment:
❑ After discovering a body in one of his apartments, a well-intentioned landlord advises Burr, "We mustn't touch *anything* until the police get here," and immediately picks up the phone to call the cops.

The Unseen (1945) 81 min. Joel McCrea, Gail Russell, Herbert Marshall, Phyllis Brooks, Elisabeth Risdon. **Screenplay by:** Hagar Wilde and Raymond Chandler. **Directed by:** Lewis Allen. **Noir Type:** Whodunit. **Noir Themes:** Woman in jeopardy, paranoia. ★½

A dark old house, a couple of murders, and a widower (McCrea) with two precocious children multiplied by an attractive new governess (Russell) should equal an interesting Gothic mystery. But director Allen's disappointing follow-up to his superior *The Uninvited* is uninteresting, uninspiring and unbearably long.

The Unsuspected (1947) 103 min. Joan Caulfield, Claude Rains, Audrey Totter, Constance Bennett, Ted North, Hurd Hatfield, Jack Lambert, Barbara Woodell. **Screenplay by:** Ranald MacDougall and Bess Meredyth. **Directed by:** Michael Curtiz. **Noir Type:** Psycho. **Noir Themes:** Woman in jeopardy, betrayal, greed. ★★★

The host of a radio murder mystery show (Rains) kills his secretary (Woodell), making it look like a suicide. Woodell's fiancé (North) shows up at Rains' home claiming to be the husband of Rains' niece (Caulfield), who supposedly died in an boating accident several weeks earlier. The imposter hopes to prove that Woodell's death was not accidental. But, unfortunately, for him, Caulfield turns up very much alive. North attempts to convince her that the reason she doesn't remember marrying him is that she has amnesia. Meanwhile, Rains, who's been slowly eliminating his family, turns his attention to Caulfield. Totter plays the wife of alcoholic Hatfield, Caulfield's former boyfriend, and Bennett is Rains' suspicious assistant. Lambert, who proves to be one of film noir's worst drivers, plays a murderer being blackmailed by Rains. The convoluted plot is difficult to follow and may require a second viewing to figure out what's really going on. But the acting is top-notch, with Rains at his deranged best, and Totter sensational as an alluring femme fatale.

Familiar Face from Television:
❏ Fred Clark (Harry Morton, George and Gracie's neighbor in *The George Burns and Gracie Allen Show*) as a homicide detective.

Memorable Noir Moments:
❏ During a game of chess, Totter tosses a hint at the pensive North. "Does it always take you so long to make a move?" she asks suggestively.
❏ Taking his cue from Zachary Scott in 1945's ***Danger Signal***, Rains cleverly tricks his trusting niece into writing a suicide note by telling her that it's for his next radio show. (See *A Kiss Before Dying* for an equally clever killer.)

The Unwritten Code (1944) 61 min. Tom Neal, Ann Savage, Roland Varno, Howard Freeman, Bobby Larson, Teddy Infuhr. **Screenplay by:** Charles Kenyon and Leslie T. White. **Directed by:** Herman Rotsten. **Noir Type:** Impersonator. **Noir Themes:** Paranoia, betrayal. ★½

After a ship carrying German prisoners of war is torpedoed by a Nazi U-boat, a brutal German corporal (Varno) steals a dying British officer's identity. In England, he feigns a war injury and takes refuge in a boarding house owned by Freeman. Neal is the American military police sergeant in charge of a nearby P.O.W. camp, and Savage is his girlfriend, a nurse's assistant at the Army hospital. Varno, who plans to break his comrades out of the camp, keeps forgetting that his arm is supposed to be paralyzed, which attracts the attention of two little kids (Larson and Infuhr) who are more observant than the grownups around them. Complete with war-time clichés ("the only good Nazi is a dead Nazi," "the only way to educate a Nazi is to kill him"), this cheapie noir is notable only for the appearance of Neal and Savage, who went on to star in the classic *Detour*.

Valerie (1957) 84 min. Sterling Hayden, Anita Ekberg, Anthony Steel, Peter Walker, John Wengraf, Iphigenie Castiglioni. **Screenplay by**: Leonard Heideman and Emmett Murphy. **Directed by**: Gerd Oswald. **Noir Type**: Trial. **Noir Themes**: Greed, paranoia, sexual hostility. ★½

Civil war veteran Hayden is charged with murdering his "foreigner" in-laws (Wengraf and Castiglioni) and attempting to kill his new wife, Ekberg. At the trial, only three witnesses are called — the handsome new minister (Steel), Hayden himself, and, the recuperating Ekberg, who also happens to be pregnant. Steel's and Ekberg's stories that Hayden abused, even tortured, his wife conflict with Hayden's own testimony. He claims that Ekberg was the town tramp, who seduced not only the minister but his own brother (Walker), and that he shot his in-laws in self-defense and his wife by accident. Who's lying? Who cares? Noir icon Hayden is wasted as a former Army interrogator, who may or may not have used some of his sinister techniques on his beautiful bride. Swedish bombshell Ekberg was married to British co-star Steel at the time.

Memorable Noir Moment:
❑ Hayden's misogynistic lawyer, who seems to know evil when he sees it, tells the jury, "I've seen much evil in my day, but there's nothing so evil as a debauched, immoral woman."

The Velvet Touch (1948) 97 min. Rosalind Russell, Leo Genn, Claire Trevor, Sydney Greenstreet, Leon Ames. **Screenplay by**: Leo Rosten and Walter Reilly. **Directed by**: John Gage. **Noir Type**: Show Biz. **Noir Themes**: Guilt, character deterioration, lust, jealousy. ★★★

Russell plays a stage actress who kills her former lover, Broadway producer Ames, by clubbing him with a statuette when he threatens to ruin her career and her relationship with her new boyfriend (Genn). It seems she's gotten away with murder when one of her co-stars (Trevor), Ames' former girlfriend, gets the blame. Guilt-stricken, Russell also must endure the constant presence of a jocular, food-loving detective (Greenstreet). Russell does a good job as the comedienne with a yen to be a dramatic actress, and Greenstreet is enjoyable as the portly police captain. Look for former screen Tarzan Lex Barker in a small role as Russell's leading man, and Martha Hyer as an understudy.

Familiar Face from Television:
❑ James Flavin (Lt. Donovan in *Man with a Camera*) as a homicide detective.

Memorable Noir Moments:
❑ Trevor, complaining about romantic rival Russell, says, "The trouble with her is she's here today and here tomorrow."
❑ Trevor, who knows that she's facing a murder charge for Russell's crime, lashes out at the actress from her hospital bed. "Where did you get your luck, Valerie?" she asks. "Or does God pity the wicked?"
❑ Not one to mince words, even with a famous actress, Genn loses patience with Russell's

snobby chitchat. "Do you mind not calling me 'darling'?" he says. "You toss affection around as though it were in mass production."

The Verdict (1946) 86 min. Sydney Greenstreet, Peter Lorre, Joan Lorring, George Coulouris, Paul Cavanagh, Morton Lowry. **Screenplay by:** Peter Milne. **Directed by:** Don Siegel. **Noir Type:** Period. **Noir Themes:** Guilt, betrayal, revenge. ★★★

In Victorian London, Scotland Yard superintendent Greenstreet is forced to resign after the man he caught and helped convict of murdering a wealthy dowager is hung and then found to have been innocent. Greenstreet's superiors appoint his arrogant rival (Coulouris) to the vacant post. When Greenstreet's friend (Lowry), the murdered woman's nephew, is killed soon afterwards, Greenstreet watches with understandable glee as his successor conducts a shoddy investigation. There's no shortage of suspects in Lowry's murder—Greenstreet's artist friend (Lorre), a member of Parliament (Cavanagh) and a nightclub entertainer (Lorring). This enjoyable locked-room mystery marked Siegel's first outing as a director and Greenstreet's and Lorre's last film appearance together. They had teamed up for nine previous movies, including the classic noirs, **The Maltese Falcon, The Mask of Dimitrios** and **Three Strangers.**

Memorable Noir Moment:
❏ Lorring, a tipsy Victorian feminist, replies to Lorre's suggestion that he's a very good man. "There's no such thing as a good man," she says.

Vertigo (1958) 127 min. James Stewart, Kim Novak, Barbara Bel Geddes, Tom Helmore. **Screenplay by:** Alec Coppel and Samuel Taylor. **Directed by:** Alfred Hitchcock. **Noir Type:** Cover-Up. **Noir Themes:** Obsession, guilt, betrayal. ★★★★

Vertigo is an offbeat film about a former cop (Stewart) who is asked by an old college chum (Helmore) to tail his wife (Novak), whom the man claims is mentally unbalanced and on the road to self-destruction. Stewart, who resigned from the police force after his fear of heights and its resulting vertigo caused the death of a fellow police officer, reluctantly takes on the case. Romantically pursued by his former fiancée (Bel Geddes), Stewart would rather follow the beautiful Novak around San Francisco. His dedication to duty pays off when Novak jumps into the Bay in an apparent suicide attempt, and he dives in after her. The ex-cop quickly falls in love with the mysterious woman, who seems to be taking on the personality of her great-grandmother, herself a suicide. Spurred on by his obsessive love, Stewart attempts to cure Novak, but tragedy strikes, leaving him an emotional vegetable. So much for the first hour. Viewers who manage to sit through the deadly slow first half, which is mostly a San Francisco area travelogue, will be rewarded for their patience during the bizarre second half, when an emotionally disturbed Stewart meets a waitress who's a dead ringer for Novak. Rated number 61 on the American Film Institute's List of America's 100 Greatest Movies and said to be Hitchcock's most personal film, this tale of impossible love is an acquired taste. Although some critics advise several viewings in order to truly appreciate it, for some viewers it may never get any better. Hitch's first choice for the role of Stewart's mystery lady was Vera Miles, unavailable because she was pregnant with hubby Gordon "Tarzan" Scott's baby.

Familiar Faces from Television:
- ❏ Ellen Corby (Grandma Walton from *The Waltons*) as a hotel manager.
- ❏ Lee Patrick (Henrietta Topper in *Topper*) as the new owner of Novak's car.
- ❏ Henry Jones (Judge Jonathan Dexter in *Phyllis*) as the coroner.
- ❏ Raymond Bailey (banker Milburn Drysdale in *The Beverly Hillbillies*) as Stewart's doctor.

The Vicious Circle (1948) 77 min. Conrad Nagel, Fritz Kortner, Reinhold Schunzel, Philip Van Zandt, Lyle Talbot, Frank Ferguson. **Screenplay by:** Heinz Herald and Guy Endore. **Directed by:** W. Lee Wilder. **Noir Type:** Trial. **Noir Themes:** Corruption, bigotry, greed, guilt. ★

This is a badly acted courtroom drama about five Jews on trial for murdering a 14-year-old girl in nineteenth century Hungary. It seems that the local baron (Schunzel) has discovered oil on the property being farmed by the accused, and this is his way of getting rid of them so he can buy the land. Nagel is the stouthearted attorney for the men, and Van Zandt is the evil special investigator in cahoots with the baron. Talbot plays an obsequious prosecutor, who gleefully takes over when his boss (Ferguson, who narrates) quits in disgust. Kortner is one of the defendants. Everyone overacts in this ridiculous, low-budget B film, also known as *The Woman in Brown*.

Familiar Faces from Television:
- ❏ Frank Cady (Doc Williams in *The Adventures of Ozzie and Harriet* and Sam Drucker in *Petticoat Junction* and *Green Acres*) as a court official.

Vicki (1953) 85 min. Jeanne Crain, Jean Peters, Elliott Reid, Richard Boone, Casey Adams, Alex D'Arcy. **Screenplay by:** Harold Greene, Dwight Taylor and Leo Townsend. **Directed by:** Harry Horner. **Noir Type:** Whodunit. **Noir Themes:** Obsession, lust, corruption, jealousy. ★★½

Boone is a homicide detective obsessed with nabbing a publicity agent (Reid) for the murder of an up-and-coming starlet (Peters). Peters' sister (Crain) is falling in love with Reid but is unsure of his innocence. Also being questioned by police are a gossip columnist (Adams) and actor (D'Arcy), who, along with Reid, are responsible for turning waitress Peters into a celebrity. A remake of the 1941 noir, *I Wake Up Screaming*, *Vicki* is an effective suspense vehicle with solid performances, especially by Crain and Boone. Yes, that weird switchboard operator is a very young Aaron Spelling before he became a successful TV producer and Tori's dad. Interestingly, Casey Adams was TV's first Ward Cleaver in the *Leave It to Beaver* pilot episode (1957).

Familiar Faces from Television:
- ❏ Carl Betz (Dr. Alex Stone in *The Donna Reed Show*) as a homicide detective.
- ❏ Burt Mustin (Fireman Gus in *Leave It to Beaver* and Mr. Quigley in *All in the Family*) as a bellboy.
- ❏ John Dehner (reporter Duke Williams in *The Roaring Twenties*) as a police captain.
- ❏ Parley Baer (Darby in *The Adventures of Ozzie and Harriet*, Mayor Stoner in *The Andy Griffith Show*) as a homicide detective.

Violated (1953) 78 min. Wim Holland, Lili Dawn, Mitchell Kowall, Vickie Carlson, William Martel, Jason Niles, Fred Lambert. **Screenplay by:** William Paul Mishkin. **Directed by:**

Walter Strate. **Noir Type:** Psycho. **Noir Themes:** Woman in jeopardy, sexual hostility, paranoia. ✷

A couple of New York detectives (Kowall and Martel), who, like the hotel dick in ***Don't Bother to Knock***, couldn't detect a monk in a convent, investigate a series of homicides committed by a psycho with a hair fetish, who gives crew cuts to his female victims after brutally stabbing them. Suspects include a fashion photographer (Holland) and a middle-aged ex-convict (Lambert), who has a thing for young girls. Dawn plays a burlesque queen who, even the snoozing viewer might notice, is a bit overweight and a tad past her prime. Carlson is a wannabe model with a front tooth problem, and Niles is a bleeding heart psychiatrist, who thinks the taxpayers' money is wasted on silly things like trials and should be used instead to educate future head shrinkers. This low-budget B bomb, also known as *New York Photographer*, has it all — atrocious acting, a hackneyed script, an inappropriate musical score, poor photography and a pretentious prologue, which reminds us that "In the darkness of indifference, evil will fester and grow. Bring it to light and it will ultimately disappear."

Memorable Noir Moment:

❑ Dialogue from the Ed Wood, Jr., school of screenwriting? When a newspaper reporter asks a policeman if the murder victim had a boyfriend, the cop replies, "A boyfriend? The landlady said she had hundreds. Friendship was her business. It could have been any one of them." Scratching his head, the wavering cop adds, "Then again, maybe not."

Violence (1947). 72 min. Michael O'Shea, Nancy Coleman, Sheldon Leonard, Peter Whitney, Emory Parnell. **Screenplay by:** Stanley Rubin and Louis Lantz. **Directed by:** Jack Bernhard. **Noir Type:** Troubled Veteran. **Noir Themes:** Woman in jeopardy, social reform, lust. ✷✷

Special agent O'Shea and reporter Coleman go undercover to expose a shady veteran's organization that has been duping ex–G.I.s into committing acts of violence by "priming them with hate." Funded by a mysterious "Mr. X," the ring (headed by Parnell, Leonard and Whitney) promises vets better housing conditions, relief from shortages and good jobs if they'll only join the organization and follow orders. It's slow going but there's an interesting gimmick that might keep the viewer interested — investigative reporter Coleman develops amnesia and gets caught up in the ring's propaganda.

Familiar Face from Television:

❑ John Hamilton (Perry White in *The Adventures of Superman*) as a doctor.

Memorable Noir Moment:

❑ Sensitivity Training Required: A newspaper headline containing two adjectives too many, states, "*Pretty Girl* Reporter Exposes Phony Group."

Violent Saturday (1955) 90 min. Victor Mature, Richard Egan, Stephen McNally, Virginia Leith, Tommy Noonan, Lee Marvin, Margaret Hayes, J. Carrol Naish, Sylvia Sidney, Ernest Borgnine. **Screenplay by:** Sydney Boehm. **Directed by:** Richard Fleischer. **Noir Type:** Heist. **Noir Themes:** Victim of fate, obsession, greed, jealousy. ✷✷✷½

Bad guys McNally, Marvin and Naish arrive in a small mining town to rob the local bank. Not realizing they're about to pull a heist in *Peyton Place*, the would-be robbers witness the dark side of small-town life while making their plans. Mature is a mining engineer who's trying to regain the respect of his little boy, who recently found out that his dad wasn't a war hero like his friend's father. Egan, the unhappy president of the mining company, whose wife (Hayes) is cheating on him, has been hitting the bottle hard lately. Sidney, the local librarian, is facing foreclosure on her mortgage, and resorts to stealing a pocketbook from a library customer. The bank manager (Noonan) is a secret peeping tom, who can't keep his eyes off a pretty nurse (Leith), who can't keep *her* eyes off of Egan. It looks like an easy score for the three hoods, but they haven't met Borgnine yet, an Amish farmer whose religious convictions will soon be put to the test. This is a marginal but interesting film noir, with an electrifying last half-hour. Marvin, who abused women in *The Big Heat*, is similarly cruel here, stepping on a little kid's hand like he was squashing a cigarette butt. Naish, who for a change isn't stereotyped as a heavily accented Italian, does well as the robber with a soft spot for kids.

Memorable Noir Moment:
❑ Egan and Hayes candidly discuss the possibility of giving their marriage another chance. "We can't change," she says. "Not us. You're an alcoholic and I'm a tramp."

Voice in the Wind (1944) 85 min. Francis Lederer, Sigrid Gurie, J. Edward Bromberg, J. Carrol Naish, Alexander Granach, David Cota. **Screenplay by:** Frederick Torberg. **Directed by:** Arthur Ripley. **Noir Type:** Amnesia. **Noir Themes:** Fatalism, betrayal. ★★

A Czech concert pianist (Lederer) and his wife (Gurie) are separated when he disobeys a Nazi directive by playing a patriotic Czech song during a recital. When he flees the country, Gurie is arrested and tortured but eventually escapes. Both wind up on the Portuguese island of Guadalupe unaware of the other's existence. Lederer, an amnesiac who's either pretending to be, or really is, mentally deficient, works for three dysfunctional seagoing brothers (Naish, Granach and Cota), who rip off refugees seeking passage to America. Meanwhile, Gurie, under Dr. Bromberg's care, lies dying in a seedy hotel room across the street from the saloon where the melancholy Lederer hangs out playing the piano. Naish, an Irish-American who made a career out of stereotyping Italians, is a guy named Luigi who can't pronounce an English word without adding the letter "a" to the end of it. This gloomy, low-budget film tries hard to be artsy fartsy but doesn't succeed.

Memorable Noir Moment:
❑ From the Stupid Nazi Department: Two German soldiers guarding a political prisoner aboard a train, sing and play the harmonica. "I am hungry," shouts one. "I am drunk," cries the other. "Heil Hitler," yells the first. "Heil Hitler," responds the second. Both break into raucous laughter, giving their handcuffed prisoner the opportunity to knock them both unconscious and escape.

Voice of the Whistler (1945) 60 min. Richard Dix, Lynn Merrick, Rhys Williams, James Cardwell. **Screenplay by:** William Castle and Wilfrid H. Pettitt. **Directed by:** William Castle. **Noir Type:** Newlywed. **Noir Themes:** Fatalism, jealousy, greed. ★★½

Dix and director Castle team up for yet another short but effective *Whistler* drama. This time around, Dix plays a wealthy industrialist, diagnosed with a fatal illness. While on vacation, Dix meets Williams, a happy-go-lucky taxi driver who diagnoses his problem as a severe cast of loneliness and introduces him to a pretty nurse (Merrick), who works in a neighborhood clinic. Dix, starving for companionship and ever the businessman, makes Merrick an offer she can't refuse — if she marries him, he'll leave her his entire fortune when he dies. Seeing dollar signs and believing that Dix has only about six months to live, Merrick dumps her true love (Cardwell), a penniless doctor, and marries the deliriously happy tycoon. Married life agrees with Dix, and six months later he's still around, much to the chagrin of Merrick, who's bored with playing housewife — in a lighthouse, no less. Then one day a determined Cardwell arrives at the couple's isolated home, ready to commit murder if necessary to win Merrick back. Dix is entertaining, as usual, as the unhappy businessman with a new lease on life, and Cardwell gives an interesting performance as the dedicated physician gone bad over a dame. For more of this enjoyable series, see *The Whistler*, *Mark of the Whistler*, *Power of the Whistler*, *Mysterious Intruder*, *Secret of the Whistler*, *The Thirteenth Hour* and *The Return of the Whistler*.

Familiar Faces from Television:

❑ John Hamilton (Perry White in *The Adventures of Superman*) as Dix's doctor.
❑ Byron Foulger (Wendell Gibbs in *Petticoat Junction*) as a henpecked husband at a flower stand.

Walk a Crooked Mile (1948) 91 min. Louis Hayward, Dennis O'Keefe, Louise Allbritton, Carl Esmond, Onslow Stevens, Raymond Burr, Art Baker, Lowell Gilmore, Charles Evans. **Screenplay by:** George Bruce. **Directed by:** Gordon Douglas. **Noir Type:** Nuclear. **Noir Themes:** Conspiracy, betrayal. ★★★

From the future director of 1951's *I Was a Communist for the F.B.I.* comes an early Red menace film, almost as good as his later one. This one has Hayward as a Scotland Yard investigator and O'Keefe as an F.B.I. agent teaming up to fight those "who walk their crooked miles along the highways and byways of free America." They're hoping to discover who's stealing atomic secrets from an American company and turning them over to Commie spies. Suspects include the company's president (Baker), a scientist (Gilmore), a physicist (Evans), and a mathematician (Esmond) and his Ph.D. girlfriend (Allbritton). Spy Stevens and his henchman (Burr) are intent on getting the vital atomic information and won't hesitate to knock off any fed or inept comrade who gets in their way. Good, solid performances help make this enjoyably camp B movie a treat. Burr also played a Red spy in 1951's **The Whip Hand**.

Familiar Faces from Television:

❑ John Hamilton (Perry White in *The Adventures of Superman*) as a special agent of the F.B.I.
❑ Frank Ferguson (Gus the ranch hand in *My Friend Flicka*) as a spy working at a laundry.
❑ Arthur Space (Doc Weaver on *Lassie* and Velvet's dad in *National Velvet*) as O'Keefe's boss.
❑ Ray Teal (Sheriff Roy Coffee in *Bonanza*) as a police sergeant at a murder scene.

Memorable Noir Moment:

❑ Hayward, while searching a Communist spy's apartment, appreciates a painting the man has been working on. "He could be a pretty fair painter," he tells O'Keefe. The F.B.I. agent can't resist a pun. "Yes," he replies, "if there wasn't so much *red* in his work."

Walk East on Beacon (1952) 98 min. George Murphy, Finlay Currie, Virginia Gilmore, Karel Stepanek, Louisa Horton, Peter Capell. **Screenplay by:** Leo Rosten, Virginia Shaler, Leonard Heideman and Emmett Murphy. **Directed by:** Alfred L. Werker. **Noir Type:** Commie. **Noir Themes:** Conspiracy, betrayal. ★★★

Murphy is an F.B.I. agent investigating an espionage case involving Commie spy Stepanek and his "American" comrades (Gillmore, Horton and Capell), who attempt to steal the design of a hi-tech calculator being developed by an elderly immigrant scientist (Currie). Holding Currie's son hostage in East Berlin, the Reds offer to release him unharmed if the scientist cooperates but threaten to kill the boy if he doesn't. Currie, not taking much stock in the promises of Party officials, contacts Murphy and his "alert and highly trained special agents." Based on a *Reader's Digest* article by F.B.I. Director J. Edgar Hoover, *Walk East*, which was shot on location in Boston, is a no-nonsense, realistic portrayal of a Russian spy operation in the U.S. at the beginning of the Cold War and the F.B.I.'s methodical response to it. Yes, it's dated, but the clichés are kept to a minimum, and future U.S. Senator Murphy and his mostly unknown colleagues help make it a fairly enjoyable film noir entry.

Memorable Noir Moments:
❏ A captured Red spy gets dramatic with unimpressed F.B.I. interrogators. "For every one of us you arrest," she brags, "there are a lot of others trained and waiting to take over."
❏ From the Some-Things-Never-Change Department: The film's narrator unknowingly describes America's future terrorism problem when he states, "The foreign espionage agent operating in this country is well aware that he enjoys a unique privilege — the freedoms guaranteed by the Bill of Rights to all loyal American citizens."

Walk Softly, Stranger (1950) 81 min. Joseph Cotten, (Alida) Valli, Spring Byington, Paul Stewart, John McIntire. **Screenplay by:** Frank Fenton. **Directed by:** Robert Stevenson. **Noir Type:** On the Run. **Noir Themes:** Greed, obsession, revenge. ★½

While hiding out after his last robbery, a small-time crook (Cotten) falls in love with a crippled girl (Valli), and decides to go straight. Complicating his plan is his on-the-run, former partner (Stewart), who shows up looking for a place to hide. McIntire is Cotten's boss at his legit factory job, and Jack Paar, before his TV heyday as the *Tonight Show* host, plays Cotten's co-worker and poker buddy. Byington (TV's *December Bride*) is Cotton's sweet old landlady. Except for a terrific car crash, this romantic melodrama is snooze material.

The Way Out (1955-British) 86 min. Gene Nelson, Mona Freeman, John Bentley, Michael Goodliffe, Charles Victor. **Screenplay by:** Montgomery Tully. **Directed by:** Montgomery Tully. **Noir Type:** On the Run. **Noir Themes:** Paranoia, betrayal. ★½

"The way out" is an escape route for criminals fleeing Great Britain. Freeman, devoted wife of killer Nelson, uses her life savings to get her cry-baby husband out of the country. Even after she learns that Nelson's story about killing a bookie accidentally is a lie, she still goes ahead with her plans to thwart English justice, placing herself and her brother (Goodliffe) in danger of being arrested as accomplices. After she purchases the route from an underworld figure (Victor), Freeman and Goodliffe take off with Nelson on a long and, for the viewer, boring ride, switching vehicles occasionally to confuse Detective Sergeant Bentley and the rest of London's finest, who attempt to track them down. American actor Nelson, who gave a good performance in *Crime Wave*, hits rock bottom in this pointless British noir (released as *Dial 999*), playing an ungrateful womanizer whose demands and temper tantrums eventually cause his downfall. Nelson later had better success as a director for such TV series as *The Rifleman*, *The Andy Griffith Show*, *Starsky and Hutch*, *Hawaii Five-O* and *Barnaby Jones*.

We Were Strangers (1949) 106 min. Jennifer Jones, John Garfield, Pedro Armendariz, Gilbert Roland. **Screenplay by**: John Huston and Peter Viertel. **Directed by**: John Huston. **Noir Type**: South of the Border. **Noir Themes**: Conspiracy, revenge, fatalism, jealousy. ★★

When her revolutionary-minded brother is murdered by the chief of the Cuban secret police (Armendariz), a vengeful bank secretary (Jones) joins the underground to overthrow the repressive regime. She teams up with Garfield, a Cuban-American who has returned to his homeland to join the fight for freedom. Garfield concocts a plan that involves digging a tunnel from Jones' home to a nearby cemetery, assassinating a high government official, and then blowing up the mourners at his funeral, killing not only the president and his cabinet but quite possibly their families — an acceptable loss according to Garfield. Meanwhile, the suspicious and lecherous Armendariz is trying to make time with Jones, who has fallen in love with Garfield. Roland, a co-conspirator and tunnel digger, would like nothing more than to play suicide bomber and drive a truck loaded with dynamite into the government palace. Conservative critics condemned the film as being blatantly pro–Communist, while the most important critics, the moviegoers, had enough sense to stay away from the box office. Even the presence of such major Hollywood icons as Garfield and Jones couldn't prevent Huston's first independent film from flopping.

The Weapon (1956-British) 80 min. Steve Cochran, Lizabeth Scott, Herbert Marshall, Jon Whiteley, Nicole Maurey, George Cole. **Screenplay by**: Fred Freiberger. **Directed by**: Val Guest. **Noir Type**: On the Run. **Noir Themes**: Victim of fate, obsession, fatalism. ★★★

After a ten-year-old boy (Whiteley) finds a gun in a bombed-out London ruin, he accidentally shoots a playmate. Thinking the cops want to arrest him, Whiteley runs away from home, leaving his American mum (Scott), the widow of a British soldier, frantic with worry. A callous American Army intelligence officer (Cochran) is called in by Scotland Yard inspector Marshall because a ballistics test shows that the gun was the weapon used to kill an American soldier a decade earlier. Cochran tries to keep the story out of the newspaper so that the murderer (Cole), "a seedy little man," won't know that he's closing in on him. Cole gets wind of the story, however, and desperately scours London for his gun and the boy who's carrying it. Along the way, the killer discovers that Cochran has tracked down a dance hall hostess (Maurey), a witness who can finger him. *The Weapon* is a dynamic British thriller with solid performances by Cochran and the always reliable Scott.

Memorable Noir Moment:

❑ The cold-hearted Cochran seems to have found his soulmate. When bar girl Maurey asks him why she should help him in his murder investigation, he tells her that she could help save a little boy's life. "Kids are dying all over," she responds cynically.

The Web (1947) 87 min. Edmond O'Brien, Ella Raines, Vincent Price, William Bendix, Howland Chamberlin. **Screenplay by**: William Bowers and Bertram Millhauser. **Directed by**: Michael Gordon. **Noir Type**: Wrong Man. **Noir Themes**: Victim of fate, guilt, greed, betrayal. ★★½

A wealthy industrialist (Price) offers a brash young attorney (O'Brien) a job as his bodyguard, claiming that a former employee (Chamberlin) who has just been released after a five-year jail term for embezzling a million dollars from Price's firm, is out for revenge. Not one to turn down an easy five grand, O'Brien accepts the position and asks his friend at homicide (Bendix) to rush through a gun permit for him. Against his better judgment, Bendix obliges, and the next evening O'Brien shoots and kills Chamberlin during what appears to be a violent attack on Price. Prompted by feelings of guilt and Bendix's suspicions that he murdered Chamberlin for the dough, O'Brien attempts to find out if he's been played for a patsy. In the process, he falls in love with Price's live-in secretary (Raines). Entertaining and, at times, suspenseful, with noir icon O'Brien and the masterful Price providing enjoyable performances.

The Well (1951) 85 min. Richard Rober, Henry (Harry) Morgan, Barry Kelley, Maidie Norman, Ernest Anderson. **Screenplay by**: Russell Rouse and Clarence Green. **Directed by**: Leo C. Popkin and Russell Rouse. **Noir Type**: Racist. **Noir Themes**: Bigotry, paranoia, child in jeopardy. ★★★

A five-year-old black girl, on her way to school, falls down a 60-foot well and within hours the peaceful town is embroiled in racial turmoil that could explode into a full-scale riot. A stranger in town (Morgan), the nephew of a construction company owner (Kelley), had been seen with the little girl before she disappeared. Rumors quickly spread in the black community that a white man killed the girl, and townspeople, both black and white, begin to get edgy. Meanwhile, the girl's parents (Norman and Anderson) wait and hope. After the sheriff (Rober) arrests Morgan, the blacks fear that the suspect will be released because he's white. Fights break out between gangs of black and white ruffians, and both camps begin to organize into small armies. How far will the violence go before the little girl is discovered? Is she dead or alive? Noir veteran Morgan is excellent as the innocent man suspected of being a child molester and murderer. Dimitri Tiomkin's score contributes greatly to the tension and excitement. This is a very progressive film for its time, bold in its handling of racism and one of only a few films noirs with black actors in major roles.

Memorable Noir Moments:

❑ An anxious Rober issues a warning to Kelley and his armed mob, who are ready to march on the blacks. "I'll shoot you down like a pack of mad dogs!" he threatens.
❑ When a group of white boys beat up a young black man, the rumor mill has it that the boys were defending a white girl he supposedly attacked. "I heard she killed herself afterwards," one whisperer is heard to say.

Wetbacks (1956) 89 min. Lloyd Bridges, Nancy Gates, John Hoyt, Barton MacLane, Harold Peary. **Screenplay by:** Peter LaRoche. **Directed by:** Hank McCune. **Noir Type:** South of the Border. **Noir Themes:** Greed, social reform. ★½

A former Coast Guard officer (Bridges), now the destitute captain of a fishing boat, gets involved with Hoyt and Peary, members of a gang that's smuggling illegal aliens into the United States from Mexico. Gates, abandoned in a small Mexican town by MacLane after a fishing excursion, is Bridges' love interest. Bridges, who went on to star in syndicated TV series *Sea Hunt*, is disappointing in this slow-moving B movie.

When Strangers Marry (1944) 67 min. Kim Hunter, Robert Mitchum, Dean Jagger.

Screenplay by: Dennis J. Cooper and Philip Yordan. **Directed by:** William Castle. **Noir Type:** Newlywed. **Noir Themes:** Victim of fate, paranoia, distrust, betrayal. ★★★

This suspenseful noir, also known as *Betrayed*, stars Hunter as a newlywed married to Jagger, whom she only recently met and whom she now suspects might be the Silk Stocking Killer being hunted by police. You can't help but sympathize with Hunter as she stumbles around in confusion and fear hoping for the best but believing the worst. Mitchum, in his first important role and his first of many films noirs, gives a solid performance as Hunter's ex-boyfriend. Although made before on-location filming became practical, the New York studio set is effectively claustrophobic and oppressing. The newlyweds' temporary refuge in an African-American jazz joint and their walk through Harlem are interesting for the time. Rhonda Fleming has a bit part as a newlywed traveling alone by train.

Familiar Faces from Television:
- ❑ Minerva Urecal (Annie in *The Adventures of Tugboat Annie* and "Mother" in *Peter Gunn*) as the couple's overnight landlady.
- ❑ Byron Foulger (Wendell Gibbs in *Petticoat Junction*), in a photograph only, as a slide-show murderer.

Memorable Noir Moment:
- ❑ In what must be a film noir first, Hunter and Jagger leave a jazz joint in Harlem and wind up face to face with a couple of black New York City motorcycle cops.

Where Danger Lives (1950) 84 min. Robert Mitchum, Faith Domergue, Claude Rains, Maureen O'Sullivan. **Screenplay by:** Charles Bennett. **Directed by:** John Farrow. **Noir Type:** Femme Fatale. **Noir Themes:** Obsession, lust, jealousy, paranoia. ★★½

Mitchum plays a hospital doctor who treats attempted suicide victim Domergue and, of course, falls in love with her, dumping his girlfriend (O'Sullivan). When he drunkenly barges into Domergue's mansion to confront her father, who he believes wants to break up the relationship, he discovers that the "father" is really her elderly husband (Rains). A fight ensues and Mitchum gets hit over the head with a fireplace poker before knocking the older man to the floor. After dousing himself with cold water, he finds that Rains is dead. Not thinking straight because of a concussion, he allows Domergue to talk him into taking a powder with her to Mexico. Their nightmare car trip ends tragically at the Mexican border after Mitchum discovers that

Domergue is a pretty sick dame. Mitchum's performance saves the film, which is nearly identical to his *Angel Face*. The part must have been a natural for the sleepy-eyed, laid-back Mitchum because for more than half of the film he walks around in a semi-comatose condition as a result of the concussion. Domergue, while quite a looker, isn't persuasive as the psychotic femme fatale.

Familiar Faces from Television:

❑ Jack Kruschen (Tully in *Hong Kong* and Sam Markowitz in *Busting Loose*) as an ambulance driver.
❑ Jack Kelly (Brother Bart in *Maverick*) as an ambulance attendant.
❑ Sherry Jackson (Terry Williams in *Make Room for Daddy* a.k.a. *The Danny Thomas Show*) as the little girl in the iron lung.
❑ Ray Teal (Sheriff Coffee in *Bonanza*) as a small-town sheriff.

Where the Sidewalk Ends (1950) 95 min. Dana Andrews, Gene Tierney, Gary Merrill, Karl Malden, Craig Stevens, Bert Freed, Neville Brand. **Screenplay by:** Ben Hecht. **Directed by:** Otto Preminger. **Noir Type:** Bad Cop. **Noir Themes:** Corruption, guilt, paranoia, fatalism. ★★★★

A detective (Dana Andrews, left) grills a gangster (Gary Merrill, right) while the hood's angry flunkies (David Wolfe, second from left, and Neville Brand) get ready to rumble in *Where the Sidewalk Ends* (20th Century–Fox, 1950).

Andrews, a two-fisted police detective warned by his boss to lay off the rough stuff, gets into a brawl with an inebriated murder suspect (Stevens, TV's *Peter Gunn*) and accidentally kills him. Already self-conscious and ashamed because he's known on both sides of the law as the son of a thief killed by police, Andrews hides the body and tries to frame Merrill, a local hood. During the investigation, he meets Stevens' estranged wife (Tierney) and falls in love with her. When Tierney's father is arrested by police lieutenant Malden for his son-in-law's murder, Andrews faces the inevitable choice — do the right thing and go to jail or continue to cover up. Freed is Andrews' understanding partner, who must hock his wife's jewelry to help his friend assuage his guilt. Andrews is outstanding in one of his best performances, and Merrill is excellent as the murderous hood. Brand gives one of his enjoyable, patented performances as a sadistic thug.

Familiar Faces from Television:

❏ Harry von Zell (the announcer of *The George Burns and Gracie Allen Show*) as an unlucky gambler, who winds up losing a lot more than he wins.
❏ Anthony George (Agent Allison in *The Untouchables* and Don Corey in *Checkmate*) as a hood accompanying Andrews to the gang's warehouse hideout.

Memorable Noir Moments:

❏ When his boss reminds him that there have been twelve complaints of assault and battery against him in one month, Andrews snarls, "From who? Hoods, dusters, mugs — a lot of nickel rats."
❏ Andrews' favorite waitress means well when she puts in a good word for him with Tierney. "He gets himself a dizzy blonde once in a while," she confides, "but that's no life."

While the City Sleeps (1956) 99 min. Dana Andrews, Rhonda Fleming, George Sanders, Howard Duff, Thomas Mitchell, Vincent Price, John Barrymore, Jr., Ida Lupino, James Craig, Sally Forrest. **Screenplay by**: Casey Robinson. **Directed by**: Fritz Lang. **Noir Type**: Psycho. **Noir Themes**: Corruption, sexual hostility, woman in jeopardy, betrayal, conspiracy. ★★★½

A news conglomerate's managers (Sanders, Mitchell and Craig) are in a dogfight for a promotion promised by the corporation's arrogant new owner (Price) to the first one who finds the deranged psycho known as the "Lipstick Killer" (Barrymore). Andrews, a hard-drinking TV commentator, who sides with newspaper editor Mitchell in the competition, is so shallow that he puts his fiancée (Forrest) in mortal danger by setting her up as a decoy to trap the killer. Then, in one of his frequent alcoholic stupors, he allows himself to be seduced by a sexy gossip columnist (Lupino), who's using him to help the newswire manager (Sanders) win the promotion. In the meantime, the photo editor (Craig) is having an affair with Price's scheming wife (Fleming), hoping she'll help him land the job. Duff is a homicide detective and Andrews' former rival for Forrest's affections. Director Lang is more interested in the anything-for-a-story ruthlessness of the scheming journalists than in the pathetic serial killer, who, even in his deranged condition, provokes more sympathy than any of the newsmen. Luckily, the confusing soap opera subplots of this somewhat talky, but interesting, film noir are offset by the veteran cast.

Memorable Noir Moment:

Media executives (Thomas Mitchell, left, Vincent Price, center, and George Sanders) look over a bulletin in *While the City Sleeps* (RKO, 1956).

❑ A tipsy Andrews informs temptress Lupino that he's as faithful to his fiancée as the day is long. She replies seductively, "This is the shortest day of the year."

The Whip Hand (1951) 82 min. Elliot Reid, Carla Balenda, Raymond Burr, Edgar Barrier, Otto Waldis. **Screenplay by:** George Bricker and Frank L. Moss. **Directed by:** William Cameron Menzies. **Noir Type:** Nuclear. **Noir Themes:** Conspiracy, paranoia, betrayal. ★★½

On a fishing trip, reporter Reid stumbles across a hotbed of Commie spies in the small town of Winnoga. Communist Waldis is an ex–Nazi bacteriologist who's using the town as an experimental center for germ warfare. Burr is the Commie henchman fronting as an innkeeper, and Barrier is the town doctor assisting Waldis. Balenda, the doctor's innocent sister, teams up with Reid to expose the nasty group. A little too long, it's still an interesting oddity — a mishmash of the *Island of Lost Souls* (1933), *Bad Day at Black Rock* (1955) and *Invasion of the Body Snatchers* (1956). Burr livens things up as the devious Commie posing as a guffawing hick. Produced by Howard Hughes, this was originally entitled *The Man He Found* and was intended to be a story about Hitler escaping to a small town in the U.S. and plotting once again to conquer the world. But, after filming was completed, Hughes reshot the movie, updating the villains to the more contemporary Russian Communists.

Familiar Face from Television:

❏ Olive Carey (Macdonald Carey's secretary in *Lock Up* and Elsie in *Mr. Adams and Eve*) as Mabel.

Memorable Noir Moments:

❏ Reid is astonished over the mysterious goings on in the small town. "What are they trying to do? he wonders. "Drop an iron curtain around Winnoga?"
❏ Mad scientist Waldis, bragging about how he's about to blow up the germ warfare compound and spread lethal bacteria across the country, is told by an unimpressed federal agent, "Aw, you talk like a crazy man."
❏ When a G-man tries to brown-nose Waldis, who has his finger on a detonator, by telling him how a scientist of his great intelligence can benefit mankind, the lunatic replies, "I *am* benefiting mankind — by ridding the world of the people that stand in the way of Communism."

Whiplash (1948) 91 min. Dane Clark, Alexis Smith, Zachary Scott, Jeffrey Lynn, Eve Arden, Alan Hale. **Screenplay by:** Harriet Frank, Maurice Geraghty and Gordon Kahn. **Directed by:** Lewis Seiler. **Noir Type:** Boxing. **Noir Themes:** Obsession, jealousy, corruption, character deterioration. ★★

Clark stars as a promising young artist who takes to the boxing ring because he feels rejected by the woman he loves (Smith). Between rounds of his championship fight at Madison Square Garden, we learn via flashback that nightclub singer Smith is married to a wheelchair-bound ex-boxer (Scott) who is living vicariously through Clark's meteoric rise to the middleweight championship. Lynn plays the doctor who operated on Scott, leaving him a bitter cripple; Arden provides the comic relief as Clark's supportive and romantically interested friend; and Hale is Clark's crusty trainer. The good acting, especially by Clark and Smith, doesn't compensate for the overly dramatic, cliché-ridden script. Before turning to acting, Clark boxed a little, and it shows during the realistic fight scenes.

Familiar Face from Television:

❏ Jimmy Dodd (the head Mouseketeer in *The Mickey Mouse Club*) as a piano player.

Memorable Noir Moments:

❏ After knowing Smith for all of six hours, the starry-eyed Clark informs her, "This is it. It's the whole show. It's what they set to music."
❏ Scott takes an exciting wheelchair ride during the unsurprising climax. (See *The Beast with Five Fingers*, *Kiss of Death*, and *The Lineup* for more wheelchair daredevilry.)

The Whipped *see* The Underworld Story

Whirlpool (1949) 97 min. Gene Tierney, Richard Conte, José Ferrer, Charles Bickford. **Screenplay by:** Ben Hecht and Andrew Solt. **Directed by:** Otto Preminger. **Noir Type:** Con Artist. **Noir Themes:** Woman in jeopardy, jealousy. ★★½

A psychiatrist's wife (Tierney) is suffering from kleptomania and insomnia. Rather than confide in her husband (Conte), she begins to see an astrologer (Ferrer) who hypnotizes her and prepares her to do his evil bidding. Ferrer, it seems, is eager to do away with a former lady friend, who wants him to return the money that he bilked from her. Bickford, the police lieutenant who arrests Tierney for murder, reluctantly agrees to work with Conte to prove her innocence. Although it's all been done before, *Whirlpool* is still enjoyable thanks to solid performances by Tierney and Bickford. Ferrer is entertaining as the pompous astrologer, but Conte is much better at portraying racketeers than psychiatrists.

Memorable Noir Moment:
❏ Ferrer disapprovingly refers to a psychiatrist's habit of recording sessions with a client as "wiretapping the subconscious."

Whispering City (1947-Canadian) 89 min. Paul Lukas, Helmut Dantine, Mary Anderson, John Pratt, Joy Lafleur. **Screenplay by**: Rian James and Leonard Lee. **Directed by**: Fyodor Otsep. **Noir Type**: Newspaper. **Noir Themes**: Woman in jeopardy, greed. ★½

Canadian newspaper reporter Anderson is assigned by her boss (Pratt) to cover the story of a once-famous actress who has been hospitalized after being hit by a truck. On her deathbed, the delirious actress talks about her fiancé's mysterious death years earlier, and Anderson decides to look into it. Her investigation leads her to a composer (Dantine) who thinks he murdered his shrewish wife (Lafleur), and a crooked, cultured attorney (Lukas), who blackmails Dantine into killing the snoopy reporter. Lukas and Dantine are capable, but the rest of the cast is undistinguished, and the ghostly scheme to frighten Lukas into confessing is ludicrous.

Whispering Footsteps (1943) 54 min. John Hubbard, Rita Quigley, Joan Blair, Charles Halton, Billy Benedict. **Screenplay by**: Dane Lussier and Gertrude Walker. **Directed by**: Howard Bretherton. **Noir Type**: Wrong Man. **Noir Themes**: Victim of fate, distrust, paranoia. ★★

Bank teller Hubbard seems to bear a striking resemblance to the strangler who's been terrorizing local townsfolk. At first, friends and neighbors give him the benefit of the doubt but, after a few more local girls are killed, they eventually turn on him. His friends (Quigley and Blair) provide alibis for him when the police think they have him trapped. But even they begin to question his innocence. Not much here, but Hubbard is appealing as the man suspected of having a Jekyll-Hyde personality.

Whistle Stop (1946) 85 min. George Raft, Ava Gardner, Tom Conway, Victor McLaglen. Jorja Curtright. **Screenplay by**: Philip Yordan. **Directed by**: Leonide Moguy. **Noir Type**: Gangster. **Noir Themes**: Obsession, greed, betrayal. ★★

Not a very exciting or even interesting Raft vehicle, *Whistle Stop* does have a plus—gorgeous Ava Gardner, one film closer to the hit film that would make her famous (*The Killers*). Here she plays a tank town girl with a yen for the big city. She tries to get Raft to run off with her, but he's too busy wasting his life "boozing and loafing and playing cards." So she goes off alone and eventually returns wearing a mink coat. She resumes her on-again, off-again love affair with the penniless bum, who still lives at home with mom and pop. When not with Raft, Gardner is cozying up to nightclub owner Conway. McLaglen plays Conway's bartender, who convinces Raft to join him in a plan to rob Conway and knock him off. Things don't work out exactly the way they planned, and they're soon up to their necks in trouble. Curtright is a gal in love with Raft, but she doesn't have what it takes to get him interested. Despite Gardner's presence (and McLaglen's wonderful trademark facial expressions), this minor film noir is wearisome.

Memorable Noir Moment:

❑ Curtright, romantically despondent over Raft, decides to forget her troubles by square dancing at a county fair to strains of *O Susanna* and *Little Brown Jug*. Her partner, in a frenzied dance fever, flings her across the floor and through a wooden railing, putting her in the intensive care unit of the hospital.

The Whistler (1944) 59 min. Richard Dix, J. Carrol Naish, Gloria Stuart, Otto Forrest. **Screenplay by:** Eric Taylor. **Directed by:** William Castle. **Noir Type:** Hit Man. **Noir Themes:** Fatalism, fear, guilt. ★★★½

"I know many things, for I walk at night." Thus speaks the narrator, the phantom-like Whistler (Forrest), as he introduces us to a nervous, middle-aged man (Dix) sitting in a tavern, waiting to hire a hit man through a local hood. The twist (by now a common one, but then fairly original) is that Dix himself, despondent and plagued by guilt over the drowning death of his wife, is the mark. Ironically, his contact is killed by police, but not before sending Dix's name and address to his hit man partner

A flophouse resident (Trevor Bardette, left) has his eye on Richard Dix's jacket in *The Whistler* (Columbia, 1944).

(Naish). When Dix gets a telegram informing him that his wife was not drowned after all but had been in a Japanese P.O.W. camp for the past two years, he tries to cancel the contract. Good luck! Dix is excellent as the desperate and dazed businessman tormented by hit man Naish, who thinks of the contract as a "wonderful psychological experiment." Stuart, Dix's faithful secretary, is, of course, in love with her boss. A clever little thriller, *The Whistler*, also a popular radio drama in the 1940s, was a big hit for William Castle, who went on to direct three more films in the Whistler series and produce and direct a number of successful B horror movies in the fifties. (See also *Mark of the Whistler, Power of the Whistler, Voice of the Whistler, Mysterious Intruder, Secret of the Whistler, The Thirteenth Hour* and *The Return of the Whistler*.) Dix starred in all of the Whistler films except the final one, **The Return of the Whistler**.

Familiar Face from Television:
❏ Billy Benedict (Whitey in the Bowery Boys movies, Skinny in the East Side Kids movies, and Toby in *The Blue Knight*) as a deaf mute engrossed in a Superman comic book.

Memorable Noir Moment:
❏ Rather than accept a generous severance, Dix's faithful butler asks to stay on with him. "Where I'm going, it will be a little cramped for the both of us," Dix says, referring to his impending demise.

White Heat (1949) 114 min. James Cagney, Virginia Mayo, Edmond O'Brien, Steve Cochran, Margaret Wycherly. **Screenplay by:** Ivan Goff and Ben Roberts. **Directed by:** Raoul Walsh. **Noir Type:** Gangster. **Noir Themes:** Greed, paranoia, betrayal. ★★★★★

Cagney shines in his role as a psychopathic, mother-fixated killer, who fears he may follow in his old man's footsteps and die "kicking and screaming in the nuthouse." In the meantime, he suffers from excruciating and debilitating headaches that can be relieved only by attention from his loving Ma (Wycherly). O'Brien, Cagney's cellmate and surrogate mother, is an undercover cop who plans their escape so he can trace the dough from Cagney's last big heist — a daring, daytime train robbery. Mayo, usually portrayed as the all–American girl next door, is sensational as Cagney's femme fatale wife. Cochran plays the gangster's rival, who is having an affair with Mayo. Cagney, who became a star with *Public Enemy* in 1931, marked his return to the genre with an explosive performance. This is an intense and explicitly violent film noir, with a climax that gives the ending of *The Godfather* a run for its money as the most memorable in the history of American crime movies.

Memorable Noir Moments:
❏ Cagney suffers one of his killer headaches on a prison work detail, and, in a surprisingly poignant moment, cellmate O'Brien gently massages the back of his neck until the pain goes away. He's rewarded with a smile and a soft touch from the murderous psychopath.
❏ In the thrilling finale, Cagney shouts one of filmdom's most famous lines: "Made it, Ma. Top of the world."

Wicked Woman (1954 77 min. Beverly Michaels, Richard Egan, Percy Helton, Evelyn Scott, Robert Osterloh. **Screenplay by:** Clarence Greene and Russell Rouse. **Directed by:** Russell Rouse. **Noir Type:** Femme Fatale. **Noir Themes:** Obsession, lust, greed. ★★★½

A psychopathic convict (James Cagney) gets a visit from his beloved ma (Margaret Wycherly) in *White Heat* (Warner Bros., 1949).

Michaels, the new femme fatale in town, is down on her luck and looking for a job. She finds one as a barmaid in a local establishment owned by alcoholic Scott and her bartender husband (Egan). With her blonde hair, tight skirts and long, sexy legs, Michaels is soon hit on by almost every man in the joint. She handles *them* with ease but has a difficult time keeping her eyes and hands off of the muscular Egan. It isn't long before they're involved in a steamy affair right under Scott's inebriated nose. Michaels wants her new lover to sell the bar to Osterloh and carry her off to Mexico, the place of her dreams, but Egan knows that Scott won't part with the place. They concoct what seems like a foolproof plan to overcome that little obstacle, but Helton, Michaels' toady next-door neighbor, gets wise to their plans and blackmails her into a romantic relationship. This is a fun outing with B movie icon Michaels a joy to watch as she provocatively slinks and wiggles her impressive body for the camera (even when she's alone in her room!). Veteran character actor Helton steals the film as the lecherous little troll who finally gets what he wants and doesn't seem to care about (or even notice) Michaels' obvious disgust.

Memorable Noir Moment:
❑ Stopping by Michaels' boarding house unexpectedly, Egan catches Helton showering her with wet, slobbering kisses. The zany fight that follows is a riot.

The Wild One (1953) 79 min. Marlon Brando, Mary Murphy, Robert Keith, Lee Marvin, Jay C. Flippen, Hugh Sanders. **Screenplay by:** John Paxton. **Directed by:** Laslo Benedek. **Noir Type:** Troubled Youth. **Noir Themes:** Lawbreaking for kicks, fatalism, sexual hostility. ★★★★

This granddaddy of biker movies stars Brando as the psychologically disturbed leader of the Black Rebels Motorcycle Club. While the gang terrorizes the citizens of a small town, the weak-willed, boozing sheriff (Keith) frets about how to handle the thugs, who go on a drunken spree of destruction and intimidation. Brando falls for the sheriff's pretty daughter (Murphy), an innocent girl confused by his schizoid behavior. One minute he's cruel and abusive, the next sympathetic, almost shy. When a former member of the Rebels (Marvin) shows up in town with his new gang, the already dangerous situation becomes explosive. In the meantime, some of the townsfolk, led by bully Sanders, are understandably upset at the sheriff's lack of action and decide to take the law into their own hands, with tragic results. Flippen plays the county sheriff, who shows up to help the ineffective Keith regain order. The film is dated, of course, but it's still highly entertaining, with Brando giving a terrific performance as the moody biker, and Keith excellent as the indecisive lawman. Look for Timothy Carey, wonderfully despicable as usual, as Marvin's right-hand man.

Familiar Faces from Television:
- Ray Teal (Sheriff Roy Coffee in *Bonanza*) as the bar-cafe owner.
- Jerry Paris (Jerry Helper on *The Dick Van Dyke Show* and Agent Flaherty in *The Untouchables*) as a gang member.
- John Doucette (Jim Weston in *Lock Up* and Captain Andrews in *The Partners*) as a motorcycle race official.

Memorable Noir Moments:
- When a girl from town finds out that the gang's name is the Black Rebels Motorcycle Club, she asks Brando, "What are you rebelling against?" "What've ya got?" he answers.
- Brando, trying to explain his wanderer's philosophy to a bewildered Murphy, says, "If you're gonna stay cool, you gotta wail. You gotta put something down. You gotta make some jive. Don't ya know what I'm talkin' about?" Murphy answers, "My father was going to take me on a fishing trip to Canada once." "Yeah?" Brando asks, waiting to hear more. "We didn't go," she answers. "Crazy," he says.

Winchester '73 (1950) 92 min. James Stewart, Shelley Winters, Dan Duryea, Stephen McNally, Millard Mitchell, Charles Drake. **Screenplay by:** Robert L. Richards and Borden Chase. **Directed by:** Anthony Mann. **Noir Type:** Horse Opera. **Noir Themes:** Revenge, obsession, betrayal. ★★★★

This tale of vengeance centers around Winchester Rifle Model 1873, "the gun that won the West," and the men who are obsessed with owning it. Its first owner (Stewart) wins it in a shooting contest in Dodge City, where he's searching for McNally, the man who murdered his father. McNally steals the rifle from Stewart, and he and his men hightail it out of town to join outlaw Duryea for a Wells Fargo heist. Meanwhile, the rifle changes hands a few more times before making its way back to Stewart, who's hot on McNally's trail. Along the way, Stewart and his partner (Mitchell) meet a saloon girl (Winters) and her cowardly boyfriend (Drake), and take time out to help the cavalry fight off a band of Apaches who want to duplicate Crazy Horse's Little Big Horn victory over Custer. *Winchester '73* was the first in a series of psychological Westerns directed by Mann and starring Stewart (see *The Man from Laramie* and *The Naked Spur*) and, like the others, it's fast-paced, suspenseful and action-packed. Stewart, McNally, Winters, Duryea and the film's many veteran character actors do a fine job. Look for a very young Tony Curtis as a soldier fighting off the Apaches.

Familiar Faces from Television:

❑ Rock Hudson (Commissioner McMillan in *McMillan and Wife*) as the Apache chief.
❑ Will Geer (Grandpa Walton in *The Waltons*) as Wyatt Earp.
❑ Jay C. Flippen (Chief Nelson in *Ensign O'Toole*) as a Cavalry sergeant.
❑ John Doucette (Jim Weston in *Lock Up* and Captain Andrews in *The Partners*) as a member of Duryea's gang.
❑ James Best (Sheriff Roscoe P. Coltrane in *The Dukes of Hazzard*) as a soldier.
❑ Ray Teal (Sheriff Roy Coffee in *Bonanza*) as the U.S. marshal who corners Duryea and his gang.
❑ John McIntire (Lt. Dan Muldoon in *Naked City* and Chris Hale in *Wagon Train*) as an Indian trader.

Memorable Noir Moments:

❑ Sensitivity Training Required: The film's opening statement, describing the Winchester '73 rifle, informs the viewer that "an Indian would sell his soul to own one."
❑ Winters seems to have Duryea pegged right when she tells him, "You're about the lowest thing I've ever seen standing in a pair of boots."

The Window (1949) 73 min. Bobby Driscoll, Arthur Kennedy, Barbara Hale, Paul Stewart, Ruth Roman. **Screenplay by:** Mel Dinelli. **Directed by:** Ted Tetzlaff. **Noir Type:** Cover-Up. **Noir Themes:** Child in jeopardy, paranoia. ★★★★

Director Tetzlaff successfully captures the grim existence of the lower working class in New York City's slums and the desperation and paranoia of a young boy whose cries for help fall only on deaf adult ears. Based on pulp fiction writer Cornell Woolrich's novelette, *The Boy Who Cried Murder*, and the more familiar folk tale, *The Boy Who Cried Wolf*, this exciting suspense thriller stars Driscoll as a young, attention-starved boy who makes up tall tales, to the annoyance of his impatient parents (Kennedy and Hale). One hot summer night he climbs out onto the fire escape to flee the miserable New York heat. Peering through his upstairs neighbors' window, he witnesses the brutal murder of a seaman, whom the bungling neighbors (Roman and Stewart) had unsuccessfully attempted to rob. When he confides in his parents, they think he's just fibbing again. So he goes on his own to the police station, where he has even less success. After a friendly cop brings him home, Driscoll's mother brings him upstairs to apologize to the murderers! Now aware that the boy witnessed their crime, the neighbors must find a way to shut him up. Excellent acting, terrific cinematography and a suspenseful script made this now-classic film noir a big financial winner for RKO. Young Driscoll, on loan to RKO from Walt Disney, won a special Academy Award (Outstanding Juvenile Actor) for his performance. As a teenager, Driscoll's career took a nose dive and he turned to drugs. Ironically, in

A murder witness (Bobby Driscoll) gets a late night visit from a sinister upstairs neighbor (Ruth Roman) in *The Window* (RKO, 1949).

1968, at age 31, he was found dead of an apparent heart attack in an abandoned New York City tenement, much like the one in the thrilling climax of *The Window*. He was buried as a John Doe in Potter's Field, and it wasn't until a year later that fingerprints identified him as the once-famous child actor.

Memorable Noir Moment:
❏ Sensitivity Training Required: Because he can't trust his son to stay at home while he's at work and his wife is spending the night at her sister's, Kennedy, this otherwise loving dad nails the boy's window shut (on an oppressive summer night) and locks him in his room.

Without Honor (1949) 69 min. Laraine Day, Dane Clark, Franchot Tone, Agnes Moorehead, Bruce Bennett. **Screenplay by:** James Poe. **Directed by:** Irving Pichel. **Noir Type:** Triangle. **Noir Themes:** Jealousy, betrayal, obsession. ★★

Good cast, poor script, unlucky viewer. Day plays a housewife who has been having an affair with a married man (Tone). He shows up at her home one day to announce that they've been found out and that he's dropping her to return to his wife (Moorehead) and children. Despondent, Day threatens suicide and half-heartedly rests a barbecue skewer over her heart. Tone tries to take it away from her and, during the struggle, is accidentally stabbed in the chest. He stumbles to the laundry room and collapses. Day plans to go to the police and confess that she's killed her lover, but her vindictive brother-in-law (Clark) arrives to announce that the private investigator he hired has provided him with evidence of her scandalous affair and that he plans to turn it over to his cuckolded brother (Bennett) and to Moorehead, who's on her way to Day's house. It's all downhill from there, as Day stumbles around in a guilt-induced fog for the rest of the film. Clark is excellent as the jealous squealer who justifies his loathsome behavior as an act of brotherly love. But neither Clark nor the rest of the capable cast can salvage this mess.

Memorable Noir Moments:
- ❑ Bennett arrives home with a surprise: one of those newfangled gadgets, a cumbersome 12-inch television set, delivered by truck and carried in by two deliverymen.
- ❑ A self-satisfied Clark consoles his brother after disclosing the news about Day's affair. "I know it hurts," he says. "Getting rid of her was like pulling out a rotten tooth. But it's out now. You still feel where it was hurting."

Witness to Murder (1954) 81 min. Barbara Stanwyck, George Sanders, Gary Merrill, Jesse White. **Screenplay by:** Chester Erskine. **Directed by:** Roy Rowland. **Noir Type:** Cover-Up. **Noir Themes:** Woman in jeopardy, victim of the law, paranoia. ★★★

An interior designer (Stanwyck) witnesses Sanders strangling a woman in the building across from hers. When Sanders sees detectives Merrill and White pull up in front of Stanwyck's apartment, he quickly hides the body in the vacant apartment next door and plays dumb when the cops arrive to investigate. Merrill and White shrug it all off as a nightmare, almost convincing Stanwyck herself. The spunky lady investigates on her own, but can only come up with circumstantial evidence that Merrill, who by now is romantically interested, writes off as coincidence and "women's intuition." Meanwhile, former Nazi bigwig Sanders decides that Stanwyck is a real danger, especially now that she's taken to hanging around with Merrill. Stanwyck is excellent in a role similar to one she played in the more famous *Sorry, Wrong Number* (1948), and Sanders wonderfully overacts.

Familiar Faces from Television:
- ❑ Claude Akins (Sheriff Elroy Lobo in two series—*B.J. and the Bear* and *Lobo*) as a uninformed cop watching a murder victim's apartment.
- ❑ Burt Mustin (Fireman Gus in *Leave It to Beaver* and Mr. Quigley in *All in the Family*) as a night watchman at a construction site.

Memorable Noir Moments:
- ❑ Sanders grabs Stanwyck and tries a romantic line before violently kissing her. "You look at me with loathing and hate," he says. "And that's just the way I want you to look at me. For in hate there is love, true love, love that gives pain and extinguishes life." "You're mad," responds Stanwyck. No kidding. (See *Gilda* and *Female on the Beach* similar romantic prose.)
- ❑ Homicide detective White compares real cops with "TV detectives" and hums the *Dragnet* theme song ("dum da dum dum"). (See *Private Hell 36* for another reference to the famous TV detective series.)

The Woman in Brown *see* **The Vicious Circle**

Woman in Hiding (1949) 92 min. Ida Lupino, Howard Duff, Stephen McNally, Peggy Dow, John Litel. **Screenplay by:** Oscar Saul. **Directed by:** Michael Gordon. **Noir Type:** Newlywed. **Noir Themes:** Women in danger, betrayal, paranoia. ★★★

Lupino stars as a newlywed whose husband (McNally) is trying to kill her so he can inherit the mill once owned by her rich father (Litel), whom he has already murdered. While fleeing town, Lupino loses control of her car, thanks to McNally's brake-tampering job, and plunges it into a creek. She escapes death but realizes that the police will not believe her story so she must "stay dead" until she finds McNally's former girlfriend (Dow), who she thinks will back up her claim that McNally is trying to kill her. Along the way, she meets a $32.50-a-week newsstand operator (Duff), an ex–G.I. who thinks she's mentally and emotionally unbalanced. A caring kind of guy (but also hoping to collect the five grand reward that McNally has offered), he notifies her husband. But he soon realizes his mistake and begins helping Lupino search for Dow. Lupino is terrific as the betrayed wife, hunted by the man she thought loved her. McNally does well as the mill manager whose madness accounts for his deluded attempts to ensure the economic survival of his town. Duff nicely underplays his role, and Dow is a pretty fair femme fatale. In real life, Duff and Lupino would marry in 1951 and divorce in 1973. This was their first of many roles together and eventually they would star in the popular but short-lived TV series *Mr. Adams and Eve*, a situation comedy based on their Hollywood experiences.

Familiar Faces from Television:
- ❑ Joe Besser ("Stinky" on *The Abbott and Costello Show* and, later, one of the Three Stooges) as a boisterous conventioneer.
- ❑ Jerry Paris (dentist Jerry Helper on *The Dick Van Dyke Show* and Agent Flaherty in *The Untouchables*) as a newsstand customer trying to remember where he saw Lupino.
- ❑ Russ Conway (Lt. Pete Kile in *Richard Diamond, Private Detective*) as a newspaper reporter.

Memorable Noir Moment:
- ❑ A newsstand owner can't understand why an intelligent guy like Duff seems to enjoy traveling around the country taking menial jobs. "I don't get the psychology of it," he says. "Look," replies Duff, "for 32.50 a week, I don't discuss psychology."

The Woman in the Window (1944) 99 min. Edward G. Robinson, Joan Bennett, Raymond Massey, Dan Duryea, Thomas E. Jackson, Arthur Loft. **Screenplay by:** Nunnally Johnson. **Directed by:** Fritz Lang. **Noir Type:** Cover-Up. **Noir Themes:** Victim of fate, character deterioration, fatalism, jealousy. ★★★★

After an evening of drinking with old friends at the men's club, a middle-aged assistant university professor (Robinson) stops to ogle a painting of a beautiful woman (Bennett) in a store window. As he stares longingly at the portrait, Bennett suddenly appears in the window reflection and, unbelievably, invites the astonished dreamer to have a couple of drinks with her. With his wife and kids out of town, Robinson gives in to temptation. They wind up at her apartment, ostensibly to view some sketches of her. Before anything can happen, though, Bennett's boyfriend (Loft) arrives and starts a fight with Robinson and attempts to choke him. Bennett hands Robinson a pair of scissors, which he uses to stab his attacker several times in the back, killing him. Rather than call the police, Robinson and Bennett decide to cover up the crime by moving the body to a rural area, miles from the apartment. As luck would have it, though, Loft turns out to have been an important financier, whose disappearance attracts wide media attention. The murdered man's bodyguard (Duryea) shows up demanding five Gs from the couple to keep his mouth shut, leaving them with only one possible alternative — murder. Massey plays Robinson's D.A. buddy, and Jackson is a homicide detective. Both are hot on the trail of the killer. Noir icons Robinson, Bennett and Duryea are as terrific in this classic film noir as they are in *Scarlet Street*, also directed by Lang. The surprise ending of *The Woman in the Window* may disappoint some viewers but cause others to applaud appreciatively. Look for Little Rascal George "Spanky" McFarland as a boy scout.

Familiar Face from Television:
❑ Robert Blake (Detective Tony Baretta in *Baretta*) as Robinson's little boy.

Memorable Noir Moment:
❑ As cops question a woman they suspect may be involved in the murder, D.A. Massey's misogynistic tendencies show when he remarks to Robinson, "She's got something on her conscience. But what woman hasn't?"

The Woman in White (1948) 109 min. Eleanor Parker, Sydney Greenstreet, Alexis Smith, Gig Young, John Emery, John Abbott. **Screenplay by:** Stephen Morehouse Avery. **Directed by:** Peter Godfrey. **Noir Type:** Period. **Noir Themes:** Woman in jeopardy, betrayal, greed. ★★★★

Parker plays dual roles in this eerie Gothic mystery set in mid-nineteenth century England. She portrays a rich young woman at the mercy of a pair of insidious con artists and a lookalike cousin (the woman in white), who has escaped from an asylum bearing evil tidings. Greenstreet (playing an Italian count!) and Emery are the bad guys. Parker's new art teacher (a foppish Young) falls in love with her and is driven away by her beautiful assistant (Smith), who fears that he will spoil Parker's upcoming marriage to Emery. Kidnapping, insanity, murder, lust. It all sounds terribly exciting, but the film doesn't live up to its potential. It does have its bright moments, though, especially Greenstreet's melodramatic, but enjoyable, portrayal of the portly villain with a lustful eye for Smith. Abbott is a roar as the hypochondriac art collector.

Familiar Face from Television:
❑ Agnes Moorehead (Endora in *Bewitched*) as Greenstreet's jewelry-loving wife.

Memorable Noir Moment:
❑ The non-violent Greenstreet, impatient with Emery's talk of murder, scoffs, "Murder is the resort of imbeciles," causing the already high-strung Abbott to utter nervously, "Murder? Oh, you couldn't. The whole house would be full of police and things."

The Woman on Pier 13 *see* I Married a Communist

The Woman on the Beach (1947) 71 min. Joan Bennett, Robert Ryan, Charles Bickford, Nan Leslie. **Screenplay by**: Frank Davis, Michael Hogan and Jean Renoir. **Directed by**: Jean Renoir. **Noir Type**: Troubled Veteran. **Noir Themes**: Betrayal, jealousy, lust. ★★

French director Jean Renoir, in his last American film, applies the noir treatment to the hackneyed triangle plot. Unfortunately, it's all atmosphere and no substance. Ryan plays a Coast Guard officer, recuperating from severe mental and emotional stress as a result of his combat experiences. One day, while horseback riding on the beach, he runs into Bennett as she collects firewood from an abandoned shipwreck. Feeling an immediate attraction to the woman, Ryan quickly drops his fiancée (Leslie), and he and Bennett begin a torrid love affair behind the back of her husband (Bickford), whom she accidentally blinded several years earlier. Once a successful artist, Bickford is now an embittered and jealous husband. Ryan believes the man is faking his blindness and goes to extremes to prove it so the guilt-stricken Bennett will feel free to leave him. But Bickford plans to hold onto his wife no matter what. Beautifully photographed but not one of Renoir's or noir icon Ryan's best.

Familiar Face from Television:

❑ Irene Ryan (Granny on *The Beverly Hillbillies*) as Leslie's best friend.

Memorable Noir Moment:

❑ Before Ryan can utter a common noir pejorative, Bennett beats him to the punch. "Go ahead," she says. "Say it. I'm a tramp. You're just finding that out?"

Woman on the Run (1950) 77 min. Ann Sheridan, Dennis O'Keefe, Robert Keith, Ross Elliott. **Screenplay by**: Alan Campbell and Norman Foster. **Directed by**: Norman Foster. **Noir Type**: Psycho. **Noir Themes**: Victim of fate, woman in jeopardy. ★★★½

Sheridan is a wife searching for her husband (Elliott), an artist who witnessed a vicious murder and is hiding out from the police and the killer. The two haven't been getting along very well lately, but Sheridan begins to discover long-lost feelings for her missing man. O'Keefe is a reporter who seems eager for the exclusive story, and Keith is the detective who has big problems keeping Sheridan in line. Sheridan does a great job as the tough, wisecracking protagonist, who always manages to stay one step ahead of the cops. There are some terrific daytime shots of San Francisco's hilly streets, a scene or two that will make you jump out of your seat, and a climactic fight during a nighttime roller coaster ride. This minor film noir succeeds thanks to clever plot twists and an excellent cast.

Familiar Face from Television:

❑ Victor Sen Yung (Hop Sing of *Bonanza*) as a dancer and friend of Sheridan and Elliott.

Memorable Noir Moment:

❑ Sensitivity Training Required: When asked by a detective if she considered getting a job since her husband took off, Sheridan replies, "Why should I? That's *his* responsibility, not mine."

A Woman's Devotion (1956) 88 min. Ralph Meeker, Janice Rule, Paul Henreid. **Screenplay by**: Robert Hill. **Directed by**: Paul Henreid. **Noir Type**: Troubled Veteran. **Noir Themes**: Paranoia, character deterioration, woman in jeopardy. ★★

Newlyweds Meeker and Rule are bumming around Acapulco when they become involved in the murders of two local women. Mexican police captain Henreid suspects that Meeker, a World War II veteran with severe mental problems, is the killer. Rule, who was unaware that Meeker had been confined to a mental hospital after the war because of "battle shock," tries to get him out of the country after the husband of one of the murdered women tries to blackmail them. Also known as *Battle Shock*, this precursor to the many movies yet to come out of Hollywood about psychotic Vietnam War veterans, is a slow-paced mystery with Meeker doing a fair job as the disturbed war hero.

A Woman's Face (1941) 105 min. Joan Crawford, Melvyn Douglas, Conrad Veidt, Albert Basserman, Marjorie Main, Richard Nichols. **Screenplay by**: Elliot Paul and Donald Ogden Stewart. **Directed by**: George Cukor. **Noir Type**: Plastic Surgery. **Noir Themes**: Child in jeopardy, paranoia, greed, betrayal. ★★★★

This highly enjoyable film begins with Crawford on trial for murder, slowly unfolding in a series of flashback testimonies by several witnesses. Bitterly paranoid and self-conscious about her badly scarred face, she turns to crime, specializing in blackmail. When plastic surgeon Douglas, the husband of one of her intended victims, offers his services, Crawford undergoes the knife. Luckily, the operation is a success and Crawford, who, according to Douglas, now has "a beautiful face and no heart," happily returns to her lover (Veidt). Veidt convinces her to participate in a crime that may be too cruel even for her — the murder of his four-year-old nephew (Nichols) — so that Veidt can inherit the family fortune. Hired by the child's grandfather (Basserman) as a governess, Crawford must deal with an overprotective and jealous housekeeper (Main), and a kid who could give Shirley Temple a run for her money in the cute department. Crawford is sensational as the lonely woman trying desperately to please her demanding lover. German actor Veidt (famous for his role as the somnambulist in the silent classic *The Cabinet of Dr. Caligari*) is wonderfully sinister, and fellow German Basserman also does an excellent job, considering he spoke no English and had to learn his lines phonetically.

Familiar Face from Television:
❑ Connie Gilchrist (Purity, pub proprietress and girlfriend of *Long John Silver*) as a member of Crawford's blackmail ring.

Memorable Noir Moment:
❑ Crawford, after more than twenty years of living with horrible facial scars caused by a fire, complains plaintively, "I want to belong to the human race."

A Woman's Secret (1949) 85 min. Maureen O'Hara, Melvyn Douglas, Gloria Grahame, Victor Jory, Jay C. Flippen. **Screenplay by**: Herman J. Mankiewicz. **Directed by**: Nicholas Ray. **Noir Type**: Whodunit. **Noir Themes**: Fatalism, victim of fate. ★½

O'Hara is a has-been singer who, along with her piano player (Douglas), discovers a bright new singing talent (Grahame) and becomes her mentor. Grahame rises to the top as singer "Estrellita," but is unhappy with her success and wants to quit. This annoys O'Hara, who confronts her behind bedroom doors. A gunshot is heard, the police arrive, and Grahame is rushed to the hospital, where it's doubtful that she'll pull through. O'Hara admits to shooting her but Douglas doesn't believe it. He tries to convince homicide detective Flippen that she couldn't possibly have done such a horrible thing and, in a series of flashbacks, tells him the whole boring story. Jory is the lawyer who has a thing for Grahame but, in a conflict of interest case if there ever was one, is representing O'Hara. It's always a pleasure to watch the delicious Grahame, one of film noir's greats, but even she can't salvage this inane story, which might leave some viewers scratching their heads in bewilderment.

Familiar Faces from Television:
❑ Bill Williams (Kit Carson in *The Adventures of Kit Carson*) as Grahame's boyfriend.
❑ Ellen Corby (Grandma Walton in *The Waltons*) as a nurse.

Memorable Noir Moment:
❑ When asked by a colleague how he knows when a suspect is telling the truth, a homicide detective shares his philosophy. "That's very simple," he says. "To me, the minute any-body's arrested, from then on he's a liar, unless he's pleading guilty, of course."

Women's Prison (1955) 80 min. Ida Lupino, Howard Duff, Jan Sterling, Cleo Moore, Audrey Totter, Phyllis Thaxter, Barry Kelley, Warren Stevens. **Screenplay by:** Crane Wilbur and Jack DeWitt. **Directed by:** Lewis Seiler. **Noir Type:** Prison. **Noir Themes:** Woman in jeopardy, victim of fate, corruption, social reform. ★★½

"Men and women behind the same walls, with only concrete and rifle bullets trying to keep them apart." The opening narration would have you believe that the sex-craved guys are climbing the walls trying to get to the dames on the other side, but it's really only Stevens, desperate to see his unjustly imprisoned wife (Totter). Lupino and Kelley are the cruel co-wardens of this almost co-ed prison. Duff (Lupino's real-life husband) is the benevolent prison doctor, who abhors the inhu-mane conditions he sees every day. Thaxter, convicted on an accidental manslaugh-ter charge, is the newcomer who goes off the deep end, and Sterling and Moore are her blonde bombshell cellmates. By the way, Stevens finally succeeds in sneaking over the wall, and it isn't long before authorities discover that Totter is pregnant (they had, after all, been kissing in the prison laundry). To save her job, the evil Lupino has no choice but to beat the pregnant inmate senseless. It's *all* pretty senseless, but it's a terrific cast and a lot of fun.

Memorable Noir Moments:
❑ Moore tells prison newcomer Thaxter about how cellmate Sterling "used to learn 'em how to talk good English." Looking to Sterling for approval, she adds, "I'm doing much better since you seen me last, ain't I?"
❑ Moore's fractured English raises its cute head once again, this time when the cons take Lupino hostage. "One squawk out of you and I'll punch a hole right through your dia-gram," she says. Smiling, Sterling gently corrects her, saying, "Diaphragm, honey."

World for Ransom (1954) 82 min. Dan Duryea, Reginald Denny, Gene Lockhart, Patric Knowles, Marian Carr, Arthur Shields, Nigel Bruce, Douglass Dumbrille. **Screenplay by:** Lindsay Hardy. **Directed by:** Robert Aldrich. **Noir Type:** Far East. **Noir Themes:** Fatalism, betrayal, sexual hostility. ★★½

Duryea, an Irish P.I. in Singapore gets involved with international terrorists led by Lockhart after they convince his friend (Knowles) to kidnap a British scientist (Shields), who holds "the secret of the hydrogen bomb." The gang plans to sell Shields to the highest bidding government, and the British Governor (Bruce), the police inspector (Dumbrille), and a stodgy officer (Denny) must rescue the hostage before any Commies can get their hands on him. Their one hope is Duryea, who knows where the terrorists have taken Shields. Duryea's only interest in the affair is to return Knowles to his wife, nightclub singer Carr, who has promised the P.I. that she'll leave her husband once she knows he's safe. Filmed with the intention of cashing in on Duryea's successful TV adventure series *China Smith* (also starring Dumbrille), the low-budget *World for Ransom* is a camp action film that is at times silly and confusing. But, as usual, Duryea is a joy to watch.

Familiar Faces from Television:
❑ Keye Luke (Master Po in *Kung Fu*) as a street photographer.
❑ Strother Martin (Aaron Donager in *Hotel de Paree* and Jimmy Stewart's cousin, R.J. Hawkins, in *Hawkins*) as a duty conscious British corporal.

The Wrong Man (1956) 105 min. Henry Fonda, Vera Miles, Anthony Quayle, Harold J. Stone, Nehemiah Persoff. **Screenplay by:** Maxwell Anderson and Angus MacPhail. **Directed by:** Alfred Hitchcock. **Noir Type:** Wrong Man. **Noir Themes:** Victim of fate, victim of the law. ★★★★

Fonda, a bass player at New York's Stork Club, is identified as the holdup man who has been robbing local business establishments. Stone is the detective who traps Fonda by having him duplicate a note written by the real stickup man — his printing is similar and he misspells the same word. Quayle is the sympathetic attorney whose faith in the unfortunate musician compensates for his inexperience. Fonda's wife (Miles) stands by her man until she cracks under the pressure and winds up a zombie in a mental institution. Persoff plays Fonda's brother-in-law, who puts up the seven thousand dollar bail money. Based on a true story, *The Wrong Man* is a bleak tale that may be too much for some sensitive viewers to sit through — it's that depressing and seemingly hopeless. Despite the almost unbelievable coincidences that have to take place for this story to work, Hitchcock, in his opening narration, swears it's all true. Fonda gives a standout, low-key performance, and Miles is sensational as his neurotic, guilt-ridden wife.

Familiar Faces from Television:
❑ Bonnie Franklin (Ann Romano in *One Day at a Time*) as the giggling young girl on the left.
❑ Werner Klemperer (Col. Klink in *Hogan's Heroes*) as Miles' psychiatrist.

Memorable Noir Moment:
❑ Stone tells Fonda one of the biggest fibs in all of film noir. "If you haven't done anything wrong," he claims, "you have nothing to fear."
❑ While his lawyer is questioning a witness, Fonda takes a look around the courtroom and what he sees is plenty discouraging: his attorney's assistant is doing a crossword puzzle, the prosecutor is enjoying a joke with a colleague, and his own sister and brother-in-law are chatting pleasantly. Adding to his depression, one of the jurors stands up and objects to a boring line of questioning.

Appendix A:
Films Noirs Listed by Director

Adreon, Franklin— The Man Is Armed; No Man's Woman; Terror at Midnight

Aldrich, Robert— Attack; Autumn Leaves; The Big Knife; Kiss Me Deadly; The Garment Jungle (uncredited, with Vincent Sherman); World for Ransom

Allen, Lewis— Appointment with Danger; A Bullet for Joey; Chicago Deadline; Desert Fury; Illegal; So Evil My Love; Suddenly; The Unseen

Anderson, Michael— Chase a Crooked Shadow

Archainbaud, George— Hunt the Man Down

Arnold, Jack— The Glass Web; Man in the Shadow; Outside the Law; The Tattered Dress

Asher, William— Shadow on the Window

Auer, John H.— The City That Never Sleeps; The Flame; Hell's Half Acre; I, Jane Doe

Baker, Roy Ward— Don't Bother to Knock; Night Without Sleep

Bare, Richard— Flaxy Martin

Beaudine, William— Murder Without Tears

Benedek, Laslo— Affair in Havana; Death of a Salesman; Port of New York; The Wild One

Berke, William— Cop Hater; Danger Zone; F.B.I. Girl; Four Boys and a Gun; Shoot to Kill

Bernhard, Jack— Blonde Ice; The Hunted; Violence

Bernds, Edwards— Calling Homicide

Bernhardt, Curtis— Conflict; High Wall; Possessed; Sirocco; A Stolen Life

Berry, John— He Ran All the Way; Tension

Biberman, Abner— The Night Runner; The Price of Fear

Birdwell, Russell— The Come-On

Birt, Daniel— The Deadly Game

Blair, George— Unmasked

Boetticher, Oscar "Budd"— Behind Locked Doors; Escape in the Fog; The Killer Is Loose; The Missing Juror; Ride Lonesome

Borzage, Frank— Moonrise

Bower, Dallas— Doorway to Suspicion

Bradley, David— Talk About a Stranger

Brahm, John— The Brasher Doubloon; Guest in the House; Hangover Square; The Locket; The Lodger; Singapore

Brooks, Richard— Crisis

Cagney, James— Short Cut to Hell

Cahn, Edward L.— Destination Murder

Castle, William— Hollywood Story; The Houston Story; Johnny Stool Pigeon; Mark of the Whistler; Mysterious Intruder; Undertow; Voice of the Whistler; When Strangers Marry; The Whistler

Chaplin, Charles— Monsieur Verdoux
Clemens, William— The Thirteenth Hour
Clifton, Elmer— The Judge
Clouzot, Henry-Georges—*Diabolique*
Clurman, Harold— Deadline at Dawn
Colmes, Walter— Accomplice
Conway, Jack— Crossroads; Illegal Entry
Corman, Roger— Teenage Doll
Cornfield, Hubert— Plunder Road; Sudden Danger
Cromwell, John— Caged; The Company She Keeps; Dead Reckoning; The Racket
Cukor, George— A Double Life; Gaslight; Keeper of the Flame; A Woman's Face
Curtiz, Michael— The Breaking Point; Casablanca; Flamingo Road; The Man in the Net; Mildred Pierce; The Unsuspected
Daniels, Harold— Date with Death; Roadblock
Dassin, Jules— Brute Force; The Naked City; Night and the City; *Rififi*; Thieves' Highway; Two Smart People
Daves, Delmer— Dark Passage; The Red House
David, Charles— Lady on a Train
de Cordova, Frederick— Her Kind of Man
Dein, Edward— Shack out on 101
De la Tour, Charles— Impulse (with Cy Endfield, uncredited); The Limping Man (with Cy Endfield, uncredited)
Del Ruth, Roy— Red Light
De Toth, Andre— Crime Wave; Dark Waters; Hidden Fear; Pitfall; Ramrod
Dickson, Paul— The Depraved
Dieterle, William— The Accused; Dark City; The Devil and Daniel Webster; Love Letters; Paid in Full; Portrait of Jennie; Rope of Sand; The Turning Point
Dmytryk, Edward— Cornered; Crossfire; The Hidden Room; Hitler's Children; Murder, My Sweet; The Sniper; So Well Remembered
Donehue, Vincent J.— Lonelyhearts
Doniger, Walter— The Steel Jungle
Douglas, Gordon— Between Midnight and Dawn; I Was a Communist for the F.B.I.; Kiss Tomorrow Goodbye; San Quentin; Walk a Crooked Mile
Dupont, E.A.— The Scarf
Duvivier, Julien— Destiny (with Reginald LeBorg); Flesh and Fantasy

Dwan, Allan— Slightly Scarlet
Endfield, Cyril— Impulse (uncredited, with Charles De Lautour); The Limping Man (uncredited, with Charles De Lautour); Try and Get Me ; The Underworld Story
Erskine, Chester— Take One False Step
Essex, Harry— I, the Jury; Mad at the World
Farrow, John— Alias Nick Beal; The Big Clock; Calcutta; His Kind of Woman; Night Has a Thousand Eyes; The Unholy Wife; Where Danger Lives
Feist, Felix E.— The Devil Thumbs a Ride; The Man Who Cheated Himself; This Woman Is Dangerous; The Threat; Tomorrow Is Another Day
Ferrer, Mel— The Secret Fury
Fisher, Terence— Blackout; Kill Me Tomorrow; Man Bait; A Stolen Face; The Unholy Four
Fleischer, Richard— Armored Car Robbery; Bodyguard; The Clay Pigeon; Compulsion; Follow Me Quietly; The Narrow Margin; Trapped; Violent Saturday
Florey, Robert— The Beast with Five Fingers; The Crooked Way; Danger Signal; Lady Gangster
Ford, Philip— Missing Women
Forde, Eugene— Backlash
Forzano, Andrea (See Joseph Losey)
Foster, Lewis R.— Crashout; The Lucky Stiff; Manhandled
Foster, Norman— Journey Into Fear (with Orson Welles, uncredited); Kiss the Blood Off My Hands; Woman on the Run
Fregonese, Hugo— Black Tuesday; Man in the Attic; One Way Street
Friedman, Seymour— I'll Get You; Loan Shark
Fuller, Samuel— The Crimson Kimono; Fixed Bayonets; House of Bamboo; Pickup on South Street; Run of the Arrow; The Steel Helmet
Gabel, Martin— The Lost Moment
Gage, John— The Velvet Touch
Garmes, Lee— Angels Over Broadway (with Ben Hecht)
Garnett, Tay— Cause for Alarm; The Postman Always Rings Twice
Gilbert, Lewis— Cast a Dark Shadow
Godfrey, Peter— Cry Wolf; Please Murder

Me; The Two Mrs. Carrolls; The Woman in White

Gordon, Michael— An Act of Murder; The Lady Gambles; The Web; Woman in Hiding

Gordon, Robert— Blind Spot

Goulding, Edmund— Nightmare Alley

Guest, Val— The Weapon

Guilfoyle, Paul— A Life at Stake

Haas, Charles— The Beat Generation; The Big Operator

Haas, Hugo— Bait; The Girl on the Bridge; Hit and Run; The Other Woman; Pickup; Strange Fascination

Haskin, Byron— The Boss; I Walk Alone; Too Late for Tears

Hathaway, Henry— Call Northside 777; The Dark Corner; Fourteen Hours; The House on 92nd Street; Kiss of Death; Niagara; Rawhide

Hawks, Howard— The Big Sleep; To Have and Have Not

Hecht, Ben— Angels Over Broadway (with Lee Garmes); Specter of the Rose

Heisler, Stuart— Among the Living; The Glass Key; I Died a Thousand Times; Smash-Up, the Story of a Woman; Storm Warning

Henreid, Paul— A Woman's Devotion

Hitchcock, Alfred— I Confess; Notorious; The Paradine Case; Rebecca; Rear Window; Shadow of a Doubt; Spellbound; Strangers on a Train; Suspicion; Vertigo; The Wrong Man

Hively, Jack— Street of Chance

Hole, William, Jr.— Hell Bound

Holt, Seth— Nowhere to Go

Hopper, Jerry— Naked Alibi

Horner, Harry— Beware, My Lovely; Vicki

Hughes, Ken— Heat Wave

Humberstone, H. Bruce— I Wake Up Screaming

Huston, John— The Asphalt Jungle; Beat the Devil; Key Largo; The Maltese Falcon; The Treasure of the Sierra Madre; We Were Strangers

Ingster, Boris— Southside 1-1000; Stranger on the Third Floor

Jackson, Pat— Shadow on the Wall

Jason, Will— Blonde Alibi

Jenkins, Patrick— The Gambler and the Lady

Juran, Nathan— The Crooked Web; Highway Dragnet

Kane, Joseph— Accused of Murder; The Crooked Circle; Hoodlum Empire; The Man Who Died Twice

Kardos, Leslie— The Strip

Karlson, Phil— The Brothers Rico; 5 Against the House; Hell's Island; Kansas City Confidential; 99 River Street; The Phenix City Story; Scandal Sheet; Tight Spot

Karn, Bill— Gang Busters

Kazan, Elia— Boomerang; On the Waterfront; Panic in the Streets

Keays, Vernon— Dangerous Intruder

Keighley, William— The Street with No Name

Keller, Harry— The Blonde Bandit; Step Down to Terror

Kern, James V.— The Second Woman

Kershner, Irvin— Stakeout on Dope Street

King, Henry— The Gunfighter

Koch, Howard W.— The Last Mile; Shield for Murder (with Edmond O'Brien)

Korda, Zoltan— The Macomber Affair

Kress, Harold F.— No Questions Asked

Kubrick, Stanley— Killer's Kiss; The Killing

Kurosawa, Akira— Stray Dog

Landers, Lew— Inner Sanctum; Man in the Dark; The Mask of Diijon; Power of the Whistler

Landres, Paul— Johnny Rocco

Lanfield, Sidney— Station West

Lang, Fritz— Beyond a Reasonable Doubt; The Big Heat; The Blue Gardenia; Clash by Night; Cloak and Dagger; Hangmen Also Die!; House by the River; Human Desire; Ministry of Fear; Rancho Notorious; Scarlet Street; Secret Beyond the Door; While the City Sleeps; The Woman in the Window

Larkin, John— Circumstantial Evidence

Laughton, Charles— The Night of the Hunter

LeBorg, Reginald— Bad Blonde; Destiny (with Julien Duvivier); Fall Guy

Lederman, D. Ross— Key Witness; The Return of the Whistler

Leisen, Mitchell— No Man of Her Own

Leonard, Robert Z.— The Bribe

Lerner, Irving— Murder by Contract
Lerner, Joseph— C-Man; Guilty By-
stander
LeRoy, Mervyn— Johnny Eager
Levin, Henry— Convicted; The Family
Secret; Night Editor; Two of a Kind
Lewin, Albert— The Picture of Dorian
Gray
Lewis, Joseph H.— The Big Combo; Cry
of the Hunted; The Falcon in San Fran-
cisco; Gun Crazy; The Halliday Brand; A
Lady Without Passport; My Name Is Julia
Ross; So Dark the Night; Terror in a Texas
Town; The Undercover Man
Litvak, Anatole— Blues in the Night;
City for Conquest; The Long Night; Out of
the Fog; The Snake Pit; Sorry, Wrong
Number
Losey, Joseph— The Big Night; The Boy
with Green Hair; The Lawless; M; The
Prowler; The Sleeping Tiger; Stranger on
the Prowl (as Andrea Forzano); Time
Without Pity
Lubin, Arthur— Impact
Lupino, Ida— The Hitch-Hiker
McCarey, Leo— My Son, John
McCarey, Ray— Strange Triangle
McCune, Hank— Wetbacks
MacDougall, Ranald— Queen Bee
McEvoy, Earl— The Killer that Stalked
New York
McGann, William— Highway West
McLaglen, Andrew V.— Man in the Vault
McGowan, Dorrell— Tokyo File 212
(with Stuart McGowan)
McGowan, Stuart— Tokyo File 212
(with Dorrell McGowan)
Machaty, Gustav— Jealousy
Mackendrick, Alexander— Sweet Smell
of Success
Mankiewicz, Joseph L.— Dragonwyck;
House of Strangers; No Way Out; Some-
where in the Night
Mann, Anthony— Border Incident; Des-
perate; Devil's Doorway; The Furies; The
Great Flamarion; He Walked by Night
(with Alfred L. Werker); The Man from
Laramie; Man of the West; The Naked
Spur; Railroaded; Raw Deal; Reign of Ter-
ror; Serenade; Side Street; Strange Imper-
sonation; T-Men; The Tall Target; Two
O'clock Courage; Winchester '73

Marin, Edwin L.— Johnny Angel; Noc-
turne; Race Street
Markle, Fletcher— Jigsaw; Night into
Morning
Marshall, George— The Blue Dahlia
Martin, Charles— Death of a Scoundrel
Maté, Rudolph— D.O.A.; The Dark Past;
Forbidden; The Green Glove; Second
Chance; Union Station
Mayer, Gerald— Dial 1119; The Sellout
Mayo, Archie— Moontide
Menzies, William Cameron— The Whip
Hand
Meredith, Burgess— The Man on the
Eiffel Tower
Milestone, Lewis— The Strange Love of
Martha Ivers
Miller, David— Sudden Fear; Twist of
Fate
Minnelli, Vincente— The Bad and the
Beautiful; Undercurrent
Moguy, Leonide— Whistle Stop
Montagne, Edward— The Man with My
Face; The Tattooed Stranger
Montgomery, Robert— Lady in the Lake;
Ride the Pink Horse
Murphy, Ralph— Never Trust a Gambler
Myers, Frank— Lost, Lonely and Vicious
Negulesco, Jean— Deep Valley; Hu-
moresque; The Mask of Dimitrios; Nobody
Lives Forever; Road House; Three
Strangers
Neill, Roy William— Black Angel
Newfield, Sam— Apology for Murder;
The Lady Confesses; Money Madness
Newman, Joseph M.— Abandoned; Dan-
gerous Crossing; Death in Small Doses;
The Human Jungle; The Outcasts of Poker
Flat; 711 Ocean Drive
Newton, Joel— Jennifer
Nosseck, Max— The Hoodlum
Nugent, Elliott— My Favorite Brunette
Oboler, Arch— The Arnelo Affair; Be-
witched
O'Brien, Edmond— Shield for Murder
(with Howard W. Koch)
O'Keefe, Dennis— Angela
Ophüls, Max—Caught; The Reckless
Moment
Oswald, Gerd— Crime of Passion; A Kiss
Before Dying; Screaming Mimi; Valerie
Otsep, Fyodor— Whispering City

Panama, Norman— The Trap
Parrish, Robert— Cry Danger
Parrish, Robert— The Mob
Pevney, Joseph— Female on the Beach; Iron Man; The Midnight Story; Playgirl; Shakedown
Pichel, Irving— Quicksand; Temptation; They Won't Believe Me; Without Honor
Pine, Willam H.— Swamp Fire
Polonsky, Abraham— Force of Evil
Popkin, Leo C.— The Well (with Russell Rouse)
Powell, Dick— Split Second
Preminger, Otto— Angel Face; Daisy Kenyon; Fallen Angel; Laura; The Man with the Golden Arm; The 13th Letter; Where the Sidewalk Ends; Whirlpool
Price, Will— Strange Bargain
Quine, Richard— Drive a Crooked Road; Pushover
Rapper, Irving— Another Man's Poison; Deception; Strange Intruder
Ratoff, Gregory— Black Magic (with Orson Welles, uncredited); Moss Rose
Ray, Nicholas— Born to Be Bad; In a Lonely Place; Johnny Guitar; Knock on Any Door; Macao (uncredited, with Josef von Sternberg); On Dangerous Ground; Party Girl; They Live by Night; A Woman's Secret
Reed, Carol— Odd Man Out; The Third Man
Reinhardt, John— The Guilty; High Tide; Open Secret
Reis, Irving— All My Sons; Crack-Up
Renoir, Jean— The Woman on the Beach
Rich, David Lowell— No Time to Be Young
Ripley, Arthur— The Chase; Voice in the Wind
Ritt, Martin— Edge of the City
Robson, Mark— Bedlam; Champion; Edge of Doom; The Harder They Fall; Isle of the Dead; Roughshod; The Seventh Victim
Rosen, Phil— The Strange Mr. Gregory
Rossen, Robert— All the King's Men; Body and Soul; Johnny O'Clock
Rotsten, Herman— The Unwritten Code
Rouse, Russell— House of Numbers; New York Confidential; The Thief; The Well (with Leo C. Popkin); Wicked Woman

Rowland, Roy— Rogue Cop; Scene of the Crime; Witness to Murder
Salkow, Sydney— Chicago Confidential
Santley, Joseph— Shadow of a Woman; A Tragedy at Midnight
Saville, Victor— The Long Wait
Schuster, Harold— Finger Man; Loophole
Searle, Francis— Cloudburst
Sears, Fred F.— Miami Exposé
Seiler, Lewis— The System; Whiplash; Women's Prison
Seiter, William A.— Make Haste to Live
Sekely, Steve— Hollow Triumph; Lady in the Death House
Selander, Lesley— Blackmail
Sewell, Vernon— Spin a Dark Web
Shane, Maxwell— City Across the River; Fear in the Night; The Naked Street; Nightmare
Sherman, George— Larceny; The Raging Tide; Secret of the Whistler; The Sleeping City
Sherman, Vincent— Affair in Trinidad; Backfire; The Damned Don't Cry; The Garment Jungle; Nora Prentiss; The Unfaithful
Sholem, Lee— Crime Against Joe; The Louisiana Hussy
Shourds, Sherry— The Big Punch
Shumlin, Herman— Confidential Agent
Siegel, Don— Baby Face Nelson; The Big Steal; Crime in the Streets; Invasion of the Body Snatchers; The Lineup; Night unto Night; Private Hell 36; Riot in Cell Block 11; The Verdict
Simon, S. Sylvan— I Love Trouble; Lust for Gold
Siodmak, Robert— Christmas Holiday; Criss Cross; Cry of the City; The Dark Mirror; The File on Thelma Jordon; Fly by Night; The Great Sinner; The Killers; Phantom Lady; Portrait of a Sinner; The Spiral Staircase; The Strange Affair of Uncle Harry; The Suspect
Sirk, Douglas— Lured; Shockproof; Sleep, My Love
Sloane, Paul— The Sun Sets at Dawn
Springsteen, R.G.— Double Jeopardy; The Red Menace; Revolt in the Big House
Stahl, John M.— Leave Her to Heaven
Stanley, Paul— Cry Tough
Stevens, George— A Place in the Sun

Stevens, Robert— The Big Caper
Stevens, Mark— Cry Vengeance; Timetable
Stevenson, Robert— I Married a Communist; The Las Vegas Story; To the Ends of the Earth; Walk Softly, Stranger
Stone, Andrew L.— A Blueprint for Murder; Cry Terror!; Highway 301; Julie; The Night Holds Terror; The Steel Trap
Strate, Walter— Violated
Sturges, John— The Capture; Jeopardy; Mystery Street; The People Against O'Hara; The Sign of the Ram
Sturges, Preston— Unfaithfully Yours
Tetzlaff, Ted— A Dangerous Profession; Gambling House; Riff-Raff; Under the Gun; The Window
Thomas Ralph— The Clouded Yellow
Thomas, William C.— Big Town; Special Agent; They Made Me a Killer
Thompson, J. Lee— Blonde Sinner
Thorpe, Richard— The Black Hand; The Unknown Man
Tourneur, Jacques— Berlin Express; Cat People; Experiment Perilous; I Walked with a Zombie; The Leopard Man; Nightfall; Out of the Past
Tully, Montgomery— The Glass Tomb; Paid to Kill; Terror Street; The Way Out
Tuttle, Frank— A Cry in the Night; Gunman in the Streets; Suspense; This Gun for Hire
Ulmer, Edgar G.— Bluebeard; Detour; Murder Is My Beat; Ruthless; Strange Illusion; The Strange Woman
Van Dyke, W.S., II— Rage in Heaven
VeSota, Bruno— Female Jungle
Victor, Phil— My Gun Is Quick (with George A. White)
Vidor, Charles— Gilda; Ladies in Retirement
Vidor, King— Beyond the Forest; Lightning Strikes Twice; Ruby Gentry
Visconti, Luchino— Ossessione
von Fritsch, Gunther— The Curse of the Cat People (with Robert Wise); Stolen Identity
von Sternberg, Josef— Macao (with Nicholas Ray); The Shanghai Gesture
Vorhaus, Bernard— The Amazing Mr. X; Bury Me Dead
Waggner, George— Sealed Lips

Wallace, Richard— The Fallen Sparrow; Framed
Walsh, Raoul— The Enforcer (uncredited); Glory Alley; High Sierra; The Man I Love; Pursued; They Drive by Night; White Heat
Webb, Robert D.— The Spider
Welles, Orson— Black Magic (uncredited, with Gregory Ratoff; Citizen Kane; Journey into Fear (uncredited, with Norman Foster); The Lady from Shanghai; Mr. Arkadin; The Stranger; Touch of Evil
Wellman, William A.— The Iron Curtain; The Ox-Bow Incident
Wendkos, Paul— The Burglar
Werker, Alfred L.— He Walked by Night (with Anthony Mann); Repeat Performance; Shock; Walk East on Beacon
White, George A.— My Gun Is Quick (with Phil Victor)
Whorf, Richard— Love from a Stranger
Wilbur, Crane— Canon City; Outside the Wall; The Story of Molly X
Wilde, Cornel— Storm Fear
Wilder, Billy— The Big Carnival; Double Indemnity; The Lost Weekend; Sunset Blvd.
Wilder, W. Lee— The Big Bluff; The Glass Alibi; Once a Thief; The Pretender; Three Steps North; The Vicious Circle
Wiles, Gordon— The Gangster
Windust, Bretaigne— The Enforcer (with Raoul Walsh)
Wise, Robert— Blood on the Moon; The Body Snatcher; Born to Kill ; The Captive City; Criminal Court; The Curse of the Cat People (with Gunther von Fritsch); The House on Telegraph Hill; I Want to Live!; Mystery in Mexico; Odds Against Tomorrow; The Set-Up
Witney, William— The Bonne Parker Story; City of Shadows
Wood, Edward D., Jr.— Jail Bait
Wood, Sam— Ivy
Wrangell, Basil— Heartaches; Philo Vance's Gamble
Wyler, William— The Desperate Hours; Detective Story; The Letter
Yarbrough, Jean— Footsteps in the Night; House of Horrors; Inside Job
Zeisler, Alfred— Alimony; Fear; Parole, Inc.
Zinnemann, Fred— Act of Violence; A Hatful of Rain

Appendix B:
Films Noirs Listed by Type

This list attempts to classify films noirs according to "type." The purpose of this classification is simply to give readers the opportunity to find films that have similar content — so they can enjoy (or avoid) more of the same. Many of the films noirs could have been classified into more than one type (e.g., the Westerns, or "Horse Operas"). *The Man from Laramie* could just as easily be called a "Payback" noir and *The Ox-Bow Incident* could fit into the "Wrong Man" category. *Act of Violence*, the story of a disabled World War II veteran seeking revenge against his commanding officer, could be classified as either "Payback" or "Troubled Veteran." Most of the types are self-explanatory but some might need explaining. "Triangle" noirs usually involve a woman who's either in love with or using one or two men. "Newlywed" noirs are films where one of the newlyweds (usually the bride) finds herself in danger after a whirlwind romance and a hasty marriage. The list is entirely subjective, but the reader may find it useful.

Adventure—Calcutta; Rope of Sand; Sirocco; To Have and Have Not

Alcoholic—*see* **Boozer**

Ambition—Citizen Kane; Death of a Salesman; Death of a Scoundrel; Humoresque; Mildred Pierce; Night and the City; Out of the Fog; Ruthless; Shakedown; Suspense; Sweet Smell of Success

Amnesia—Blackout; The Clay Pigeon; The Crooked Way; Fall Guy; High Wall; The Long Wait; Love Letters; Man in the Dark; Power of the Whistler; The Scarf; Somewhere in the Night; Spellbound; Street of Chance; Two O'clock Courage; Voice in the Wind

Asylum—Bedlam; Behind Locked Doors; Fly by Night; The Secret Fury; The Snake Pit; Strange Illusion

Bad Cop—Murder Is My Beat; Night Editor; No Questions Asked; Private Hell 36; The Prowler; Pushover; Roadblock; Rogue Cop; The Sellout; Shield for Murder; Timetable; Touch of Evil; Where the Sidewalk Ends

Blackmail—The Arnelo Affair; Crossroads; The Deadly Game; F.B.I. Girl; The Girl on the Bridge; Man Bait; The Mask of Dimitrios; Moontide; The Reckless Moment; Ride the Pink Horse

Boozer—Black Angel; Blind Spot; Guilty Bystander; Illegal; The Lost Weekend; Night into Morning; Night Without Sleep; Smash-Up, the Story of a Woman; Time Without Pity

Boxing—The Big Punch; Body and Soul; Champion; City for Conquest; The Crooked Circle; Glory Alley; The Harder They Fall; Iron Man; The Set-Up; Whiplash

Combat—Attack; Fixed Bayonets; The Steel Helmet

Comedy—Angels Over Broadway; Beat the Devil; Lady on a Train; Monsieur Verdoux; My Favorite Brunette; Unfaithfully Yours

Commie—I Married a Communist; I Was a Communist for the FBI; The Iron Curtain; My Son John; Pickup on South Street; The Red Menace; Walk East on Beacon

Con Artist—The Amazing Mr. X; Cast a Dark Shadow; The Come-On; Danger Signal; Fallen Angel; Female on the Beach; Larceny; Nightmare Alley; Nobody Lives Forever; Two of a Kind; Two Smart People; Whirlpool

Cover-Up—The Accused; All My Sons; The Blue Gardenia; Criminal Court; The Family Secret; Fear; The Glass Tomb; Inner Sanctum; Man in the Shadow; The Man Who Cheated Himself; Mr. Arkadin; Moonrise; Never Trust a Gambler; Quicksand; The Red House; Shock; Strange Bargain; The Strange Love of Martha Ivers; Vertigo; The Window; Witness to Murder; The Woman in the Window

Drugs—*see* **Narcotics**

Fantasy—Alias Nick Beal; The Boy with Green Hair; The Curse of the Cat People; The Devil and Daniel Webster; Flesh and Fantasy; Night Has a Thousand Eyes; The Picture of Dorian Gray; Portrait of Jennie; Repeat Performance; Three Strangers

Far East—House of Bamboo; Forbidden; Macao; The Shanghai Gesture; Singapore; Stray Dog; Tokyo File 212; World for Ransom

Femme Fatale—Alimony; Angel Face; Another Man's Poison; Angela; Apology for Murder; Bad Blonde; The Blonde Bandit; Blonde Ice; Born to Be Bad; Crime of Passion; The Damned Don't Cry; The Depraved; Detour; Double Indemnity; The File on Thelma Jordon; Flaxy Martin; Framed; The Great Flamarion; Guest in the House; Heat Wave; Hell's Island; Human Desire; Impulse; Ivy; The Killers; The Lady from Shanghai; Leave Her to Heaven; A Life at Stake; The Locket; The Louisiana Hussy; The Macomber Affair; No Man's Woman; *Ossessione*; Out of the Past; Portrait of a Sinner; The Postman Always Rings Twice; Queen Bee; Ruby Gentry; Scarlet Street; Secret of the Whistler; Shockproof; Spin a Dark Web; Strange Triangle; The Strange Woman; Temptation; Tension; Too Late for Tears; The Unholy Wife; Where Danger Lives; Wicked Woman

Fugitive—*see* **On the Run**

Gambling—Force of Evil; The Gambler and the Lady; The Great Sinner; The Lady Gambles; The Las Vegas Story; Miami Exposé

Gangster—Baby Face Nelson; The Bonnie Parker Story; The Big Combo; The Black Hand; Black Tuesday; The Brothers Rico; City of Shadows; Cry of the City; The Gangster; Her Kind of Man; High Sierra; Highway 301; Hoodlum Empire; The Houston Story; I Died a Thousand Times; Johnny Eager; Johnny O'clock; Key Largo; Kiss of Death; Kiss Tomorrow Goodbye; Lady Gangster; The Naked Street; Party Girl; The Racket; 711 Ocean Drive; Slightly Scarlet; The System; The Third Man; Tight Spot; The Trap; The Turning Point; Whistle Stop; White Heat

Gold Fever—Bait; Lust for Gold; The Treasure of the Sierra Madre

Heist—Armored Car Robbery; The Asphalt Jungle; The Big Caper; Criss Cross; Drive a Crooked Road; 5 Against the House; Hell Bound; Kansas City Confidential; The Killing; Man in the Vault; The Man Is Armed; Oddman Out; Odds Against Tomorrow; Plunder Road; *Rififi*; Violent Saturday

High Seas—A Blueprint for Murder; The Breaking Point; Dangerous Crossing; Johnny Angel; Raging Tide

Hit Man—Accused of Murder; The Enforcer; Murder by Contract; New York Confidential; Paid to Kill; The Pretender; Short Cut to Hell; Sorry, Wrong Number; This Gun for Hire; The Whistler

Horror—The Beast with Five Fingers;

The Body Snatcher; Cat People; House of Horrors; I Walked with a Zombie; The Leopard Man

Horse Opera—Blood on the Moon; Devil's Doorway; The Furies; The Gunfighter; The Halliday Brand; Johnny Guitar; The Man from Laramie; Man of the West; The Naked Spur; The Outcasts of Poker Flat; The Ox-Bow Incident; Pursued; Ramrod; Rancho Notorious; Rawhide; Ride Lonesome; Roughshod; Run of the Arrow; Station West; Terror in a Texas Town; Winchester '73

Hostage—Cry Terror!; The Dark Past; The Desperate Hours; Dial 1119; He Ran All the Way; The Hitch-Hiker; The Night Holds Terror; Shadow on the Window; Storm Fear; Suddenly

Impersonator—Chase a Crooked Shadow; Dark Waters; Date with Death; Hollow Triumph; The House on Telegraph Hill; Invasion of the Body Snatchers; Key Witness; Mark of the Whistler; My Name Is Julia Ross; The Narrow Margin; Nora Prentiss; No Man of Her Own; Rear Window; Sealed Lips; Stolen Identity; The Strange Mr. Gregory; The Unwritten Code

Jailbird—The Company She Keeps; Crime Wave; Destiny; The Hoodlum; The Hunted; Inside Job; Outside the Wall; Tomorrow Is Another Day; *see also* **Prison**

Mexico—*see* **South of the Border**

Missing Person—Accomplice; Backfire; Berlin Express; Conflict; Jennifer; Lured; Missing Women; Mysterious Intruder; The Return of the Whistler; The Seventh Victim

Narcotics—A Hatful of Rain; Johnny Stool Pigeon; The Lineup; The Man Who Died Twice; The Man with the Golden Arm; Port of New York; Stakeout on Dope Street; To the Ends of the Earth

Nazi—The Fallen Sparrow; Hangmen Also Die!; Hitler's Children; The House on 92nd Street; Journey into Fear; Ministry of Fear; The Stranger

Nuclear—A Bullet for Joey; Cloak and Dagger; Shack out on 101; Split Second; The Thief; Walk a Crooked Mile; The Whip Hand

Newlywed—Autumn Leaves; The Big Bluff; Cause for Alarm; Christmas Holiday; Cry Wolf; Gaslight; The Glass Alibi; High-

way West; Rebecca; Secret Beyond the Door; Shadow of a Woman; Specter of the Rose; Strange Fascination; Suspicion; Undercurrent; Voice of the Whistler; When Strangers Marry; Woman in Hiding

Newspaper—The Big Carnival; Big Town; Captive City; Chicago Deadline; Kill Me Tomorrow; Lonelyhearts; Scandal Sheet; The Underworld Story; Whispering City

Nightmare—Crack-Up; Escape in the Fog; Fear in the Night; Manhandled; Nightmare

On the Run—The Big Clock; The Burglar; Clouded Yellow; Confidential Agent; Crashout; Cry of the Hunted; Deep Valley; Desperate; The Green Glove; Gun Crazy; Gunman in the Streets; Hell's Half Acre; Nightfall; Nowhere to Go; Raw Deal; Side Street; Special Agent; The Steel Trap; Stranger on the Prowl; They Live by Night; They Made Me a Killer; Undertow; Walk Softly, Stranger; The Way Out; The Weapon

Plastic Surgery—Dark Passage; Jail Bait; A Stolen Face; Strange Impersonation; A Woman's Face

Payback—Between Midnight and Dawn; The Big Heat; The Big Night; Cloudburst; Cornered; Cry Danger; Cry Vengeance; D.O.A.; Dark City; Destination Murder; Gambling House; The Hidden Room; I Walk Alone; The Killer Is Loose; Loan Shark; Mad at the World; Make Haste to Live; The Mask of Diijon; The Missing Juror; On Dangerous Ground; Once a Thief; Race Street; Shoot to Kill; Talk About a Stranger; Thieves' Highway; The Threat; The Unknown Man

Period—Black Magic; Bluebeard; Dragonwyck; Experiment Perilous; Hangover Square; House by the River; Ladies in Retirement; The Lodger; The Lost Moment; Love from a Stranger; Man in the Attic; Moss Rose; Reign of Terror; So Evil My Love; The Spiral Staircase; The Suspect; The Tall Target; The Verdict; The Woman in White

Plague—Isle of the Dead; The Killer that Stalked New York; Panic in the Streets

Police Procedural—C-Man; Calling Homicide; Cop Hater; Detective Story;

Follow Me Quietly; Footsteps in the Night; He Walked by Night; The Human Jungle; Murder Without Tears; Mystery Street; The Naked City; Scene of the Crime; Sudden Danger; The Tattooed Stranger; The Undercover Man; Union Station

Politics—All the King's Men; The Boss; Flamingo Road; The Phenix City Story; So Well Remembered

Prison—Blonde Sinner; Brute Force; Caged; Canon City; Convicted; Gang Busters; House of Numbers; The Last Mile; Revolt in the Big House; Riot in Cell Block 11; San Quentin; The Steel Jungle; The Story of Molly X; Under the Gun; Women's Prison; *see also* **Jailbird**

Private Eye—The Big Sleep; Blackmail; The Brasher Doubloon; The Dark Corner; The Falcon in San Francisco; High Tide; I Love Trouble; I, the Jury; Kiss Me Deadly; Lady in the Lake; The Maltese Falcon; Murder, My Sweet; My Gun Is Quick; Philo Vance's Gamble; Riff-Raff; The Spider

Psycho—The Beat Generation; Beware, My Lovely; Bewitched; Born to Kill; A Cry in the Night; Dangerous Intruder; The Devil Thumbs a Ride; Don't Bother to Knock; A Double Life; Julie; A Kiss Before Dying; M; Money Madness; Naked Alibi; The Night of the Hunter; The Night Runner; Rage in Heaven; Railroaded; Screaming Mimi; Shadow of a Doubt; The Sniper; Step Down to Terror; Strangers on a Train; The Two Mrs. Carrolls; The Unsuspected; Violated; While the City Sleeps; Woman on the Run

Racist—Crossfire; Jigsaw; The Lawless; No Way Out; Open Secret; Storm Warning; The Well

Religion—Edge of Doom; I Confess; Johnny Rocco; Red Light

Show Biz—The Bad and the Beautiful; The Big Knife; Blues in the Night; Doorway to Suspicion; Heartaches; Hollywood Story; In a Lonely Place; The Other Woman; Serenade; The Strip; Sunset Blvd.; The Velvet Touch

Soap Opera—Caught; Clash by Night; Daisy Kenyon; House of Strangers; The Man I Love; Night unto Night; Paid in Full; The Sign of the Ram

South of the Border—The Big Steal; The Bribe; The Capture; Crisis; His Kind of Woman; Jeopardy; A Lady Without Passport; Mystery in Mexico; One Way Street; Second Chance ; We Were Strangers; Wetbacks

Trial—An Act of Murder; Compulsion; I, Jane Doe; Knock on Any Door; Please Murder Me; The Tattered Dress; Valerie; The Vicious Circle

Triangle—Affair in Havana; Beyond the Forest; Casablanca; The City That Never Sleeps; Deception; Desert Fury; *Diabolique*; The Flame; Gilda; The Glass Web; Impact; Jealousy; The Judge; Killer's Kiss; The Letter; Lightning Strikes Twice; Pickup; Pitfall; A Place in the Sun; Playgirl; Possessed; Road House; Sleep, My Love; The Sleeping Tiger; The Strange Affair of Uncle Harry; Sudden Fear; They Drive by Night; This Woman Is Dangerous; Twist of Fate; The Unfaithful; Without Honor

Troubled Veteran—Act of Violence; The Chase; Kiss the Blood Off My Hands; The Long Night; Niagara; Strange Intruder; Swamp Fire; Three Steps North; Try and Get Me; Violence; The Woman on the Beach; A Woman's Devotion

Troubled Youth—City Across the River; Crime in the Streets; Cry Tough; Four Boys and a Gun; Fourteen Hours; Lost, Lonely and Vicious; No Time to Be Young; Teenage Doll; The Wild One

Good Twin, Bad Twin—Among the Living; The Dark Mirror; The Guilty; Hit and Run; A Stolen Life

Undercover—Abandoned; Affair in Trinidad; Appointment with Danger; Border Incident; Crooked Web; Death in Small Doses; Finger Man; I'll Get You ; Illegal Entry; The Mob; Notorious; Outside the Law; Parole, Inc; The Sleeping City; Southside 1-1000; The Street with No Name; T-Men; Trapped

Union—The Big Operator; Chicago Confidential; Edge of the City; The Garment Jungle; On the Waterfront

Western—*see* **Horse Opera**

Whodunit—Backfire; Backlash; Beyond a Reasonable Doubt; Blonde Alibi; Bury Me Dead; The Crimson Kimono; Danger Zone; A Dangerous Profession; Dead Reckoning; Deadline at Dawn; Female Jungle;

The Glass Key; Hunt the Man Down; I Wake Up Screaming; Keeper of the Flame; The Lady Confesses; Laura; The Limping Man; The Midnight Story; The Lucky Stiff; Nocturne; The Paradine Case; The Second Woman; So Dark the Night; Take One False Step; The 13th Letter; A Tragedy at Midnight; The Unholy Four; The Unseen; Vicki; A Woman's Secret

Wrong Man—The Blue Dahlia; Bodyguard; Boomerang; Call Northside 777; Circumstantial Evidence; Crime Against Joe; Double Jeopardy; Highway Dragnet; Loophole; The Man in the Net; The Man on the Eiffel Tower; The Man with My Face; 99 River Street; The People Against O'Hara; Phantom Lady; The Price of Fear; Shadow on the Wall; Stranger on the Third Floor; The Sun Sets at Dawn; Terror Street; They Won't Believe Me; The Thirteenth Hour; Unmasked; The Web; Whispering Footsteps; The Wrong Man

Wrong Woman—Hidden Fear; I Want to Live; Lady in the Death House; Terror at Midnight

Appendix C:
Films Noirs Listed by Year of Release

1940
Angels Over Broadway
City for Conquest
The Letter
Rebecca
Stranger on the Third Floor
They Drive by Night

1941
Among the Living
Blues in the Night
Citizen Kane
The Devil and Daniel Webster
High Sierra
Highway West
I Wake Up Screaming
Ladies in Retirement
The Maltese Falcon
Out of the Fog
Rage in Heaven
Sealed Lips
The Shanghai Gesture
Suspicion
A Woman's Face

1942
Casablanca
Cat People
Crossroads
Fly by Night
The Glass Key
Hitler's Children

Johnny Eager
Journey into Fear
Keeper of the Flame
Lady Gangster
Moontide
Ossessione
Street of Chance
This Gun for Hire
A Tragedy at Midnight

1943
Flesh and Fantasy
Hangmen Also Die!
I Walked with a Zombie
The Leopard Man
The Ox-Bow Incident
The Seventh Victim
Shadow of a Doubt
Whispering Footsteps

1944
Bluebeard
Christmas Holiday
The Curse of the Cat People
Dark Waters
Destiny
Double Indemnity
Experiment Perilous
Gaslight
Guest in the House
Lady in the Death House
Laura

The Lodger
Mark of the Whistler
The Mask of Dimitrios
Ministry of Fear
The Missing Juror
Murder, My Sweet
Phantom Lady
The Suspect
To Have and Have Not
The Unwritten Code
Voice in the Wind
When Strangers Marry
The Whistler
The Woman in the Window

1945
Apology for Murder
Bewitched
The Body Snatcher
Circumstantial Evidence
Confidential Agent
Conflict
Cornered
Danger Signal
Dangerous Intruder
Detour
Escape in the Fog
The Falcon in San Francisco
Fallen Angel
The Fallen Sparrow
The Great Flamarion
Hangover Square
The House on 92nd Street
Isle of the Dead
Jealousy
Johnny Angel
The Lady Confesses
Lady on a Train
Leave Her to Heaven
The Lost Weekend
Love Letters
Mildred Pierce
My Name Is Julia Ross
The Picture of Dorian Gray
Power of the Whistler
Scarlet Street
Spellbound
The Spider
The Strange Affair of Uncle Harry
Strange Illusion
The Strange Mr. Gregory
Two O'clock Courage

The Unseen
Voice of the Whistler

1946
Accomplice
The Beast with Five Fingers
Bedlam
The Big Sleep
Black Angel
Blonde Alibi
The Blue Dahlia
The Chase
Cloak and Dagger
Crack-Up
Criminal Court
The Dark Corner
The Dark Mirror
Deadline at Dawn
Deception
Fallen Angel
Fear
Gilda
The Glass Alibi
Her Kind of Man
House of Horrors
Humoresque
Inside Job
The Killers
The Man I Love
The Mask of Diijon
Mysterious Intruder
Night Editor
Nobody Lives Forever
Nocturne
Notorious
The Postman Always Rings Twice
San Quentin
Secret of the Whistler
Shadow of a Woman
Shock
So Dark the Night
Somewhere in the Night
The Specter of the Rose
The Spiral Staircase
A Stolen Life
Strange Impersonation
The Strange Love of Martha Ivers
Strange Triangle
The Strange Woman
The Stranger
Suspense
Swamp Fire

Temptation
Three Strangers
Two Smart People
Undercurrent
The Verdict
Whistle Stop

1947
The Arnelo Affair
Backlash
Big Town
Blackmail
Blind Spot
Body and Soul
Boomerang
Born to Kill
The Brasher Doubloon
Brute Force
Bury Me Dead
Calcutta
Crossfire
Cry Wolf
Daisy Kenyon
Dark Passage
Dead Reckoning
Deep Valley
Desert Fury
Desperate
The Devil Thumbs a Ride
A Double Life
Dragonwyck
Fall Guy
Fear in the Night
Framed
The Gangster
The Guilty
Heartaches
High Tide
High Wall
I Love Trouble
I Walk Alone
Ivy
Johnny O'Clock
Key Witness
Kiss of Death
Lady in the Lake
The Locket
The Long Night
The Lost Moment
Love from a Stranger
Lured
The Macomber Affair

Monsieur Verdoux
Moss Rose
My Favorite Brunette
Nightmare Alley
Nora Prentiss
Odd Man Out
Out of the Past
Outside the Wall
Philo Vance's Gamble
Possessed
The Pretender
Pursued
Railroaded
Ramrod
The Red House
Repeat Performance
Ride the Pink Horse
Riff-Raff
Shoot to Kill
Singapore
Smash-Up, the Story of a Woman
So Well Remembered
They Won't Believe Me
The Thirteenth Hour
The Two Mrs. Carrolls
The Unfaithful
Unfaithfully Yours
The Unsuspected
Violence
The Web
Whispering City
The Woman on the Beach

1948
The Accused
An Act of Murder
All My Sons
The Amazing Mr. X
Behind Locked Doors
Berlin Express
The Big Clock
The Big Punch
Blonde Ice
Blood on the Moon
Bodyguard
The Bonnie Parker Story
The Boy with Green Hair
Call Northside 777
Canon City
Cry of the City
The Dark Past
The Flame

Force of Evil
He Walked by Night
Hollow Triumph
The Hunted
I, Jane Doe
Inner Sanctum
The Iron Curtain
Key Largo
Kiss the Blood Off My Hands
The Lady from Shanghai
Larceny
Money Madness
Moonrise
Mystery in Mexico
The Naked City
Night Has a Thousand Eyes
Open Secret
Pitfall
Portrait of Jennie
Race Street
Raw Deal
The Return of the Whistler
Road House
Ruthless
Secret Beyond the Door
The Sign of the Ram
Sleep, My Love
The Snake Pit
So Evil My Love
Sorry, Wrong Number
Station West
The Street with No Name
T-Men
To the Ends of the Earth
The Treasure of the Sierra Madre
The Velvet Touch
The Vicious Circle
Walk a Crooked Mile
Whiplash
The Woman in White

1949
Abandoned
Act of Violence
Alias Nick Beal
Alimony
All the King's Men
Beyond the Forest
The Big Steal
Black Magic
Border Incident
The Bribe

Caught
Champion
Chicago Deadline
City Across the River
The Clay Pigeon
C-Man
Criss Cross
The Crooked Way
A Dangerous Profession
Flamingo Road
Flaxy Martin
Follow Me Quietly
The Great Sinner
The Green Glove
The Hidden Room
House of Strangers
Illegal Entry
Impact
Jigsaw
Johnny Stool Pigeon
The Judge
Knock on Any Door
The Lady Gambles
The Lucky Stiff
Lust for Gold
The Man on the Eiffel Tower
Manhandled
Night unto Night
The Paradine Case
Parole, Inc
Port of New York
The Reckless Moment
Red Light
The Red Menace
Reign of Terror
Roughshod
Scene of the Crime
The Set-Up
Shockproof
Special Agent
The Story of Molly X
Strange Bargain
Stray Dog
Take One False Step
Tension
They Live by Night
They Made Me a Killer
Thieves' Highway
The Third Man
The Threat
Too Late for Tears
Trapped

The Undercover Man
Undertow
We Were Strangers
Whirlpool
White Heat
The Window
Without Honor
Woman in Hiding
A Woman's Secret

1950
Armored Car Robbery
The Asphalt Jungle
Backfire
Between Midnight and Dawn
The Black Hand
The Blonde Bandit
Born to Be Bad
The Breaking Point
Caged
The Capture
The Company She Keeps
Convicted
Crisis
D.O.A
The Damned Don't Cry
Dark City
Destination Murder
Devil's Doorway
Dial 1119
Edge of Doom
The File on Thelma Jordon
The Furies
Gambling House
Guilty Bystander
Gun Crazy
The Gunfighter
Gunman in the Streets
Highway 301
House by the River
Hunt the Man Down
I Married a Communist
In a Lonely Place
The Killer that Stalked New York
Kiss Tomorrow Goodbye
A Lady Without Passport
The Lawless
The Man Who Cheated Himself
Mystery Street
New York Confidential
Night and the City
No Man of Her Own

No Way Out
Once a Thief
One Way Street
Paid in Full
Panic in the Streets
Quicksand
The Secret Fury
711 Ocean Drive
Shadow on the Wall
Shakedown
Side Street
The Sleeping City
Southside 1-1000
Storm Warning
The Sun Sets at Dawn
Sunset Blvd
The Tattooed Stranger
Try and Get Me
The Turning Point
The Underworld Story
Union Station
Unmasked
Walk Softly, Stranger
Where Danger Lives
Where the Sidewalk Ends
Winchester '73
Woman on the Run

1951
Another Man's Poison
Appointment with Danger
The Big Carnival
The Big Night
Cause for Alarm
Cloudburst
The Clouded Yellow
Cry Danger
Danger Zone
Death of a Salesman
Detective Story
The Enforcer
F.B.I. Girl
The Family Secret
Fixed Bayonets
Fourteen Hours
The Girl on the Bridge
He Ran All the Way
His Kind of Woman
Hollywood Story
The Hoodlum
The House on Telegraph Hill
I Was a Communist for the F.B.I

Iron Man
Lightning Strikes Twice
M
The Man With My Face
Missing Women
The Mob
Never Trust a Gambler
Night into Morning
No Questions Asked
The People Against O'Hara
Pickup
A Place in the Sun
The Prowler
The Racket
The Raging Tide
Rawhide
Roadblock
The Scarf
The Second Woman
The Sellout
Sirocco
The Steel Helmet
Strangers on a Train
The Strip
The Tall Target
The 13th Letter
Three Steps North
Tokyo File 212
Tomorrow Is Another Day
Two of a Kind
Under the Gun
The Unknown Man
The Well
The Whip Hand

1952
Affair in Trinidad
The Bad and the Beautiful
Beware, My Lovely
The Captive City
Clash by Night
Don't Bother to Knock
The Gambler and the Lady
Glory Alley
Hoodlum Empire
I'll Get You
Kansas City Confidential
The Las Vegas Story
Loan Shark
Macao
Man Bait
My Son John

The Narrow Margin
Night Without Sleep
On Dangerous Ground
The Outcasts of Poker Flat
Rancho Notorious
Ruby Gentry
Scandal Sheet
The Sniper
The Steel Trap
A Stolen Face
Strange Fascination
Stranger on the Prowl
Sudden Fear
Talk About a Stranger
The Thief
This Woman Is Dangerous
Walk East on Beacon

1953
Angel Face
Bad Blonde
Beat the Devil
The Big Heat
The Blue Gardenia
A Blueprint for Murder
The City That Never Sleeps
Cry of the Hunted
Dangerous Crossing
Forbidden
The Glass Web
The Hitch-Hiker
I Confess
I, the Jury
Jennifer
Jeopardy
The Limping Man
Man in the Attic
Man in the Dark
Murder Without Tears
The Naked Spur
Niagara
99 River Street
Pickup on South Street
Second Chance
Split Second
Stolen Identity
The System
Terror Street
The Unholy Four
Vicki
Wicked Woman
The Wild One

1954
Bait
Blackout
Crime Wave
Cry Vengeance
Doorway to Suspicion
Drive a Crooked Road
Heat Wave
Hell's Half Acre
Highway Dragnet
Human Desire
The Human Jungle
Jail Bait
Johnny Guitar
A Life at Stake
The Long Wait
Loophole
Make Haste to Live
On the Waterfront
The Other Woman
Paid to Kill
Playgirl
Private Hell 36
Pushover
Rear Window
Riot in Cell Block 11
Rogue Cop
Shield for Murder
The Sleeping Tiger
Suddenly
Twist of Fate
Violated
Witness to Murder
World for Ransom

1955
Angela
The Big Bluff
The Big Combo
The Big Knife
Black Tuesday
A Bullet for Joey
Cast a Dark Shadow
City of Shadows
Crashout
The Crooked Web
The Deadly Game
The Desperate Hours
Diabolique
Double Jeopardy
Female on the Beach
Finger Man

5 Against the House
Gang Busters
The Glass Tomb
Hell's Island
House of Bamboo
I Died a Thousand Times
Illegal
Impulse
Killer's Kiss
Kiss Me Deadly
Mad at the World
The Man from Laramie
The Man with the Golden Arm
Mr. Arkadin
Murder Is My Beat
The Naked Alibi
The Naked Street
The Night Holds Terror
The Night of the Hunter
No Man's Woman
The Phenix City Story
Queen Bee
Rififi
Shack out on 101
Sudden Danger
Tight Spot
Violent Saturday
The Way Out
Women's Prison

1956
Accused of Murder
Attack
Autumn Leaves
Beyond a Reasonable Doubt
Blonde Sinner
The Boss
Calling Homicide
The Come-On
Crime Against Joe
Crime in the Streets
A Cry in the Night
Death of a Scoundrel
The Female Jungle
The Harder They Fall
The Houston Story
Invasion of the Body Snatchers
Julie
The Killer Is Loose
The Killing
A Kiss Before Dying
Man in the Vault

The Man Is Armed
Miami Exposé
Nightfall
Nightmare
Outside the Law
Please Murder Me
The Price of Fear
Serenade
Slightly Scarlet
Spin a Dark Web
The Steel Jungle
Storm Fear
Strange Intruder
Terror at Midnight
Timetable
The Weapon
Wetbacks
While the City Sleeps
A Woman's Devotion
The Wrong Man

1957
Affair in Havana
Baby Face Nelson
The Big Caper
The Brothers Rico
The Burglar
Chase a Crooked Shadow
Chicago Confidential
Crime of Passion
Death in Small Doses
The Depraved
Edge of the City
Footsteps in the Night
Four Boys and a Gun
The Garment Jungle
The Halliday Brand
A Hatful of Rain
Hell Bound
Hidden Fear
Hit and Run
House of Numbers
Kill Me Tomorrow
Man in the Shadow
The Midnight Story
My Gun Is Quick
Night Runner
No Time to Be Young

Plunder Road
Run of the Arrow
Shadow on the Window
Short Cut to Hell
Sweet Smell of Success
The Tattered Dress
Teenage Doll
Time Without Pity
The Unholy Wife
Valerie

1958
Cop Hater
The Crooked Circle
Cry Terror!
I Want to Live!
Johnny Rocco
The Lineup
Lonelyhearts
Lost, Lonely and Vicious
Man of the West
The Man Who Died Twice
Murder by Contract
Nowhere to Go
Party Girl
Revolt in the Big House
Rope of Sand
Screaming Mimi
Stakeout on Dope Street
Step Down to Terror
Terror in a Texas Town
Touch of Evil
Vertigo

1959
The Beat Generation
The Big Operator
Compulsion
The Crimson Kimono
Cry Tough
Date with Death
The Last Mile
The Louisiana Hussy
The Man in the Net
Odds Against Tomorrow
Portrait of a Sinner
Ride Lonesome
The Trap

Appendix D:
How to Build an Affordable
Film Noir Video Library

Building a film noir video library can be an expensive project. But it doesn't have to be. Try some of the suggestions below and you'll see what I mean.

RECORDING FROM TV

If you're fortunate enough to have access to cable or satellite TV, check out TMC (Turner Movie Classics) and AMC (American Movie Classics), both of which are usually part of the provider's basic (read that cheapest) package. The Mystery Channel and The Western Channel, a part of the STARZ package, is usually provided at an extra cost. Together the stations have been broadcasting anywhere from twenty to thirty films noirs each month. All it takes are some blank tapes, which can be purchased cheaply at discount stores, and the discipline to remember to set your recorder. In 2001, I recorded almost three hundred films noirs from these channels.

To ensure that I would remember to record all scheduled films noirs (I forgot some anyway!), each month I created a simple calendar on my computer, typing in the name of the film, the station on which it would be shown, the time it started, and its length. Then on the appropriate days, I set my recorder to start five or ten minutes before the film was due to begin and to stop five or ten minutes after it was due to end. (TMC is exceptionally diligent in keeping to an exact schedule, but be sure to add some time when recording from other channels, especially AMC, which has begun placing commercials in their films).

To create your own calendar, check your cable or satellite company's monthly guide for film schedules or visit the following helpful Web sites:

- TV-now.com: http://www.tv-now.com/stars/filmnoir.htm and http://www.tv-now.com/stars/mystery.htm
- Turner Classic Movies: http://www.turnerclassicmovies.com
- American Movie Classics: http://www.amctv.com
- The Mystery Channel and the Western Channel: http://www.starzsuperpak.com/

500

I always record at the middle (LP) speed (never at the slower SLP, which results in poor quality). This allows me to record two films on each tape The quality is satisfactory because the picture from my satellite transmission is excellent. A package of eight tapes costs me $10 in a discount store. That works out to $1.25 per tape or sixty-three cents per movie! During the twelve-month period I mentioned earlier, I recorded approximately three hundred films, so my cost was around $189. For purists who wouldn't think of recording anything at less than SP, or if your VCR only has two speeds, it would have cost about $378 to record only one film on each tape.

Now, what happens if you're like me and forget to record some films? Don't kick yourself too hard because many of the films seem to show up a couple of times a year, sometimes more often, especially on the Mystery Channel and the Western Channel. Be prepared, though, because there will come a time when you'll have all of the films noirs that you're ever going to get from TV, and you may feel the need to own some of those wonderful film noir rarities. Or suppose you don't have cable or satellite TV or a kindly relative or good friend who does? Then sign up for one now if they're available in your area, or the film noir passion in you will have to be satisfied elsewhere.*

THE INTERNET AND OTHER PLACES

The Internet is a terrific place for those who want to continue their search for hard-to-find films noirs. The Internet auction site e-Bay brings together buyers and sellers of just about everything, including film noir videos. Immediately after registering at e-Bay.com, you should go to http://www.pages.ebay.com/sitemap.html and select "Movies." Then select "Search only in **Movies**" and "Search titles **and** descriptions" and enter the key word "film noir." You'll find pages and pages of films being offered for sale by individuals and companies. I suggest you wait until the last minute before making a bid on an item. During my first visit, I got into a bidding war for "Gun Crazy" and wound up paying $54 for it. If I had been patient and waited to bid until just before the auction was due to end, I might have been able to get it for much less. My bids on other films turned out to be more successful (i.e., cheaper). In addition, I was able to build my own network of sellers and eventually purchased a number of films noirs from several of them. You can do the same. Send sellers your "wish list" and when they e-mail you with the list of films that they have, negotiate, negotiate, negotiate, especially if you're making a large purchase. If they quote $15 for each film, offer them $10 (nicely, of course). You may be pleasantly surprised. Be aware that quality varies, especially with the rarer films.

Most people are happy with the deals they make on e-Bay, but occasionally problems occur. Remember, when you send money to people who are selling videos or anything else, you're trusting that they'll honor their part of the agreement to send you the promised merchandise in good condition. Most people are honest, but there are always the occasional few who try to rip people off. Order just one video first, and if there are no problems, you probably can feel safe in ordering more from that same seller. E-Bay has wisely placed a "feedback forum" on its web site where you can read what other buyers have to say about sellers. (Sellers can do the same for their buyers, so keep to your part of the deal, too). In addition, e-Bay has services to help you in case you're involved in a dispute with a seller. I've purchased a number of items on e-Bay and have had only one bad experience. If you feel uncomfortable about ordering merchandise online, see the next option.

Listed below are the online video dealers I dealt with while writing *Film Noir Guide*:

• Life Is a Movie.Com: http://www.lifeisamovie.com (Christine was a pleasure to work with)
• Englewood Entertainment: http://www.englewd.com

*All web address and e-mails are current as of this writing.

- Videoflicks.com: http://www.videoflicks.com
- Sinister Cinema: http://www.sinistercinema.com
- Best Video (rentals only): http://www.bestvideo.com
- Entertainment Studios.com: http://entertainmentstudios.com
- Reel.com: http://www.reel.com
- Amazon.com: http://www.amazon.com
- For other sources of film noir videos online, try the Video Addict Collectors Search Engines: http://videoaddicts.com

Other sites of interest:

- Eddie Brandt's Saturday Matinee Video has a good collection of films noirs for rent and for sale. They have no web address, but their snail mail is: 5006 Vineland Ave., North Hollywood, CA 91601. Telephone numbers are (818) 506-4242 and (818) 506-7722
- Check out this terrific web site dedicated to film noir. They've got a large collection of noirs and a monthly trivia contest, which can win you a free video. They even have on occasion guest authors to participate in on-line round table discussions: http://noirfilm.com
- Send an e-mail to filmnoirfilms@hotmail.com for a neat little film noir newsletter. Bob has one of the largest film noir collections in the country.
- Classic Images, the monthly periodical, also has a web site that may prove interesting to fans of other classic genres as well as film noir: (http://www.classicimages.com). Several of the newspaper's advertisers have a good collection of films noirs: Darker Image Videos,* Box 479 Medway, ME 04460 (e-mail: Darker Imagevid@webtv.net); Teakwood Video, PMB 206, 7954 Transit Road, Williamsville, NY 14221; The Movie Man, 5036 Coldwater Cyn., Apt. 206, Sherman Oaks, CA 91423

JUST HOW FANATICAL ARE YOU ANYWAY?

Most film noir fans will be satisfied with the first method described in this chapter (recording from TV). After all, the price is certainly right. However, there are those, like myself, who simply *must* have every film noir that's available. While money may be no object for *some* of our fellow fanatics, it is for the rest of us. A combination of all of the above methods will ensure that you wind up with an impressive film noir collection without breaking your bank account, but, with the term "affordable" being relative, understand that you can expect to spend three or four thousand dollars if you want to purchase every film noir covered in this book. Hopefully, your family will be as understanding about your fanaticism as my wonderful wife, Doreen, is about mine.

---

*By the way, the very knowledgeable Charles P. Mitchell of Darker Images Videos, which specializes in film noir, is also the author of a number of books on film: *A Guide to Charlie Chan Films* (1999, Greenwood); *Screen Sirens Scream* (2000, McFarland); *A Guide to Apocalyptic Cinema* (2001, Greenwood); *The Complete H.P. Lovecraft Filmography* (2001, Greenwood); *The Devil On Screen: Feature Films Worldwide 1913–2000* (2001, McFarland) and *The Hitler Filmography: 1940–2000* (2002, McFarland).

Annotated Bibliography

Alpi, Deborah Lazaroff. *Robert Siodmak.* Jefferson, N.C.: McFarland, 1998. Alpi has written the definitive biography of the famous director. She includes an informative chapter on his films noirs and a filmography by date.

Billingsley, Kenneth Lloyd. *Hollywood Party: How Communism Seduced the American Film Industry in the 1930s and 1940s.* Roseville, Calif.: Forum (Prima Publishing), 2000. Billingsley tells "the other side of the story" about how the Communist Party infiltrated Hollywood, leading to the infamous blacklist.

Bogdanovich, Peter. *Who the Devil Made It: Conversations with Legendary Film Directors.* New York: Ballantine Books, 1998. A fascinating compilation of Bogdanovich's interviews with Hollywood's best-known directors, including film noir contributors Robert Aldrich, Allan Dwan, Alfred Hitchcock, Fritz Lang, Joseph H. Lewis, Leo McCarey, Otto Preminger, Don Siegel, Josef von Sternberg, Edgar G. Ulmer and Raoul Wash. Wow.

Buhle, Paul, and Dave Wagner. *Radical Hollywood: The Untold Story Behind America's Favorite Movies.* New York: New Press, 2002. Was your favorite movie actor a Communist? How about that director or screenwriter? This book about the Hollywood Left contains an informative chapter entitled, "Politics and Mythology of Film Art — The Film Noir."

Clarens, Carlos, and updated by Foster Hirsch. *Crime Movies: An Illustrated History of the Gangster Genre from D.W. Griffith to Pulp Fiction.* New York: Da Capo Press, 1997. An enjoyable history of the genre, including many films noirs and a nice collection of photos.

Cocchi, John. *Second Feature: The Best of the 'B' Films.* Secaucus, N.J.: Carol Publishing Group (Citadel Press), 1991. Luckily for the reader, Cocchi went hog wild with the photographs in this enjoyable look at B films from the thirties through the eighties, broken down by genre. Films noirs can be found in the Mystery and Crime section.

Condor, Paul, and Jim Sangster. *The Complete Hitchcock.* London: Virgin Publishing, 1999. A popular look at the master's films, including some interesting trivia at the end of each chapter.

Cotten, Joseph. *Vanity Will Get You Somewhere: An Autobiography.* Lincoln, Neb.: toExcel Press (iUniverse.com, Inc.), 2000. Interesting autobiography and reminiscences of the star of the film noir classic *Shadow of a Doubt.*

Donati, William. *Ida Lupino: A Biography.* Lexington: University Press of Kentucky, 1995. Enjoyable bio of the noir icon.

Douglas, Kirk. *The Ragman's Son: An Auto-*

biography. New York: Pocket Books (Simon & Schuster), 1989. The noir icon's fascinating life in his own words.

Duncan, Paul. *Film Noir: Films of Trust and Betrayal*. Harpenden, England: Pocket Essentials, 2000. In this little paperback book, Duncan includes an introduction and synopses-analyses of twenty-five films noirs. The remaining hundreds of films contain credits and one-line plot descriptions. He also lists post-noirs, neo-noirs and foreign noirs, and includes several pages of reference materials. Duncan's introduction is entertaining and informative, but his one-or two-line descriptions are not helpful to fans trying to decide whether or not to spend money on a video. The endings of the twenty-five films are revealed.

Fishgall, Gary. *Against Type: The Biography of Burt Lancaster*. New York: Scribner, 1995. A comprehensive bio of the Hollywood leading man and film noir icon. The filmography includes seventy-two of his films.

Gifford, Barry. *Out of the Past: Adventures in Film Noir*. Jackson: University Press of Mississippi, 2001. Formerly *The Devil Thumbs a Ride & Other Unforgettable Films* (New York: Grove Press, 1988). Gifford takes a humorous, personal approach in his analyses of more than 100 films, most of them noirs, some neo-noirs, and others from various genres. It's entertaining and informally written, but Gifford obviously feels no remorse about disclosing the films' endings.

Gorman, Ed, Lee Server and Martin H. Greenberg, eds. *The Big Book of Noir*. New York: Carroll & Graf, 1998. Informative essays cover not only film noir but also fiction, comic book noir and radio and TV noir. Includes a chapter on one hundred essential films noirs (The Black List).

Hannsberry, Karen Burroughs. *Femme Noir: Bad Girls of Film*. Jefferson, N.C.: McFarland, 1998. Hannberry provides short, but in-depth, bios and noir filmographies for 49 actresses. Almost everyone is here, from the best known (such as Lauren Bacall, Joan Bennett, Joan

Crawford, Gloria Grahame, Ida Lupino, Barbara Stanwyck) to many lesser-known character actresses (Jeanne Crain, Rosemary De Camp, Sally Forrest, Helen Walker). A big treat for film noir fans.

Harvey, James. *Movie Love in the Fifties*. New York: Knopf, 2001. Harvey covers Hollywood in the late forties, the fifties and the early sixties, with chapters of interest to the film noir fan.

Hill, Ona L. *Raymond Burr: A Film, Radio, and Television Biography*. Jefferson, N.C.: McFarland, 1994; reprinted 1999. The ultimate Burr biography, it includes an exhaustive list of his radio and television shows and a Perry Mason Episode Guide with plot summaries and cast lists.

Hirsch, Foster. *Detours and Lost Weekend: A Map of Neo-Noir*. New York: Limelight Edition (Proscenium), 1999. Great stuff about how film noir from the classic period metamorphosed into neo-noir.

_____. *Film Noir: The Dark Side of the Screen*. New York: Da Capo Press, 1981. An entertaining overview of film noir loaded with terrific photographs.

Jarlett, Franklin. *Robert Ryan: A Biography and Critical Filmography*. Jefferson, N.C.: McFarland, 1990; reprinted 1997. A detailed look at the life and career of the noir icon.

Jarvis, Everett Grant, revised and updated by Lois Johe. *Final Curtain: Deaths of Noted Movie and Television Personalities*, 9th ed. Secaucus, N.J.: Citadel Press (Carol Publishing Group), 1998. Find out when and how your favorite movie and TV performers died, where they're interred, their original names, and who is related to whom.

Kaplan, E. Ann, ed. *Women in Film Noir*. London: British Film Institute, 1998. A revised and expanded edition of the 1978 book, this contains scholarly essays, from mostly a feminist point of view, on classic and post/neo-noir.

Leff, Leonard J., and Jerold L. Simmons. *Dame in the Kimono: Hollywood, Censorship, and the Production Code*. Lexington: University Press of Kentucky, 2001. A fascinating account of the infamous Production Code and Tinseltown censorship, with chapters on *The Postman Always Rings Twice* and *Detective Story*.

Lyons, Arthur. *Death on the Cheap: The Lost B Movies of Film Noir*. New York: Da Capo Press, 2000. Lyons writes exclusively on what he calls the "lost films," that is, hard- or impossible-to-find B-noirs. His first six chapters are devoted to an interesting history of film noir in general and the B-movie in particular. The remainder of the book contains synopses of 139 films (with revealed endings), and a listing of hundreds of others by year and by studio. The book is helpful to the film noir student in that Lyons' lists include nearly 100 films not mentioned in other film noir reference books. Written informally and humorously, it's for the student and fan alike.

Maxfield, James F. *The Fatal Woman: Sources of Male Anxiety in American Film Noir, 1941–1991*. Cranbury, N.J.: Associated University Presses (Farleigh Dickinson), 1997. Maxfield deals with the psychological threat of the femme fatale to the male protagonist in seven films noirs from the classic period and seven post/neo-noirs. For serious fans and the film student.

McGilligan, Patrick, and Paul Buhle. *Tender Comrades: A Backstory of the Hollywood Blacklist*. New York: St. Martin's Griffin, 1999. Interviews with blacklisted Hollywood figures, including Jeff Corey, Lionel Stander, Abraham Polonsky and Jules Dassin.

Meyer, David N. *A Girl and a Gun: The Complete Guide to Film Noir on Video*. New York: Avon, 1998. Meyer's book contains a useful introduction and enjoyable synopses and analyses of more than one hundred films. He strays from the classic period (1940–59) and includes a number of post-noirs and neo-noirs. Meyer also includes a list (now outdated) of thirteen films noirs not available on VHS or DVD, two pages on how to rent or purchase videos by mail and on the Internet, and a recommended reading list. Meyer refrains from divulging the endings.

Muller, Eddie. *Dark City: The Lost World of Film Noir*. New York: St. Martin's Griffin, 1998. Another well-done overview of film noir. Highly enjoyable. Great photos.

_____. *Dark City Dames: The Wicked Woman on Film Noir*. New York: Regan Books (Harper Collins), 2001. Muller writes about six of film noir's most famous femmes (Jane Greer, Audrey Totter, Marie Windsor, Evelyn Keyes, Coleen Gray, Ann Savage). Highly recommended.

Palmer, R. Barton. *Hollywood's Dark Cinema: The American Film Noir*. New York: Twayne (Simon & Schuster Macmillan), 1994. Another scholarly but readable look at film noir, with detailed plot synopses (revealing the endings) and analyses of eleven noirs from the classic period and three neo-noirs.

Parish, James Robert. *Prison Pictures from Hollywood: Plots, Critiques, Casts, and Credits for 293 Releases*. Jefferson, N.C.: McFarland, 1991; reprinted 2000. The title says it all. Covers the prison noirs but gives away the endings. Enjoyable.

Phillips, Gene D. *Creatures of Darkness: Raymond Chandler, Detective Fiction, and Film Noir*. Lexington: University Press of Kentucky, 2000. Everything you ever wanted to know about the famous mystery writer, his novels and his screenplays.

Roberts, Jerry, ed. *Mitchum in His Own Words*. New York: Limelight Edition (Proscenium), 2000. A series of interviews with the actor.

Schlossheimer, Michael. *Gunmen and Gangsters*. Jefferson, N.C.: McFarland, 2002. Entertaining and informative biographies and filmographies of Hollywood tough guys (William Bendix, Charles Bickford, Ward Bond, Broderick Crawford, Brian Donlevy, Paul Douglas, William Gargan, Barton MacLane and Lloyd Nolan), all of whom appeared in a number of films noirs.

Schwartz, Ronald. *Noir, Now and Then: Film Noir Originals and Remakes (1944–1999)*. Westport, Conn.: Greenwood Press, 2001. Schwartz provides an interesting and entertaining comparison of thirty-four classic noirs (and one French post-noir) with their remakes (e.g., 1944's *Murder, My Sweet* with the 1975 remake, *Farewell, My Lovely*). A fun read but only one photograph and, yes, he does give away the endings.

Selby, Spencer. *Dark City: The Film Noir.* Jefferson, N.C.: McFarland, 1984; reprinted 1997. Selby writes in great detail about twenty-five films noirs and lists 465 others, providing one- or two-sentence descriptions for each. He includes five helpful appendices—"Off-Genre" and Other Films Noirs, Chronology of the Film Noir, Totals by Studio or Releasing Company, Directors' Filmographies, and Bibliography of Works Cited. Of value to the film noir student and the fan. Selby discloses the endings of the twenty-five films he analyzes.

Server, Lee. *Robert Mitchum: "Baby, I Don't Care."* New York: St. Martin's Press, 2001. An entertaining and valuable biography of the noir icon.

Silver, Alain, and Elizabeth Ward, eds. *Film Noir: An Encyclopedic Reference to the American Style.* Woodstock, N.Y.: Overlook Press, 1979; 3rd ed., 1992. Long considered "the Bible" of film noir, this is an invaluable work for the serious student because of its in-depth analyses of hundreds of films useful appendices. Written before home VCRs made access to many of these films noir an easy task, some of the contributors, perhaps relying on faulty memories, are way off in their plot synopses. Warning: Endings are revealed.

_____, and James Ursini, eds. *Film Noir Reader*, 5th ed. New York: Limelight Edition (Proscenium), 1999.

_____, and _____. *Film Noir Reader 2.* New York: Limelight Edition (Proscenium), 1999. Silver and Ursini have amassed a most impressive and important collection of essays on film noir. While especially useful to the film noir student, the average fan might also enjoy delving into these interesting books.

_____, _____, and Robert Porfirio, eds. *Film Noir Reader 3: Interviews with Film-makers of the Classic Noir Period.* New York: Limelight Edition (Proscenium), 2002. A collection of interviews with eight noir directors (Andre De Toth, Edward Dmytryk, Samuel Fuller, Fritz Lang, Joseph H. Lewis, Otto Preminger, Billy Wilder and Robert Wise), and other filmmakers, including actresses Lizabeth Scott and Claire Trevor. Definitely fan-friendly.

Sklar, Robert. *City Boys: Cagney— Bogart— Garfield.* Princeton, N.J.: Princeton University Press, 1992. In his usual entertaining fashion, Sklar traces the careers of three of film noir's bad boys.

Spoto, Donald. *The Art of Alfred Hitchcock: Fifty Years of His Motion Pictures*, 2nd ed. New York: Anchor Books (Random House), 1992. Synopses and interesting analyses of the master's best-known films, including all of his films noirs. Lot of nice photos. Film endings are revealed.

Stephens, Michael L. *Film Noir: A Comprehensive, Illustrated Reference to Movies, Terms and Persons.* Jefferson, N.C.: McFarland, 1995. Stephens includes short synopses (with revealed endings) and analyses of hundreds of film noir titles and brief biographies and filmographies of film noir actors, actresses, directors, screenwriters, cinematographers, art directors, composers and others. Mainly of interest to film historians and serious students of film noir. Stephens mentions in his introduction that his synopses were obtained from numerous sources. Unfortunately, many of the same plot errors that appear in those sources are repeated here.

Thompson, Peggy, and Saeko Usukawa. *Hard-Boiled: Great Lines from Classic Noir Films.* San Francisco: Chronicle Books, 1996. "A collection of over 300 lines from nearly 150 of the wickedest films," this entertaining book was written with the noir fan in mind. It's loaded with beautiful black- and-white glossy photographs and color poster reproductions.

Walker, Alexander. *Bette Davis.* New York: Applause Books, 1986. This enjoyable biography includes a Davis filmography (1931 to 1974).

Williams, Lucy Chase. *The Complete Films of Vincent Price*. Secaucus, N.J.: Citadel Press (Carol Publishing Group), 1998. The films of noir icon and horror master Price. Filled with many wonderful photographs.

Yablonsky, Lewis. *George Raft*. Lincoln, Nebraska: iUniverse.com, 2001). An interesting biography of the famous actor, who's remembered mostly for his gangster roles.

Young, Jordan R. *Reel Characters*. Beverly Hills, Calif.: Moonstone, 1986. Bios, photos and filmographies of twelve veteran character actors, including such familiar noir faces as Elisha Cook, Jr., Iris Adrian, Sam Jaffe, John Qualen, Charles Lane, John Carradine, Burt Mustin and George Chandler. Nicely done.

Index

Numbers in **boldface** refer to pages with photographs.